Mae™

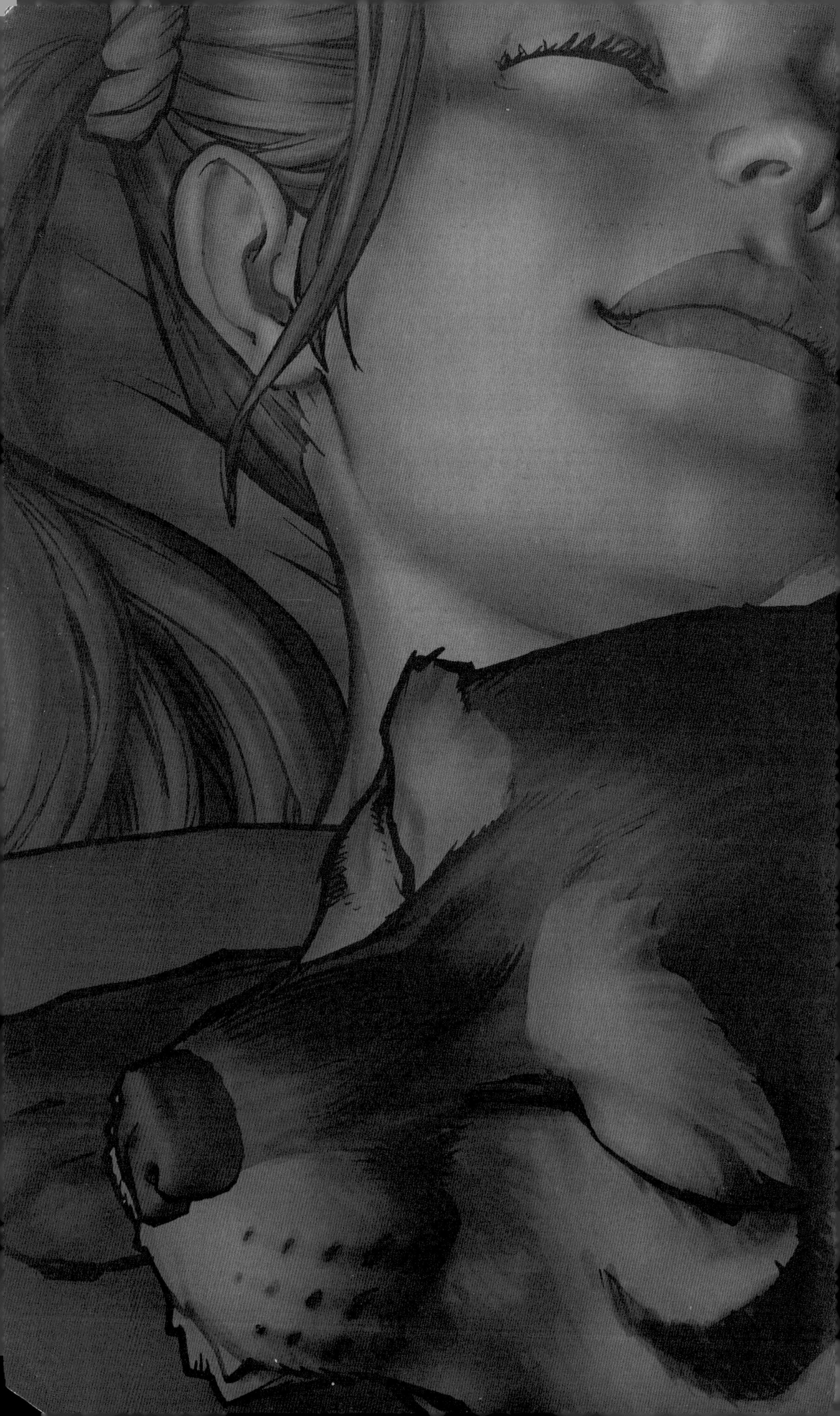

Mae™

VOLUME ONE

STORY AND ART GENE HA

COLORS ROSE McCLAIN AND WESLEY HARTMAN

ART, CHAPTER 6 PAULINA GANUCHEAU

COLORS, CHAPTER 6 KENDALL GOODE

LETTERS ZANDER CANNON

COVER ART AND CHAPTER BREAKS GENE HA

Dark Horse Books

PRESIDENT AND PUBLISHER
MIKE RICHARDSON

EDITOR
DANIEL CHABON

ASSISTANT EDITOR
CARDNER CLARK

DESIGNER
DAVID NESTELLE

DIGITAL ART TECHNICIAN
CHRISTIANNE GOUDREAU

Neil Hankerson Executive Vice President • Tom Weddle Chief Financial Officer • Randy Stradley Vice President of Publishing • Michael Martens Vice President of Book Trade Sales • Matt Parkinson Vice President of Marketing • David Scroggy Vice President of Product Development • Dale LaFountain Vice President of Information Technology • Cara Niece Vice President of Production and Scheduling • Nick McWhorter Vice President of Media Licensing • Ken Lizzi General Counsel • Dave Marshall Editor in Chief • Davey Estrada Editorial Director • Scott Allie Executive Senior Editor • Chris Warner Senior Books Editor • Cary Grazzini Director of Specialty Projects • Lia Ribacchi Art Director • Vanessa Todd Director of Print Purchasing • Matt Dryer Director of Digital Art and Prepress • Mark Bernardi Director of Digital Publishing • Sarah Robertson Director of Product Sales • Michael Gombos Director of International Publishing and Licensing

Published by Dark Horse Books
A division of Dark Horse Comics, Inc.
10956 SE Main Street
Milwaukie, OR 97222

First edition: January 2017
ISBN 978-1-50670-146-2

10 9 8 7 6 5 4 3 2 1
Printed in China

International Licensing: (503) 905-2377
Comic Shop Locator Service: (888) 266-4226

This volume collects the Dark Horse Comics series *Mae* #1–#6.

ONE

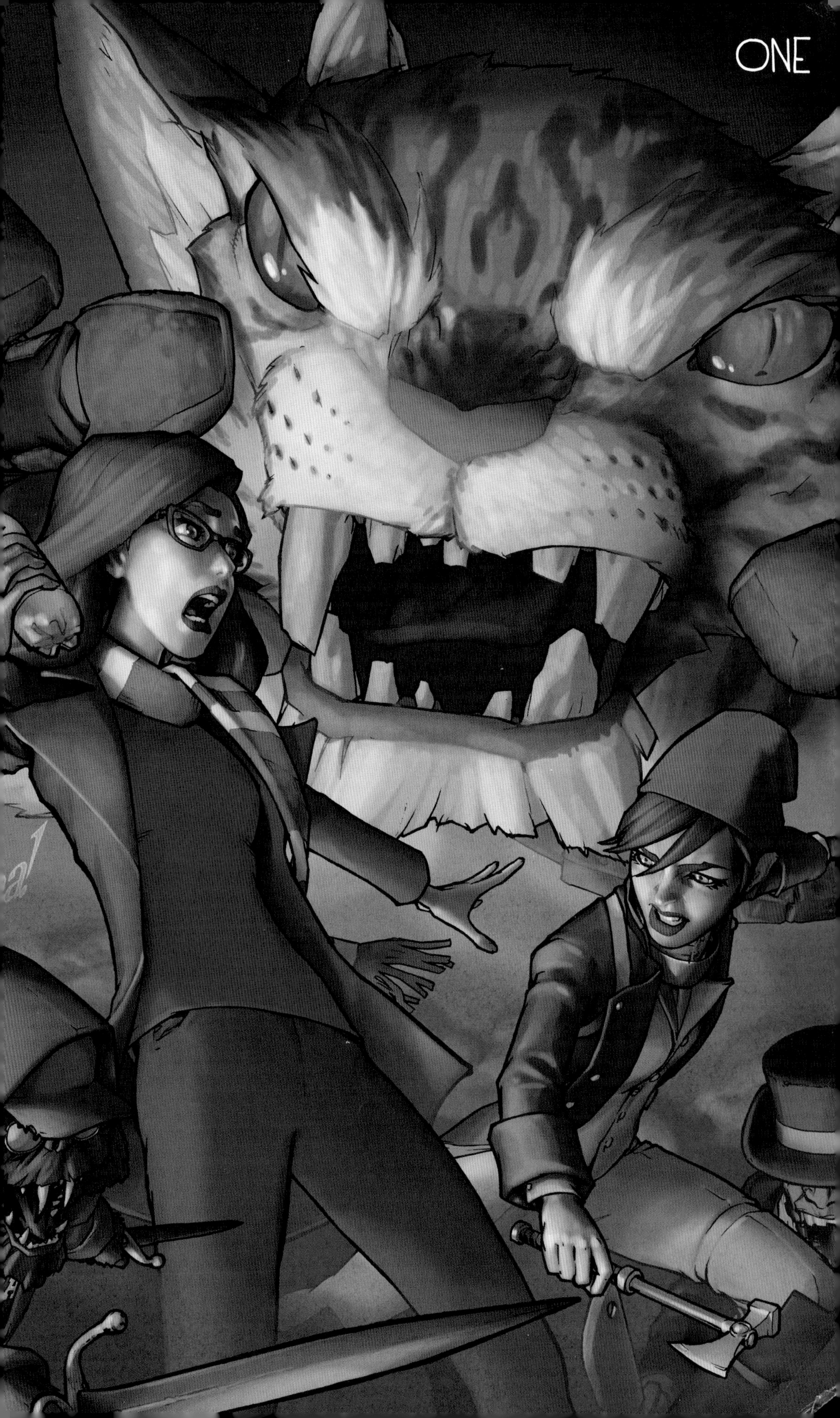

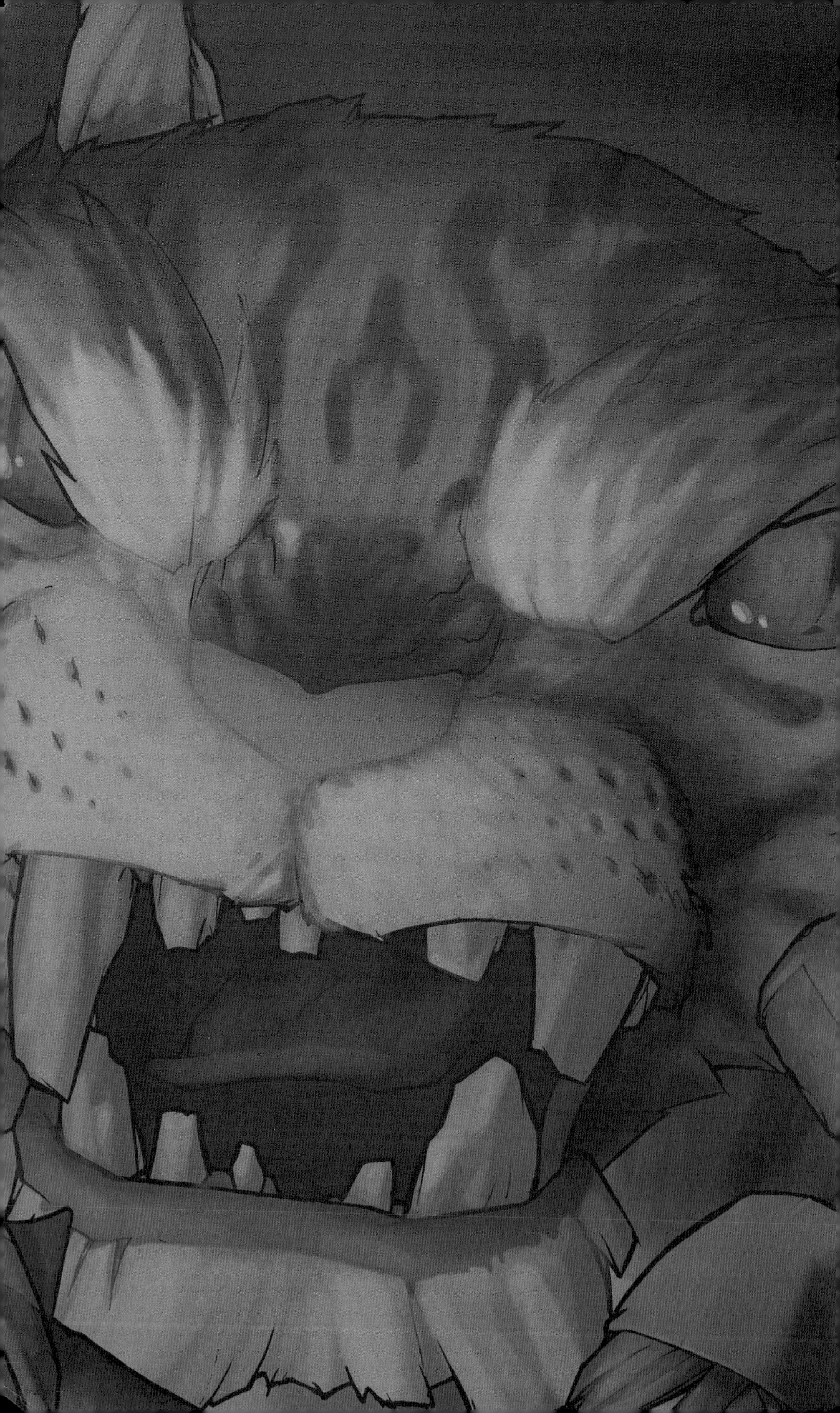

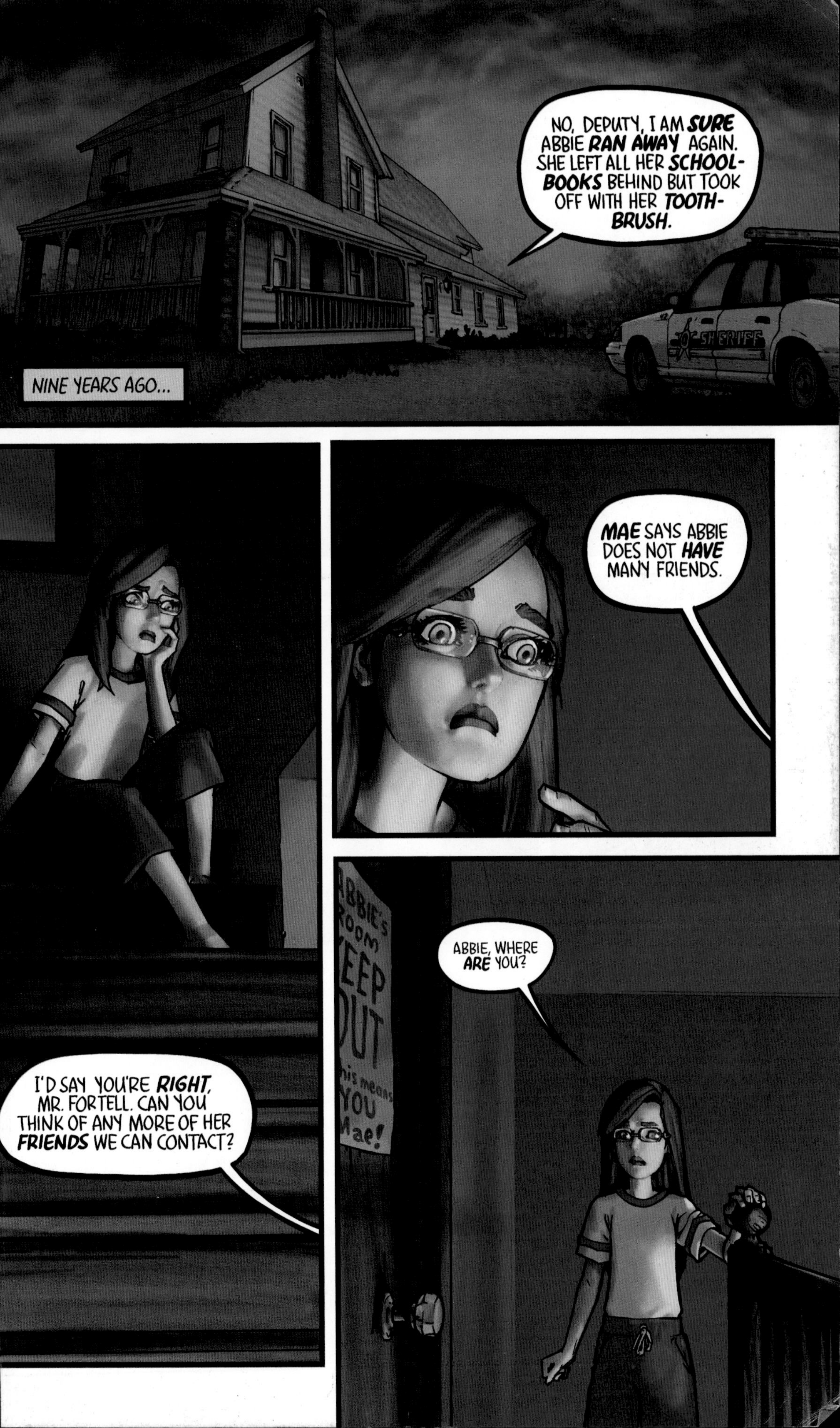

NINE YEARS AGO...
NO, DEPUTY, I AM **SURE** ABBIE **RAN AWAY** AGAIN. SHE LEFT ALL HER **SCHOOL-BOOKS** BEHIND BUT TOOK OFF WITH HER **TOOTH-BRUSH**.
SHERIFF
I'D SAY YOU'RE **RIGHT**, MR. FORTELL. CAN YOU THINK OF ANY MORE OF HER **FRIENDS** WE CAN CONTACT?
MAE SAYS ABBIE DOES NOT **HAVE** MANY FRIENDS.
YOU Mae!
ABBIE, WHERE **ARE** YOU?

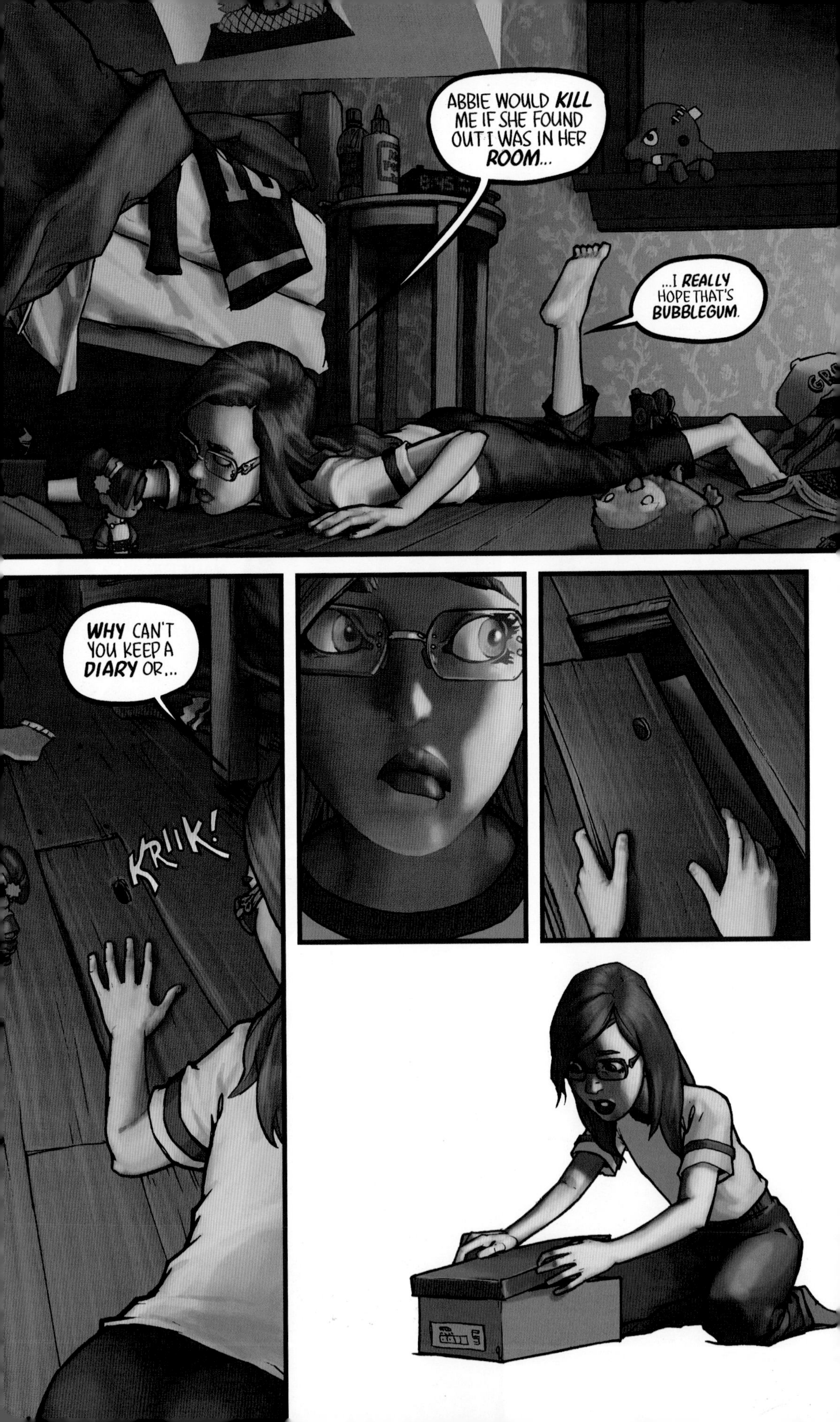
ABBIE WOULD KILL ME IF SHE FOUND OUT I WAS IN HER ROOM...
...I REALLY HOPE THAT'S BUBBLEGUM.
WHY CAN'T YOU KEEP A DIARY OR...
KRIIK!

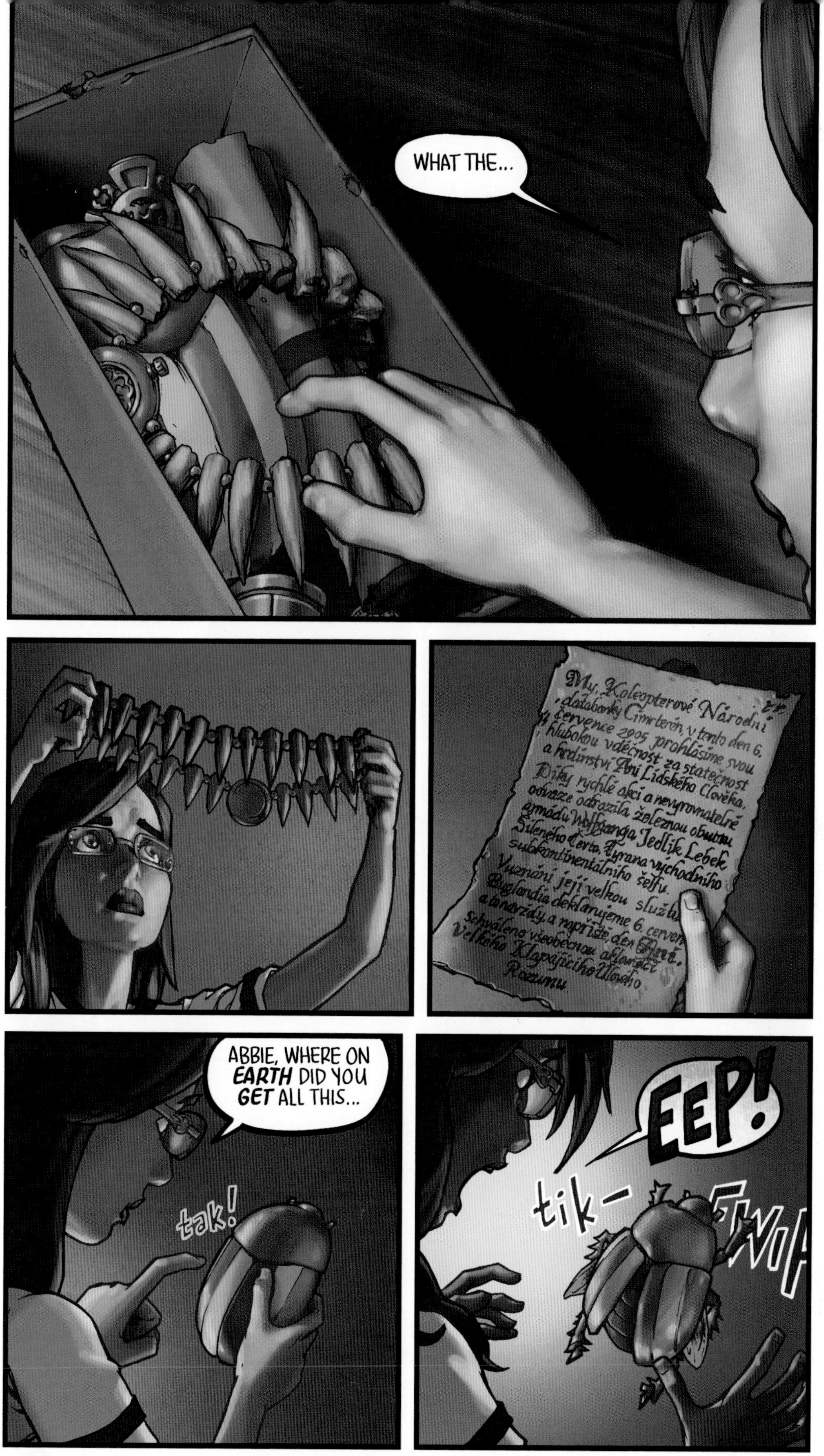
WHAT THE...
My, Koleopterové Národní
databanky Cimrterón, v tento den 6.
července 2905 prohlašime svou
hlubokou vděčnost za statečnost
a hrdinství Ani Lidského Člověka.
Díky rychlé akci a nevyrovnatelné
odvaze odrazila železnou obutou
armádu Wolfganga Jedlík Lebek
Šíleného Čerta, tyrana východního
subkontinentálního šelfu.
Vuznání její velkou služ
Buglandia deklarujeme 6. červen
a tanarzdy a napříště, den Ani.
Schváleno všeobecnou aklamací
Velkého Klapajícího Úlového
Rozumu
ABBIE, WHERE ON **EARTH** DID YOU **GET** ALL THIS...
tak!
EEP!
tik -

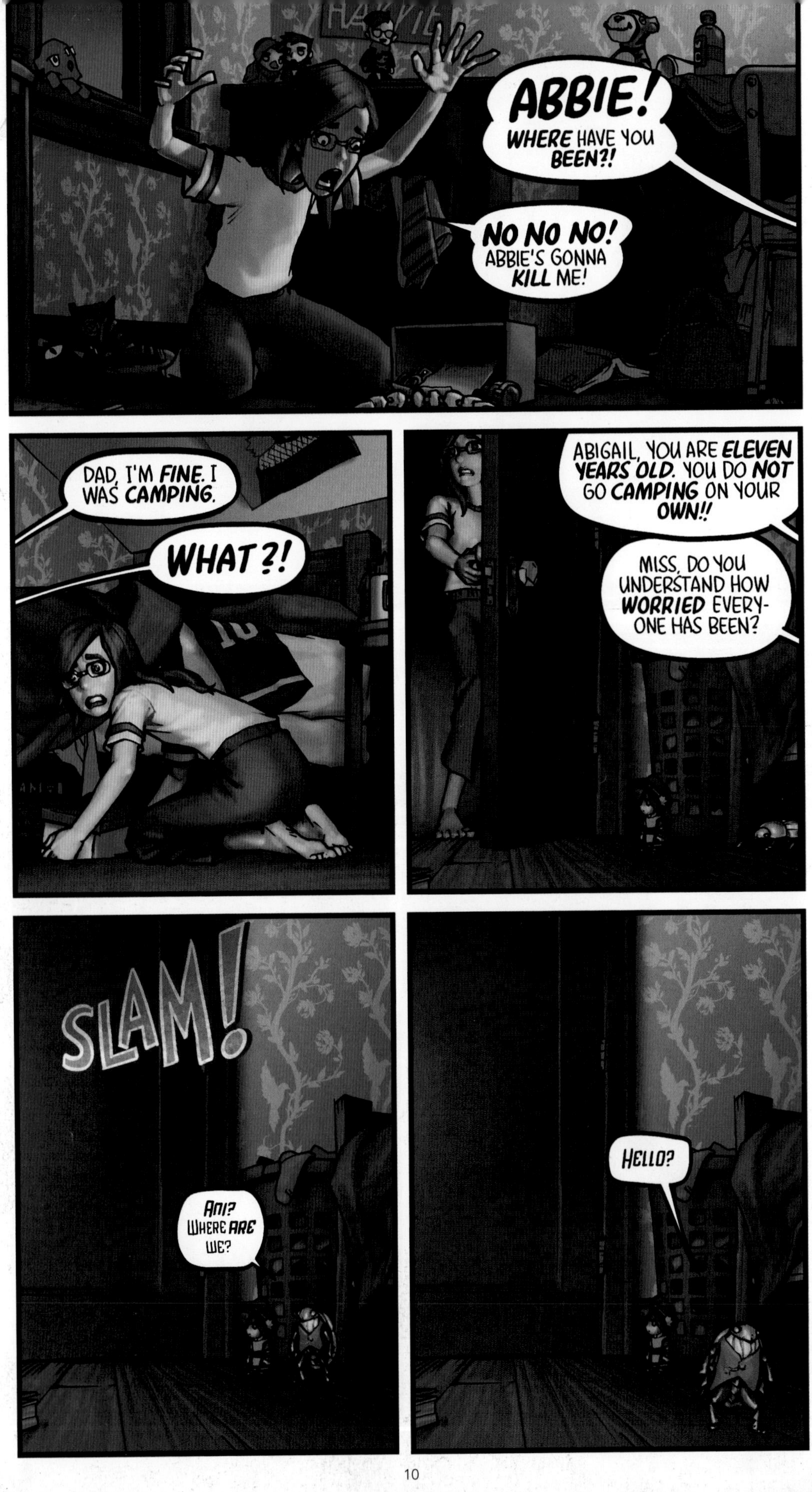
ABBIE! WHERE HAVE YOU BEEN?!
NO NO NO! ABBIE'S GONNA KILL ME!
DAD, I'M FINE. I WAS CAMPING.
WHAT?!
ABIGAIL, YOU ARE ELEVEN YEARS OLD. YOU DO NOT GO CAMPING ON YOUR OWN!!
MISS, DO YOU UNDERSTAND HOW WORRIED EVERY-ONE HAS BEEN?
SLAM!
ANI? WHERE ARE WE?
HELLO?

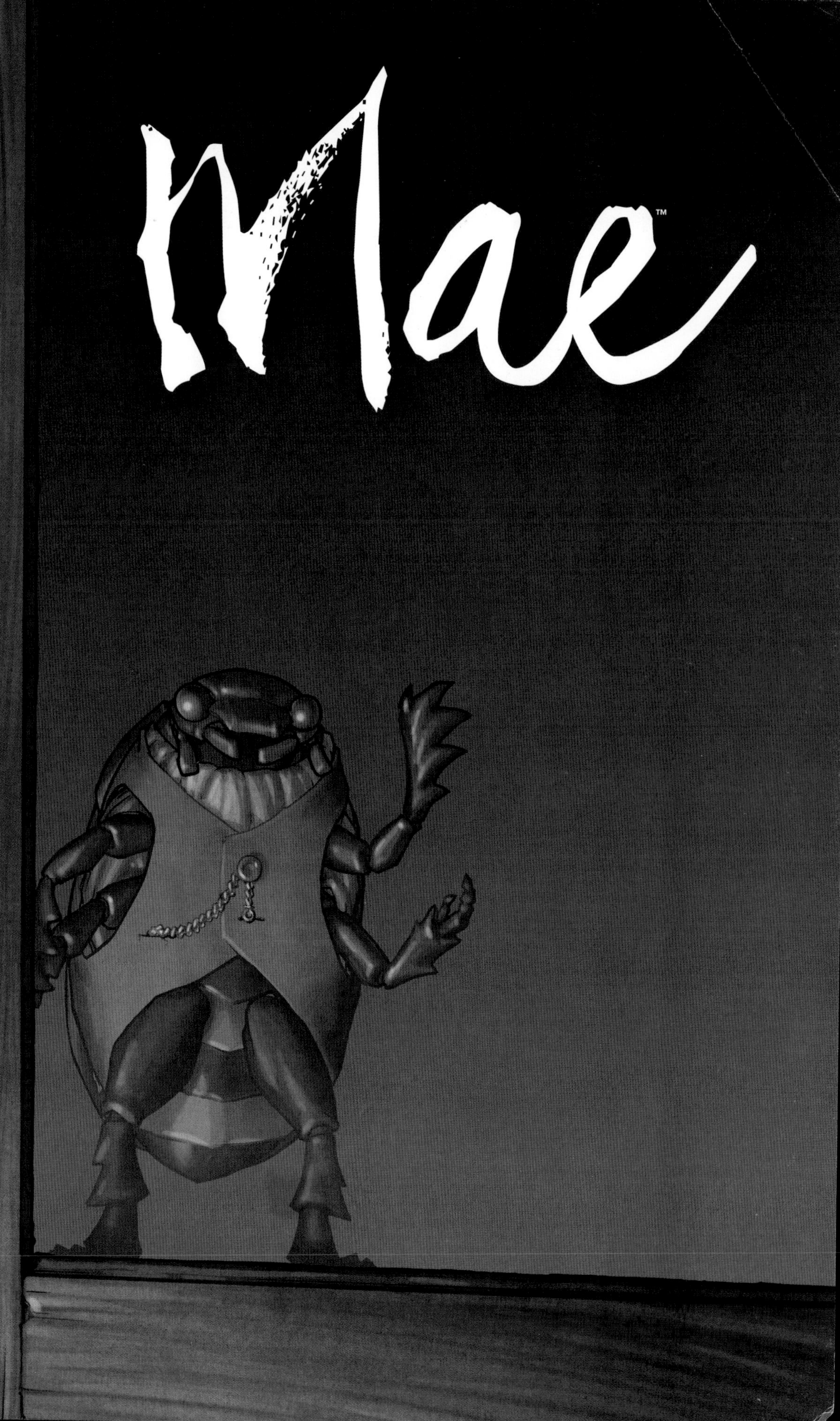
Mae™

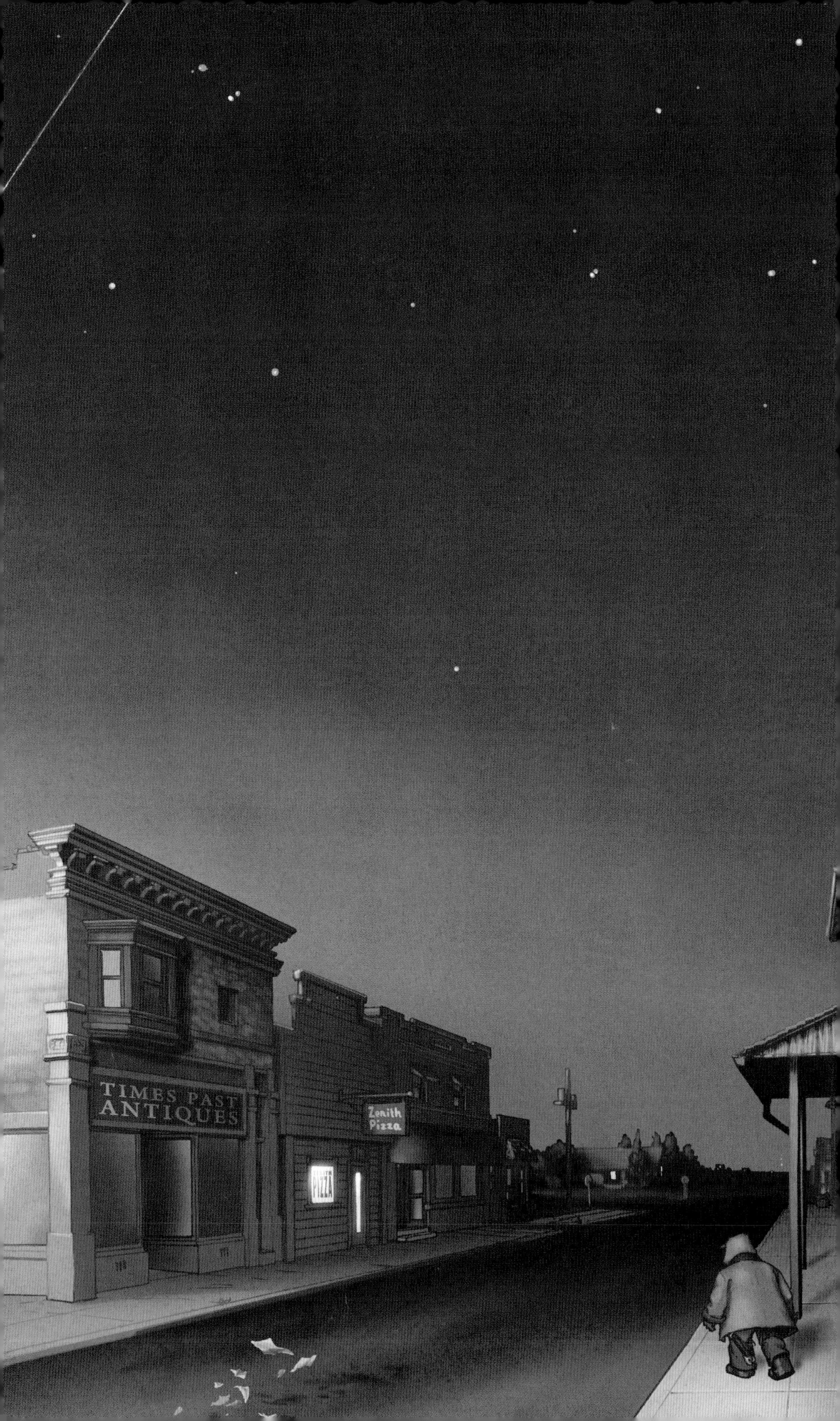
TIMES PAST
ANTIQUES
Zenith
Pizza
PIZZA

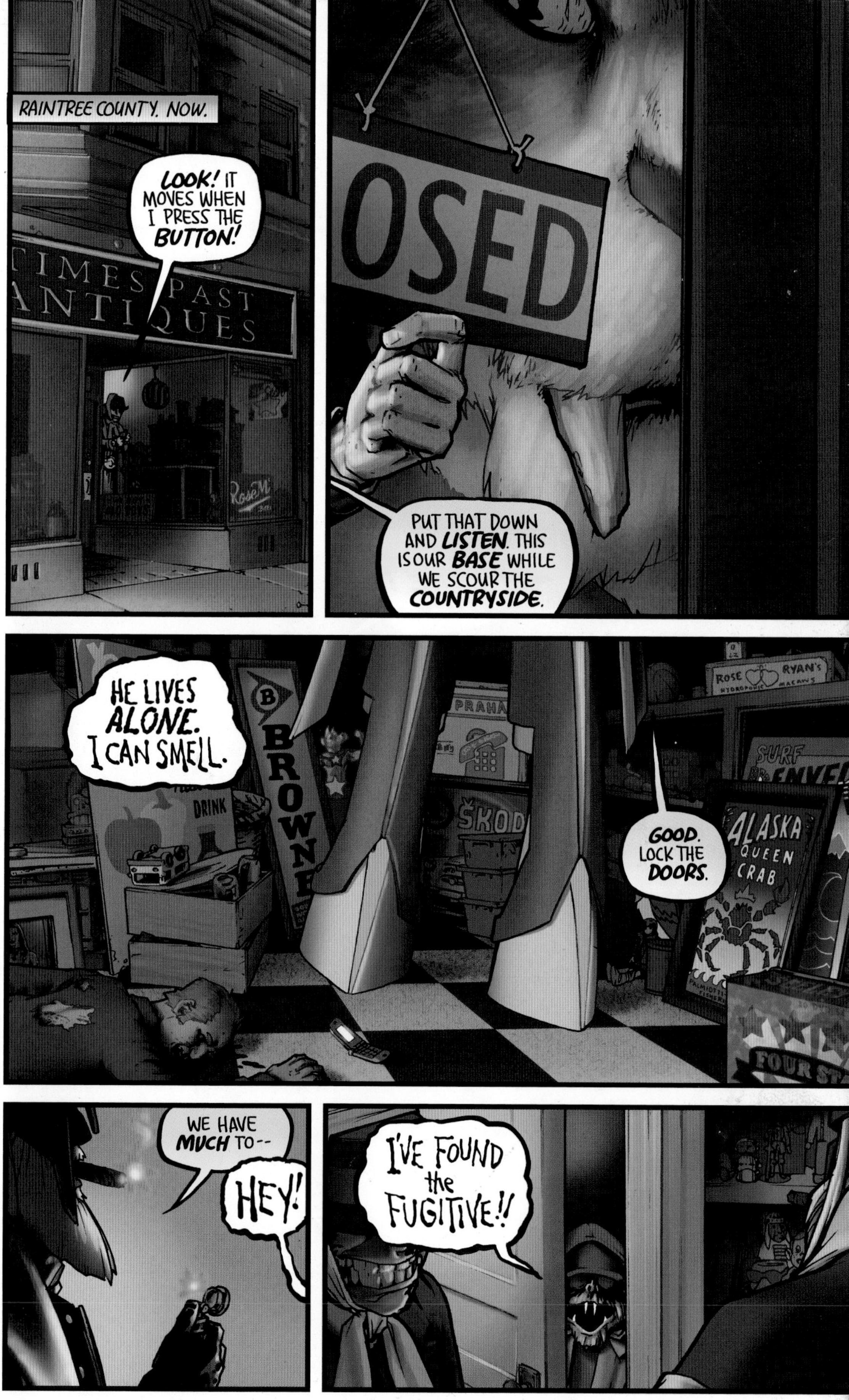
RAINTREE COUNTY. NOW.
LOOK! IT MOVES WHEN I PRESS THE BUTTON!
TIMES PAST ANTIQUES
OSED
PUT THAT DOWN AND LISTEN. THIS IS OUR BASE WHILE WE SCOUR THE COUNTRYSIDE.
HE LIVES ALONE. I CAN SMELL.
GOOD. LOCK THE DOORS.
ALASKA QUEEN CRAB
WE HAVE MUCH TO--
HEY!
I'VE FOUND the FUGITIVE!!

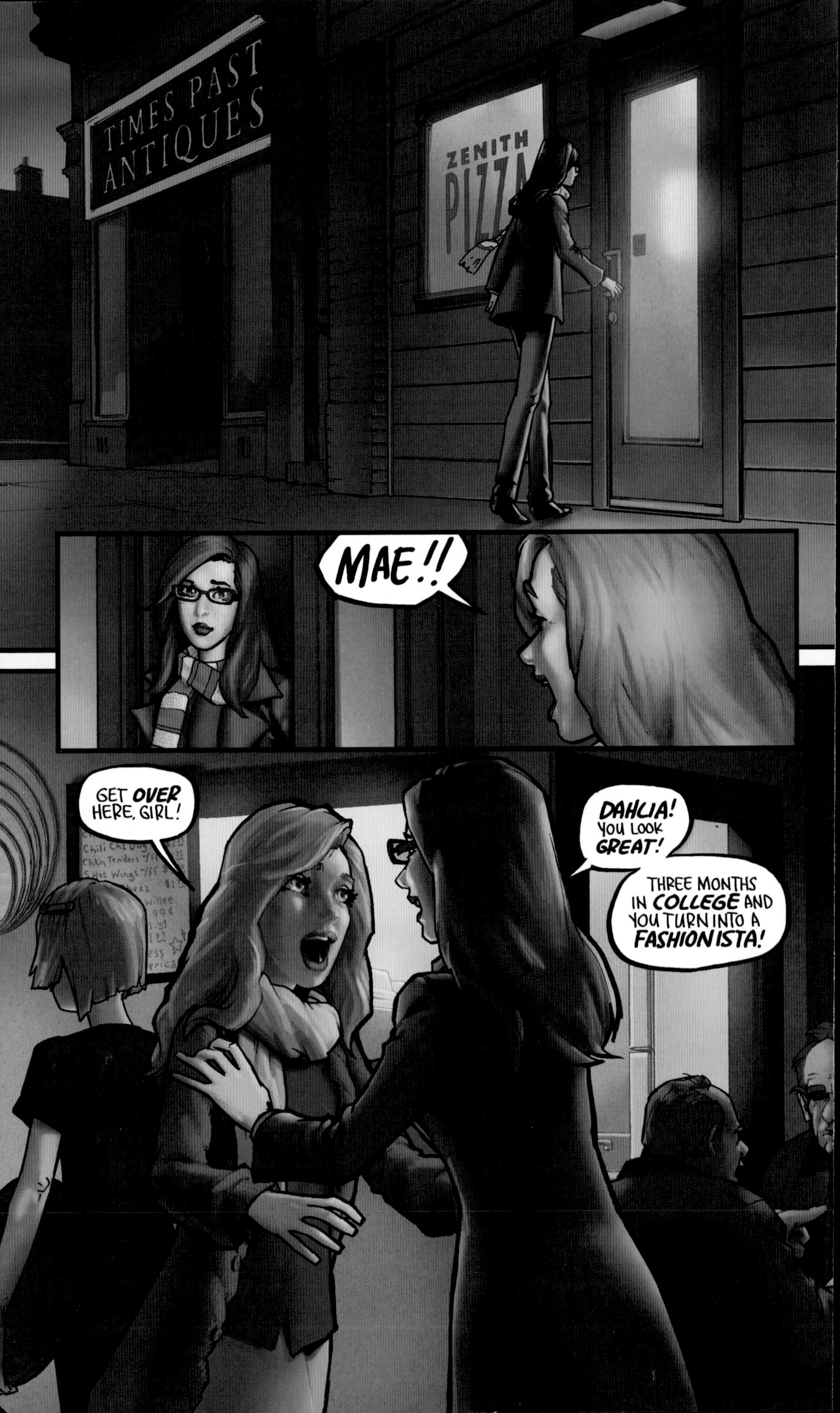
TIMES PAST ANTIQUES
ZENITH PIZZA
MAE!!
GET OVER HERE, GIRL!
DAHLIA! YOU LOOK GREAT!
THREE MONTHS IN COLLEGE AND YOU TURN INTO A FASHIONISTA!

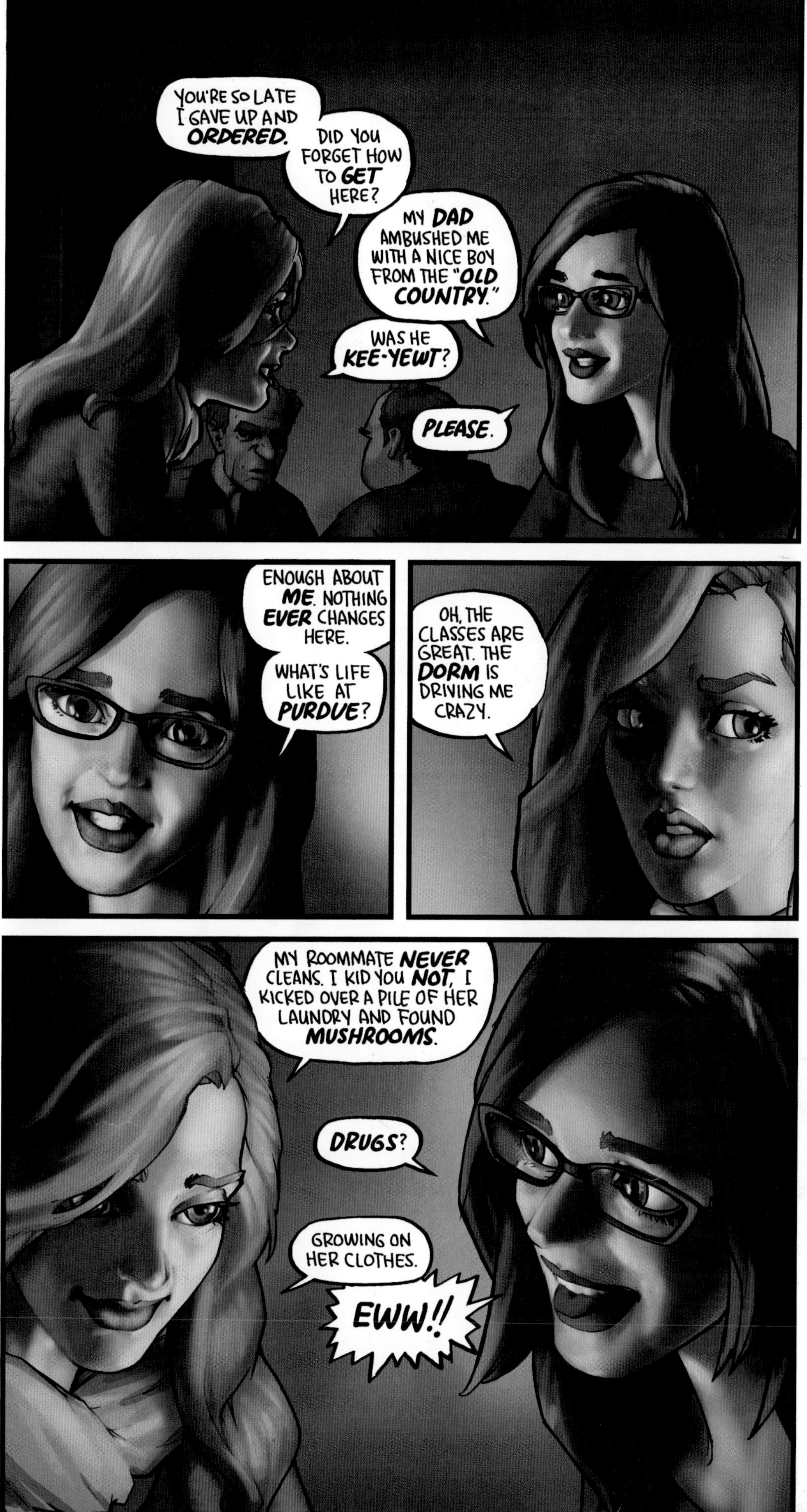
YOU'RE SO LATE I GAVE UP AND ORDERED.
DID YOU FORGET HOW TO GET HERE?
MY DAD AMBUSHED ME WITH A NICE BOY FROM THE "OLD COUNTRY."
WAS HE KEE-YEWT?
PLEASE.
ENOUGH ABOUT ME. NOTHING EVER CHANGES HERE.
WHAT'S LIFE LIKE AT PURDUE?
OH, THE CLASSES ARE GREAT. THE DORM IS DRIVING ME CRAZY.
MY ROOMMATE NEVER CLEANS. I KID YOU NOT, I KICKED OVER A PILE OF HER LAUNDRY AND FOUND MUSHROOMS.
DRUGS?
GROWING ON HER CLOTHES.
EWW!!

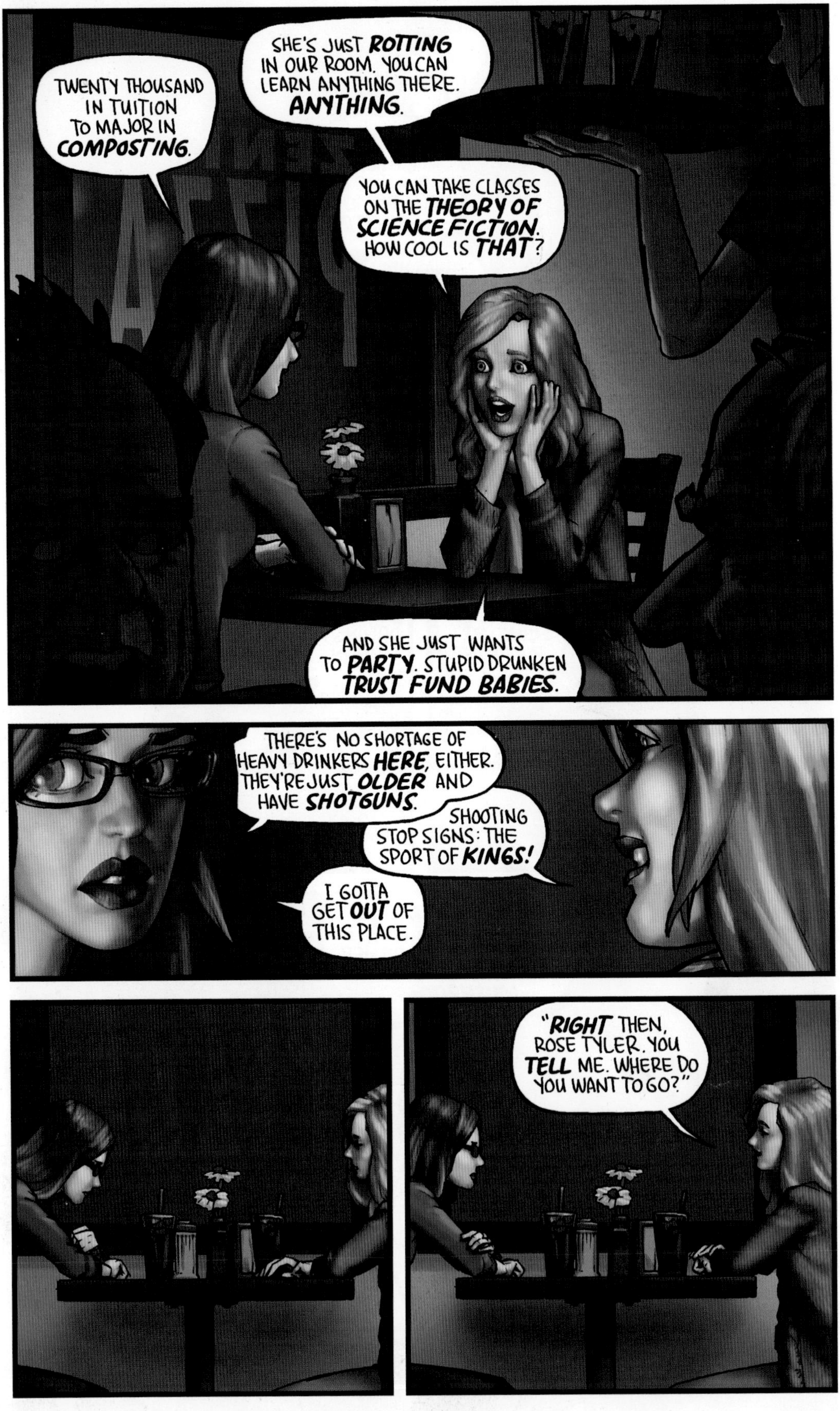
TWENTY THOUSAND IN TUITION TO MAJOR IN COMPOSTING.
SHE'S JUST ROTTING IN OUR ROOM. YOU CAN LEARN ANYTHING THERE. ANYTHING.
YOU CAN TAKE CLASSES ON THE THEORY OF SCIENCE FICTION. HOW COOL IS THAT?
AND SHE JUST WANTS TO PARTY. STUPID DRUNKEN TRUST FUND BABIES.
THERE'S NO SHORTAGE OF HEAVY DRINKERS HERE, EITHER. THEY'RE JUST OLDER AND HAVE SHOTGUNS.
SHOOTING STOP SIGNS: THE SPORT OF KINGS!
I GOTTA GET OUT OF THIS PLACE.
"RIGHT THEN, ROSE TYLER. YOU TELL ME. WHERE DO YOU WANT TO GO?"

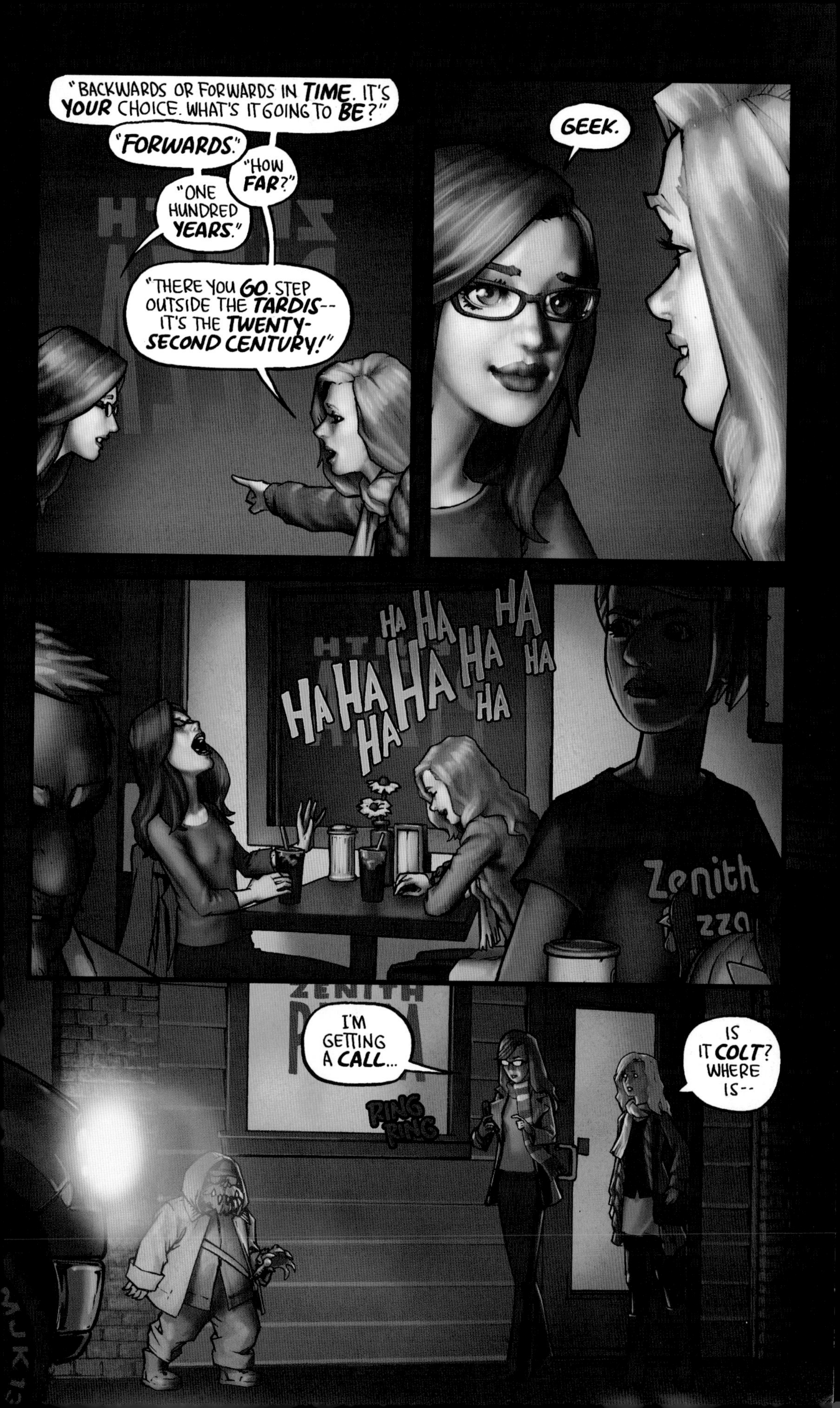
"BACKWARDS OR FORWARDS IN TIME. IT'S YOUR CHOICE. WHAT'S IT GOING TO BE?"
"FORWARDS."
"HOW FAR?"
"ONE HUNDRED YEARS."
"THERE YOU GO. STEP OUTSIDE THE TARDIS-- IT'S THE TWENTY-SECOND CENTURY!"
GEEK.
HA HA HA HA HA HA HA HA HA HA HA
Zenith
I'M GETTING A CALL...
RING RING
IS IT COLT? WHERE IS--
MJK13

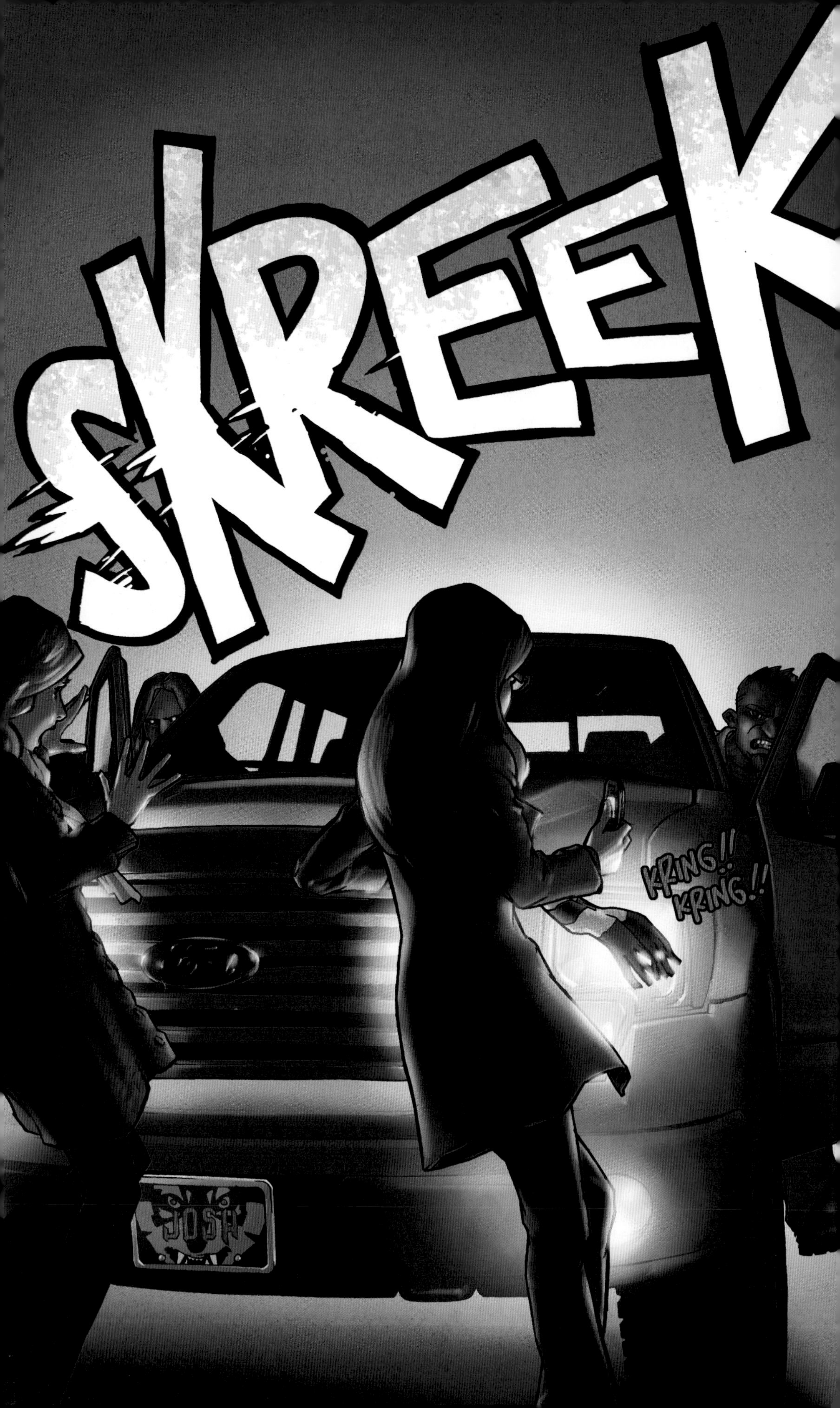
SKREEK
KRING!! KRING!!
JOSH

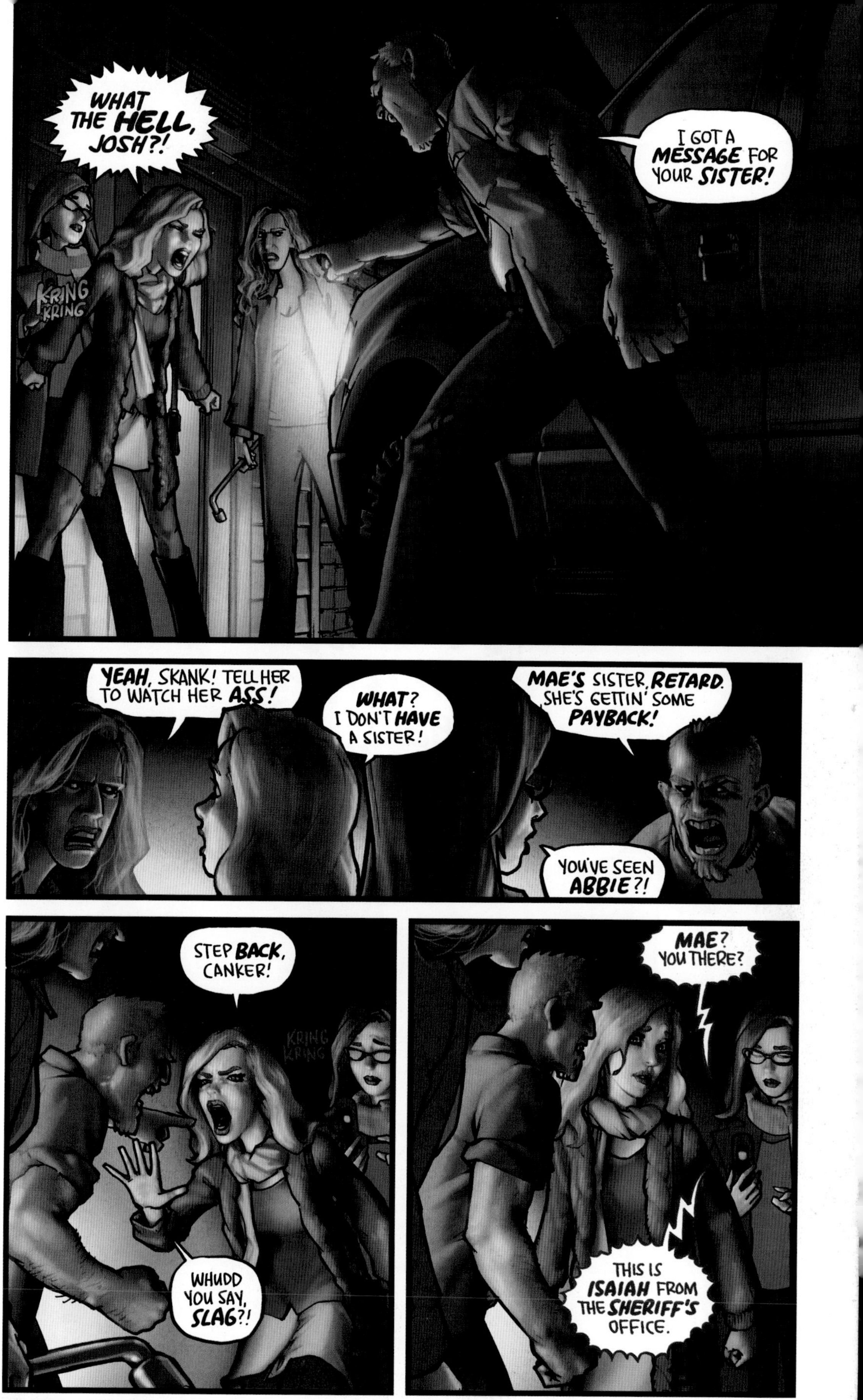

WHAT THE HELL, JOSH?!
I GOT A MESSAGE FOR YOUR SISTER!
KRING KRING
YEAH, SKANK! TELL HER TO WATCH HER ASS!
WHAT? I DON'T HAVE A SISTER!
MAE'S SISTER, RETARD. SHE'S GETTIN' SOME PAYBACK!
YOU'VE SEEN ABBIE?!
STEP BACK, CANKER!
KRING KRING
WHUDD YOU SAY, SLAG?!
MAE? YOU THERE?
THIS IS ISAIAH FROM THE SHERIFF'S OFFICE.

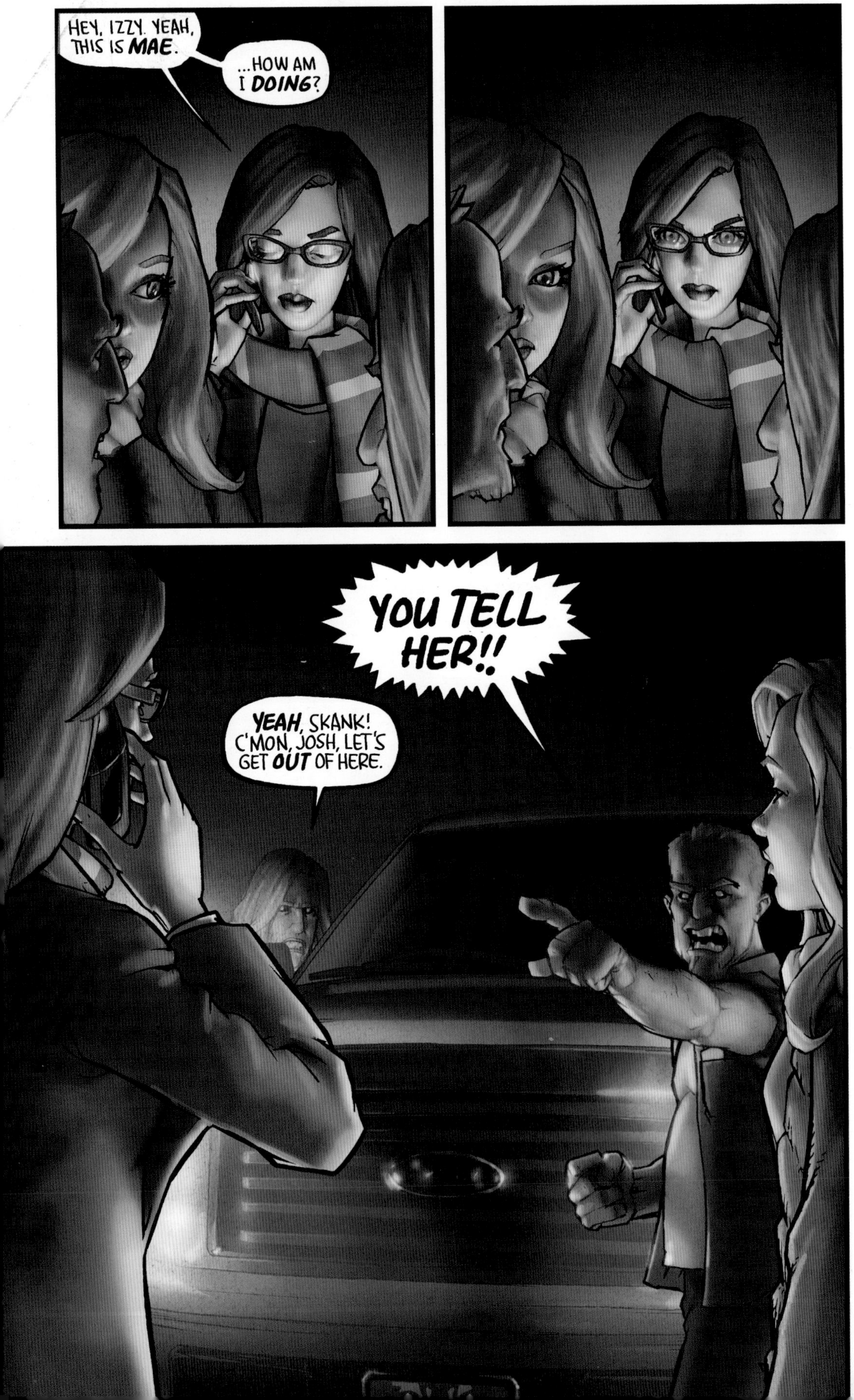
HEY, IZZY. YEAH, THIS IS MAE.
...HOW AM I DOING?
YOU TELL HER!!
YEAH, SKANK! C'MON, JOSH, LET'S GET OUT OF HERE.

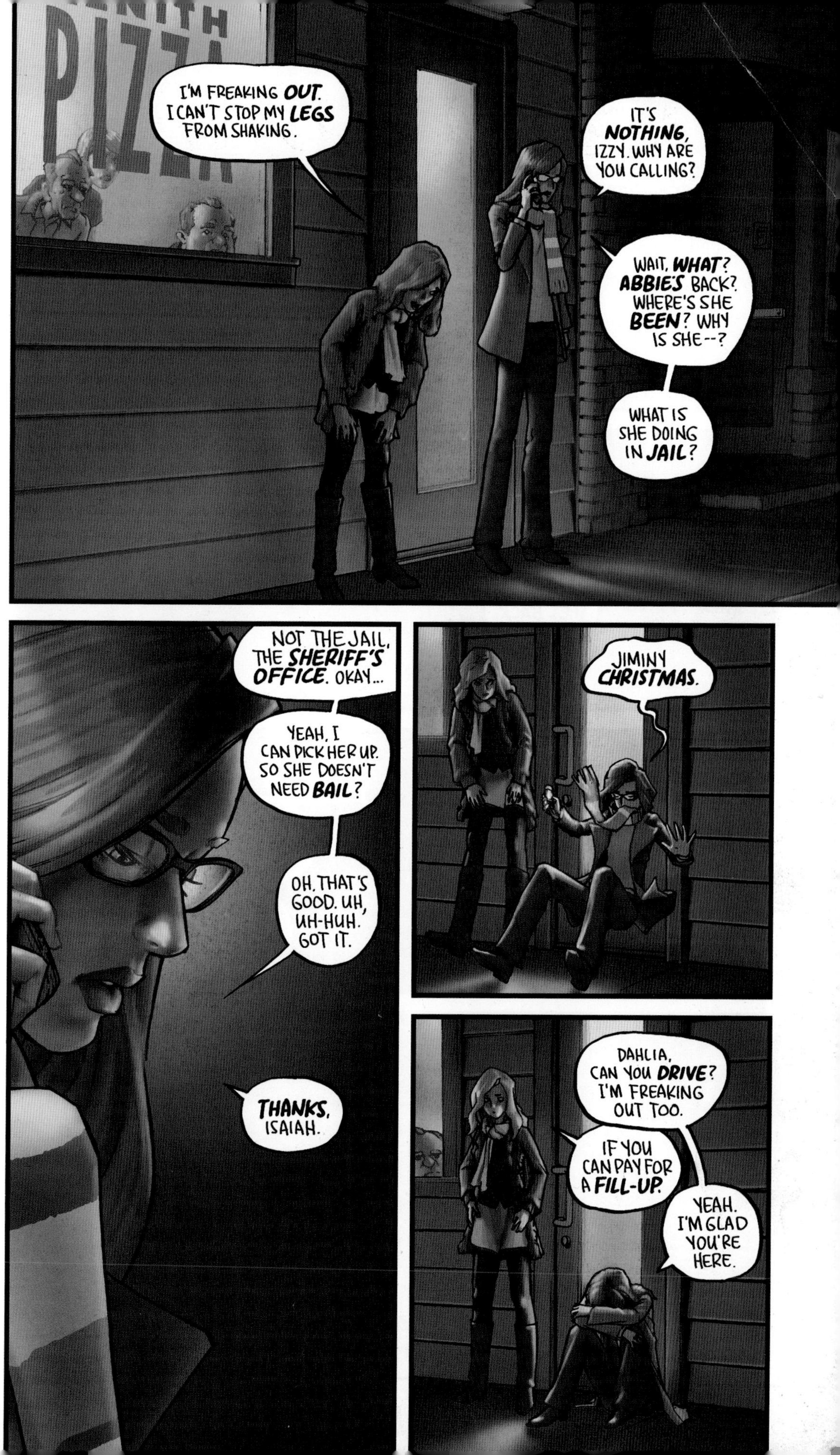
PIZZA
I'M FREAKING OUT. I CAN'T STOP MY LEGS FROM SHAKING.
IT'S NOTHING, IZZY. WHY ARE YOU CALLING?
WAIT, WHAT? ABBIE'S BACK? WHERE'S SHE BEEN? WHY IS SHE--?
WHAT IS SHE DOING IN JAIL?
NOT THE JAIL, THE SHERIFF'S OFFICE. OKAY...
YEAH, I CAN PICK HER UP. SO SHE DOESN'T NEED BAIL?
OH, THAT'S GOOD. UH, UH-HUH. GOT IT.
THANKS, ISAIAH.
JIMINY CHRISTMAS.
DAHLIA, CAN YOU DRIVE? I'M FREAKING OUT TOO.
IF YOU CAN PAY FOR A FILL-UP.
YEAH. I'M GLAD YOU'RE HERE.

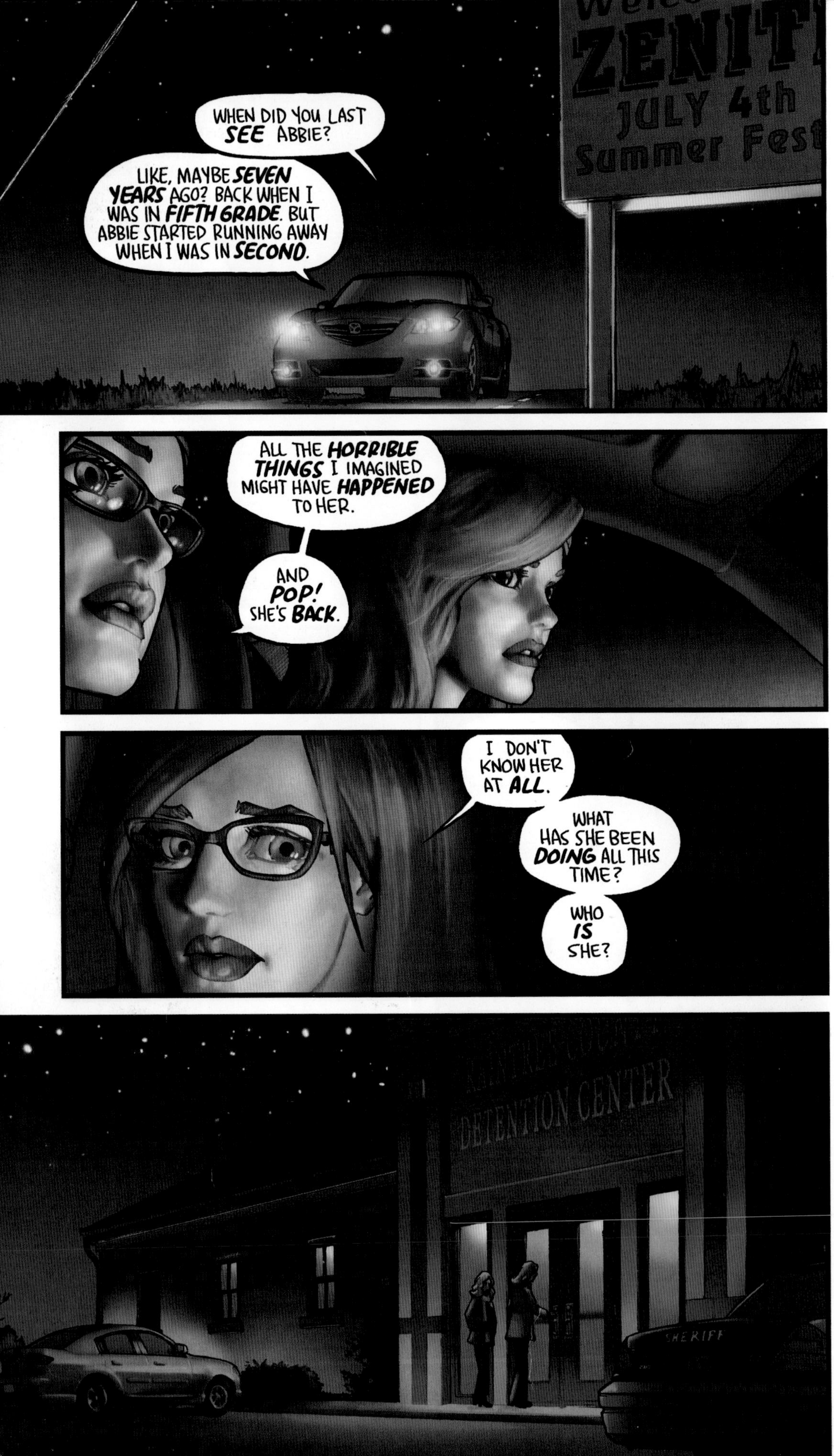

JULY 4th
WHEN DID YOU LAST SEE ABBIE?
LIKE, MAYBE SEVEN YEARS AGO? BACK WHEN I WAS IN FIFTH GRADE. BUT ABBIE STARTED RUNNING AWAY WHEN I WAS IN SECOND.
ALL THE HORRIBLE THINGS I IMAGINED MIGHT HAVE HAPPENED TO HER.
AND POP! SHE'S BACK.
I DON'T KNOW HER AT ALL.
WHAT HAS SHE BEEN DOING ALL THIS TIME?
WHO IS SHE?
DETENTION CENTER
SHERIFF

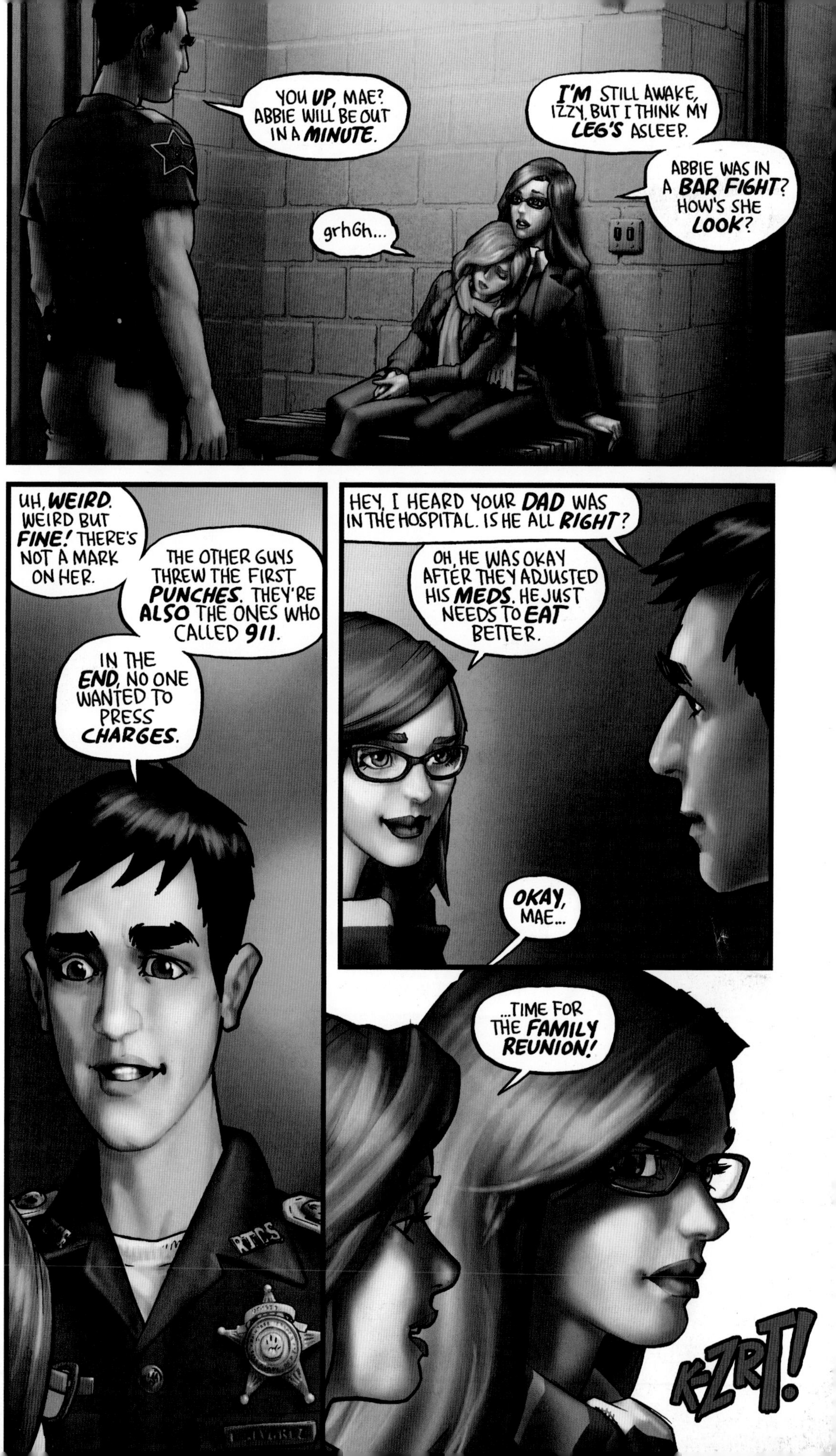

YOU UP, MAE? ABBIE WILL BE OUT IN A MINUTE.
I'M STILL AWAKE, IZZY, BUT I THINK MY LEG'S ASLEEP.
ABBIE WAS IN A BAR FIGHT? HOW'S SHE LOOK?
grhGh...
UH, WEIRD. WEIRD BUT FINE! THERE'S NOT A MARK ON HER.
THE OTHER GUYS THREW THE FIRST PUNCHES. THEY'RE ALSO THE ONES WHO CALLED 911.
IN THE END, NO ONE WANTED TO PRESS CHARGES.
HEY, I HEARD YOUR DAD WAS IN THE HOSPITAL. IS HE ALL RIGHT?
OH, HE WAS OKAY AFTER THEY ADJUSTED HIS MEDS. HE JUST NEEDS TO EAT BETTER.
OKAY, MAE...
...TIME FOR THE FAMILY REUNION!
K-ZRRT!

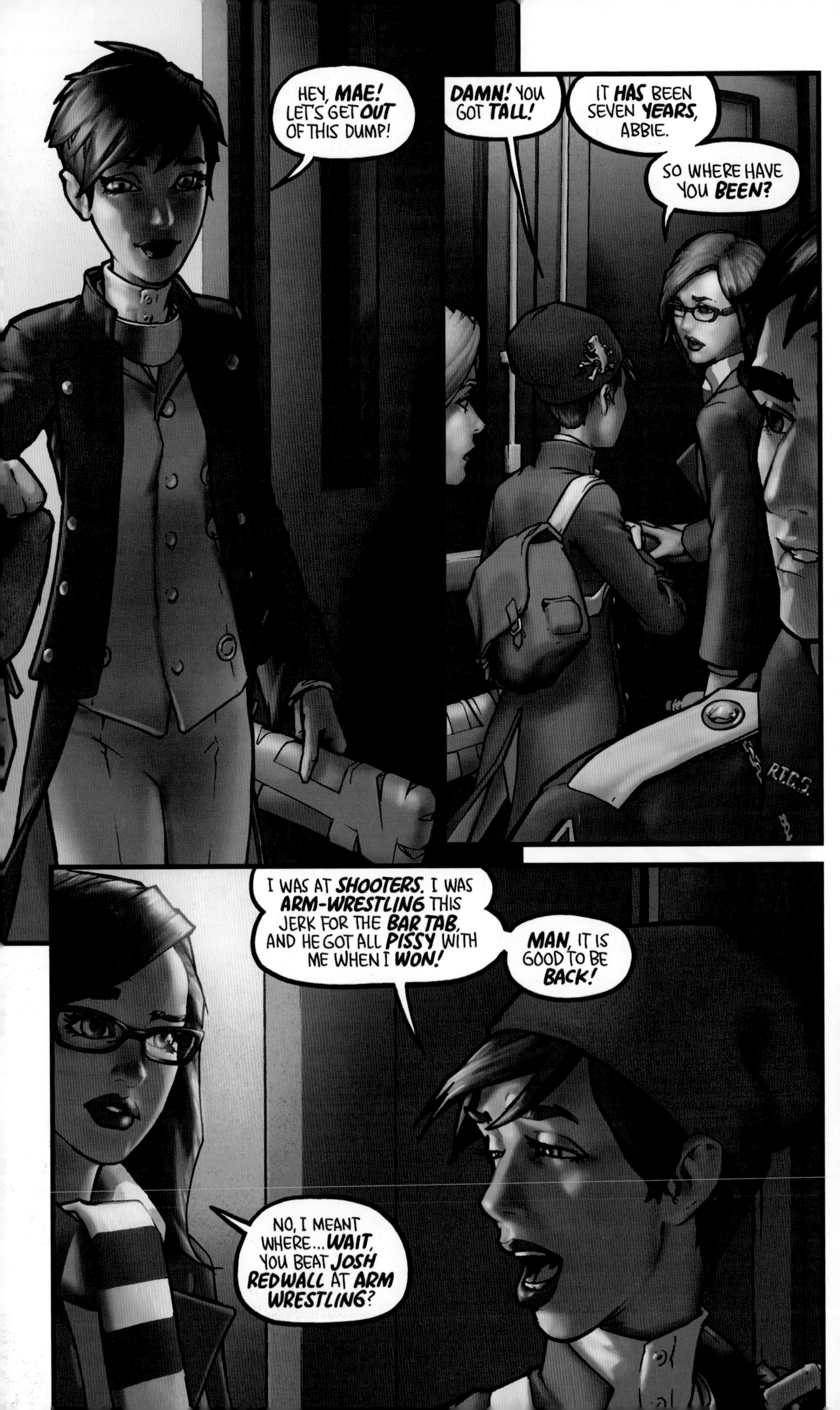

HEY, MAE! LET'S GET OUT OF THIS DUMP!
DAMN! YOU GOT TALL!
IT HAS BEEN SEVEN YEARS, ABBIE.
SO WHERE HAVE YOU BEEN?
R.I.C.S.
I WAS AT SHOOTERS. I WAS ARM-WRESTLING THIS JERK FOR THE BAR TAB, AND HE GOT ALL PISSY WITH ME WHEN I WON!
MAN, IT IS GOOD TO BE BACK!
NO, I MEANT WHERE... WAIT, YOU BEAT JOSH REDWALL AT ARM WRESTLING?

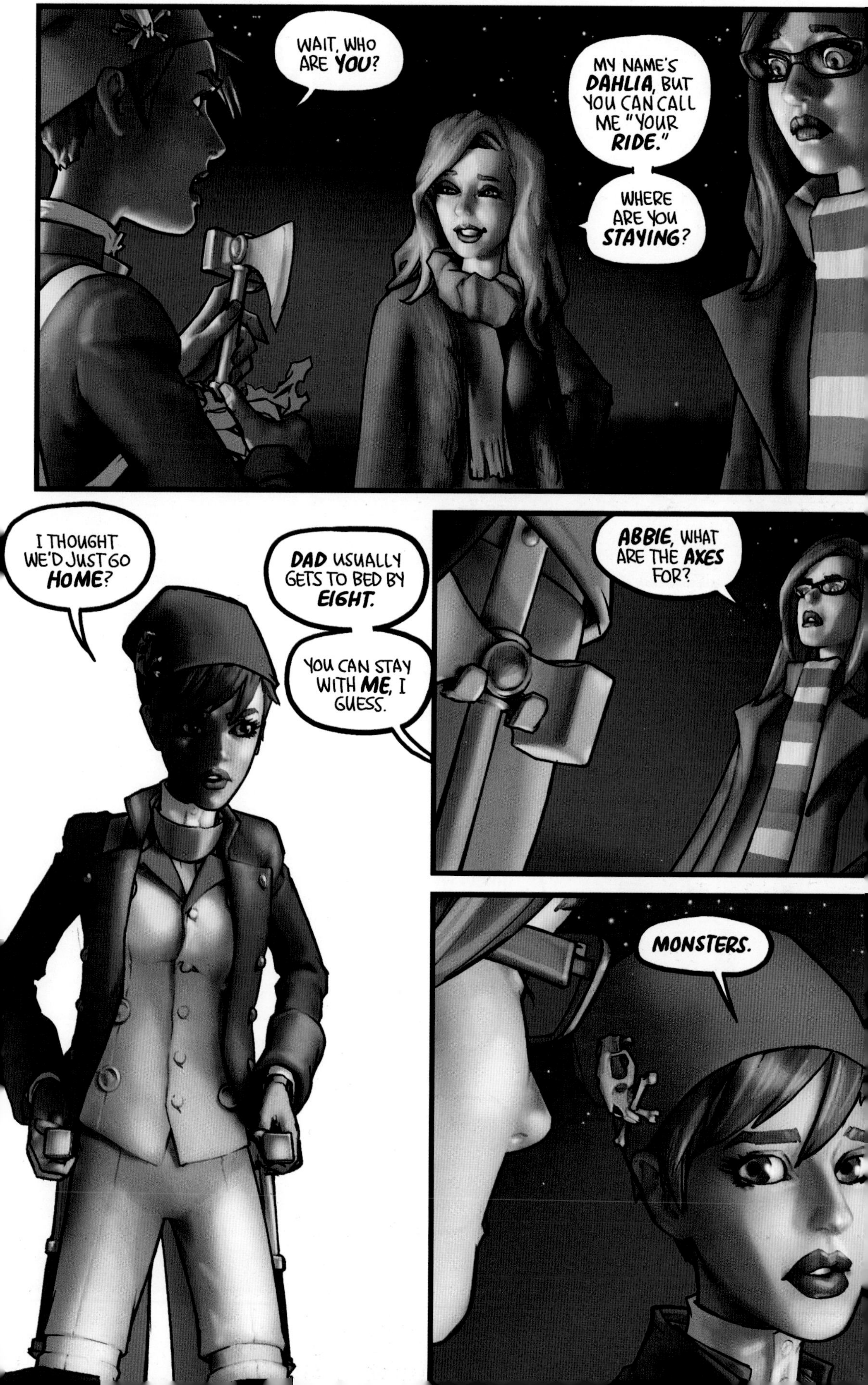
WAIT, WHO ARE YOU?
MY NAME'S DAHLIA, BUT YOU CAN CALL ME "YOUR RIDE."
WHERE ARE YOU STAYING?
I THOUGHT WE'D JUST GO HOME?
DAD USUALLY GETS TO BED BY EIGHT.
YOU CAN STAY WITH ME, I GUESS.
ABBIE, WHAT ARE THE AXES FOR?
MONSTERS.

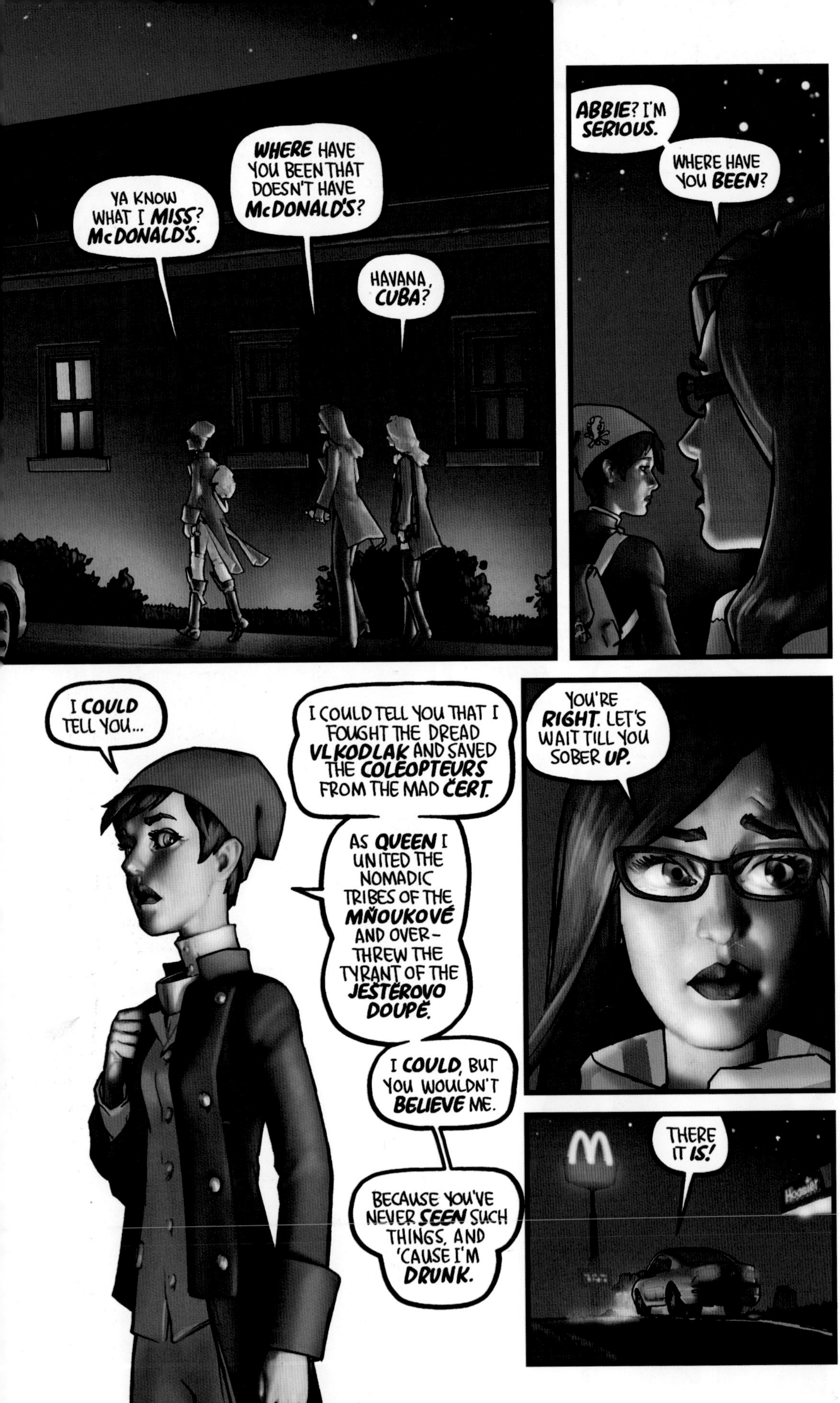
YA KNOW WHAT I MISS? McDONALD'S.
WHERE HAVE YOU BEEN THAT DOESN'T HAVE McDONALD'S?
HAVANA, CUBA?
ABBIE? I'M SERIOUS.
WHERE HAVE YOU BEEN?
I COULD TELL YOU...
I COULD TELL YOU THAT I FOUGHT THE DREAD VLKODLAK AND SAVED THE COLEOPTEURS FROM THE MAD ČERT.
AS QUEEN I UNITED THE NOMADIC TRIBES OF THE MŇOUKOVÉ AND OVER-THREW THE TYRANT OF THE JEŠTĚROVO DOUPĚ.
I COULD, BUT YOU WOULDN'T BELIEVE ME.
BECAUSE YOU'VE NEVER SEEN SUCH THINGS, AND 'CAUSE I'M DRUNK.
YOU'RE RIGHT. LET'S WAIT TILL YOU SOBER UP.
THERE IT IS!

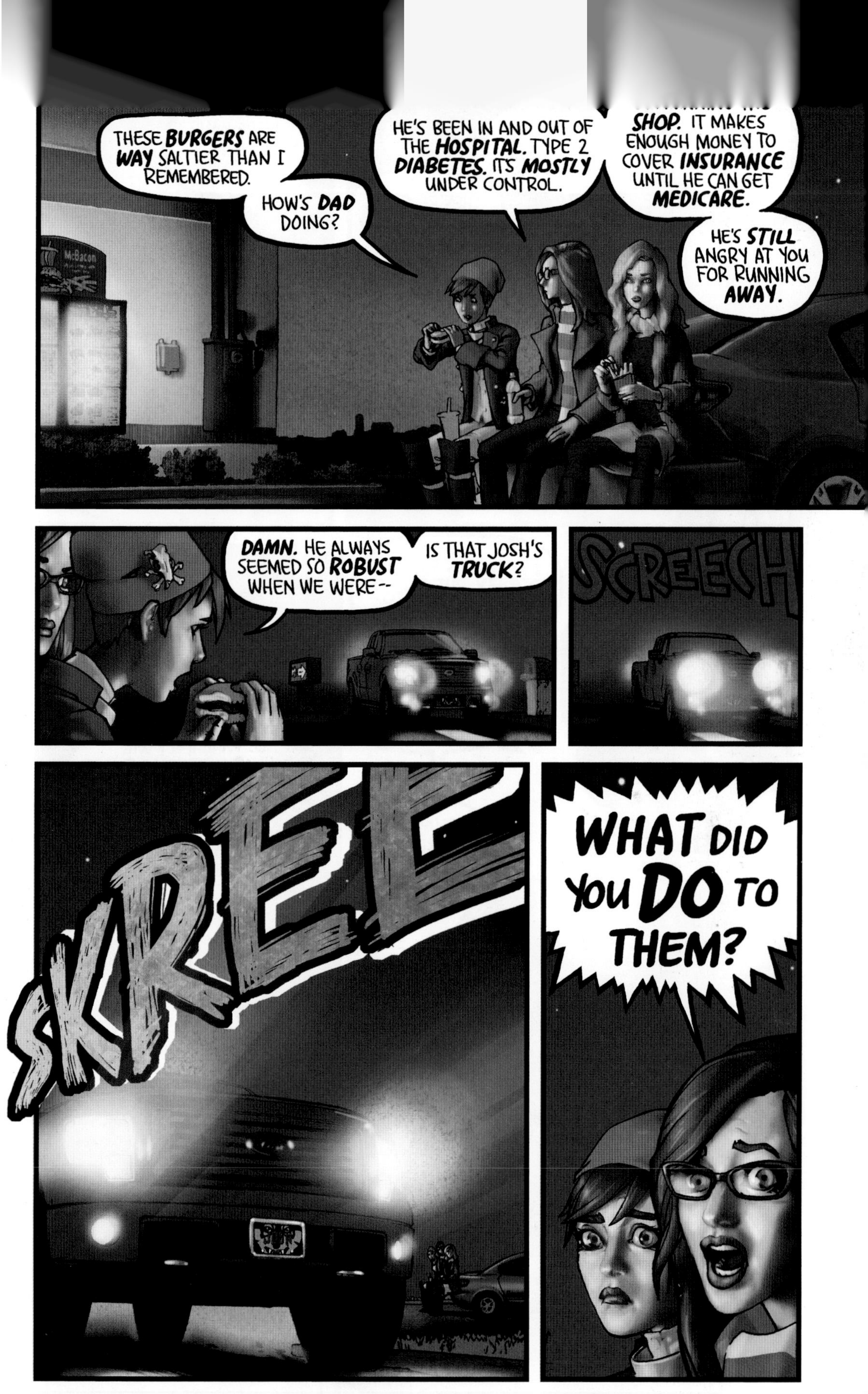
THESE BURGERS ARE WAY SALTIER THAN I REMEMBERED.
McBacon
HOW'S DAD DOING?
HE'S BEEN IN AND OUT OF THE HOSPITAL. TYPE 2 DIABETES. IT'S MOSTLY UNDER CONTROL.
SHOP. IT MAKES ENOUGH MONEY TO COVER INSURANCE UNTIL HE CAN GET MEDICARE.
HE'S STILL ANGRY AT YOU FOR RUNNING AWAY.
DAMN. HE ALWAYS SEEMED SO ROBUST WHEN WE WERE--
IS THAT JOSH'S TRUCK?
SCREECH
SKREE
WHAT DID YOU DO TO THEM?

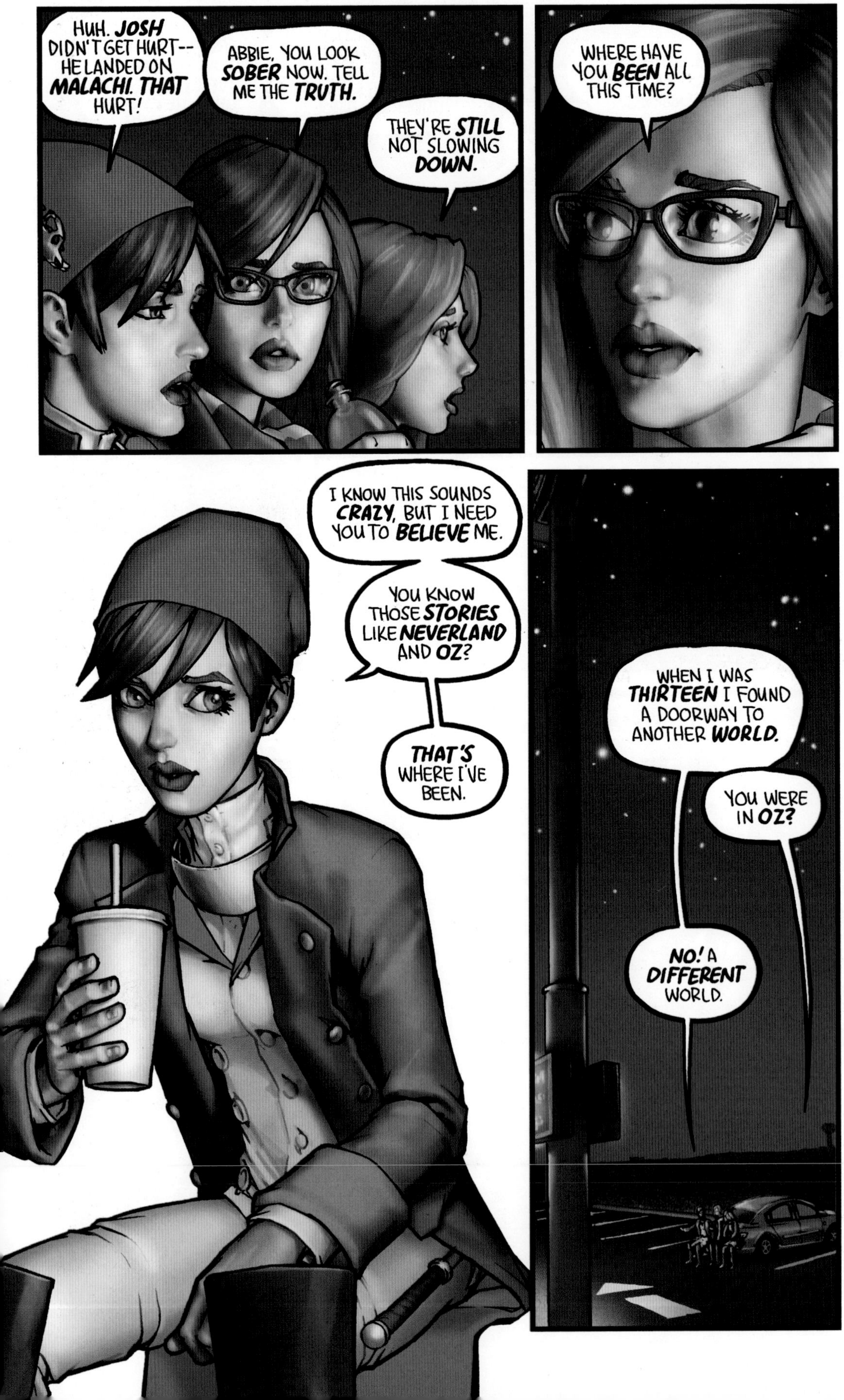
HUH. JOSH DIDN'T GET HURT-- HE LANDED ON MALACHI. THAT HURT!
ABBIE, YOU LOOK SOBER NOW. TELL ME THE TRUTH.
THEY'RE STILL NOT SLOWING DOWN.
WHERE HAVE YOU BEEN ALL THIS TIME?
I KNOW THIS SOUNDS CRAZY, BUT I NEED YOU TO BELIEVE ME.
YOU KNOW THOSE STORIES LIKE NEVERLAND AND OZ?
THAT'S WHERE I'VE BEEN.
WHEN I WAS THIRTEEN I FOUND A DOORWAY TO ANOTHER WORLD.
YOU WERE IN OZ?
NO! A DIFFERENT WORLD.

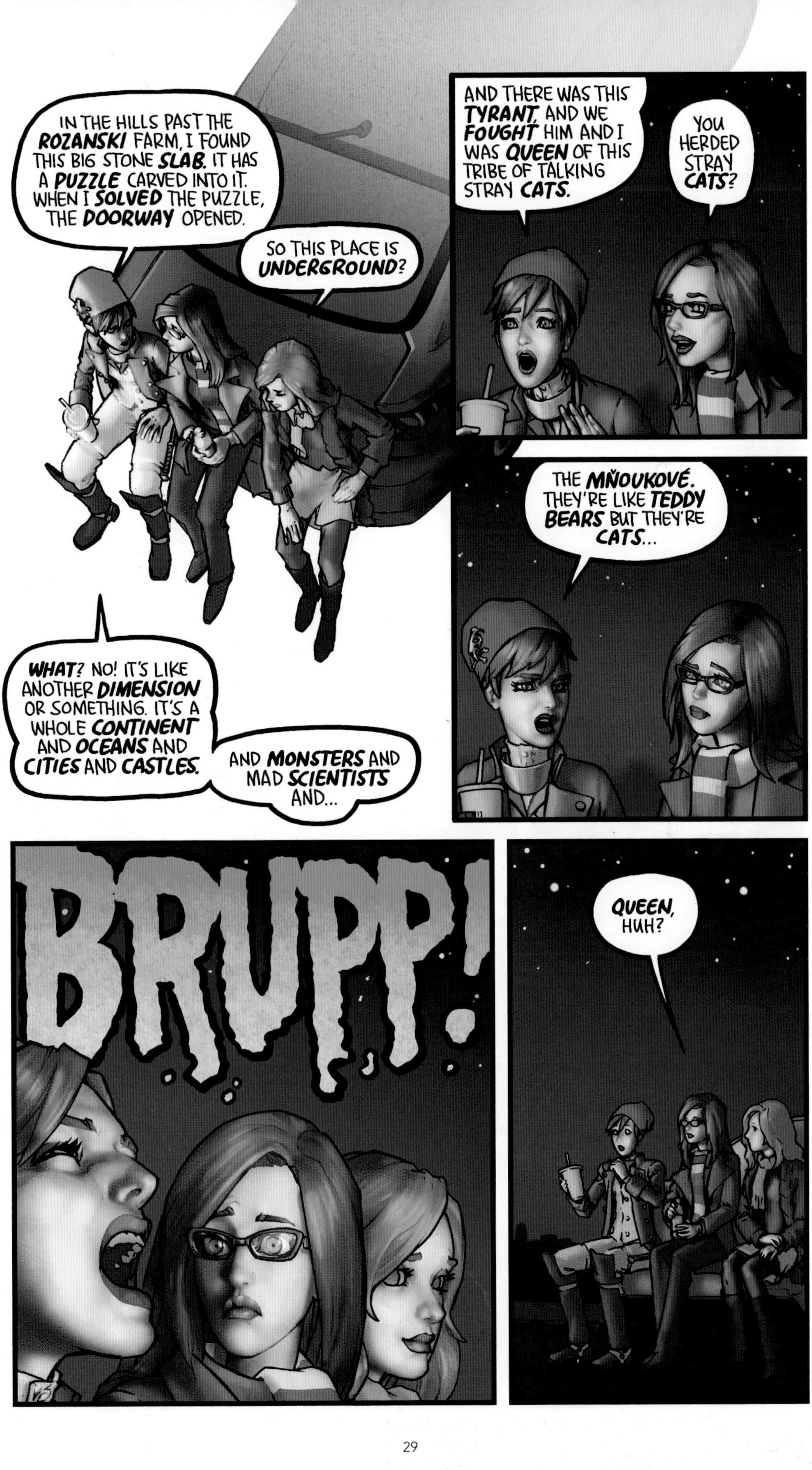
IN THE HILLS PAST THE ROZANSKI FARM, I FOUND THIS BIG STONE SLAB. IT HAS A PUZZLE CARVED INTO IT. WHEN I SOLVED THE PUZZLE, THE DOORWAY OPENED.
SO THIS PLACE IS UNDERGROUND?
WHAT? NO! IT'S LIKE ANOTHER DIMENSION OR SOMETHING. IT'S A WHOLE CONTINENT AND OCEANS AND CITIES AND CASTLES.
AND MONSTERS AND MAD SCIENTISTS AND...
AND THERE WAS THIS TYRANT, AND WE FOUGHT HIM AND I WAS QUEEN OF THIS TRIBE OF TALKING STRAY CATS.
YOU HERDED STRAY CATS?
THE MŇOUKOVÉ. THEY'RE LIKE TEDDY BEARS BUT THEY'RE CATS...
BRUPP!
QUEEN, HUH?

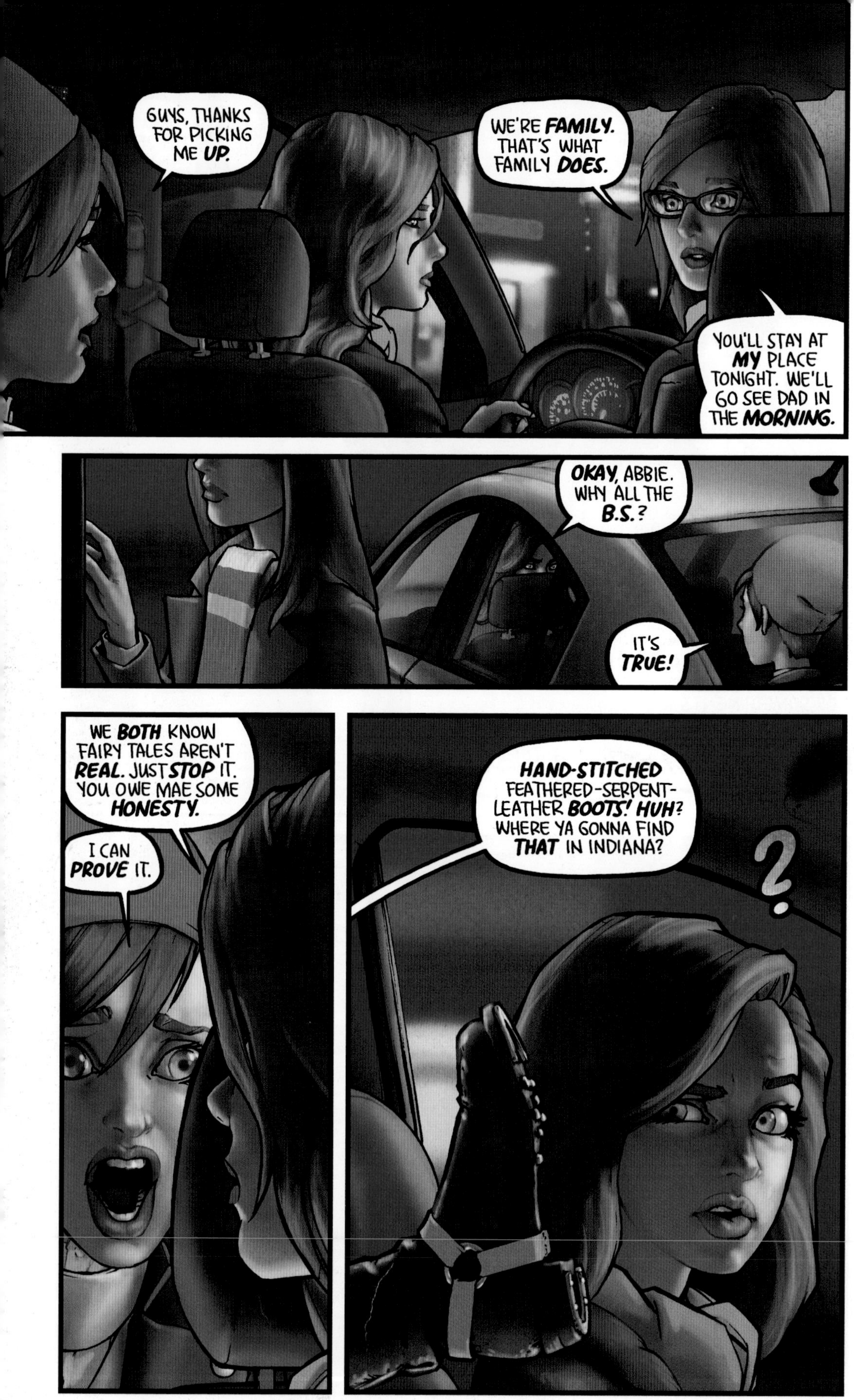
GUYS, THANKS FOR PICKING ME UP.
WE'RE FAMILY. THAT'S WHAT FAMILY DOES.
YOU'LL STAY AT MY PLACE TONIGHT. WE'LL GO SEE DAD IN THE MORNING.
OKAY, ABBIE. WHY ALL THE B.S.?
IT'S TRUE!
WE BOTH KNOW FAIRY TALES AREN'T REAL. JUST STOP IT. YOU OWE MAE SOME HONESTY.
I CAN PROVE IT.
HAND-STITCHED FEATHERED-SERPENT-LEATHER BOOTS! HUH? WHERE YA GONNA FIND THAT IN INDIANA?
?

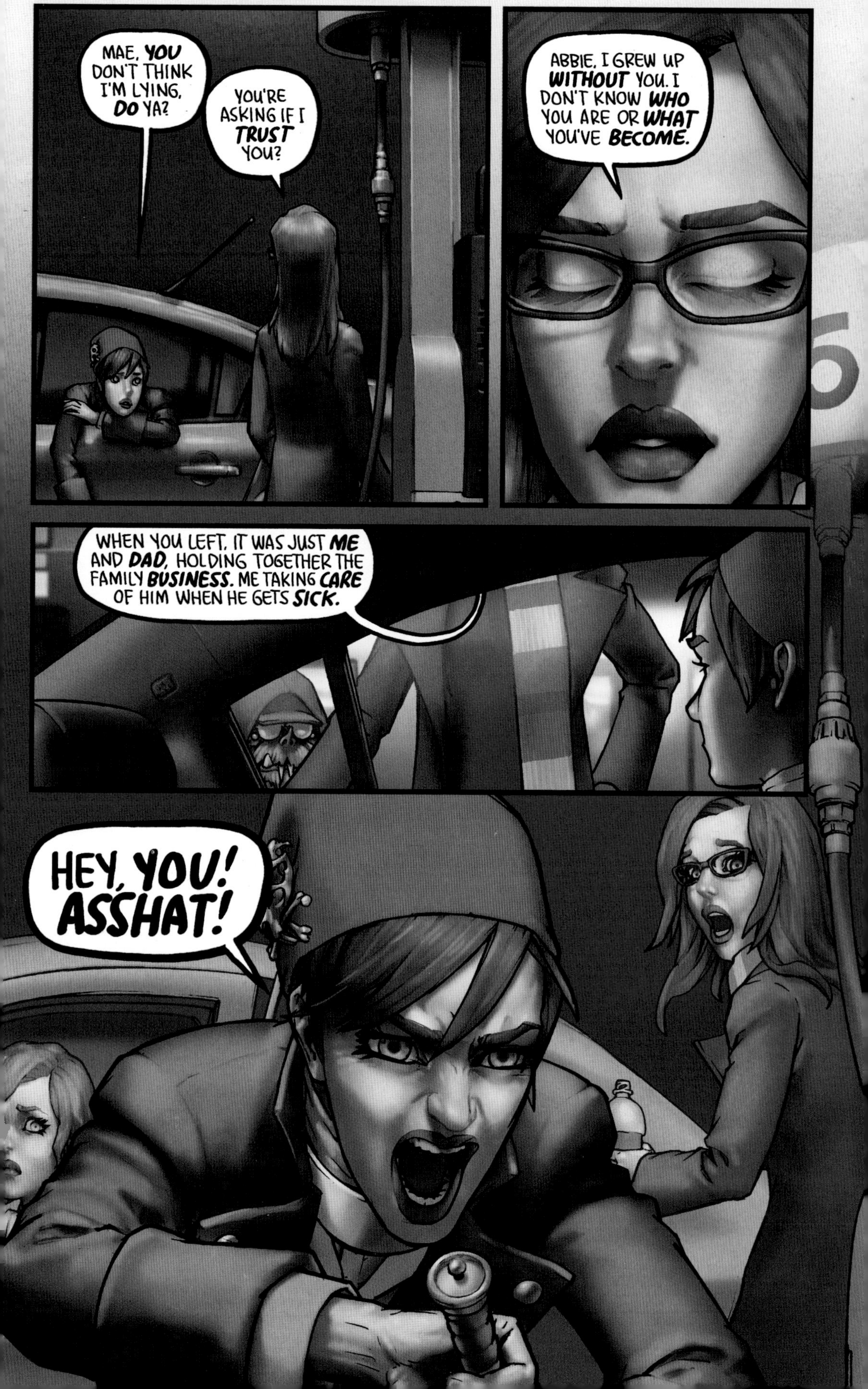
MAE, YOU DON'T THINK I'M LYING, DO YA?
YOU'RE ASKING IF I TRUST YOU?
ABBIE, I GREW UP WITHOUT YOU. I DON'T KNOW WHO YOU ARE OR WHAT YOU'VE BECOME.
WHEN YOU LEFT, IT WAS JUST ME AND DAD, HOLDING TOGETHER THE FAMILY BUSINESS. ME TAKING CARE OF HIM WHEN HE GETS SICK.
HEY, YOU! ASSHAT!

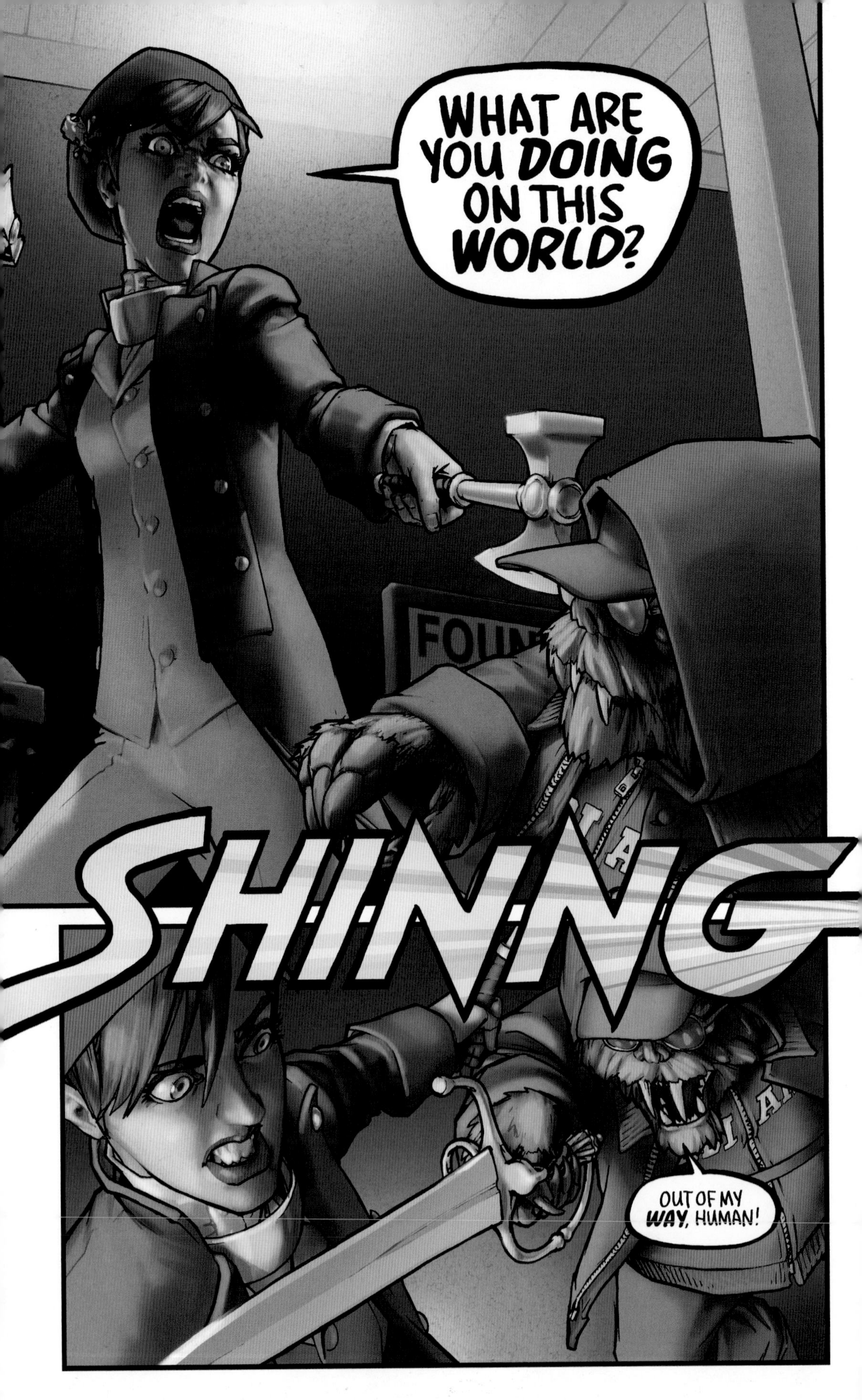
WHAT ARE YOU DOING ON THIS WORLD?
SHING
OUT OF MY WAY, HUMAN!

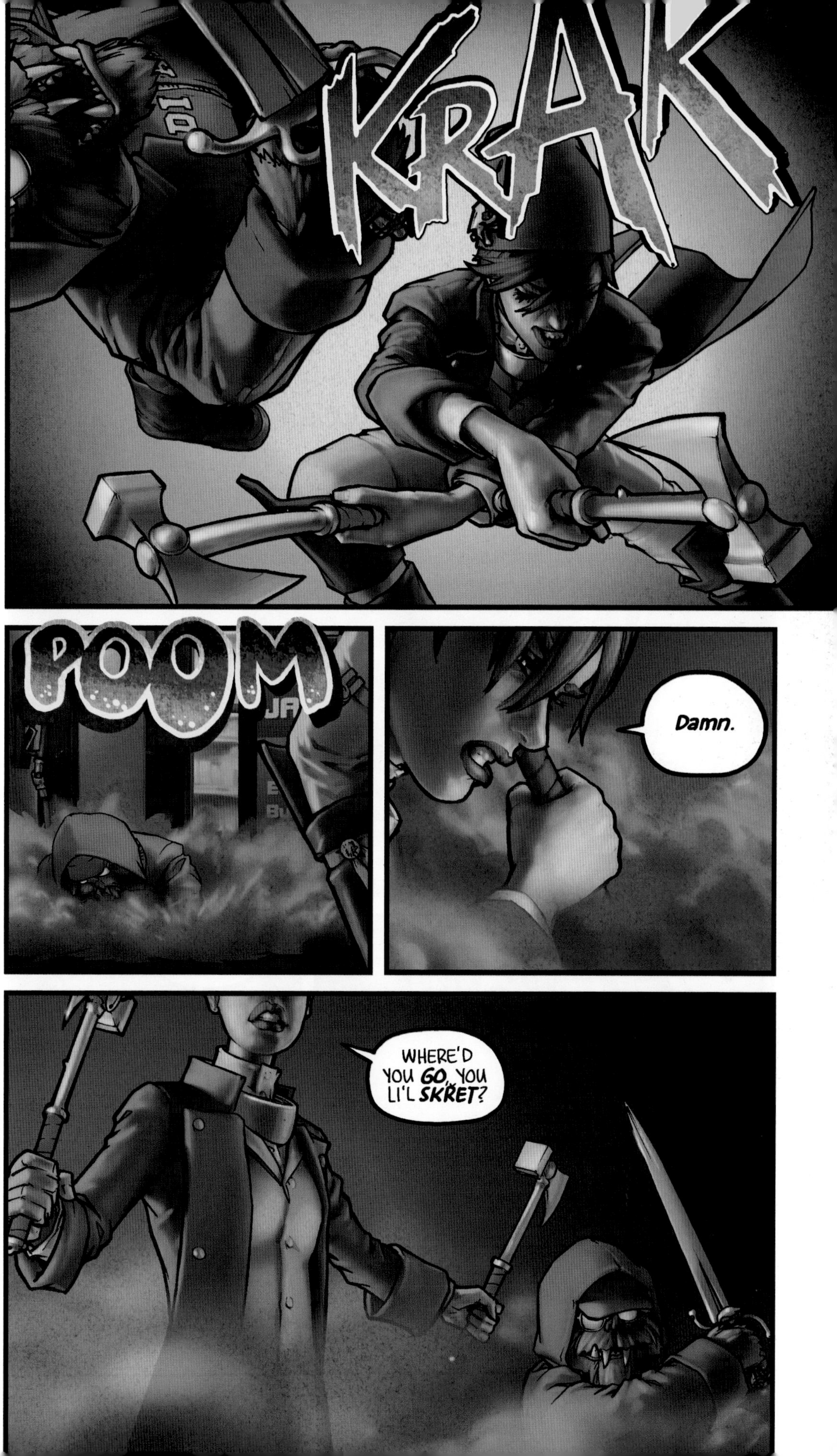
KRAK
POOM
Damn.
WHERE'D YOU GO, YOU LI'L SKRET?

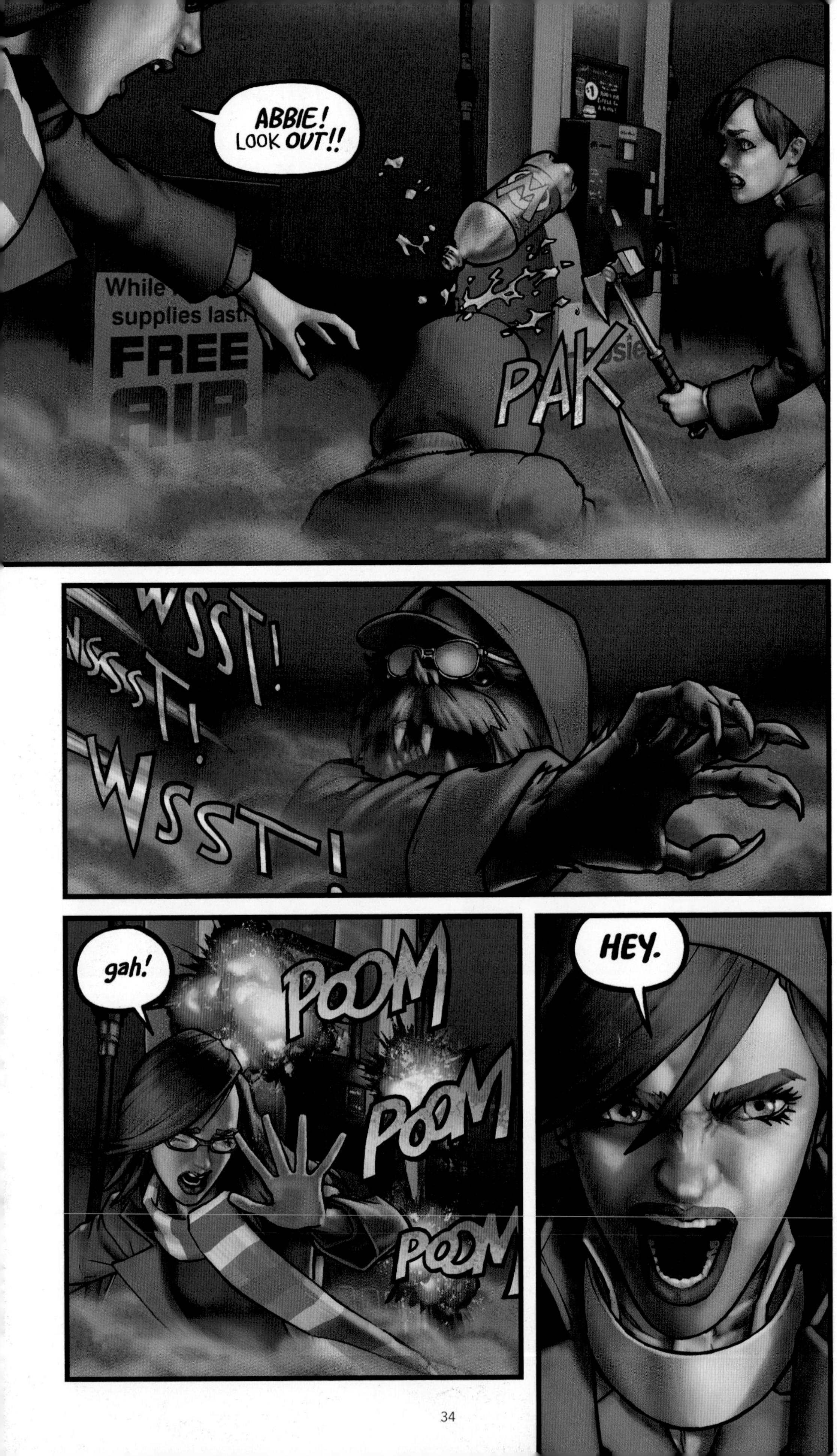
ABBIE! LOOK OUT!!
While supplies last!
FREE AIR
PAK
WSST!
WSSST!
WSST!
gah!
POOM
POOM
POOM
HEY.

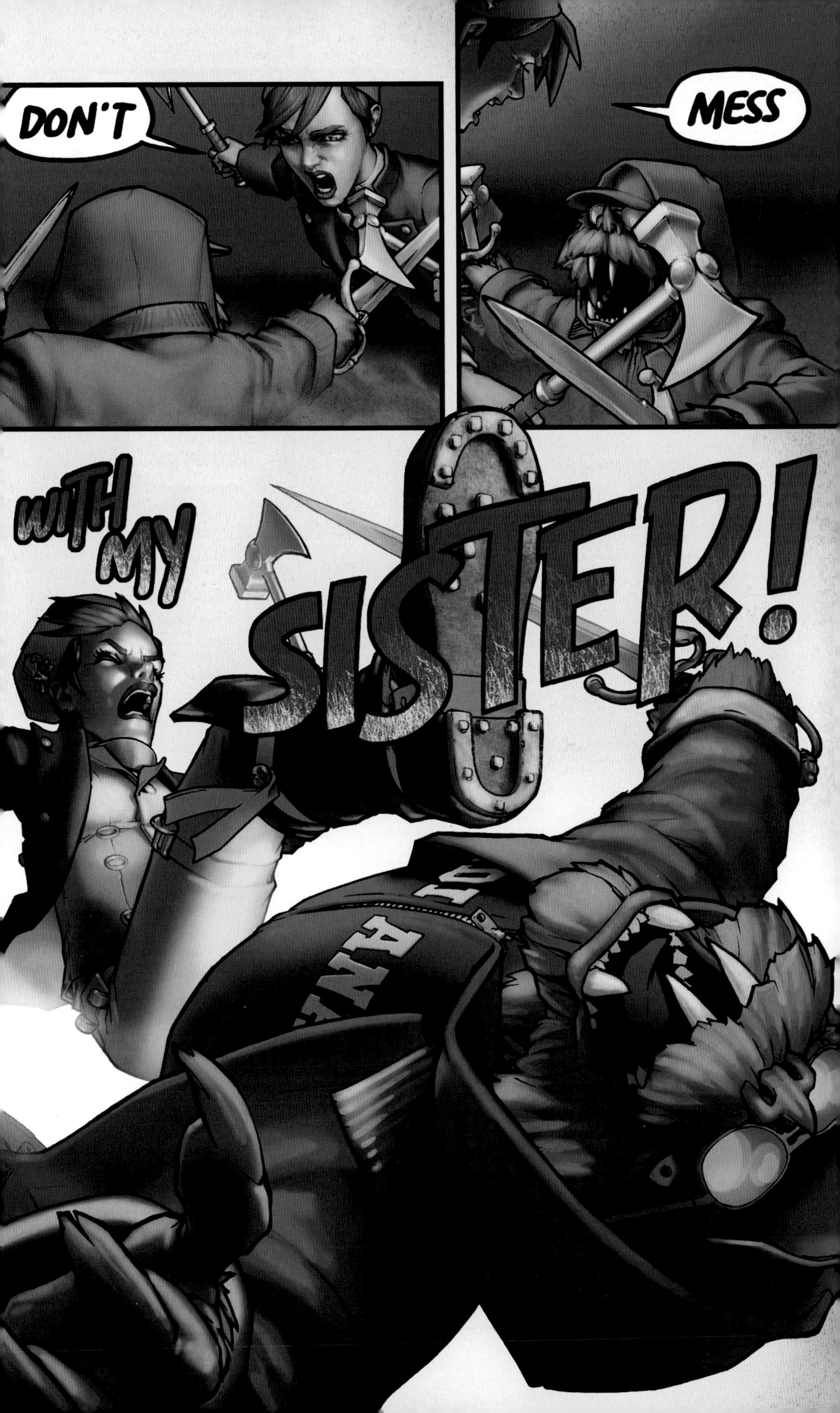
DON'T
MESS
WITH MY SISTER!

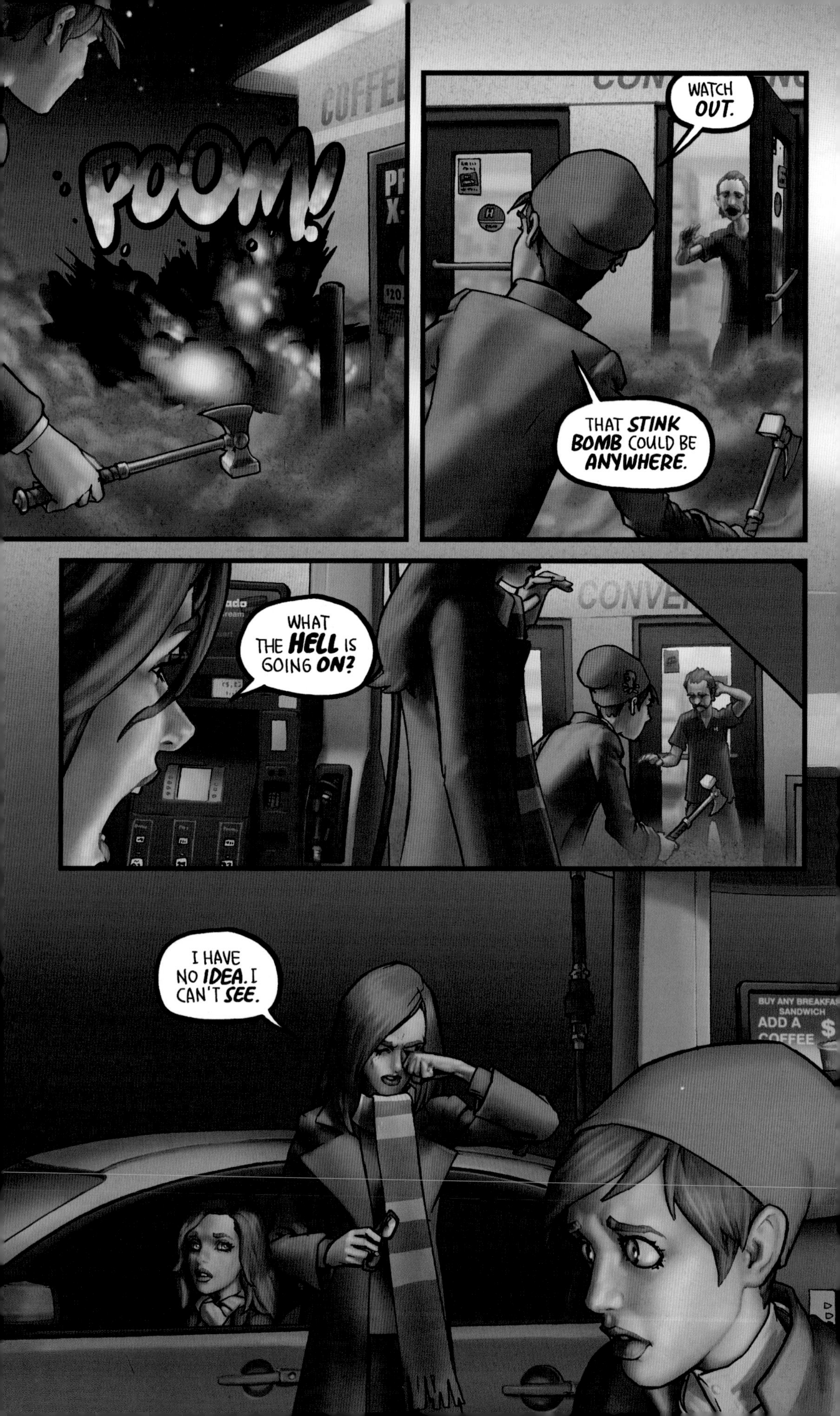
COFFEE
POOM!
WATCH OUT.
THAT STINK BOMB COULD BE ANYWHERE.
WHAT THE HELL IS GOING ON?
I HAVE NO IDEA. I CAN'T SEE.
BUY ANY BREAKFA
SANDWICH
ADD A
COFFEE

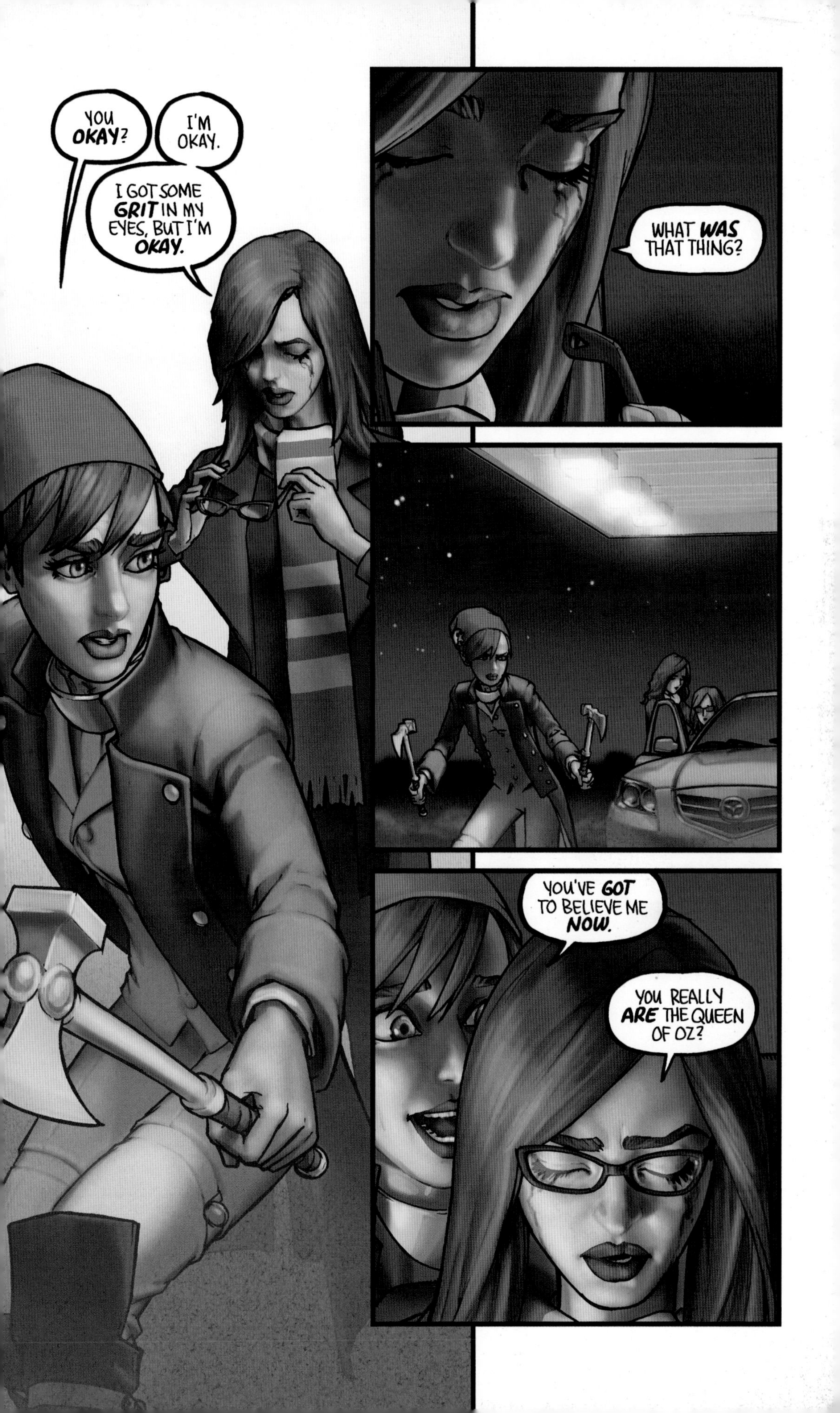
YOU OKAY?
I'M OKAY.
I GOT SOME GRIT IN MY EYES, BUT I'M OKAY.
WHAT WAS THAT THING?
YOU'VE GOT TO BELIEVE ME NOW.
YOU REALLY ARE THE QUEEN OF OZ?

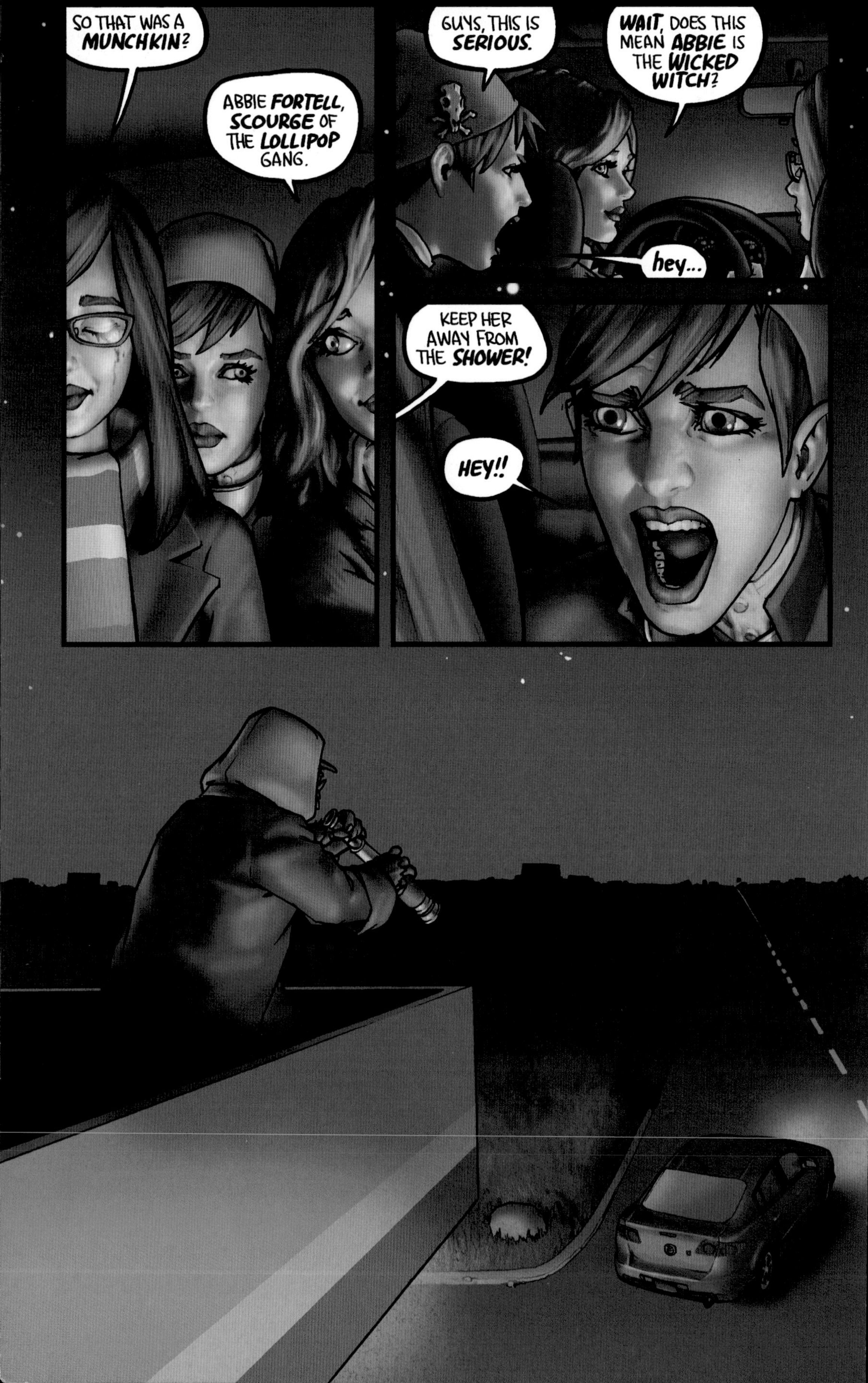
SO THAT WAS A MUNCHKIN?
ABBIE FORTELL, SCOURGE OF THE LOLLIPOP GANG.
GUYS, THIS IS SERIOUS.
WAIT, DOES THIS MEAN ABBIE IS THE WICKED WITCH?
hey...
KEEP HER AWAY FROM THE SHOWER!
HEY!!

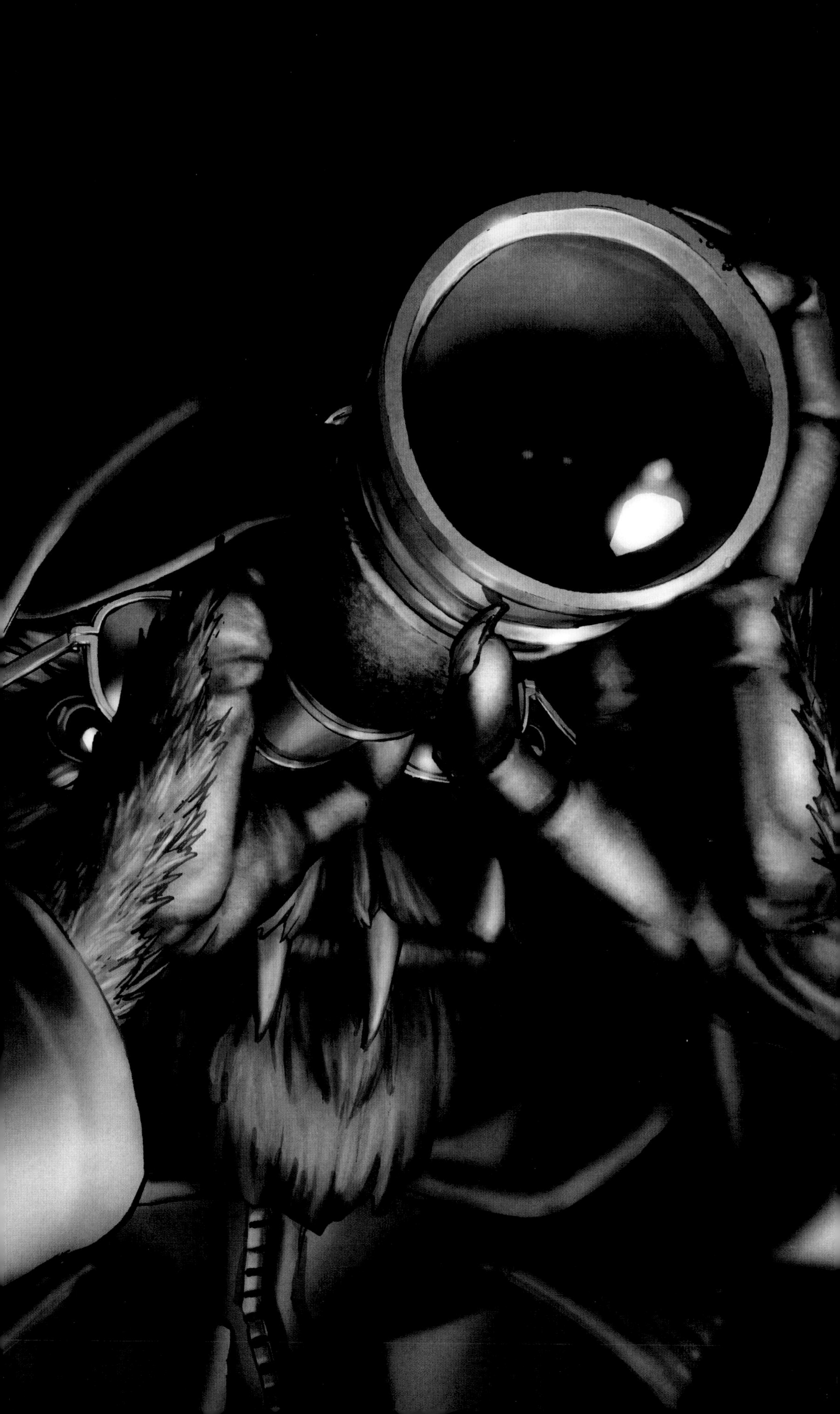

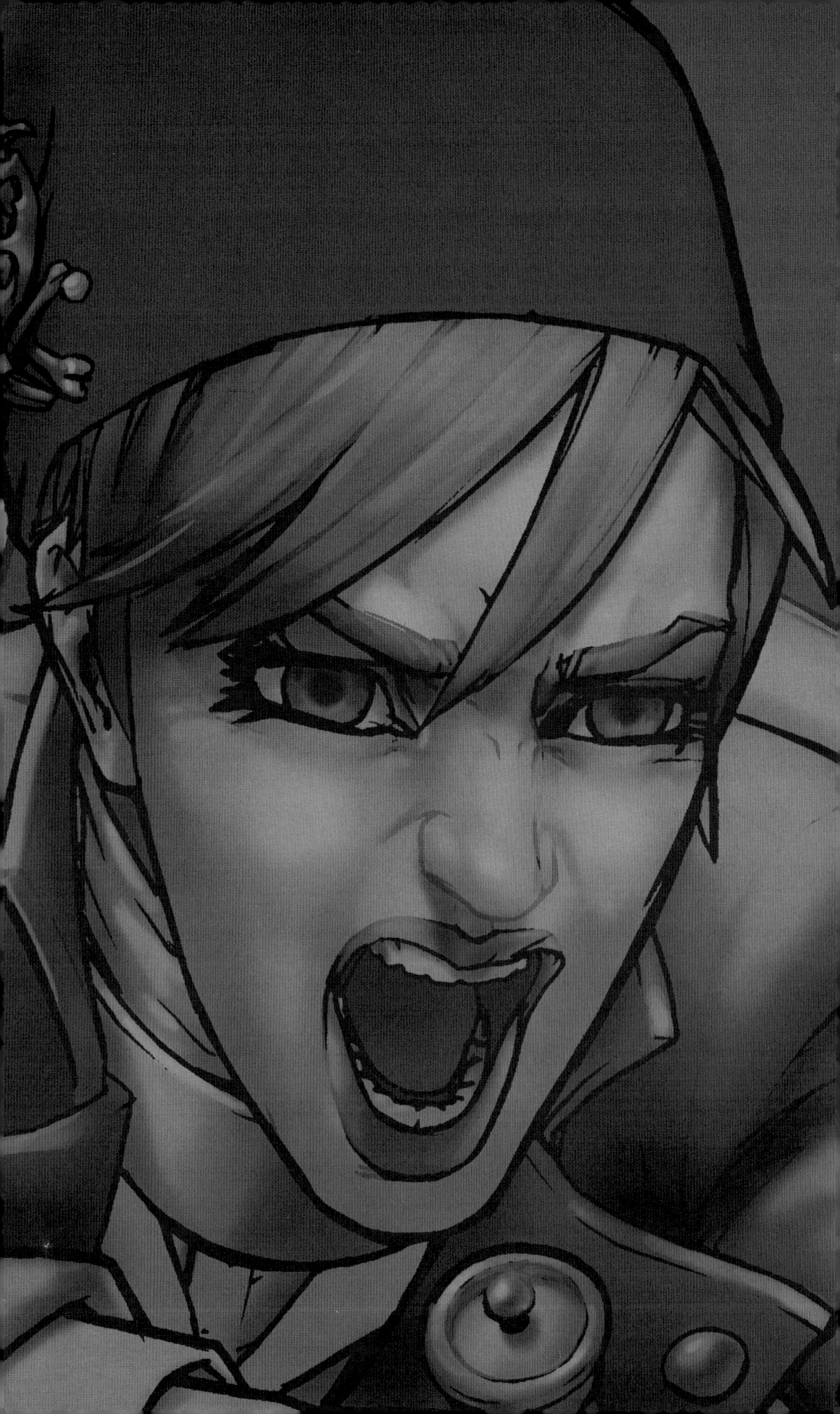

TWO

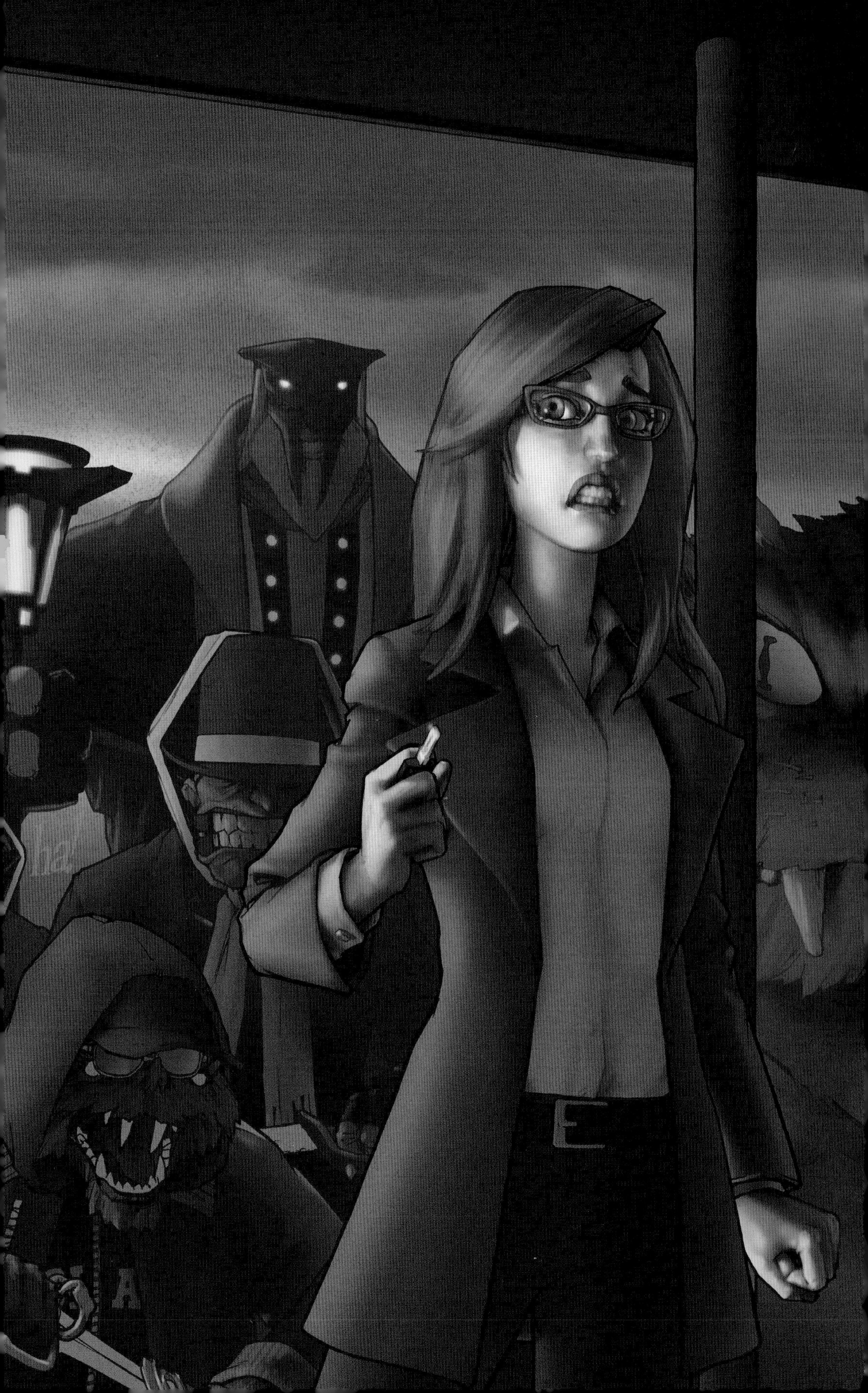

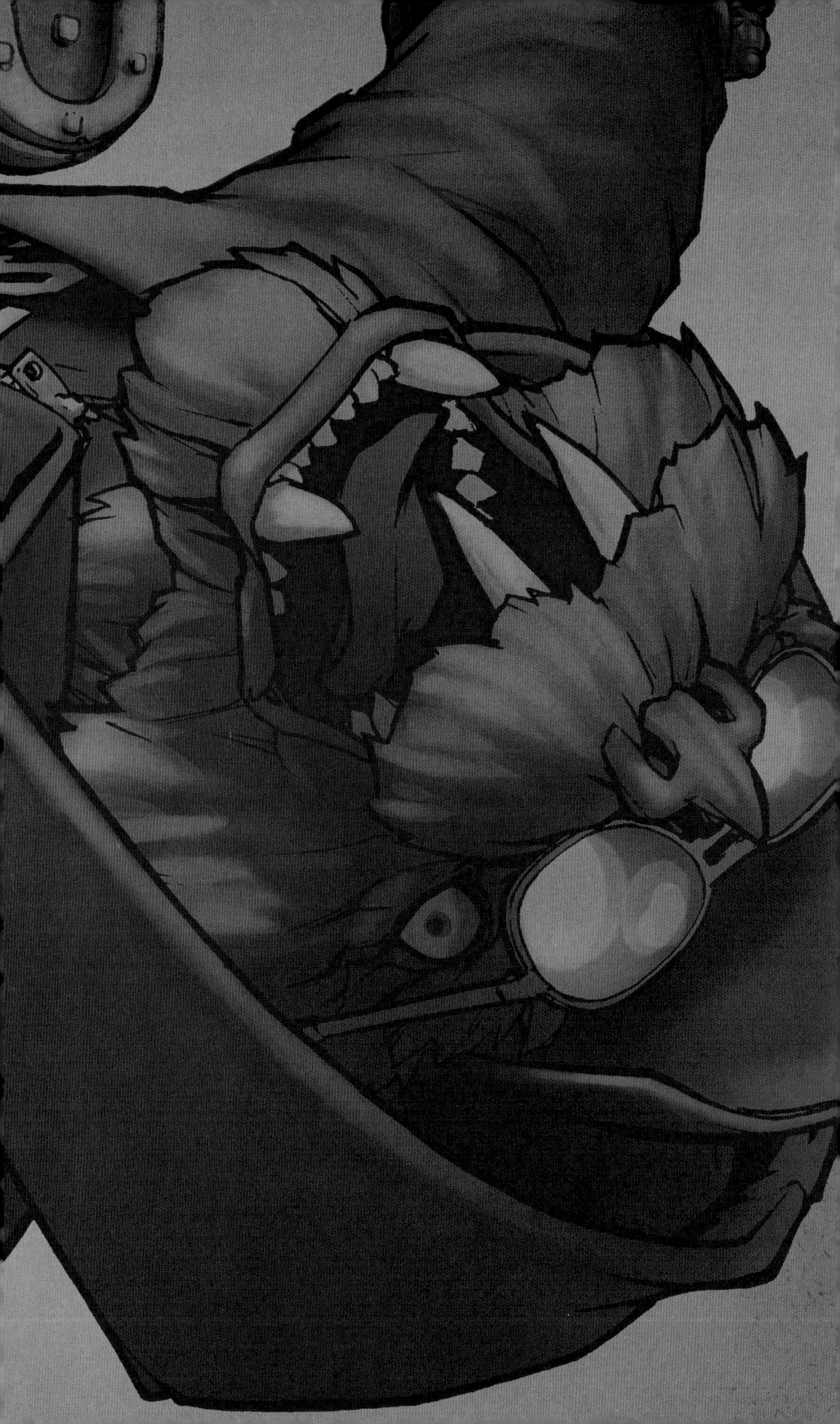

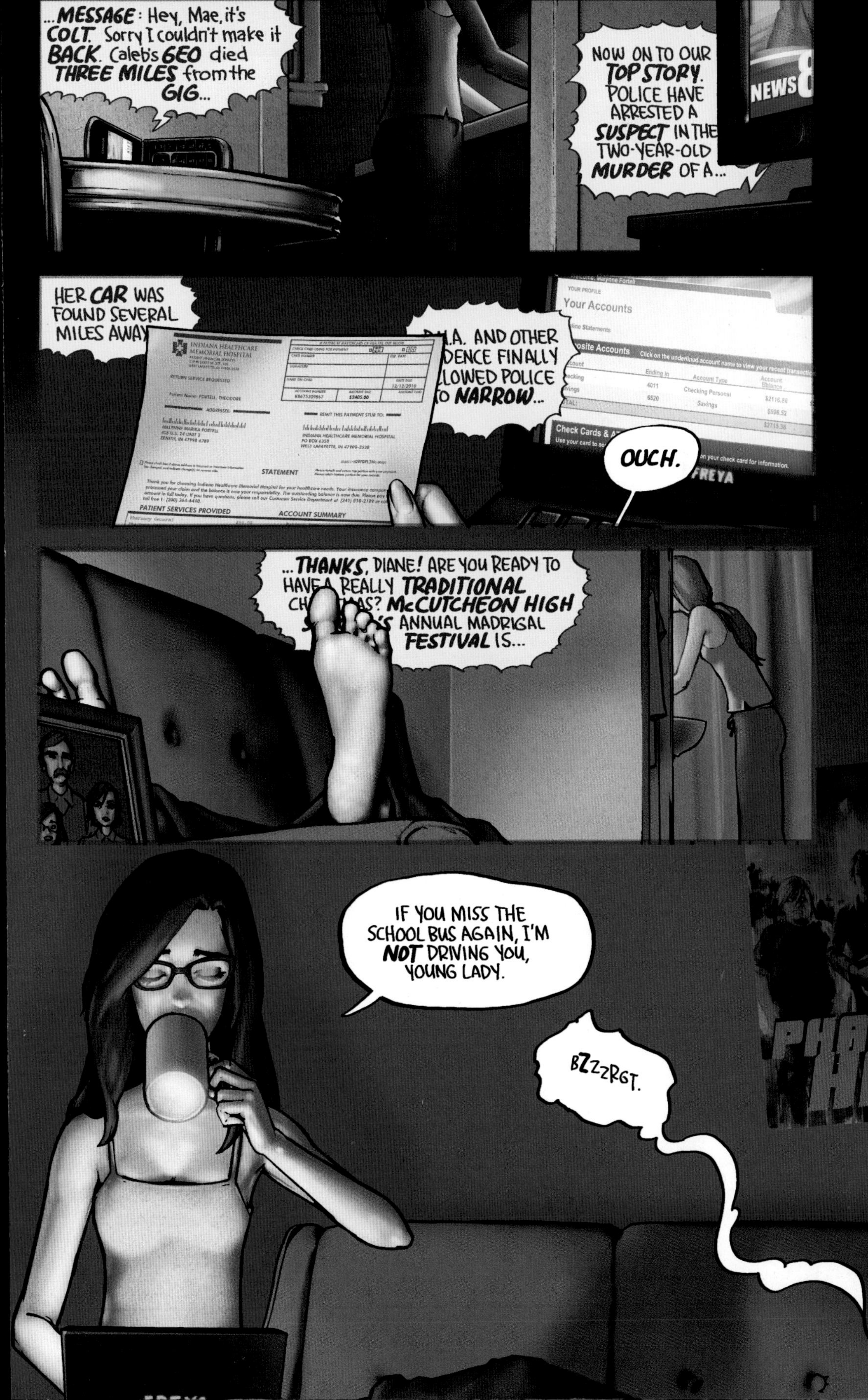
...MESSAGE: Hey, Mae, it's COLT. Sorry I couldn't make it BACK. Caleb's GEO died THREE MILES from the GIG...
NOW ON TO OUR TOP STORY. POLICE HAVE ARRESTED A SUSPECT IN THE TWO-YEAR-OLD MURDER OF A...
NEWS 8
HER CAR WAS FOUND SEVERAL MILES AWAY
INDIANA HEALTHCARE MEMORIAL HOSPITAL
STATEMENT
PATIENT SERVICES PROVIDED
ACCOUNT SUMMARY
Your Accounts
OUCH.
FREYA
...THANKS, DIANE! ARE YOU READY TO HAVE A REALLY TRADITIONAL
'S ANNUAL MADRIGAL FESTIVAL IS...
IF YOU MISS THE SCHOOL BUS AGAIN, I'M NOT DRIVING YOU, YOUNG LADY.
BZZZRGT.

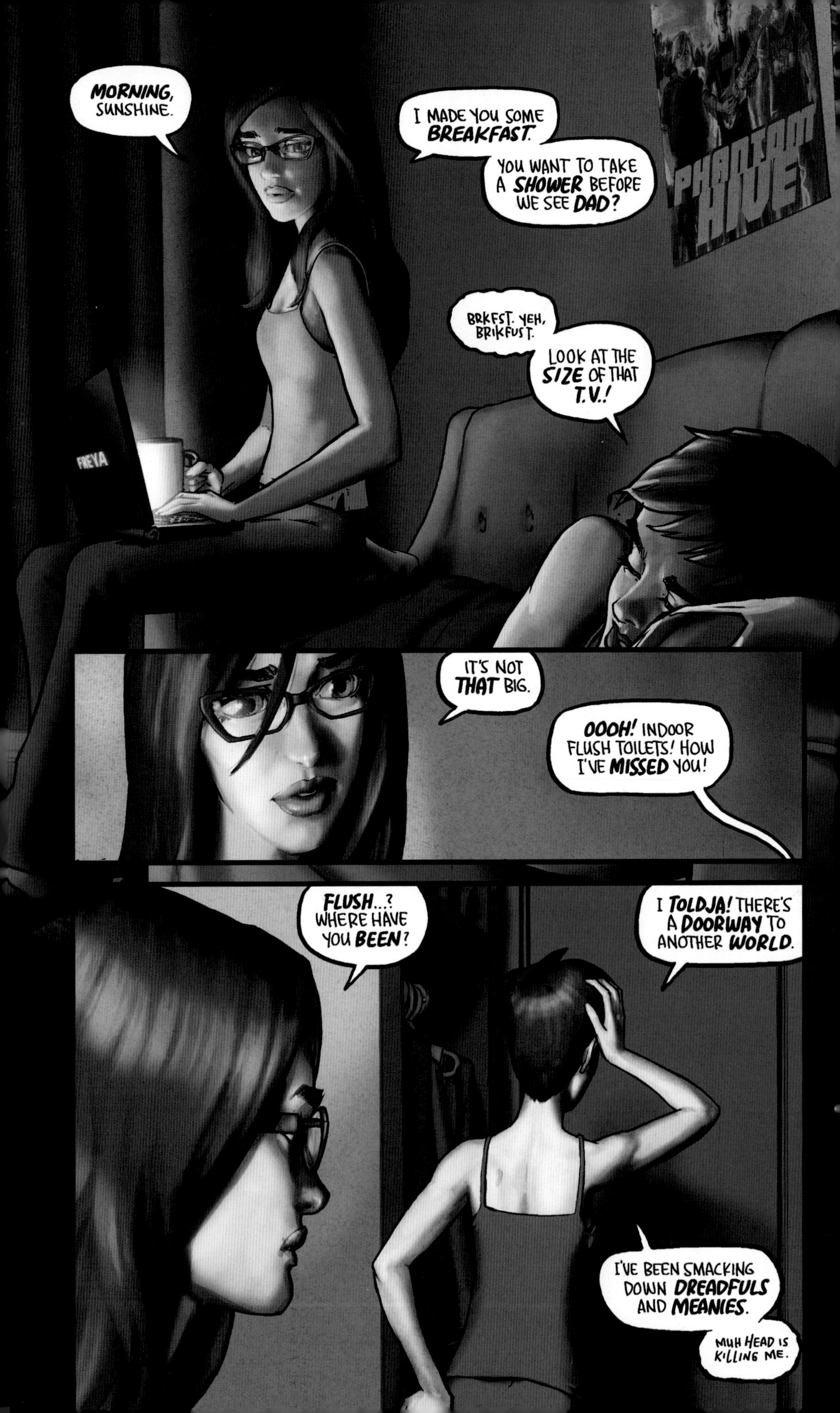
MORNING, SUNSHINE.
I MADE YOU SOME BREAKFAST.
YOU WANT TO TAKE A SHOWER BEFORE WE SEE DAD?
PHANTOM HIVE
BRKFST. YEH, BRIKFUST.
LOOK AT THE SIZE OF THAT T.V.!
FREYA
IT'S NOT THAT BIG.
OOOH! INDOOR FLUSH TOILETS! HOW I'VE MISSED YOU!
FLUSH...? WHERE HAVE YOU BEEN?
I TOLDJA! THERE'S A DOORWAY TO ANOTHER WORLD.
I'VE BEEN SMACKING DOWN DREADFULS AND MEANIES.
MUH HEAD IS KILLING ME.

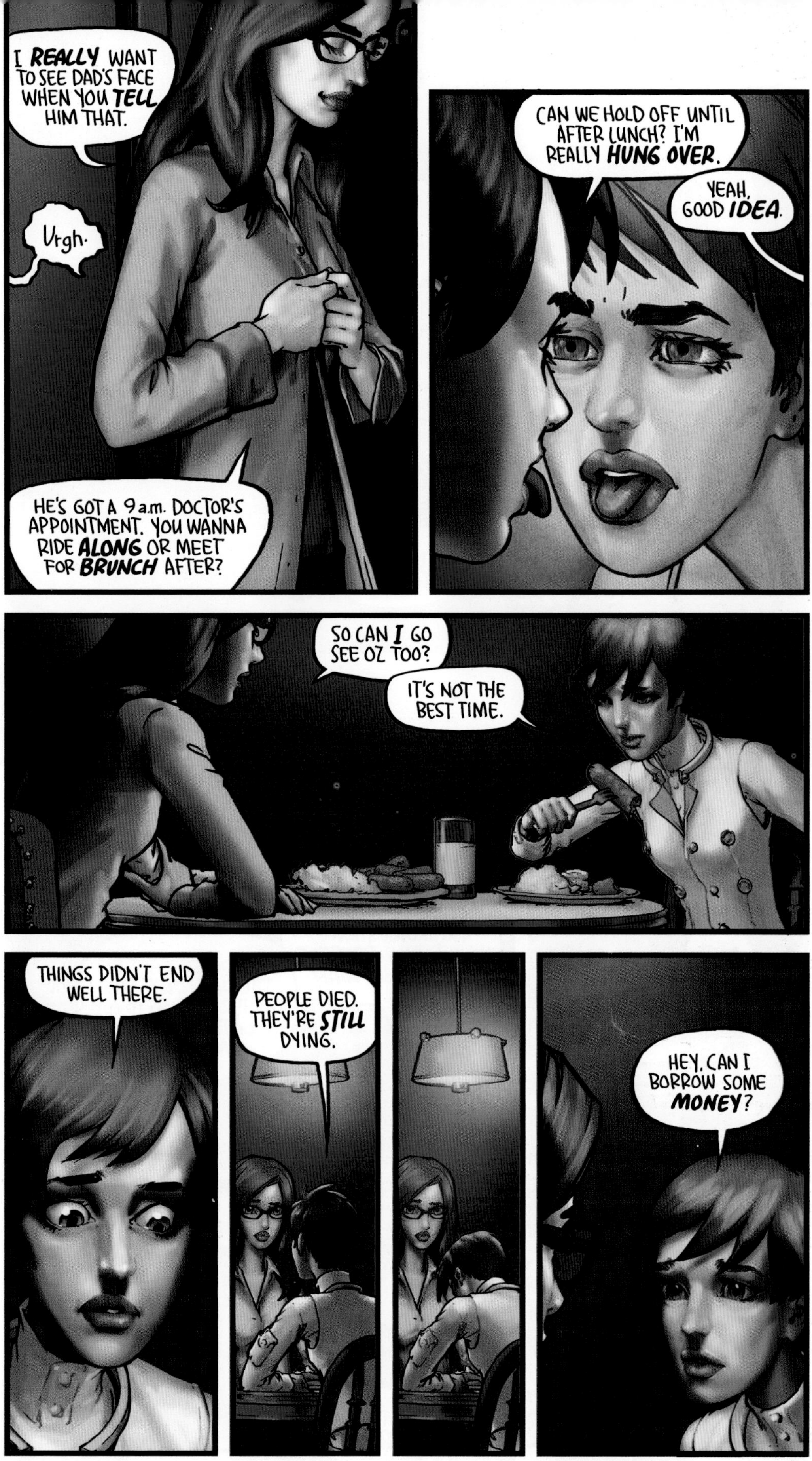

I REALLY WANT TO SEE DAD'S FACE WHEN YOU TELL HIM THAT.
Urgh.
HE'S GOT A 9 a.m. DOCTOR'S APPOINTMENT. YOU WANNA RIDE ALONG OR MEET FOR BRUNCH AFTER?
CAN WE HOLD OFF UNTIL AFTER LUNCH? I'M REALLY HUNG OVER.
YEAH, GOOD IDEA.
SO CAN I GO SEE OZ TOO?
IT'S NOT THE BEST TIME.
THINGS DIDN'T END WELL THERE.
PEOPLE DIED. THEY'RE STILL DYING.
HEY, CAN I BORROW SOME MONEY?

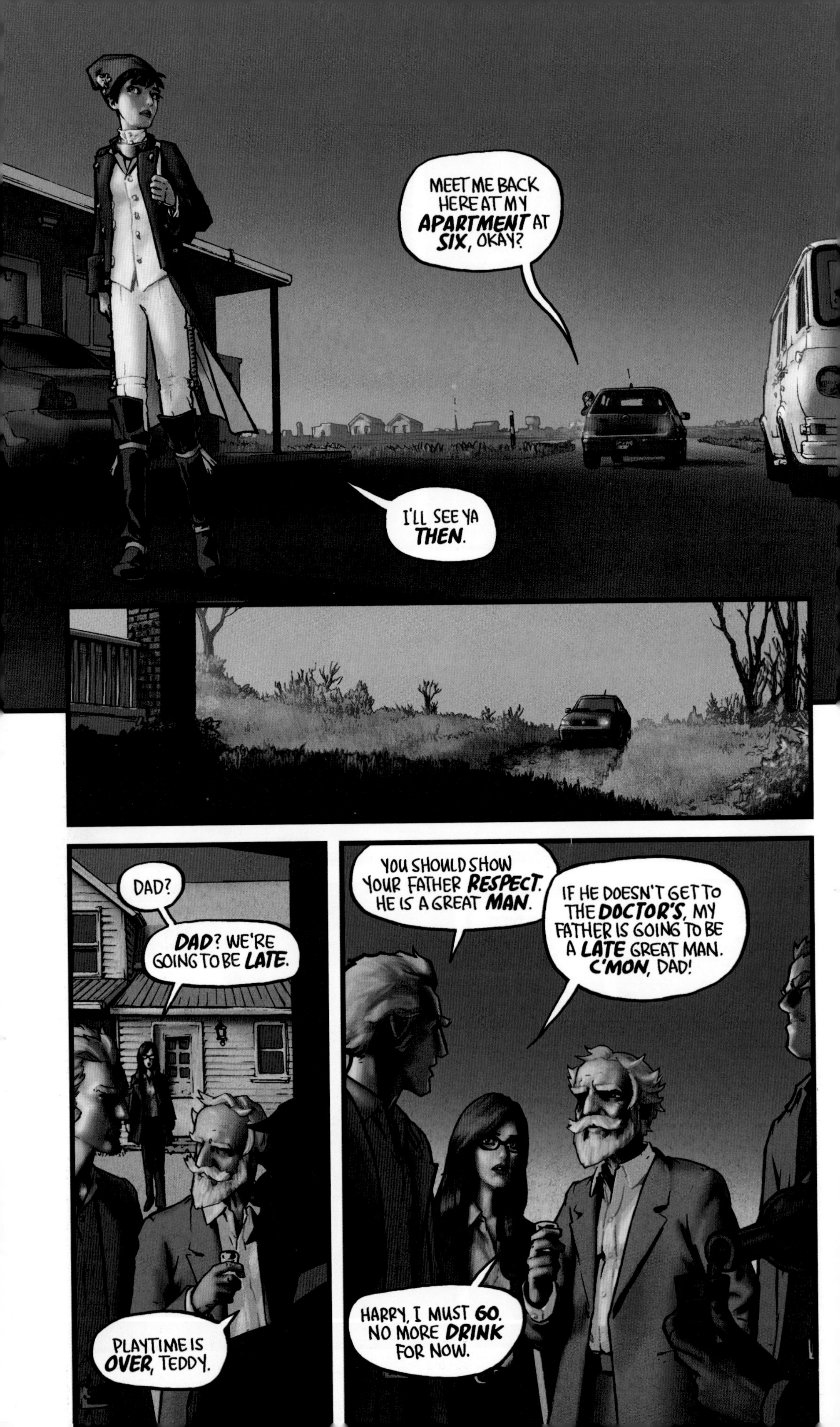
MEET ME BACK HERE AT MY APARTMENT AT SIX, OKAY?
I'LL SEE YA THEN.
DAD?
DAD? WE'RE GOING TO BE LATE.
PLAYTIME IS OVER, TEDDY.
YOU SHOULD SHOW YOUR FATHER RESPECT. HE IS A GREAT MAN.
IF HE DOESN'T GET TO THE DOCTOR'S, MY FATHER IS GOING TO BE A LATE GREAT MAN. C'MON, DAD!
HARRY, I MUST GO. NO MORE DRINK FOR NOW.

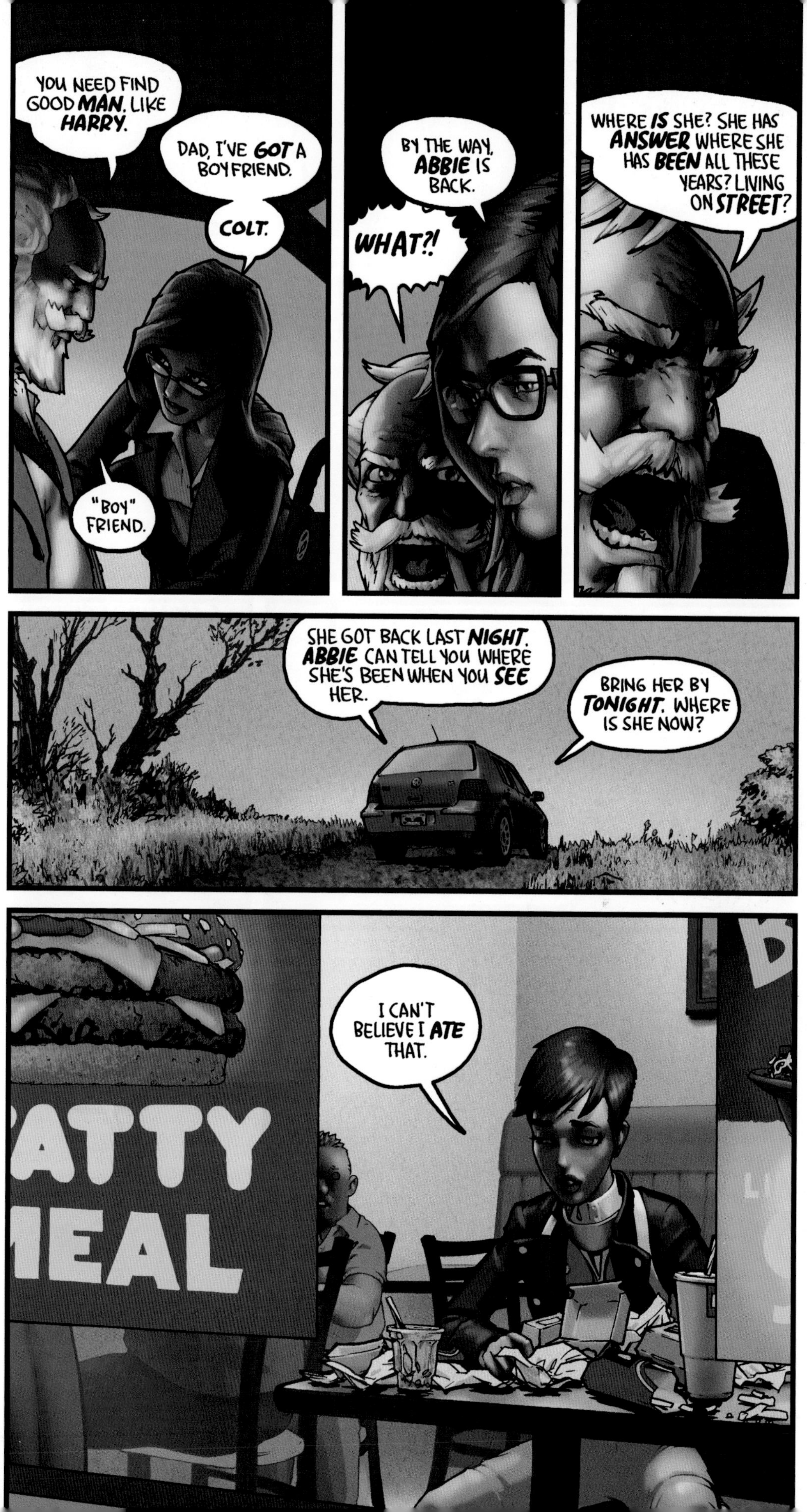
YOU NEED FIND GOOD MAN, LIKE HARRY.
DAD, I'VE GOT A BOYFRIEND.
COLT.
"BOY" FRIEND.
BY THE WAY, ABBIE IS BACK.
WHAT?!
WHERE IS SHE? SHE HAS ANSWER WHERE SHE HAS BEEN ALL THESE YEARS? LIVING ON STREET?
SHE GOT BACK LAST NIGHT. ABBIE CAN TELL YOU WHERE SHE'S BEEN WHEN YOU SEE HER.
BRING HER BY TONIGHT. WHERE IS SHE NOW?
I CAN'T BELIEVE I ATE THAT.
ATTY
MEAL

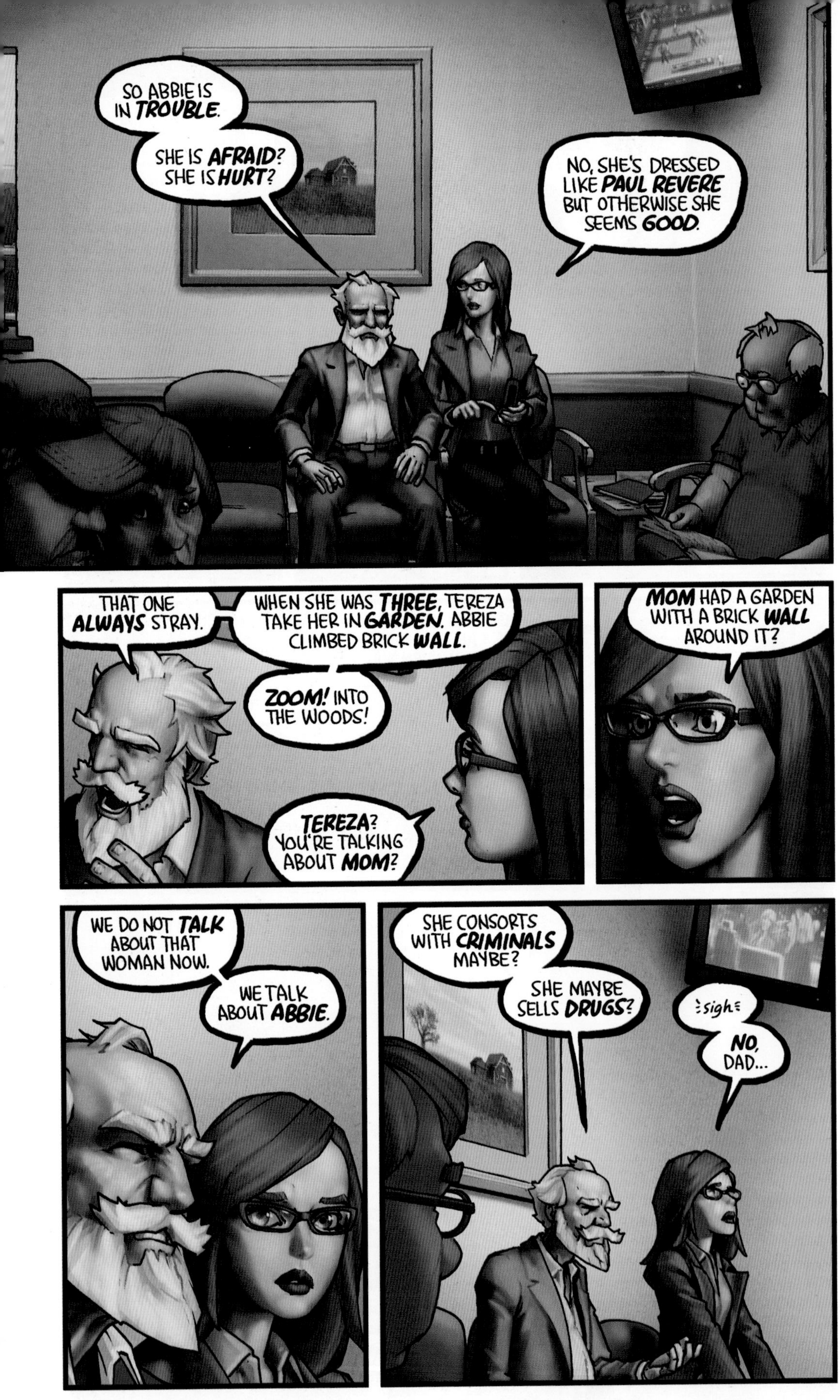
SO ABBIE IS IN TROUBLE.
SHE IS AFRAID? SHE IS HURT?
NO, SHE'S DRESSED LIKE PAUL REVERE BUT OTHERWISE SHE SEEMS GOOD.
THAT ONE ALWAYS STRAY.
WHEN SHE WAS THREE, TEREZA TAKE HER IN GARDEN. ABBIE CLIMBED BRICK WALL.
ZOOM! INTO THE WOODS!
TEREZA? YOU'RE TALKING ABOUT MOM?
MOM HAD A GARDEN WITH A BRICK WALL AROUND IT?
WE DO NOT TALK ABOUT THAT WOMAN NOW.
WE TALK ABOUT ABBIE.
SHE CONSORTS WITH CRIMINALS MAYBE?
SHE MAYBE SELLS DRUGS?
sigh
NO, DAD...

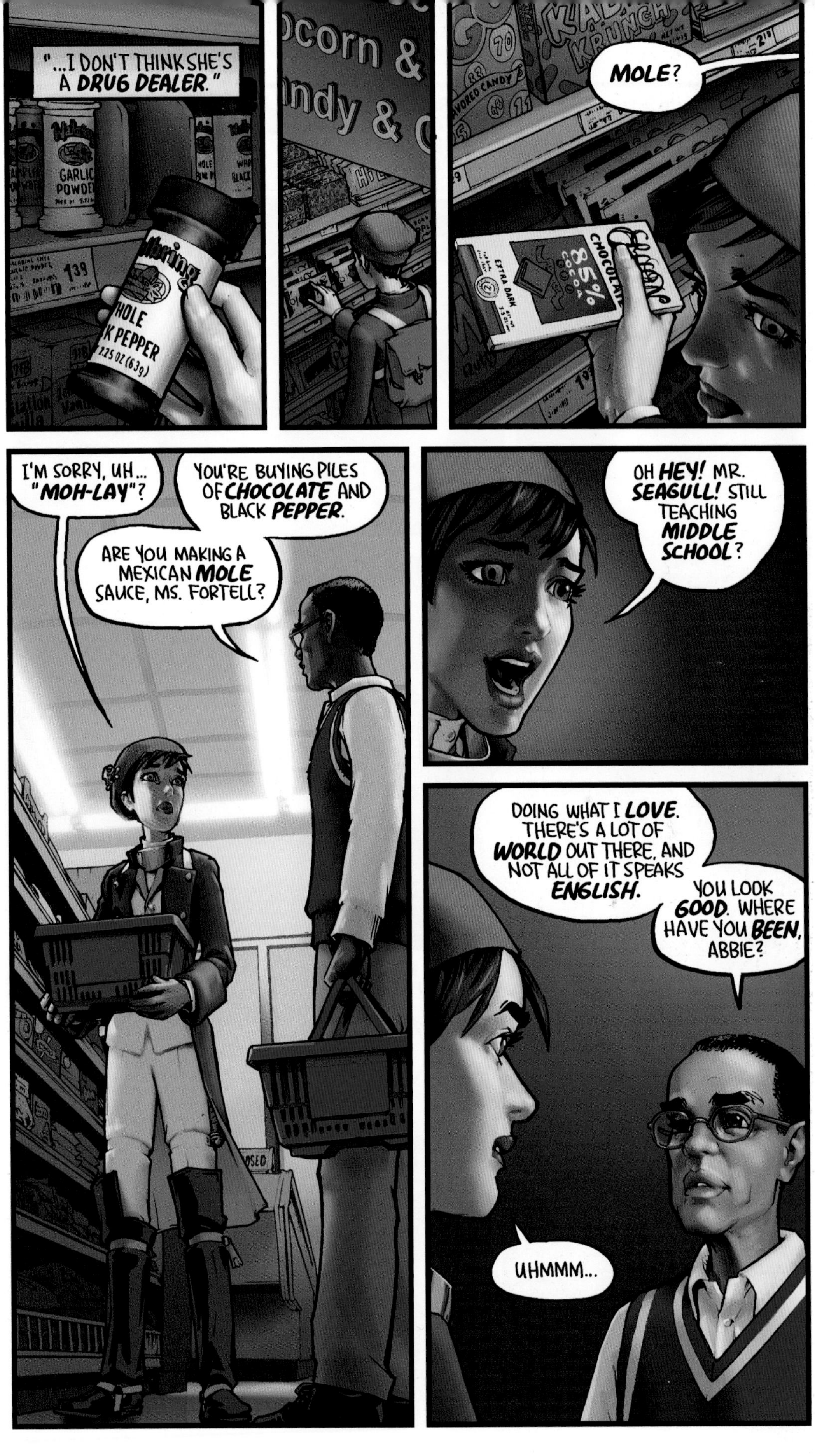
"...I DON'T THINK SHE'S A DRUG DEALER."
MOLE?
I'M SORRY, UH... "MOH-LAY"?
YOU'RE BUYING PILES OF CHOCOLATE AND BLACK PEPPER.
ARE YOU MAKING A MEXICAN MOLE SAUCE, MS. FORTELL?
OH HEY! MR. SEAGULL! STILL TEACHING MIDDLE SCHOOL?
DOING WHAT I LOVE. THERE'S A LOT OF WORLD OUT THERE, AND NOT ALL OF IT SPEAKS ENGLISH.
YOU LOOK GOOD. WHERE HAVE YOU BEEN, ABBIE?
UHMMM...

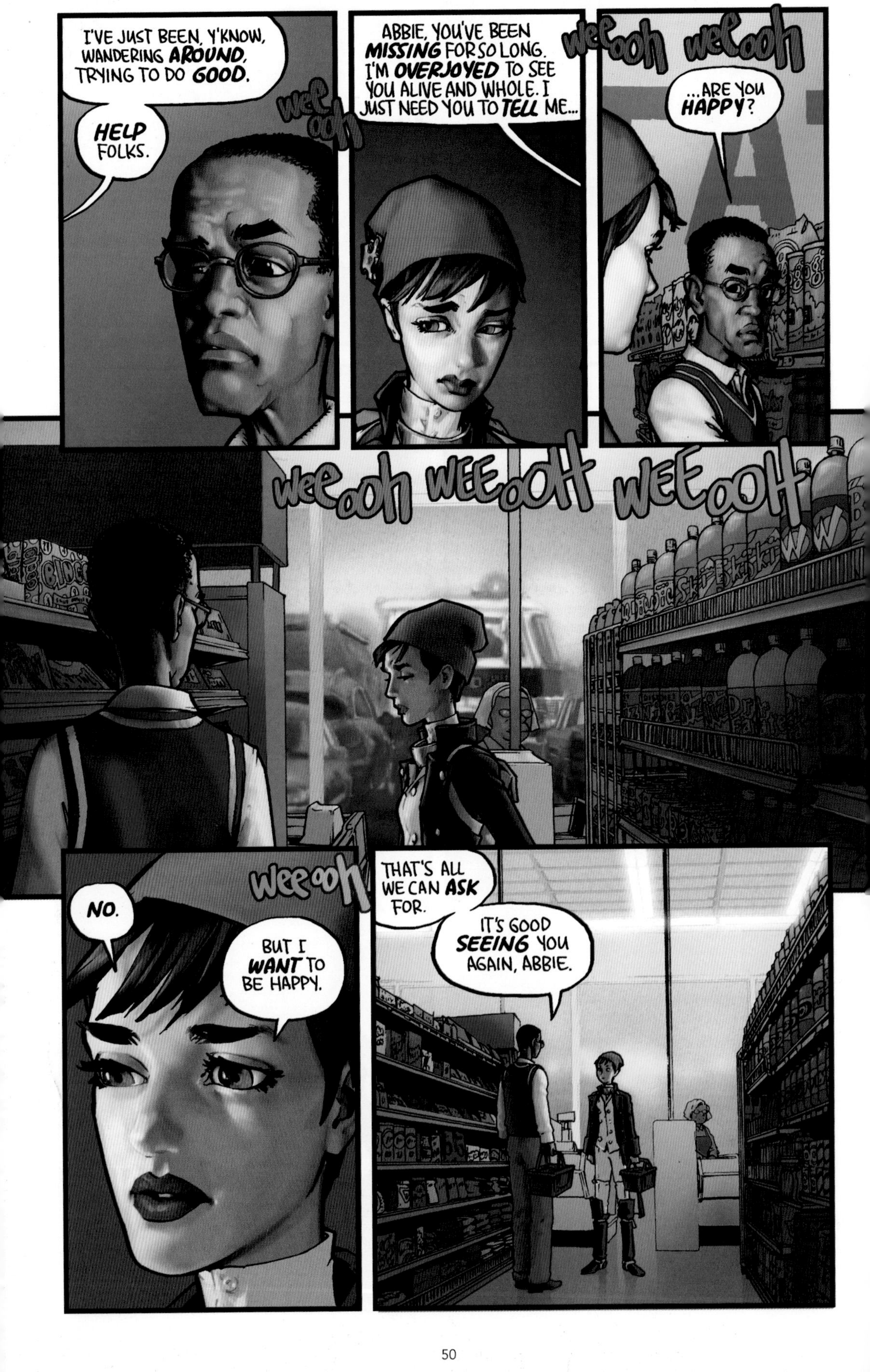
I'VE JUST BEEN, Y'KNOW, WANDERING AROUND, TRYING TO DO GOOD.
HELP FOLKS.
WEE OOH
ABBIE, YOU'VE BEEN MISSING FOR SO LONG. I'M OVERJOYED TO SEE YOU ALIVE AND WHOLE. I JUST NEED YOU TO TELL ME...
WEEOOH WEEOOH
...ARE YOU HAPPY?
WEEOOH WEEOOH WEEOOH
WEEOOH
NO.
BUT I WANT TO BE HAPPY.
THAT'S ALL WE CAN ASK FOR.
IT'S GOOD SEEING YOU AGAIN, ABBIE.

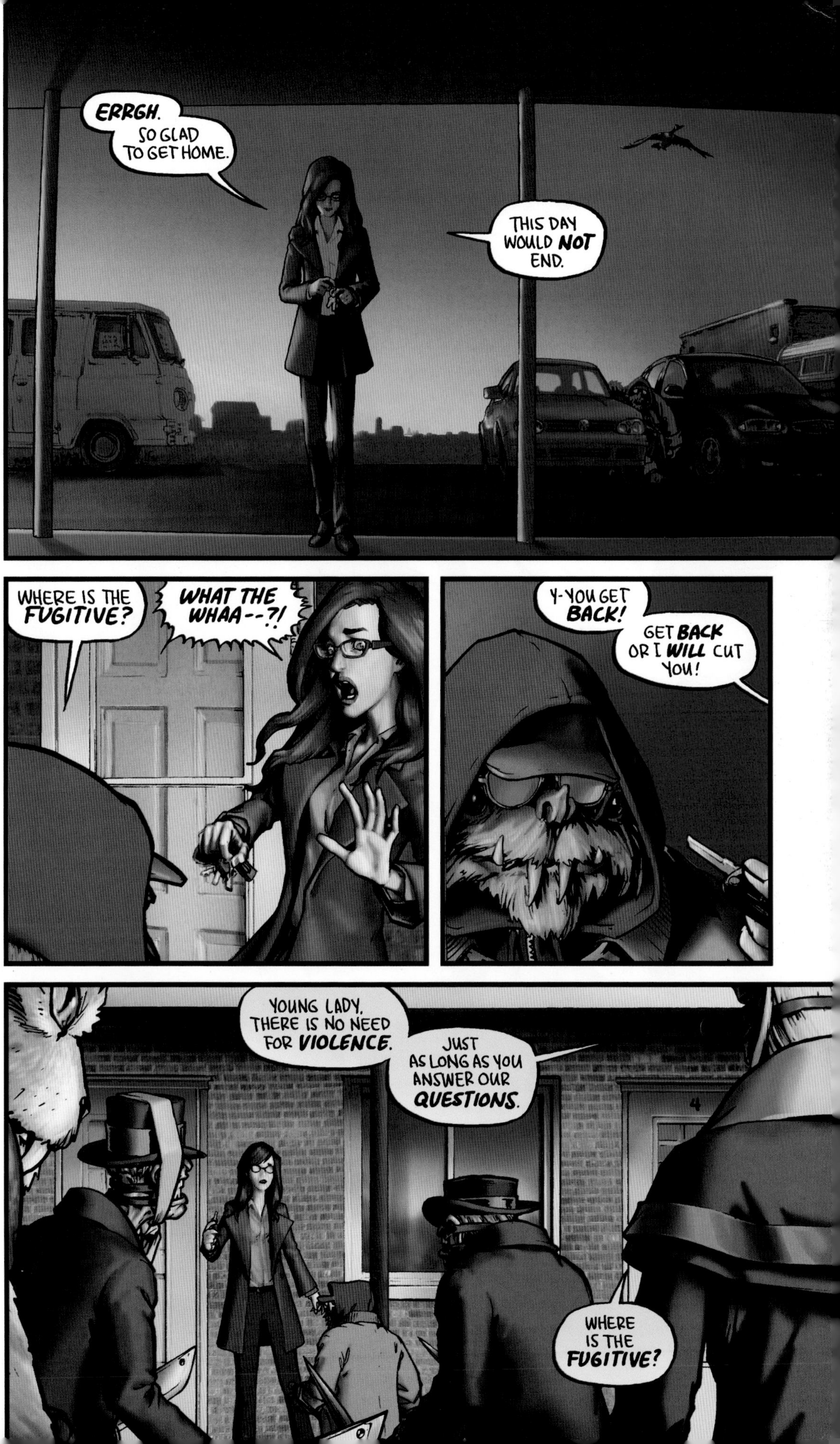
ERRGH. SO GLAD TO GET HOME.
THIS DAY WOULD NOT END.
WHERE IS THE FUGITIVE?
WHAT THE WHAA--?!
Y-YOU GET BACK!
GET BACK OR I WILL CUT YOU!
YOUNG LADY, THERE IS NO NEED FOR VIOLENCE.
JUST AS LONG AS YOU ANSWER OUR QUESTIONS.
WHERE IS THE FUGITIVE?

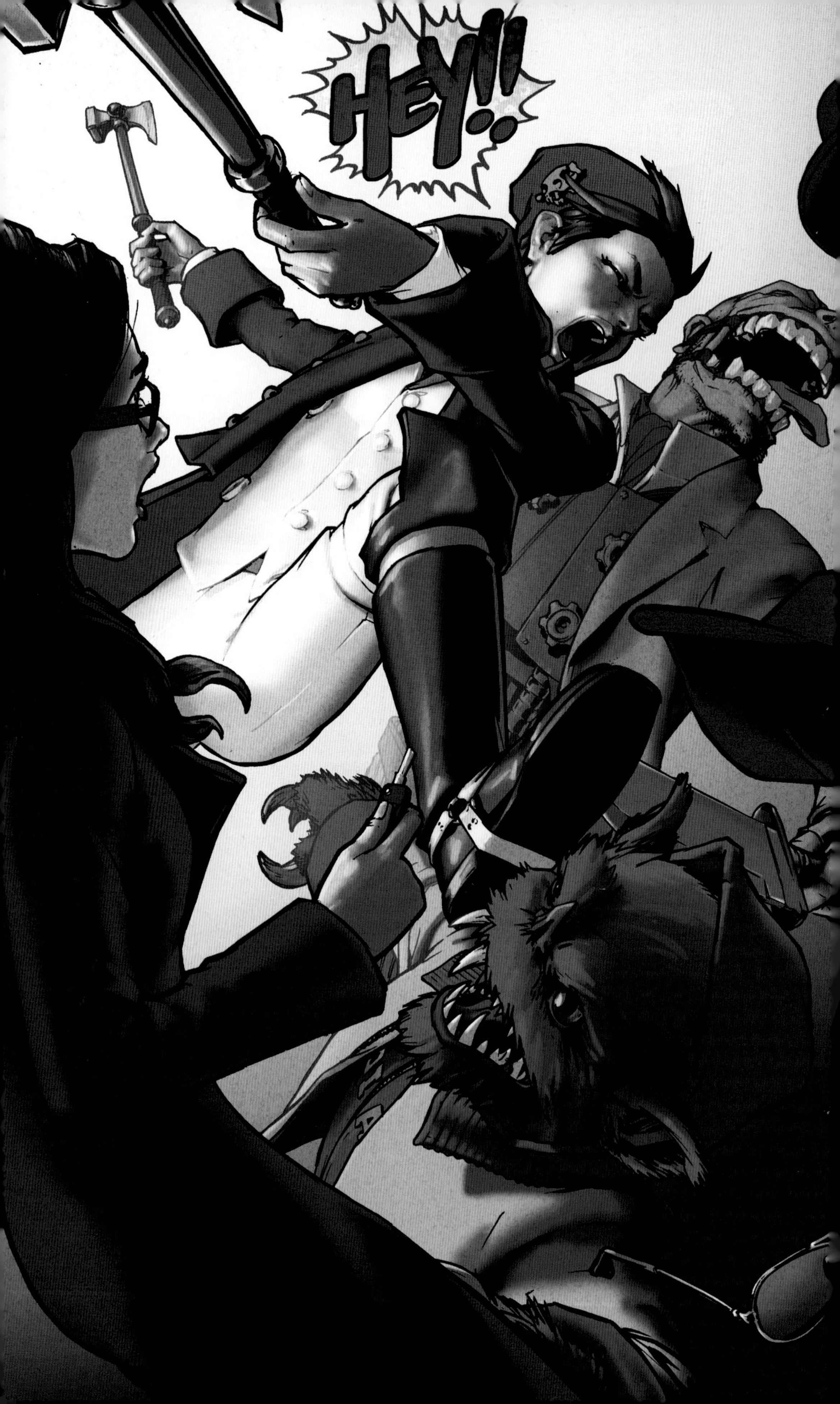
HEY!!

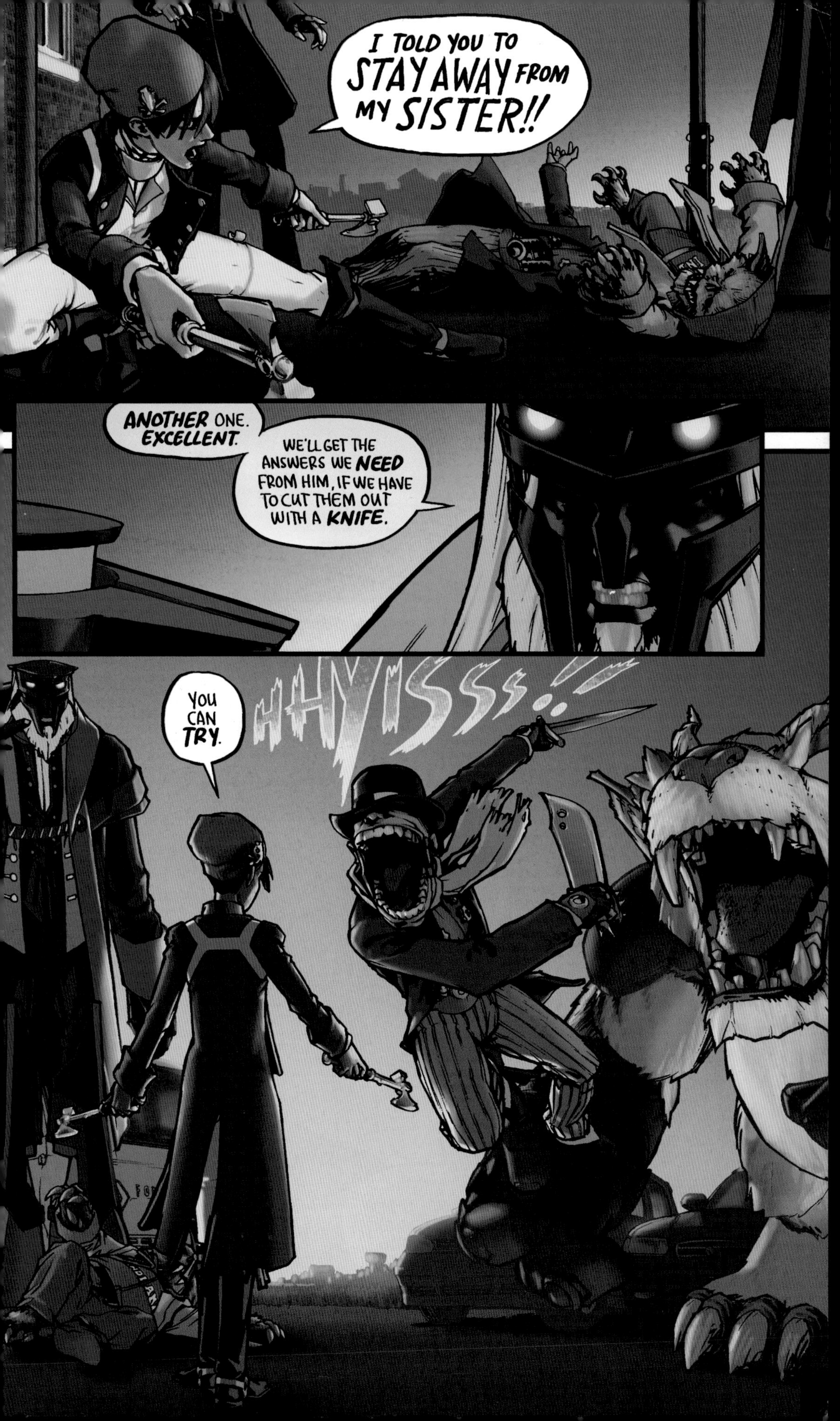
I TOLD YOU TO STAY AWAY FROM MY SISTER!!
ANOTHER ONE. EXCELLENT.
WE'LL GET THE ANSWERS WE NEED FROM HIM, IF WE HAVE TO CUT THEM OUT WITH A KNIFE.
YOU CAN TRY.
HHYISSSS!!

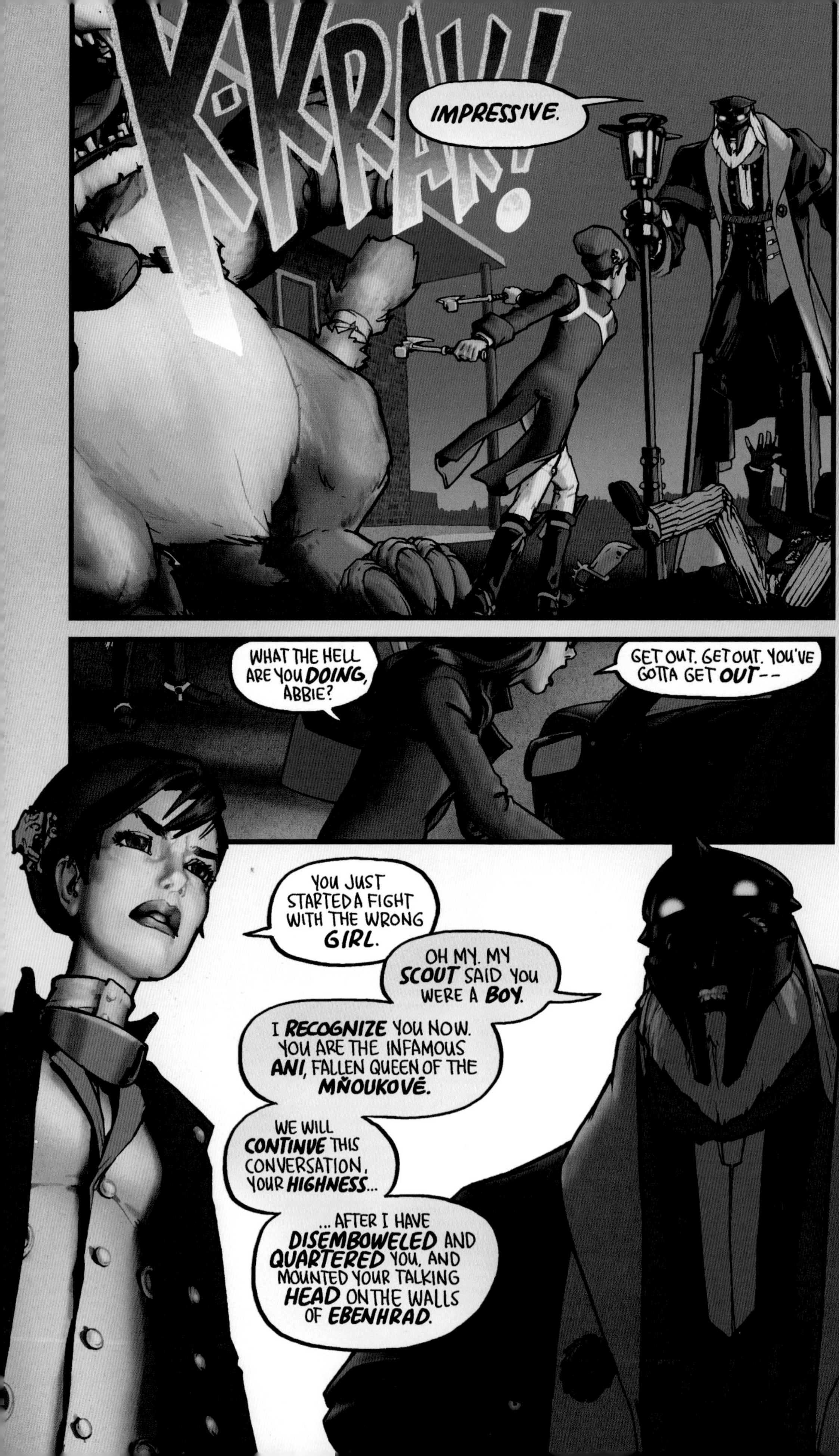
KKRAK!
IMPRESSIVE.
WHAT THE HELL ARE YOU DOING, ABBIE?
GET OUT. GET OUT. YOU'VE GOTTA GET OUT--
YOU JUST STARTED A FIGHT WITH THE WRONG GIRL.
OH MY. MY SCOUT SAID YOU WERE A BOY.
I RECOGNIZE YOU NOW. YOU ARE THE INFAMOUS ANI, FALLEN QUEEN OF THE MŇOUKOVĚ.
WE WILL CONTINUE THIS CONVERSATION, YOUR HIGHNESS...
...AFTER I HAVE DISEMBOWELED AND QUARTERED YOU, AND MOUNTED YOUR TALKING HEAD ON THE WALLS OF EBENHRAD.

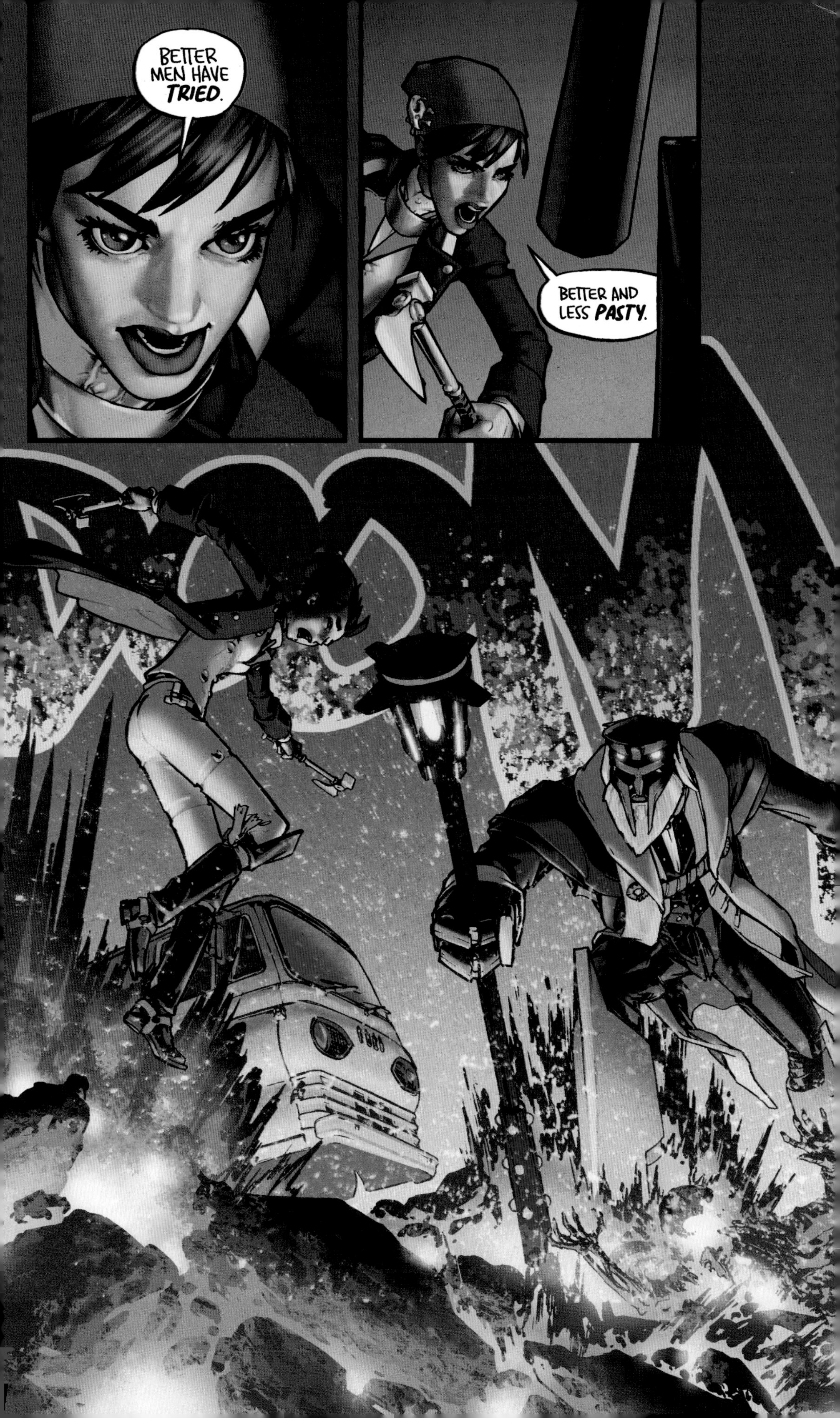
BETTER MEN HAVE TRIED.
BETTER AND LESS PASTY.

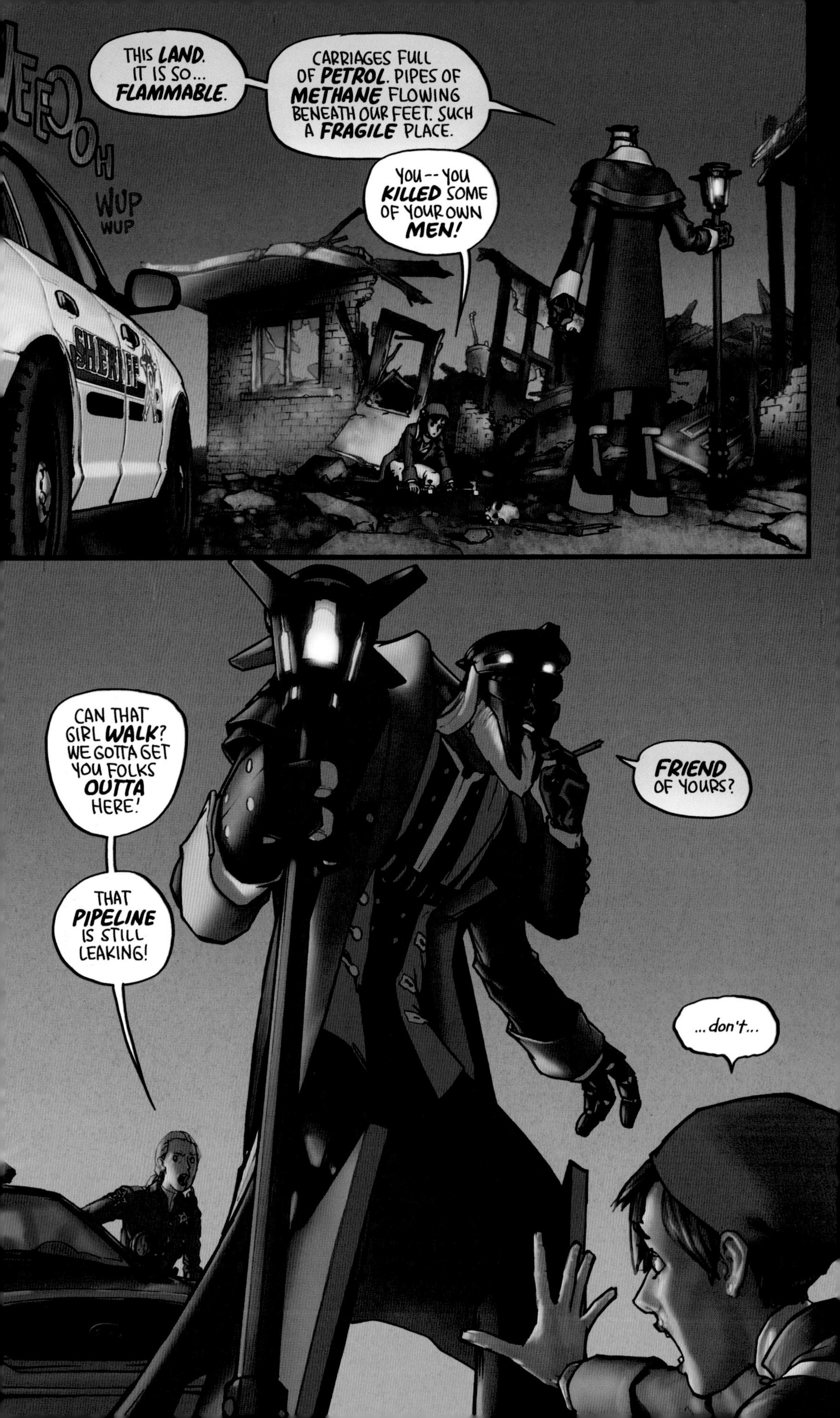
WEEOOOH
WUP WUP
THIS LAND. IT IS SO... FLAMMABLE.
CARRIAGES FULL OF PETROL. PIPES OF METHANE FLOWING BENEATH OUR FEET. SUCH A FRAGILE PLACE.
SHERIFF
YOU--YOU KILLED SOME OF YOUR OWN MEN!
CAN THAT GIRL WALK? WE GOTTA GET YOU FOLKS OUTTA HERE!
THAT PIPELINE IS STILL LEAKING!
FRIEND OF YOURS?
...don't...

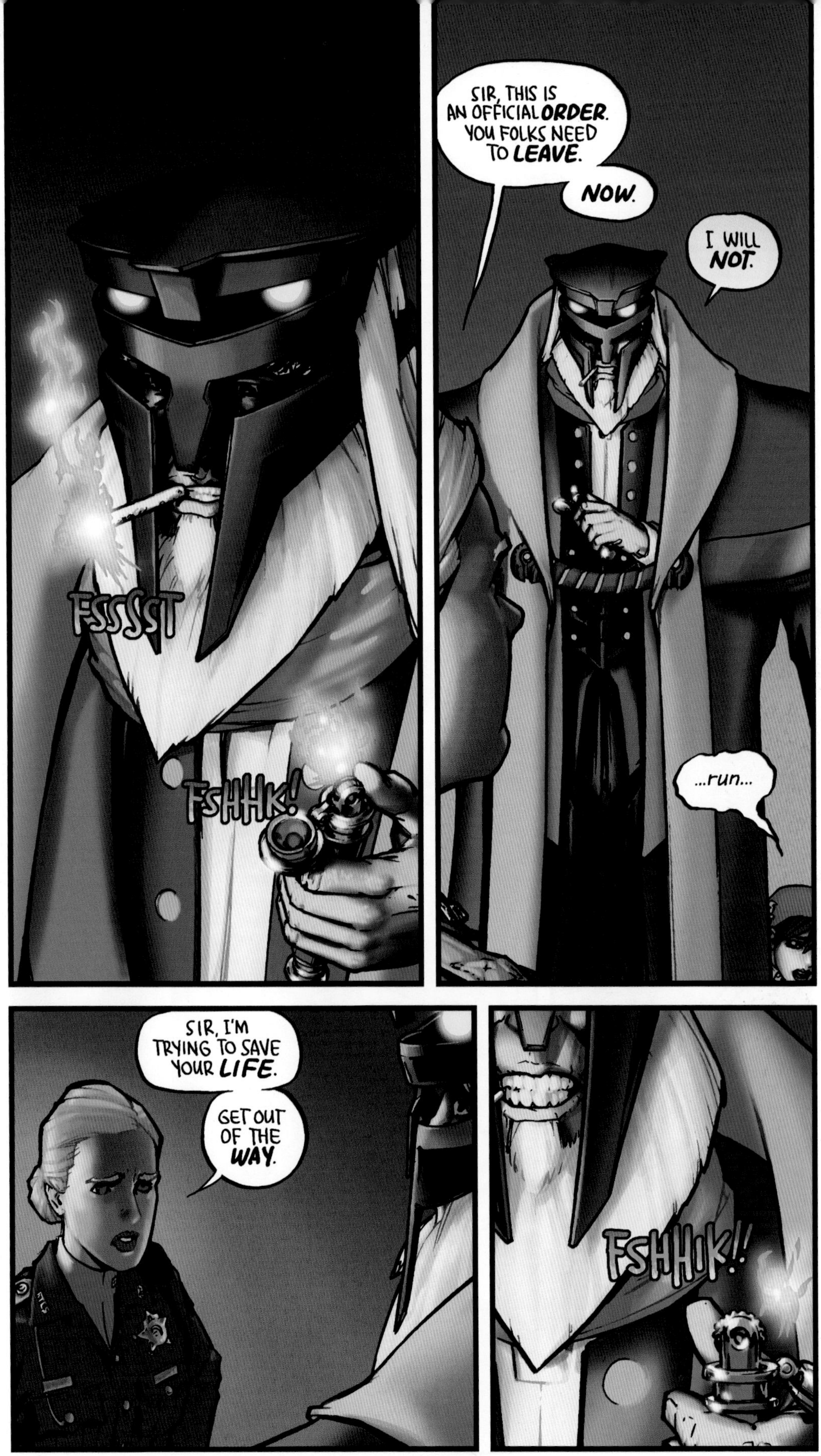
FSSSST
FSHHK!
SIR, THIS IS AN OFFICIAL ORDER. YOU FOLKS NEED TO LEAVE.
NOW.
I WILL NOT.
...run...
SIR, I'M TRYING TO SAVE YOUR LIFE.
GET OUT OF THE WAY.
FSHHK!!

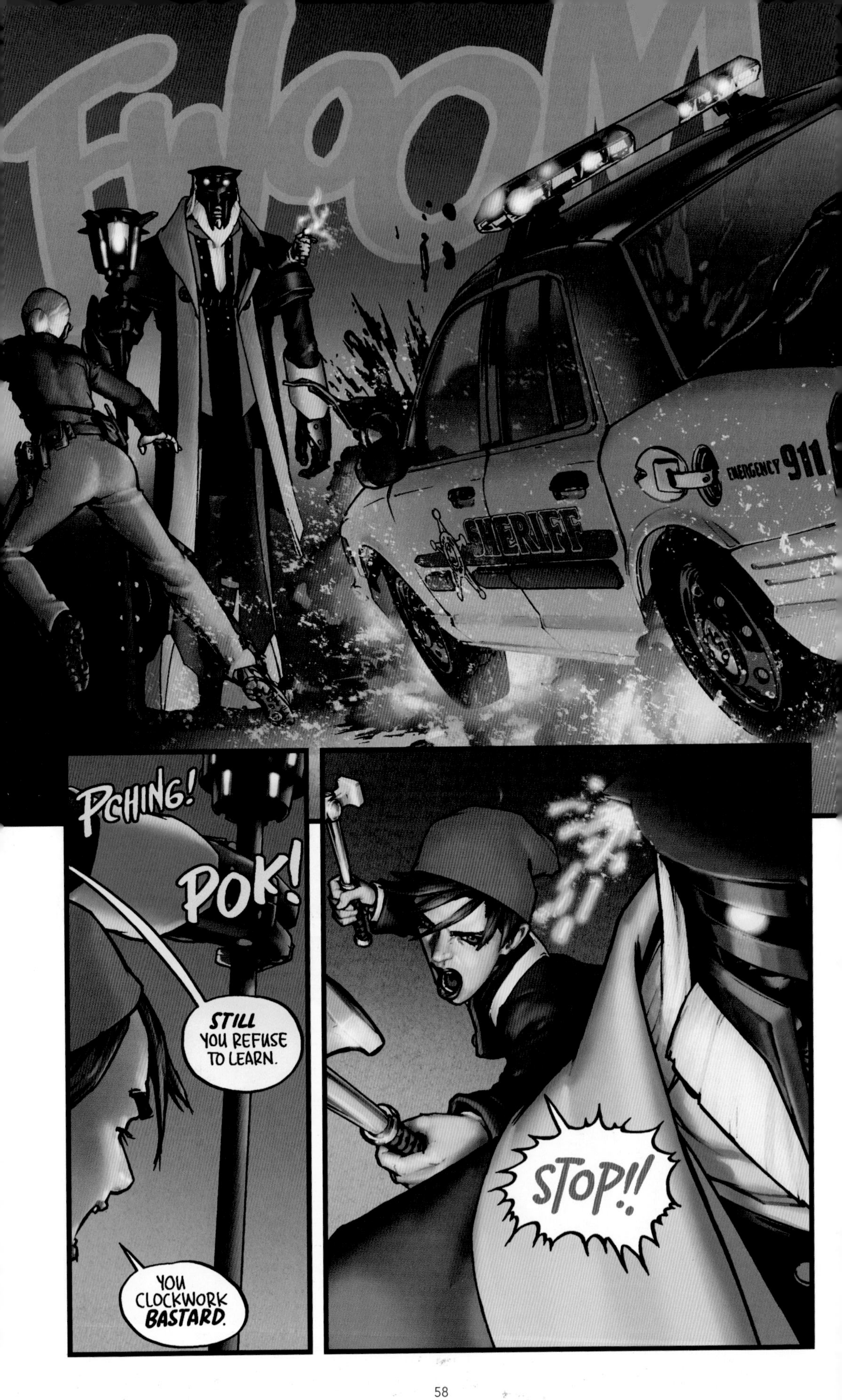
FWOOM
SHERIFF
EMERGENCY 911
PCHING!
POK!
STILL YOU REFUSE TO LEARN.
YOU CLOCKWORK BASTARD.
STOP!!

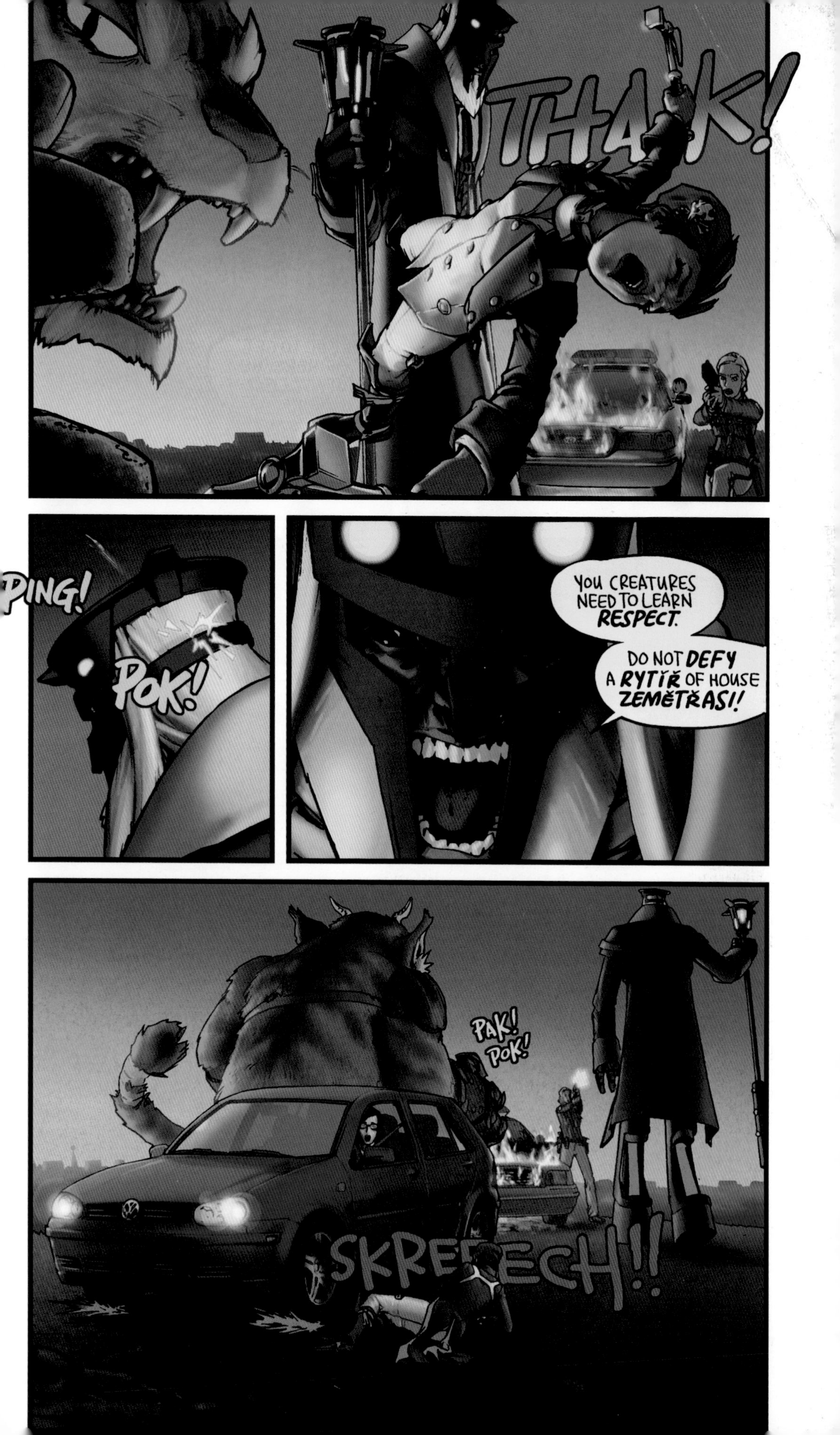
THAK!
PING!
POK!
YOU CREATURES NEED TO LEARN RESPECT.
DO NOT DEFY A RYTÍŘ OF HOUSE ZEMĚTŘASI!
PAK! POK!
SKREEECH!!

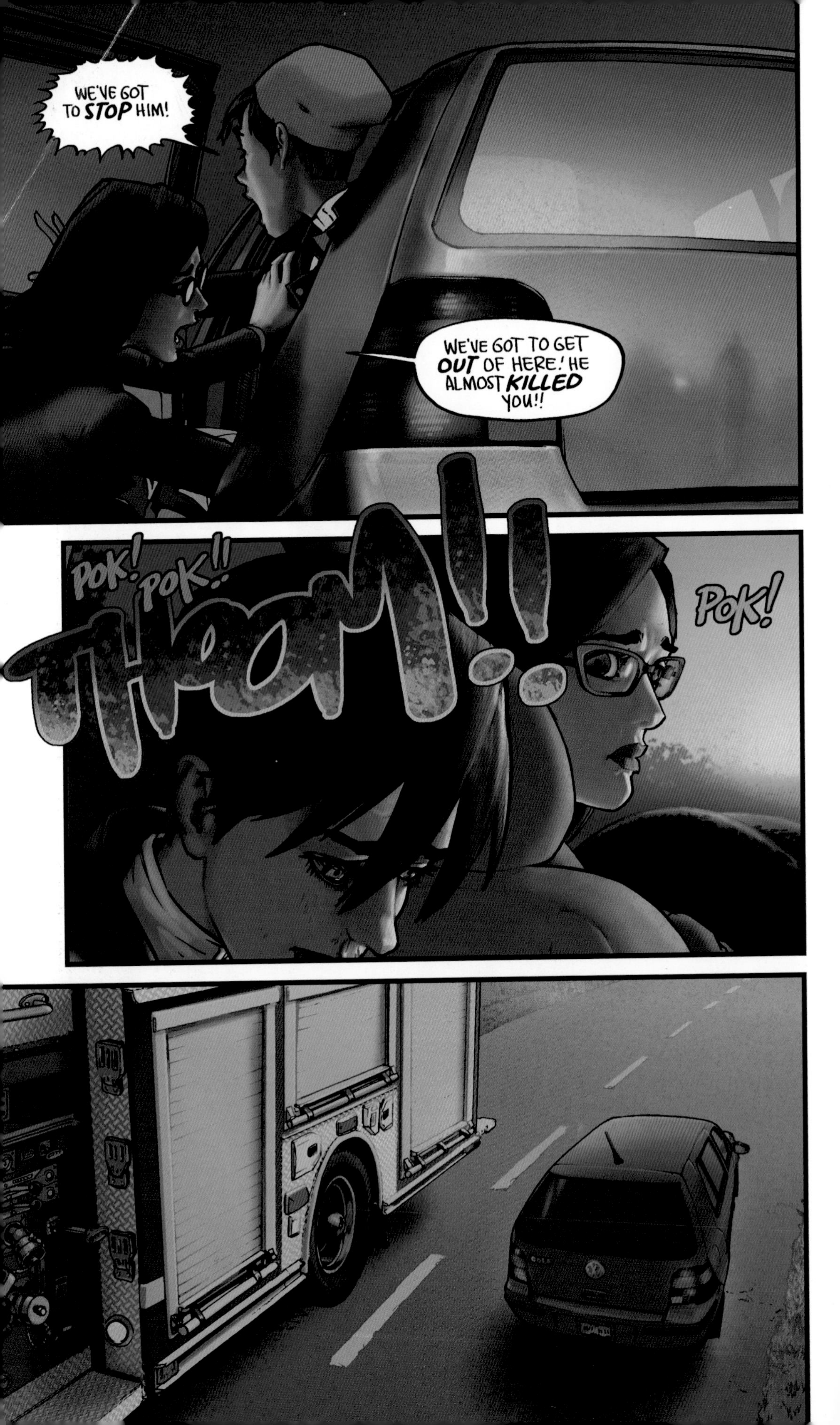
WE'VE GOT TO STOP HIM!
WE'VE GOT TO GET OUT OF HERE! HE ALMOST KILLED YOU!!
POK! POK!!
THOOM!!
POK!

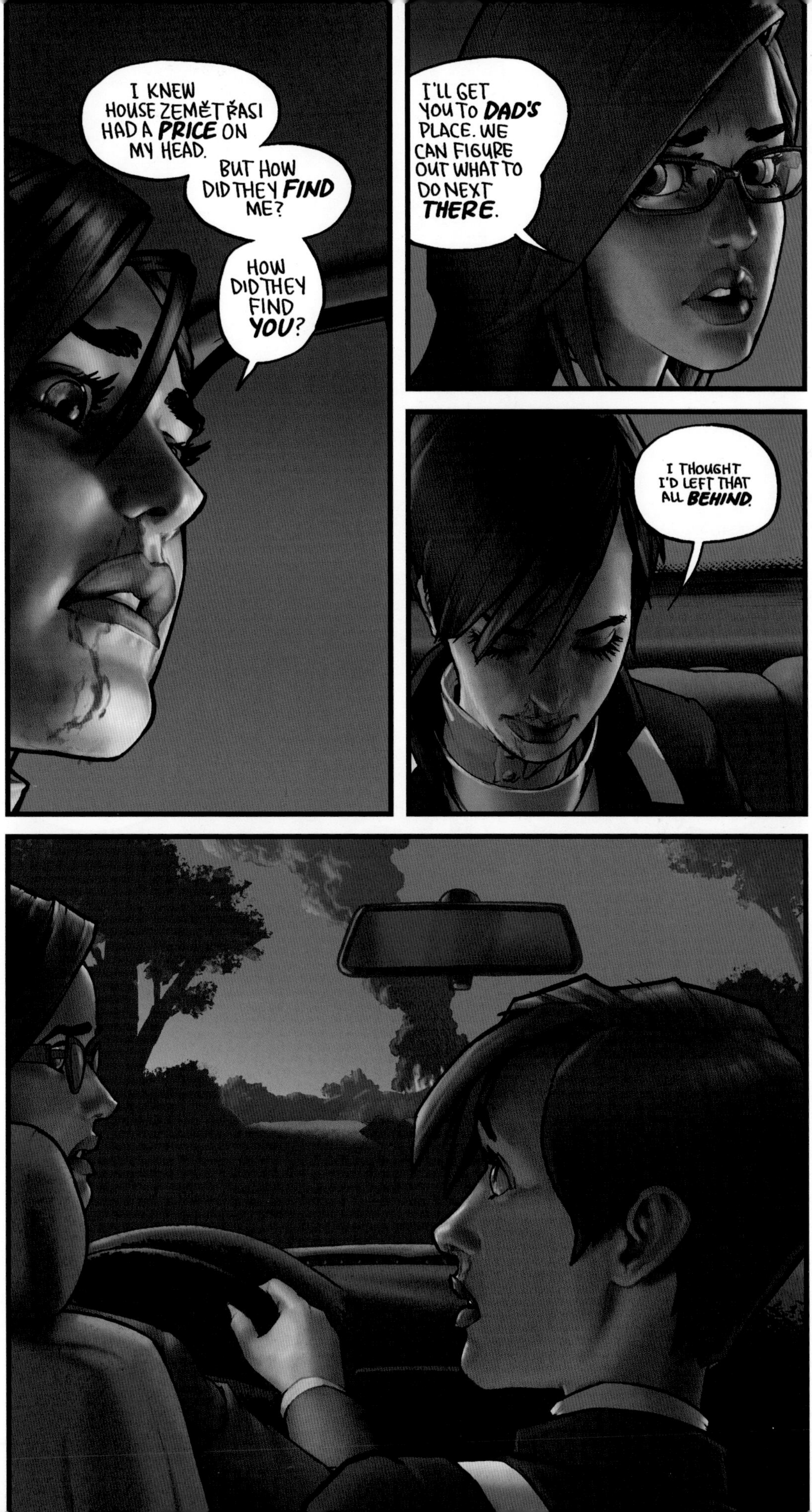
I KNEW HOUSE ZEMĚTŘASI HAD A PRICE ON MY HEAD.
BUT HOW DID THEY FIND ME?
HOW DID THEY FIND YOU?
I'LL GET YOU TO DAD'S PLACE. WE CAN FIGURE OUT WHAT TO DO NEXT THERE.
I THOUGHT I'D LEFT THAT ALL BEHIND.

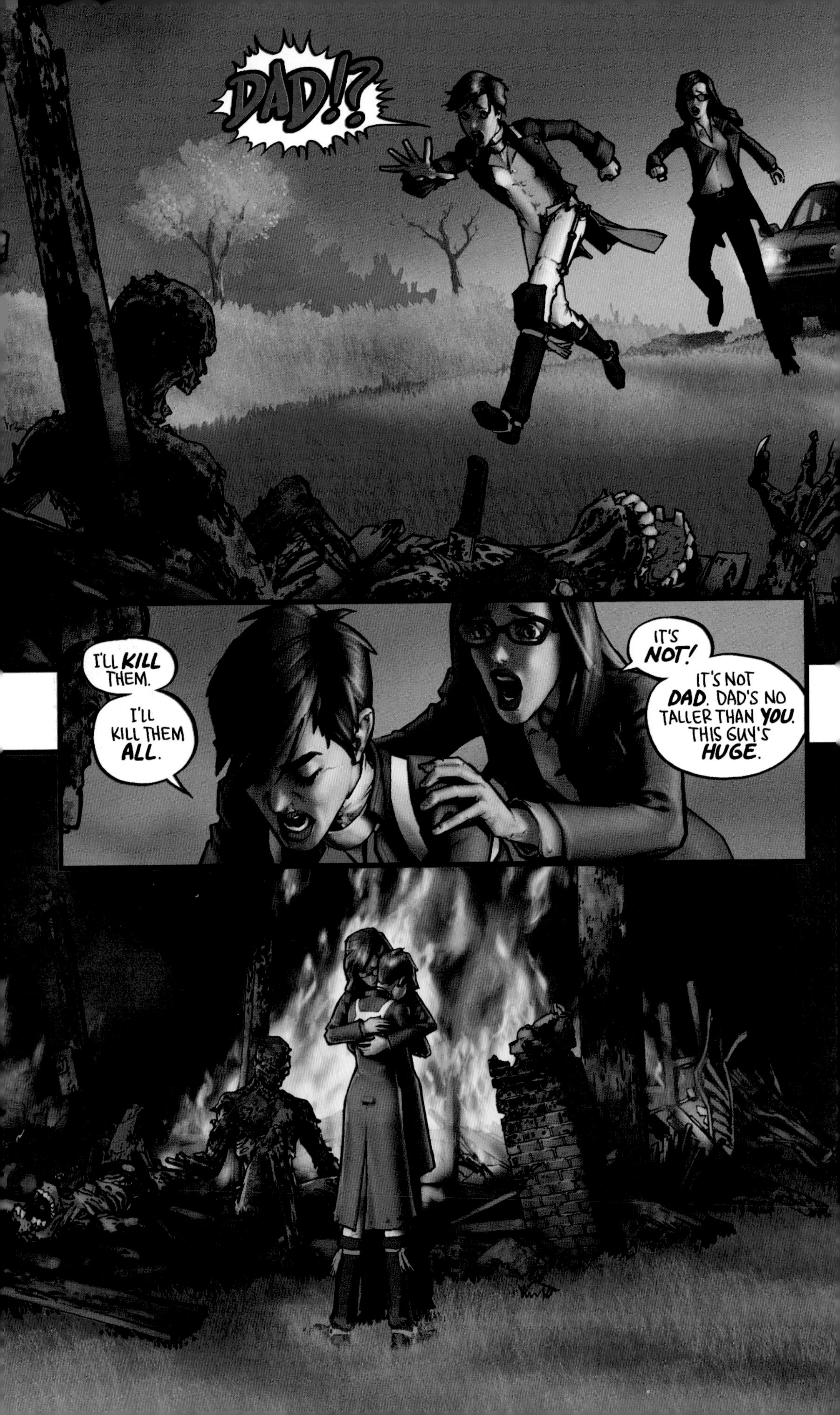
DAD!?
I'LL KILL THEM.
I'LL KILL THEM ALL.
IT'S NOT!
IT'S NOT DAD. DAD'S NO TALLER THAN YOU. THIS GUY'S HUGE.

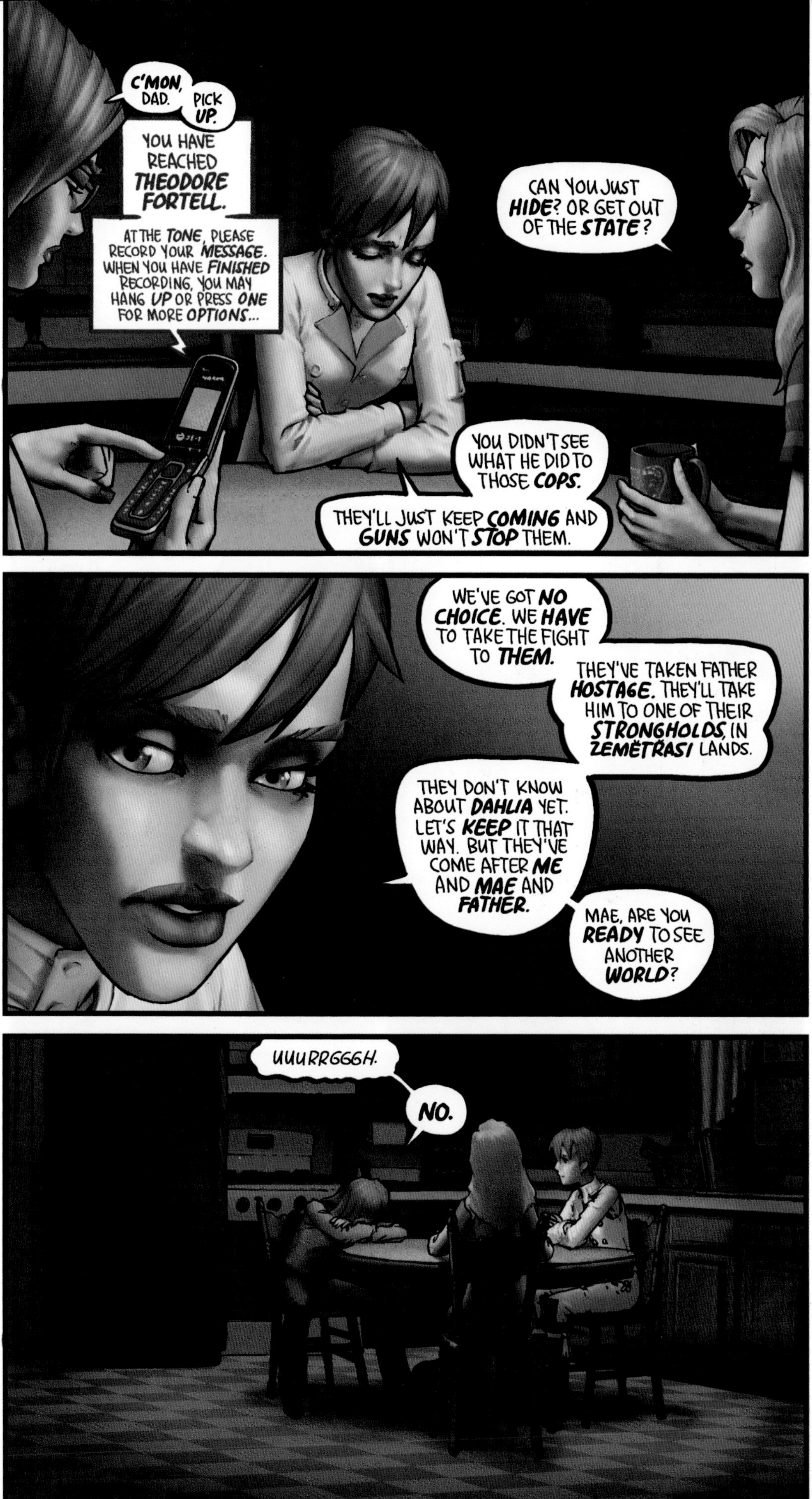
C'MON, DAD.
PICK UP.
YOU HAVE REACHED THEODORE FORTELL.
AT THE TONE, PLEASE RECORD YOUR MESSAGE. WHEN YOU HAVE FINISHED RECORDING, YOU MAY HANG UP OR PRESS ONE FOR MORE OPTIONS...
CAN YOU JUST HIDE? OR GET OUT OF THE STATE?
YOU DIDN'T SEE WHAT HE DID TO THOSE COPS.
THEY'LL JUST KEEP COMING AND GUNS WON'T STOP THEM.
WE'VE GOT NO CHOICE. WE HAVE TO TAKE THE FIGHT TO THEM.
THEY'VE TAKEN FATHER HOSTAGE. THEY'LL TAKE HIM TO ONE OF THEIR STRONGHOLDS, IN ZEMËTRASI LANDS.
THEY DON'T KNOW ABOUT DAHLIA YET. LET'S KEEP IT THAT WAY. BUT THEY'VE COME AFTER ME AND MAE AND FATHER.
MAE, ARE YOU READY TO SEE ANOTHER WORLD?
UUURRGGGH.
NO.

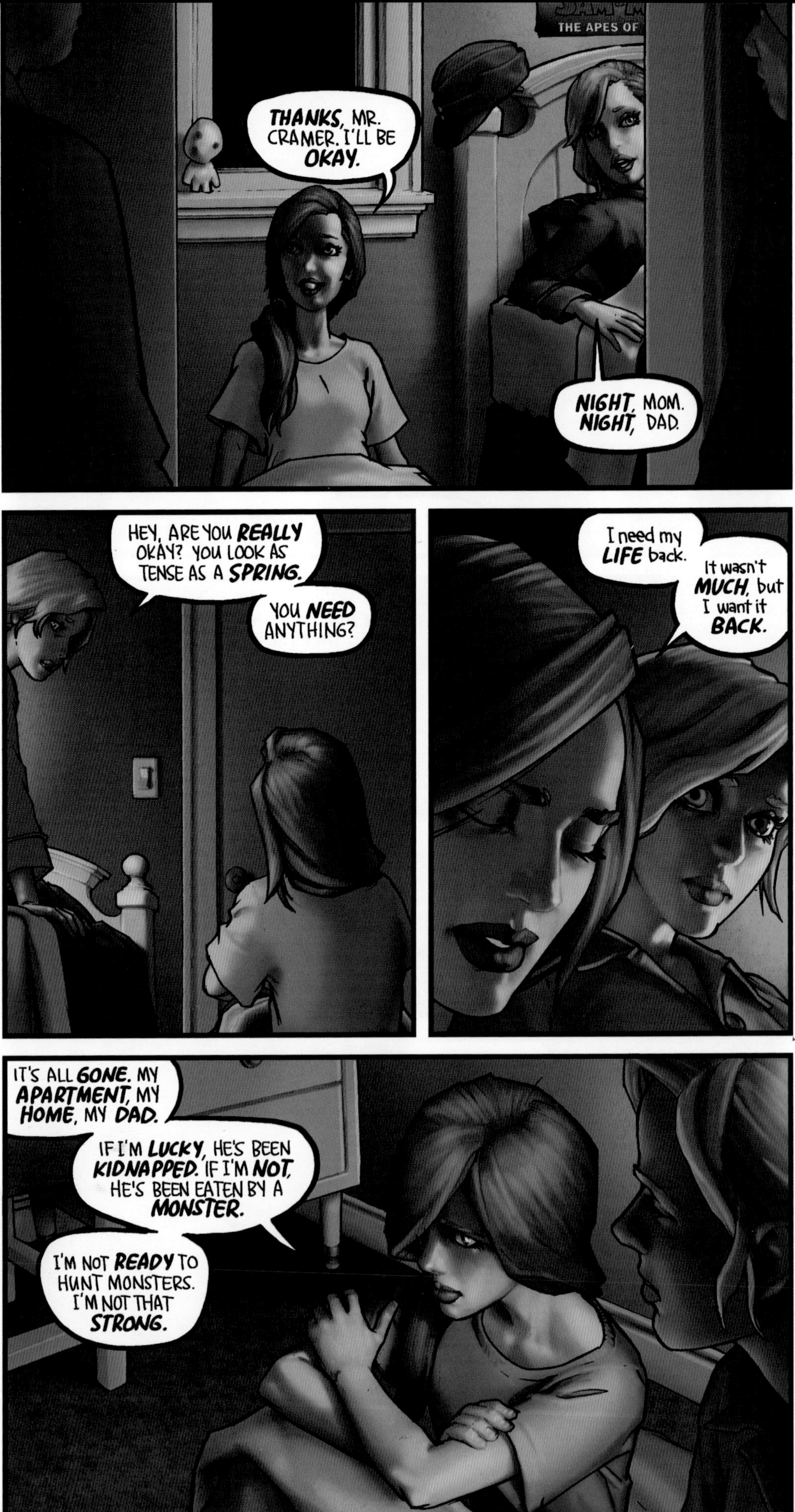
THE APES OF
THANKS, MR. CRAMER. I'LL BE OKAY.
NIGHT, MOM. NIGHT, DAD.
HEY, ARE YOU REALLY OKAY? YOU LOOK AS TENSE AS A SPRING.
YOU NEED ANYTHING?
I need my LIFE back.
It wasn't MUCH, but I want it BACK.
IT'S ALL GONE. MY APARTMENT, MY HOME, MY DAD.
IF I'M LUCKY, HE'S BEEN KIDNAPPED. IF I'M NOT, HE'S BEEN EATEN BY A MONSTER.
I'M NOT READY TO HUNT MONSTERS. I'M NOT THAT STRONG.

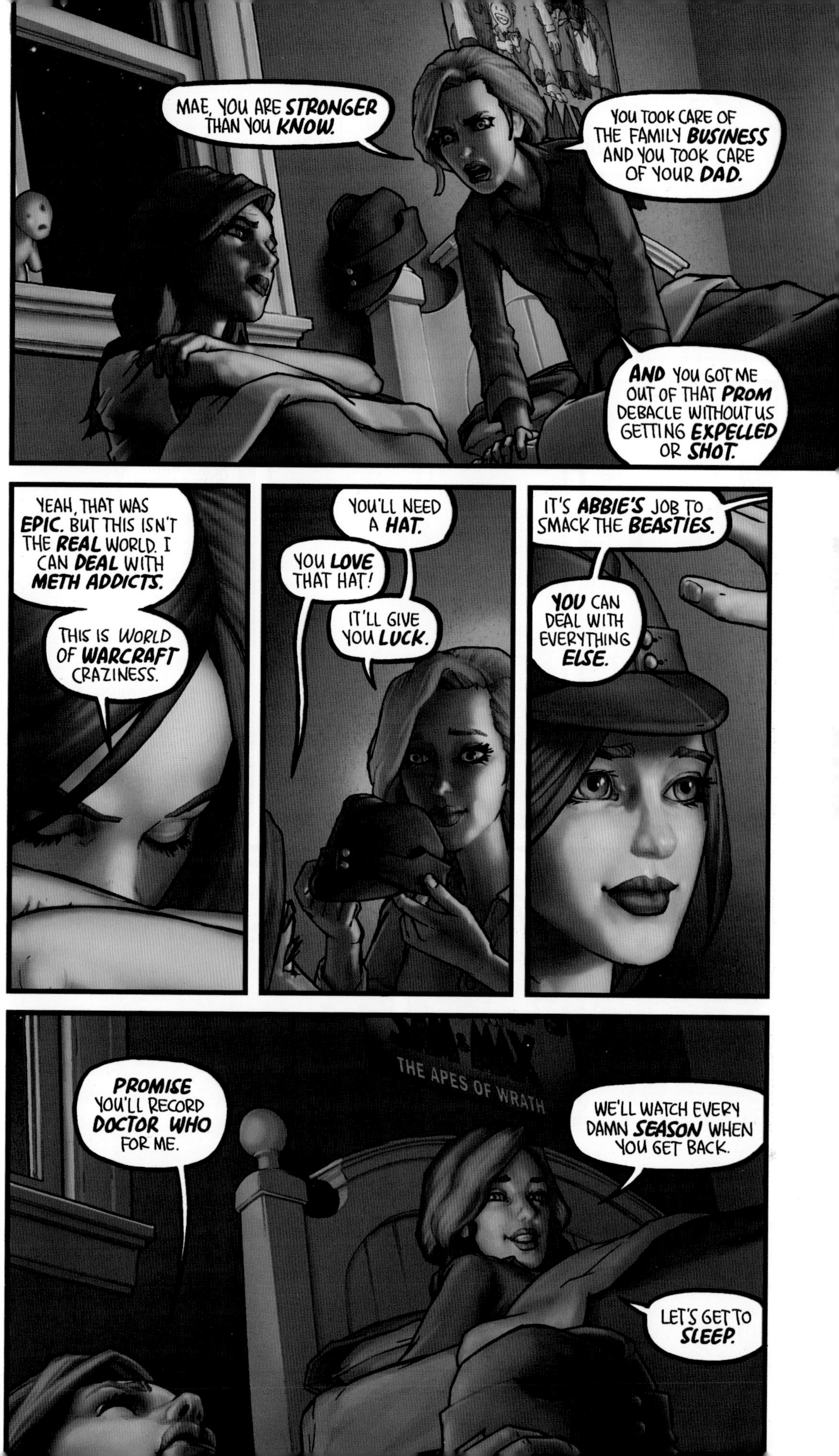
MAE, YOU ARE STRONGER THAN YOU KNOW.
YOU TOOK CARE OF THE FAMILY BUSINESS AND YOU TOOK CARE OF YOUR DAD.
AND YOU GOT ME OUT OF THAT PROM DEBACLE WITHOUT US GETTING EXPELLED OR SHOT.
YEAH, THAT WAS EPIC. BUT THIS ISN'T THE REAL WORLD. I CAN DEAL WITH METH ADDICTS.
THIS IS WORLD OF WARCRAFT CRAZINESS.
YOU'LL NEED A HAT.
YOU LOVE THAT HAT!
IT'LL GIVE YOU LUCK.
IT'S ABBIE'S JOB TO SMACK THE BEASTIES.
YOU CAN DEAL WITH EVERYTHING ELSE.
THE APES OF WRATH
PROMISE YOU'LL RECORD DOCTOR WHO FOR ME.
WE'LL WATCH EVERY DAMN SEASON WHEN YOU GET BACK.
LET'S GET TO SLEEP.

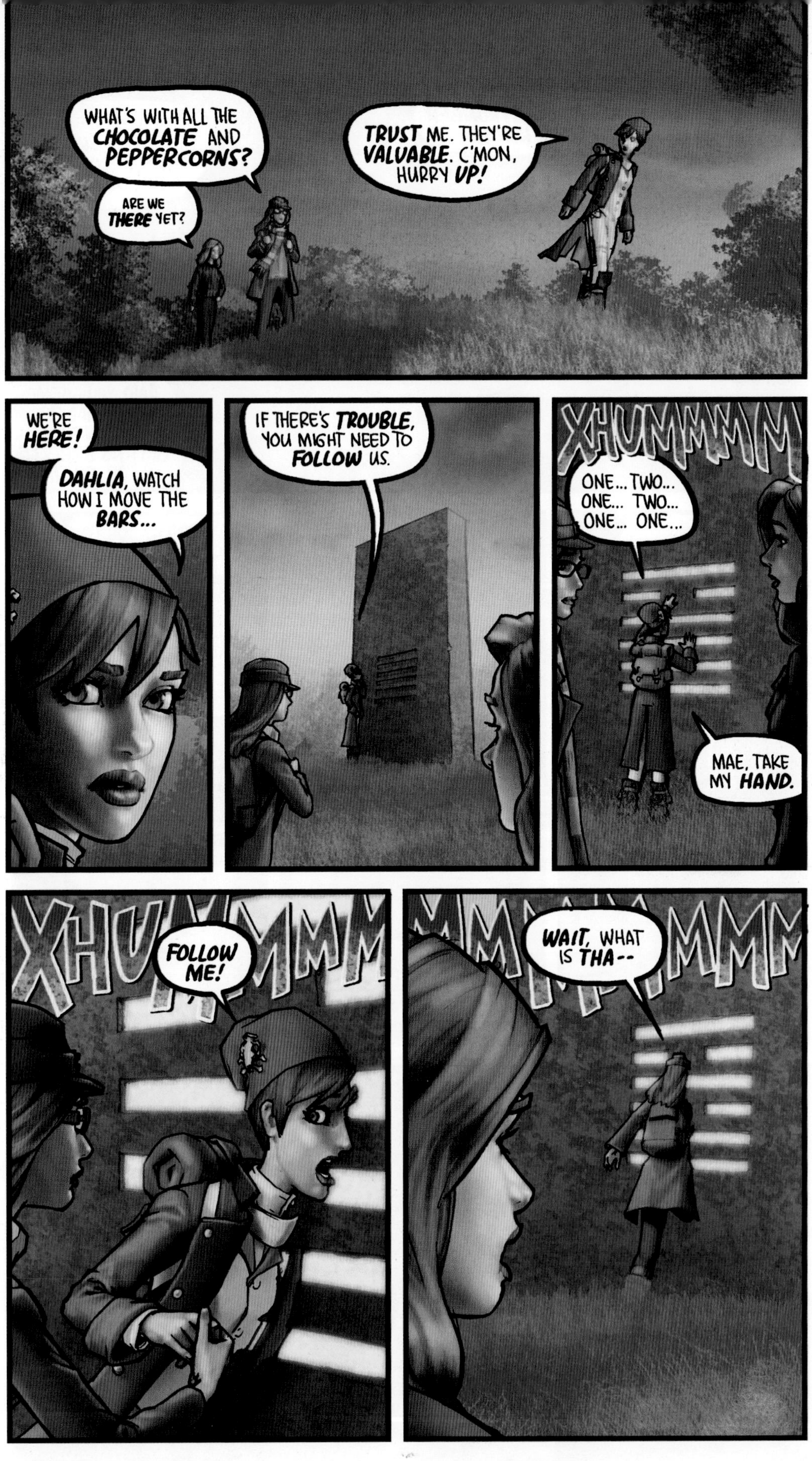

WHAT'S WITH ALL THE CHOCOLATE AND PEPPERCORNS?
ARE WE THERE YET?
TRUST ME. THEY'RE VALUABLE. C'MON, HURRY UP!
WE'RE HERE!
DAHLIA, WATCH HOW I MOVE THE BARS...
IF THERE'S TROUBLE, YOU MIGHT NEED TO FOLLOW US.
XHUMMMM
ONE... TWO... ONE... TWO... ONE... ONE...
MAE, TAKE MY HAND.
XHUMMMM
FOLLOW ME!
MMMMMMM
WAIT, WHAT IS THA--

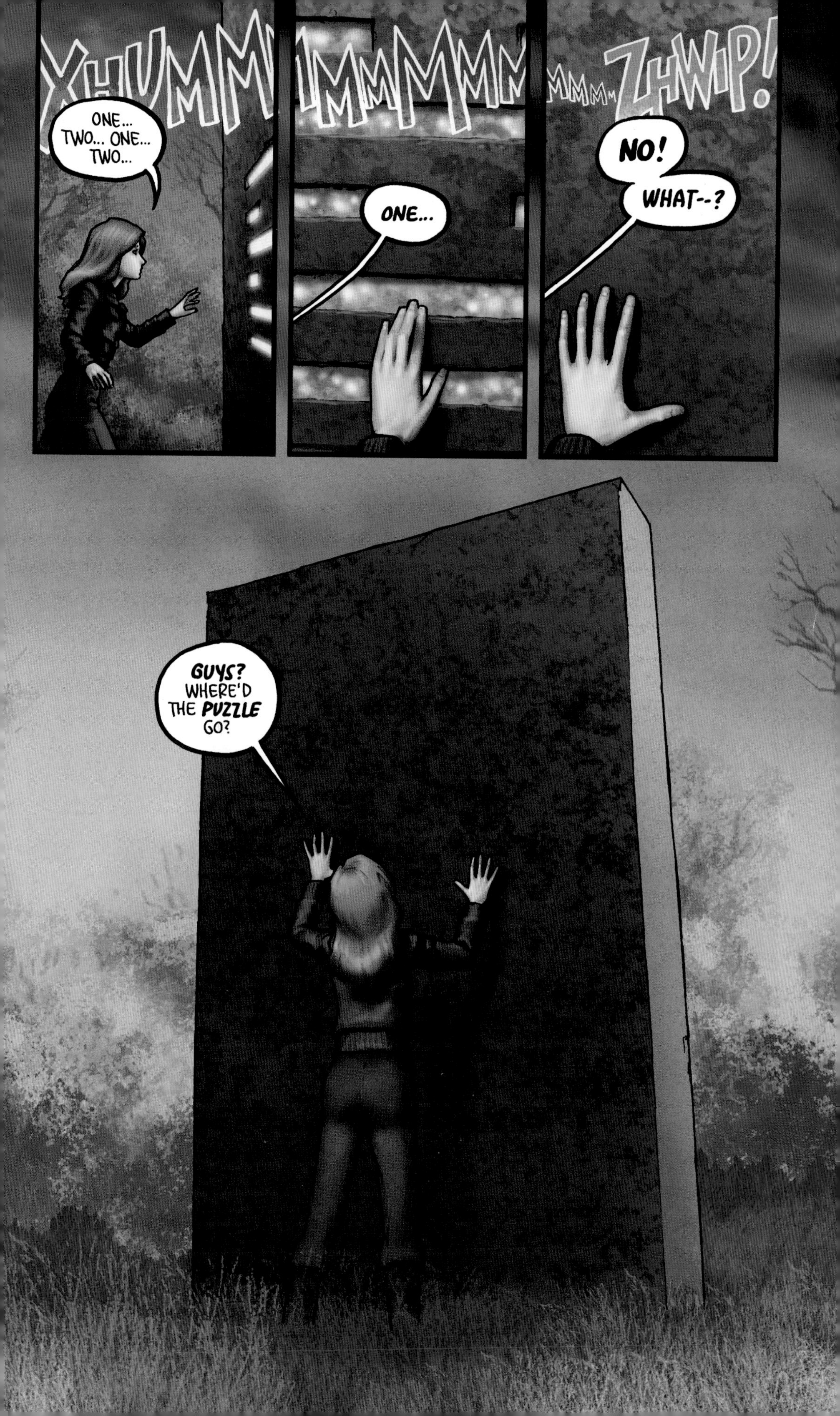
XHUMMMMMMMMMMMMMMMMM
ONE... TWO... ONE... TWO...
ONE...
ZHWIP!
NO!
WHAT--?
GUYS? WHERE'D THE PUZZLE GO?

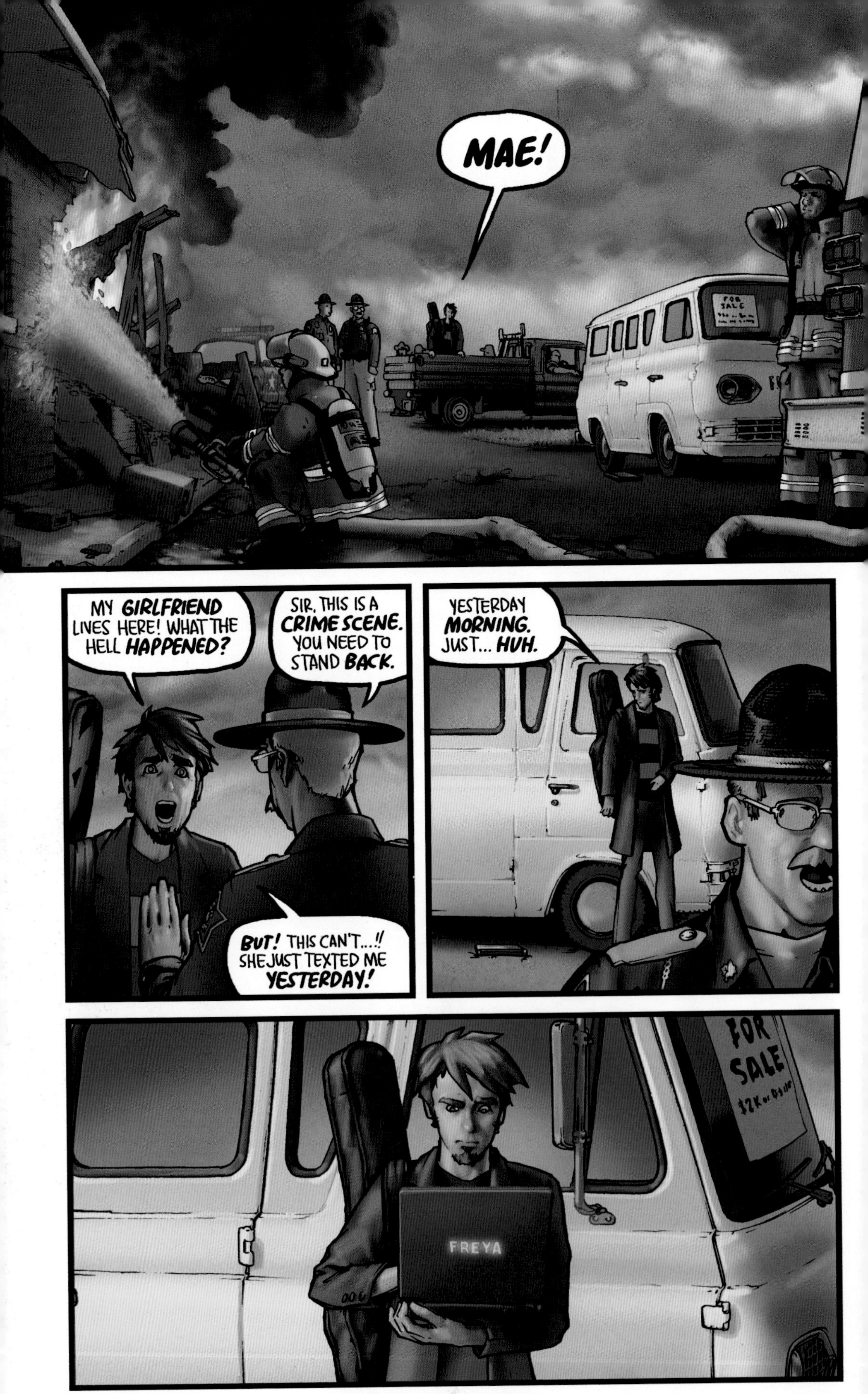
MAE!
FOR SALE
MY GIRLFRIEND LIVES HERE! WHAT THE HELL HAPPENED?
SIR, THIS IS A CRIME SCENE. YOU NEED TO STAND BACK.
BUT! THIS CAN'T...!! SHE JUST TEXTED ME YESTERDAY!
YESTERDAY MORNING. JUST... HUH.
FOR SALE
FREYA

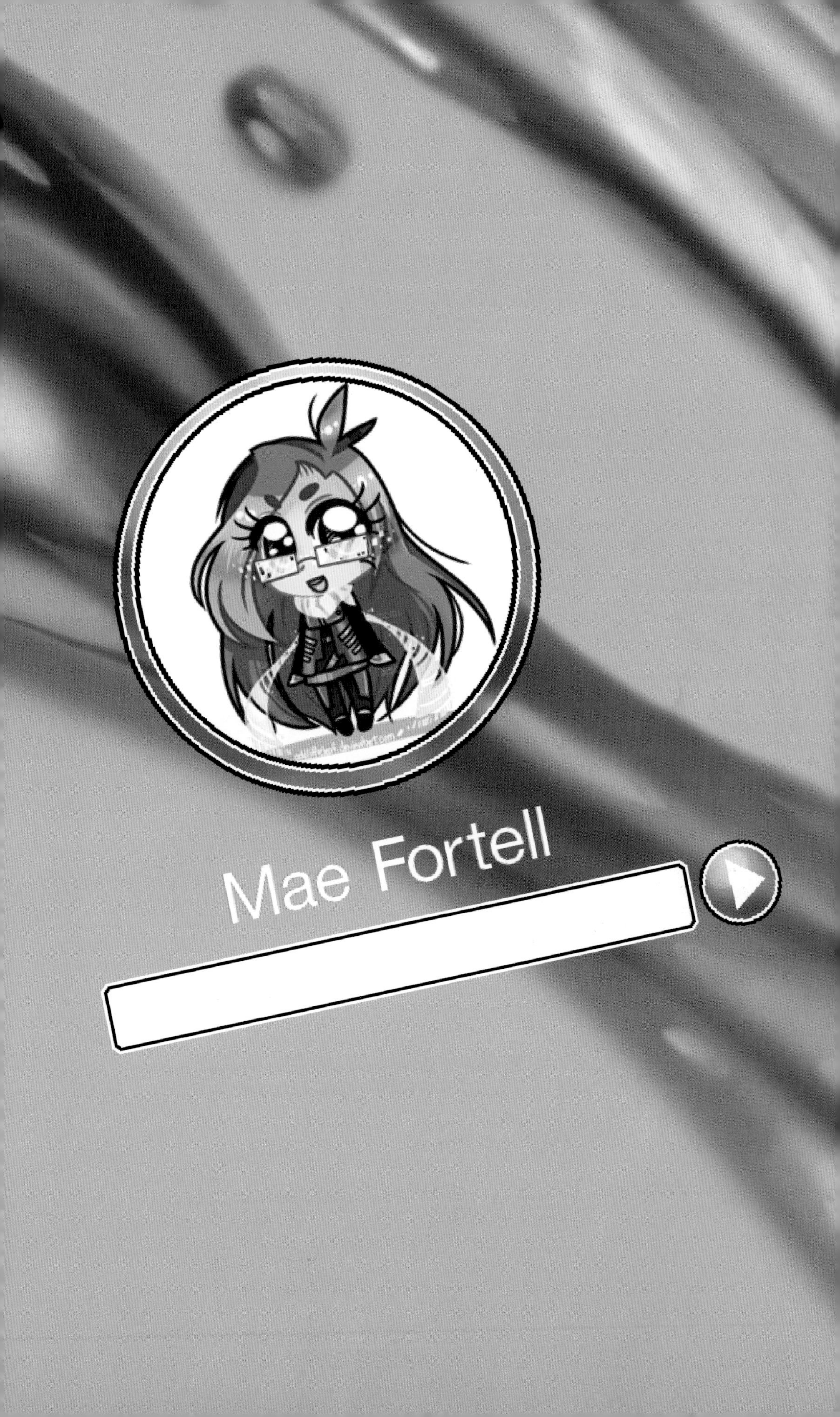
Mae Fortell

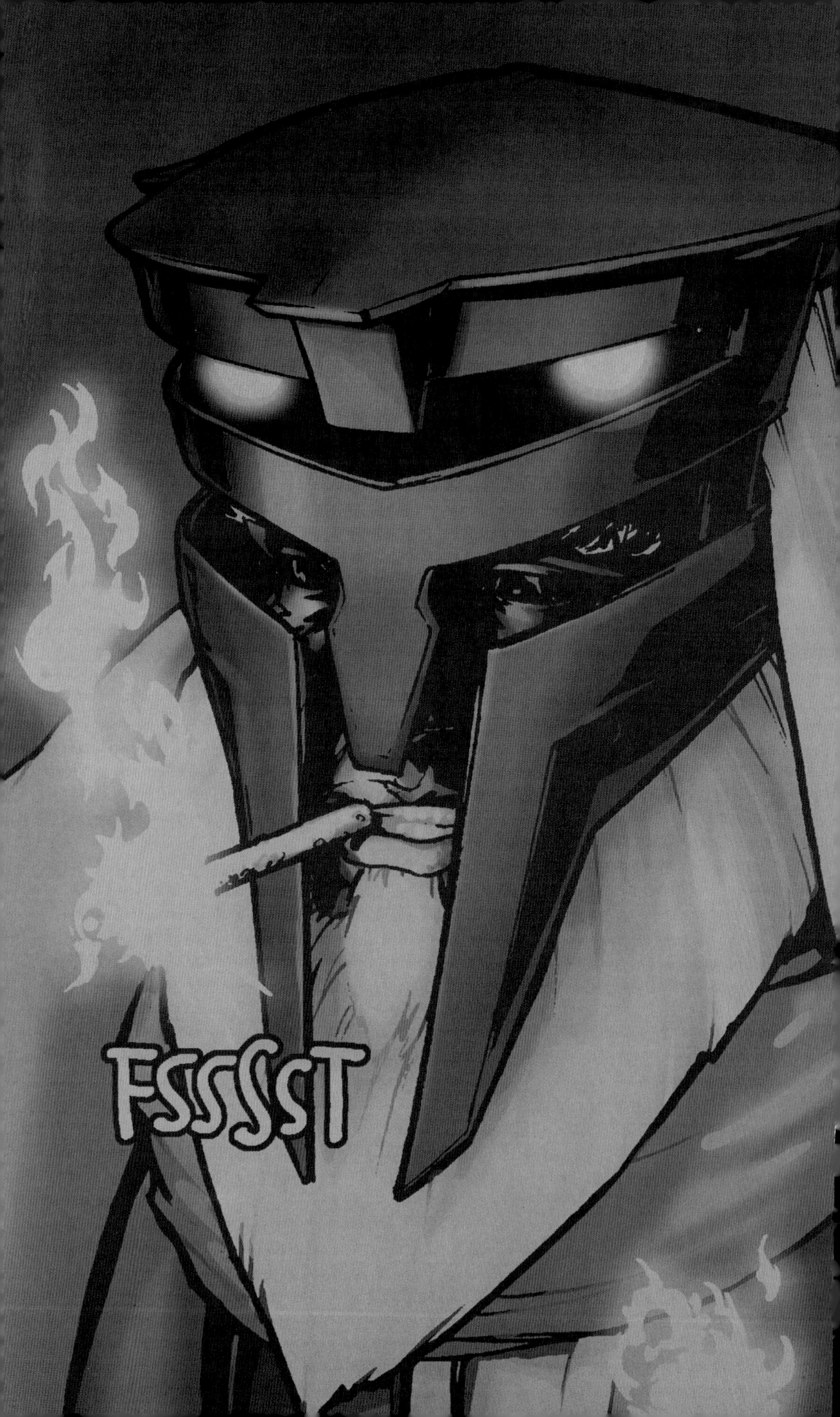
FSSSST

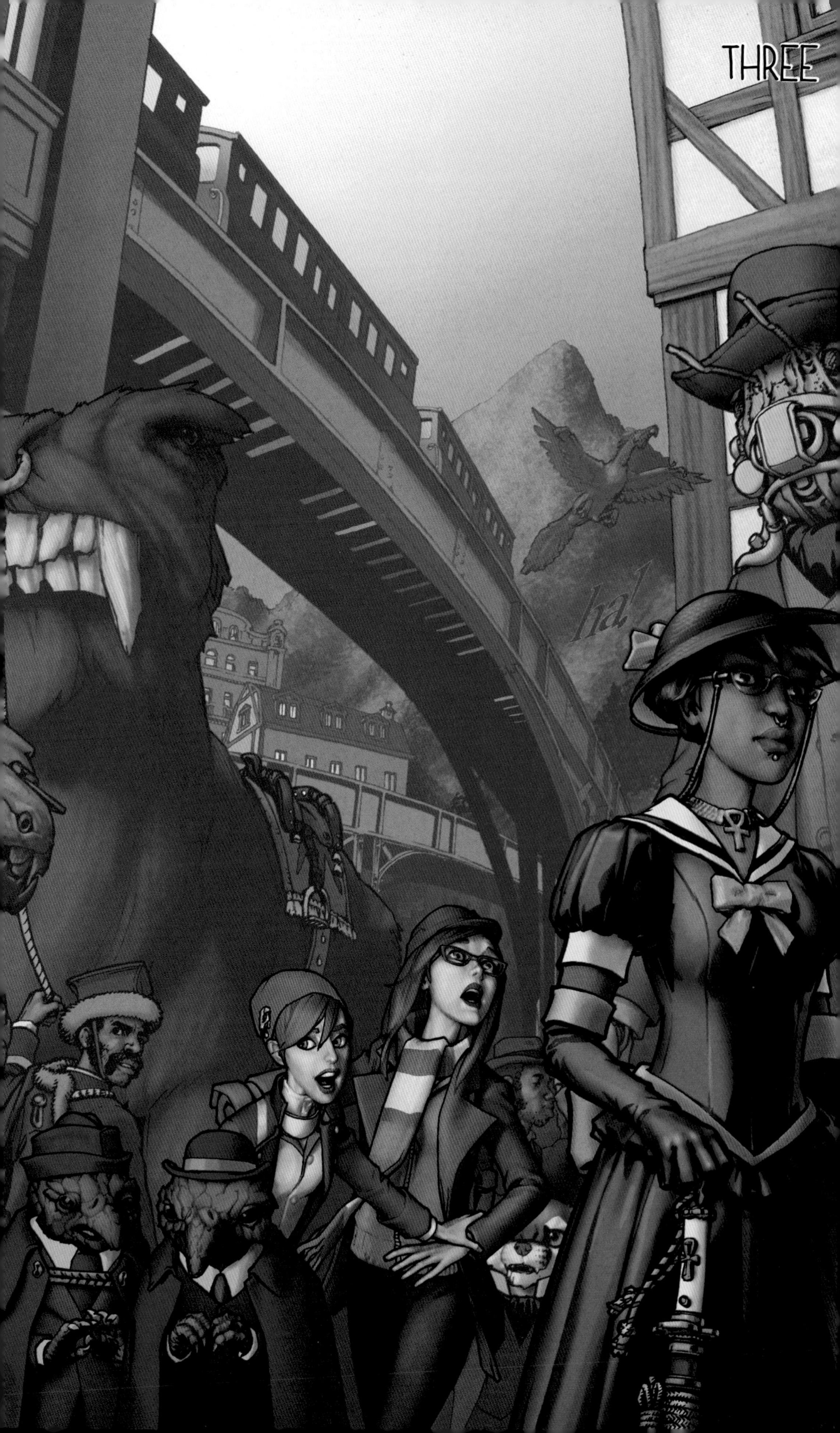
THREE
ha!

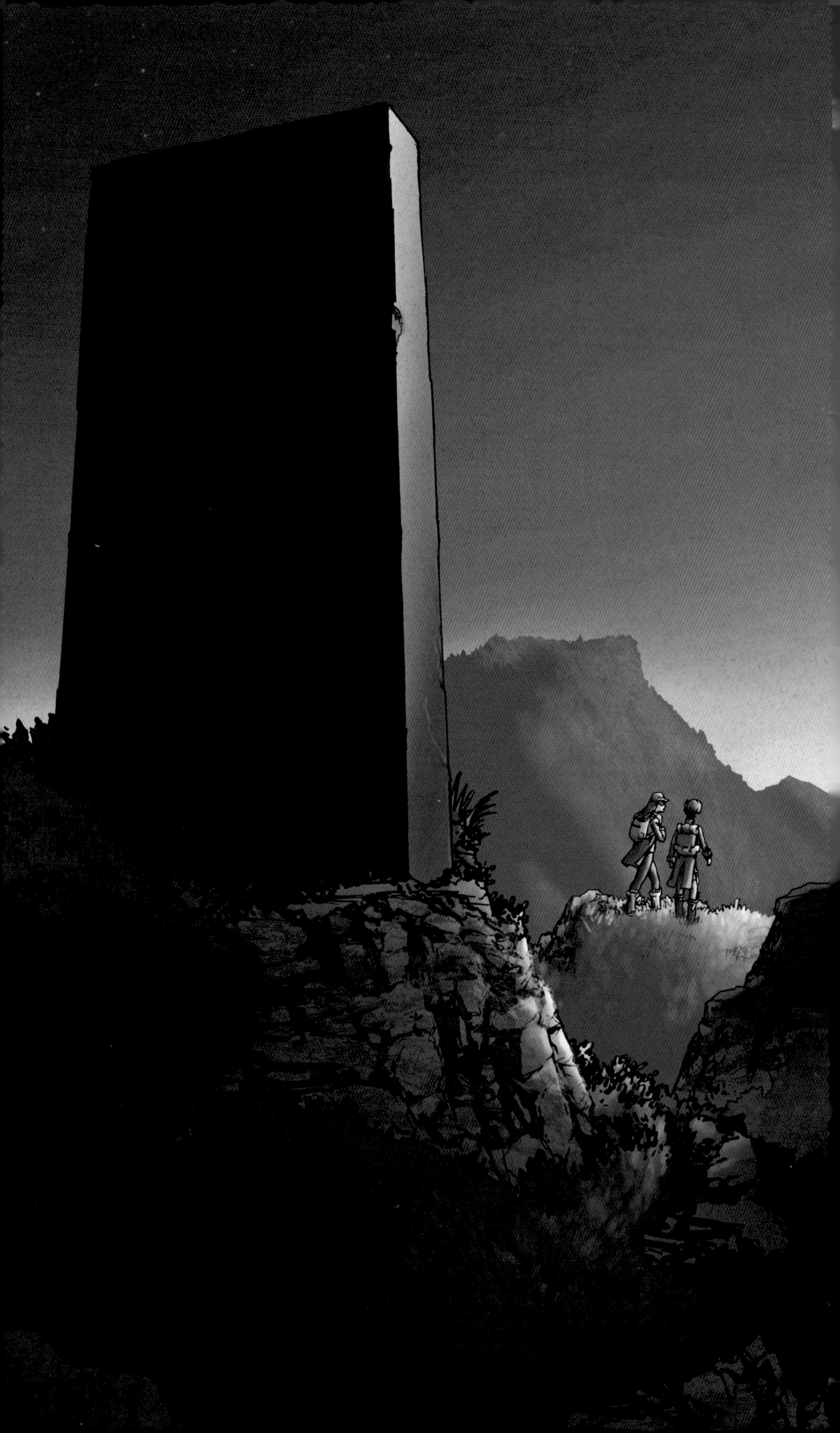

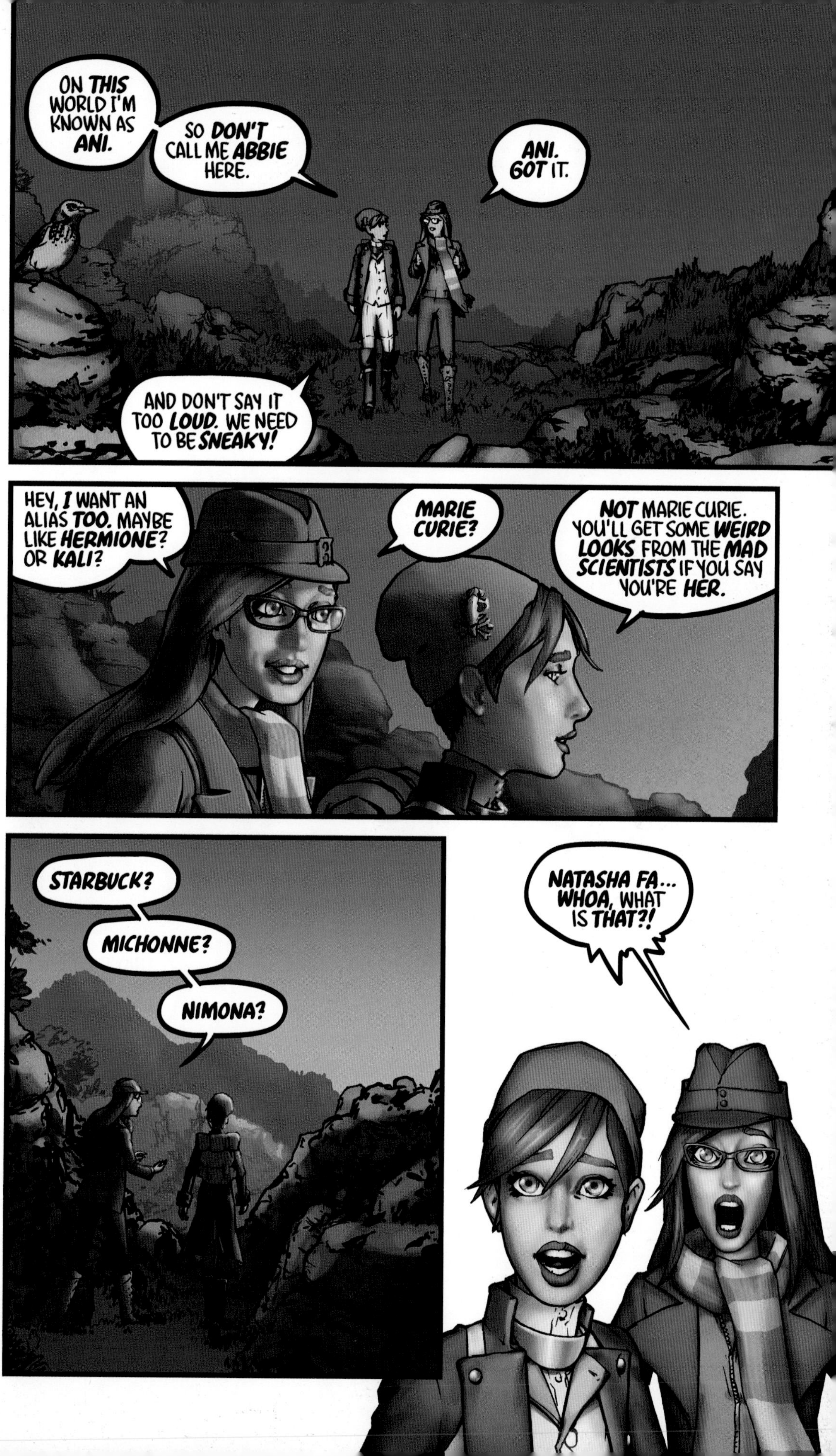

ON THIS WORLD I'M KNOWN AS ANI.
SO DON'T CALL ME ABBIE HERE.
ANI. GOT IT.
AND DON'T SAY IT TOO LOUD. WE NEED TO BE SNEAKY!
HEY, I WANT AN ALIAS TOO. MAYBE LIKE HERMIONE? OR KALI?
MARIE CURIE?
NOT MARIE CURIE. YOU'LL GET SOME WEIRD LOOKS FROM THE MAD SCIENTISTS IF YOU SAY YOU'RE HER.
STARBUCK?
MICHONNE?
NIMONA?
NATASHA FA... WHOA, WHAT IS THAT?!

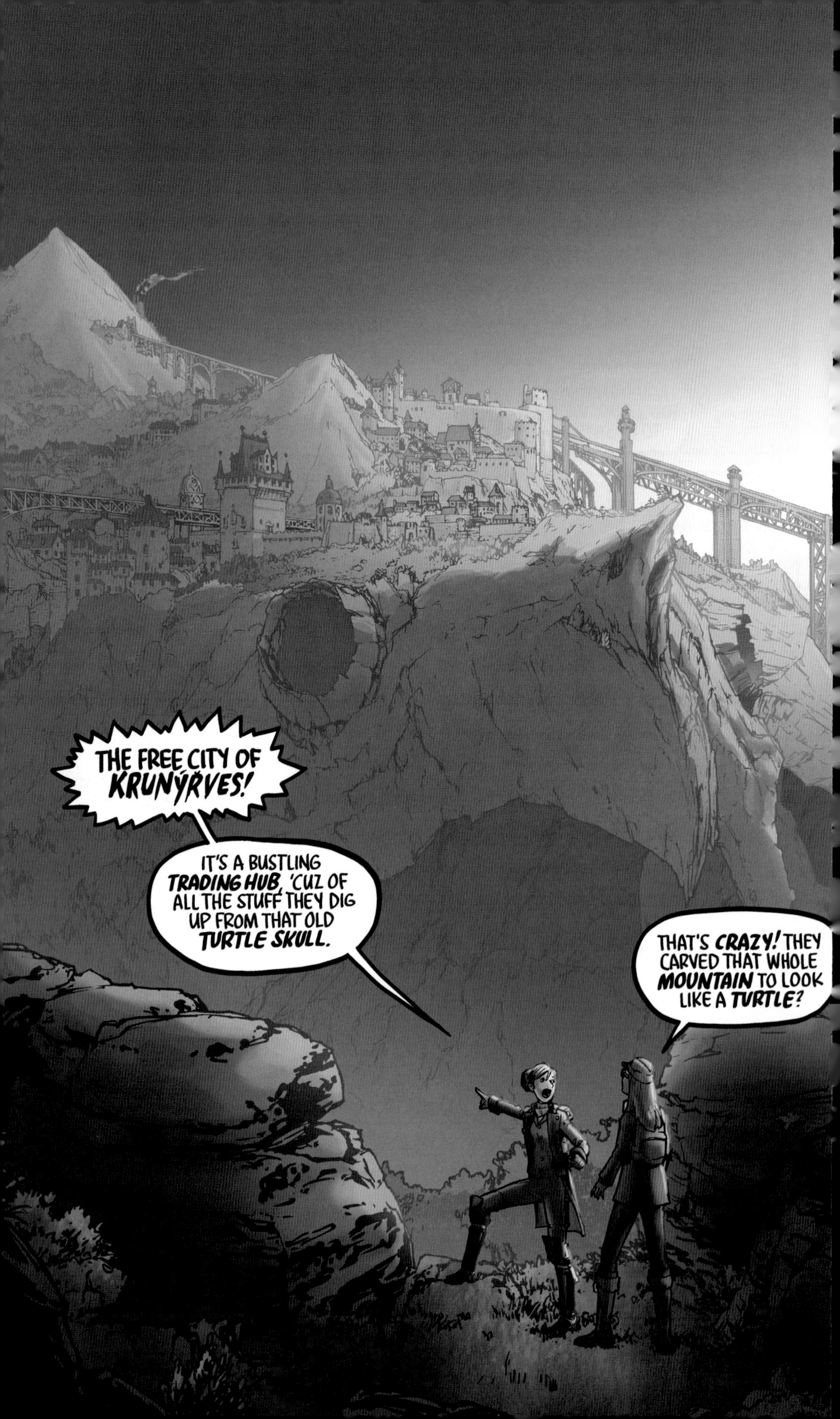
THE FREE CITY OF KRUNÝRVES!
IT'S A BUSTLING TRADING HUB, 'CUZ OF ALL THE STUFF THEY DIG UP FROM THAT OLD TURTLE SKULL.
THAT'S CRAZY! THEY CARVED THAT WHOLE MOUNTAIN TO LOOK LIKE A TURTLE?

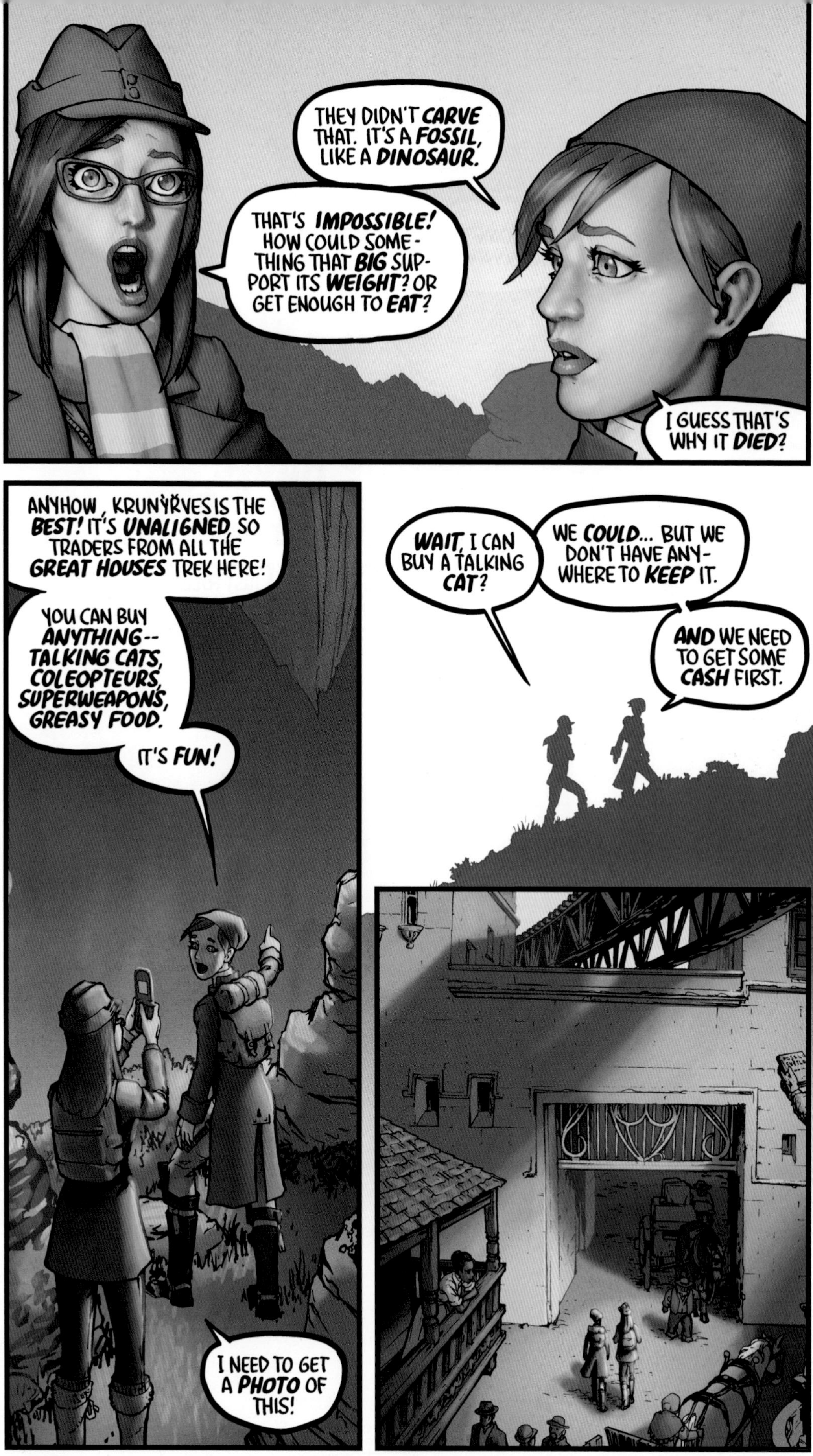
THEY DIDN'T CARVE THAT. IT'S A FOSSIL, LIKE A DINOSAUR.
THAT'S IMPOSSIBLE! HOW COULD SOME-THING THAT BIG SUP-PORT ITS WEIGHT? OR GET ENOUGH TO EAT?
I GUESS THAT'S WHY IT DIED?
ANYHOW, KRUNÝŘVES IS THE BEST! IT'S UNALIGNED, SO TRADERS FROM ALL THE GREAT HOUSES TREK HERE!
YOU CAN BUY ANYTHING-- TALKING CATS, COLEOPTEURS, SUPERWEAPONS, GREASY FOOD.
IT'S FUN!
I NEED TO GET A PHOTO OF THIS!
WAIT, I CAN BUY A TALKING CAT?
WE COULD... BUT WE DON'T HAVE ANY-WHERE TO KEEP IT.
AND WE NEED TO GET SOME CASH FIRST.

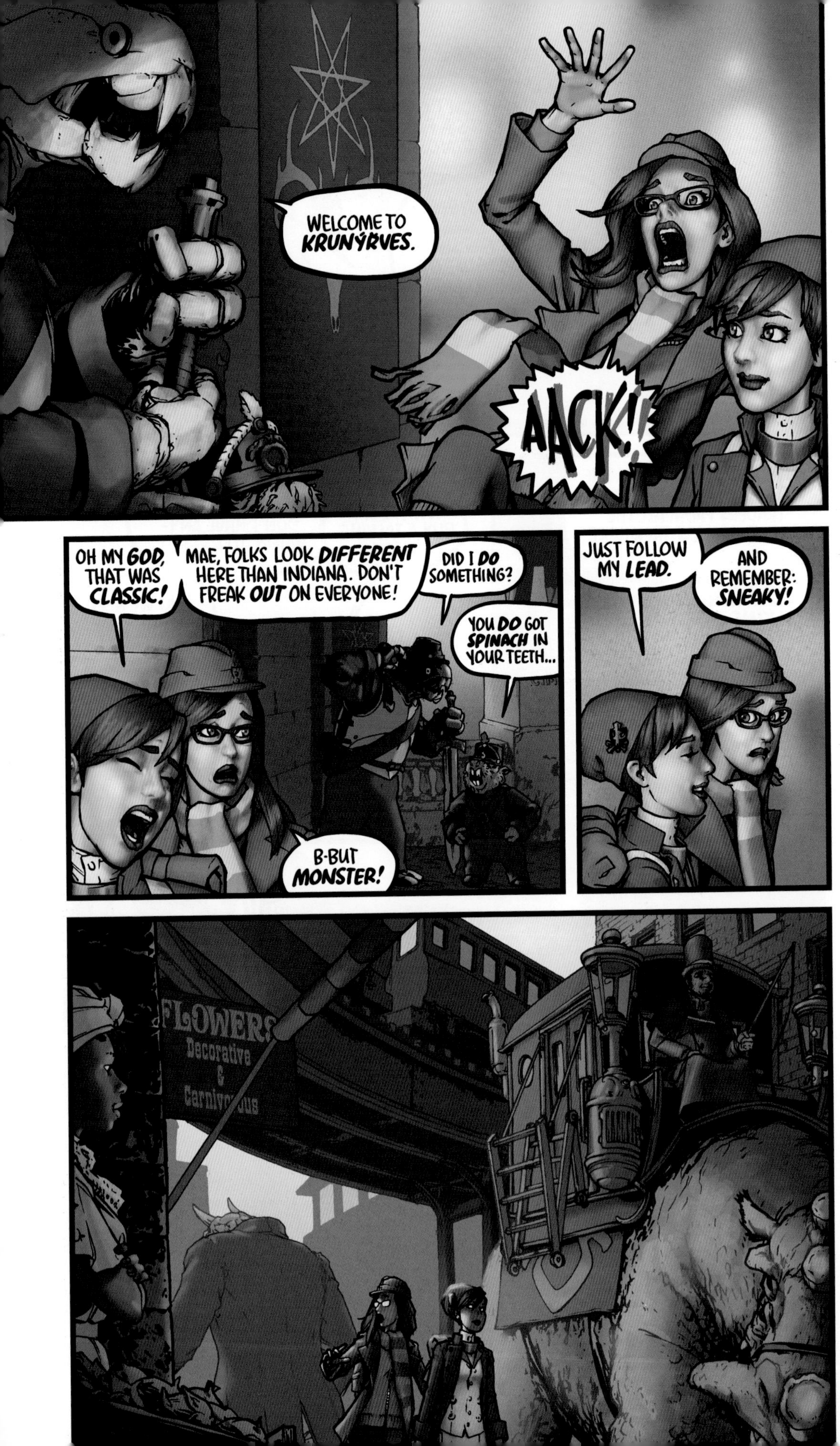
WELCOME TO KRUNÝRVES.
AACK!!
OH MY GOD, THAT WAS CLASSIC!
MAE, FOLKS LOOK DIFFERENT HERE THAN INDIANA. DON'T FREAK OUT ON EVERYONE!
DID I DO SOMETHING?
YOU DO GOT SPINACH IN YOUR TEETH...
B-BUT MONSTER!
JUST FOLLOW MY LEAD.
AND REMEMBER: SNEAKY!
FLOWERS
Decorative & Carnivorous

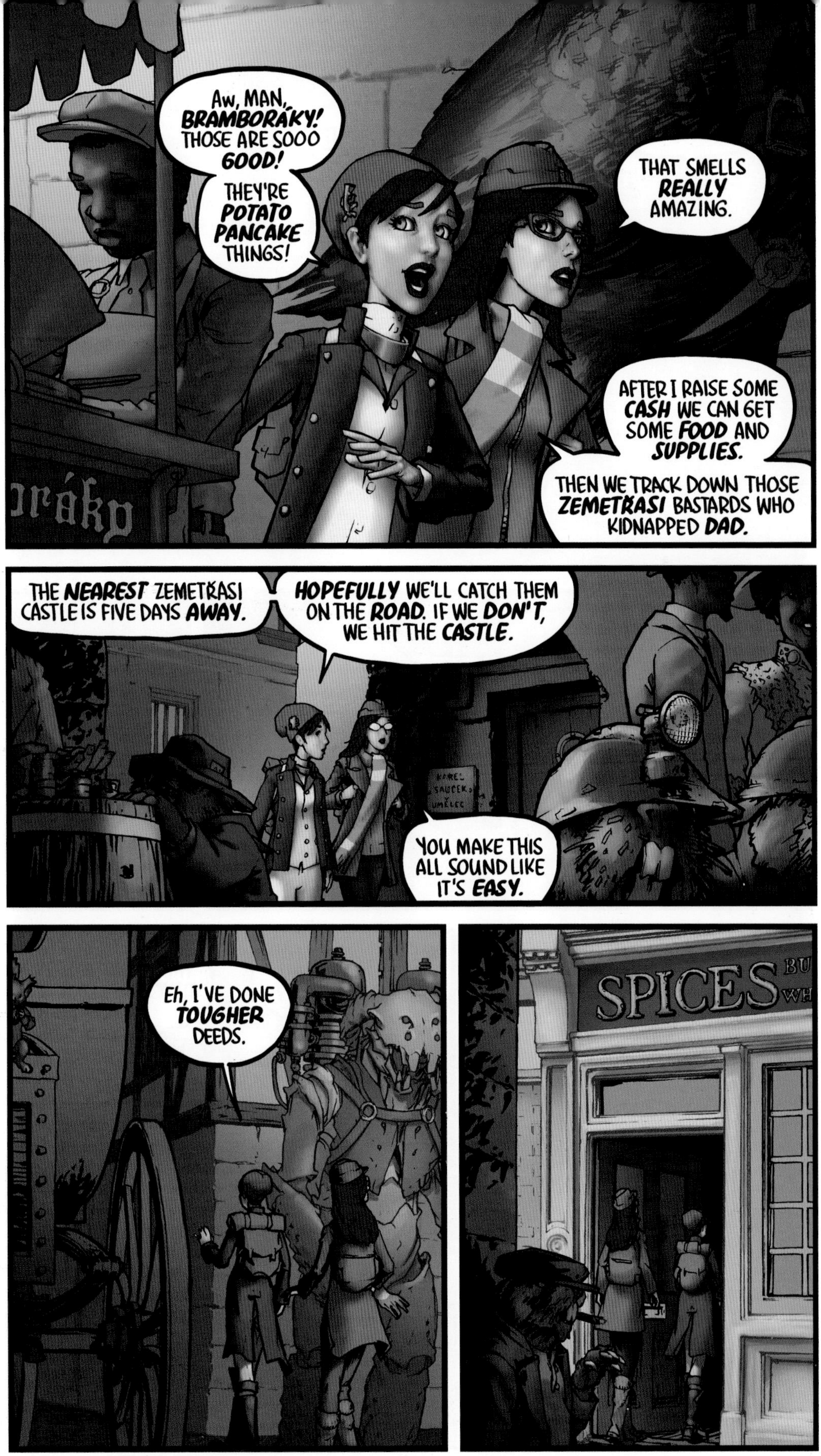
Aw, MAN, BRAMBORÁKY! THOSE ARE SOOO GOOD!
THEY'RE POTATO PANCAKE THINGS!
THAT SMELLS REALLY AMAZING.
AFTER I RAISE SOME CASH WE CAN GET SOME FOOD AND SUPPLIES.
THEN WE TRACK DOWN THOSE ZEMETŘASI BASTARDS WHO KIDNAPPED DAD.
THE NEAREST ZEMETŘASI CASTLE IS FIVE DAYS AWAY.
HOPEFULLY WE'LL CATCH THEM ON THE ROAD. IF WE DON'T, WE HIT THE CASTLE.
YOU MAKE THIS ALL SOUND LIKE IT'S EASY.
Eh, I'VE DONE TOUGHER DEEDS.
SPICES

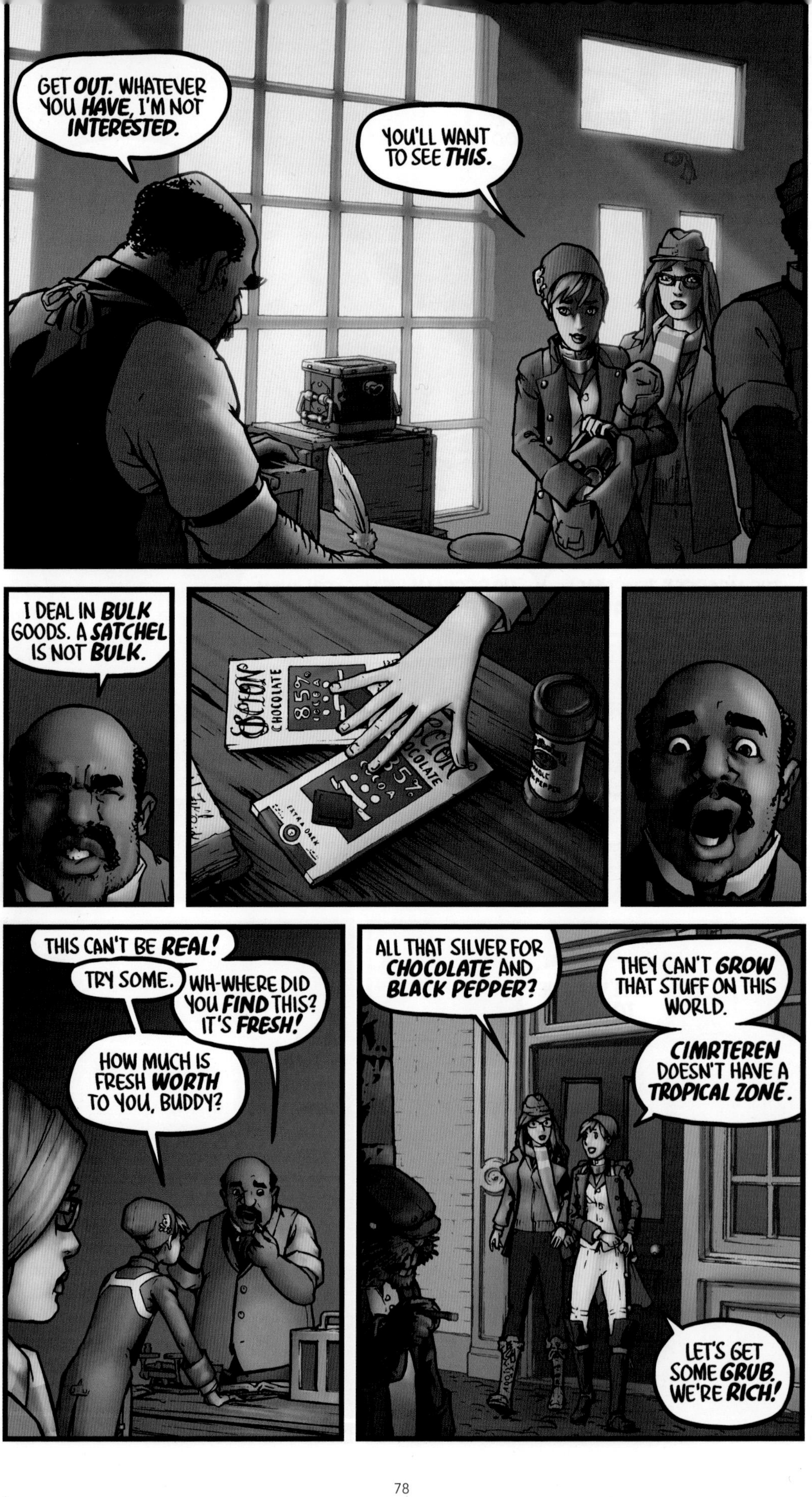
GET OUT. WHATEVER YOU HAVE, I'M NOT INTERESTED.
YOU'LL WANT TO SEE THIS.
I DEAL IN BULK GOODS. A SATCHEL IS NOT BULK.
THIS CAN'T BE REAL!
TRY SOME.
WH-WHERE DID YOU FIND THIS? IT'S FRESH!
HOW MUCH IS FRESH WORTH TO YOU, BUDDY?
ALL THAT SILVER FOR CHOCOLATE AND BLACK PEPPER?
THEY CAN'T GROW THAT STUFF ON THIS WORLD.
CIMRTEREN DOESN'T HAVE A TROPICAL ZONE.
LET'S GET SOME GRUB. WE'RE RICH!

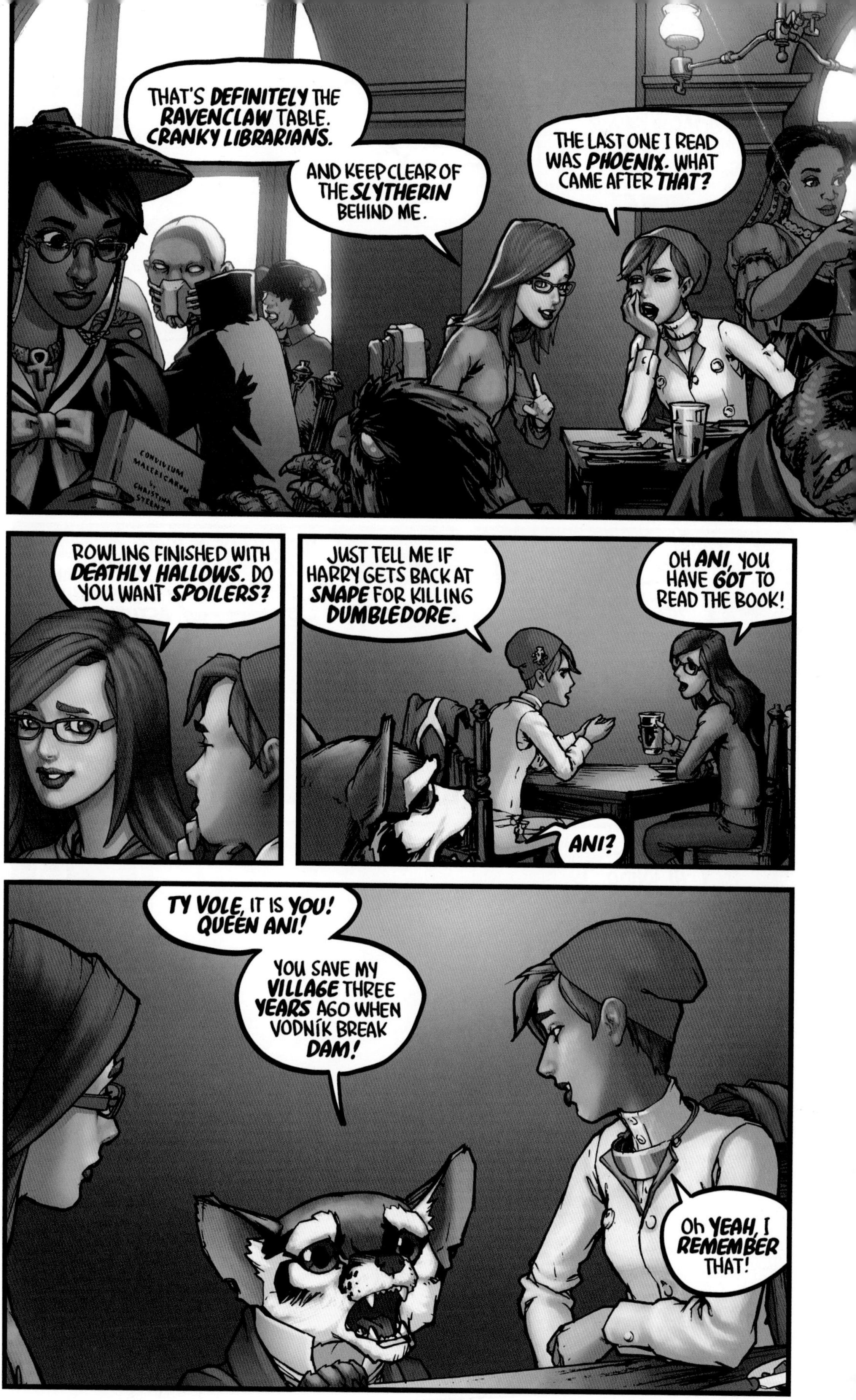
THAT'S DEFINITELY THE RAVENCLAW TABLE. CRANKY LIBRARIANS.
AND KEEP CLEAR OF THE SLYTHERIN BEHIND ME.
THE LAST ONE I READ WAS PHOENIX. WHAT CAME AFTER THAT?
CONVIVIUM MALEFICARUM by CHRISTINA STEENZ
ROWLING FINISHED WITH DEATHLY HALLOWS. DO YOU WANT SPOILERS?
JUST TELL ME IF HARRY GETS BACK AT SNAPE FOR KILLING DUMBLEDORE.
OH ANI, YOU HAVE GOT TO READ THE BOOK!
ANI?
TY VOLE, IT IS YOU! QUEEN ANI!
YOU SAVE MY VILLAGE THREE YEARS AGO WHEN VODNÍK BREAK DAM!
Oh YEAH, I REMEMBER THAT!

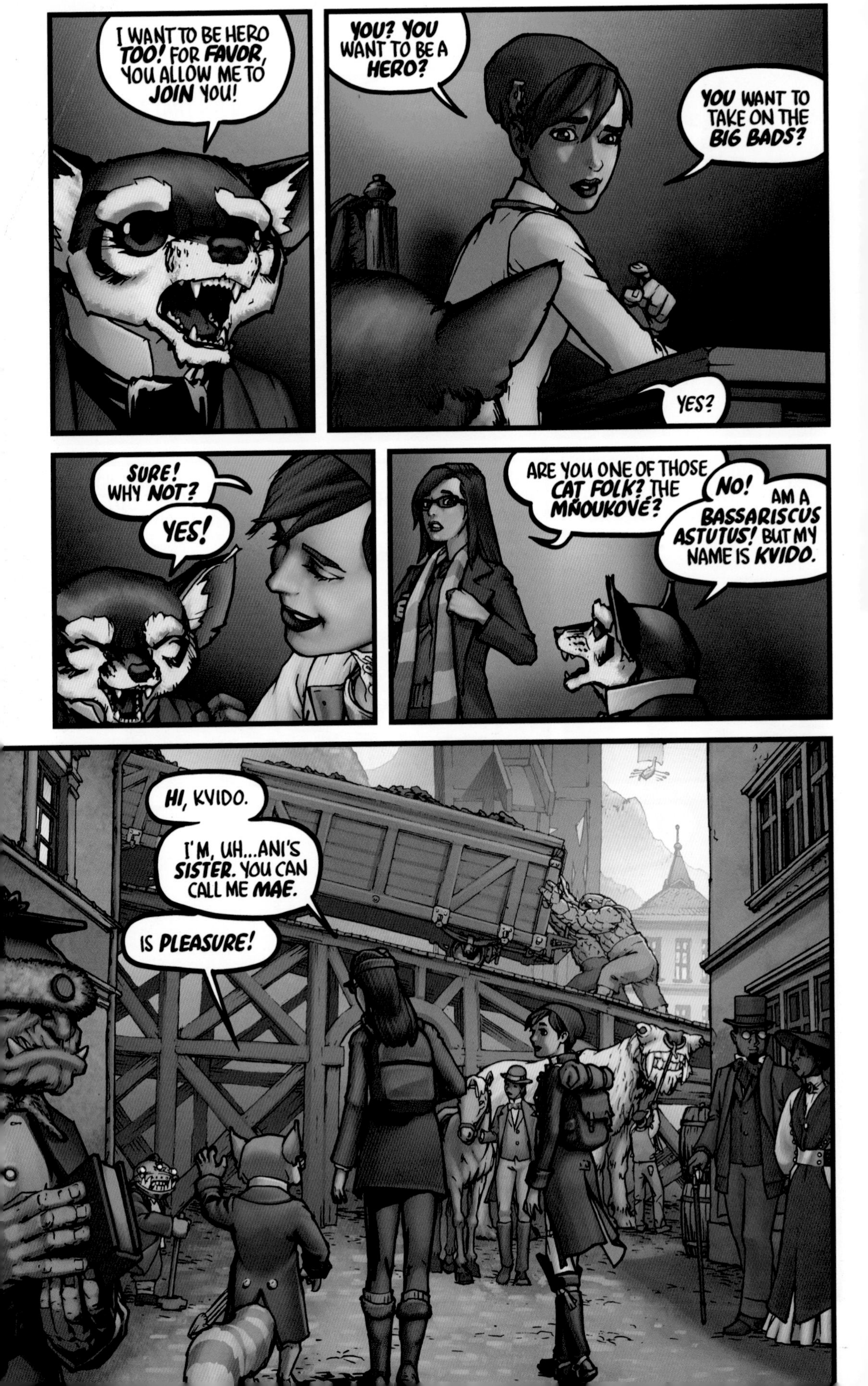
I WANT TO BE HERO TOO! FOR FAVOR, YOU ALLOW ME TO JOIN YOU!
YOU? YOU WANT TO BE A HERO?
YOU WANT TO TAKE ON THE BIG BADS?
YES?
SURE! WHY NOT?
YES!
ARE YOU ONE OF THOSE CAT FOLK? THE MŇOUKOVÉ?
NO!
AM A BASSARISCUS ASTUTUS! BUT MY NAME IS KVIDO.
HI, KVIDO.
I'M, UH...ANI'S SISTER. YOU CAN CALL ME MAE.
IS PLEASURE!

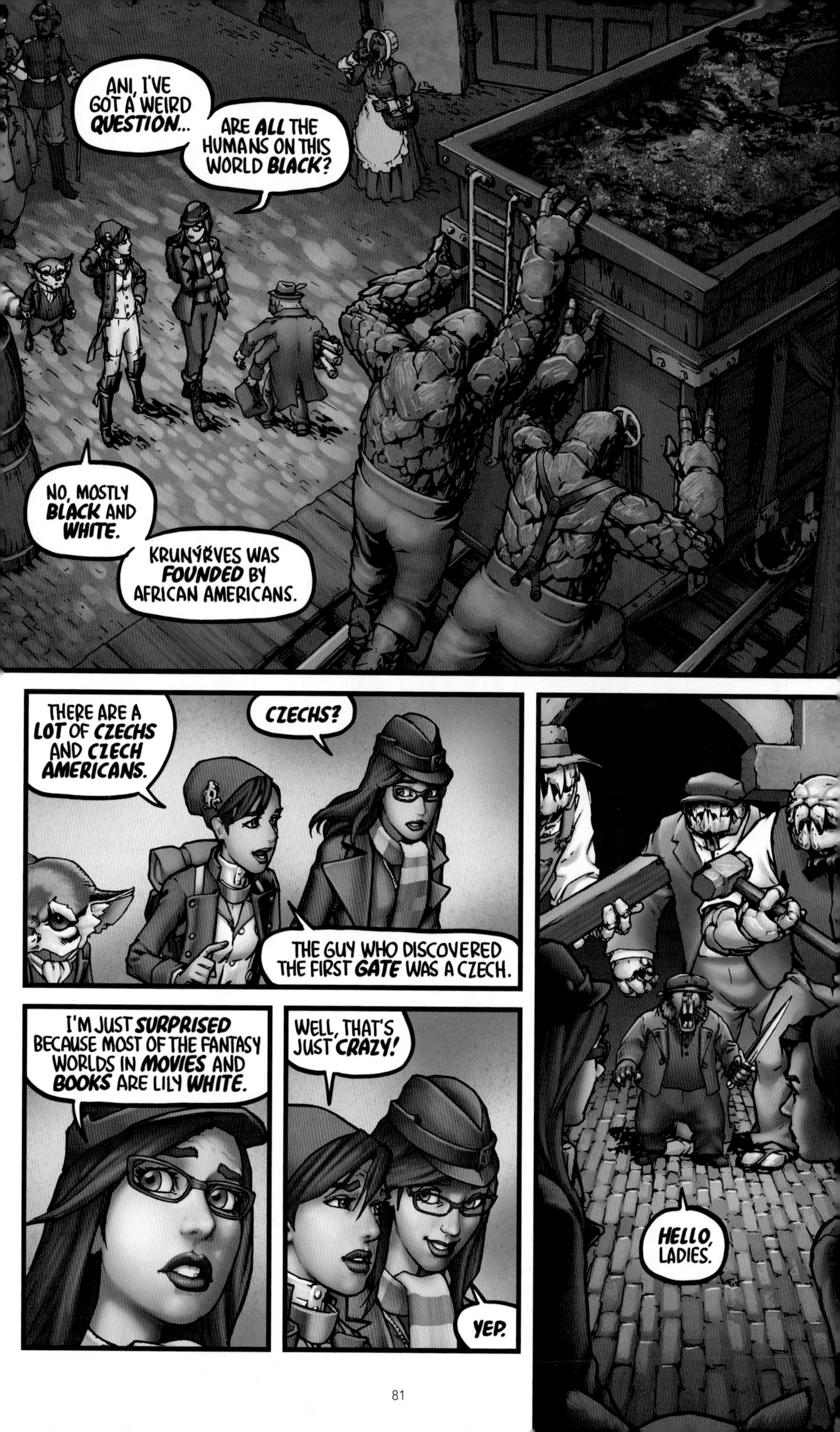
ANI, I'VE GOT A WEIRD QUESTION...
ARE ALL THE HUMANS ON THIS WORLD BLACK?
NO, MOSTLY BLACK AND WHITE.
KRUNÝŘVES WAS FOUNDED BY AFRICAN AMERICANS.
THERE ARE A LOT OF CZECHS AND CZECH AMERICANS.
CZECHS?
THE GUY WHO DISCOVERED THE FIRST GATE WAS A CZECH.
I'M JUST SURPRISED BECAUSE MOST OF THE FANTASY WORLDS IN MOVIES AND BOOKS ARE LILY WHITE.
WELL, THAT'S JUST CRAZY!
YEP.
HELLO, LADIES.

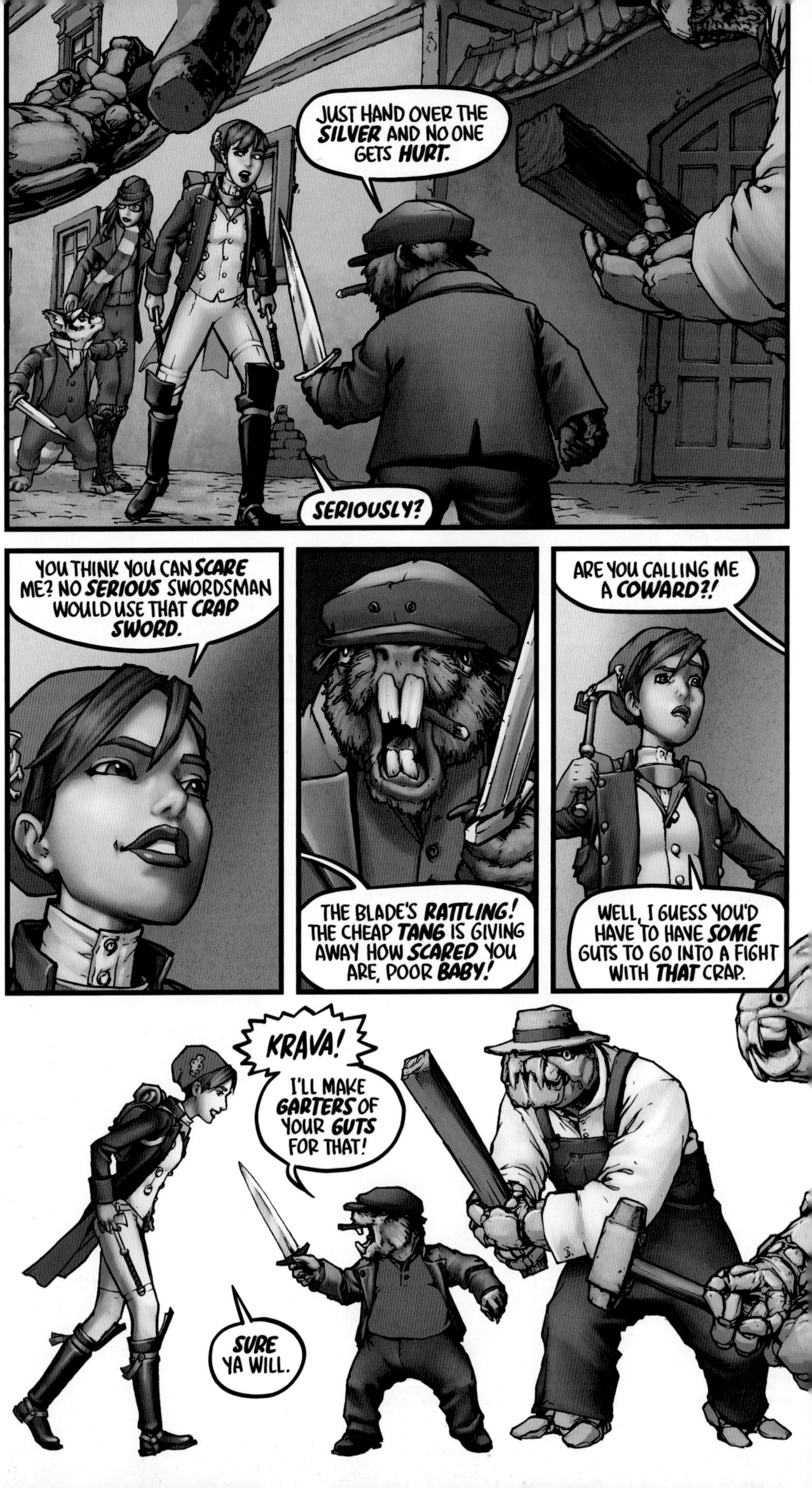
JUST HAND OVER THE SILVER AND NO ONE GETS HURT.
SERIOUSLY?
YOU THINK YOU CAN SCARE ME? NO SERIOUS SWORDSMAN WOULD USE THAT CRAP SWORD.
THE BLADE'S RATTLING! THE CHEAP TANG IS GIVING AWAY HOW SCARED YOU ARE, POOR BABY!
ARE YOU CALLING ME A COWARD?!
WELL, I GUESS YOU'D HAVE TO HAVE SOME GUTS TO GO INTO A FIGHT WITH THAT CRAP.
KRAVA!
I'LL MAKE GARTERS OF YOUR GUTS FOR THAT!
SURE YA WILL.

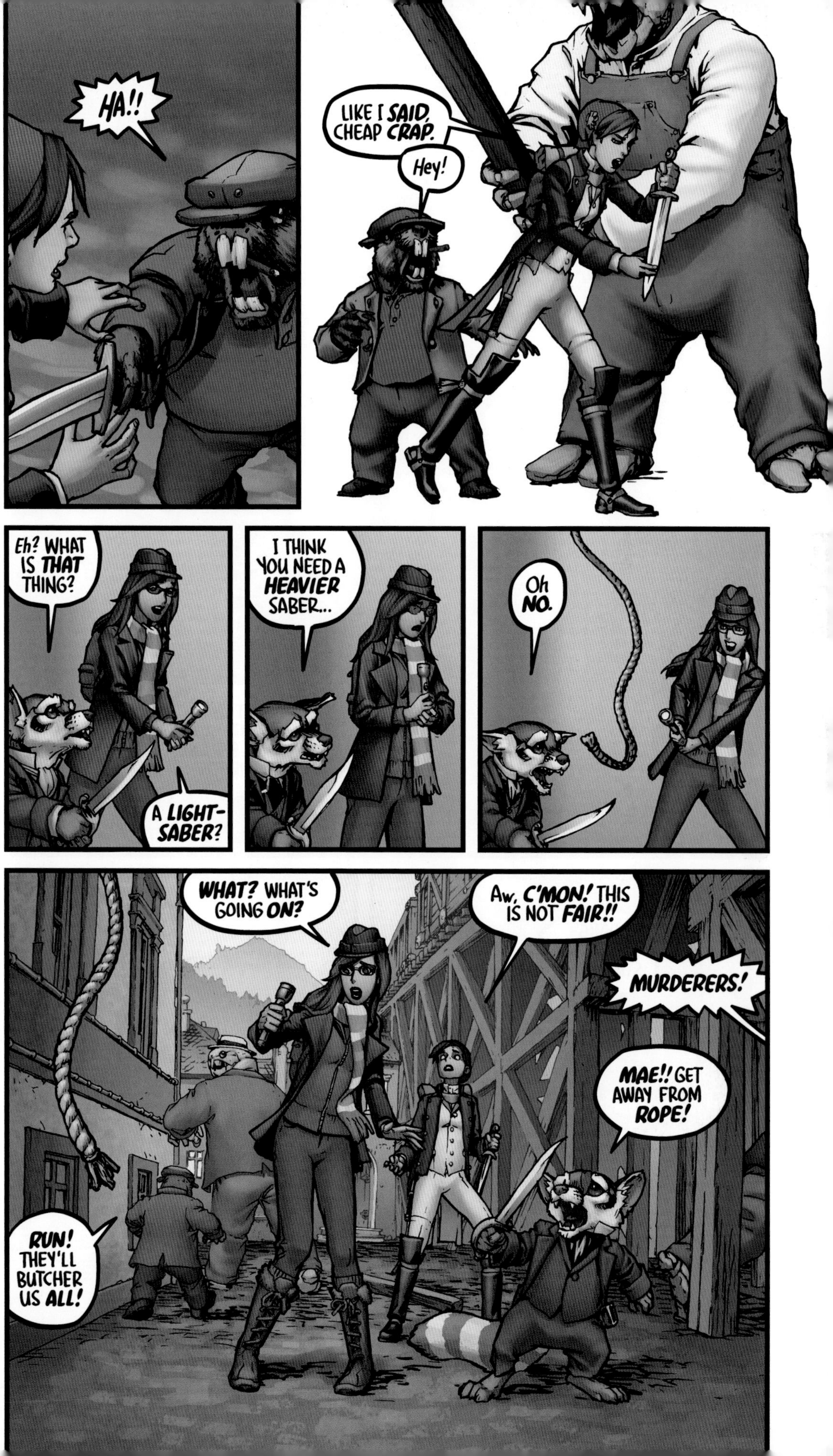
HA!!
LIKE I SAID, CHEAP CRAP.
Hey!
Eh? WHAT IS THAT THING?
A LIGHT-SABER?
I THINK YOU NEED A HEAVIER SABER...
Oh NO.
WHAT? WHAT'S GOING ON?
Aw, C'MON! THIS IS NOT FAIR!!
MURDERERS!
MAE!! GET AWAY FROM ROPE!
RUN! THEY'LL BUTCHER US ALL!

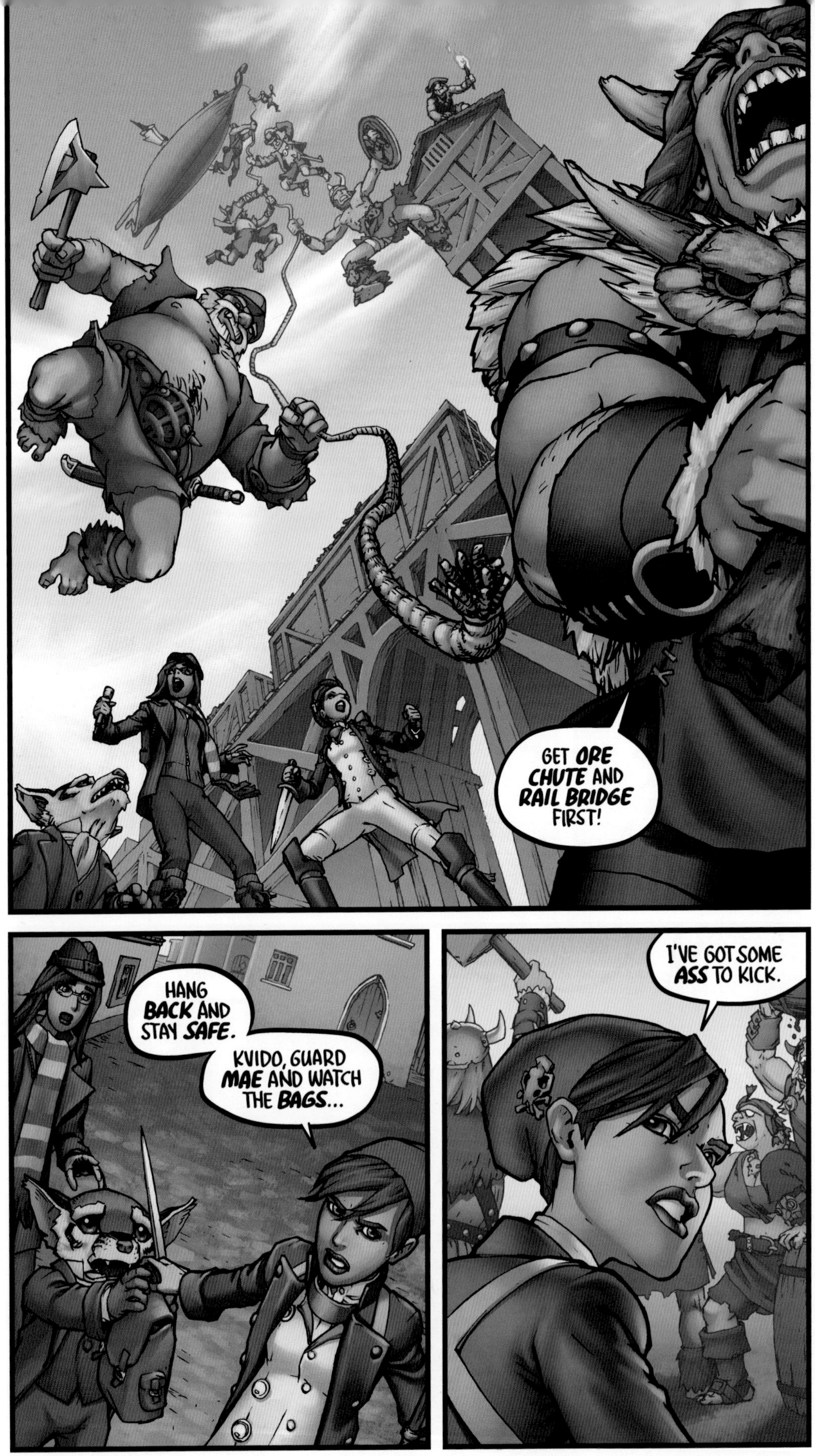
GET **ORE CHUTE** AND **RAIL BRIDGE** FIRST!
HANG **BACK** AND STAY **SAFE**.
KVIDO, GUARD **MAE** AND WATCH THE **BAGS**...
I'VE GOT SOME **ASS** TO KICK.

TY VOLE!!

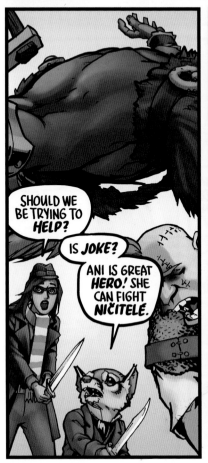

SHOULD WE BE TRYING TO *HELP?*

IS *JOKE?*

ANI IS GREAT *HERO!* SHE CAN FIGHT *NIČITELE.*

WE *HELP* BY STAY OUT OF *TROUBLE.*

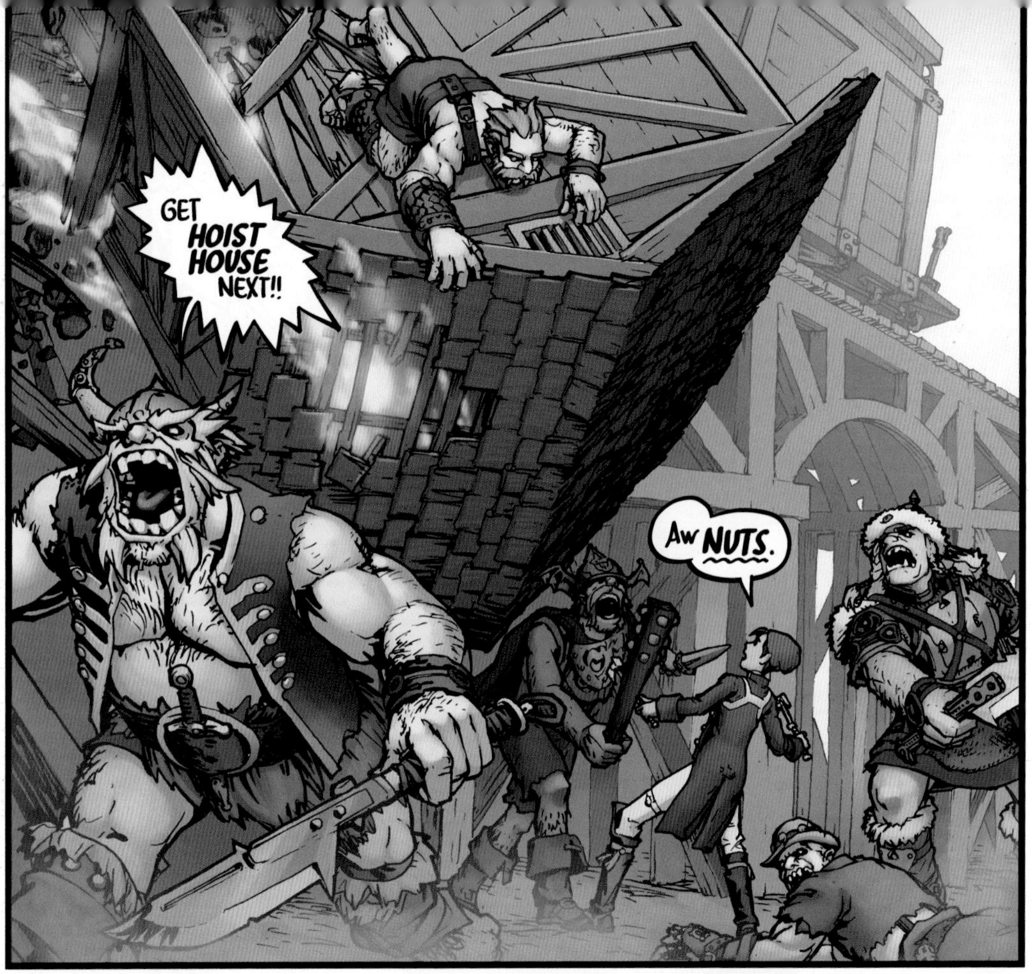
GET HOIST HOUSE NEXT!!
Aw NUTS.

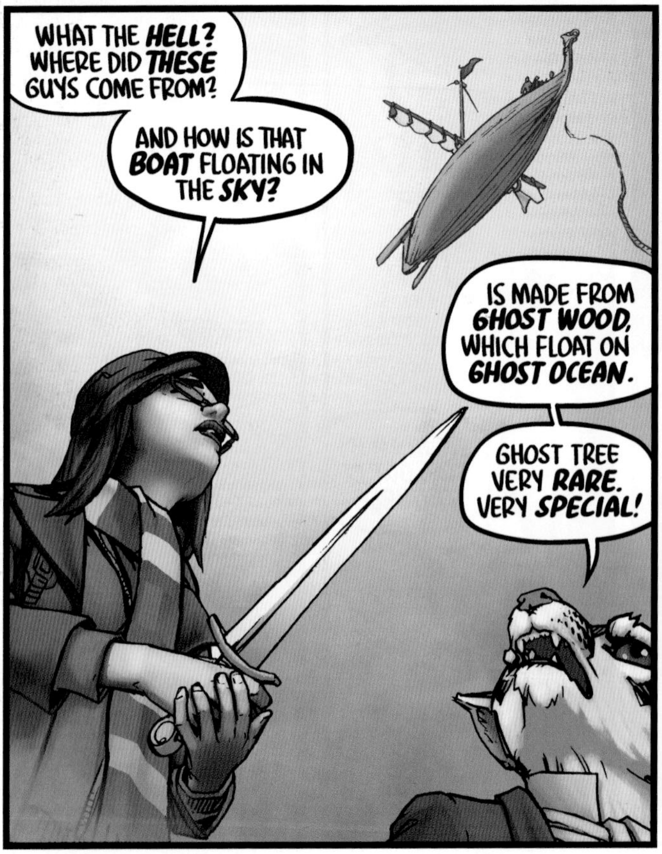
WHAT THE HELL? WHERE DID THESE GUYS COME FROM?
AND HOW IS THAT BOAT FLOATING IN THE SKY?
IS MADE FROM GHOST WOOD, WHICH FLOAT ON GHOST OCEAN.
GHOST TREE VERY RARE. VERY SPECIAL!

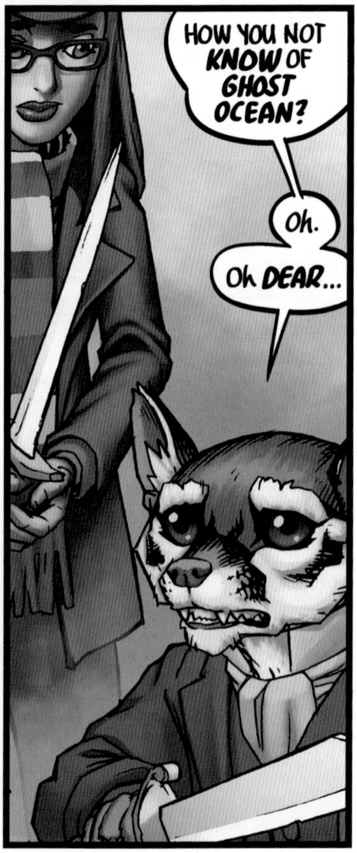
HOW YOU NOT KNOW OF GHOST OCEAN?
Oh.
Oh DEAR...

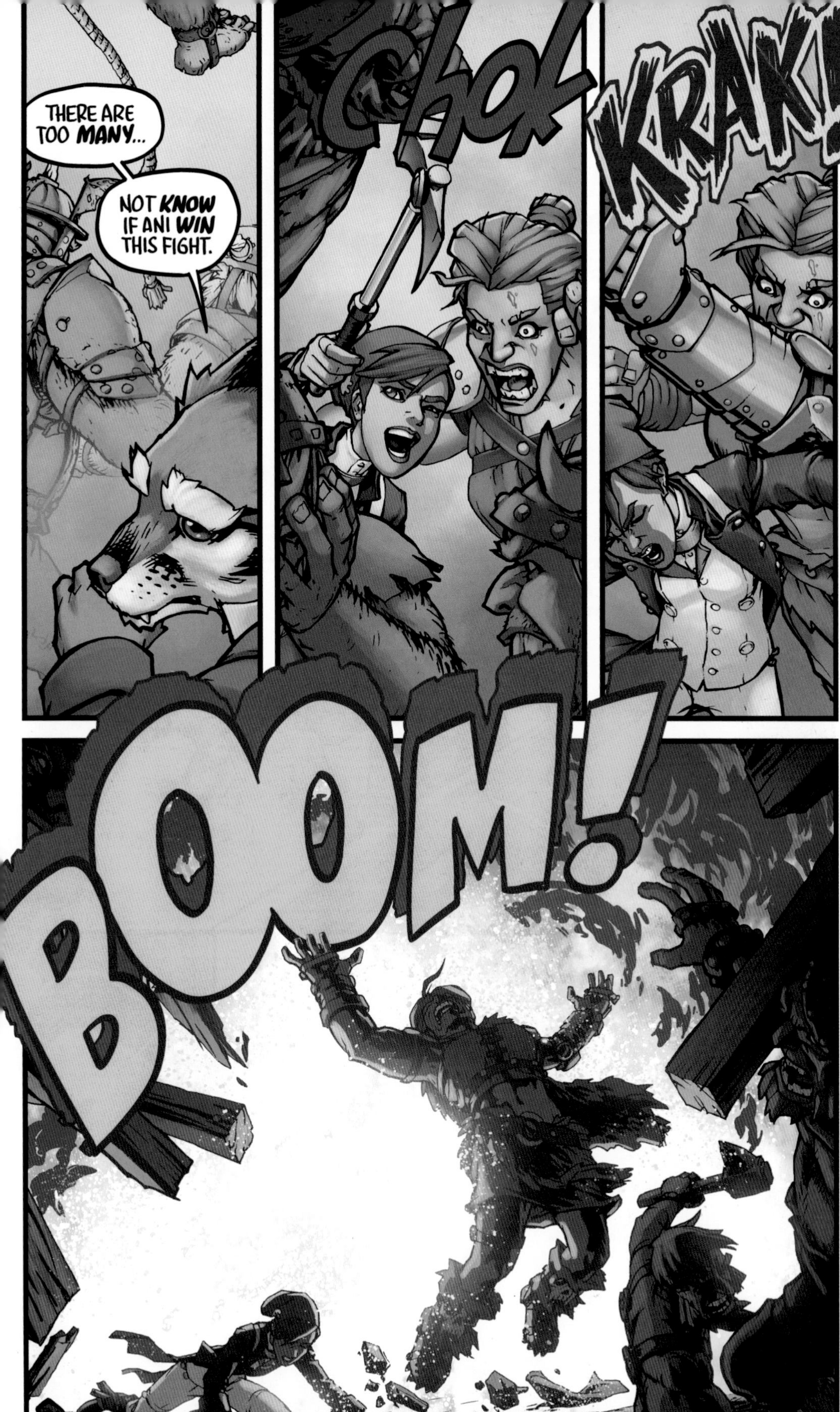
THERE ARE TOO **MANY**...
NOT **KNOW** IF ANI **WIN** THIS FIGHT.
CHOK!
KRAK!
BOOM!

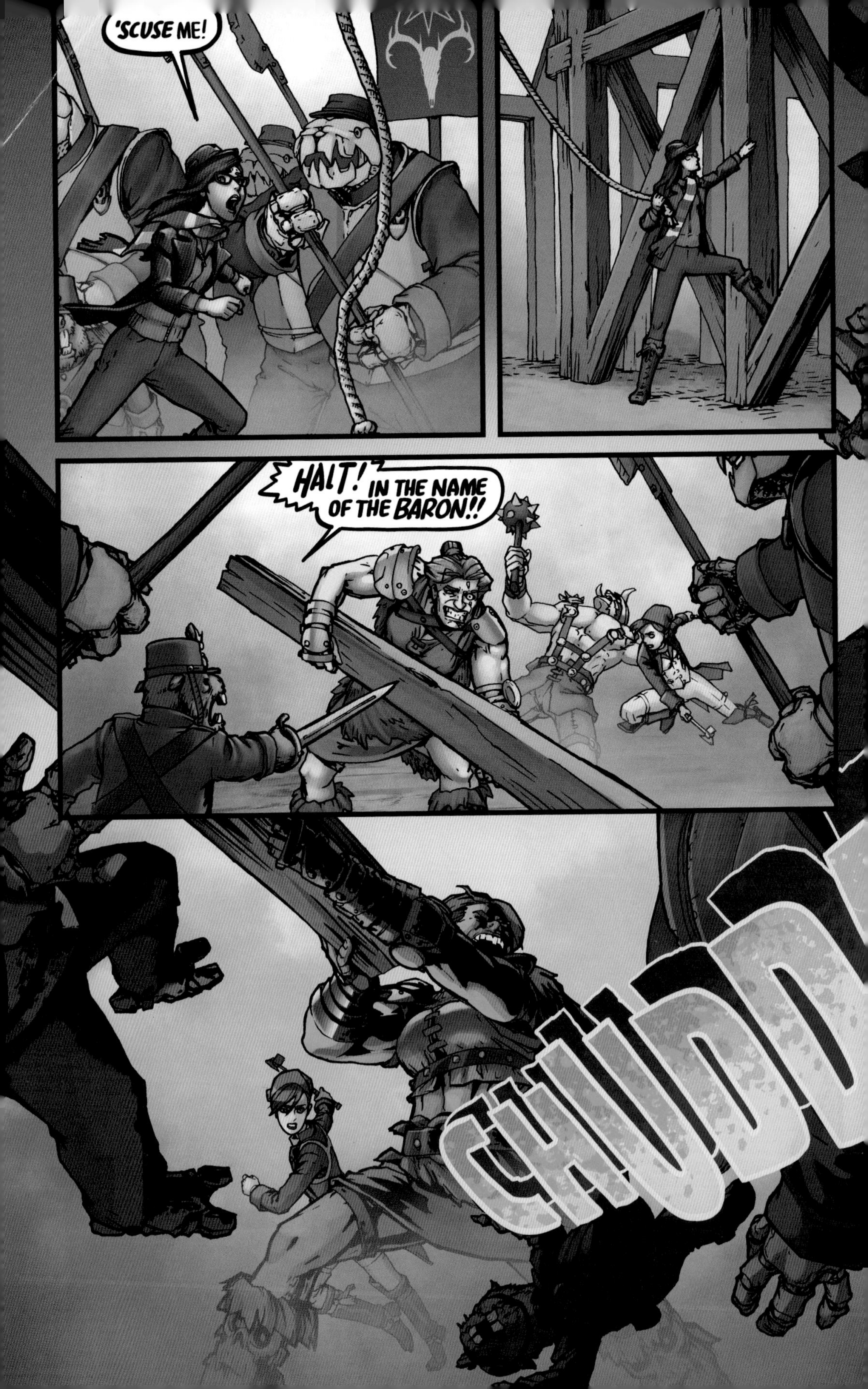
'SCUSE ME!
HALT! IN THE NAME OF THE BARON!!
CHUDD

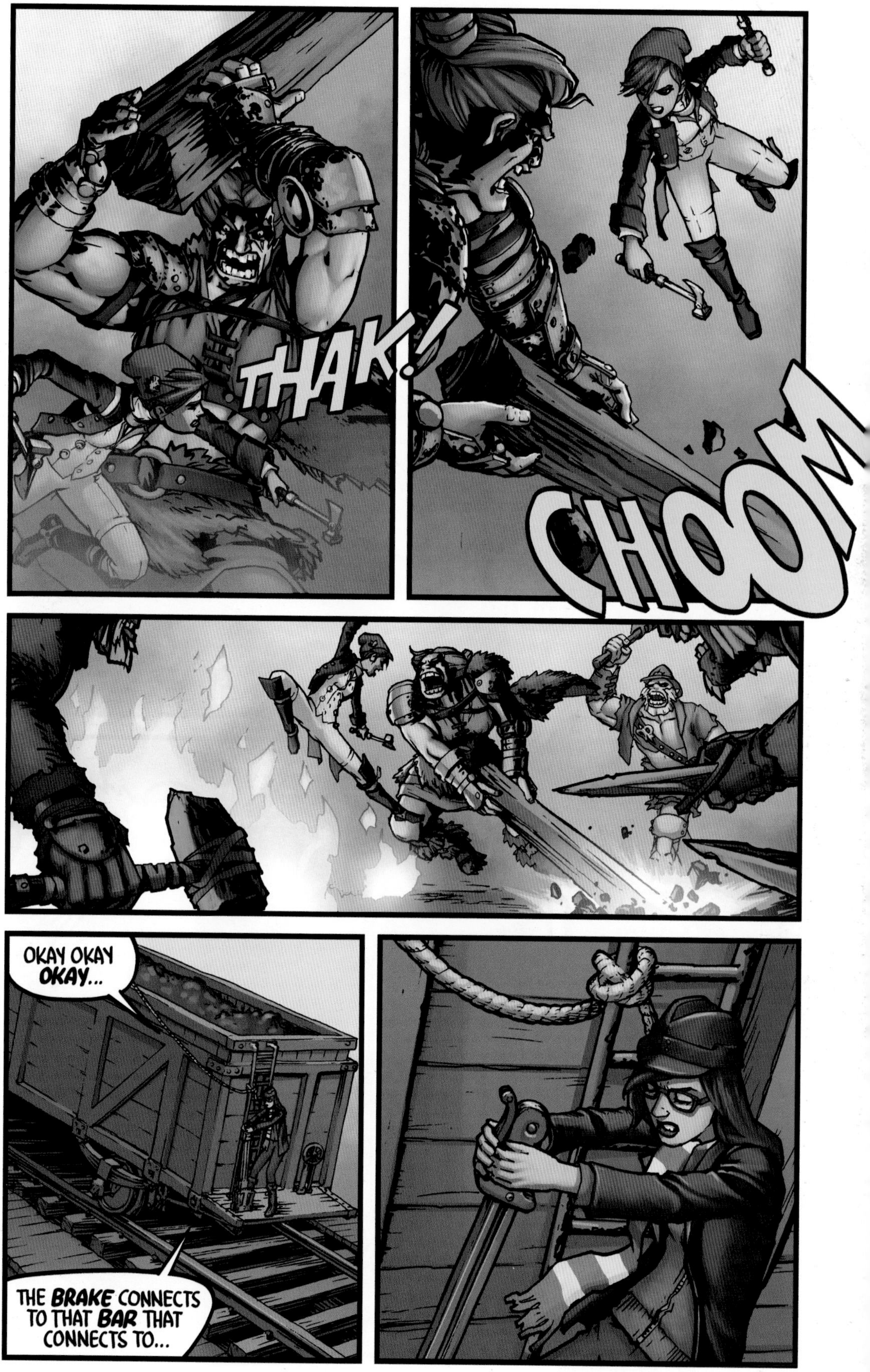
THAK!
CHOOM
OKAY OKAY OKAY...
THE BRAKE CONNECTS TO THAT BAR THAT CONNECTS TO...

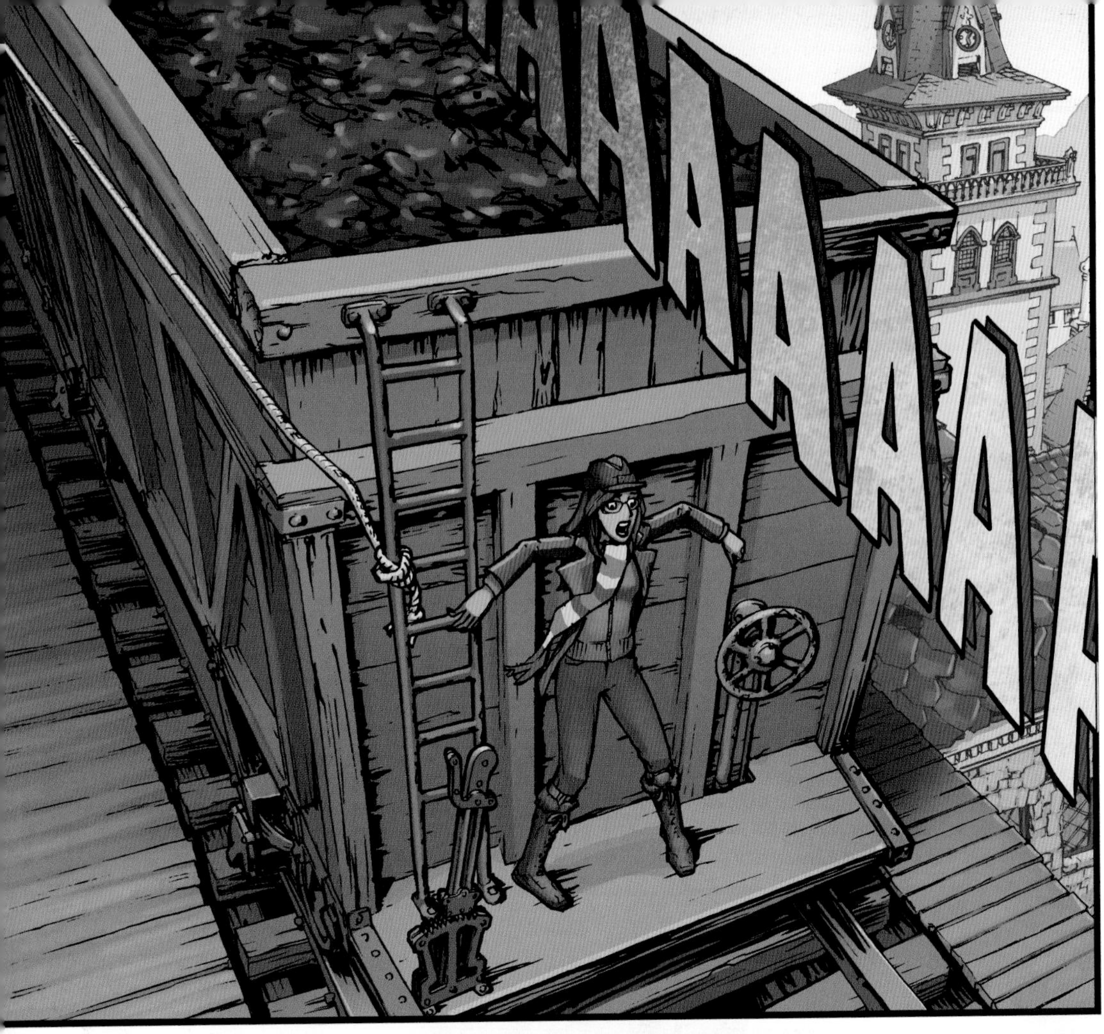

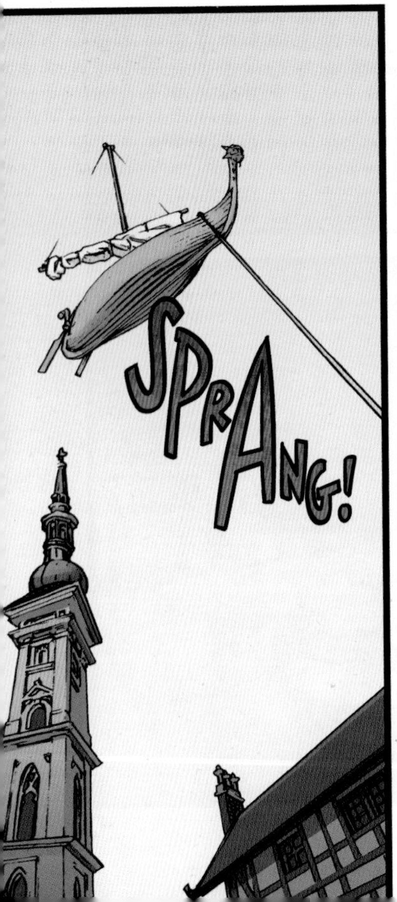
SPRANG!

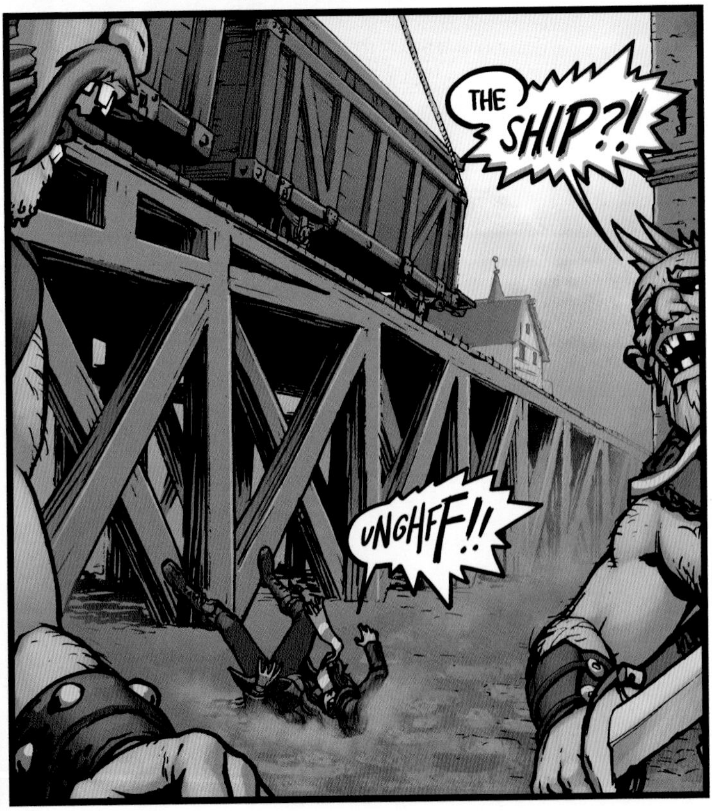
THE SHIP?!
UNGHFF!!

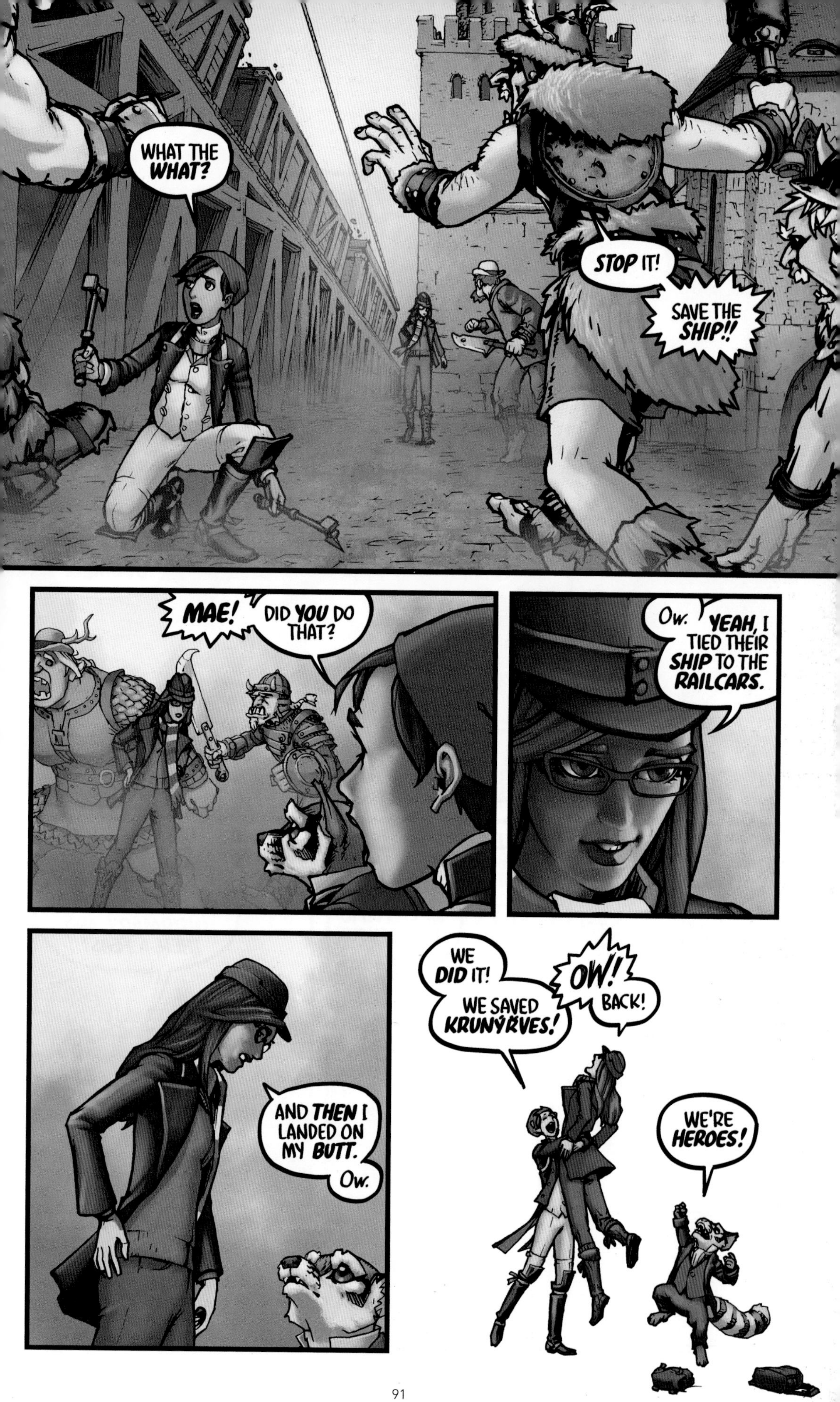
WHAT THE WHAT?
STOP IT!
SAVE THE SHIP!!
MAE!
DID YOU DO THAT?
Ow. YEAH, I TIED THEIR SHIP TO THE RAILCARS.
AND THEN I LANDED ON MY BUTT. Ow.
WE DID IT!
WE SAVED KRUNÝŘVES!
OW!! BACK!
WE'RE HEROES!

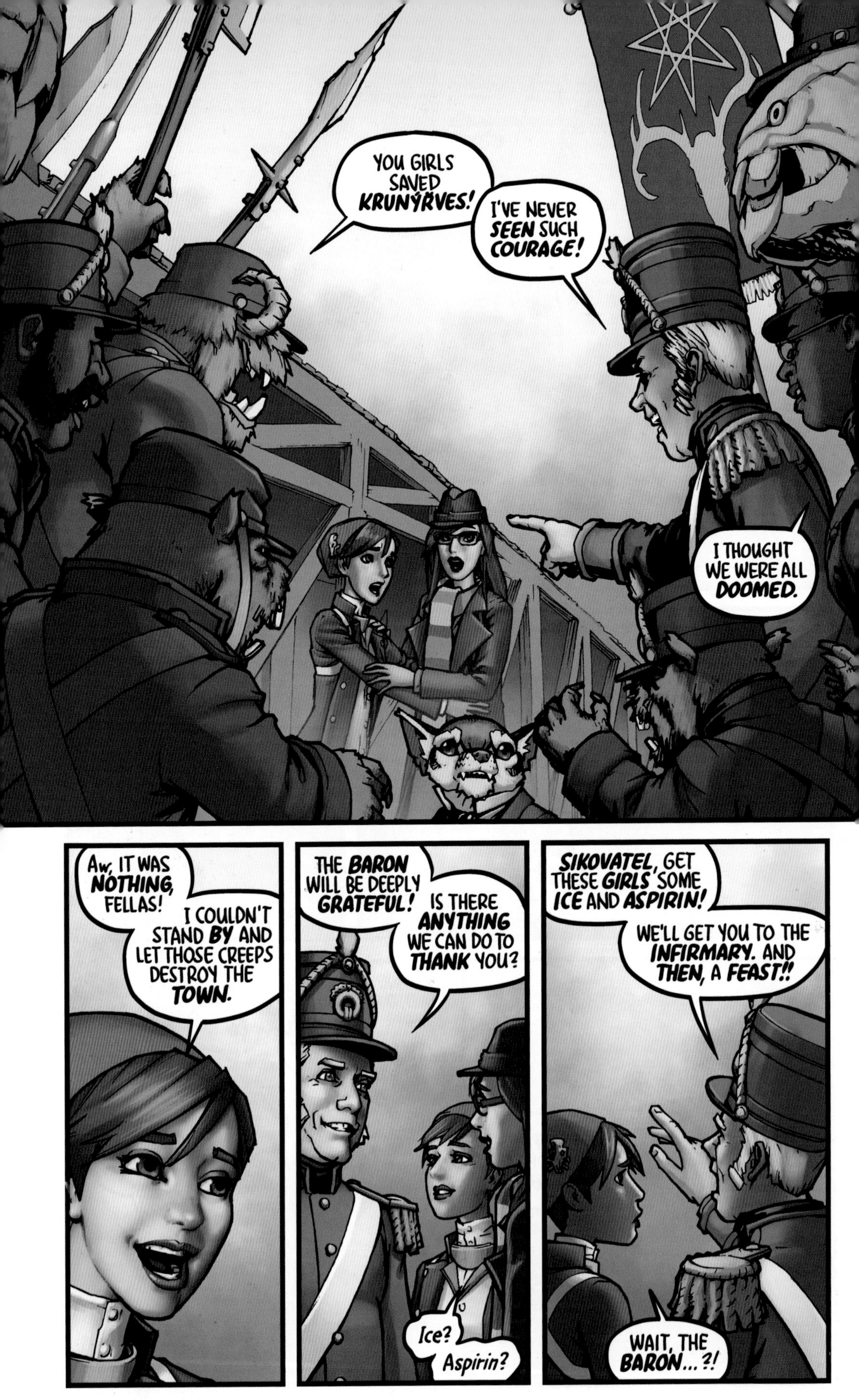
YOU GIRLS SAVED KRUNÝRVES!
I'VE NEVER SEEN SUCH COURAGE!
I THOUGHT WE WERE ALL DOOMED.
Aw, IT WAS NOTHING, FELLAS!
I COULDN'T STAND BY AND LET THOSE CREEPS DESTROY THE TOWN.
THE BARON WILL BE DEEPLY GRATEFUL!
IS THERE ANYTHING WE CAN DO TO THANK YOU?
Ice?
Aspirin?
SIKOVATEL, GET THESE GIRLS SOME ICE AND ASPIRIN!
WE'LL GET YOU TO THE INFIRMARY. AND THEN, A FEAST!!
WAIT, THE BARON...?!

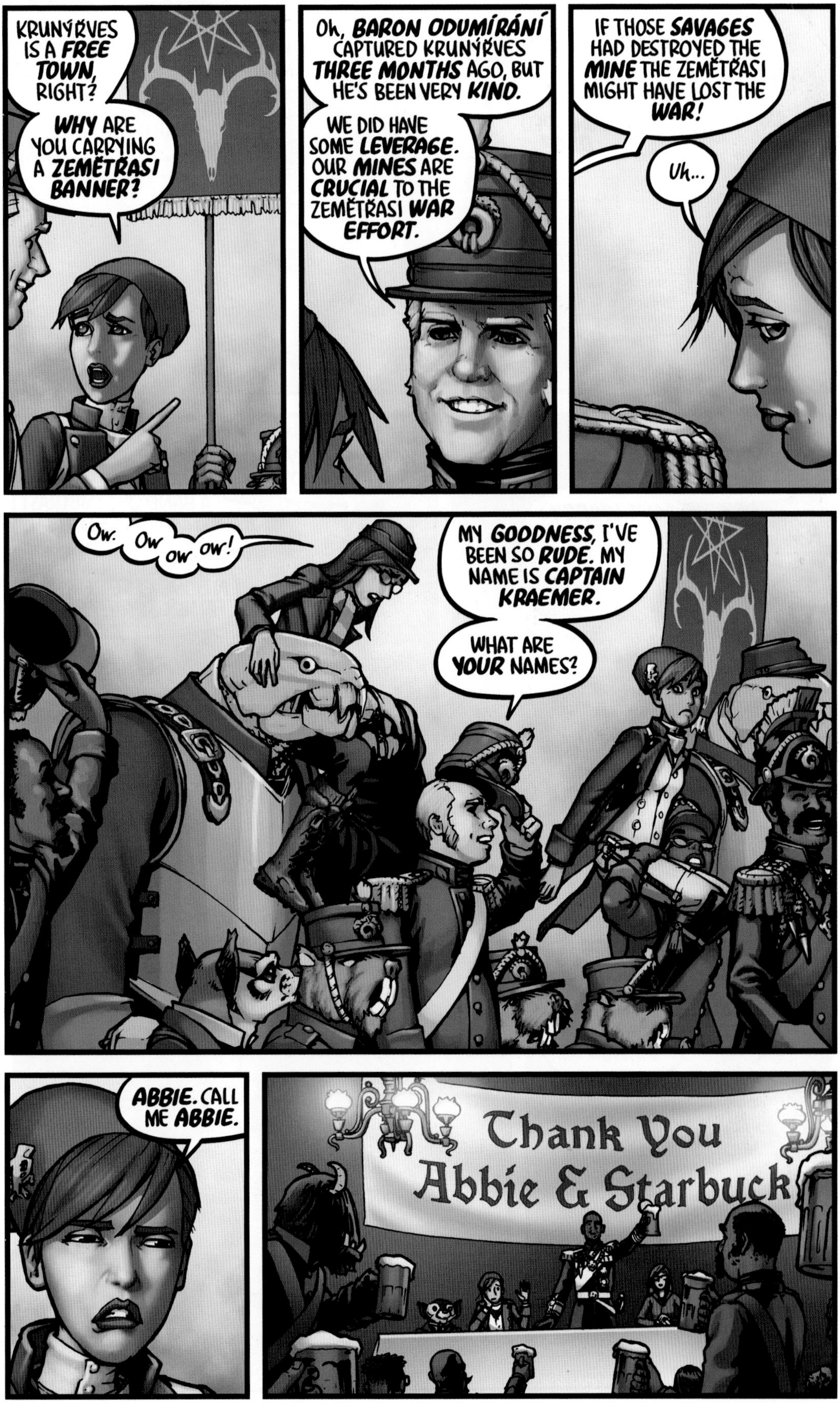
KRUNÝŘVES IS A FREE TOWN, RIGHT?
WHY ARE YOU CARRYING A ZEMĚTŘASI BANNER?
Oh, BARON ODUMÍRÁNÍ CAPTURED KRUNÝŘVES THREE MONTHS AGO, BUT HE'S BEEN VERY KIND.
WE DID HAVE SOME LEVERAGE. OUR MINES ARE CRUCIAL TO THE ZEMĚTŘASI WAR EFFORT.
IF THOSE SAVAGES HAD DESTROYED THE MINE THE ZEMĚTŘASI MIGHT HAVE LOST THE WAR!
Uh...
Ow. Ow ow ow!
MY GOODNESS, I'VE BEEN SO RUDE. MY NAME IS CAPTAIN KRAEMER.
WHAT ARE YOUR NAMES?
ABBIE. CALL ME ABBIE.
Thank You Abbie & Starbuck

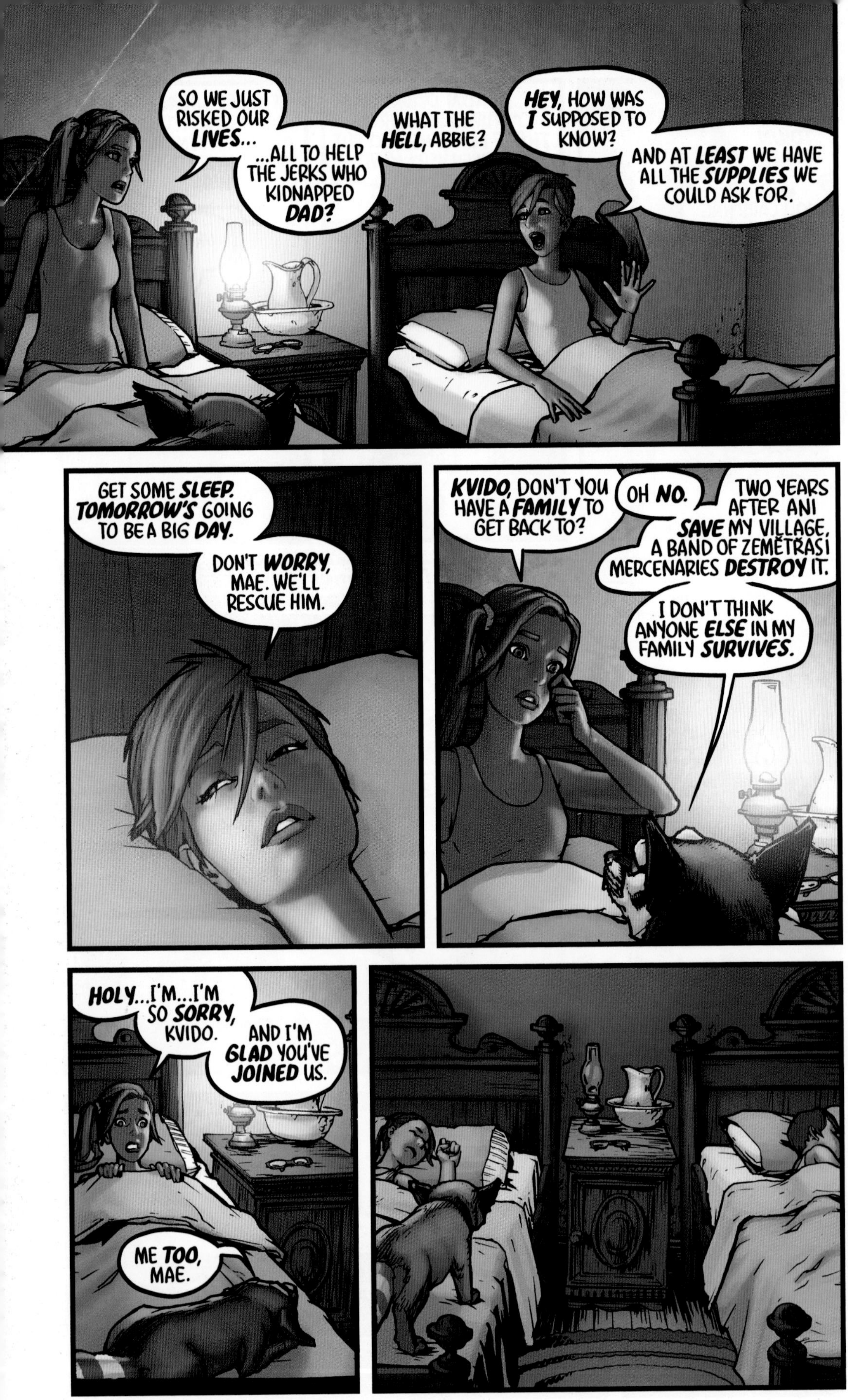
SO WE JUST RISKED OUR LIVES...
...ALL TO HELP THE JERKS WHO KIDNAPPED DAD?
WHAT THE HELL, ABBIE?
HEY, HOW WAS I SUPPOSED TO KNOW?
AND AT LEAST WE HAVE ALL THE SUPPLIES WE COULD ASK FOR.
GET SOME SLEEP. TOMORROW'S GOING TO BE A BIG DAY.
DON'T WORRY, MAE. WE'LL RESCUE HIM.
KVIDO, DON'T YOU HAVE A FAMILY TO GET BACK TO?
OH NO.
TWO YEARS AFTER ANI SAVE MY VILLAGE, A BAND OF ZEMĚTRASI MERCENARIES DESTROY IT.
I DON'T THINK ANYONE ELSE IN MY FAMILY SURVIVES.
HOLY...I'M...I'M SO SORRY, KVIDO.
AND I'M GLAD YOU'VE JOINED US.
ME TOO, MAE.

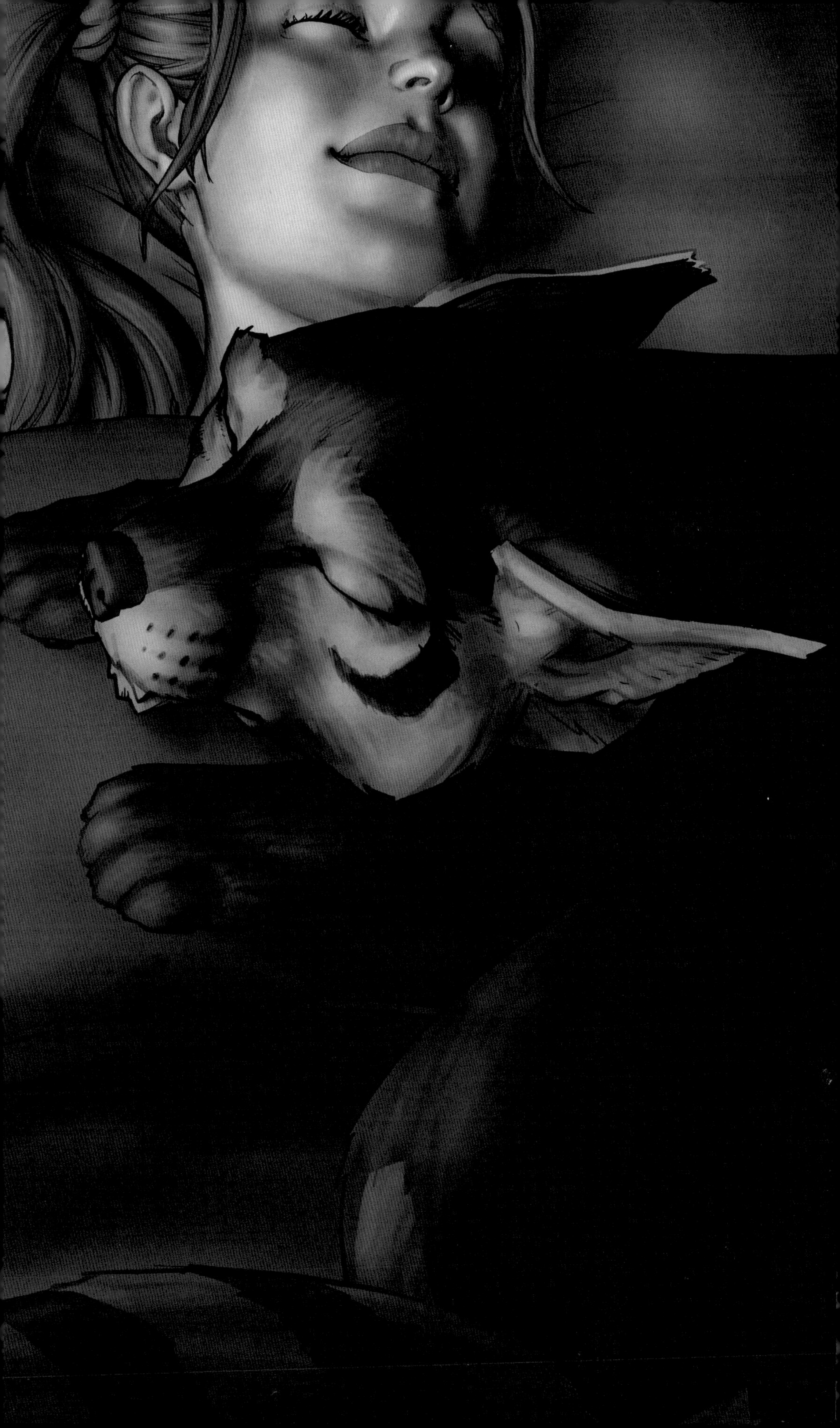

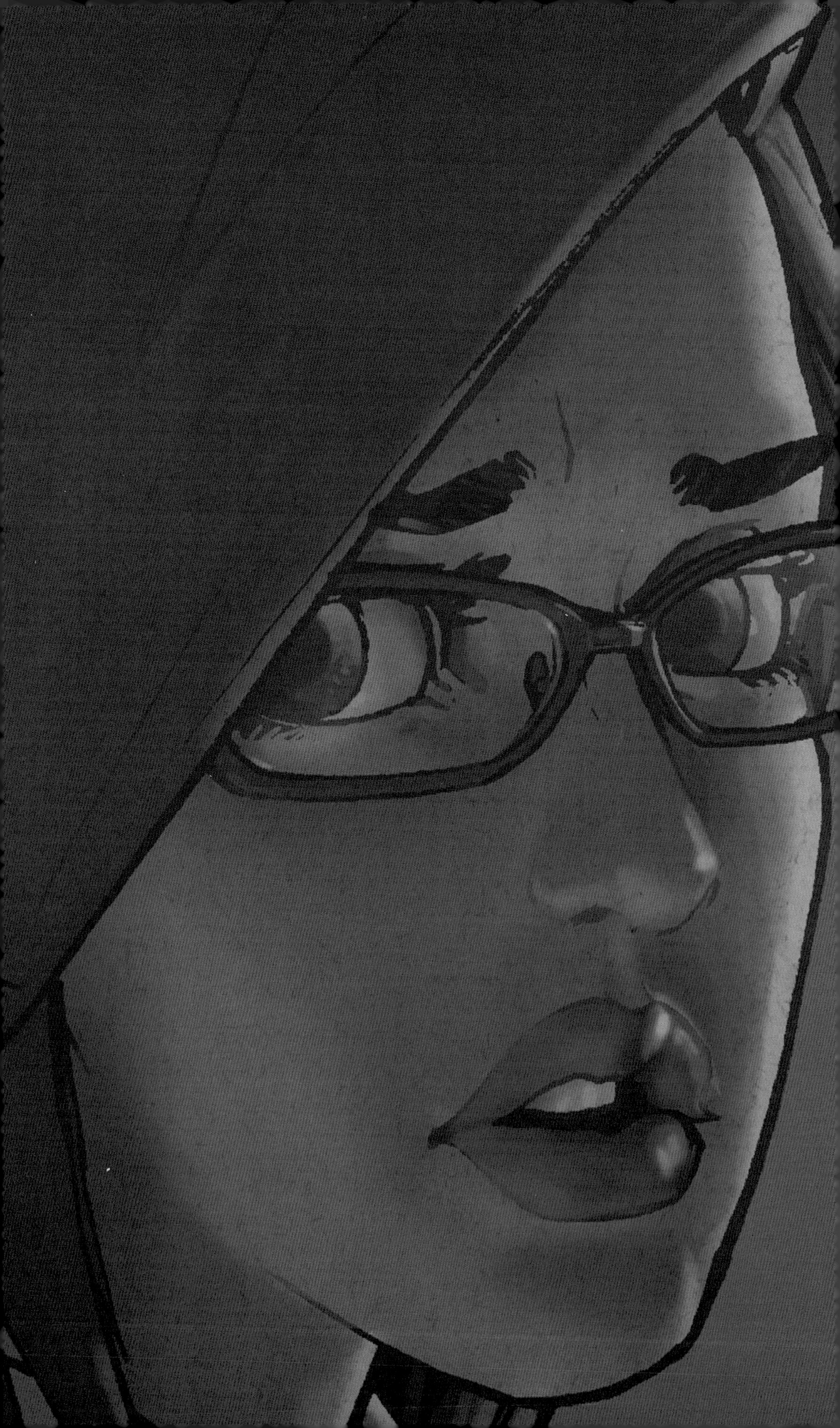

FOUR

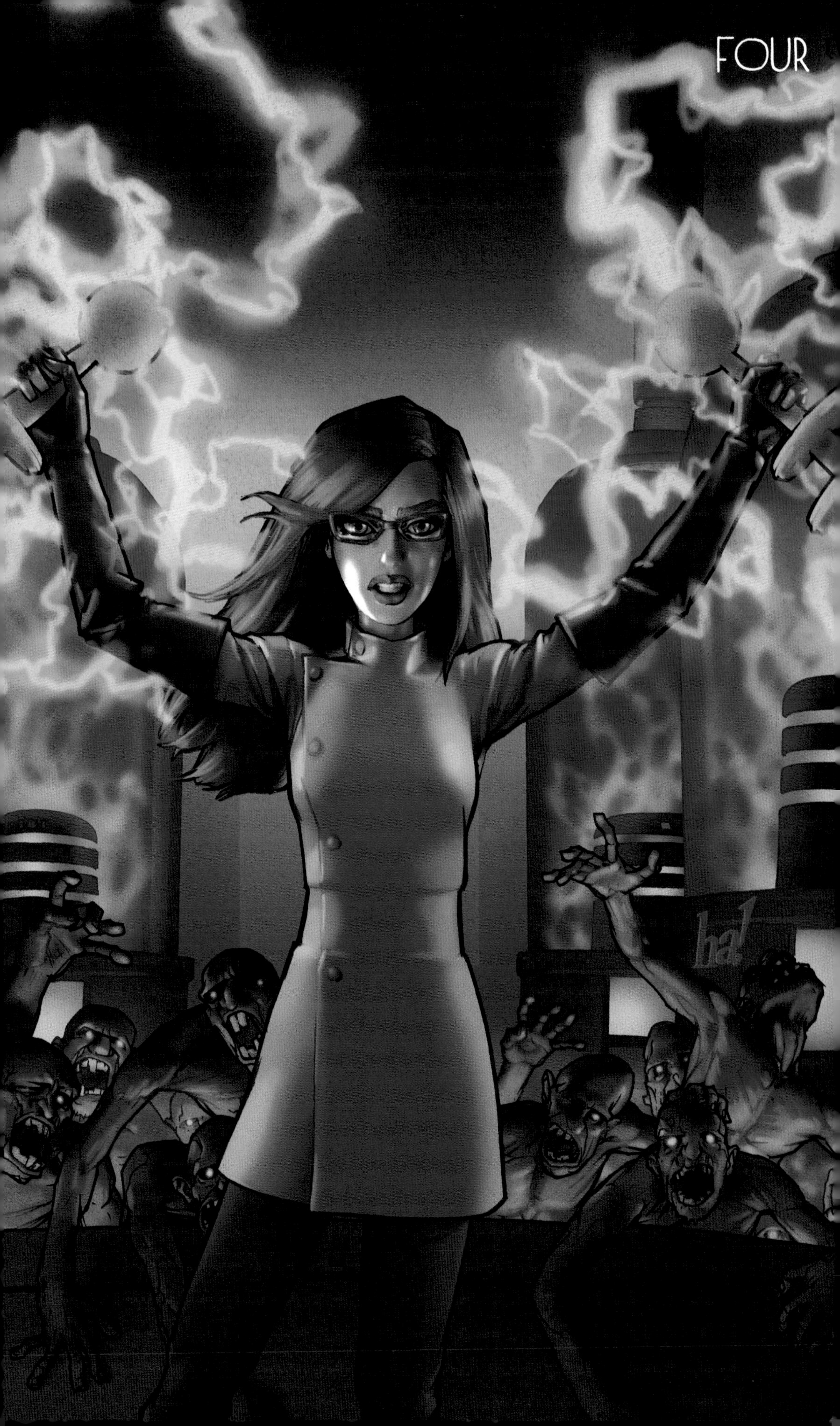
ha!

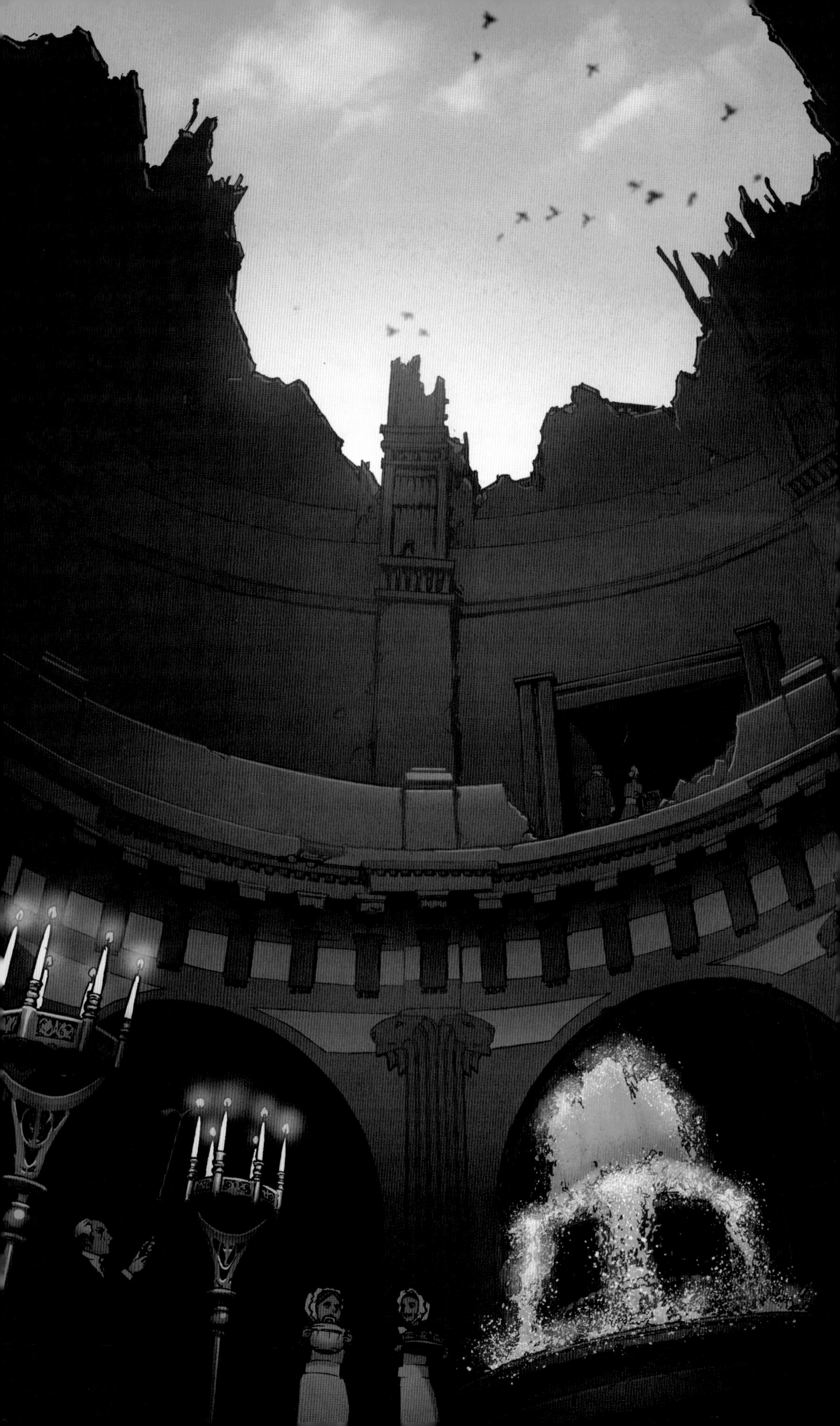

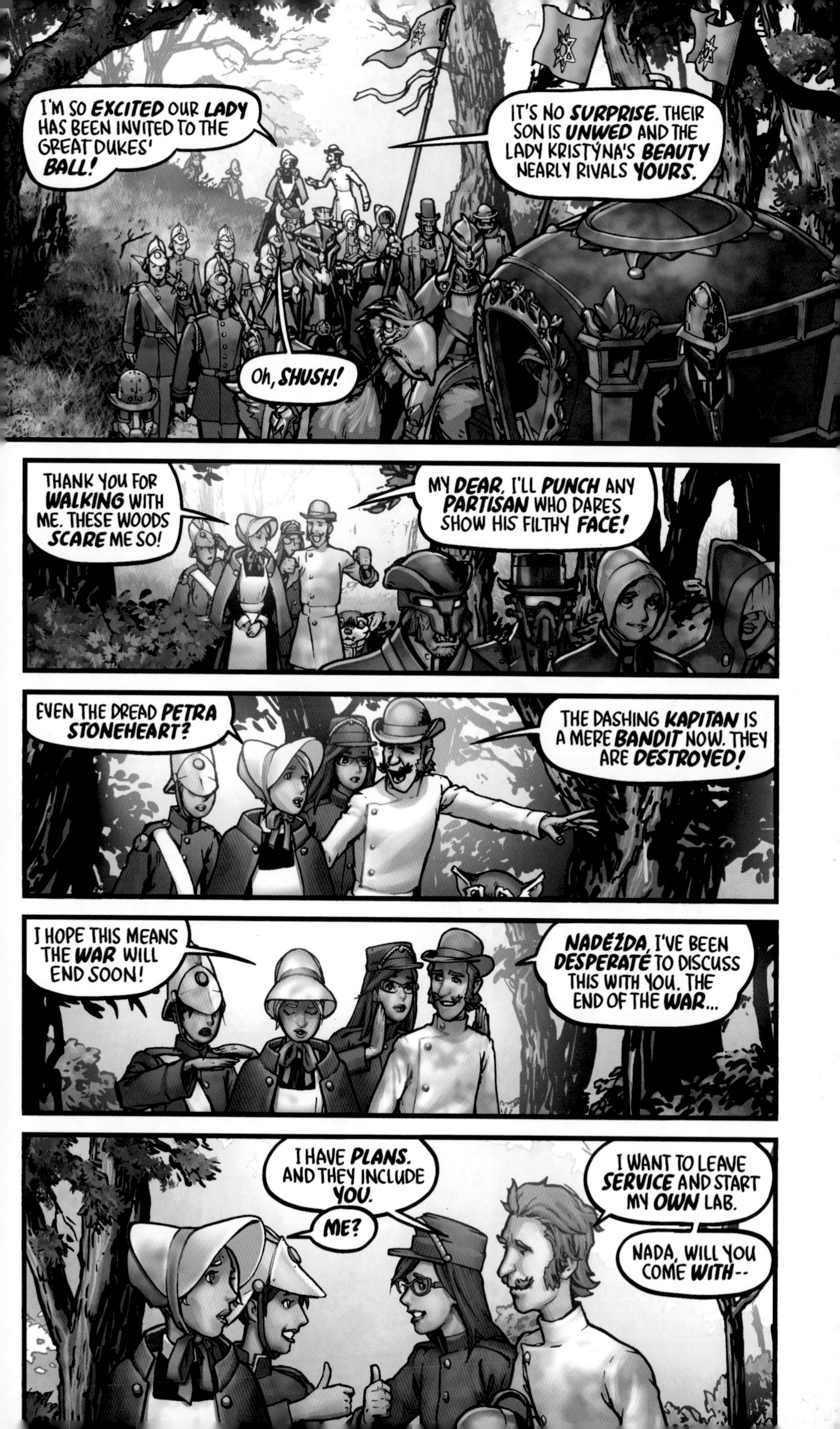
I'M SO EXCITED OUR LADY HAS BEEN INVITED TO THE GREAT DUKES' BALL!
IT'S NO SURPRISE. THEIR SON IS UNWED AND THE LADY KRISTÝNA'S BEAUTY NEARLY RIVALS YOURS.
Oh, SHUSH!
THANK YOU FOR WALKING WITH ME. THESE WOODS SCARE ME SO!
MY DEAR, I'LL PUNCH ANY PARTISAN WHO DARES SHOW HIS FILTHY FACE!
EVEN THE DREAD PETRA STONEHEART?
THE DASHING KAPITAN IS A MERE BANDIT NOW. THEY ARE DESTROYED!
I HOPE THIS MEANS THE WAR WILL END SOON!
NADĚŽDA, I'VE BEEN DESPERATE TO DISCUSS THIS WITH YOU. THE END OF THE WAR...
I HAVE PLANS. AND THEY INCLUDE YOU.
ME?
I WANT TO LEAVE SERVICE AND START MY OWN LAB.
NADA, WILL YOU COME WITH--

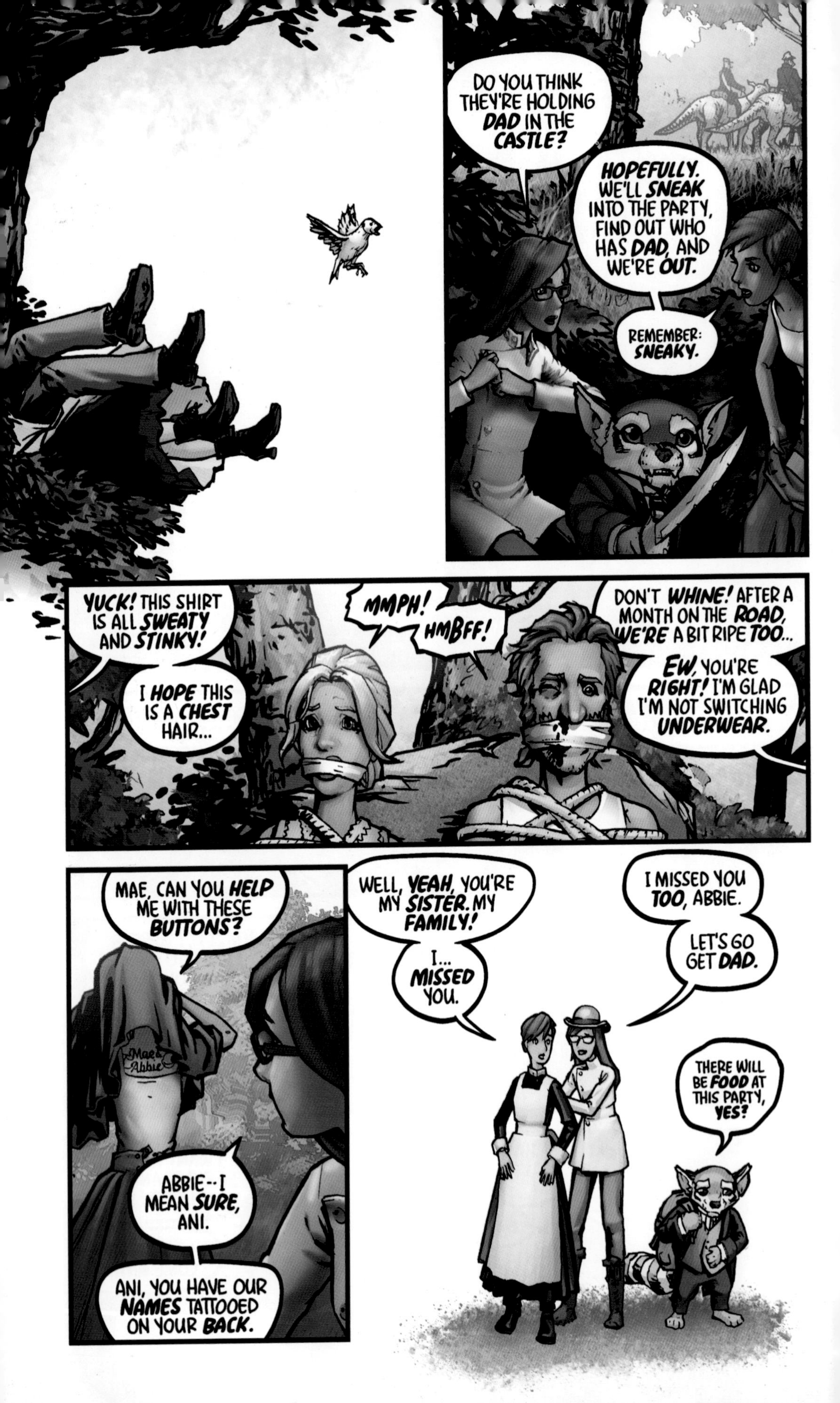
DO YOU THINK THEY'RE HOLDING DAD IN THE CASTLE?
HOPEFULLY. WE'LL SNEAK INTO THE PARTY, FIND OUT WHO HAS DAD, AND WE'RE OUT.
REMEMBER: SNEAKY.
YUCK! THIS SHIRT IS ALL SWEATY AND STINKY!
I HOPE THIS IS A CHEST HAIR...
MMPH!
HMBFF!
DON'T WHINE! AFTER A MONTH ON THE ROAD, WE'RE A BIT RIPE TOO...
EW, YOU'RE RIGHT! I'M GLAD I'M NOT SWITCHING UNDERWEAR.
MAE, CAN YOU HELP ME WITH THESE BUTTONS?
Mae Abbie
ABBIE--I MEAN SURE, ANI.
ANI, YOU HAVE OUR NAMES TATTOOED ON YOUR BACK.
WELL, YEAH, YOU'RE MY SISTER. MY FAMILY!
I... MISSED YOU.
I MISSED YOU TOO, ABBIE.
LET'S GO GET DAD.
THERE WILL BE FOOD AT THIS PARTY, YES?

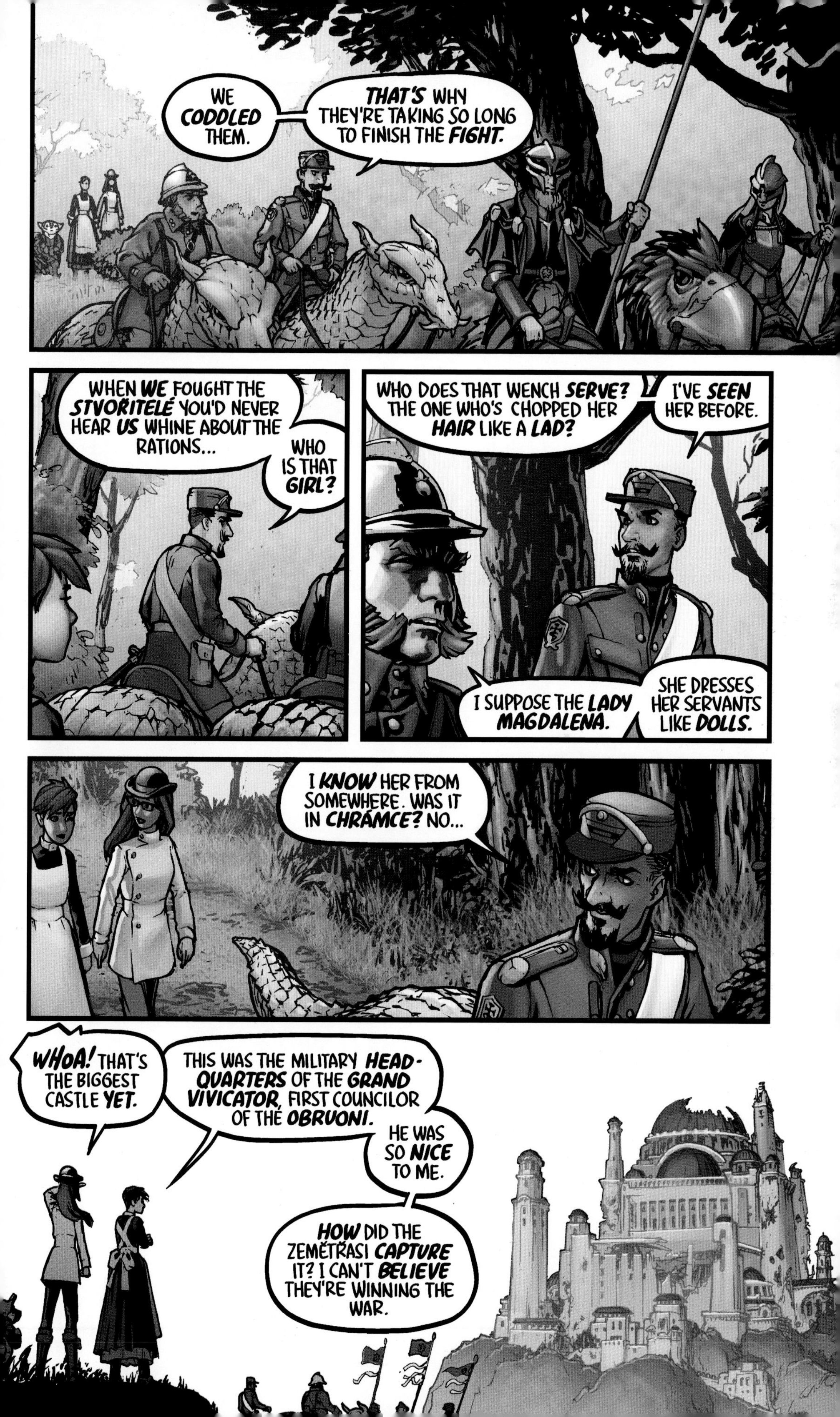
WE CODDLED THEM.
THAT'S WHY THEY'RE TAKING SO LONG TO FINISH THE FIGHT.
WHEN WE FOUGHT THE STVOŘITELÉ YOU'D NEVER HEAR US WHINE ABOUT THE RATIONS...
WHO IS THAT GIRL?
WHO DOES THAT WENCH SERVE? THE ONE WHO'S CHOPPED HER HAIR LIKE A LAD?
I'VE SEEN HER BEFORE.
I SUPPOSE THE LADY MAGDALENA.
SHE DRESSES HER SERVANTS LIKE DOLLS.
I KNOW HER FROM SOMEWHERE. WAS IT IN CHRÁMCE? NO...
WHOA! THAT'S THE BIGGEST CASTLE YET.
THIS WAS THE MILITARY HEAD-QUARTERS OF THE GRAND VIVICATOR, FIRST COUNCILOR OF THE OBRUONI.
HE WAS SO NICE TO ME.
HOW DID THE ZEMĚTŘASI CAPTURE IT? I CAN'T BELIEVE THEY'RE WINNING THE WAR.

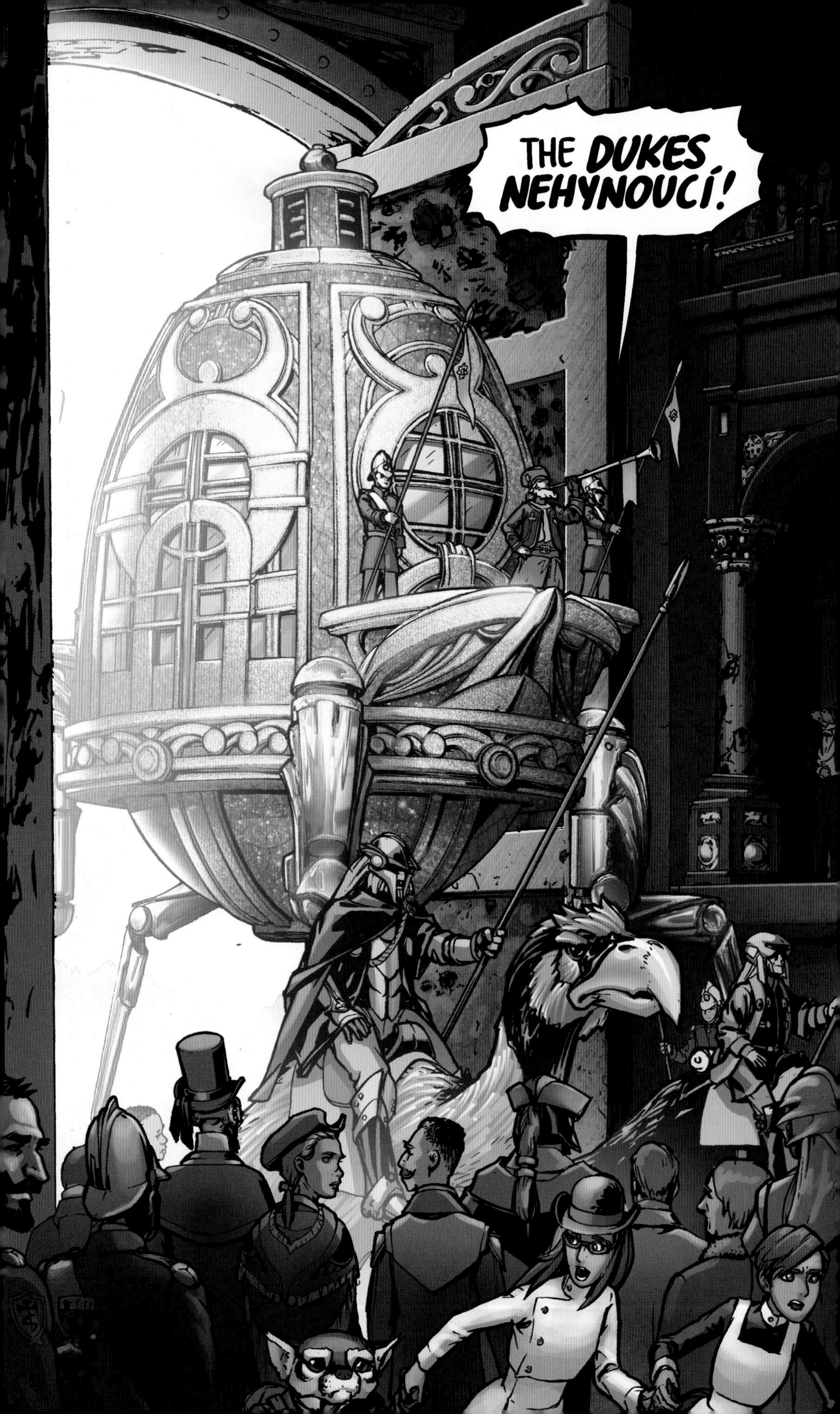
THE DUKES NEHYNOUCÍ!

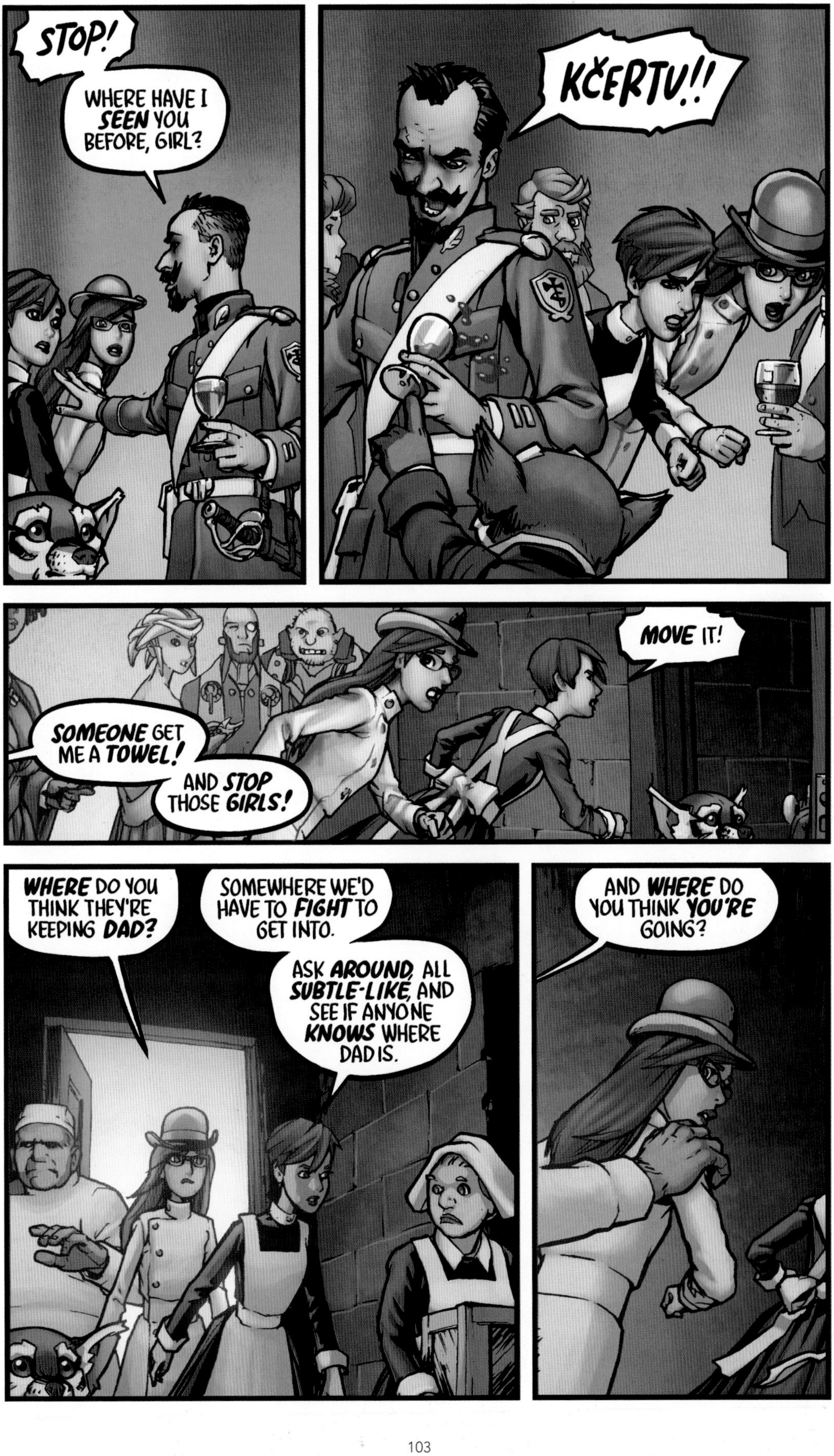
STOP!
WHERE HAVE I SEEN YOU BEFORE, GIRL?
KČERTU!!
MOVE IT!
SOMEONE GET ME A TOWEL!
AND STOP THOSE GIRLS!
WHERE DO YOU THINK THEY'RE KEEPING DAD?
SOMEWHERE WE'D HAVE TO FIGHT TO GET INTO.
ASK AROUND, ALL SUBTLE-LIKE, AND SEE IF ANYONE KNOWS WHERE DAD IS.
AND WHERE DO YOU THINK YOU'RE GOING?

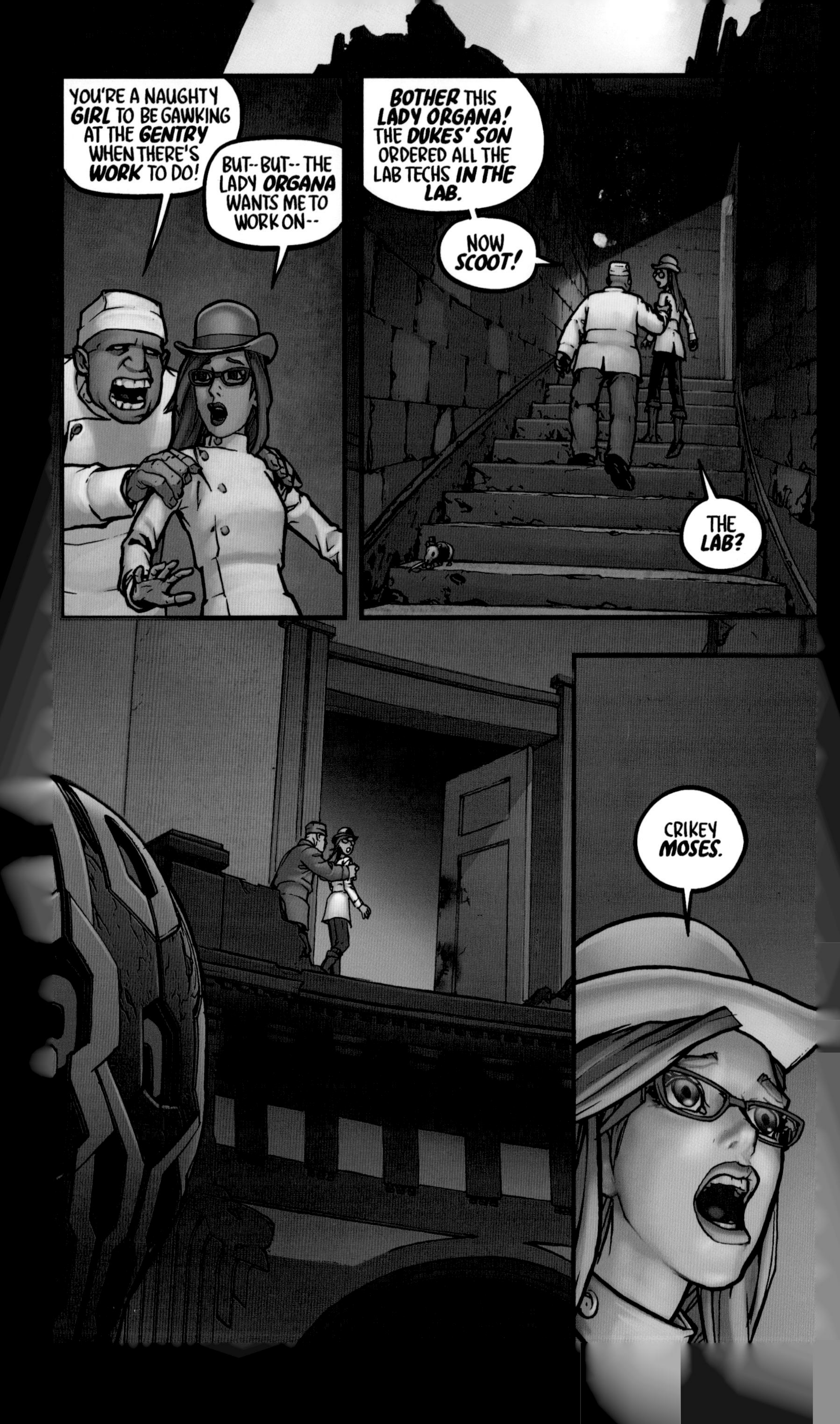
YOU'RE A NAUGHTY GIRL TO BE GAWKING AT THE GENTRY WHEN THERE'S WORK TO DO!
BUT--BUT-- THE LADY ORGANA WANTS ME TO WORK ON--
BOTHER THIS LADY ORGANA! THE DUKES' SON ORDERED ALL THE LAB TECHS IN THE LAB.
NOW SCOOT!
THE LAB?
CRIKEY MOSES.

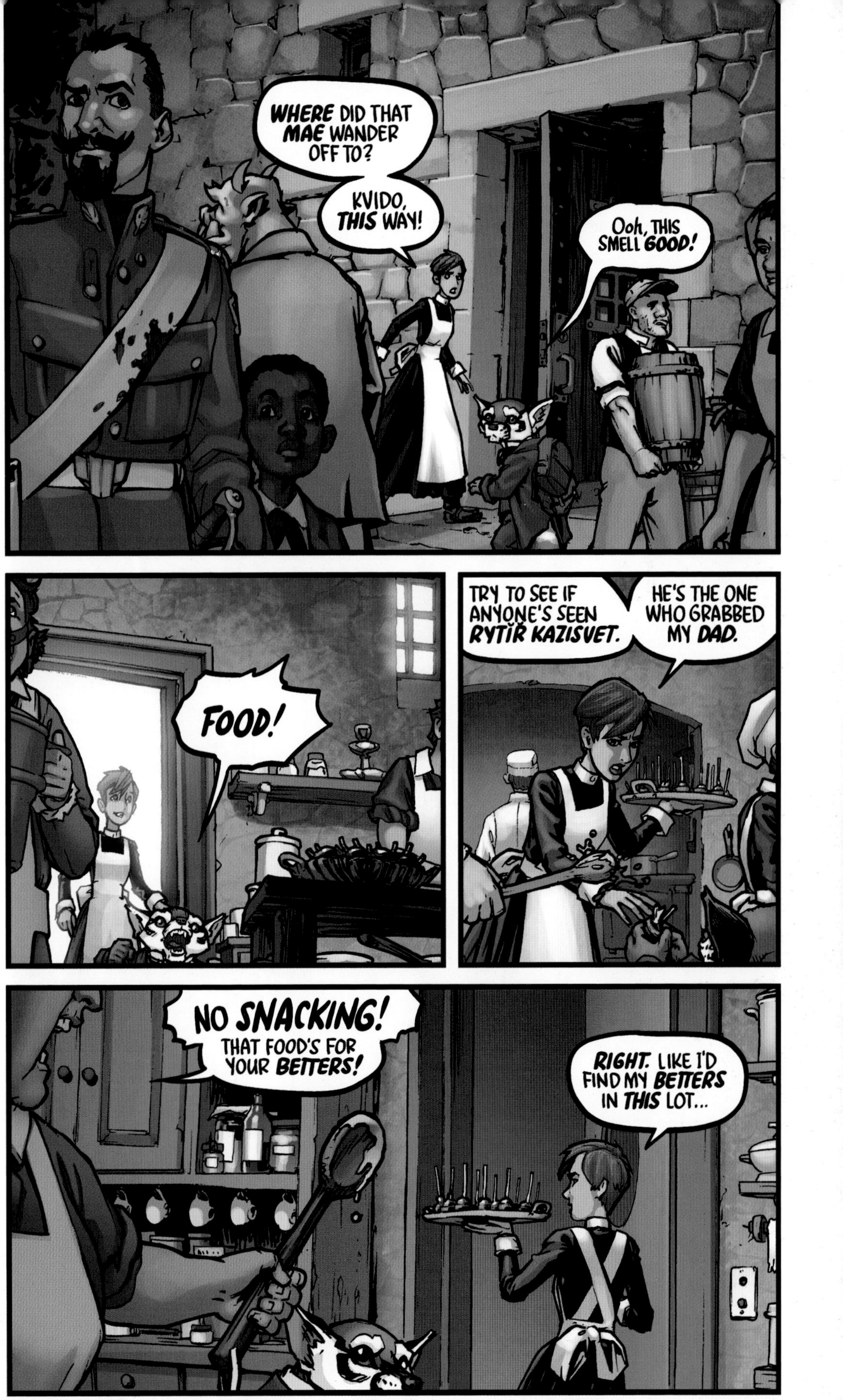
WHERE DID THAT MAE WANDER OFF TO?
KVIDO, THIS WAY!
Ooh, THIS SMELL GOOD!
FOOD!
TRY TO SEE IF ANYONE'S SEEN RYTÍŘ KAZISVET.
HE'S THE ONE WHO GRABBED MY DAD.
NO SNACKING! THAT FOOD'S FOR YOUR BETTERS!
RIGHT. LIKE I'D FIND MY BETTERS IN THIS LOT...

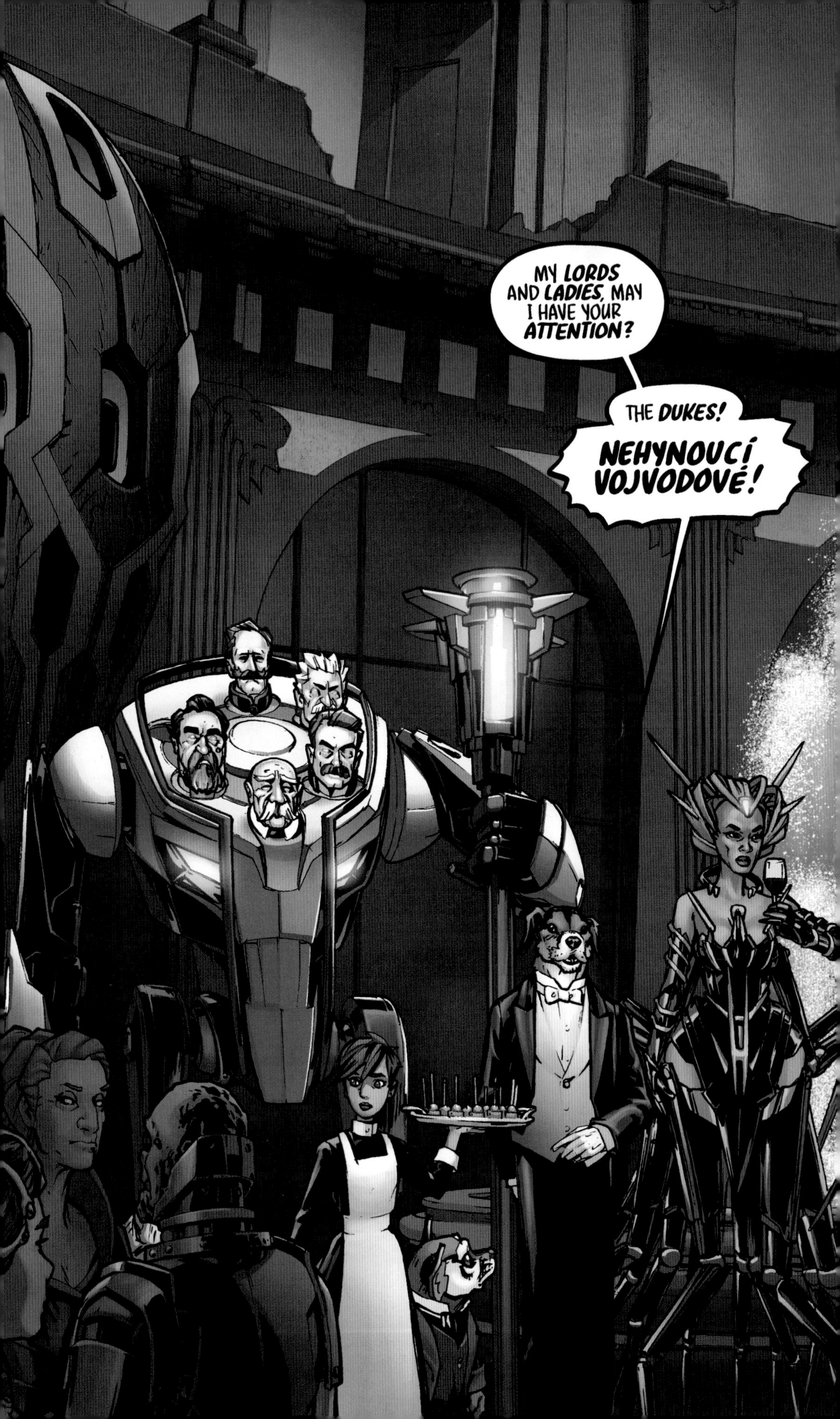
MY LORDS AND LADIES, MAY I HAVE YOUR ATTENTION?
THE DUKES!
NEHYNOUCÍ VOJVODOVÉ!

MY **FRIENDS**, HOW THE TIDE HAS **TURNED!** A FEW YEARS AGO THE HOUSES OF THE **ZEMĚTŘASI** WERE **DIVIDED**, AND THE **OBRUONI LEVIATHANS** INVADED OUR LANDS.

MANY EXPECTED THE ZEMĚTŘASI CAPITAL **ITSELF** TO FALL.

BUT **TONIGHT** WE CELEBRATE IN THIS **MIGHTIEST FORTRESS** OF THE OBRUONI!

M'LADY, HAVE YOU SEEN **RYTÍŘ KAZISVĚT?** I HAVE A **MESSAGE** FOR HIM.

WHY ARE YOU **TALKING**, PEASANT?

NOT **ALL** ZEMĚTŘASI THOUGHT THIS WAR **WISE**. SOME **STILL** DOUBT OUR FINAL VICTORY.

THEY ARE **COWARDS** AND **FOOLS**.

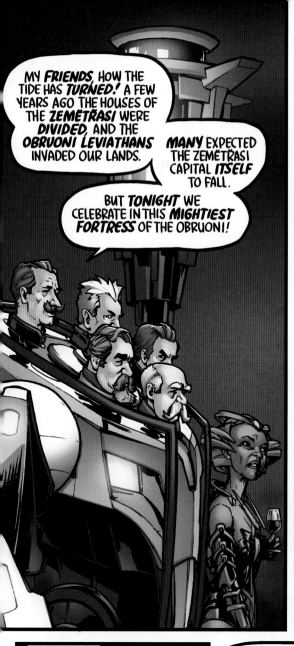

OR WORSE. **TRAITORS**.

I KINDA **FORGOT** WHAT **JERKS** THE HIGH AND MIGHTY CAN BE.

ANY SIGN OF **MAE** YET?

NOT **SEEN** MAE. **SORRY!**

ALL ENEMIES SHALL FALL BEFORE ZEMĚTŘASI **VALOR** AND ZEMĚTŘASI **SCIENCE**.

WE FEAR **NO** FOE, NOT EVEN THE **GRAND VIVICATOR** HIMSELF...

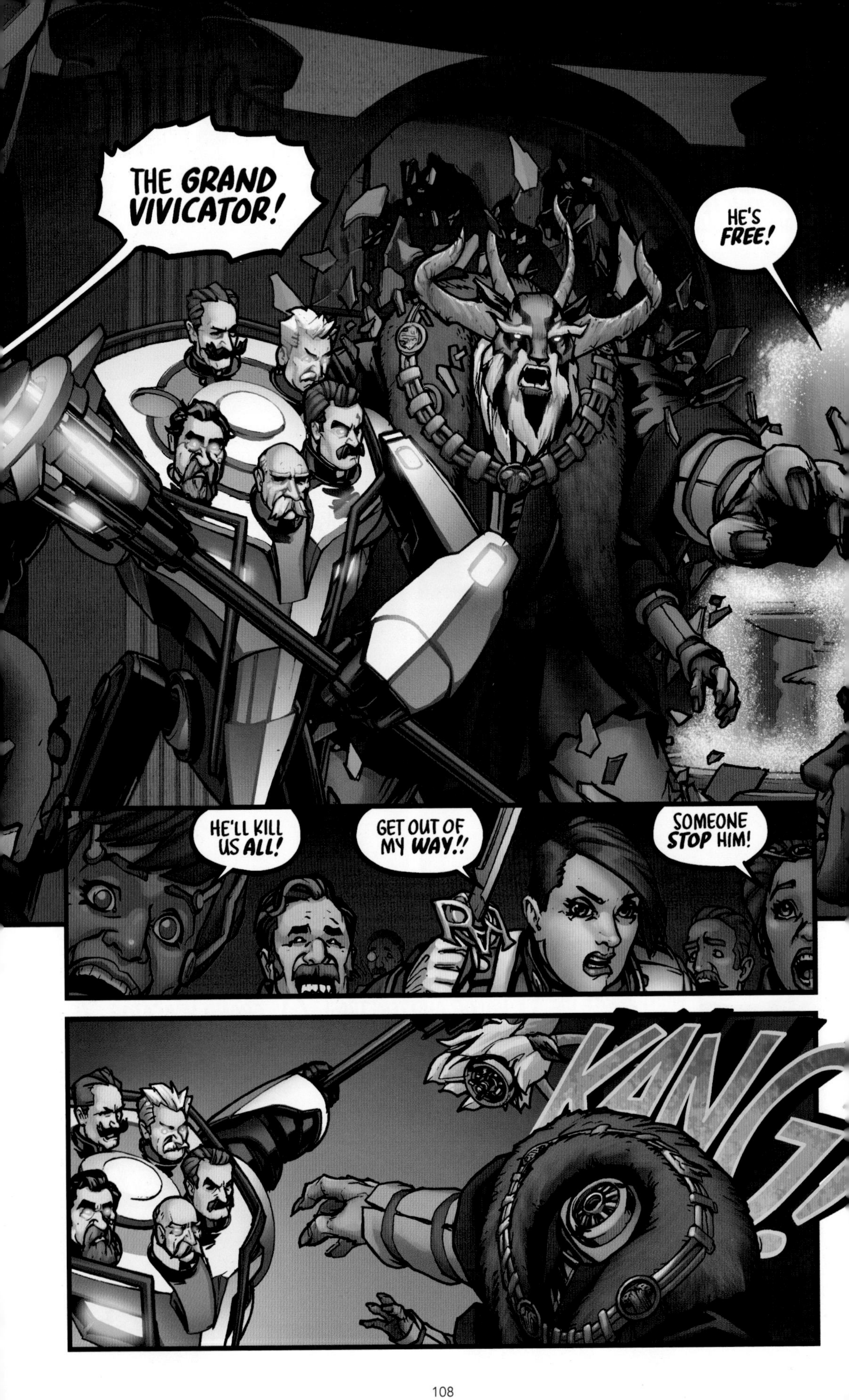
THE GRAND VIVICATOR!
HE'S FREE!
HE'LL KILL US ALL!
GET OUT OF MY WAY!!
SOMEONE STOP HIM!
KANG

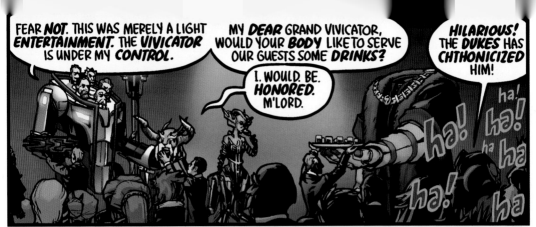

FEAR **NOT**. THIS WAS MERELY A LIGHT **ENTERTAINMENT**. THE **VIVICATOR** IS UNDER MY **CONTROL**.

MY **DEAR** GRAND VIVICATOR, WOULD YOUR **BODY** LIKE TO SERVE OUR GUESTS SOME **DRINKS**?

I. WOULD. BE. **HONORED**. M'LORD.

HILARIOUS! THE **DUKES** HAS **CHTHONICIZED** HIM!

ha! ha! ha! ha! ha! ha!

TO **HOUSE ZEMĚTŘASI**, AND WE THE **LUPIČVRAKŮ** WHO SHALL ONCE AGAIN **RULE** IT!

HURRAH!!

ZEMĚTŘASI **SCIENCE** HAS YET **ANOTHER** WONDER FOR US TODAY.

THIS **STRONGHOLD** HELD A **STOREHOUSE** OF ARTIFACTS, THE LOST **TECHNOLOGY** OF THE **ANCIENTS**.

BEYOND THE UNDER-STANDING OF OBRUONI **TECHNOCRATS**, BUT NOT TO **US**.

VIVICATOR, HAVE YOU ANY FURTHER **USE** FOR THAT BODY?

NONE. **WHATSOEVER**. MY DEAR. DUKES.

GOOD...

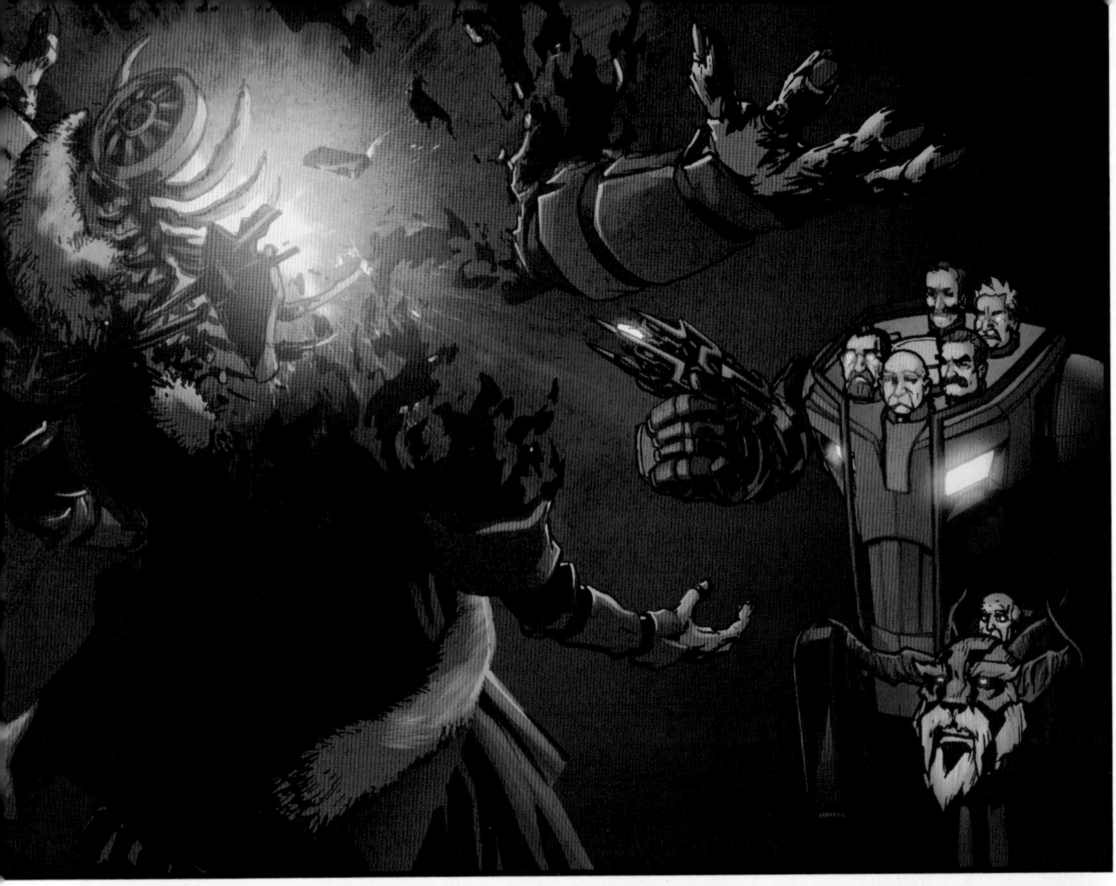

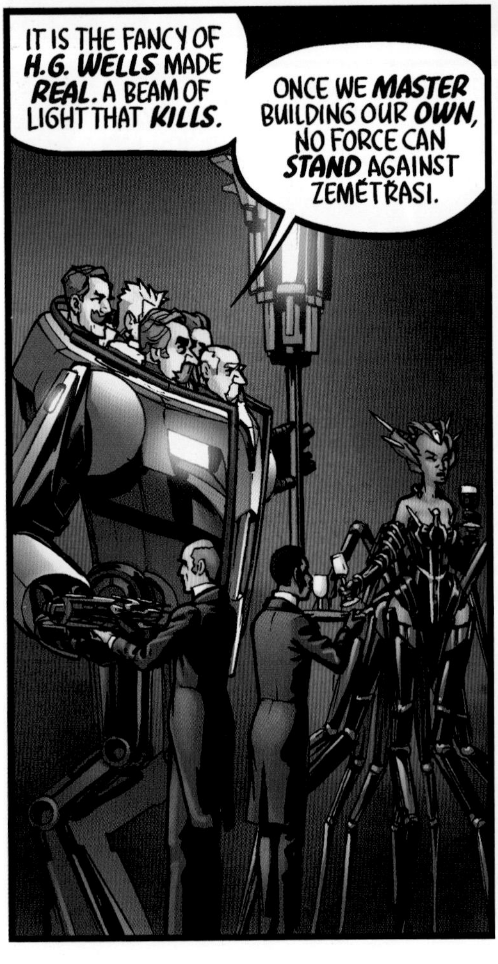
IT IS THE FANCY OF H.G. WELLS MADE REAL. A BEAM OF LIGHT THAT KILLS.
ONCE WE MASTER BUILDING OUR OWN, NO FORCE CAN STAND AGAINST ZEMËTRASI.

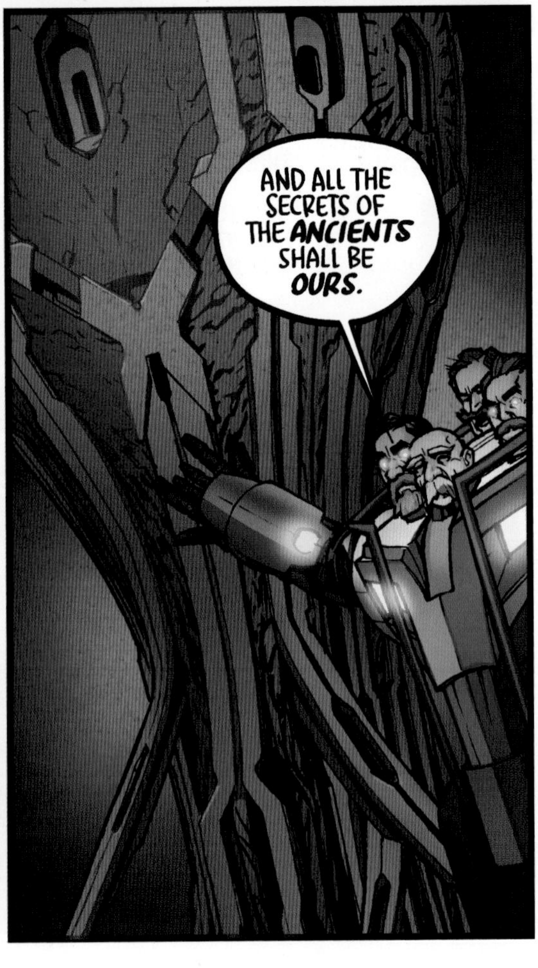
AND ALL THE SECRETS OF THE ANCIENTS SHALL BE OURS.

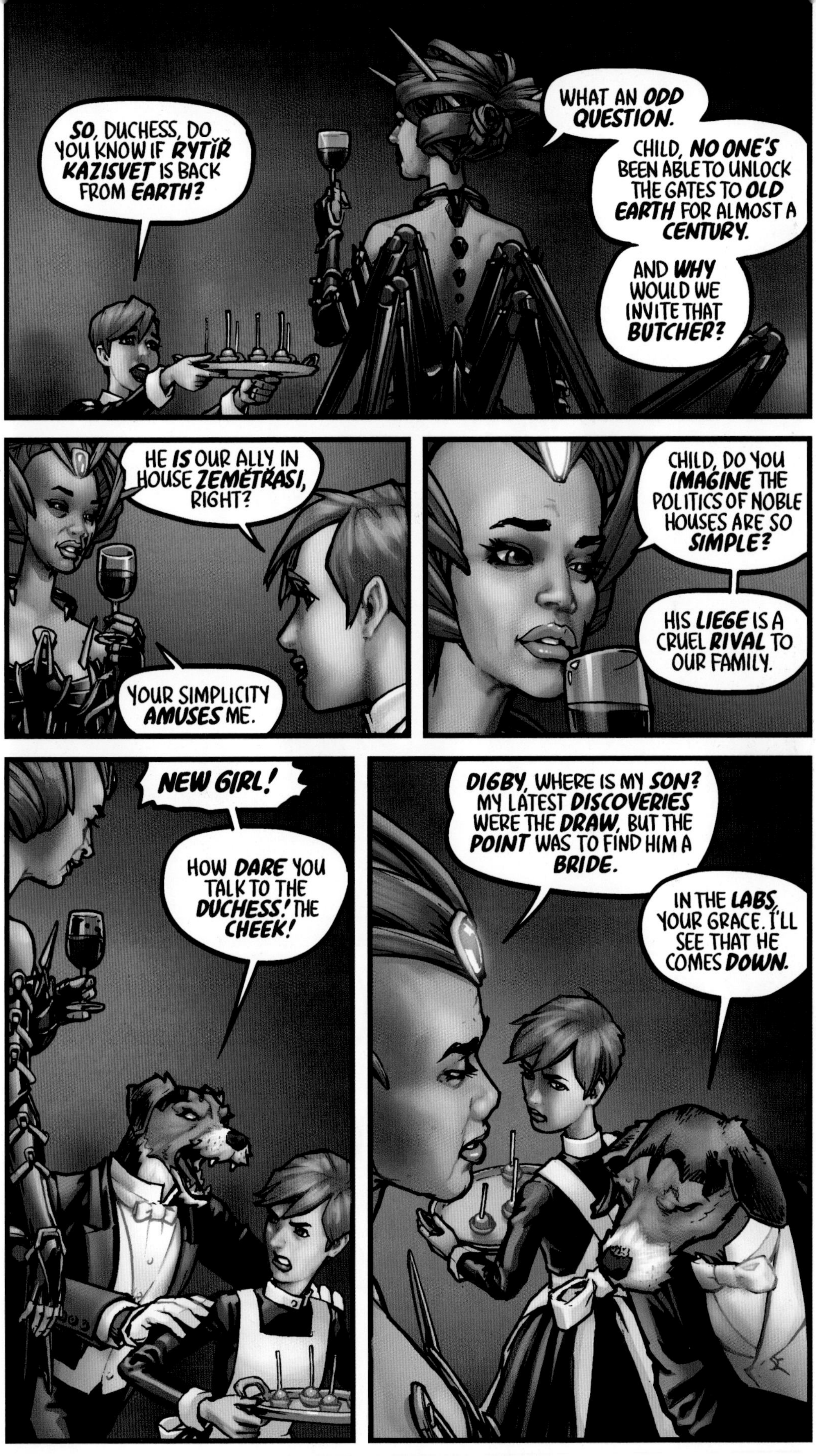
SO, DUCHESS, DO YOU KNOW IF RYTÍŘ KAZISVET IS BACK FROM EARTH?
WHAT AN ODD QUESTION.
CHILD, NO ONE'S BEEN ABLE TO UNLOCK THE GATES TO OLD EARTH FOR ALMOST A CENTURY.
AND WHY WOULD WE INVITE THAT BUTCHER?
HE IS OUR ALLY IN HOUSE ZEMĚTŘASI, RIGHT?
YOUR SIMPLICITY AMUSES ME.
CHILD, DO YOU IMAGINE THE POLITICS OF NOBLE HOUSES ARE SO SIMPLE?
HIS LIEGE IS A CRUEL RIVAL TO OUR FAMILY.
NEW GIRL!
HOW DARE YOU TALK TO THE DUCHESS! THE CHEEK!
DIGBY, WHERE IS MY SON? MY LATEST DISCOVERIES WERE THE DRAW, BUT THE POINT WAS TO FIND HIM A BRIDE.
IN THE LABS, YOUR GRACE. I'LL SEE THAT HE COMES DOWN.

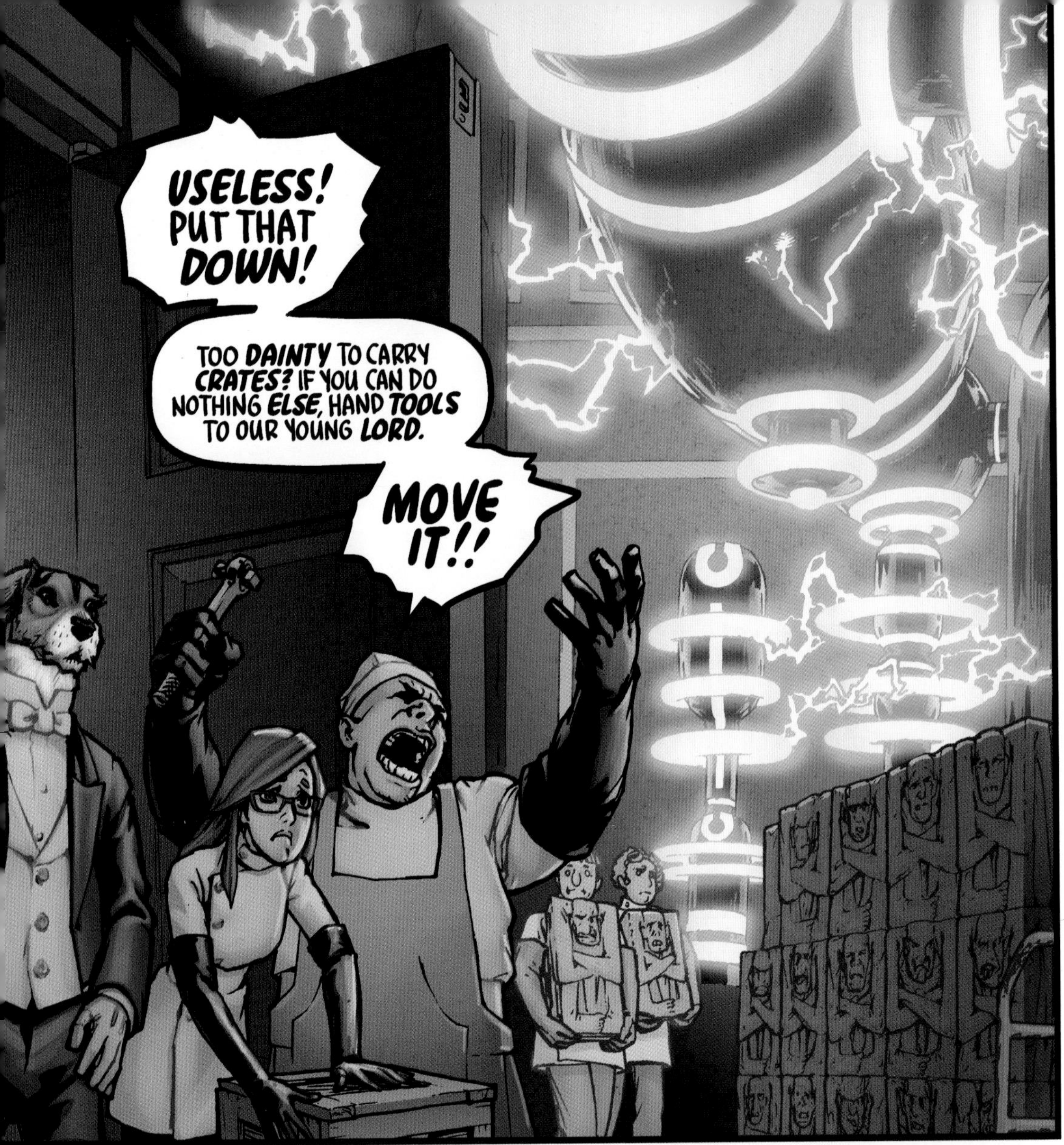
USELESS! PUT THAT DOWN!
TOO DAINTY TO CARRY CRATES? IF YOU CAN DO NOTHING ELSE, HAND TOOLS TO OUR YOUNG LORD.
MOVE IT!!

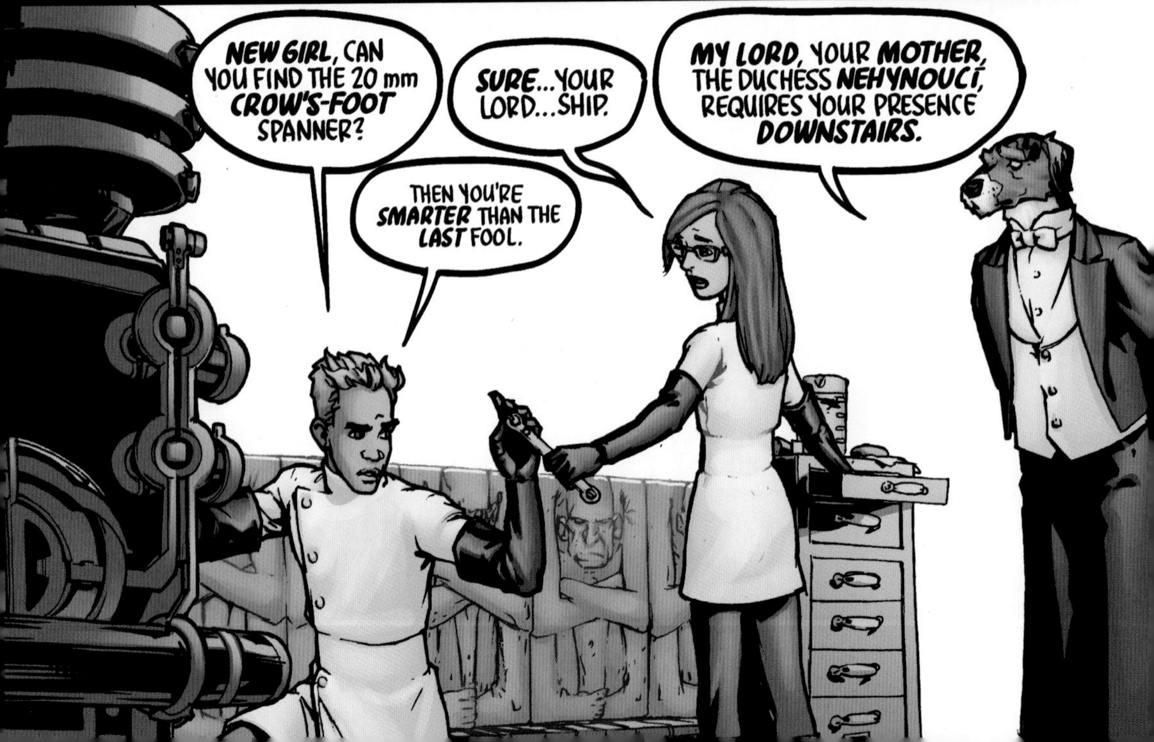
NEW GIRL, CAN YOU FIND THE 20 mm CROW'S-FOOT SPANNER?
SURE...YOUR LORD...SHIP.
THEN YOU'RE SMARTER THAN THE LAST FOOL.
MY LORD, YOUR MOTHER, THE DUCHESS NEHYNOUCÍ, REQUIRES YOUR PRESENCE DOWNSTAIRS.

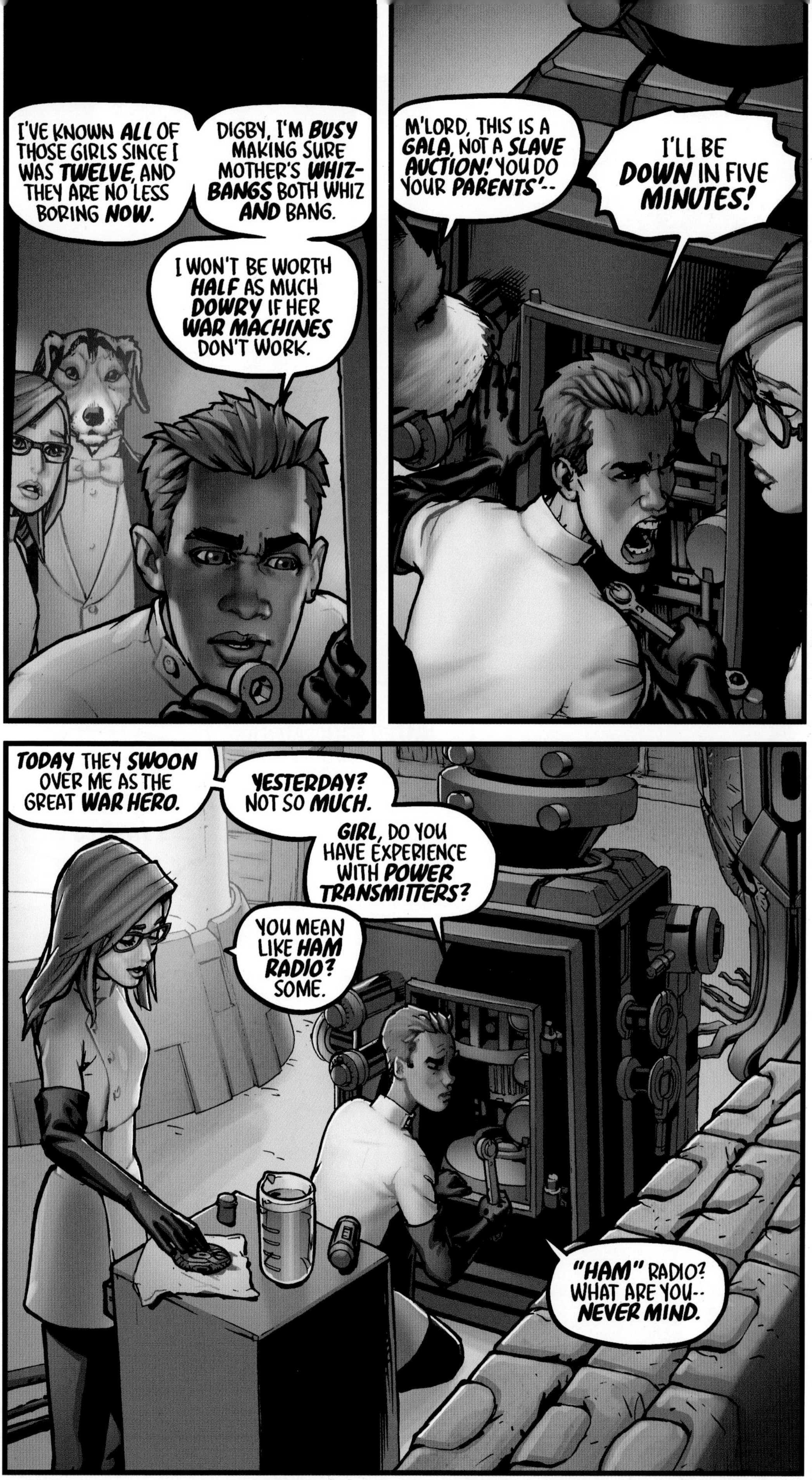
I'VE KNOWN ALL OF THOSE GIRLS SINCE I WAS TWELVE, AND THEY ARE NO LESS BORING NOW.
DIGBY, I'M BUSY MAKING SURE MOTHER'S WHIZ-BANGS BOTH WHIZ AND BANG.
I WON'T BE WORTH HALF AS MUCH DOWRY IF HER WAR MACHINES DON'T WORK.
M'LORD, THIS IS A GALA, NOT A SLAVE AUCTION! YOU DO YOUR PARENTS'--
I'LL BE DOWN IN FIVE MINUTES!
TODAY THEY SWOON OVER ME AS THE GREAT WAR HERO.
YESTERDAY? NOT SO MUCH.
GIRL, DO YOU HAVE EXPERIENCE WITH POWER TRANSMITTERS?
YOU MEAN LIKE HAM RADIO? SOME.
"HAM" RADIO? WHAT ARE YOU-- NEVER MIND.

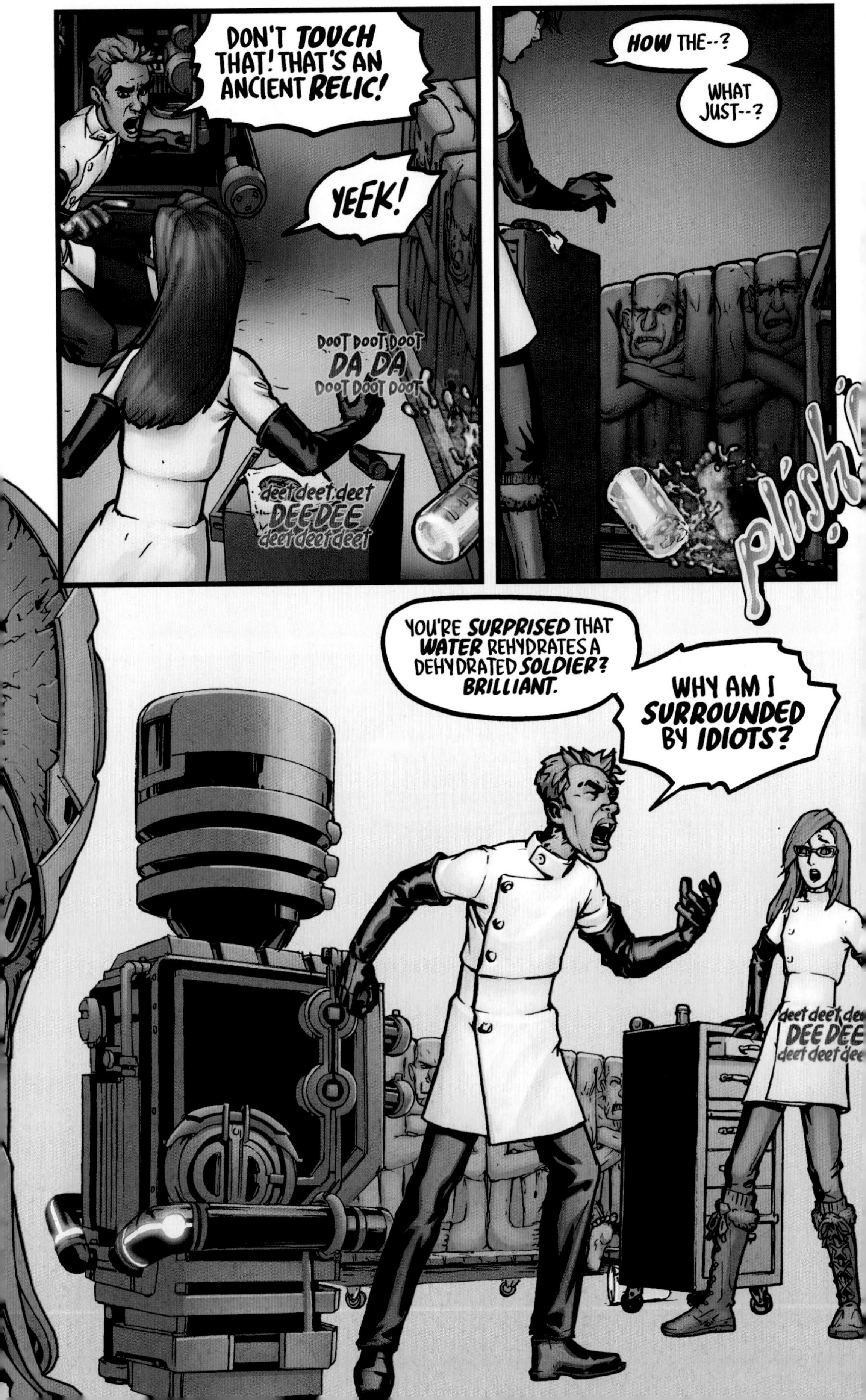
DON'T TOUCH THAT! THAT'S AN ANCIENT RELIC!
YEEK!
DOOT DOOT DOOT DA DA DOOT DOOT DOOT
deet deet deet DEE DEE deet deet deet
HOW THE--?
WHAT JUST--?
plish!
YOU'RE SURPRISED THAT WATER REHYDRATES A DEHYDRATED SOLDIER? BRILLIANT.
WHY AM I SURROUNDED BY IDIOTS?
DEE DEE

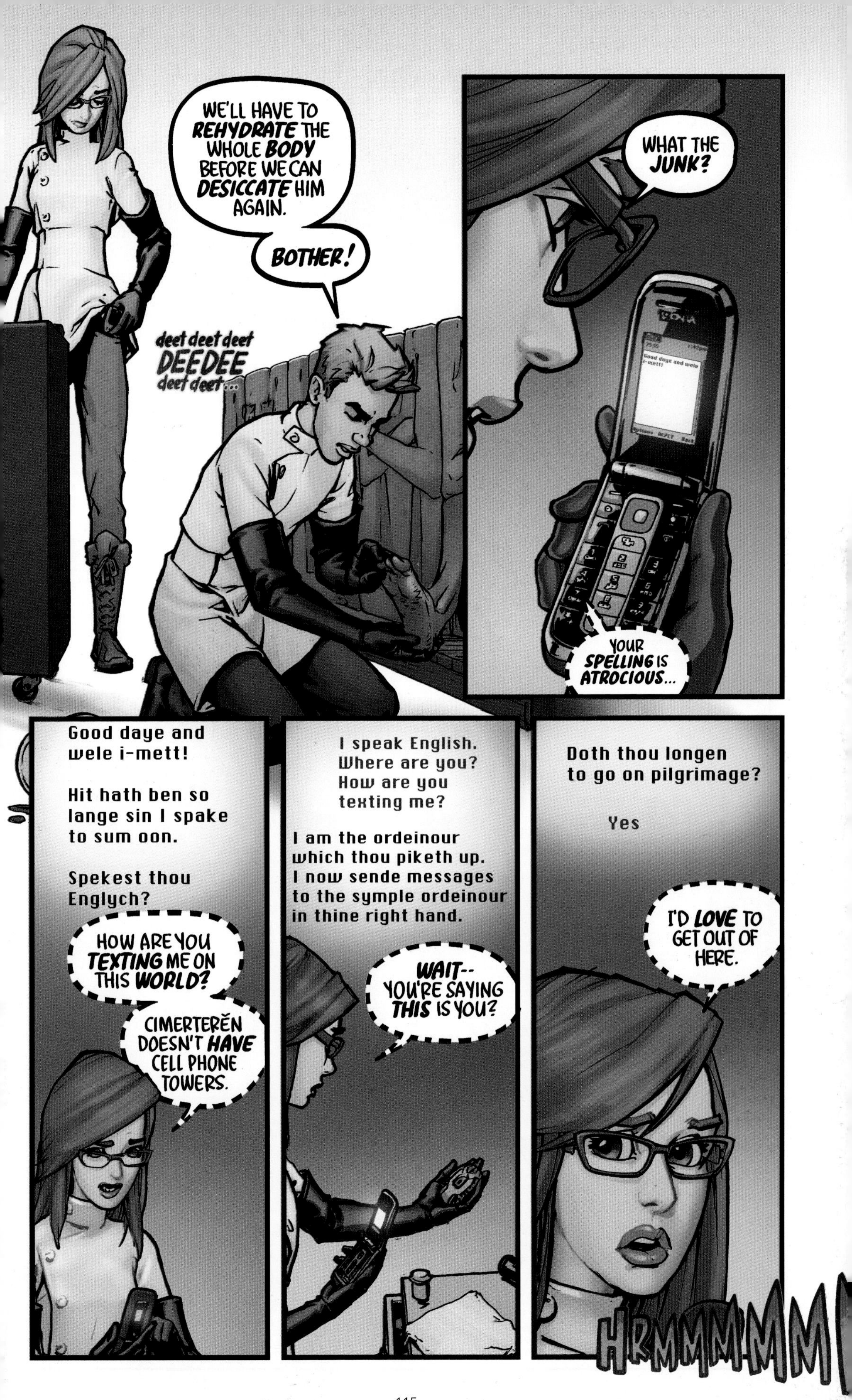
WE'LL HAVE TO REHYDRATE THE WHOLE BODY BEFORE WE CAN DESICCATE HIM AGAIN.
BOTHER!
deet deet deet DEEDEE deet deet...
WHAT THE JUNK?
Good daye and wele i-mett!
YOUR SPELLING IS ATROCIOUS...
Good daye and wele i-mett!
Hit hath ben so lange sin I spake to sum oon.
Spekest thou Englych?
HOW ARE YOU TEXTING ME ON THIS WORLD?
CIMERTERĔN DOESN'T HAVE CELL PHONE TOWERS.
I speak English. Where are you? How are you texting me?
I am the ordeinour which thou piketh up. I now sende messages to the symple ordeinour in thine right hand.
WAIT-- YOU'RE SAYING THIS IS YOU?
Doth thou longen to go on pilgrimage?
Yes
I'D LOVE TO GET OUT OF HERE.
HRMMMMMM

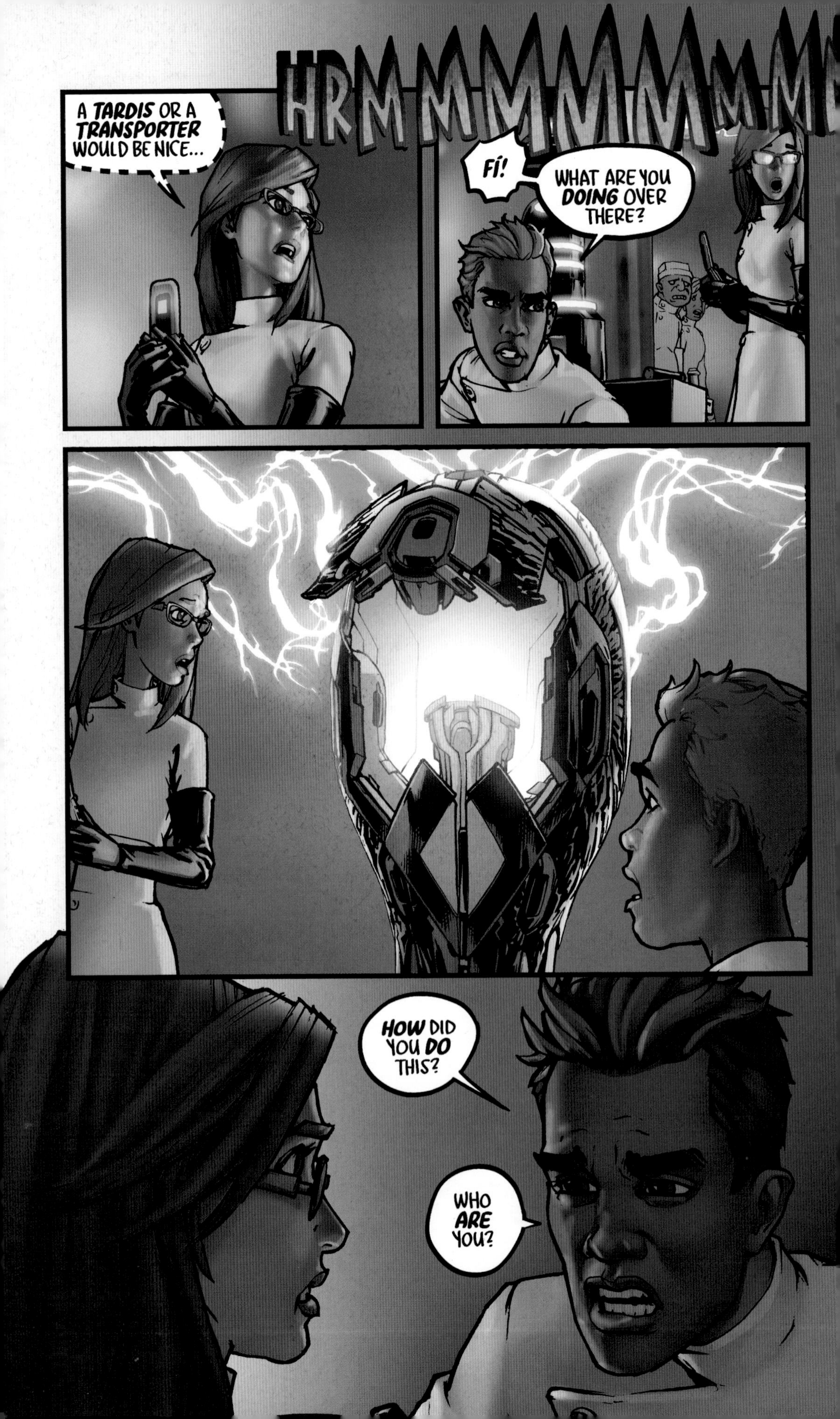
HRMMMMMMMMMM
A TARDIS OR A TRANSPORTER WOULD BE NICE...
FÍ!
WHAT ARE YOU DOING OVER THERE?
HOW DID YOU DO THIS?
WHO ARE YOU?

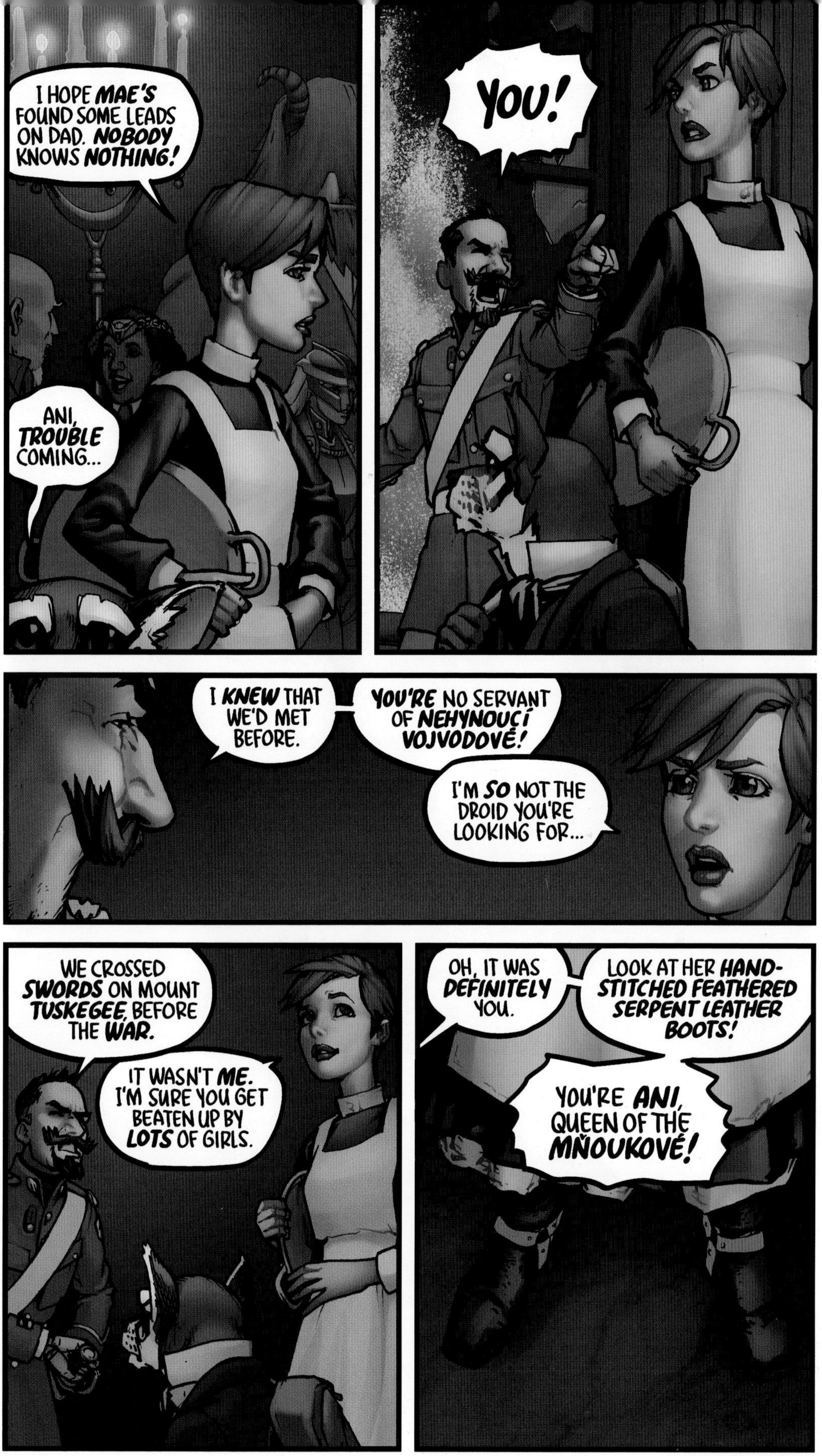
I HOPE MAE'S FOUND SOME LEADS ON DAD. NOBODY KNOWS NOTHING!
ANI, TROUBLE COMING...
YOU!
I KNEW THAT WE'D MET BEFORE.
YOU'RE NO SERVANT OF NEHYNOUCÍ VOJVODOVÉ!
I'M SO NOT THE DROID YOU'RE LOOKING FOR...
WE CROSSED SWORDS ON MOUNT TUSKEGEE, BEFORE THE WAR.
IT WASN'T ME. I'M SURE YOU GET BEATEN UP BY LOTS OF GIRLS.
OH, IT WAS DEFINITELY YOU.
LOOK AT HER HAND-STITCHED FEATHERED SERPENT LEATHER BOOTS!
YOU'RE ANI, QUEEN OF THE MŇOUKOVÉ!

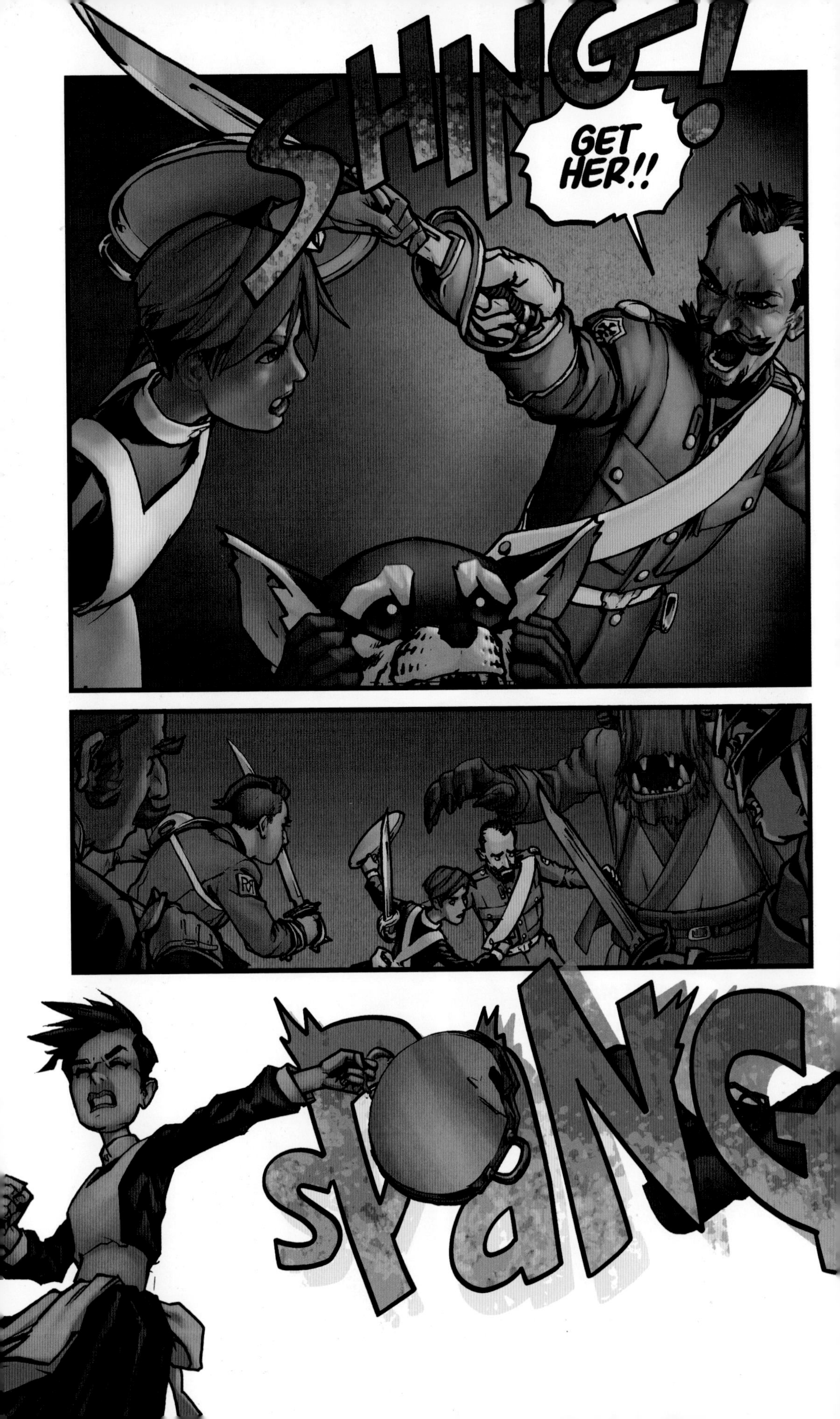
SHING-!
GET HER!!
SPANG

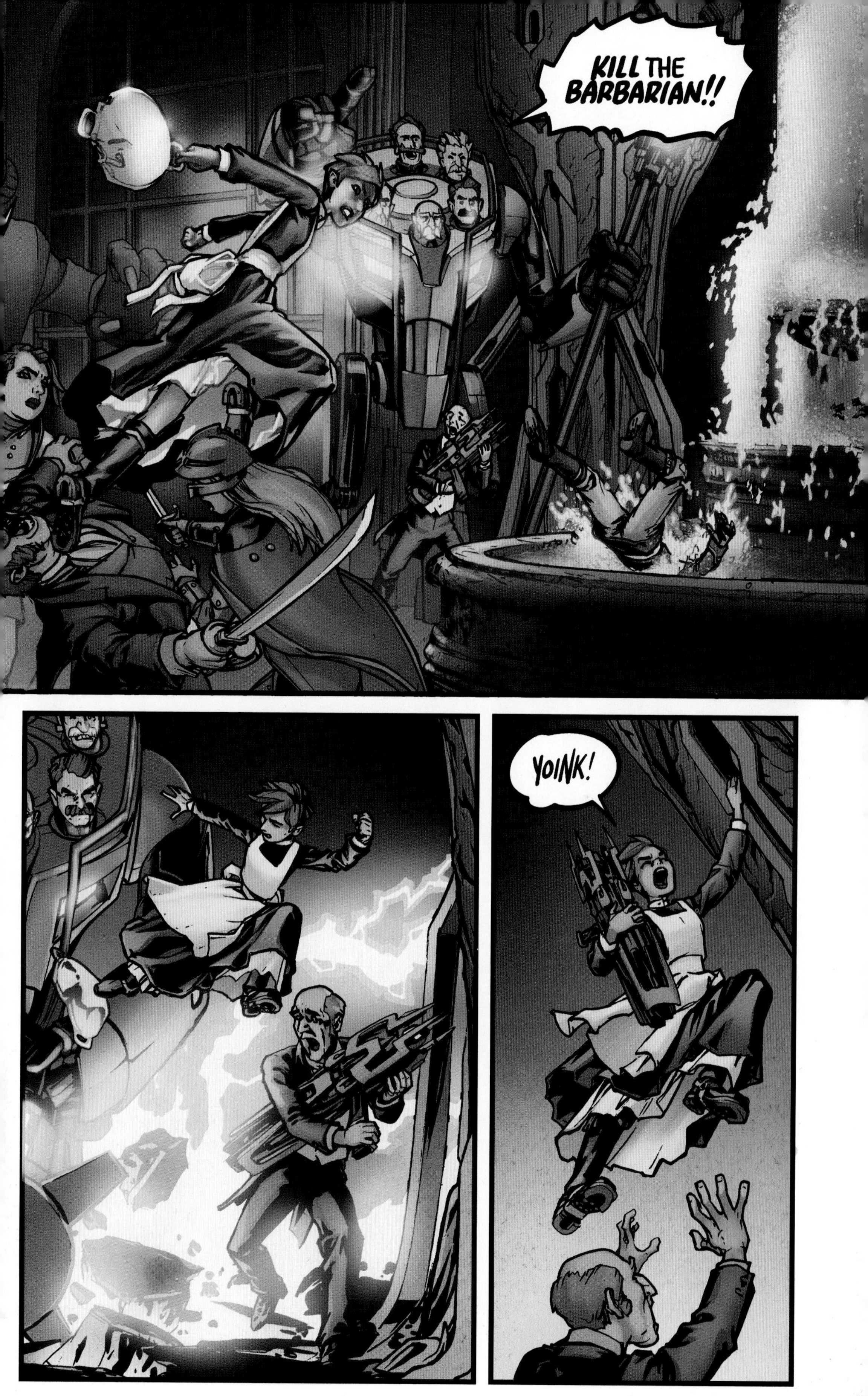
KILL THE BARBARIAN!!
YOINK!

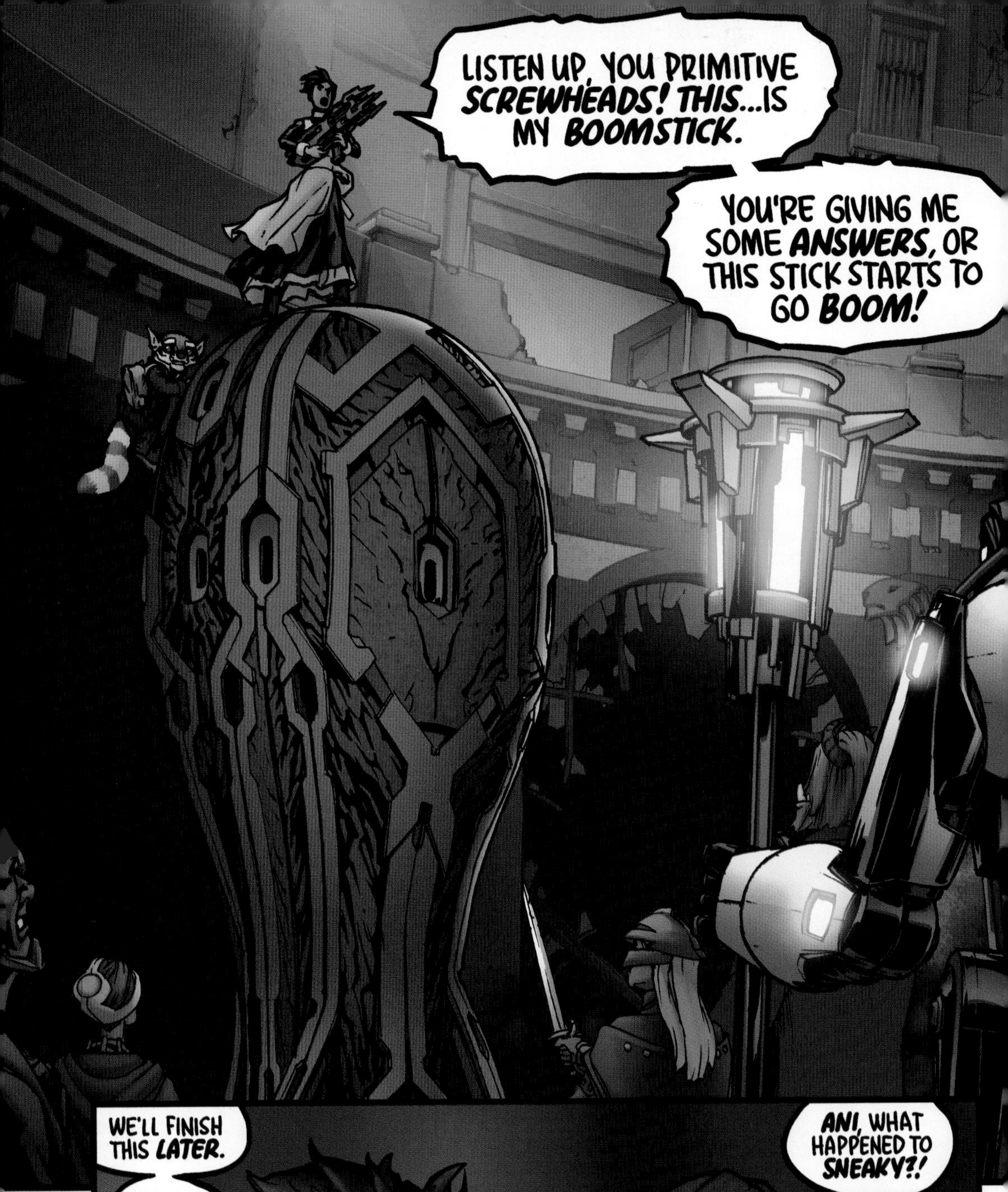
LISTEN UP, YOU PRIMITIVE SCREWHEADS! THIS...IS MY BOOMSTICK.
YOU'RE GIVING ME SOME ANSWERS, OR THIS STICK STARTS TO GO BOOM!

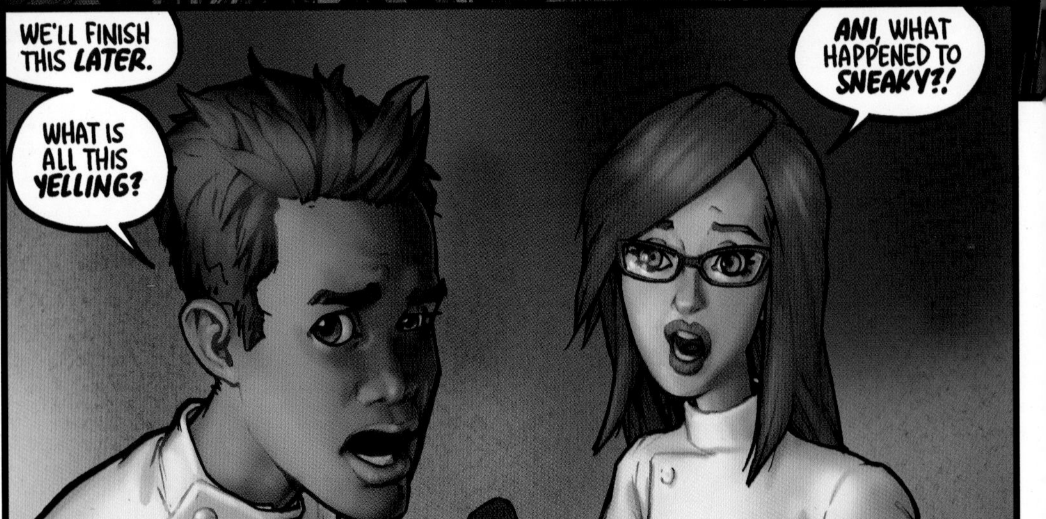
WE'LL FINISH THIS LATER.
WHAT IS ALL THIS YELLING?
ANI, WHAT HAPPENED TO SNEAKY?!

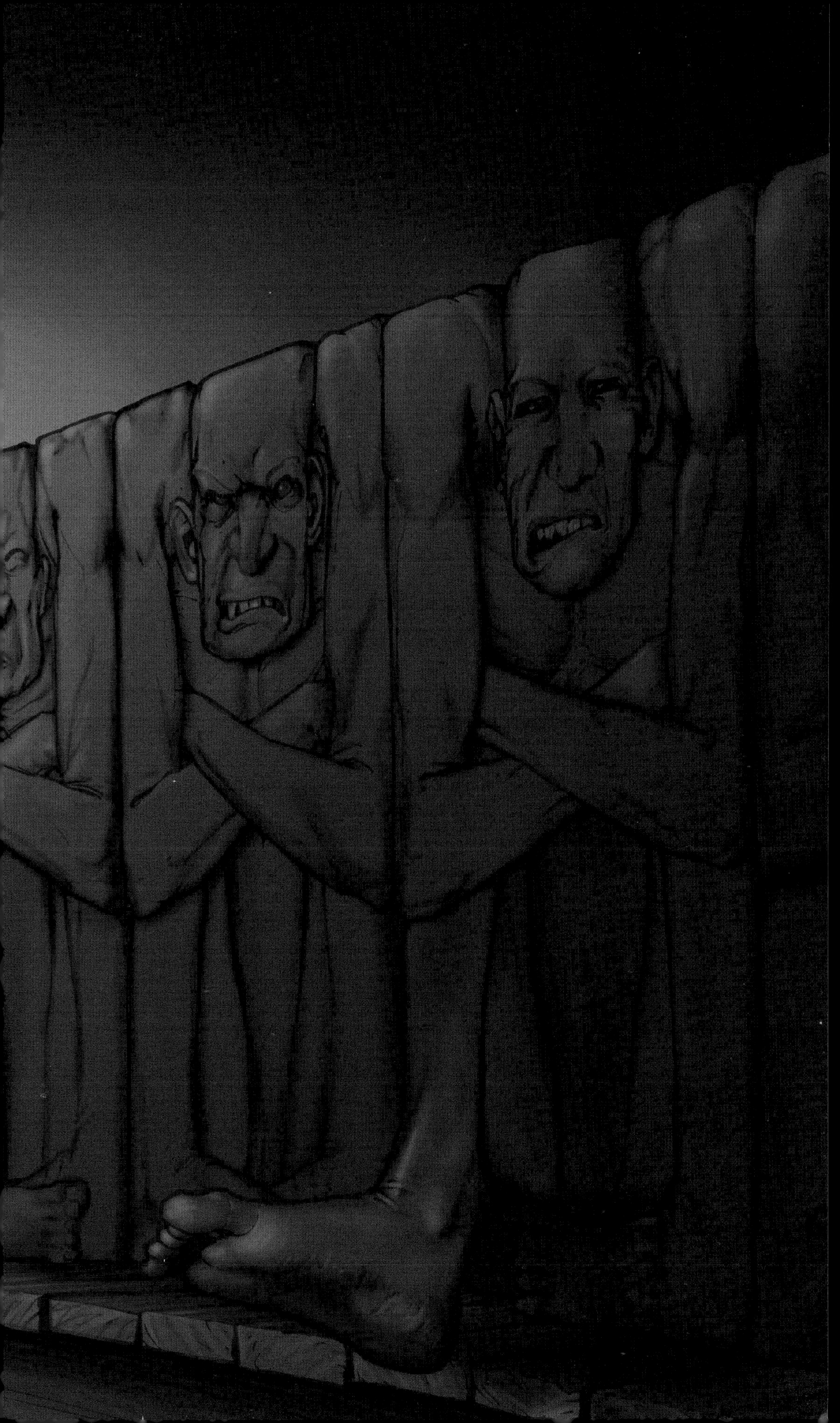

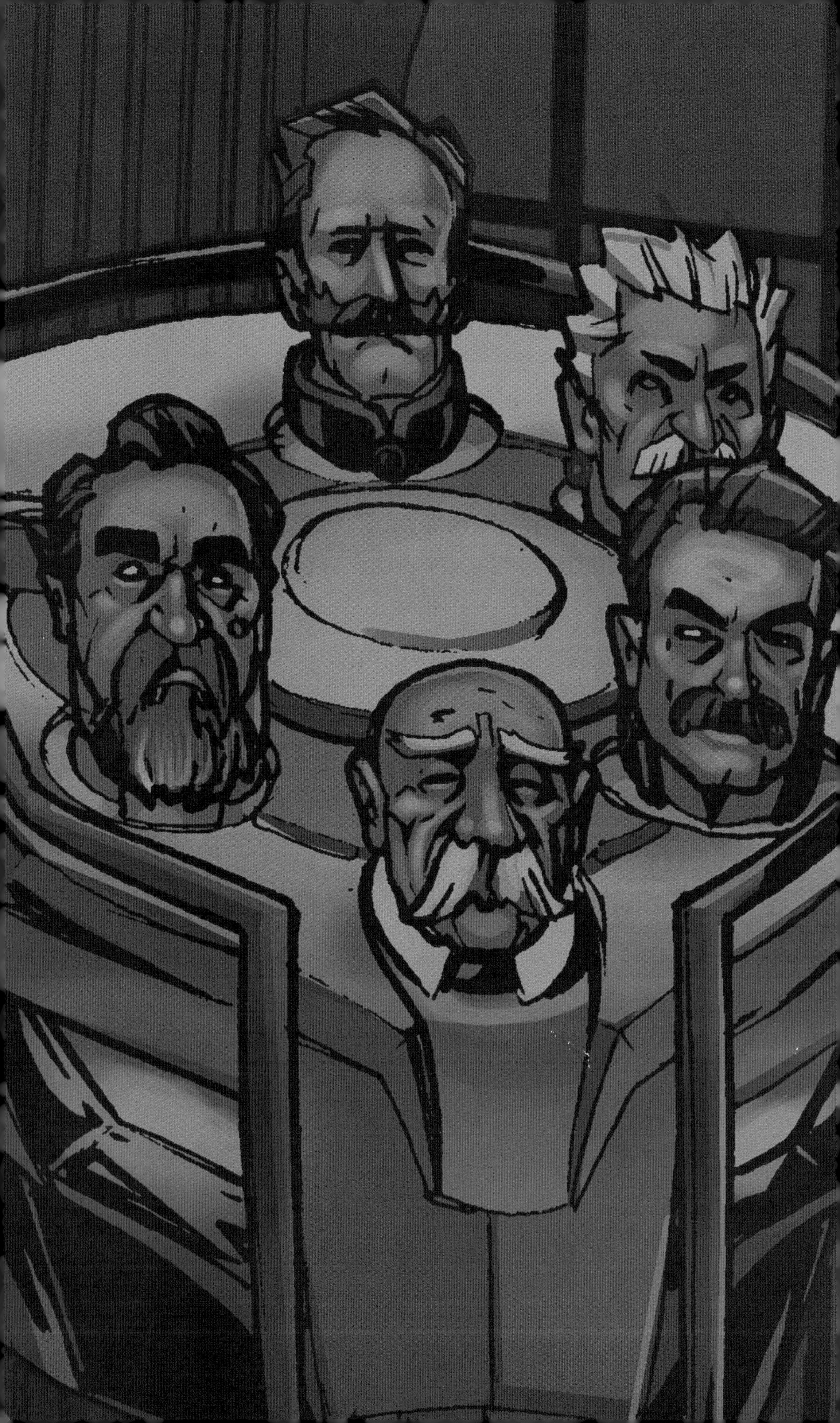

FIVE

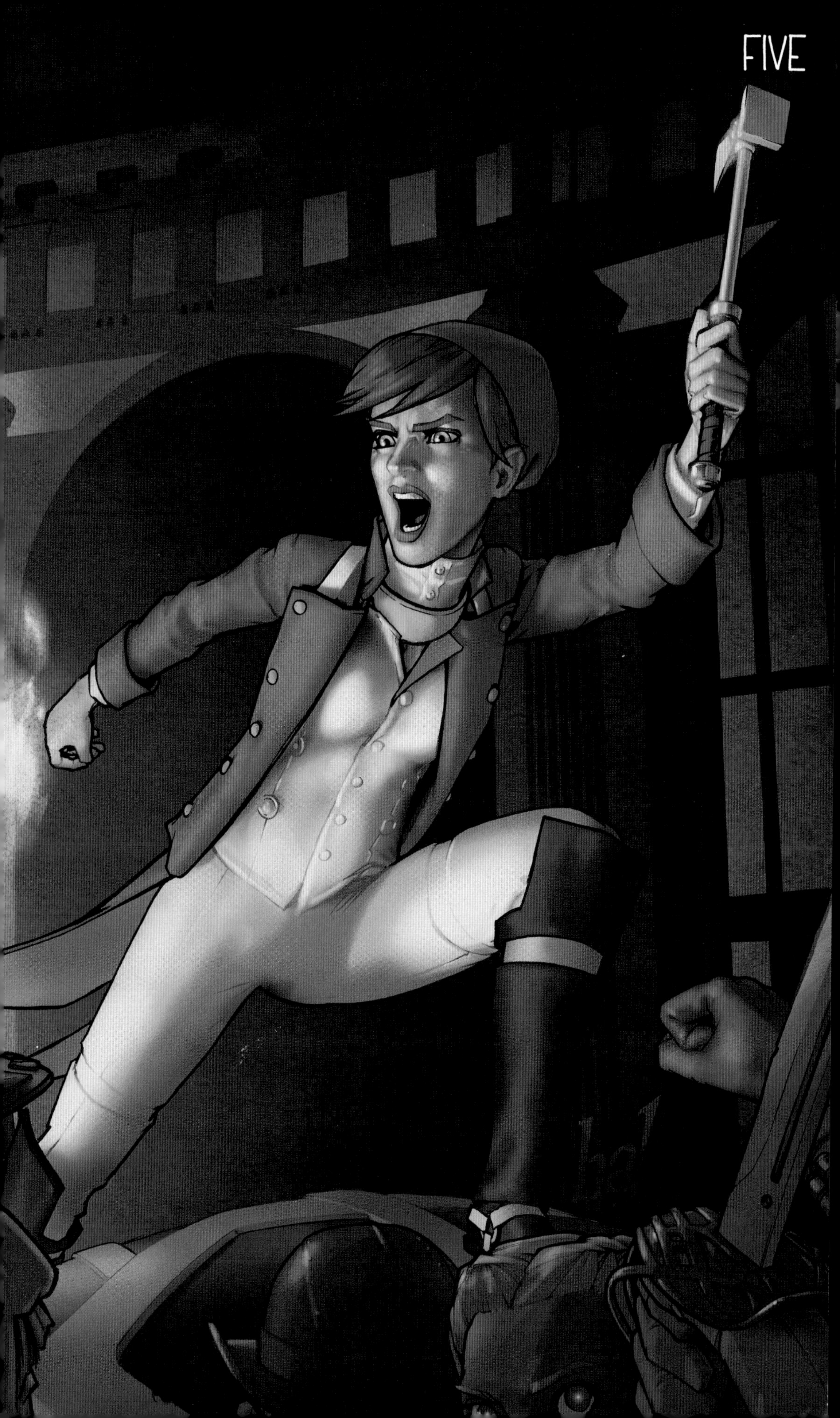

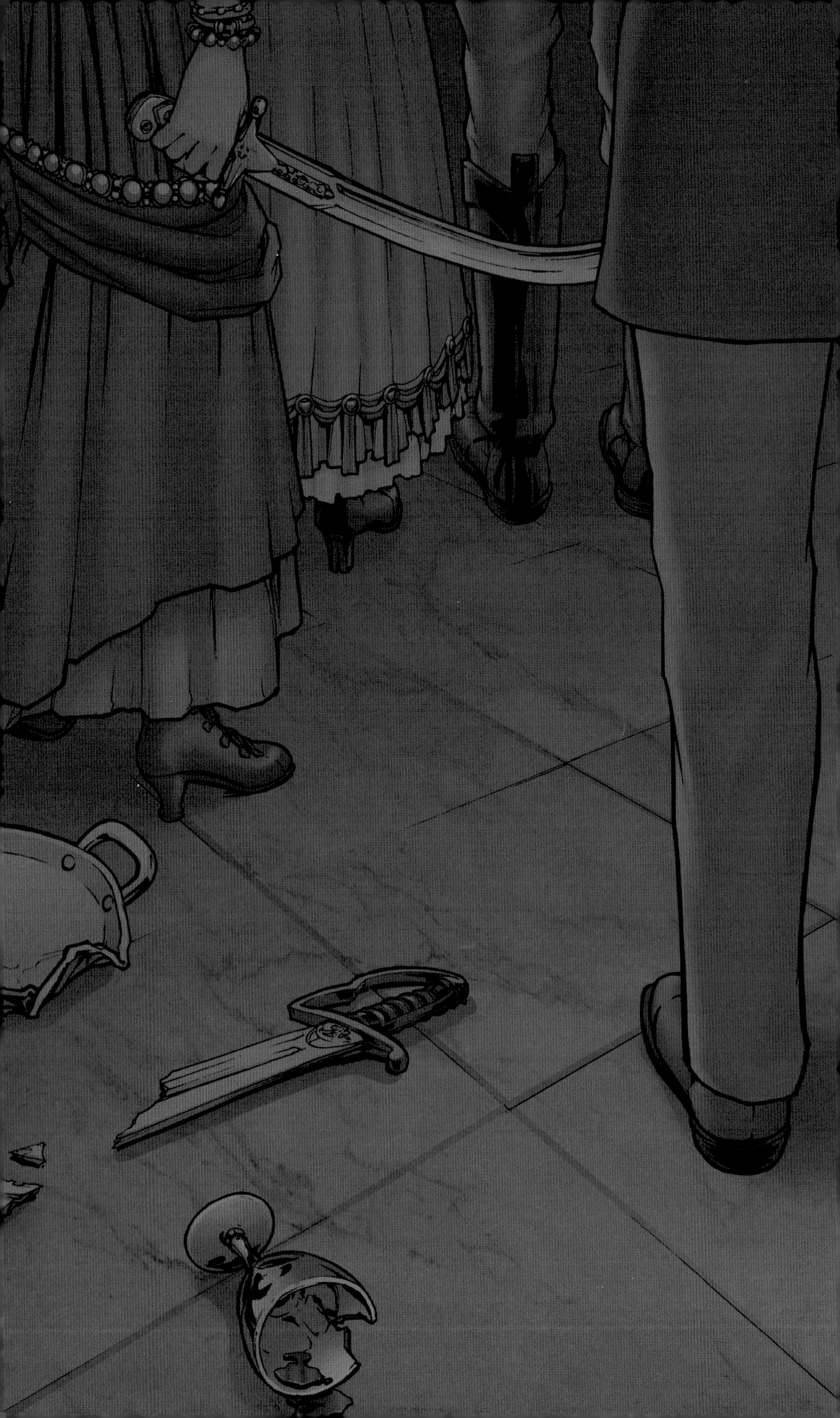

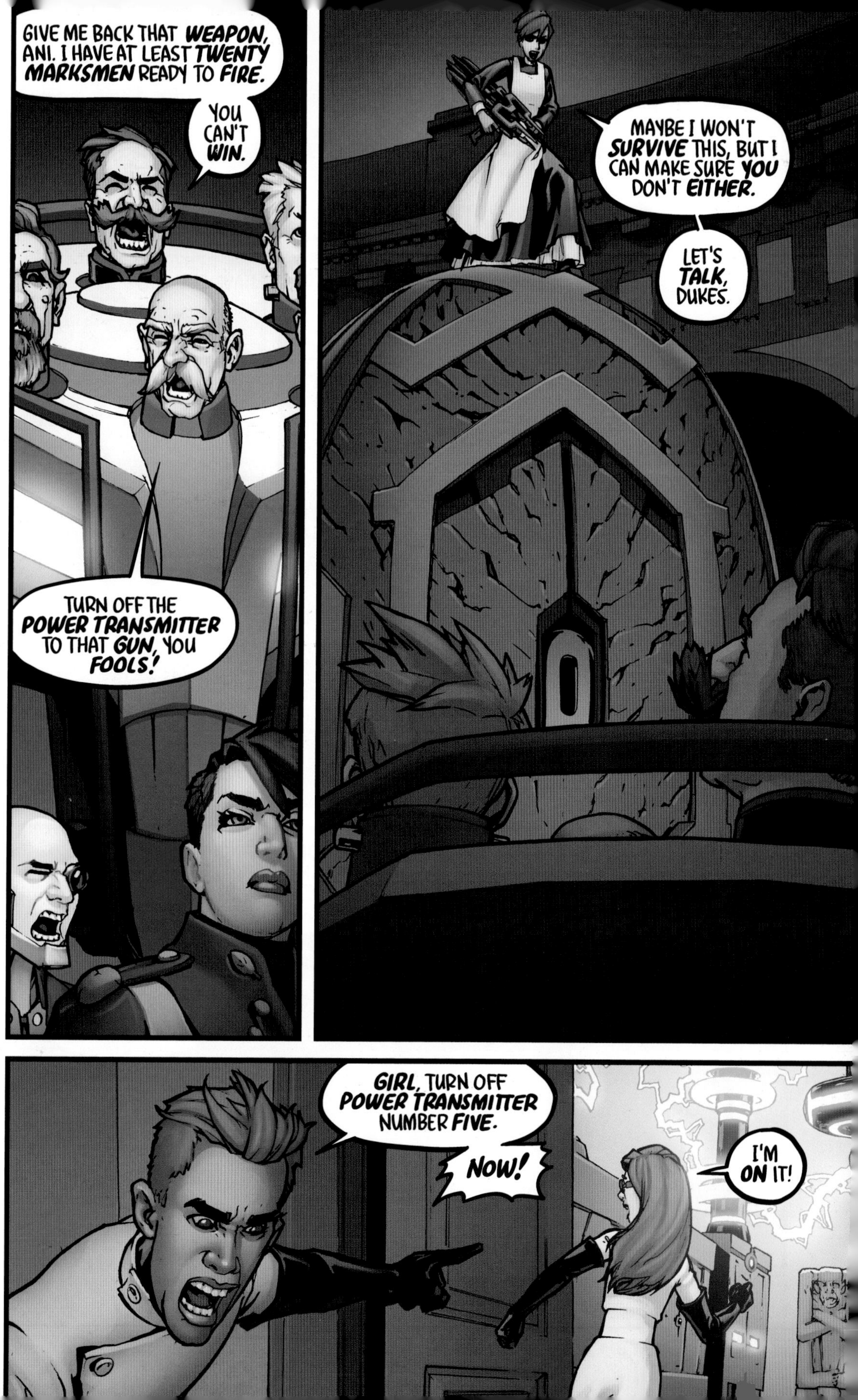
GIVE ME BACK THAT WEAPON, ANI. I HAVE AT LEAST TWENTY MARKSMEN READY TO FIRE.
YOU CAN'T WIN.
TURN OFF THE POWER TRANSMITTER TO THAT GUN, YOU FOOLS!
MAYBE I WON'T SURVIVE THIS, BUT I CAN MAKE SURE YOU DON'T EITHER.
LET'S TALK, DUKES.
GIRL, TURN OFF POWER TRANSMITTER NUMBER FIVE.
NOW!
I'M ON IT!

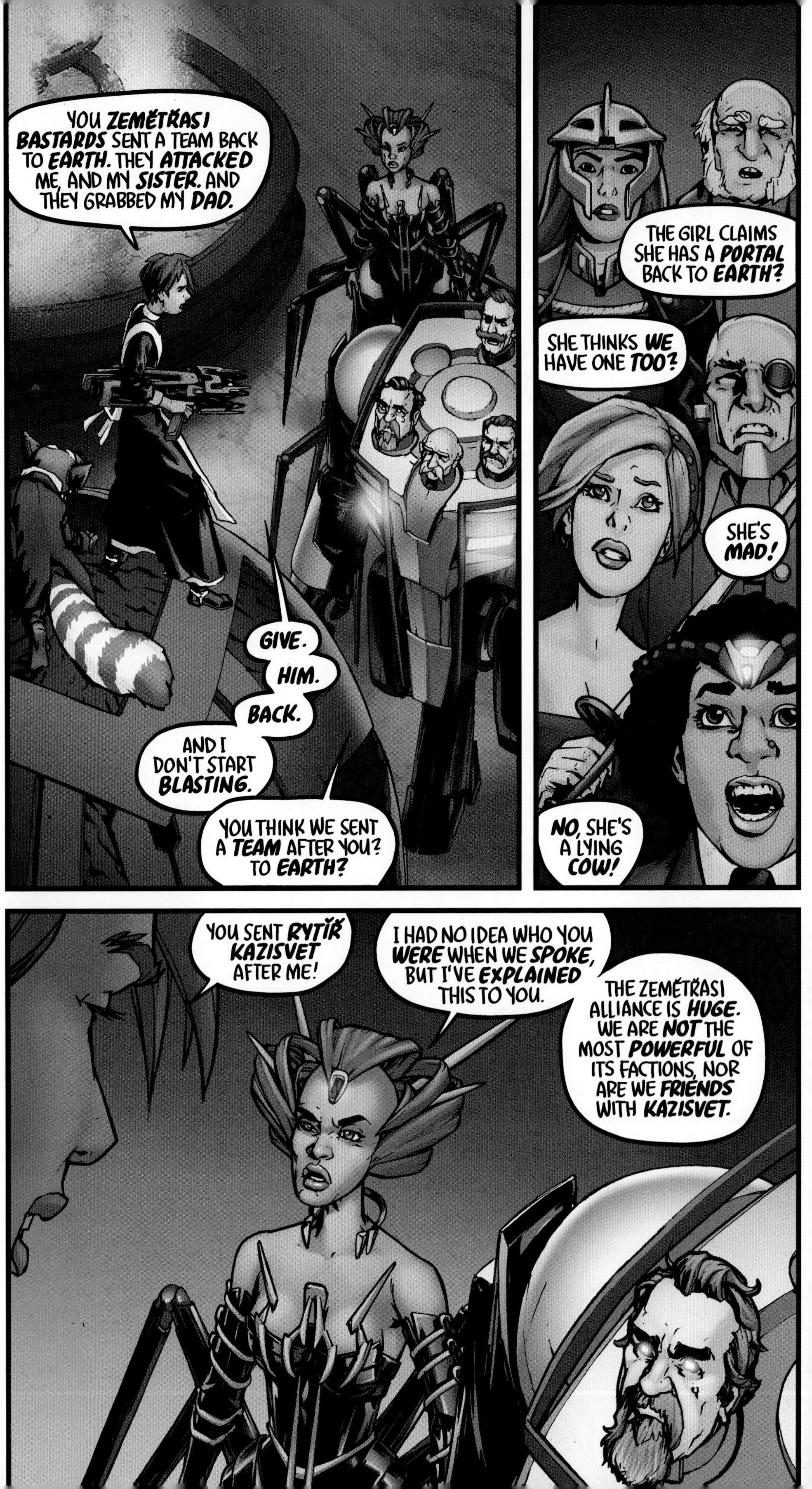
YOU ZEMĚTŘASI BASTARDS SENT A TEAM BACK TO EARTH. THEY ATTACKED ME, AND MY SISTER. AND THEY GRABBED MY DAD.
GIVE.
HIM.
BACK.
AND I DON'T START BLASTING.
YOU THINK WE SENT A TEAM AFTER YOU? TO EARTH?
THE GIRL CLAIMS SHE HAS A PORTAL BACK TO EARTH?
SHE THINKS WE HAVE ONE TOO?
SHE'S MAD!
NO, SHE'S A LYING COW!
YOU SENT RYTÍŘ KAZISVET AFTER ME!
I HAD NO IDEA WHO YOU WERE WHEN WE SPOKE, BUT I'VE EXPLAINED THIS TO YOU.
THE ZEMĚTŘASI ALLIANCE IS HUGE. WE ARE NOT THE MOST POWERFUL OF ITS FACTIONS, NOR ARE WE FRIENDS WITH KAZISVET.

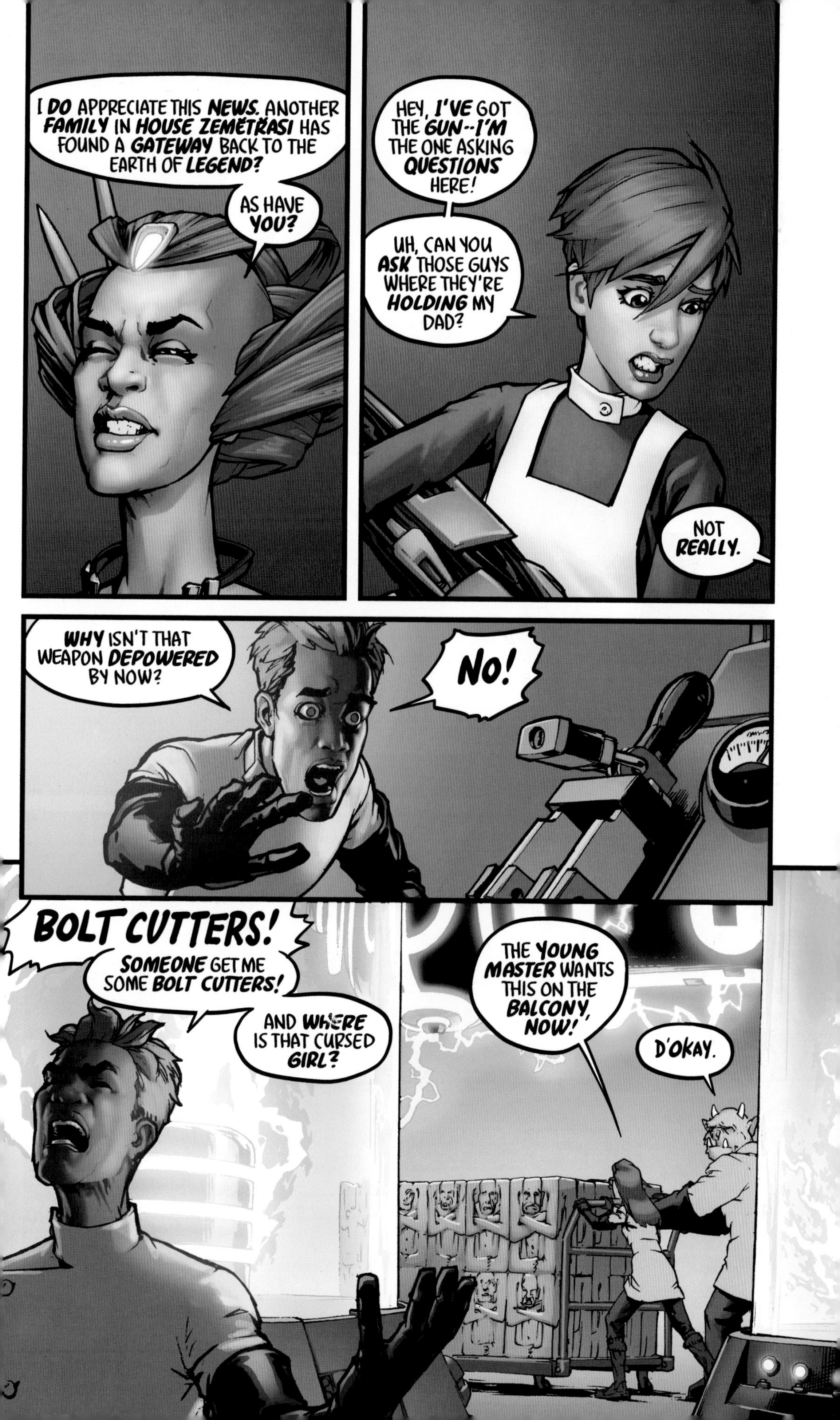
I DO APPRECIATE THIS NEWS. ANOTHER FAMILY IN HOUSE ZEMĔTRASI HAS FOUND A GATEWAY BACK TO THE EARTH OF LEGEND?
AS HAVE YOU?
HEY, I'VE GOT THE GUN--I'M THE ONE ASKING QUESTIONS HERE!
UH, CAN YOU ASK THOSE GUYS WHERE THEY'RE HOLDING MY DAD?
NOT REALLY.
WHY ISN'T THAT WEAPON DEPOWERED BY NOW?
NO!
BOLT CUTTERS!
SOMEONE GET ME SOME BOLT CUTTERS!
AND WHERE IS THAT CURSED GIRL?
THE YOUNG MASTER WANTS THIS ON THE BALCONY, NOW!
D'OKAY.

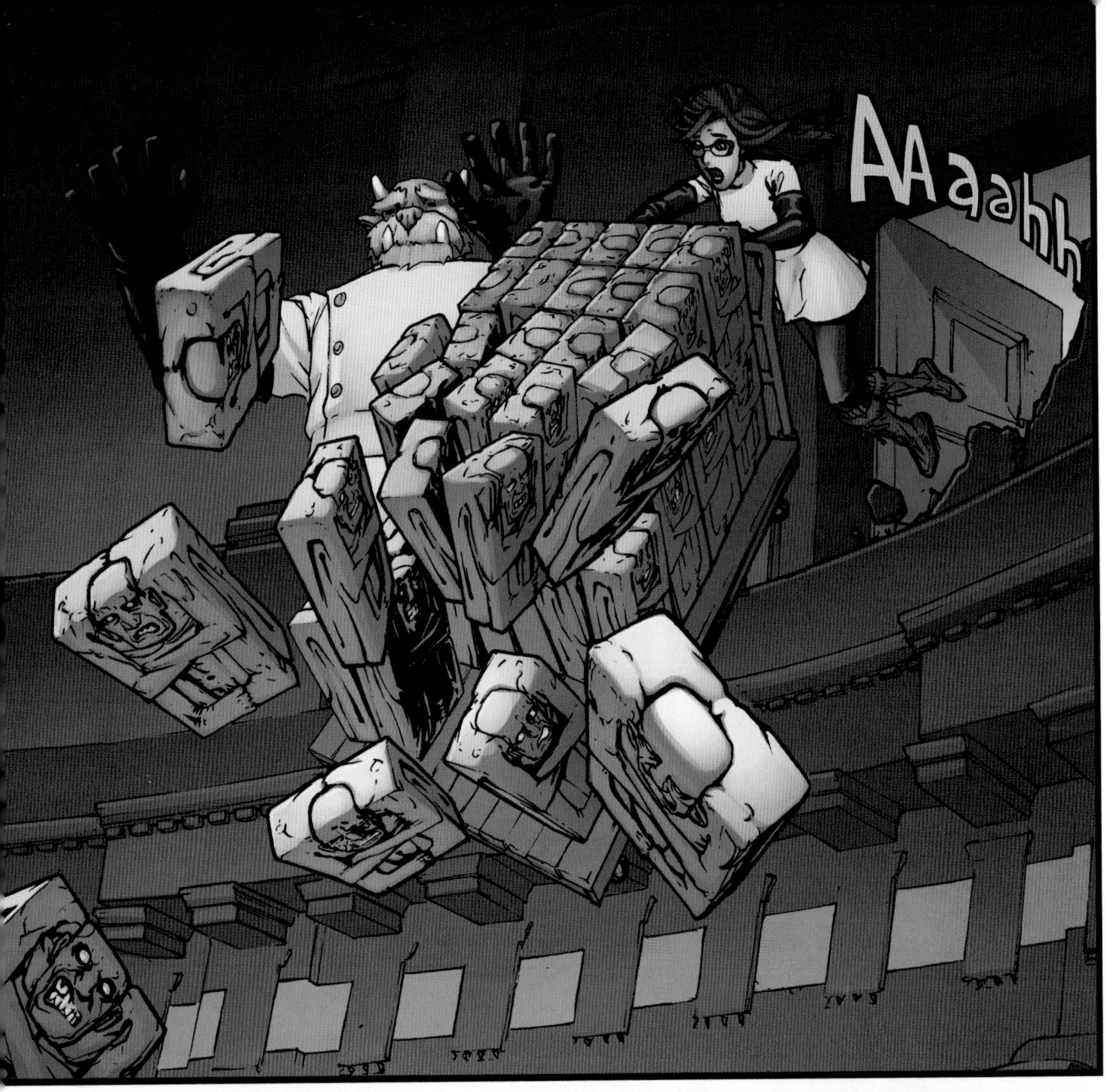
AAaahh

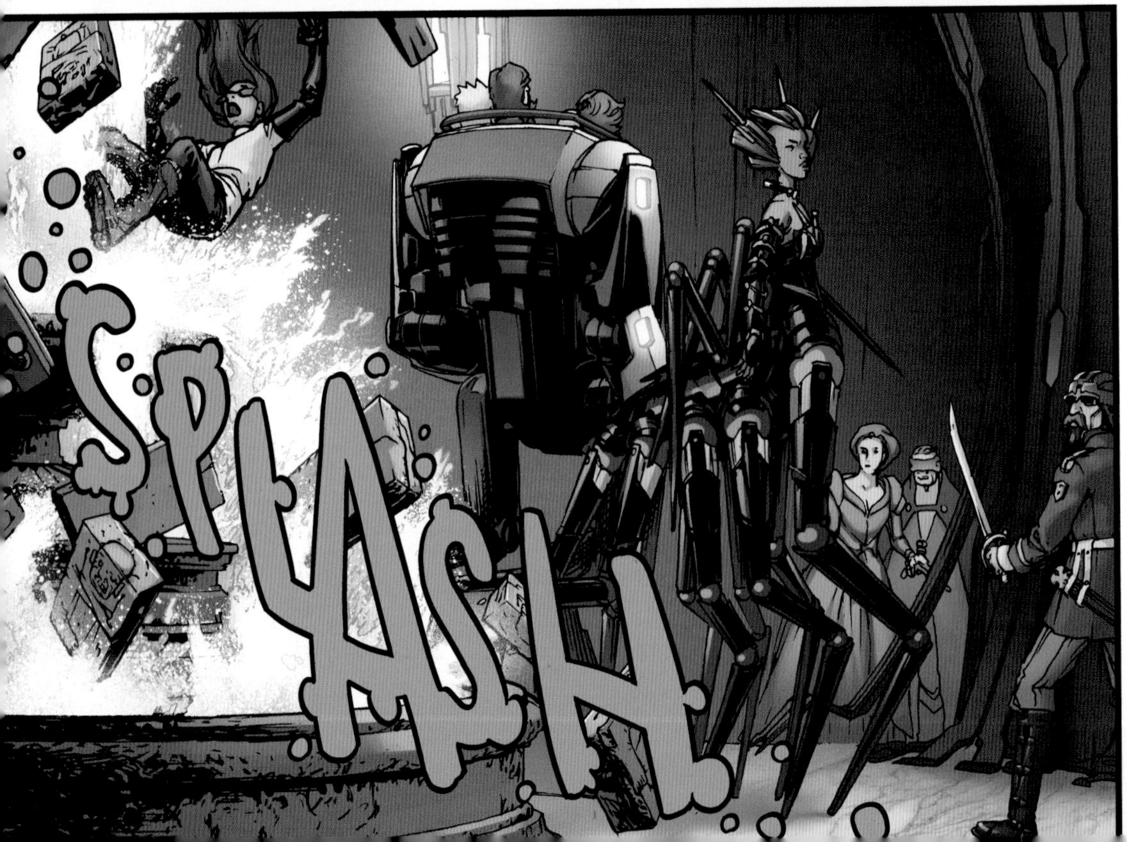
SPLASH!!

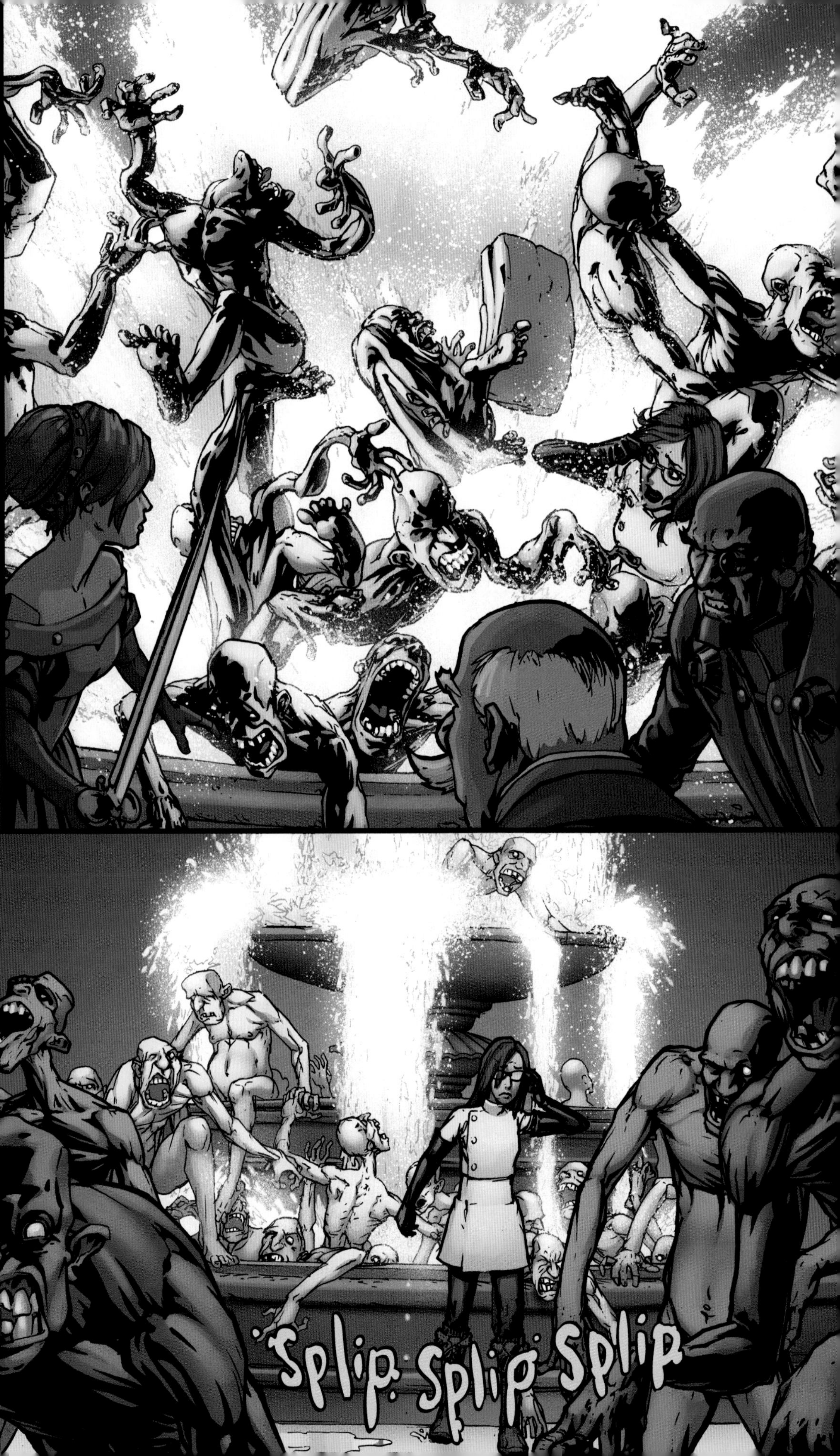
Splip Splip Splip

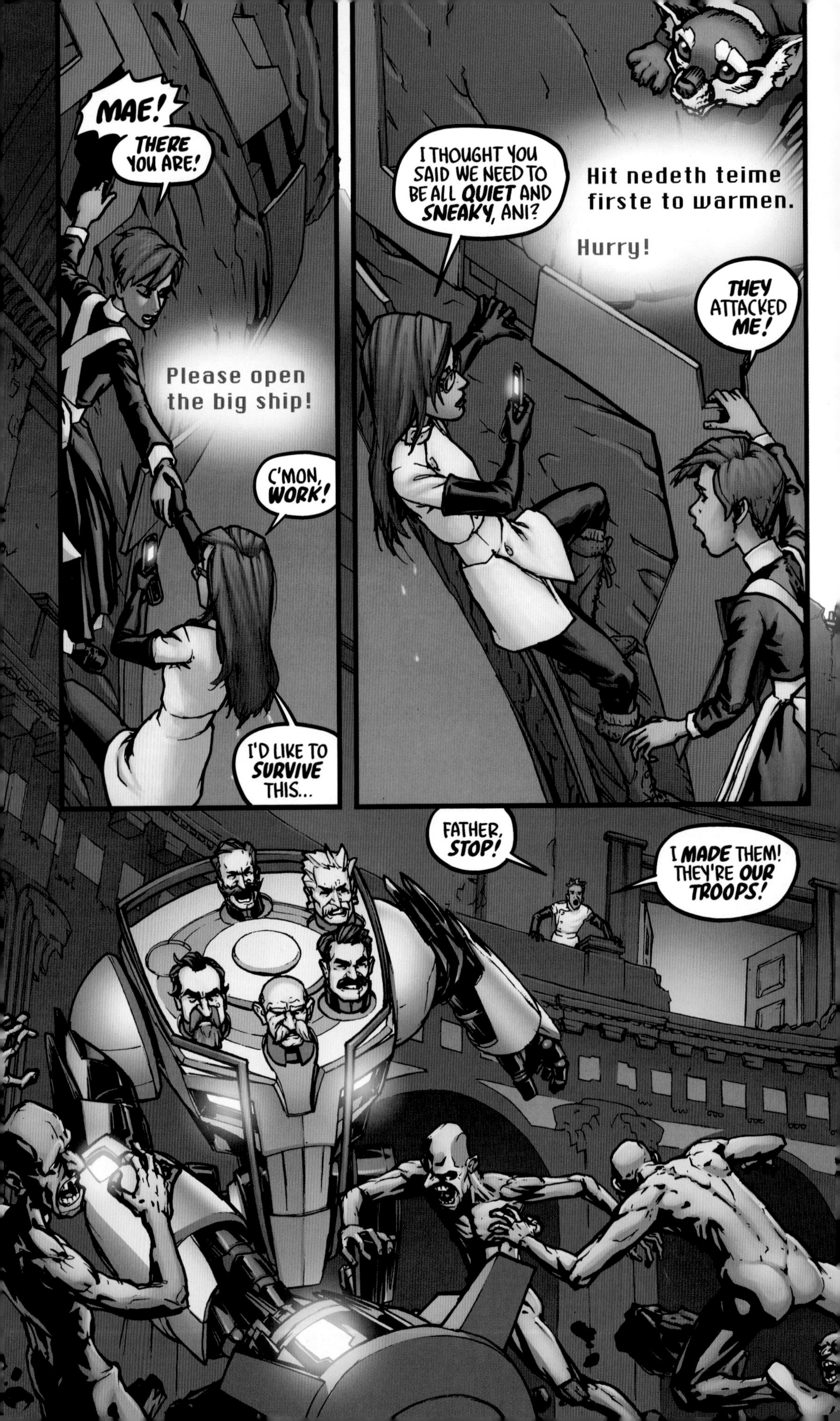
MAE!
THERE YOU ARE!
Please open the big ship!
C'MON, WORK!
I'D LIKE TO SURVIVE THIS...
I THOUGHT YOU SAID WE NEED TO BE ALL QUIET AND SNEAKY, ANI?
Hit nedeth teime firste to warmen.
Hurry!
THEY ATTACKED ME!
FATHER, STOP!
I MADE THEM! THEY'RE OUR TROOPS!

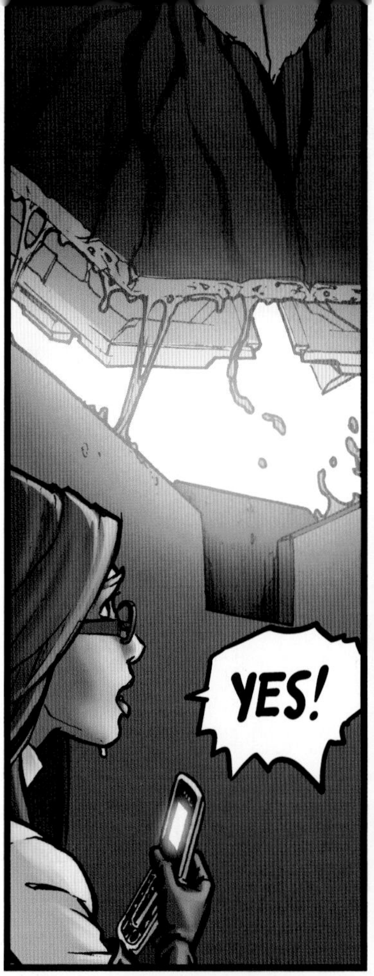
YES!

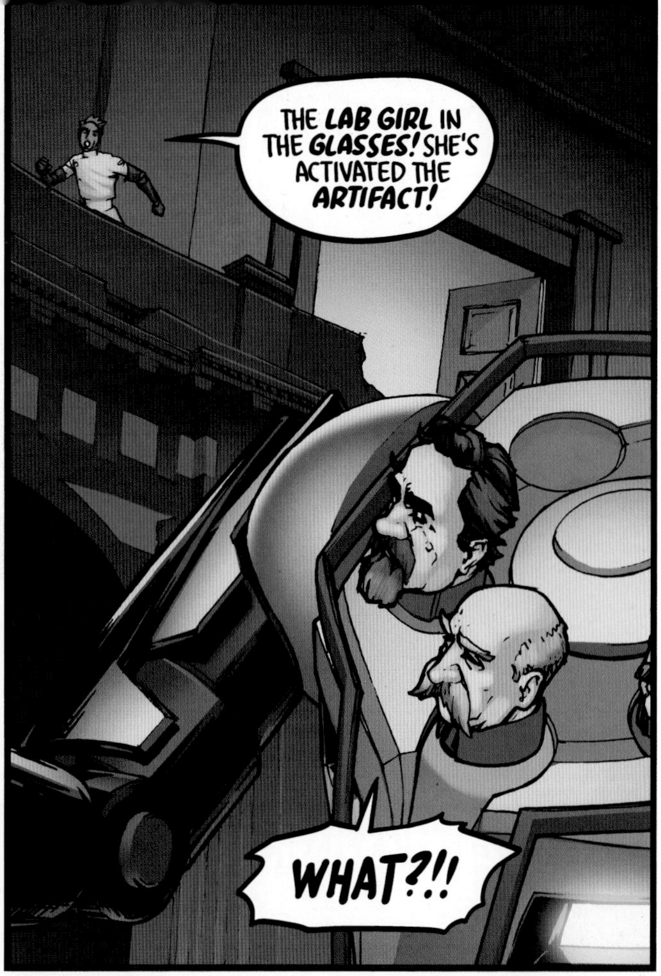
THE LAB GIRL IN THE GLASSES! SHE'S ACTIVATED THE ARTIFACT!
WHAT?!!

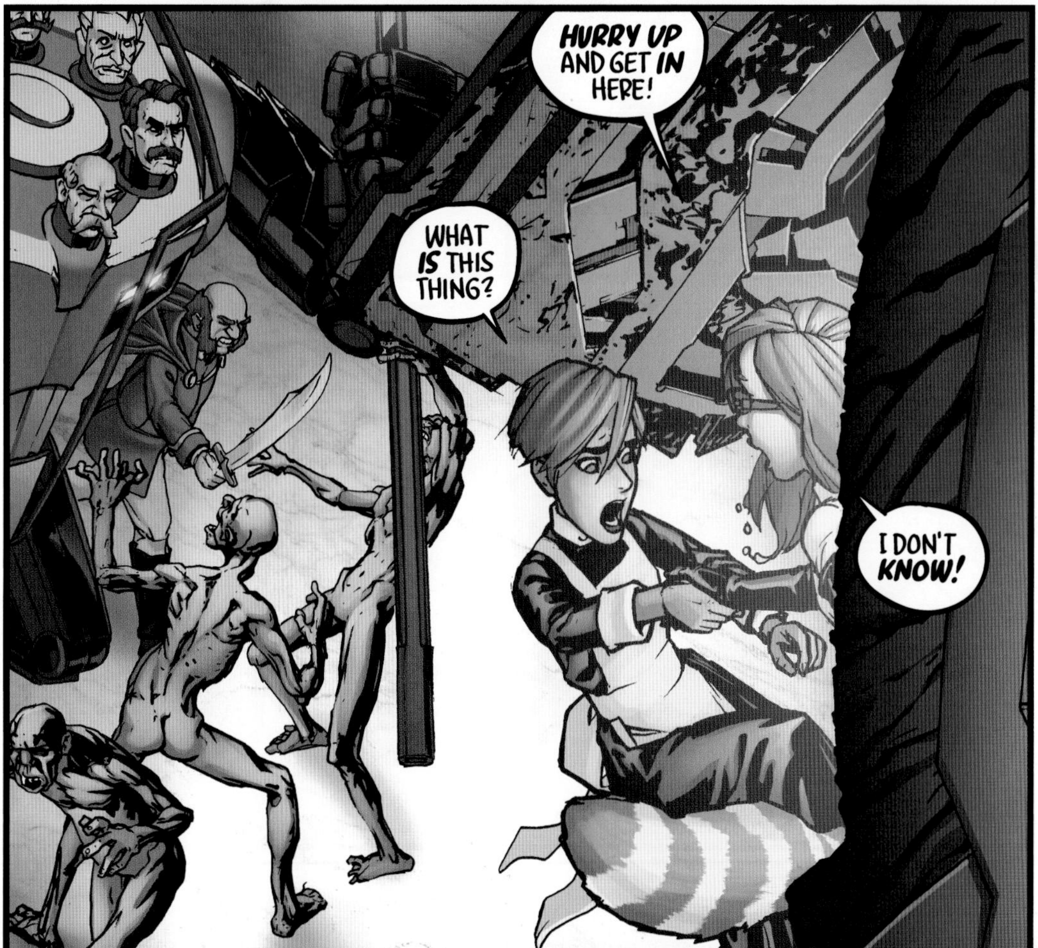
HURRY UP AND GET IN HERE!
WHAT IS THIS THING?
I DON'T KNOW!

SHUMPF!!
NO!
HOW ARE WE GETTING OUT OF THIS?
KTHOOM
Let's roll!
To turnen?
aAAaaAAAA
VWHIZZZHHHH
GREAT, I'M GONNA DIE IN A COUNTY FAIR VOMIT COMET!

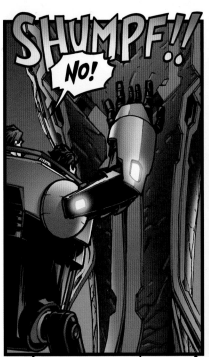

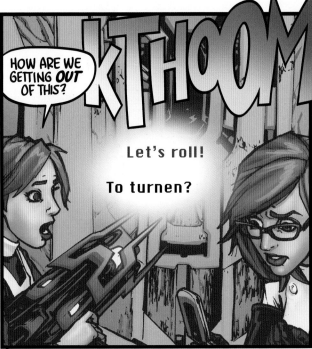

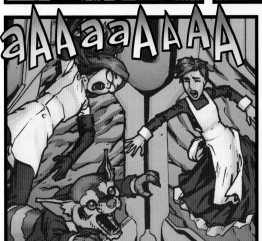

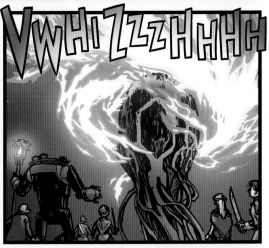

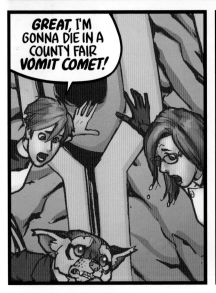

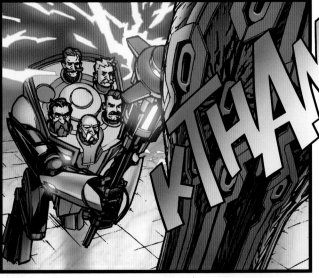

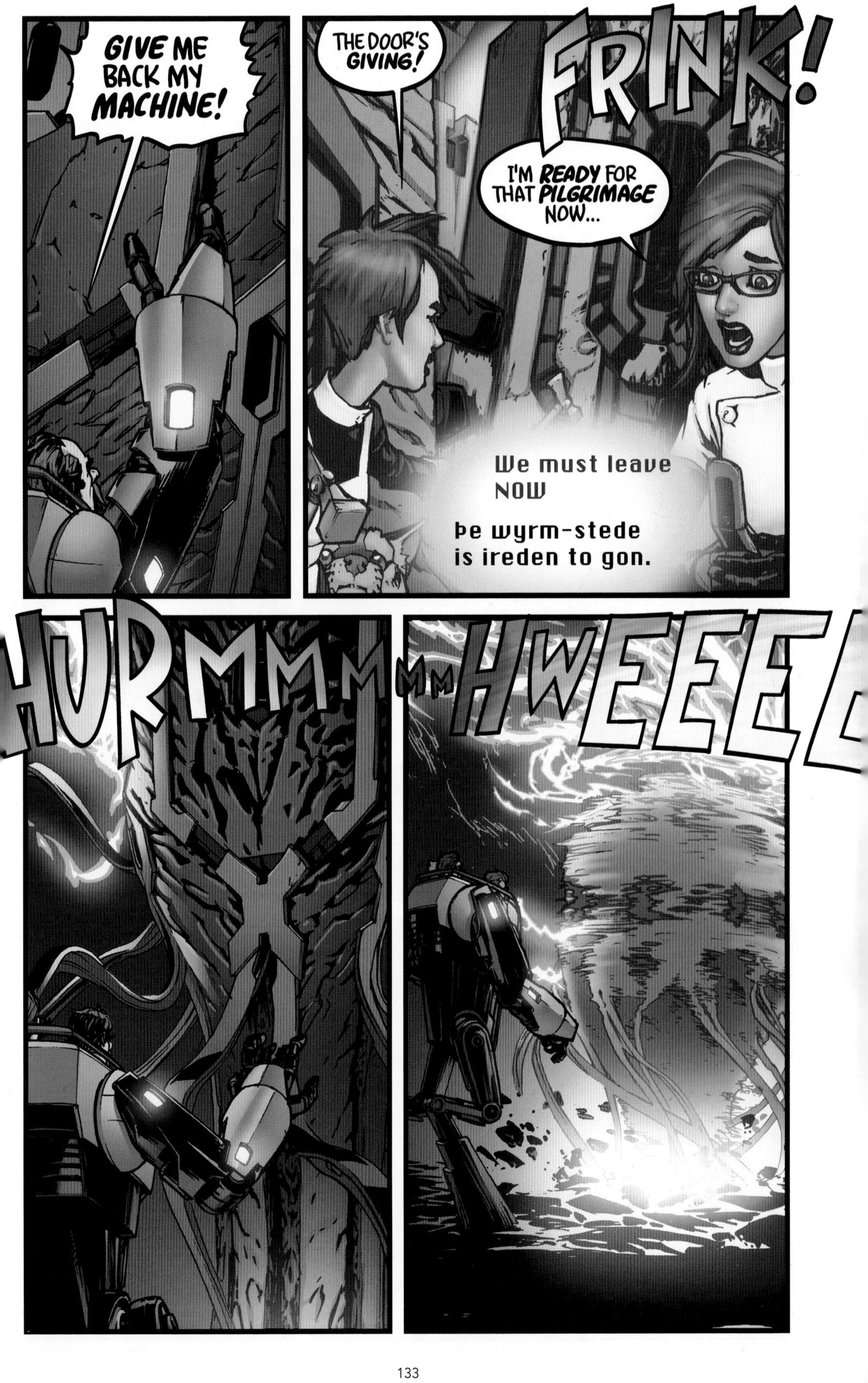
GIVE ME BACK MY MACHINE!
THE DOOR'S GIVING!
FRINK!
I'M READY FOR THAT PILGRIMAGE NOW...
We must leave NOW
þe wyrm-stede is ireden to gon.
HURMMMMMM
HWEEEE

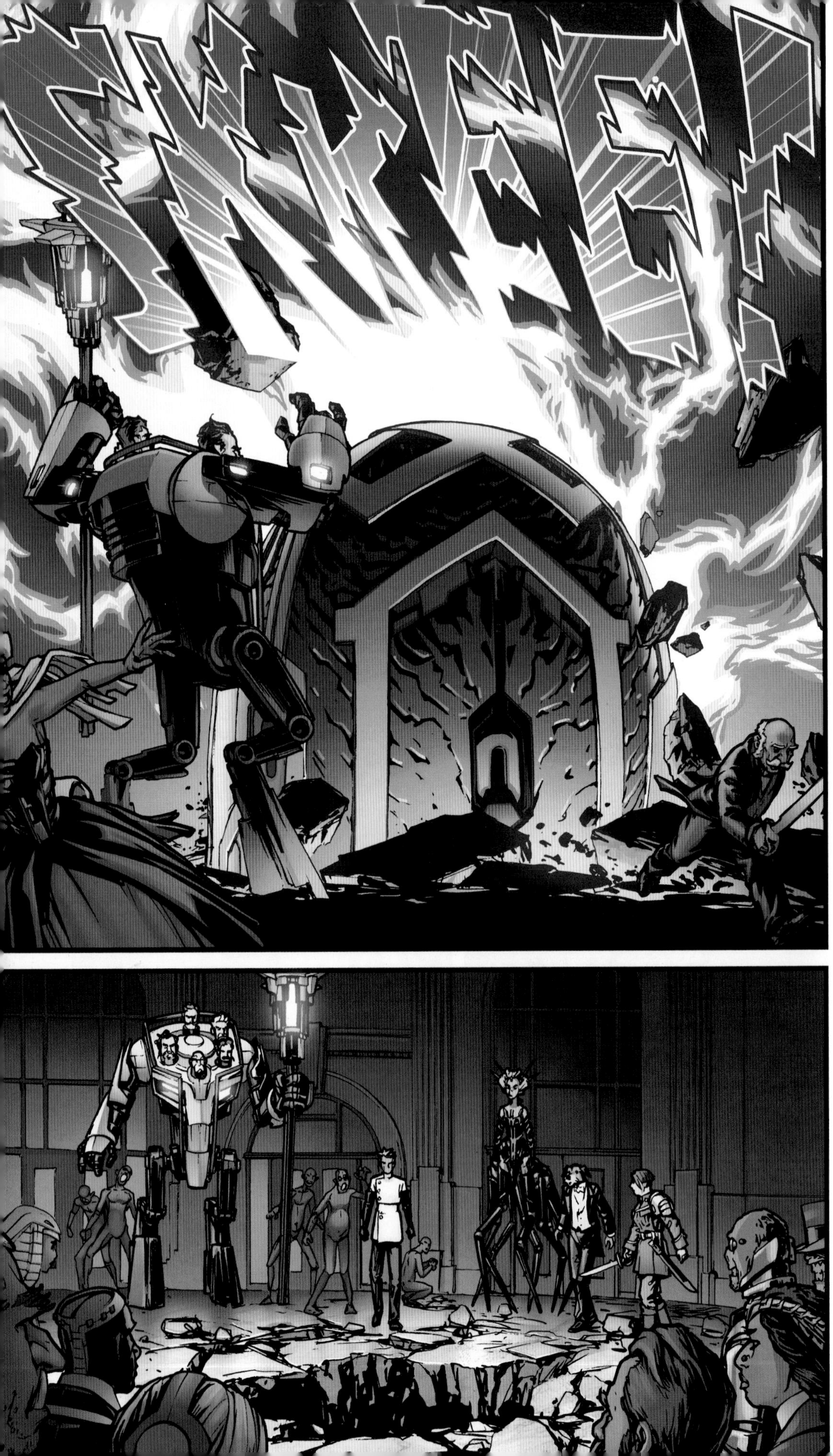

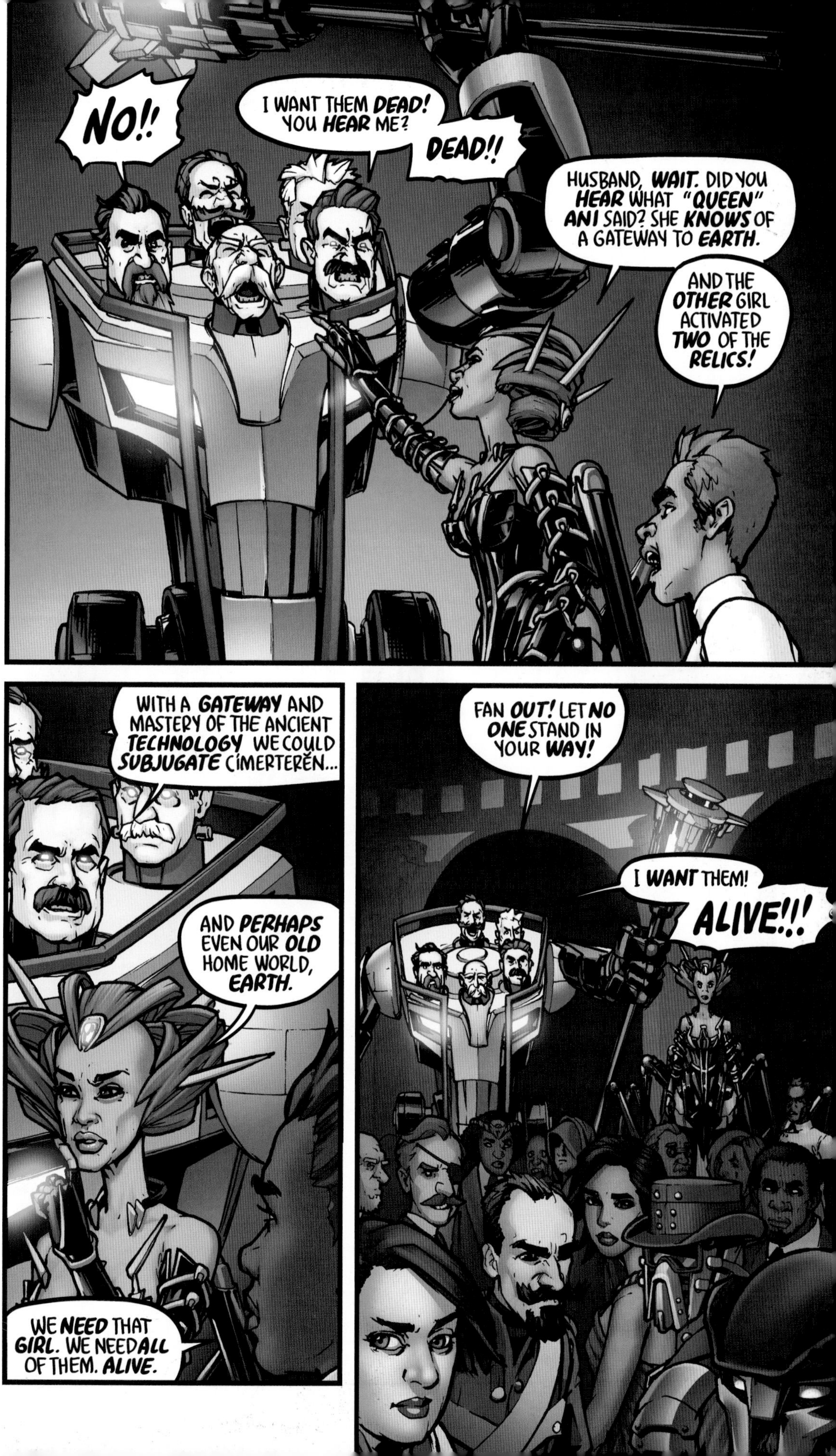
NO!!
I WANT THEM DEAD! YOU HEAR ME?
DEAD!!
HUSBAND, WAIT. DID YOU HEAR WHAT "QUEEN" ANI SAID? SHE KNOWS OF A GATEWAY TO EARTH.
AND THE OTHER GIRL ACTIVATED TWO OF THE RELICS!
WITH A GATEWAY AND MASTERY OF THE ANCIENT TECHNOLOGY WE COULD SUBJUGATE CÍMERTERĚN...
AND PERHAPS EVEN OUR OLD HOME WORLD, EARTH.
WE NEED THAT GIRL. WE NEED ALL OF THEM. ALIVE.
FAN OUT! LET NO ONE STAND IN YOUR WAY!
I WANT THEM!
ALIVE!!!

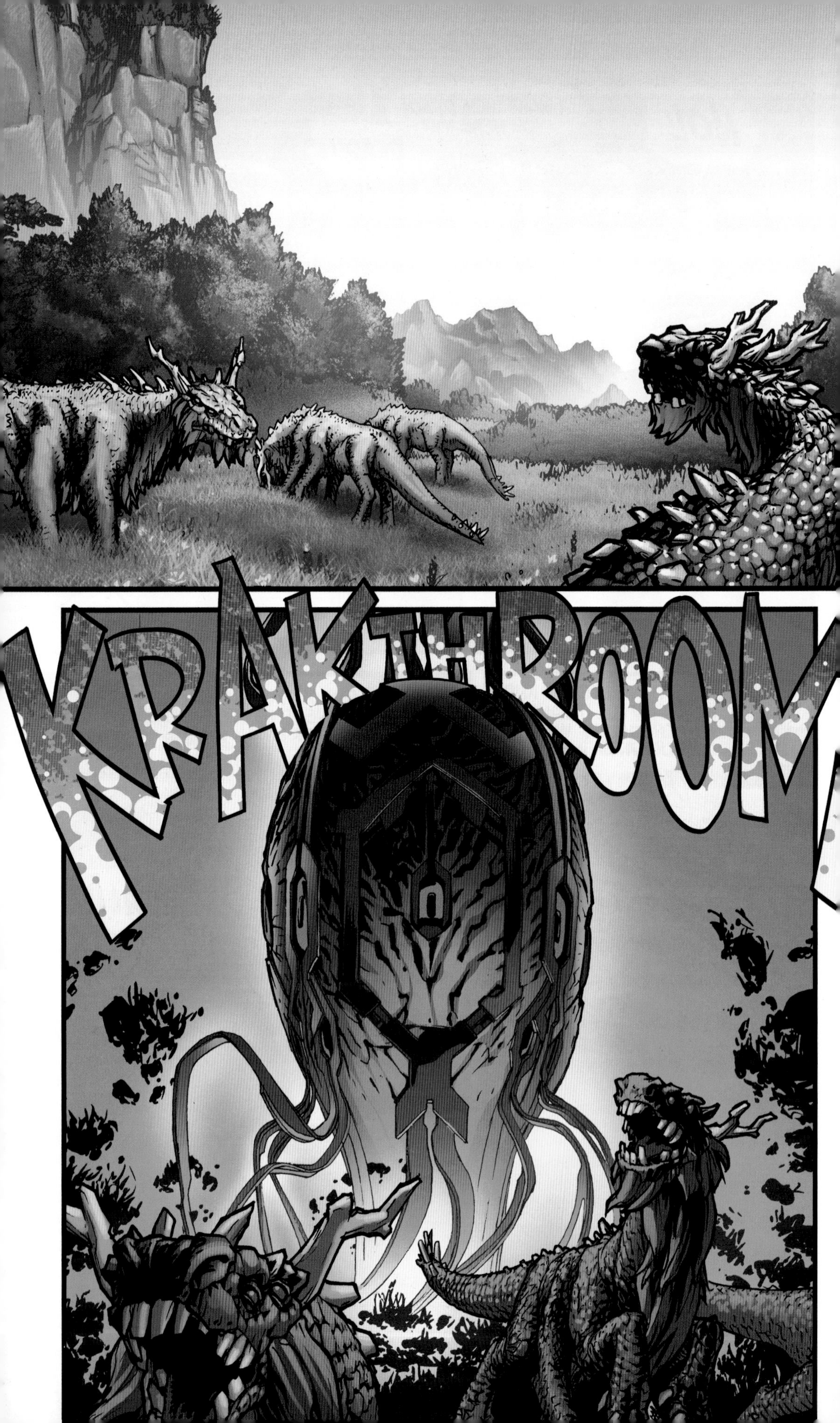
KRAKTHROOM

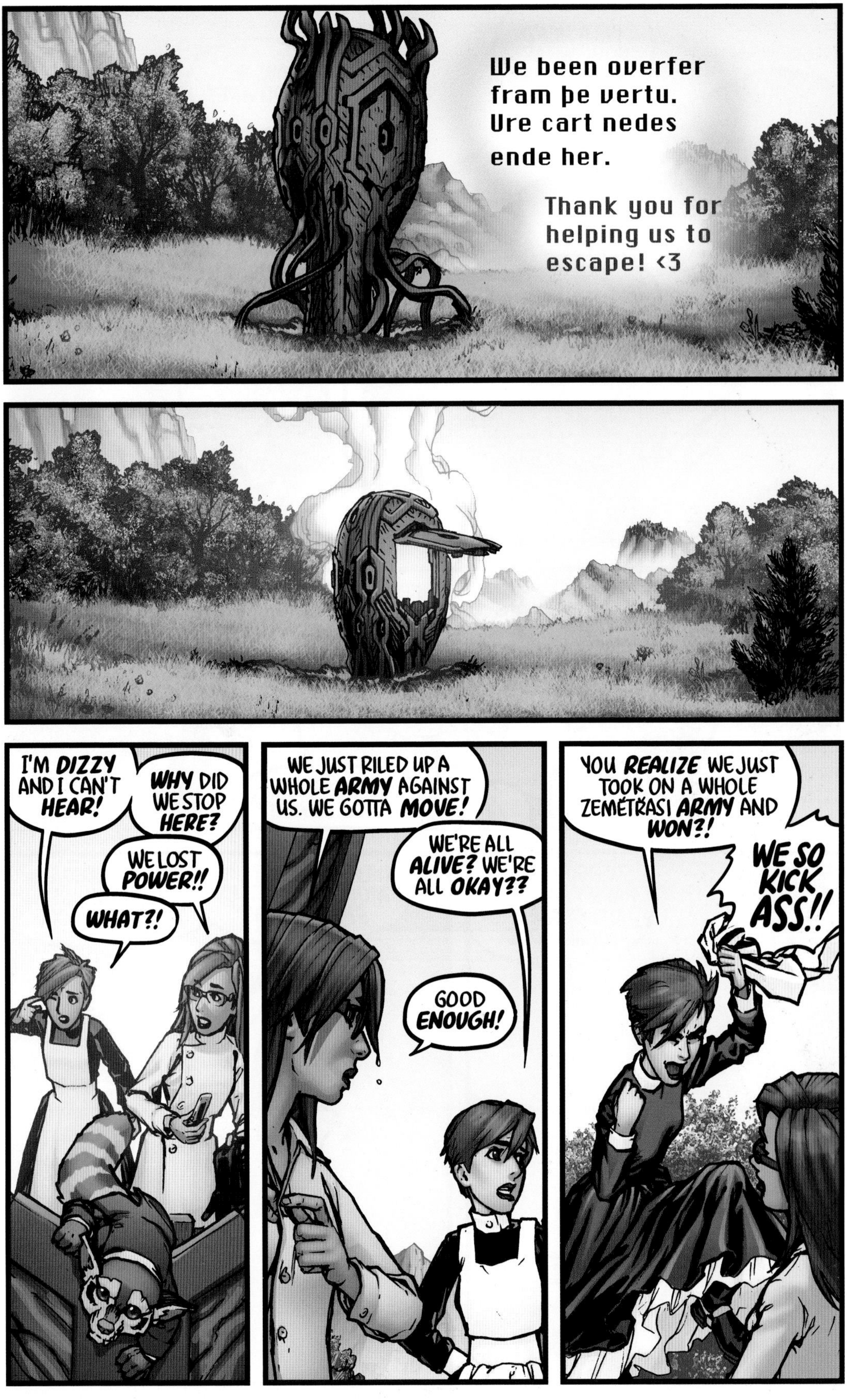
We been overfer fram þe vertu. Ure cart nedes ende her.
Thank you for helping us to escape! <3
I'M DIZZY AND I CAN'T HEAR!
WHY DID WE STOP HERE?
WE LOST POWER!!
WHAT?!
WE JUST RILED UP A WHOLE ARMY AGAINST US. WE GOTTA MOVE!
WE'RE ALL ALIVE? WE'RE ALL OKAY??
GOOD ENOUGH!
YOU REALIZE WE JUST TOOK ON A WHOLE ZEMĚTŘASI ARMY AND WON?!
WE SO KICK ASS!!

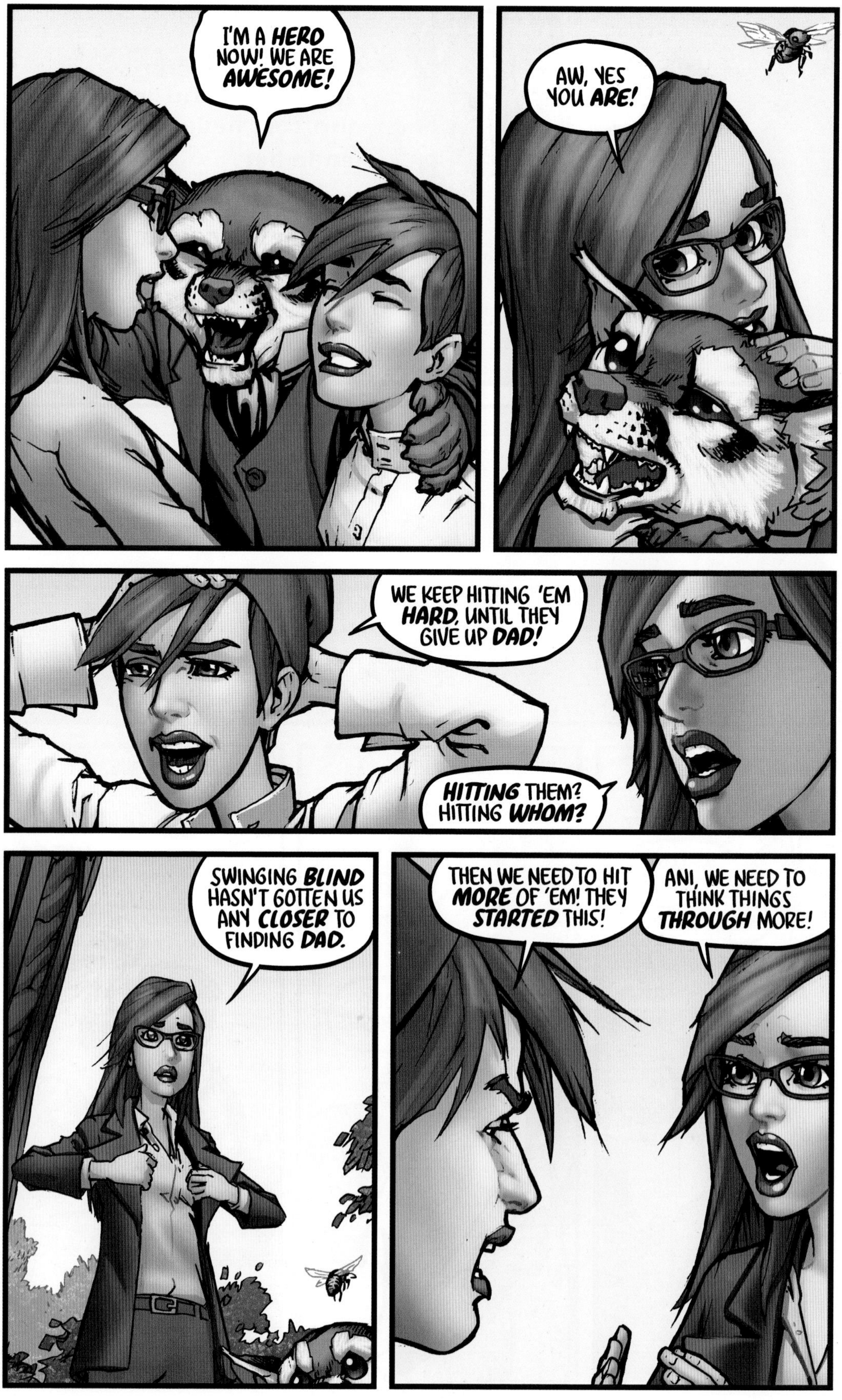

I'M A HERO NOW! WE ARE AWESOME!
AW, YES YOU ARE!
WE KEEP HITTING 'EM HARD, UNTIL THEY GIVE UP DAD!
HITTING THEM? HITTING WHOM?
SWINGING BLIND HASN'T GOTTEN US ANY CLOSER TO FINDING DAD.
THEN WE NEED TO HIT MORE OF 'EM! THEY STARTED THIS!
ANI, WE NEED TO THINK THINGS THROUGH MORE!

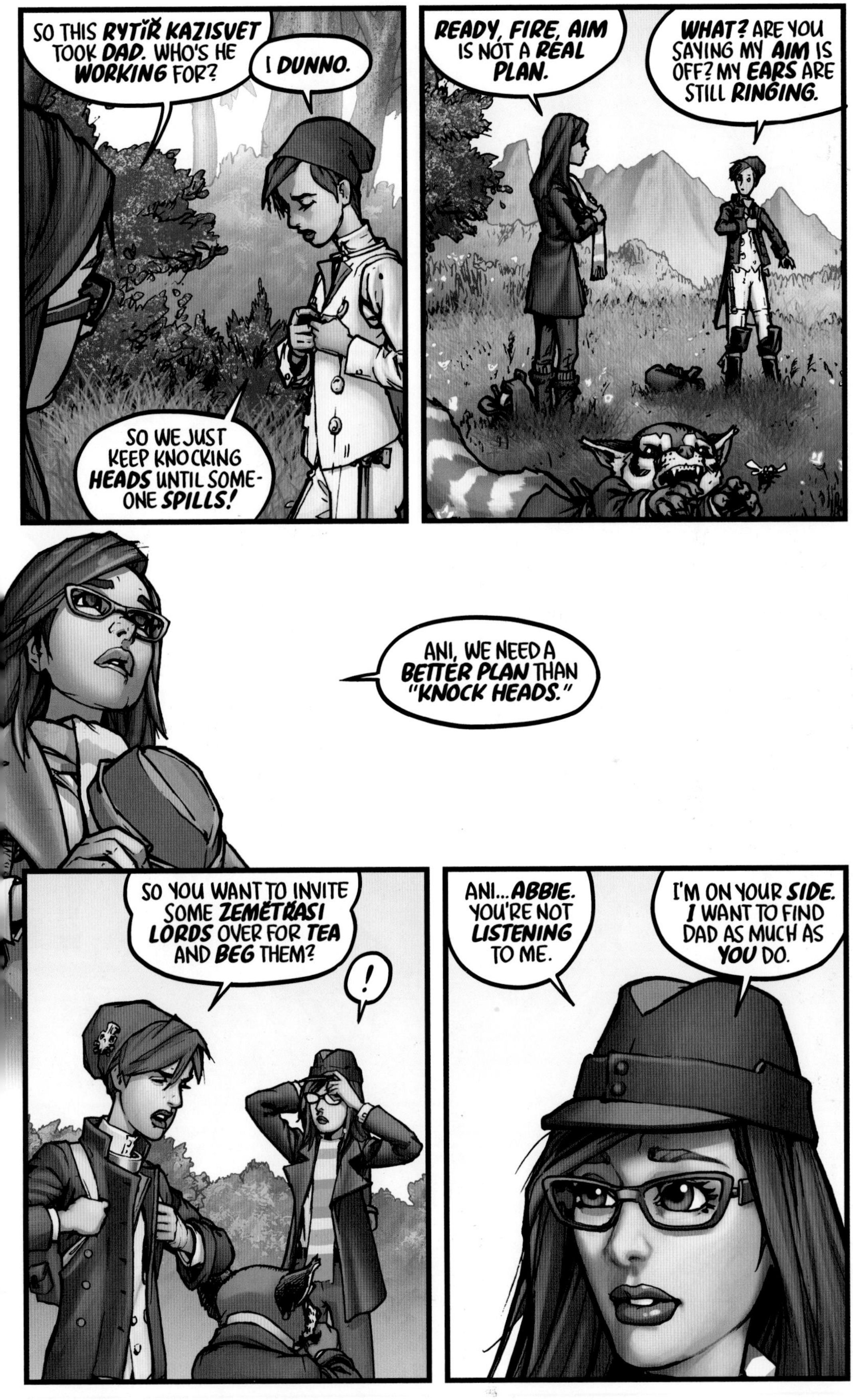
SO THIS RYTÍŘ KAZISVET TOOK DAD. WHO'S HE WORKING FOR?
I DUNNO.
SO WE JUST KEEP KNOCKING HEADS UNTIL SOME-ONE SPILLS!
READY, FIRE, AIM IS NOT A REAL PLAN.
WHAT? ARE YOU SAYING MY AIM IS OFF? MY EARS ARE STILL RINGING.
ANI, WE NEED A BETTER PLAN THAN "KNOCK HEADS."
SO YOU WANT TO INVITE SOME ZEMĚTŘASI LORDS OVER FOR TEA AND BEG THEM?
!
ANI... ABBIE. YOU'RE NOT LISTENING TO ME.
I'M ON YOUR SIDE. I WANT TO FIND DAD AS MUCH AS YOU DO.

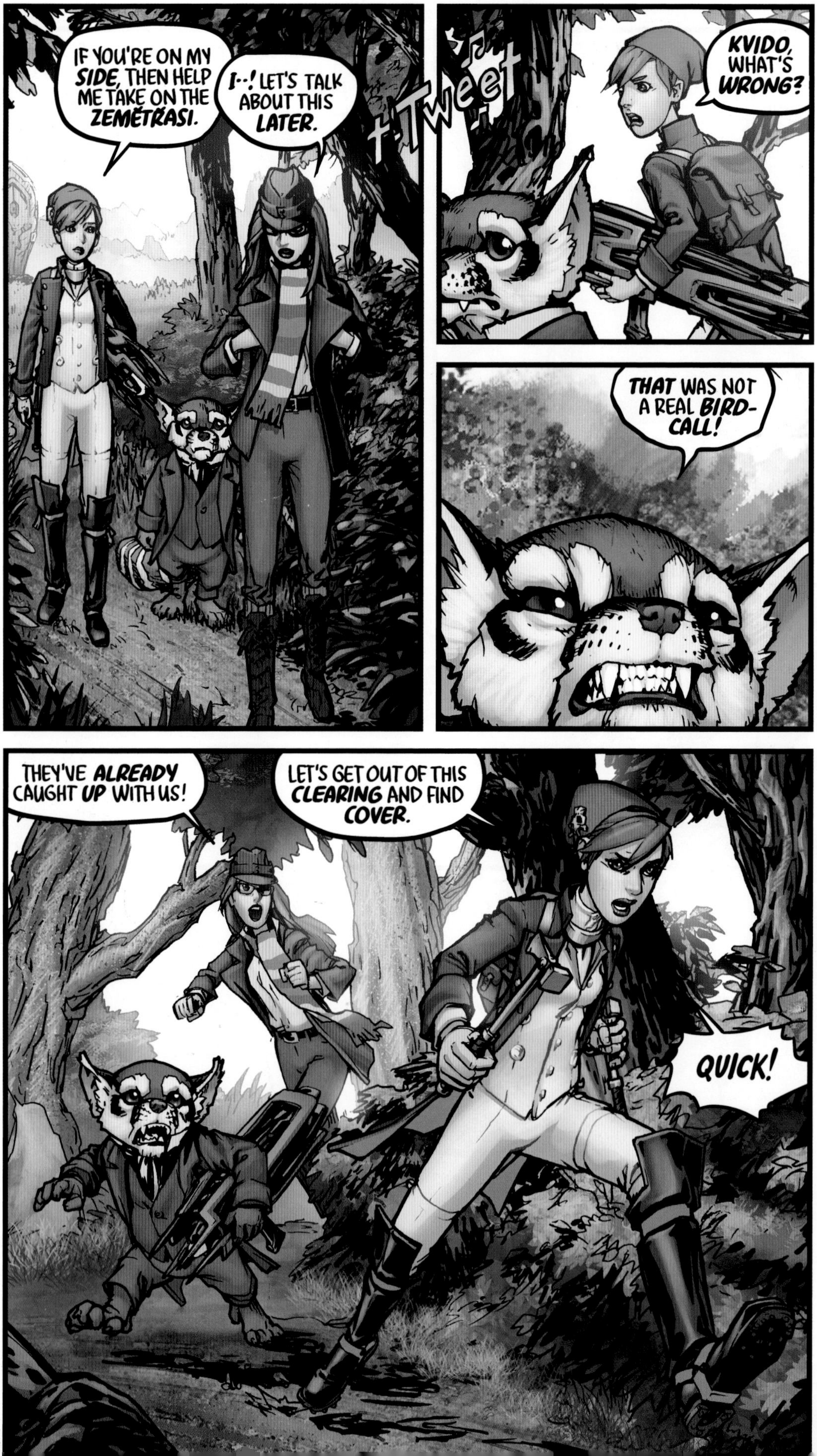
IF YOU'RE ON MY SIDE, THEN HELP ME TAKE ON THE ZEMĚTŘASI.
I--! LET'S TALK ABOUT THIS LATER.
TWEET
KVIDO, WHAT'S WRONG?
THAT WAS NOT A REAL BIRD-CALL!
THEY'VE ALREADY CAUGHT UP WITH US!
LET'S GET OUT OF THIS CLEARING AND FIND COVER.
QUICK!

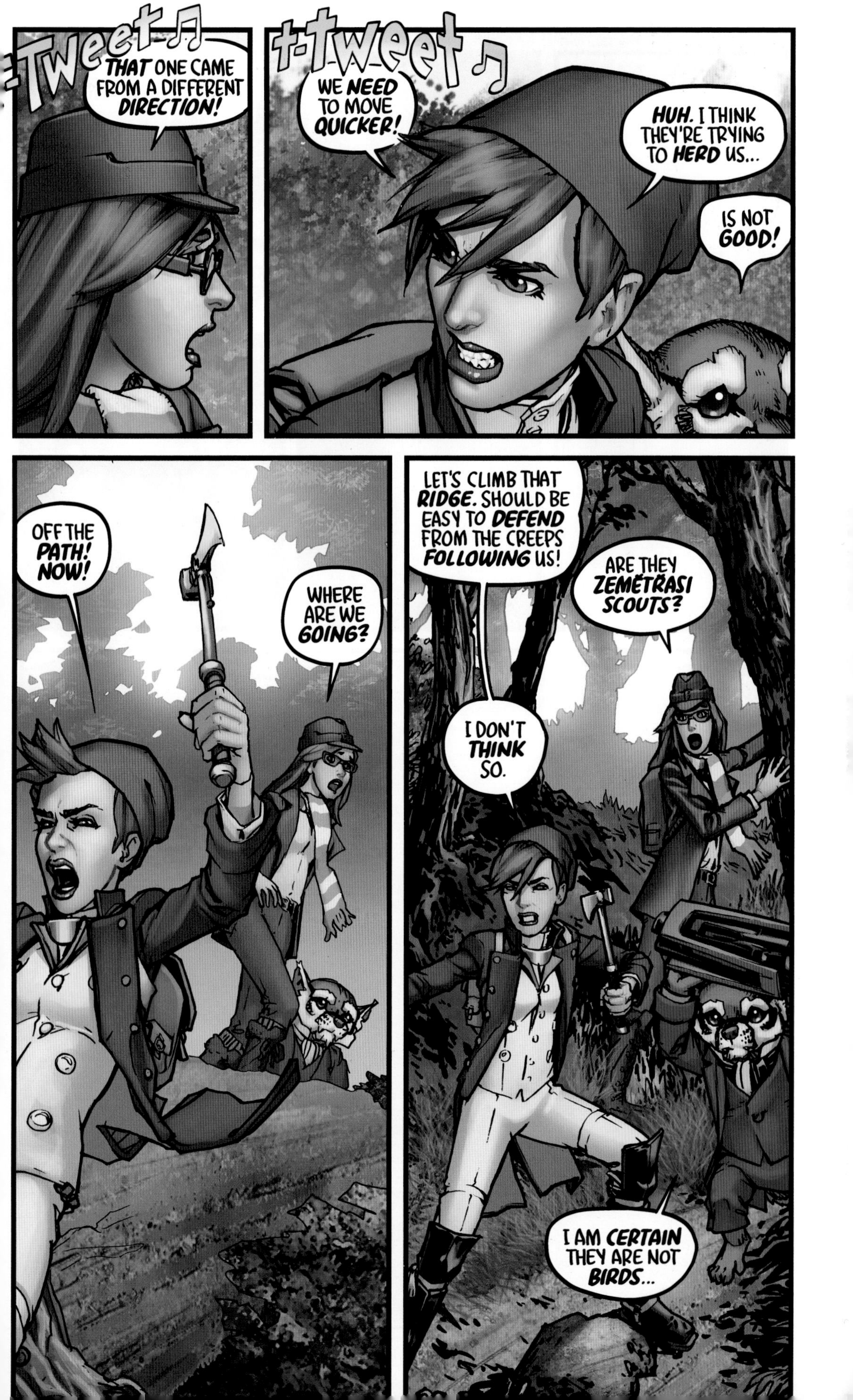
TWEET ♫
THAT ONE CAME FROM A DIFFERENT DIRECTION!
T-TWEET ♫
WE NEED TO MOVE QUICKER!
HUH. I THINK THEY'RE TRYING TO HERD US...
IS NOT GOOD!
OFF THE PATH! NOW!
WHERE ARE WE GOING?
LET'S CLIMB THAT RIDGE. SHOULD BE EASY TO DEFEND FROM THE CREEPS FOLLOWING US!
ARE THEY ZEMĒTRASI SCOUTS?
I DON'T THINK SO.
I AM CERTAIN THEY ARE NOT BIRDS...

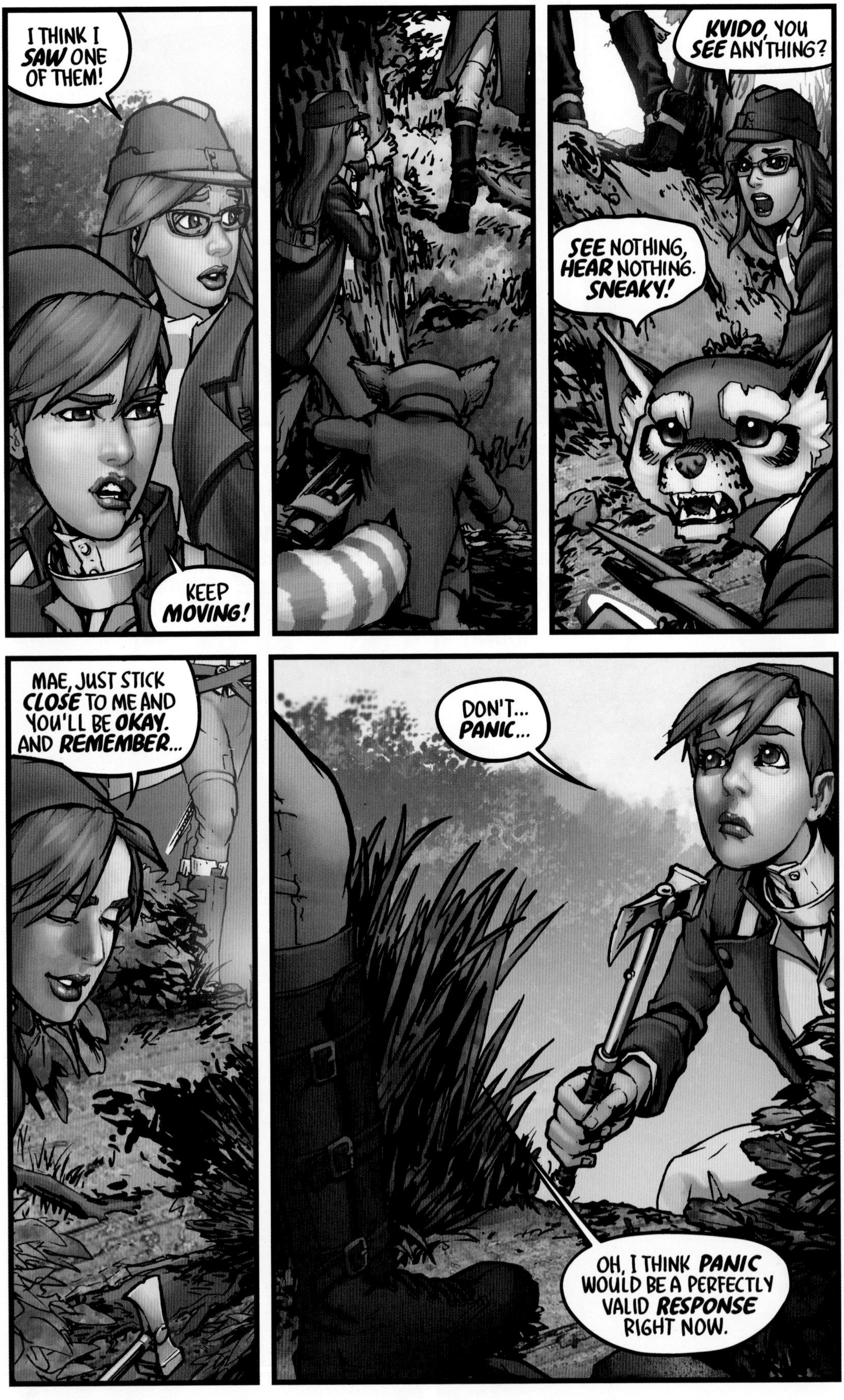

I THINK I SAW ONE OF THEM!
KEEP MOVING!
KVIDO, YOU SEE ANYTHING?
SEE NOTHING, HEAR NOTHING. SNEAKY!
MAE, JUST STICK CLOSE TO ME AND YOU'LL BE OKAY. AND REMEMBER...
DON'T... PANIC...
OH, I THINK PANIC WOULD BE A PERFECTLY VALID RESPONSE RIGHT NOW.

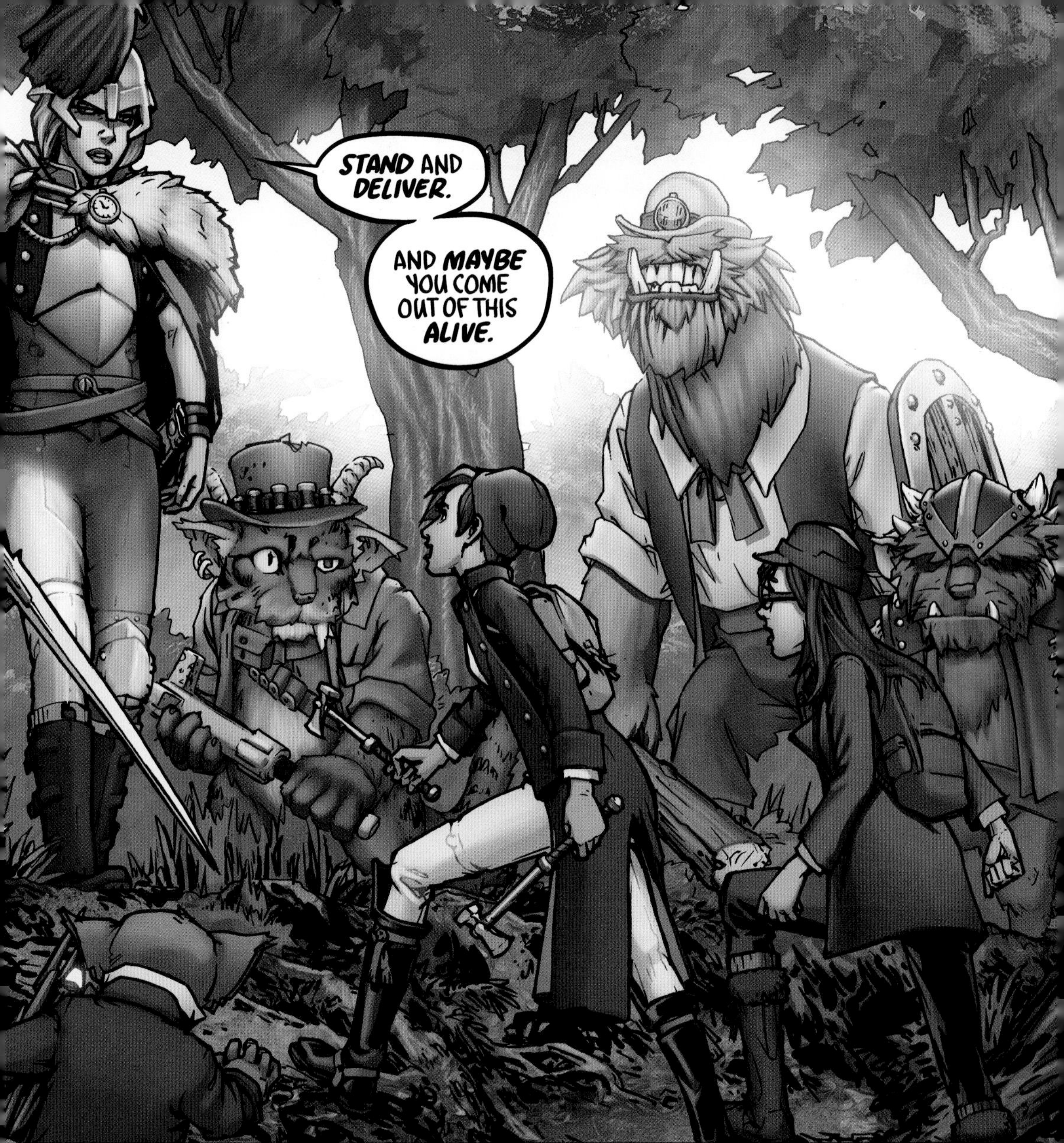
STAND AND **DELIVER.**
AND **MAYBE** YOU COME OUT OF THIS **ALIVE.**

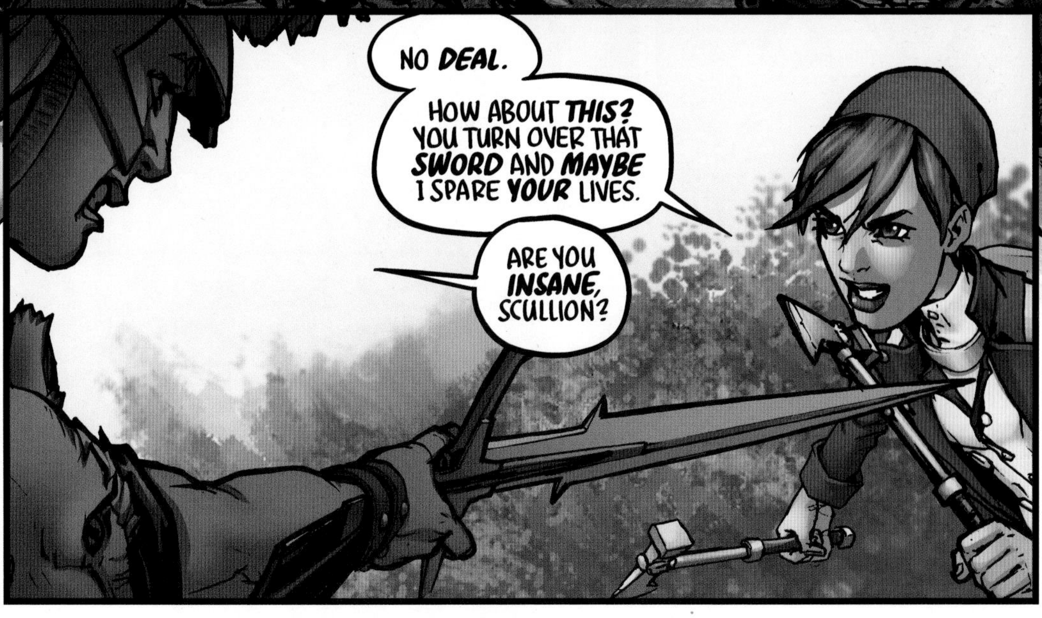
NO **DEAL.**
HOW ABOUT **THIS?** YOU TURN OVER THAT **SWORD** AND **MAYBE** I SPARE **YOUR** LIVES.
ARE YOU **INSANE,** SCULLION?

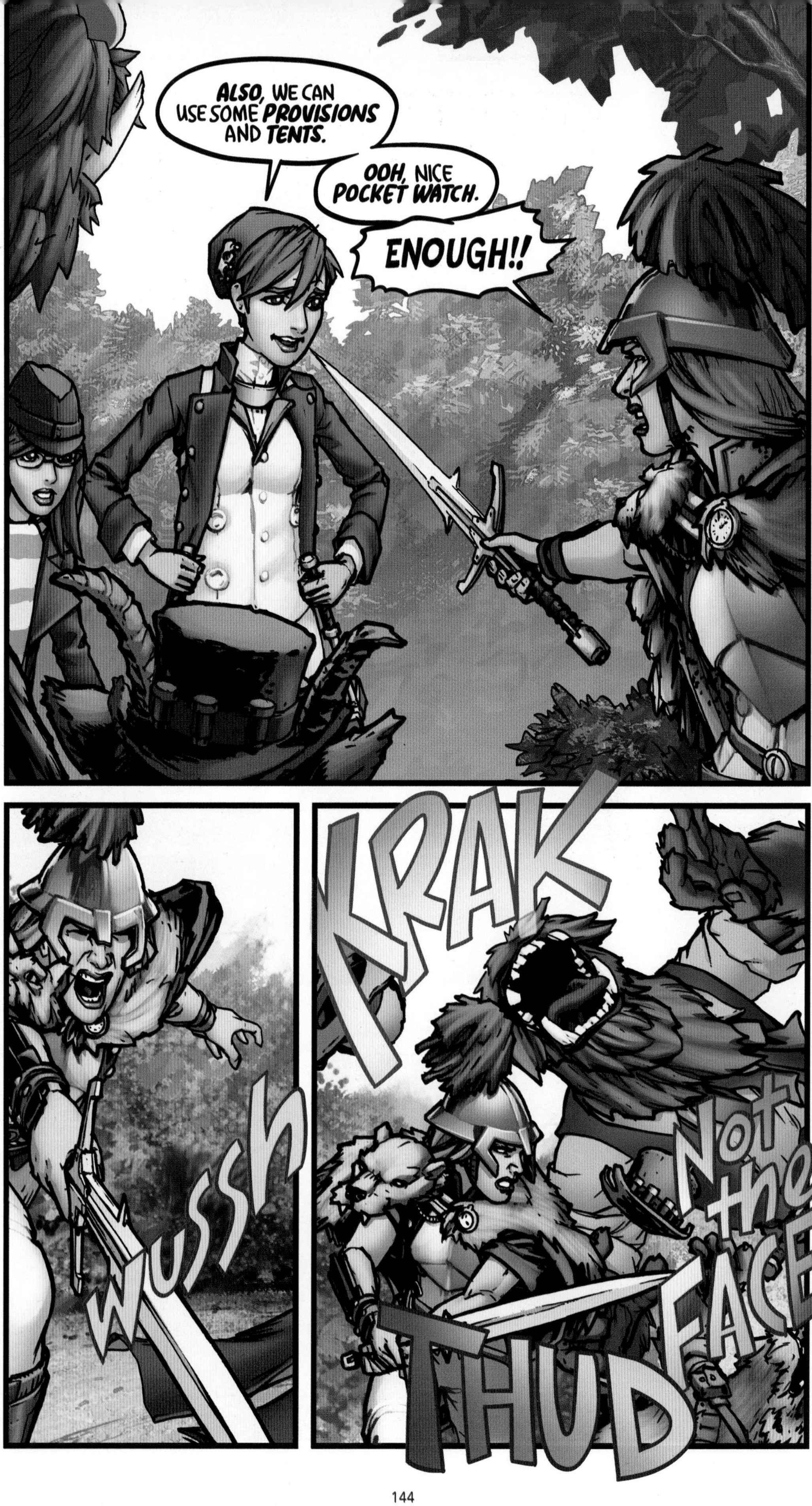
ALSO, WE CAN USE SOME PROVISIONS AND TENTS.
OOH, NICE POCKET WATCH.
ENOUGH!!
WUSSH
KRAK
Not the FACE
THUD

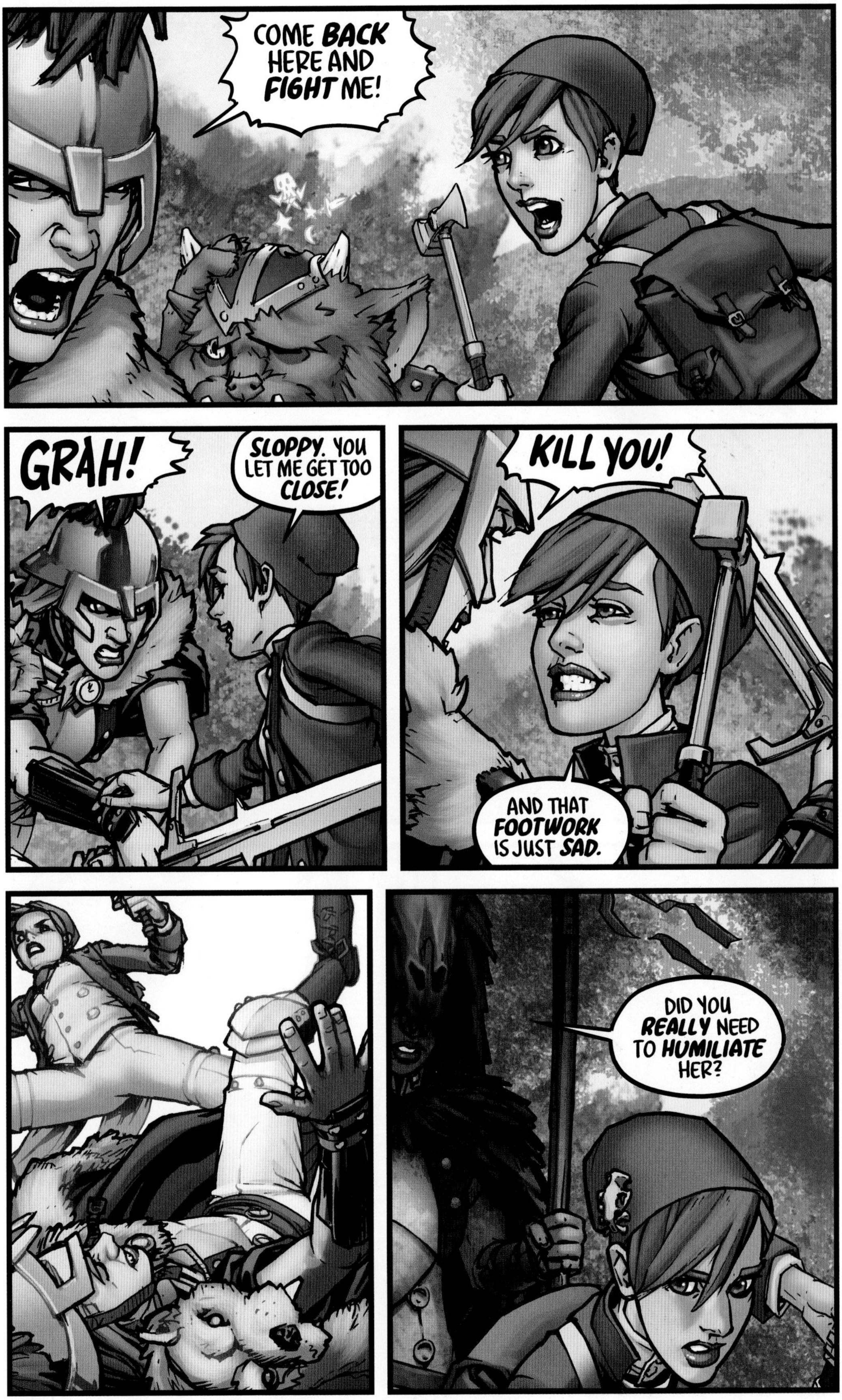
COME BACK HERE AND FIGHT ME!
GRAH!
SLOPPY. YOU LET ME GET TOO CLOSE!
KILL YOU!
AND THAT FOOTWORK IS JUST SAD.
DID YOU REALLY NEED TO HUMILIATE HER?

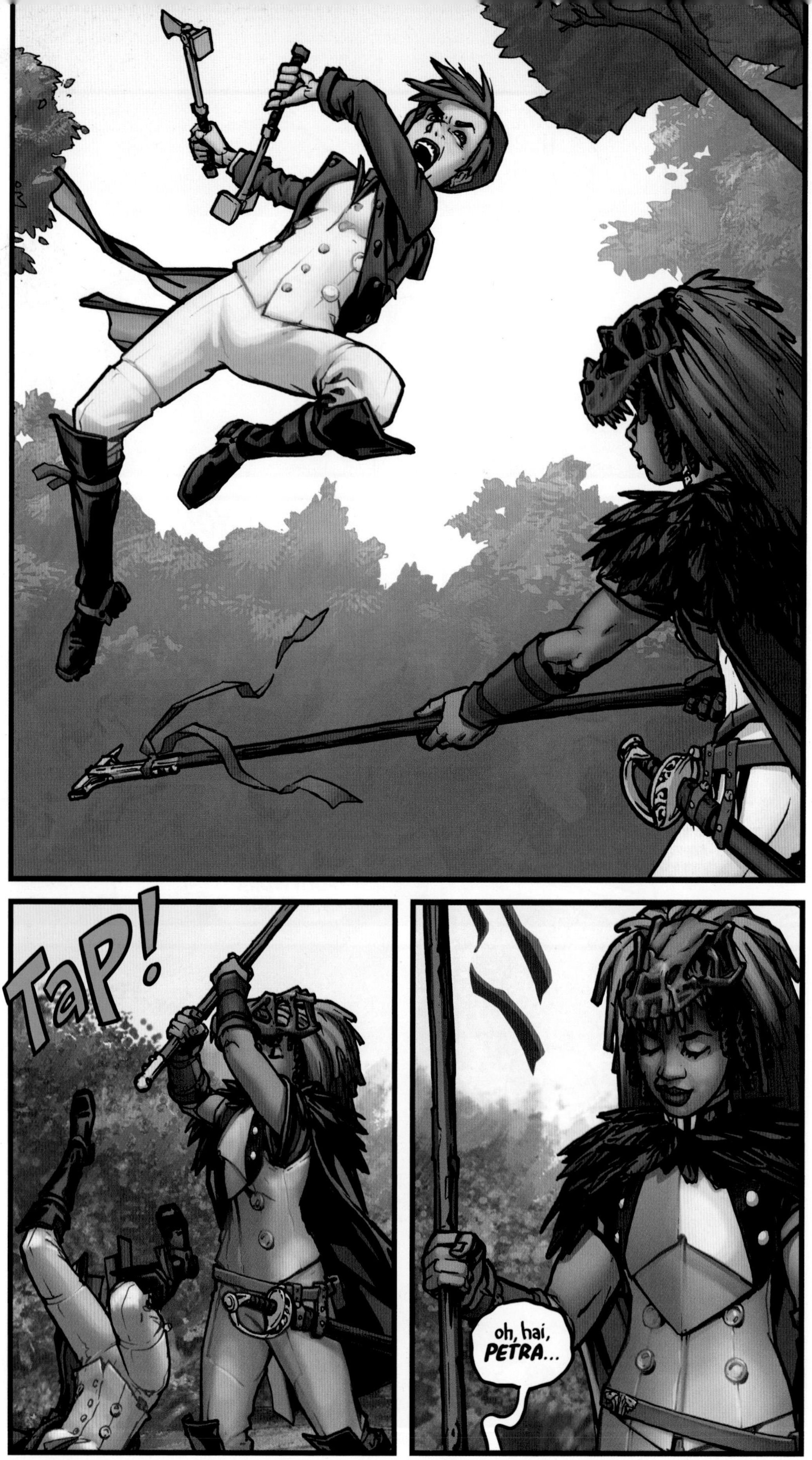
TAP!
oh, hai, PETRA...

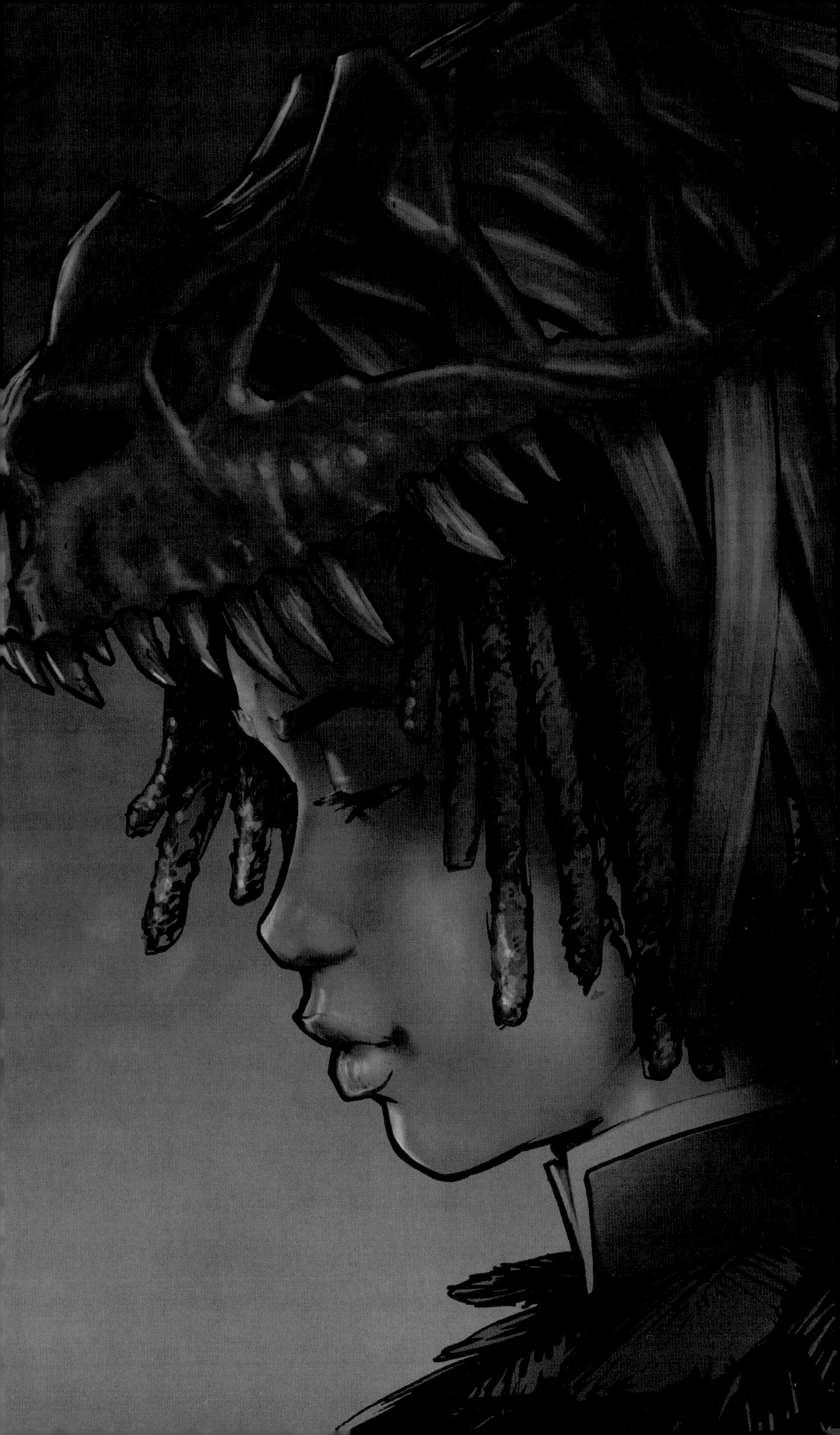

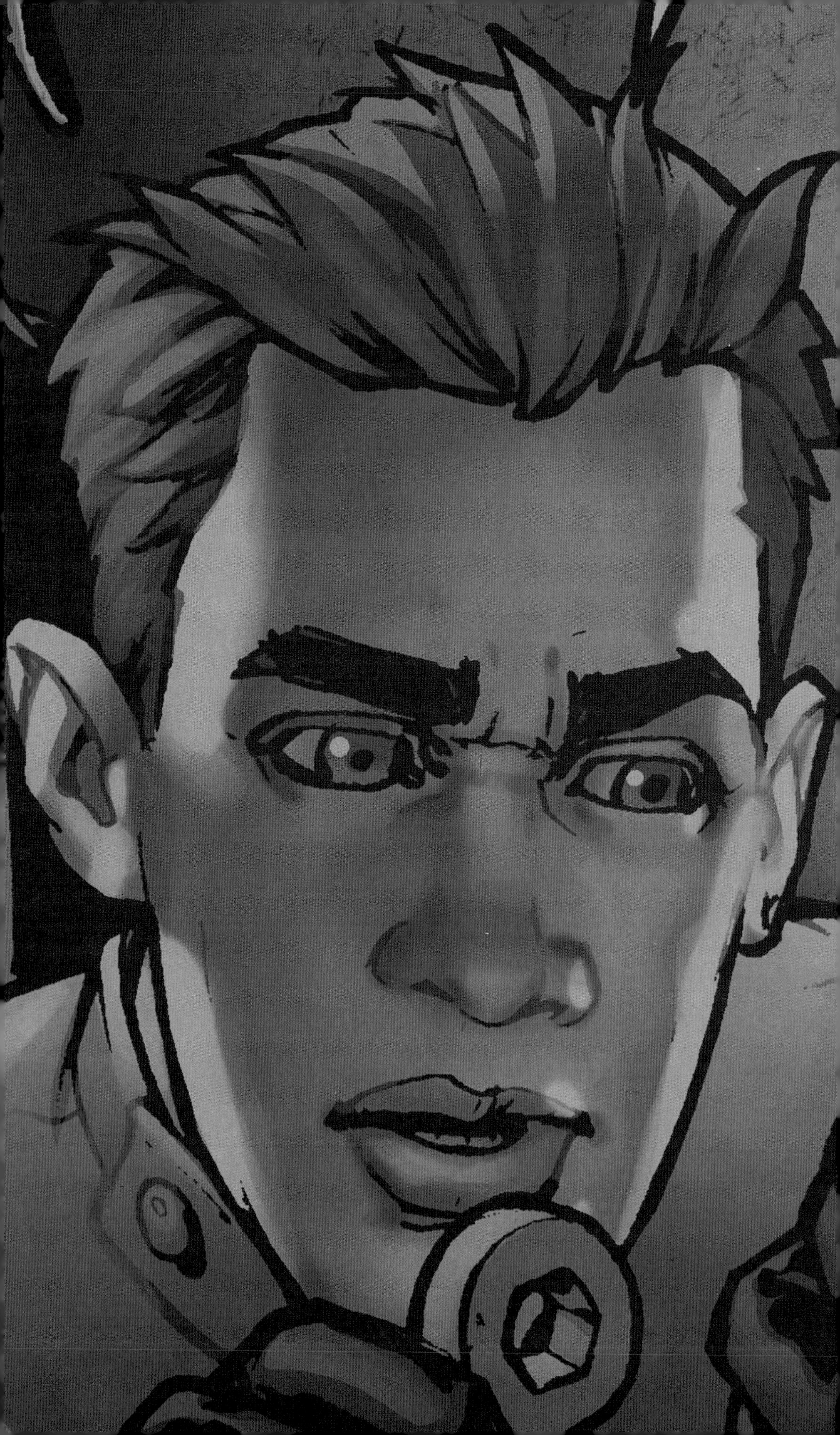

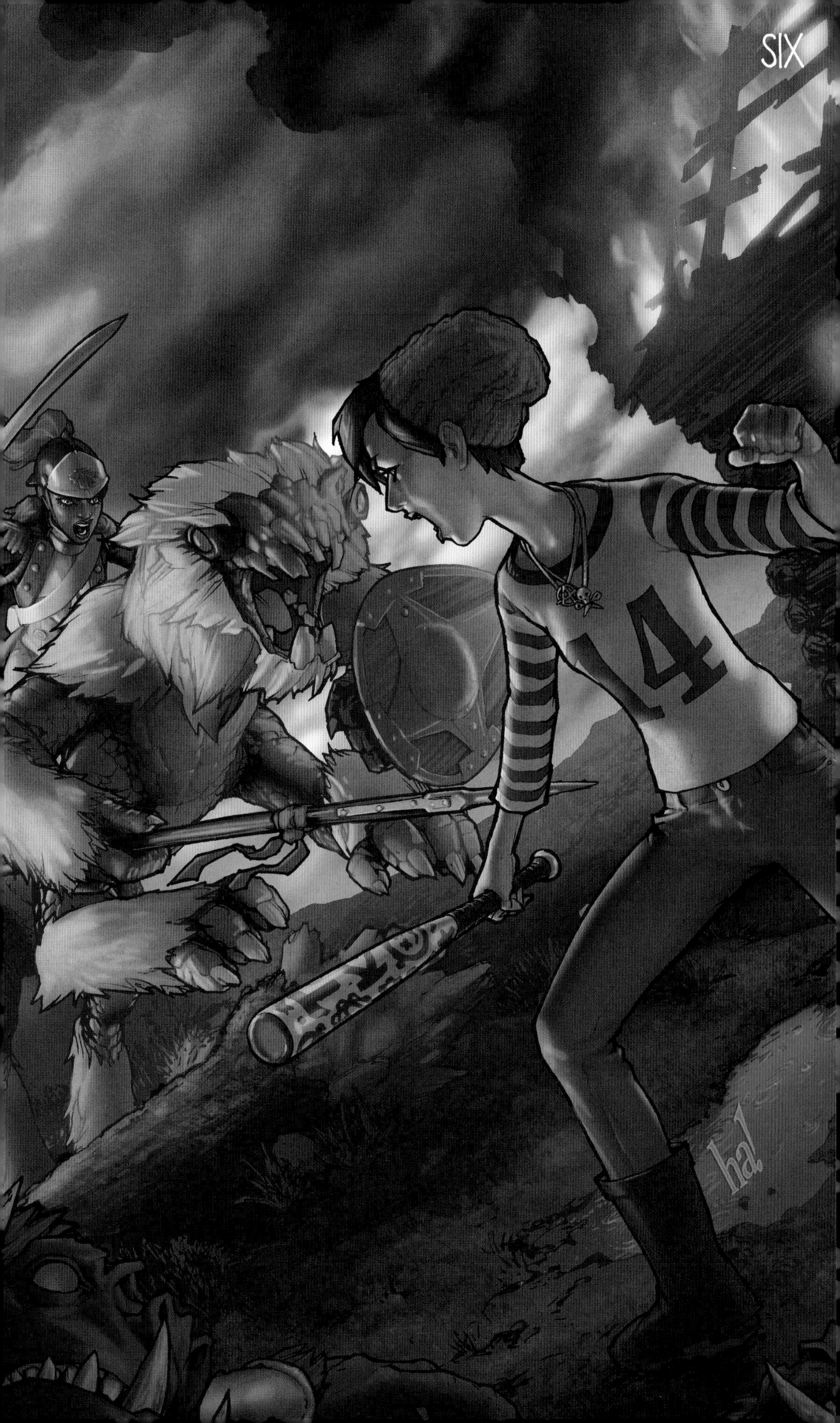
SIX
ha!

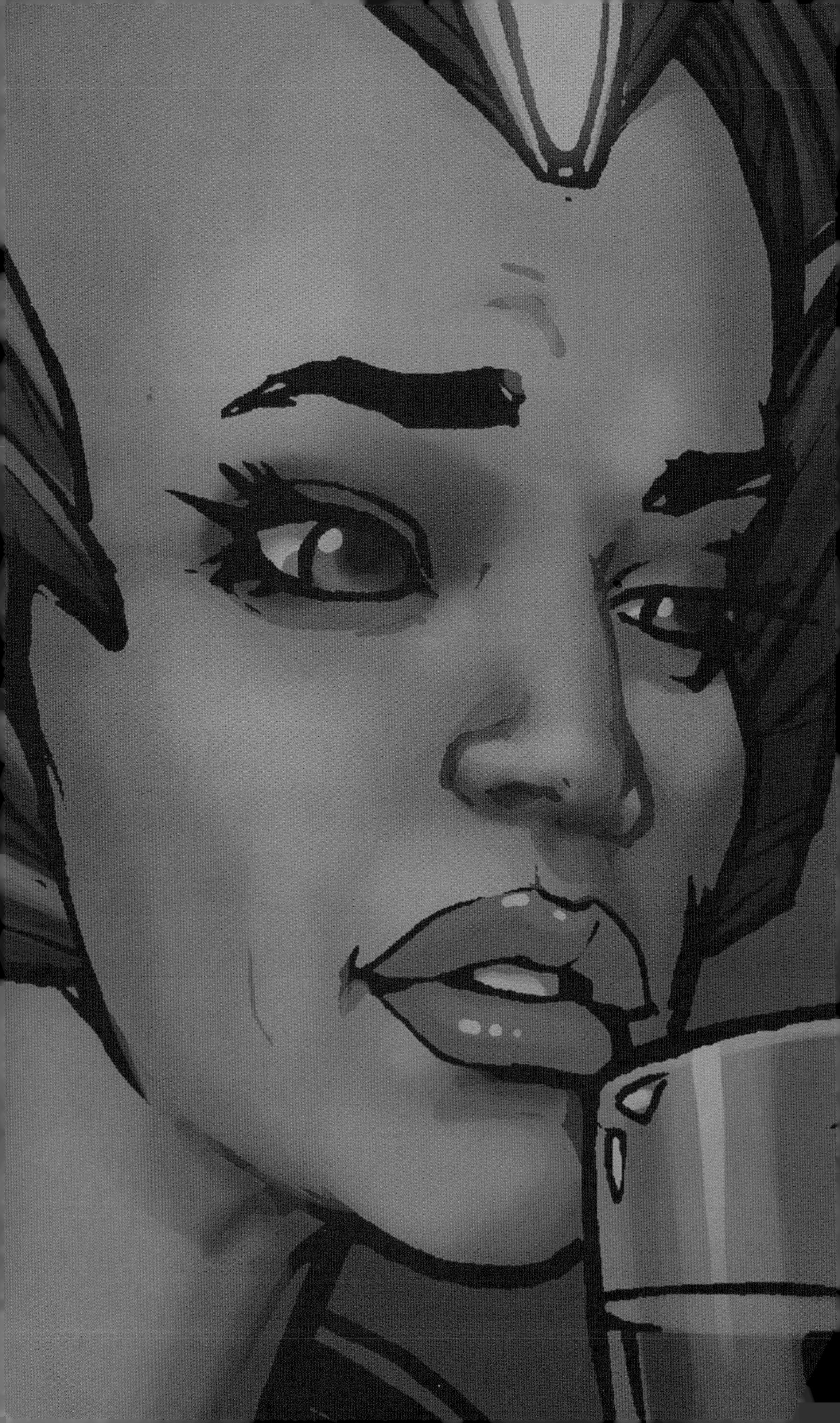

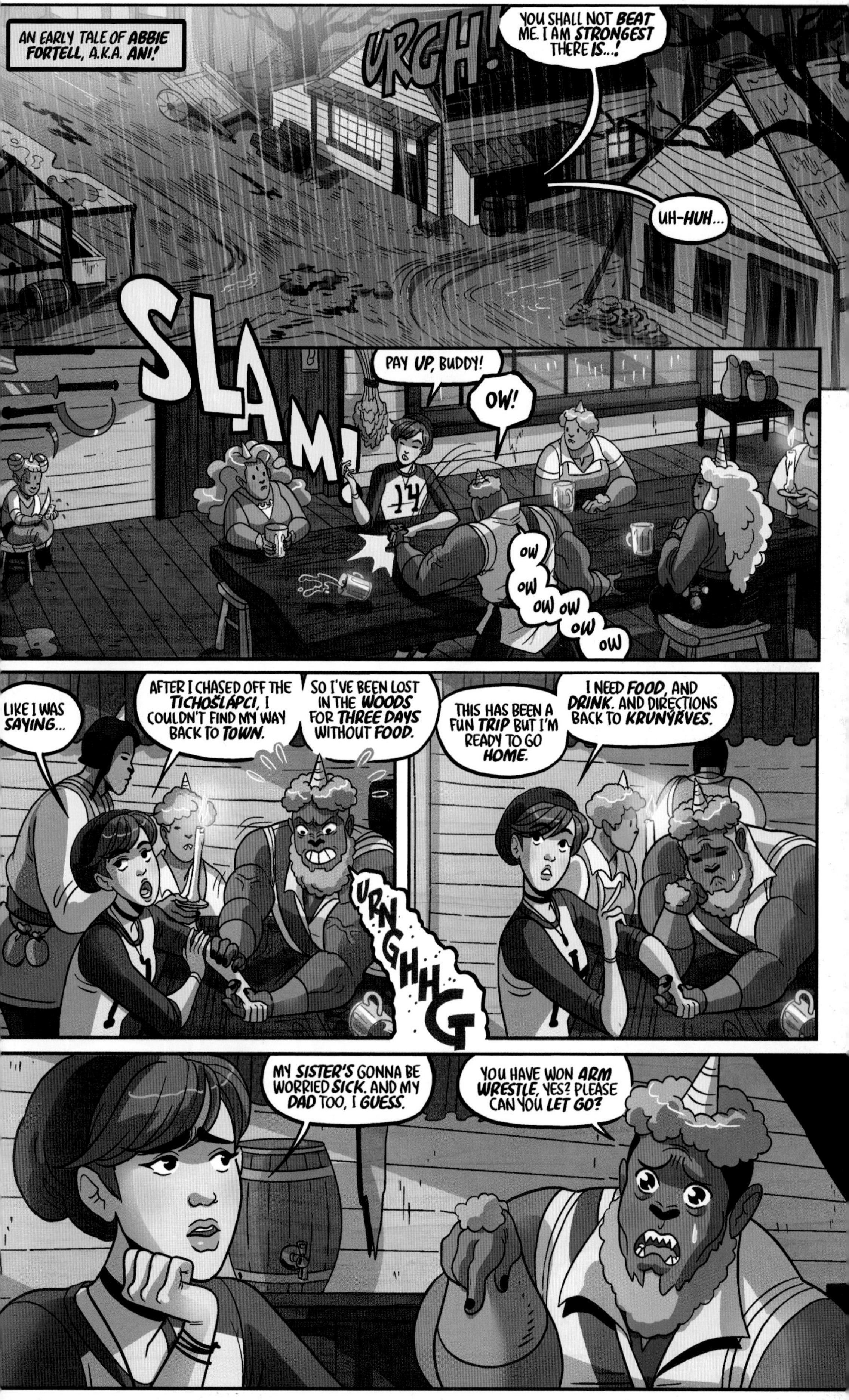
AN EARLY TALE OF ABBIE FORTELL, A.K.A. ANI!
URGH!
YOU SHALL NOT BEAT ME. I AM STRONGEST THERE IS...!
UH-HUH...
SLAM!
PAY UP, BUDDY!
OW!
OW OW OW OW OW OW
LIKE I WAS SAYING...
AFTER I CHASED OFF THE TICHOŠLÁPCI, I COULDN'T FIND MY WAY BACK TO TOWN.
SO I'VE BEEN LOST IN THE WOODS FOR THREE DAYS WITHOUT FOOD.
URNGHHG
THIS HAS BEEN A FUN TRIP BUT I'M READY TO GO HOME.
I NEED FOOD, AND DRINK. AND DIRECTIONS BACK TO KRUNÝŘVES.
MY SISTER'S GONNA BE WORRIED SICK. AND MY DAD TOO, I GUESS.
YOU HAVE WON ARM WRESTLE, YES? PLEASE CAN YOU LET GO?

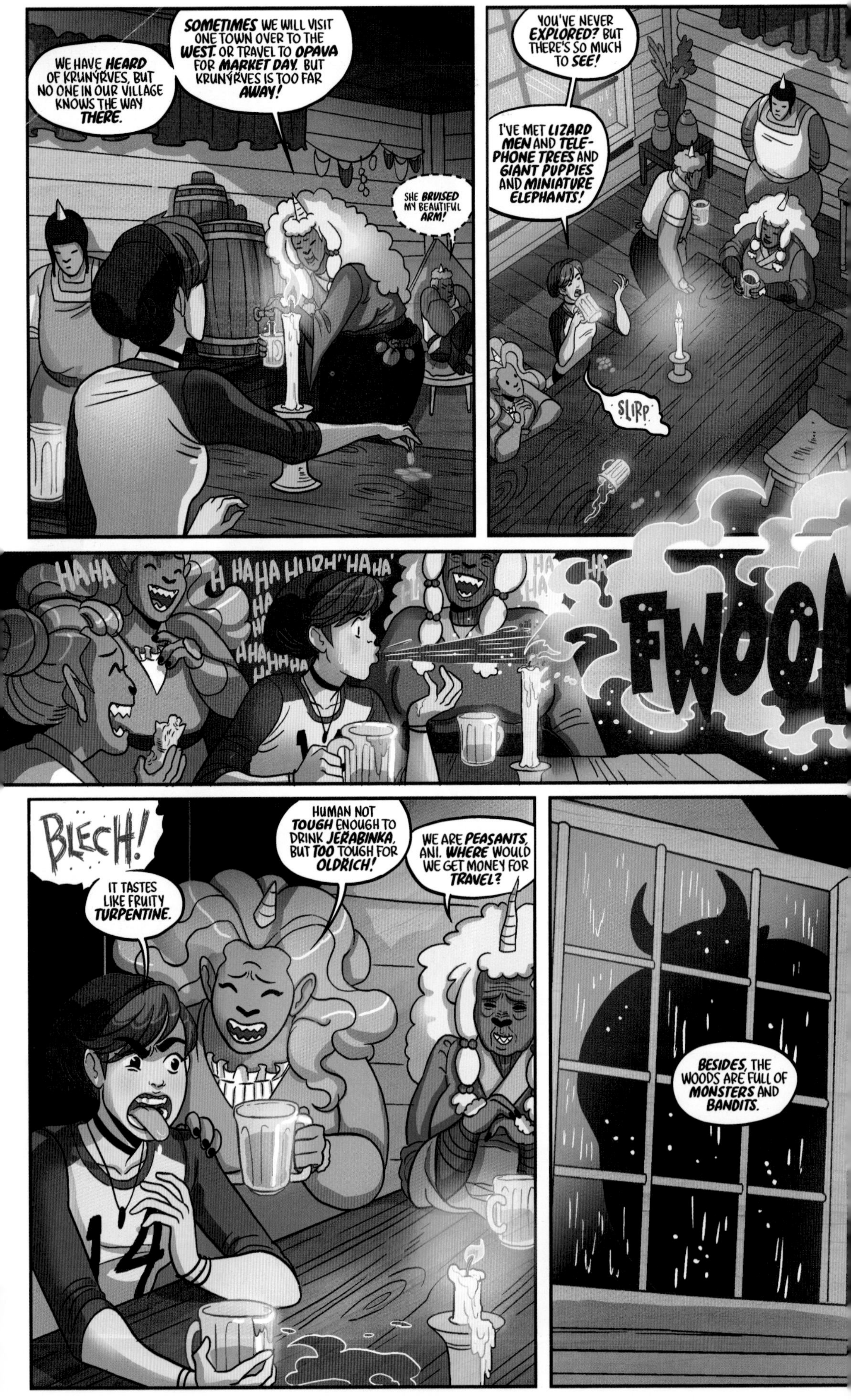
WE HAVE HEARD OF KRUNÝRVES, BUT NO ONE IN OUR VILLAGE KNOWS THE WAY THERE.
SOMETIMES WE WILL VISIT ONE TOWN OVER TO THE WEST. OR TRAVEL TO OPAVA FOR MARKET DAY. BUT KRUNÝRVES IS TOO FAR AWAY!
SHE BRUISED MY BEAUTIFUL ARM!
YOU'VE NEVER EXPLORED? BUT THERE'S SO MUCH TO SEE!
I'VE MET LIZARD MEN AND TELEPHONE TREES AND GIANT PUPPIES AND MINIATURE ELEPHANTS!
SLIRP
HAHA
HAHA HURH HAHA
FWOO
BLECH!
IT TASTES LIKE FRUITY TURPENTINE.
HUMAN NOT TOUGH ENOUGH TO DRINK JEŘABINKA, BUT TOO TOUGH FOR OLDRICH!
WE ARE PEASANTS, ANI. WHERE WOULD WE GET MONEY FOR TRAVEL?
BESIDES, THE WOODS ARE FULL OF MONSTERS AND BANDITS.

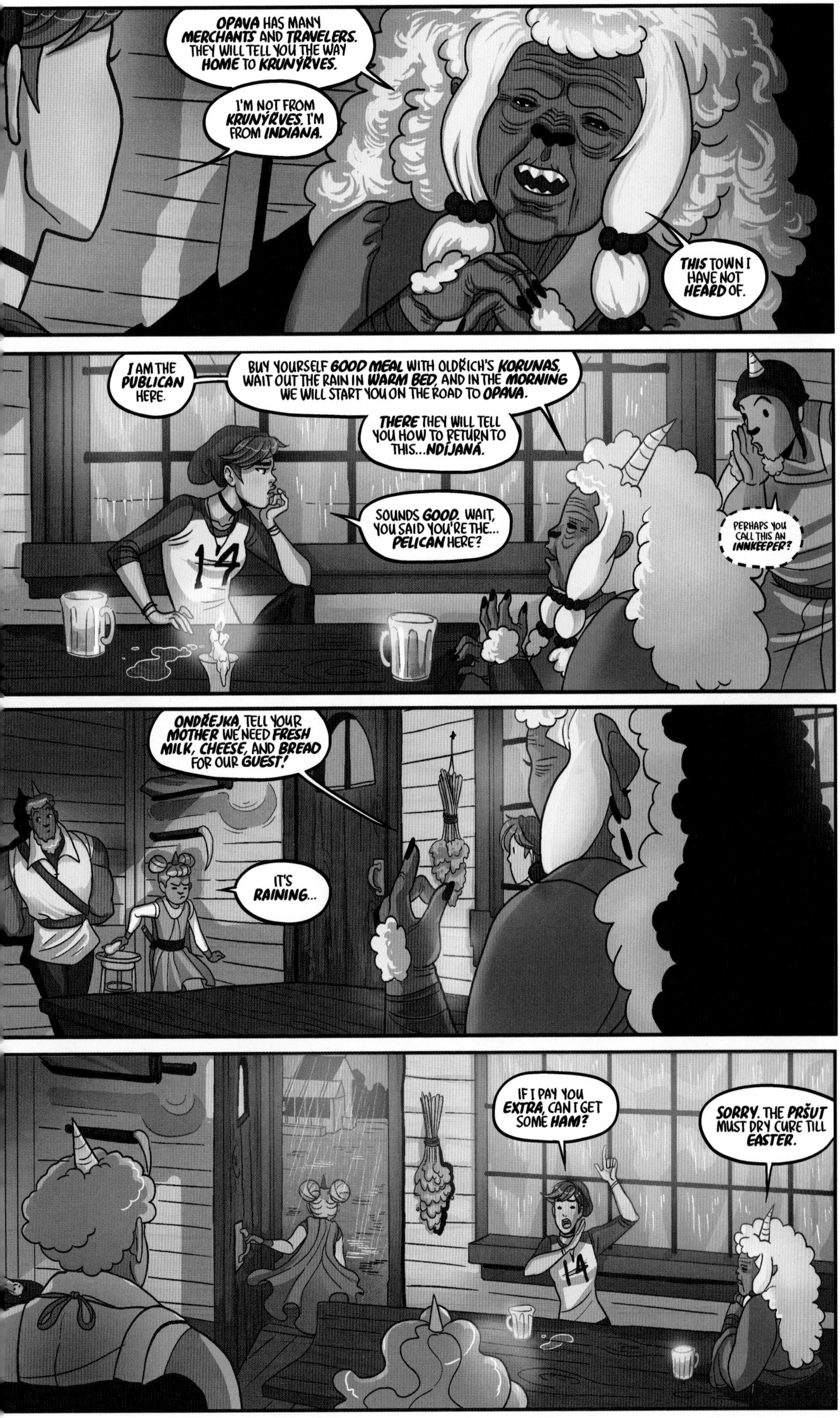
OPAVA HAS MANY MERCHANTS AND TRAVELERS. THEY WILL TELL YOU THE WAY HOME TO KRUNÝŘVES.
I'M NOT FROM KRUNÝŘVES. I'M FROM INDIANA.
THIS TOWN I HAVE NOT HEARD OF.
I AM THE PUBLICAN HERE.
BUY YOURSELF GOOD MEAL WITH OLDŘICH'S KORUNAS, WAIT OUT THE RAIN IN WARM BED, AND IN THE MORNING WE WILL START YOU ON THE ROAD TO OPAVA.
THERE THEY WILL TELL YOU HOW TO RETURN TO THIS...NDÍJANÁ.
SOUNDS GOOD. WAIT, YOU SAID YOU'RE THE... PELICAN HERE?
PERHAPS YOU CALL THIS AN INNKEEPER?
ONDŘEJKA, TELL YOUR MOTHER WE NEED FRESH MILK, CHEESE, AND BREAD FOR OUR GUEST!
IT'S RAINING...
IF I PAY YOU EXTRA, CAN I GET SOME HAM?
SORRY. THE PRŠUT MUST DRY CURE TILL EASTER.

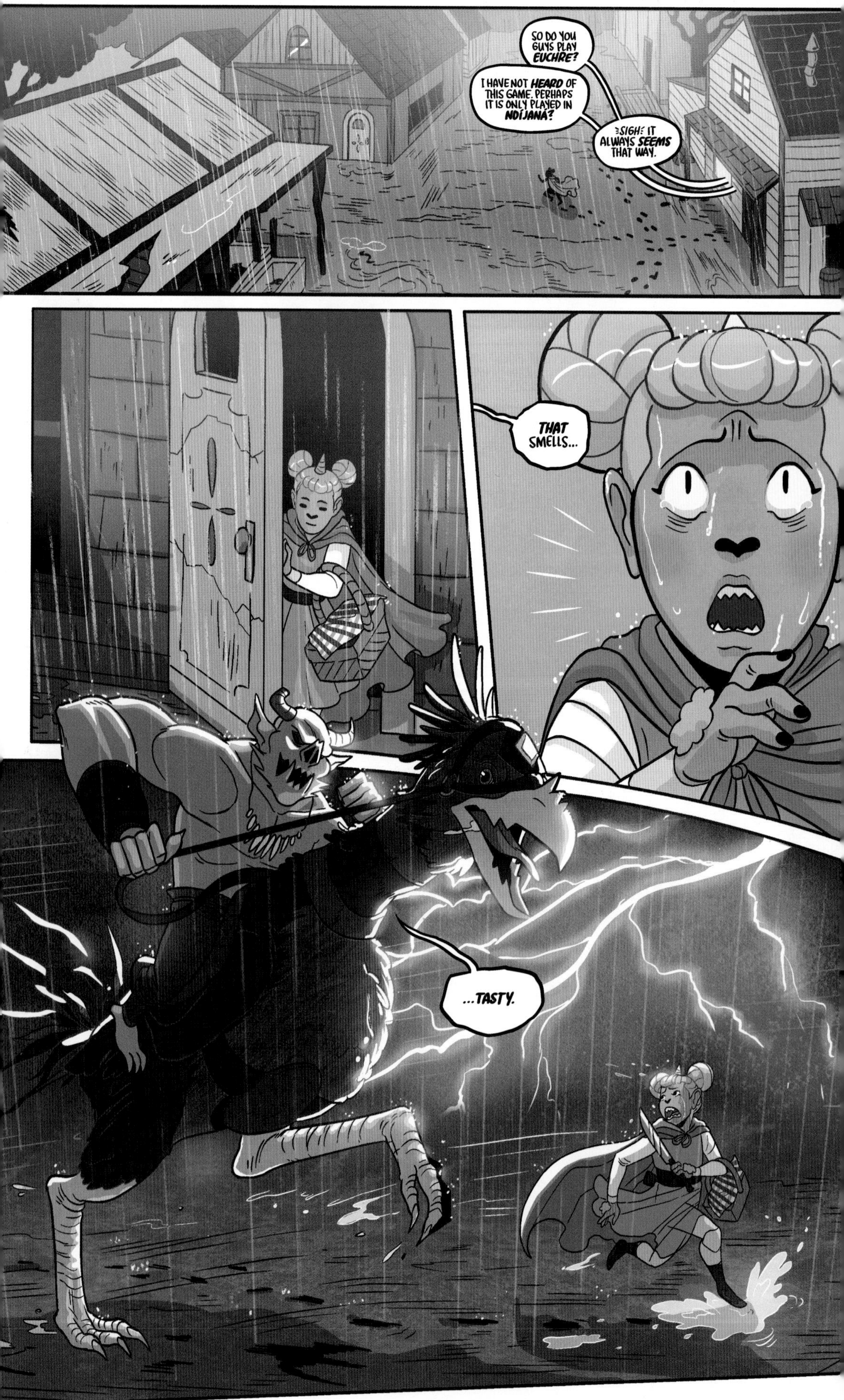
SO DO YOU GUYS PLAY EUCHRE?
I HAVE NOT HEARD OF THIS GAME. PERHAPS IT IS ONLY PLAYED IN NDÍJANÁ?
SIGH IT ALWAYS SEEMS THAT WAY.
THAT SMELLS...
...TASTY.

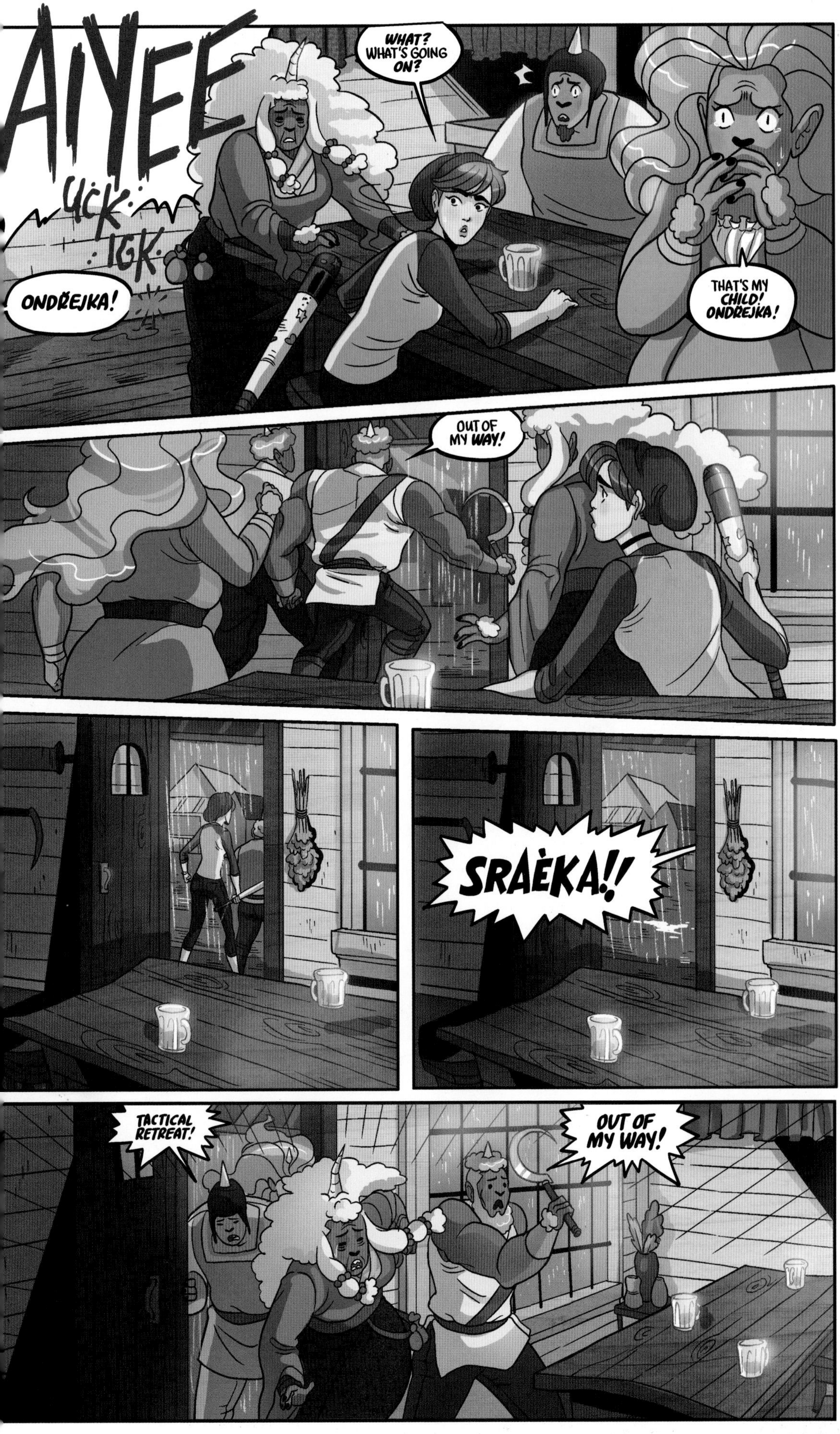
AIYEE
UCK
IGK
ONDŘEJKA!
WHAT? WHAT'S GOING ON?
THAT'S MY CHILD! ONDŘEJKA!
OUT OF MY WAY!
SRAĖKA!!
TACTICAL RETREAT!
OUT OF MY WAY!

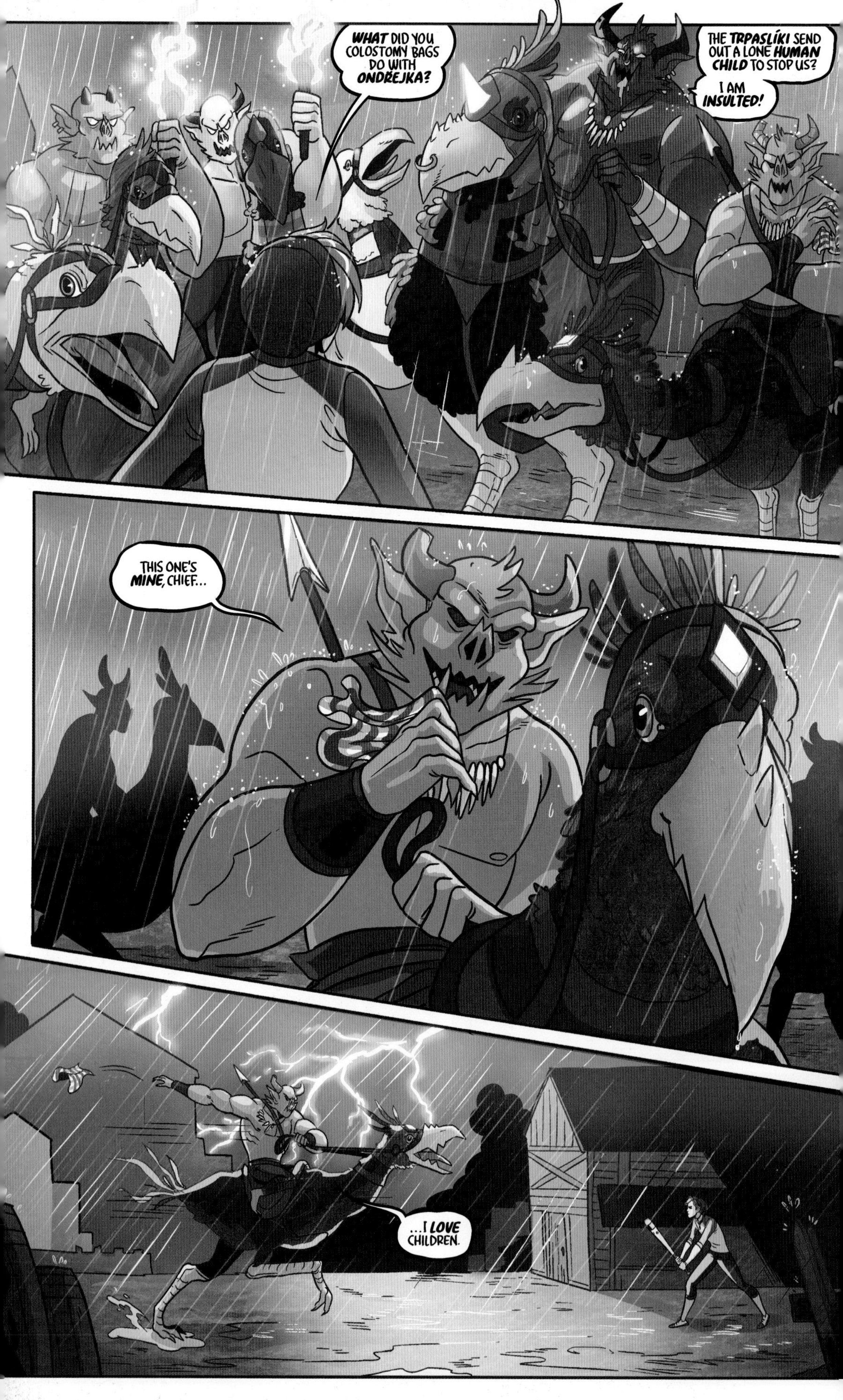
WHAT DID YOU COLOSTOMY BAGS DO WITH ONDREJKA?
THE TRPASLÍKI SEND OUT A LONE HUMAN CHILD TO STOP US?
I AM INSULTED!
THIS ONE'S MINE, CHIEF...
...I LOVE CHILDREN.

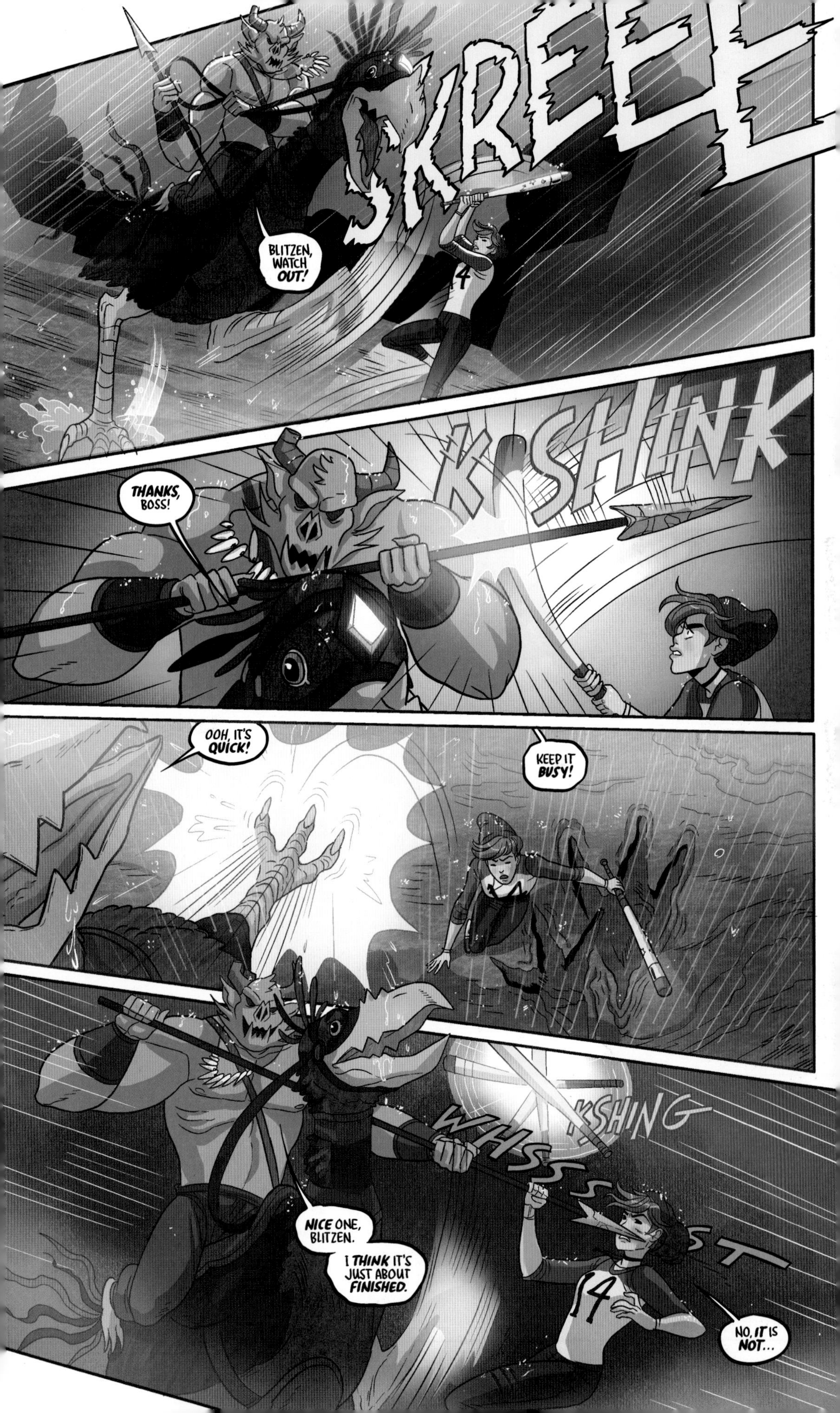
SKREEE
BLITZEN, WATCH OUT!
K'SHINK
THANKS, BOSS!
OOH, IT'S QUICK!
KEEP IT BUSY!
K'SHING
WHSSSSST
NICE ONE, BLITZEN.
I THINK IT'S JUST ABOUT FINISHED.
NO, IT IS NOT...

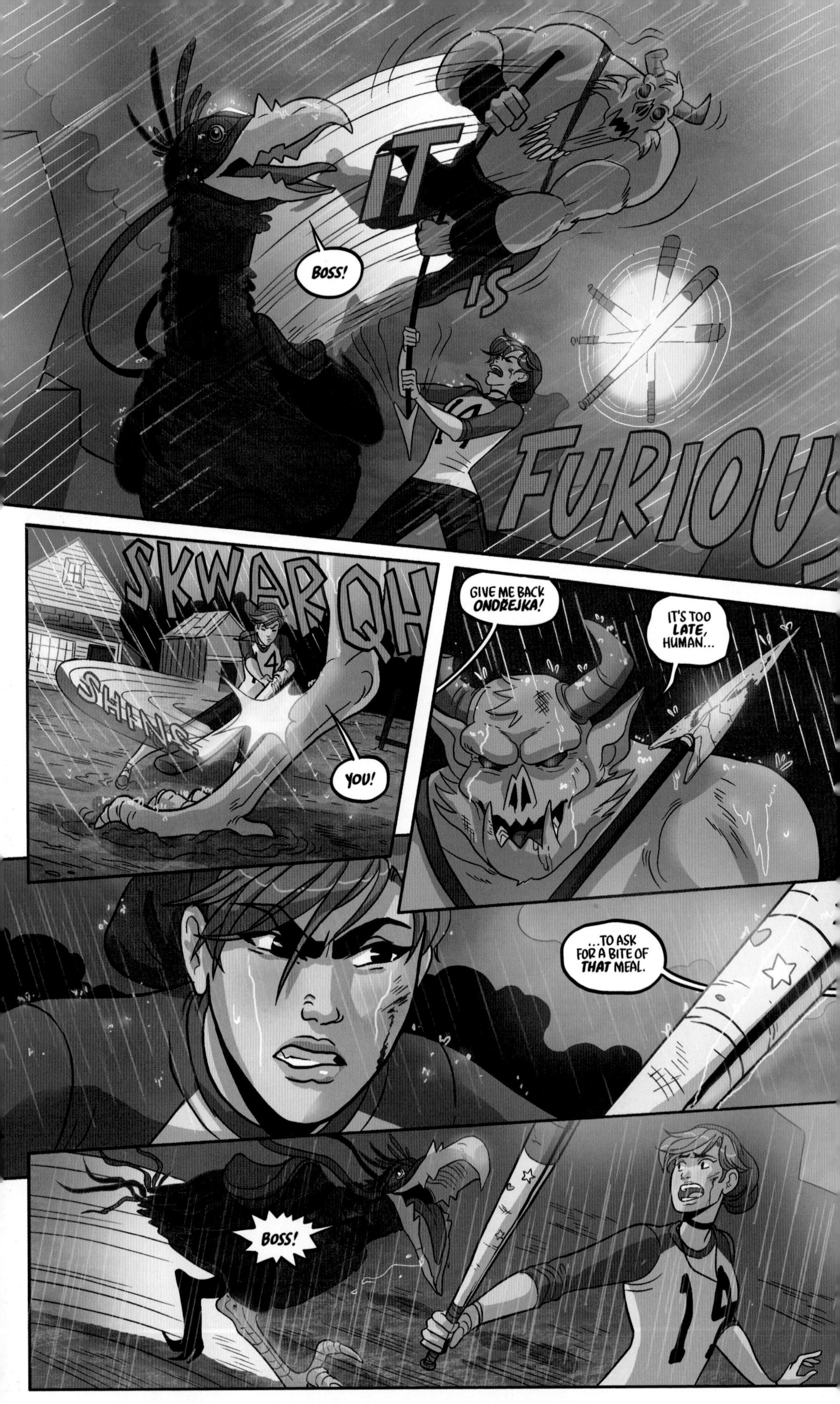
IT
BOSS!
IS
FURIOUS
SKWARQH
SHING
YOU!
GIVE ME BACK ONDREJKA!
IT'S TOO LATE, HUMAN...
...TO ASK FOR A BITE OF THAT MEAL.
BOSS!

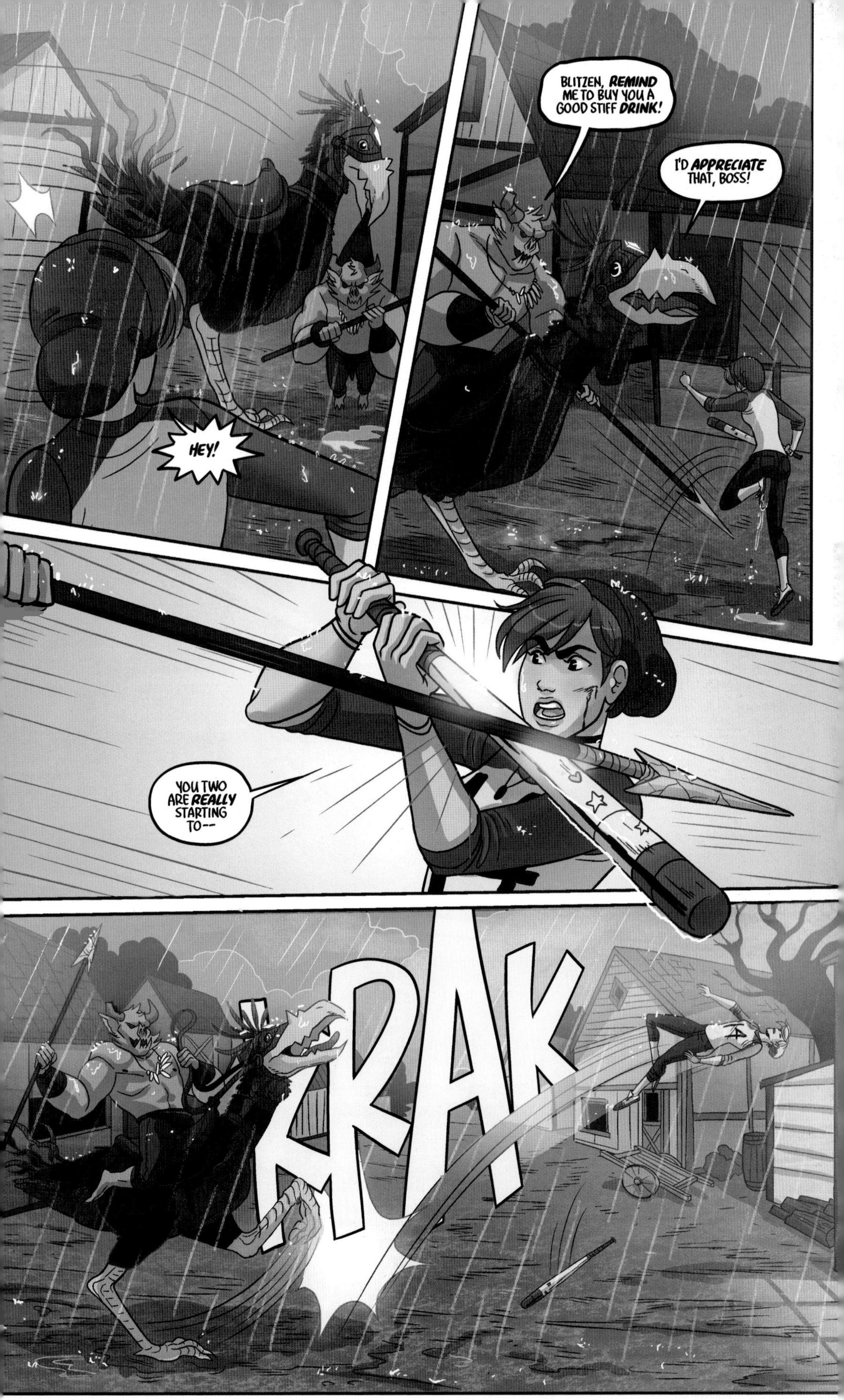
BLITZEN, REMIND ME TO BUY YOU A GOOD STIFF DRINK!
I'D APPRECIATE THAT, BOSS!
HEY!
YOU TWO ARE REALLY STARTING TO--
KRAK

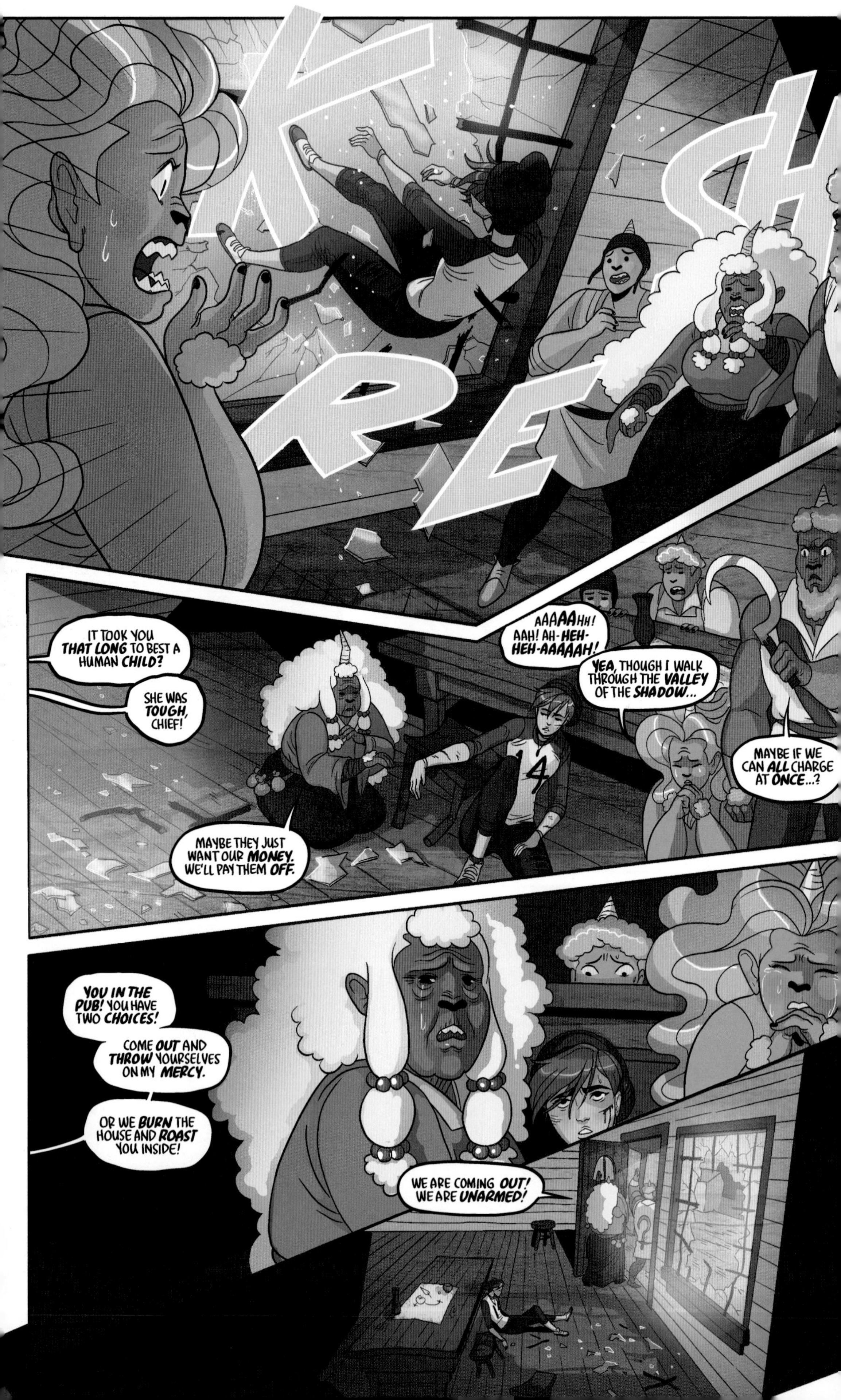
KRESH
IT TOOK YOU THAT LONG TO BEST A HUMAN CHILD?
SHE WAS TOUGH, CHIEF!
AAAAAHH! AAH! AH-HEH-HEH-AAAAAH!
YEA, THOUGH I WALK THROUGH THE VALLEY OF THE SHADOW...
MAYBE IF WE CAN ALL CHARGE AT ONCE...?
MAYBE THEY JUST WANT OUR MONEY. WE'LL PAY THEM OFF.
YOU IN THE PUB! YOU HAVE TWO CHOICES!
COME OUT AND THROW YOURSELVES ON MY MERCY.
OR WE BURN THE HOUSE AND ROAST YOU INSIDE!
WE ARE COMING OUT! WE ARE UNARMED!

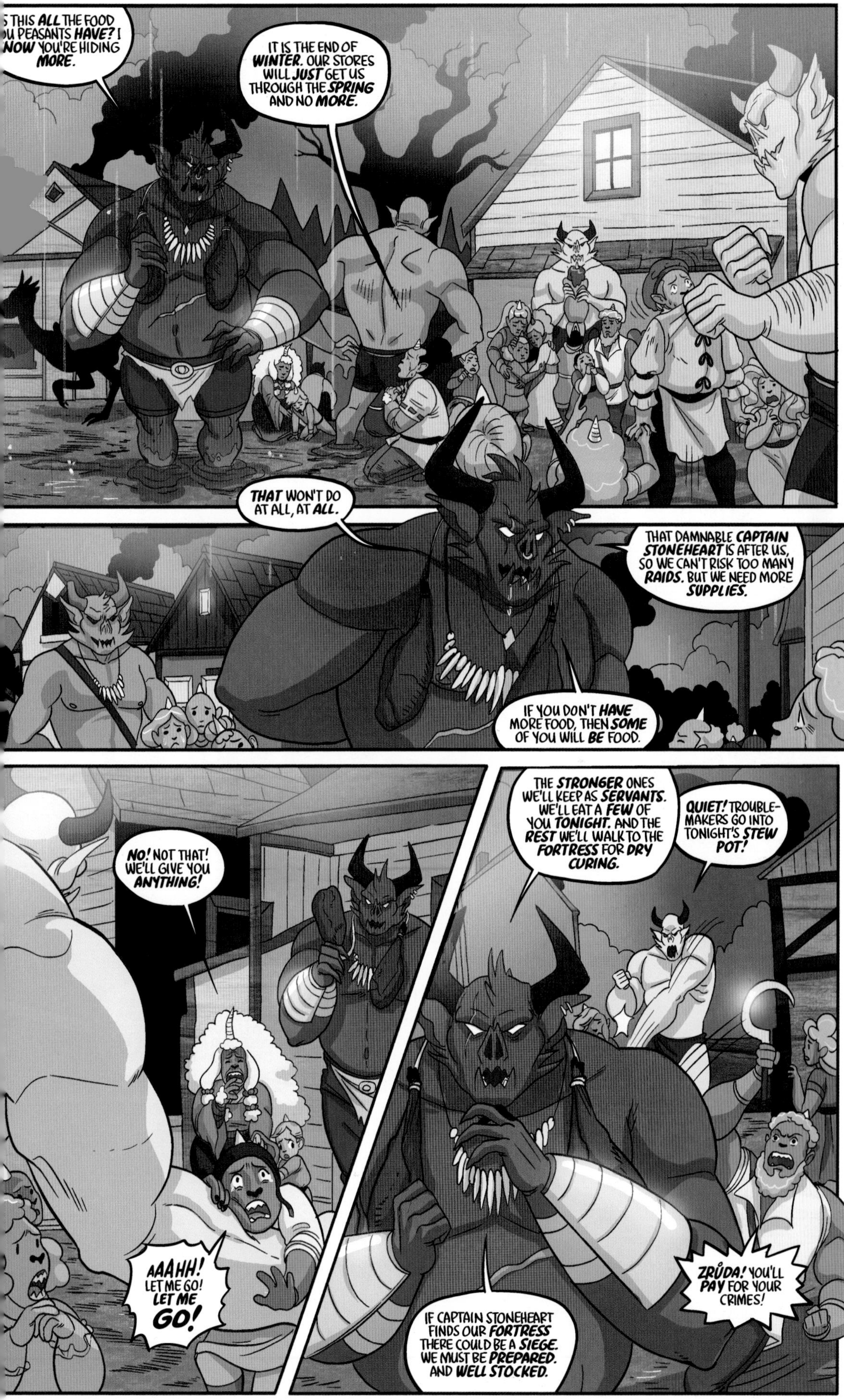
S THIS ALL THE FOOD OU PEASANTS HAVE? I NOW YOU'RE HIDING MORE.
IT IS THE END OF WINTER. OUR STORES WILL JUST GET US THROUGH THE SPRING AND NO MORE.
THAT WON'T DO AT ALL, AT ALL.
THAT DAMNABLE CAPTAIN STONEHEART IS AFTER US, SO WE CAN'T RISK TOO MANY RAIDS. BUT WE NEED MORE SUPPLIES.
IF YOU DON'T HAVE MORE FOOD, THEN SOME OF YOU WILL BE FOOD.
NO! NOT THAT! WE'LL GIVE YOU ANYTHING!
AAAHH! LET ME GO! LET ME GO!
THE STRONGER ONES WE'LL KEEP AS SERVANTS. WE'LL EAT A FEW OF YOU TONIGHT. AND THE REST WE'LL WALK TO THE FORTRESS FOR DRY CURING.
QUIET! TROUBLE-MAKERS GO INTO TONIGHT'S STEW POT!
ZRŮDA! YOU'LL PAY FOR YOUR CRIMES!
IF CAPTAIN STONEHEART FINDS OUR FORTRESS THERE COULD BE A SIEGE. WE MUST BE PREPARED. AND WELL STOCKED.

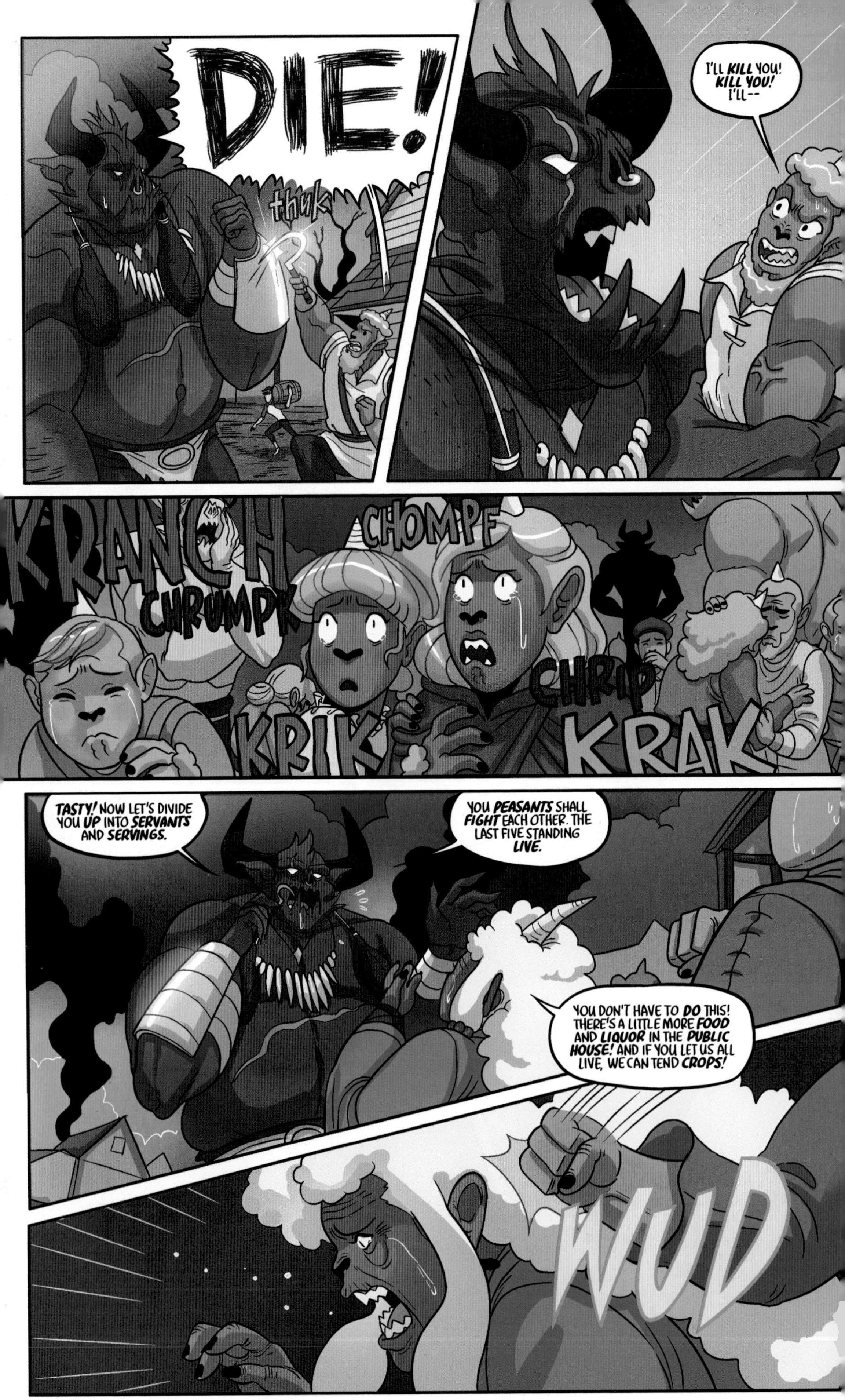

DIE!
thuk
I'LL KILL YOU! KILL YOU! I'LL--
KRANCH
CHOMPF
CHRUMPK
CHRIP
KRIK
KRAK
TASTY! NOW LET'S DIVIDE YOU UP INTO SERVANTS AND SERVINGS.
YOU PEASANTS SHALL FIGHT EACH OTHER. THE LAST FIVE STANDING LIVE.
YOU DON'T HAVE TO DO THIS! THERE'S A LITTLE MORE FOOD AND LIQUOR IN THE PUBLIC HOUSE! AND IF YOU LET US ALL LIVE, WE CAN TEND CROPS!
WUD

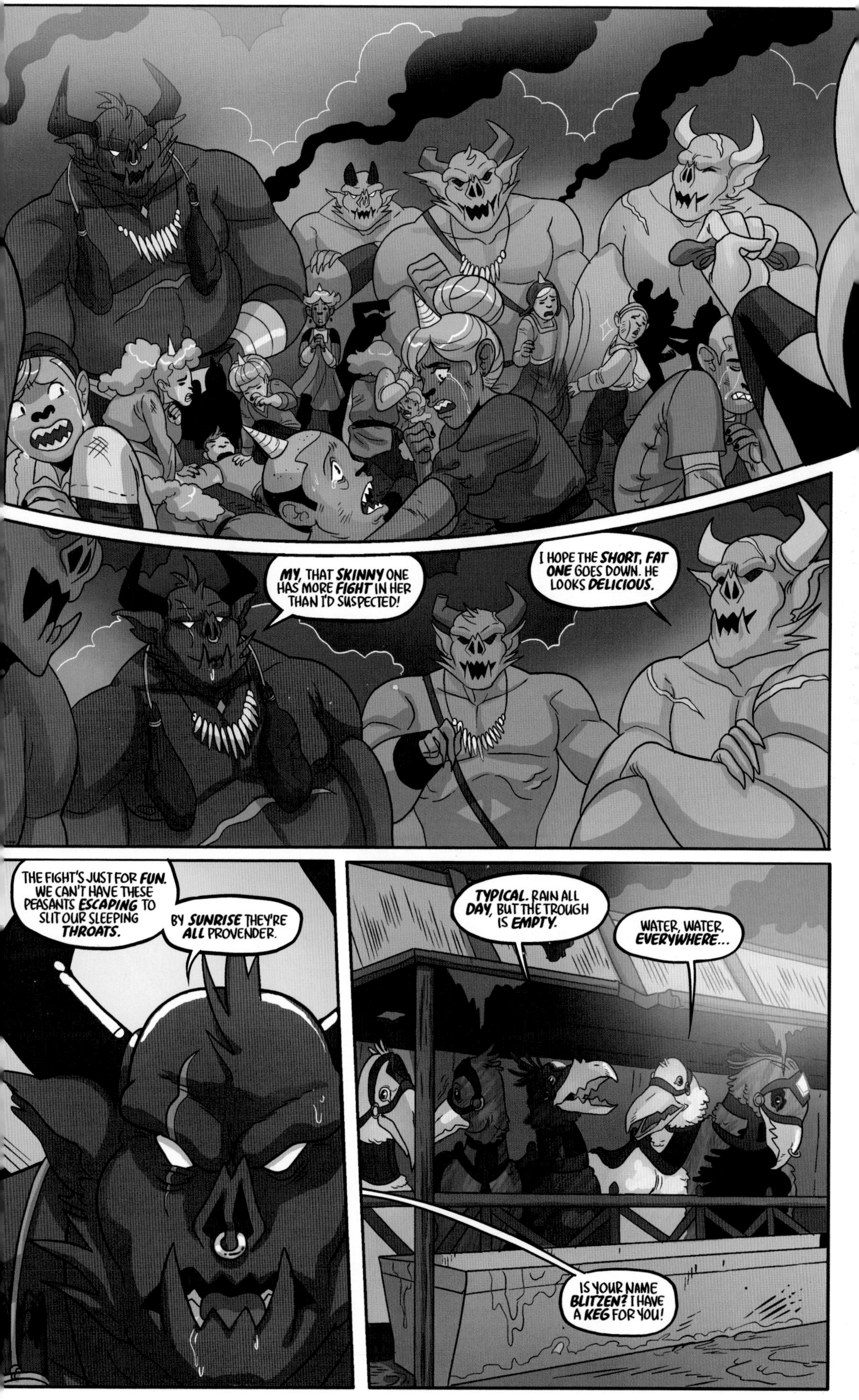
MY, THAT SKINNY ONE HAS MORE FIGHT IN HER THAN I'D SUSPECTED!
I HOPE THE SHORT, FAT ONE GOES DOWN. HE LOOKS DELICIOUS.
THE FIGHT'S JUST FOR FUN. WE CAN'T HAVE THESE PEASANTS ESCAPING TO SLIT OUR SLEEPING THROATS.
BY SUNRISE THEY'RE ALL PROVENDER.
TYPICAL. RAIN ALL DAY, BUT THE TROUGH IS EMPTY.
WATER, WATER, EVERYWHERE...
IS YOUR NAME BLITZEN? I HAVE A KEG FOR YOU!

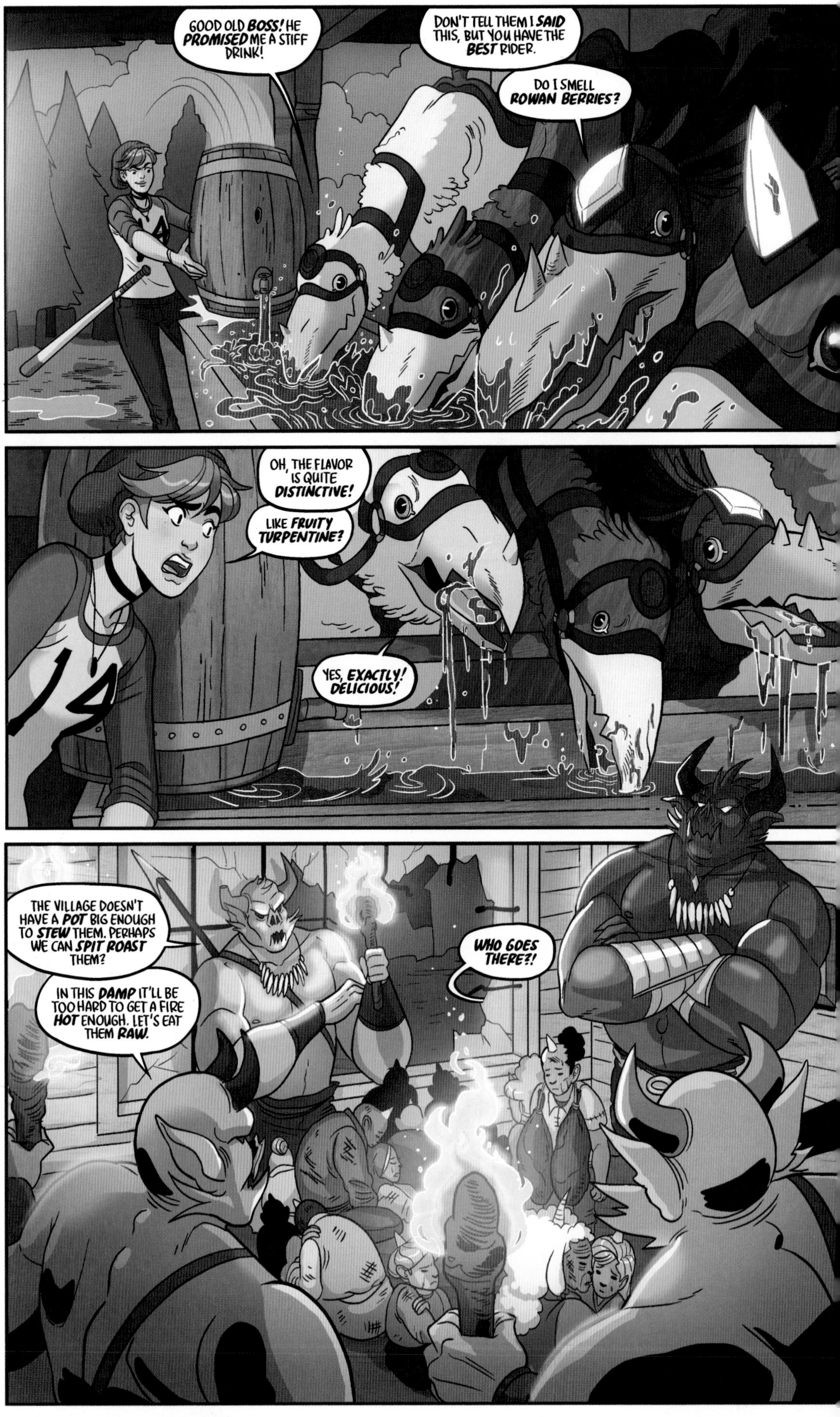
GOOD OLD BOSS! HE PROMISED ME A STIFF DRINK!
DON'T TELL THEM I SAID THIS, BUT YOU HAVE THE BEST RIDER.
DO I SMELL ROWAN BERRIES?
OH, THE FLAVOR IS QUITE DISTINCTIVE!
LIKE FRUITY TURPENTINE?
YES, EXACTLY! DELICIOUS!
THE VILLAGE DOESN'T HAVE A POT BIG ENOUGH TO STEW THEM. PERHAPS WE CAN SPIT ROAST THEM?
IN THIS DAMP IT'LL BE TOO HARD TO GET A FIRE HOT ENOUGH. LET'S EAT THEM RAW.
WHO GOES THERE?!

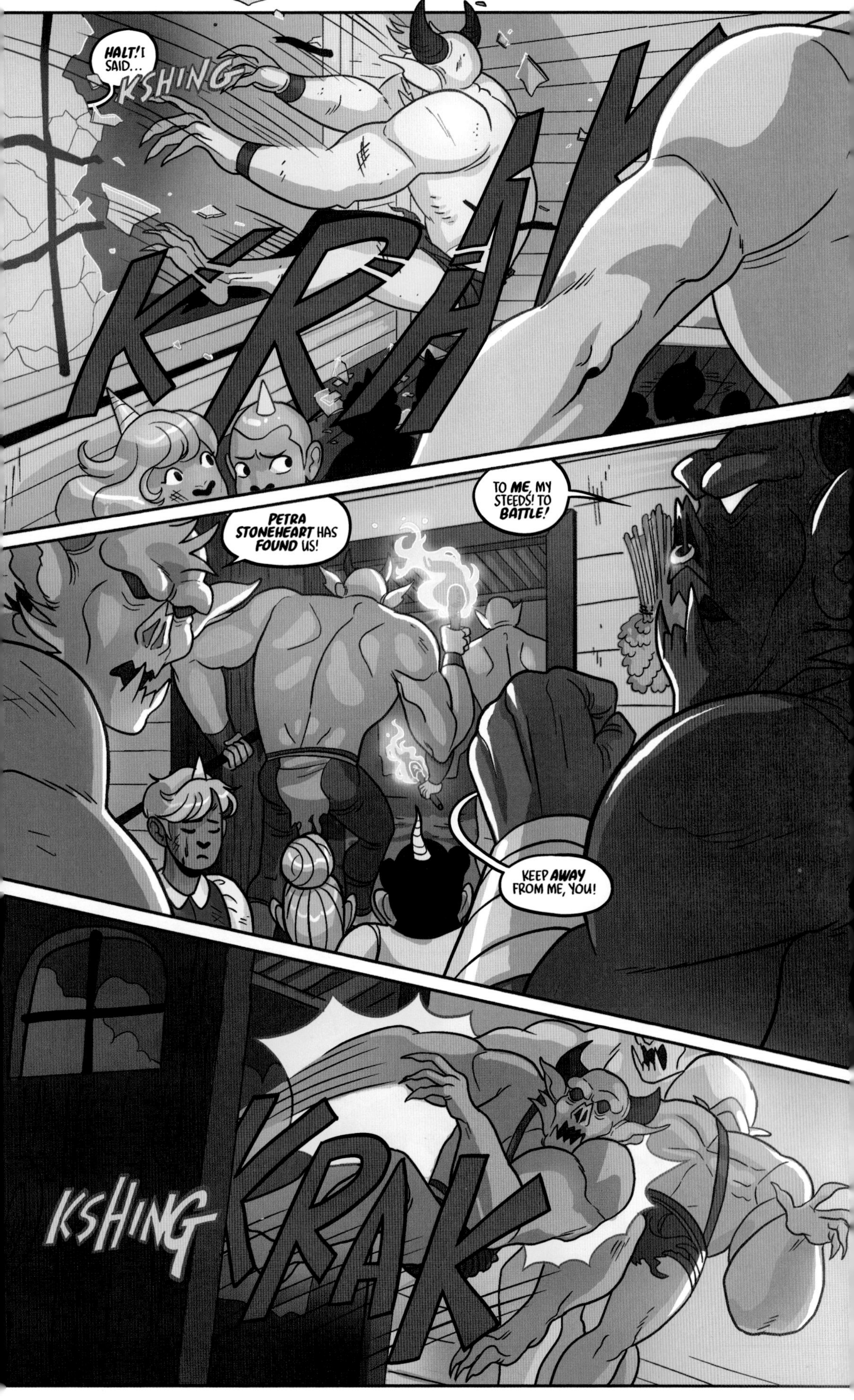
HALT! I SAID...
KSHING
KRAK
TO ME, MY STEEDS! TO BATTLE!
PETRA STONEHEART HAS FOUND US!
KEEP AWAY FROM ME, YOU!
KSHING
KRAK

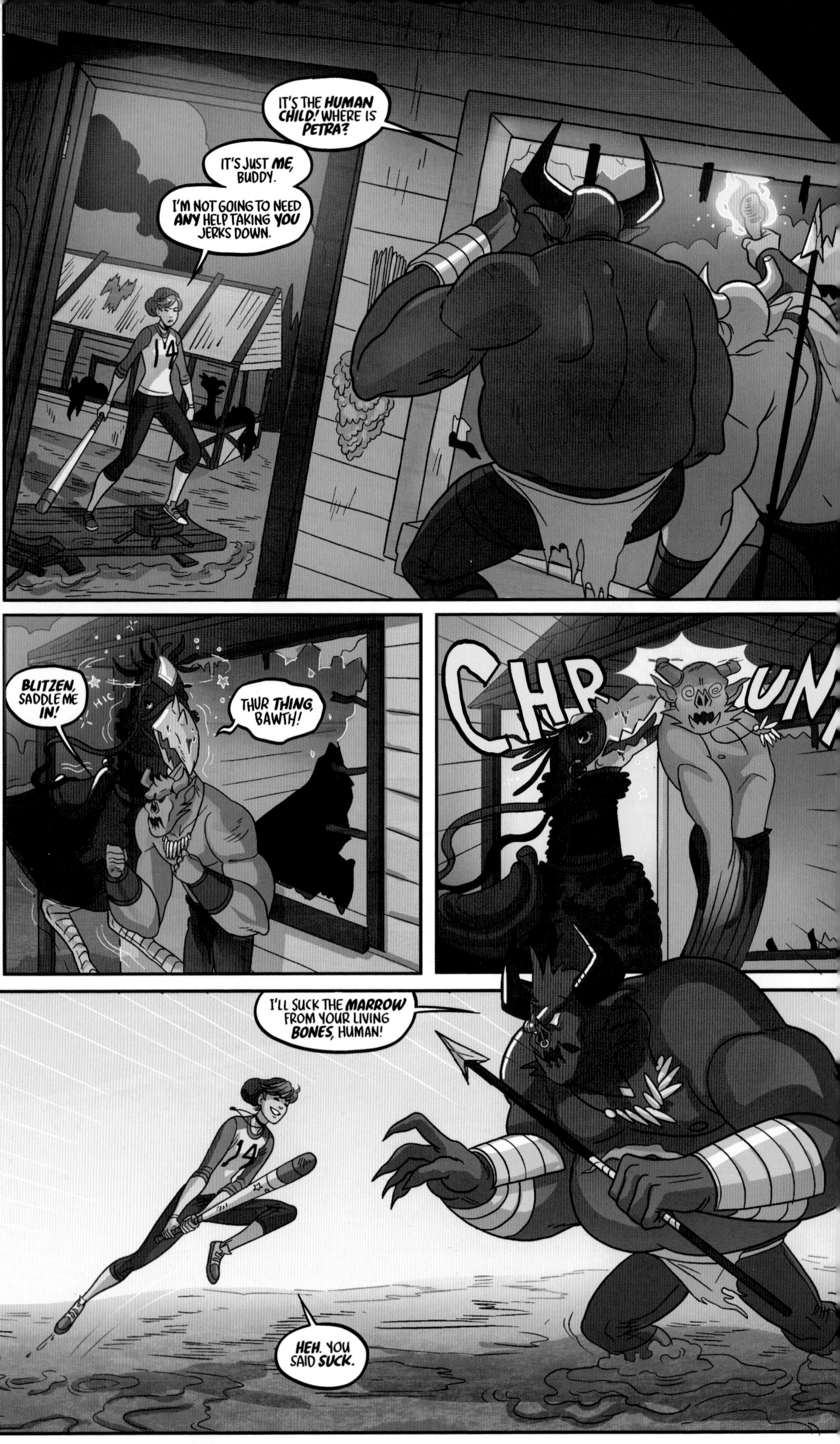
IT'S THE **HUMAN CHILD!** WHERE IS **PETRA?**
IT'S JUST **ME**, BUDDY.
I'M NOT GOING TO NEED **ANY** HELP TAKING **YOU** JERKS DOWN.
BLITZEN, SADDLE ME **IN!**
HIC
THUR **THING**, BAWTH!
CHR
UN
I'LL SUCK THE **MARROW** FROM YOUR LIVING **BONES**, HUMAN!
HEH. YOU SAID **SUCK**.

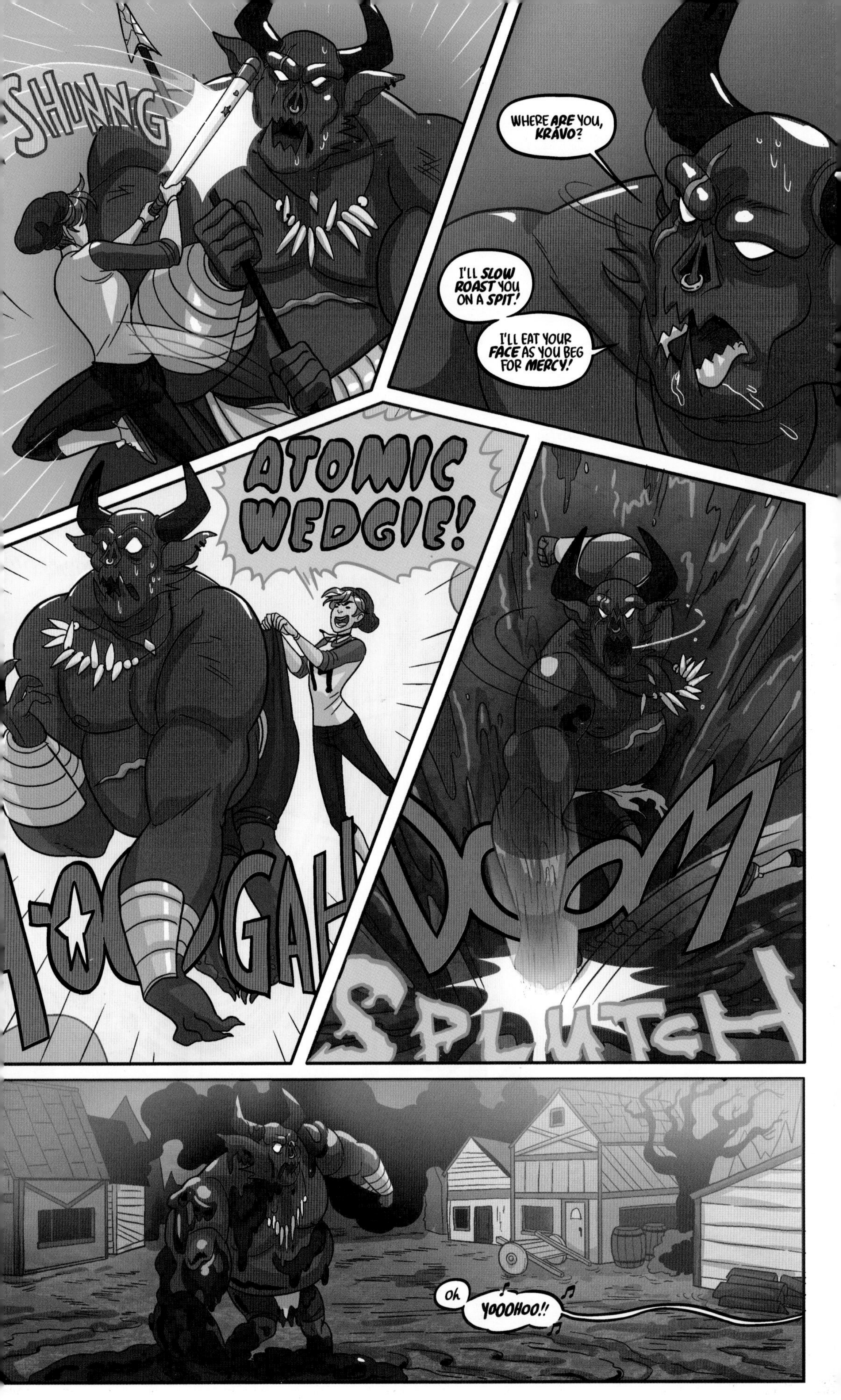
SHINNG
WHERE ARE YOU, KRAVO?
I'LL SLOW ROAST YOU ON A SPIT!
I'LL EAT YOUR FACE AS YOU BEG FOR MERCY!
ATOMIC WEDGIE!
AOOGAH
DOOM
SPLUTCH
Oh
YOOOHOO!!

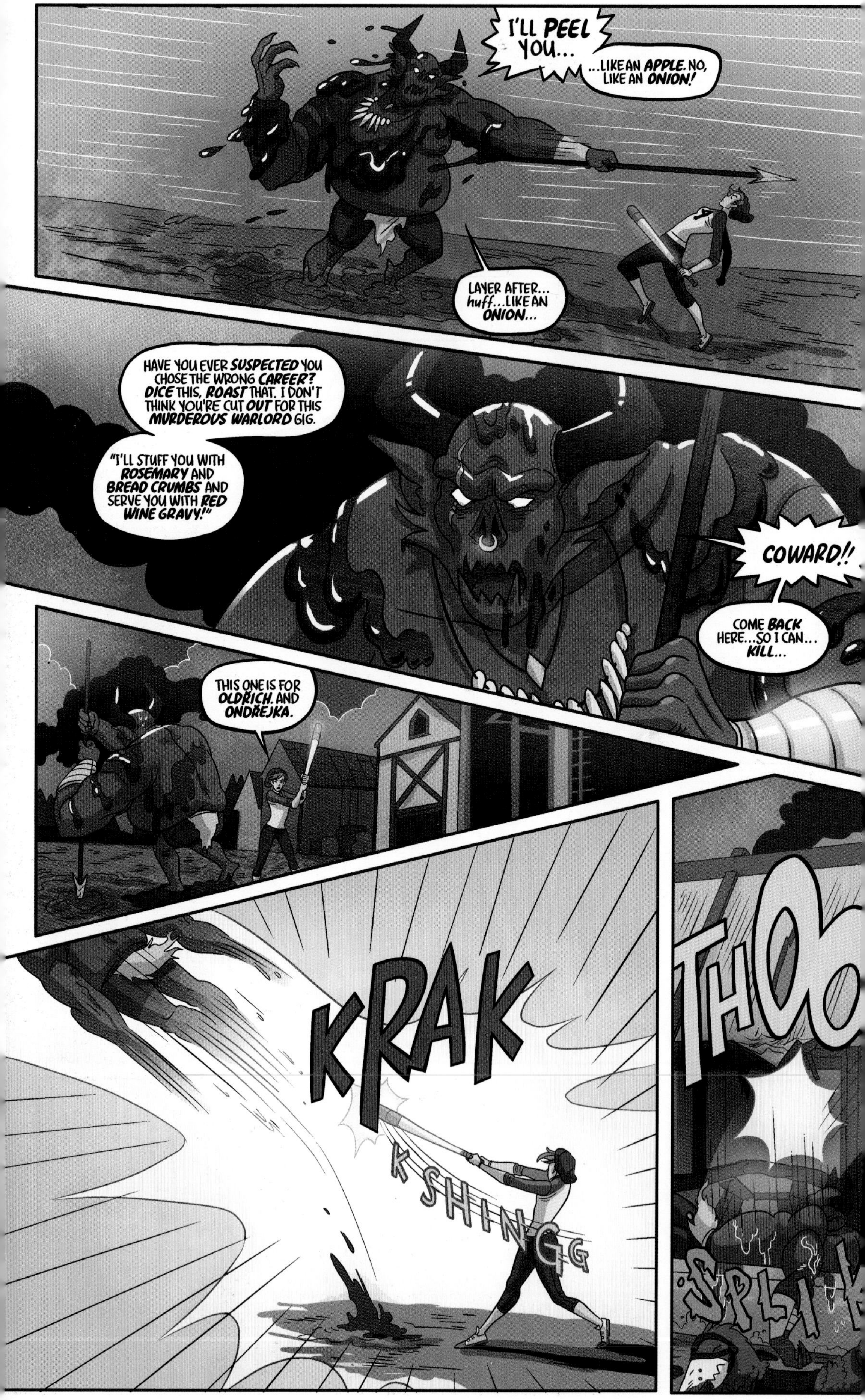
I'LL PEEL YOU...
...LIKE AN APPLE. NO, LIKE AN ONION!
LAYER AFTER... huff...LIKE AN ONION...
HAVE YOU EVER SUSPECTED YOU CHOSE THE WRONG CAREER? DICE THIS, ROAST THAT. I DON'T THINK YOU'RE CUT OUT FOR THIS MURDEROUS WARLORD GIG.
"I'LL STUFF YOU WITH ROSEMARY AND BREAD CRUMBS AND SERVE YOU WITH RED WINE GRAVY!"
COWARD!!
COME BACK HERE...SO I CAN... KILL...
THIS ONE IS FOR OLDŘICH. AND ONDŘEJKA.
KRAK
KSHINGG
THOO
SPLI

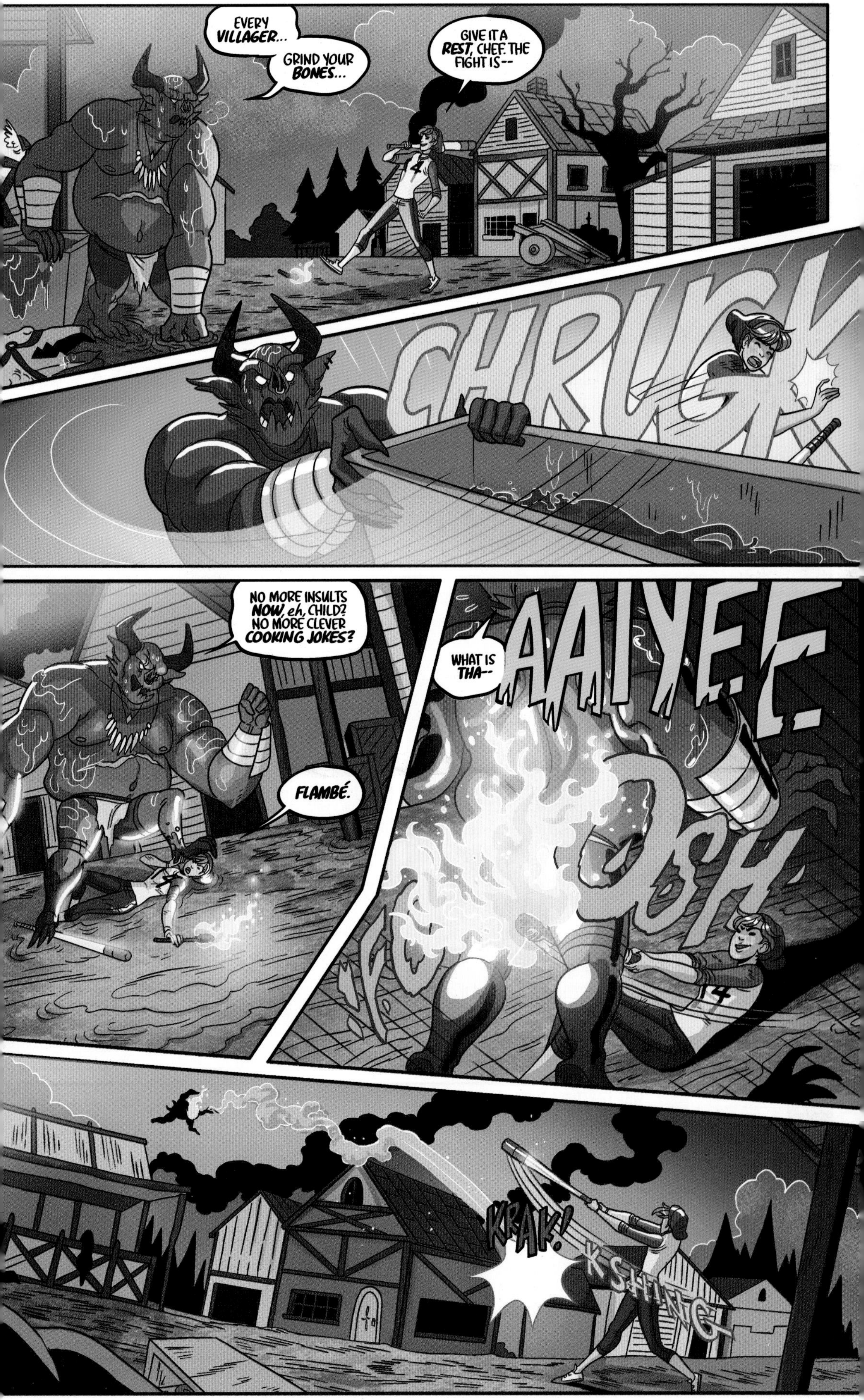
EVERY VILLAGER...
GRIND YOUR BONES...
GIVE IT A REST, CHEF. THE FIGHT IS--
CHRUSK
NO MORE INSULTS NOW, eh, CHILD? NO MORE CLEVER COOKING JOKES?
FLAMBÉ.
WHAT IS THA--
AAIYEE!
FOOSH
KRAK!
KSHING

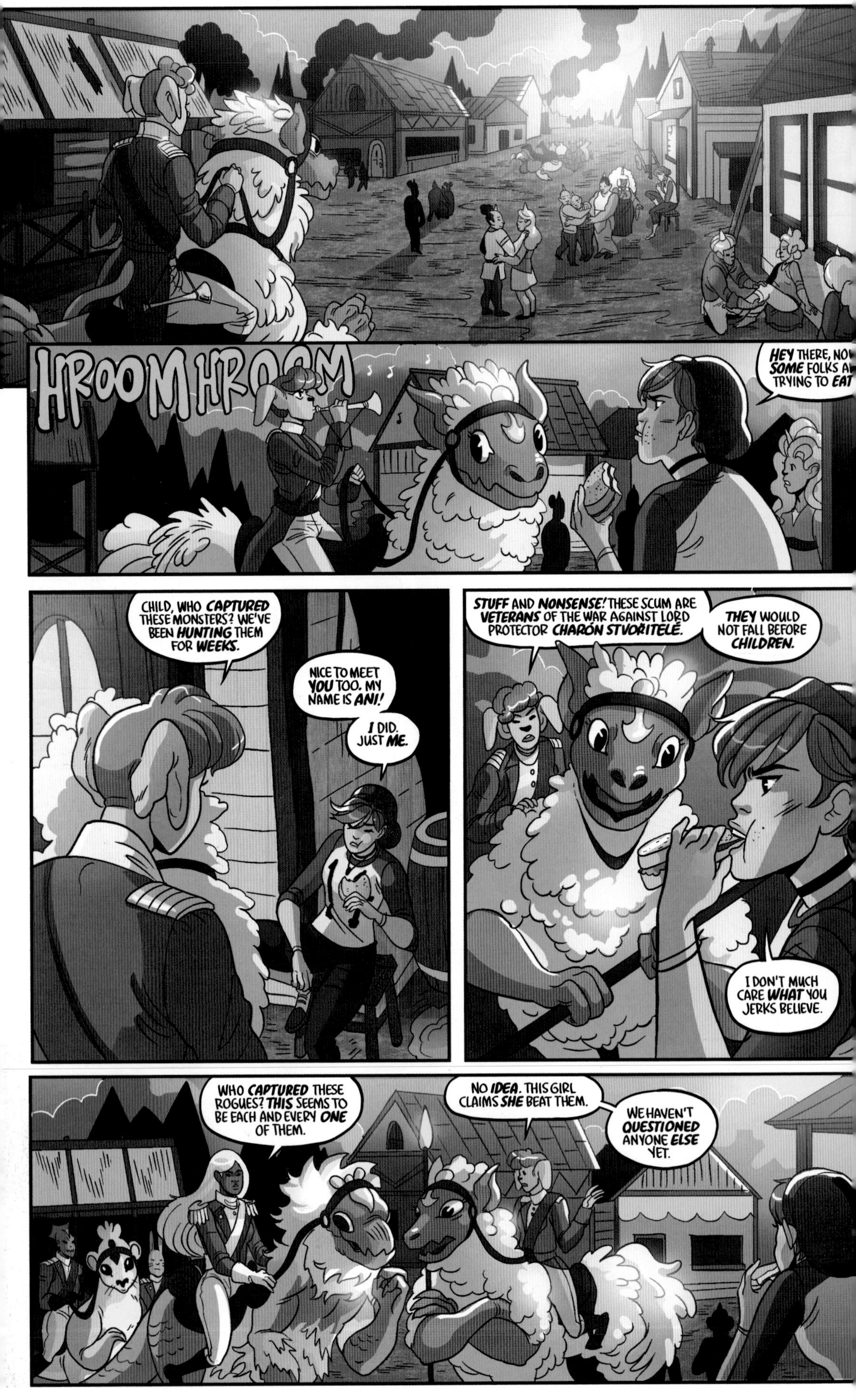
HROOM HROOM
HEY THERE, NO
SOME FOLKS A
TRYING TO EAT
CHILD, WHO CAPTURED THESE MONSTERS? WE'VE BEEN HUNTING THEM FOR WEEKS.
NICE TO MEET YOU TOO. MY NAME IS ANI!
I DID. JUST ME.
STUFF AND NONSENSE! THESE SCUM ARE VETERANS OF THE WAR AGAINST LORD PROTECTOR CHARÓN STVOŘITELÉ.
THEY WOULD NOT FALL BEFORE CHILDREN.
I DON'T MUCH CARE WHAT YOU JERKS BELIEVE.
WHO CAPTURED THESE ROGUES? THIS SEEMS TO BE EACH AND EVERY ONE OF THEM.
NO IDEA. THIS GIRL CLAIMS SHE BEAT THEM.
WE HAVEN'T QUESTIONED ANYONE ELSE YET.

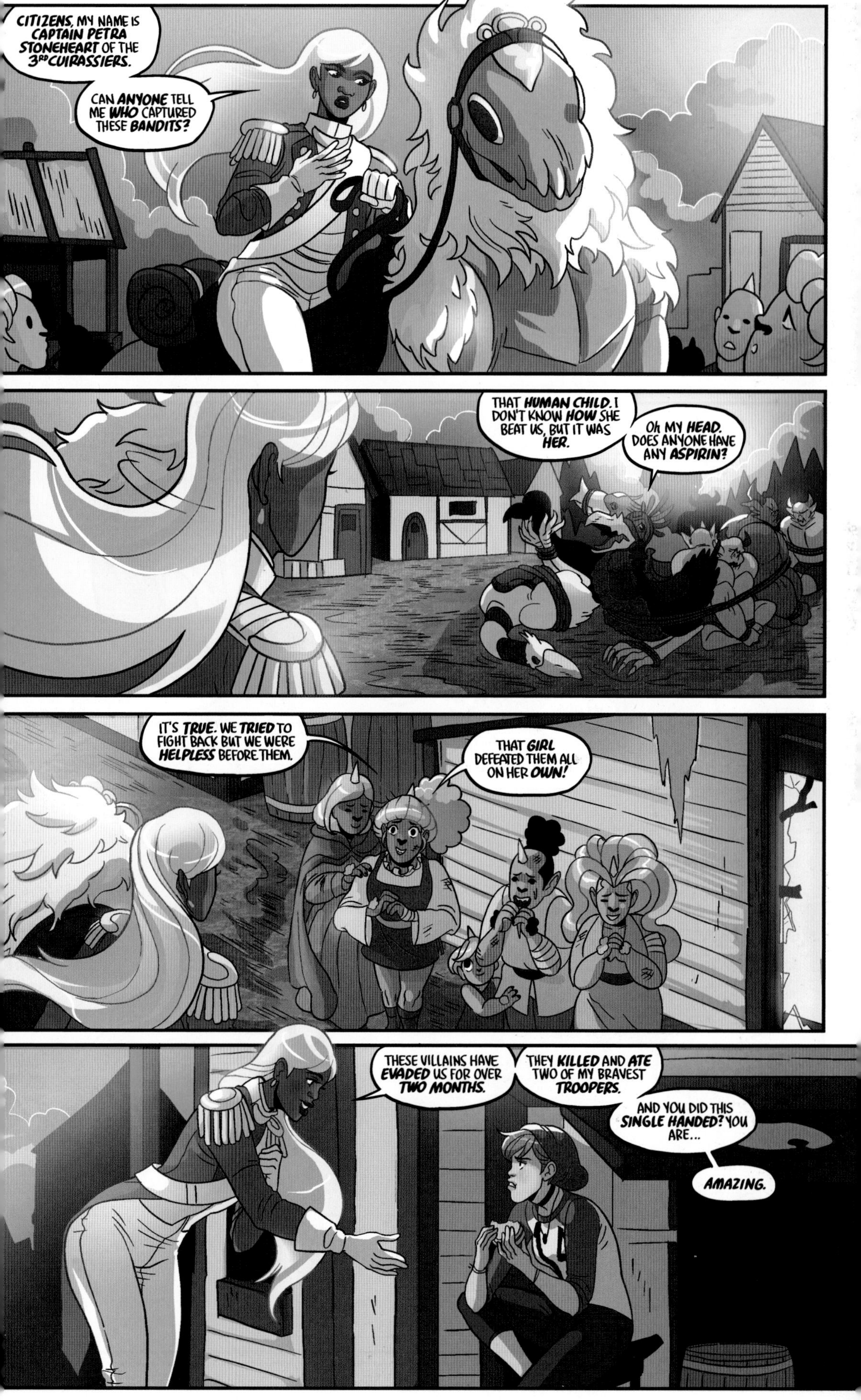
CITIZENS, MY NAME IS CAPTAIN PETRA STONEHEART OF THE 3RD CUIRASSIERS.
CAN ANYONE TELL ME WHO CAPTURED THESE BANDITS?
THAT HUMAN CHILD. I DON'T KNOW HOW SHE BEAT US, BUT IT WAS HER.
Oh MY HEAD. DOES ANYONE HAVE ANY ASPIRIN?
IT'S TRUE. WE TRIED TO FIGHT BACK BUT WE WERE HELPLESS BEFORE THEM.
THAT GIRL DEFEATED THEM ALL ON HER OWN!
THESE VILLAINS HAVE EVADED US FOR OVER TWO MONTHS.
THEY KILLED AND ATE TWO OF MY BRAVEST TROOPERS.
AND YOU DID THIS SINGLE HANDED? YOU ARE...
AMAZING.

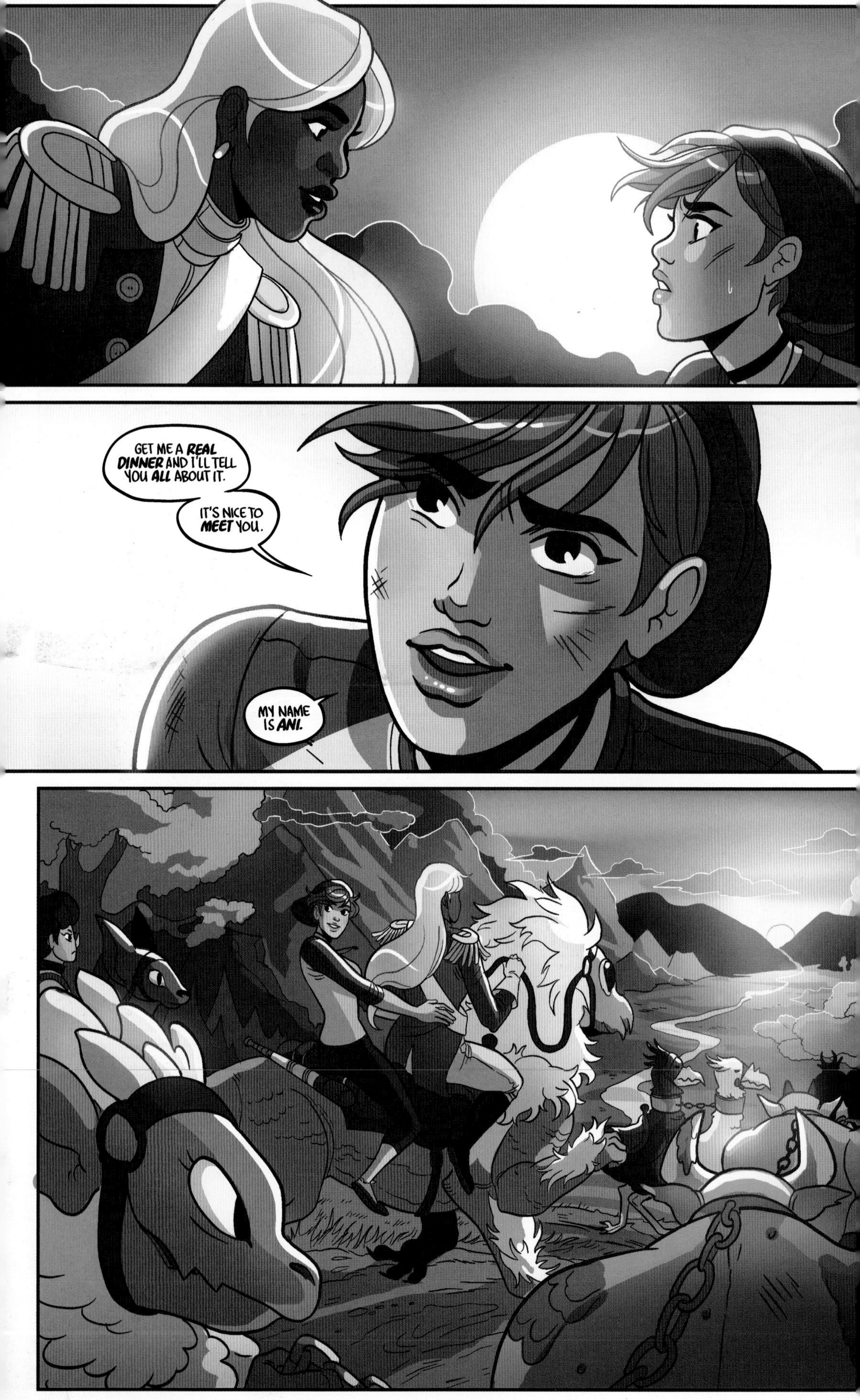
GET ME A REAL DINNER AND I'LL TELL YOU ALL ABOUT IT.
IT'S NICE TO MEET YOU.
MY NAME IS ANI.

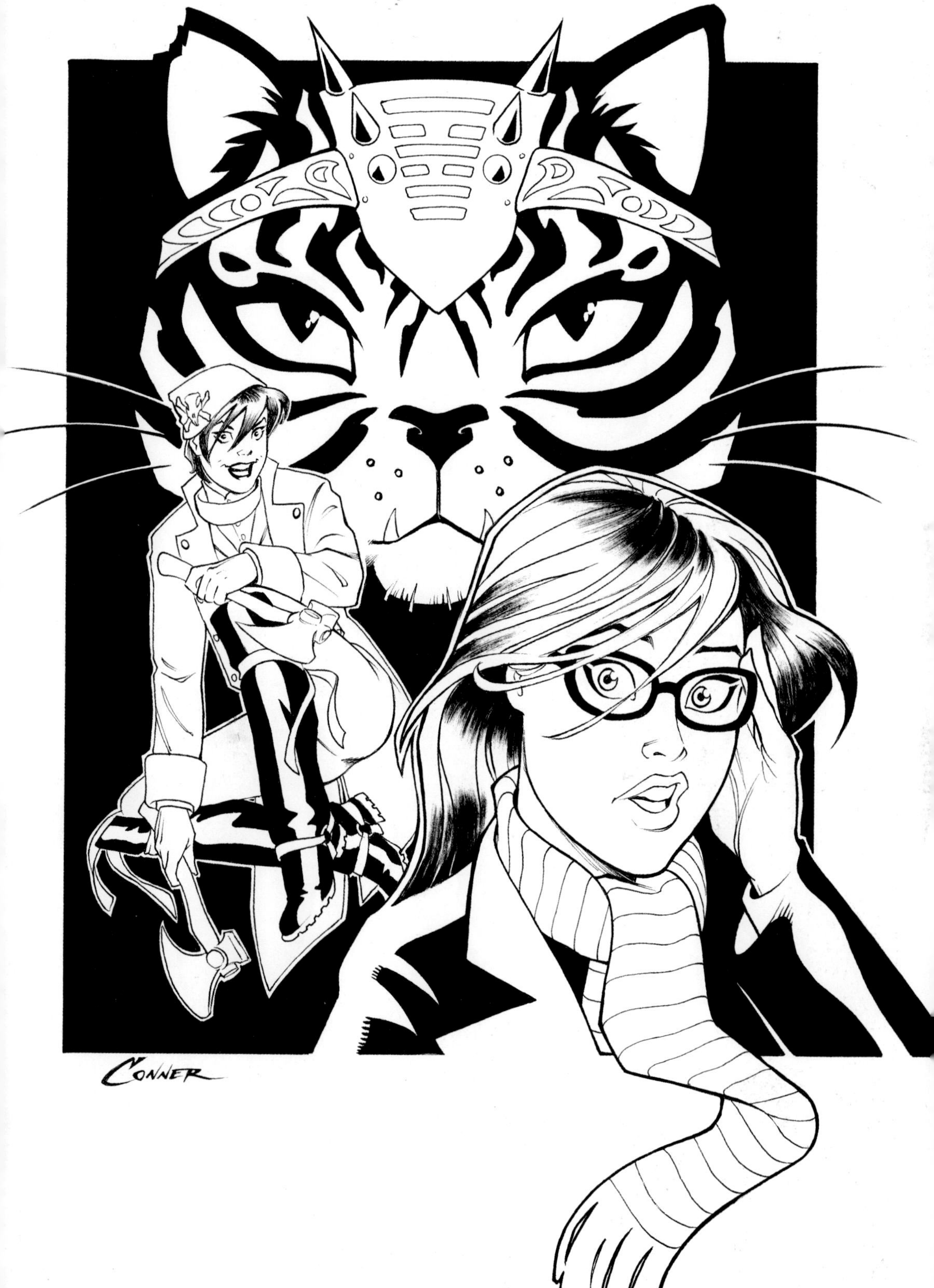
CONNER

AMANDA CONNER

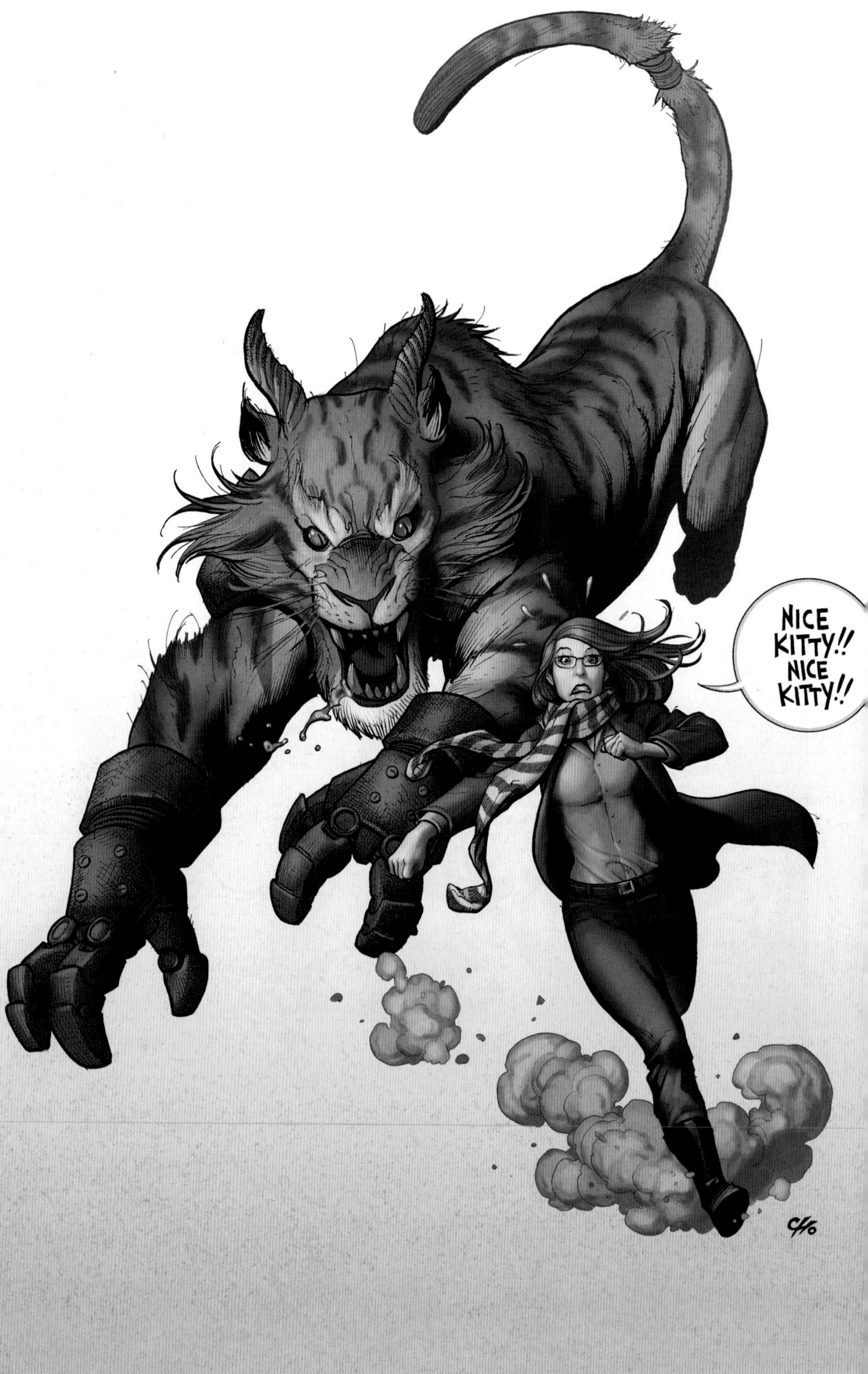
NICE KITTY!! NICE KITTY!!
CHO

FRANK CHO

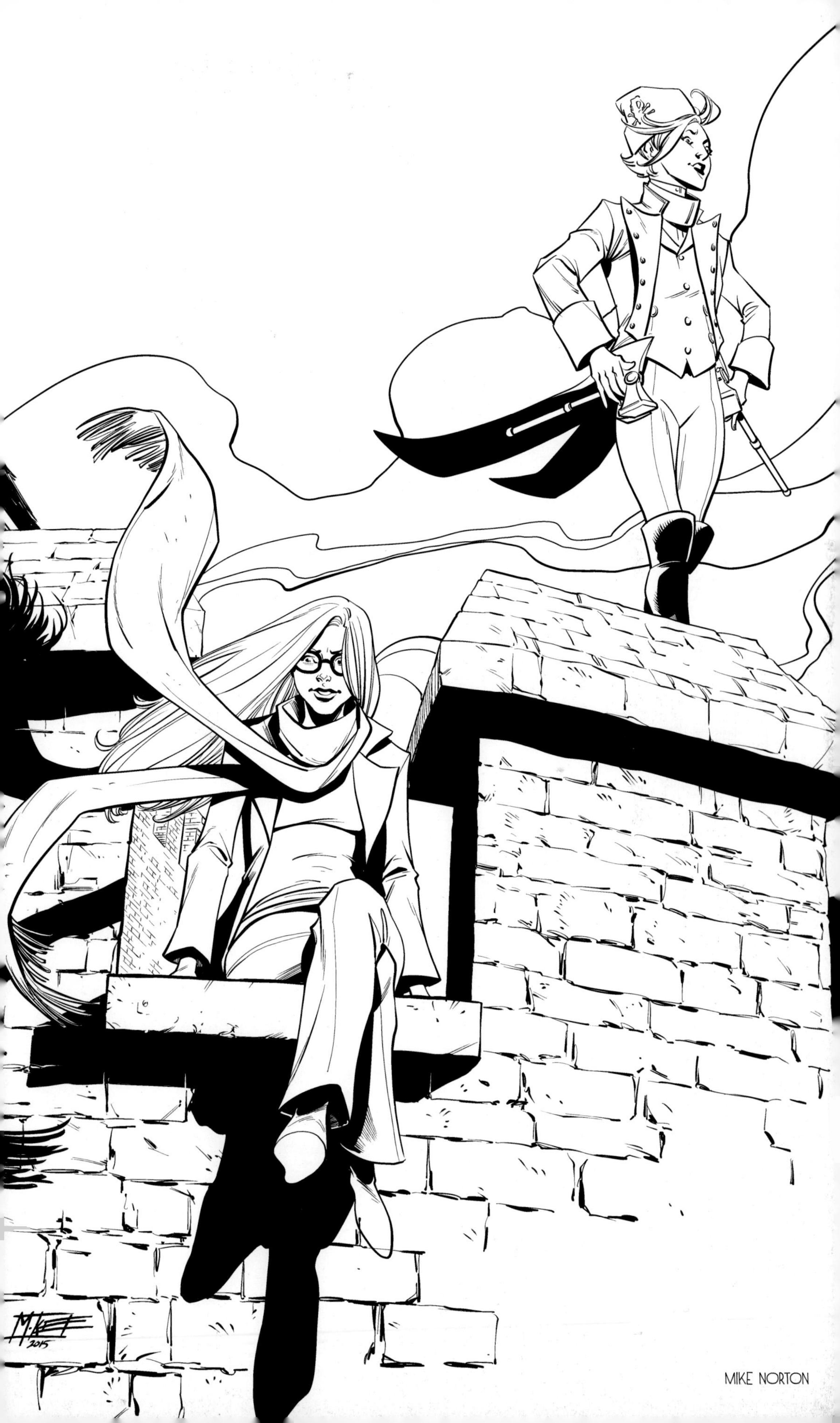

MIKE NORTON

BRANDON GRAHAM

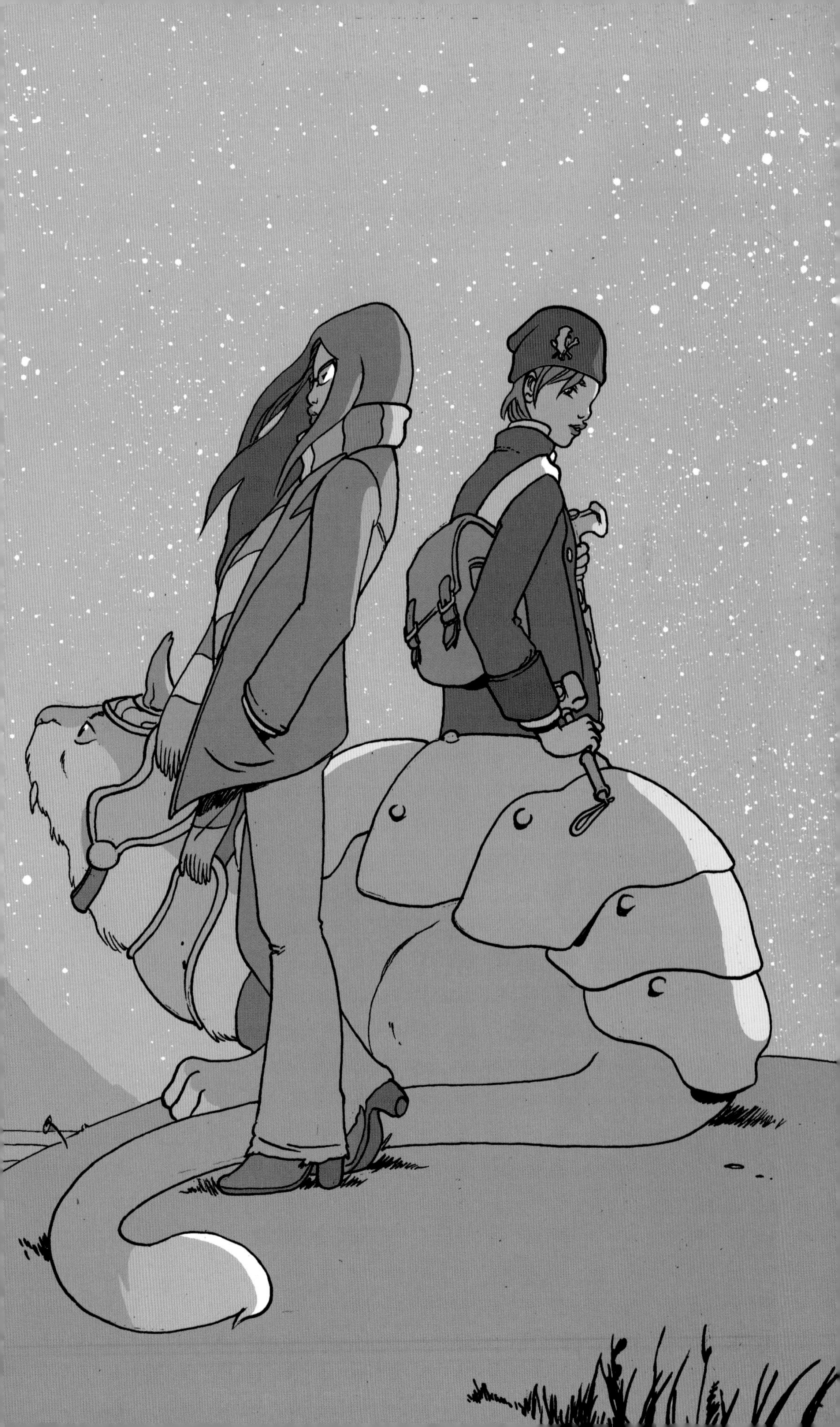

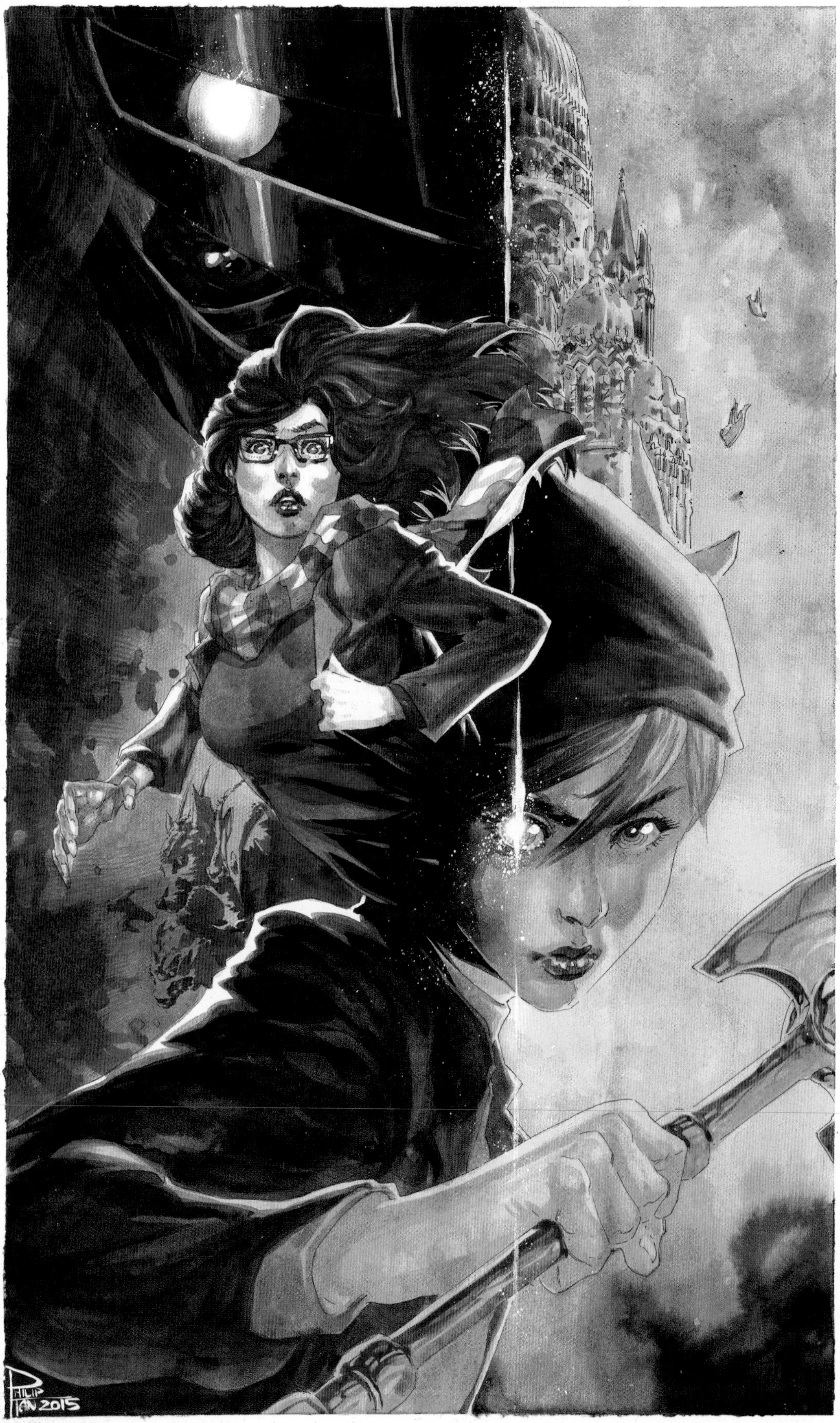
PHILIP TAN 2015

PHILIP TAN

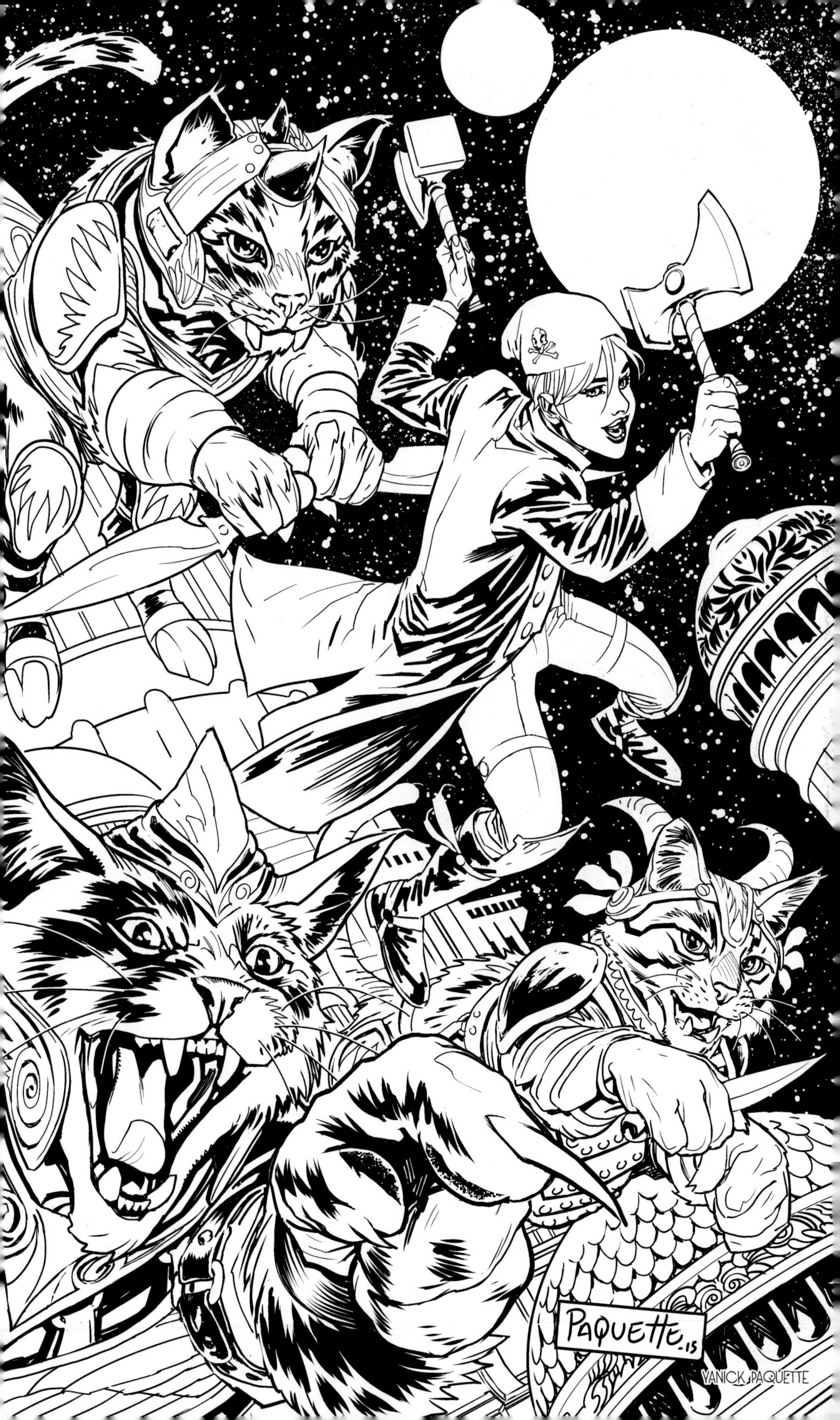
PAQUETTE.15
VANICK PAQUETTE

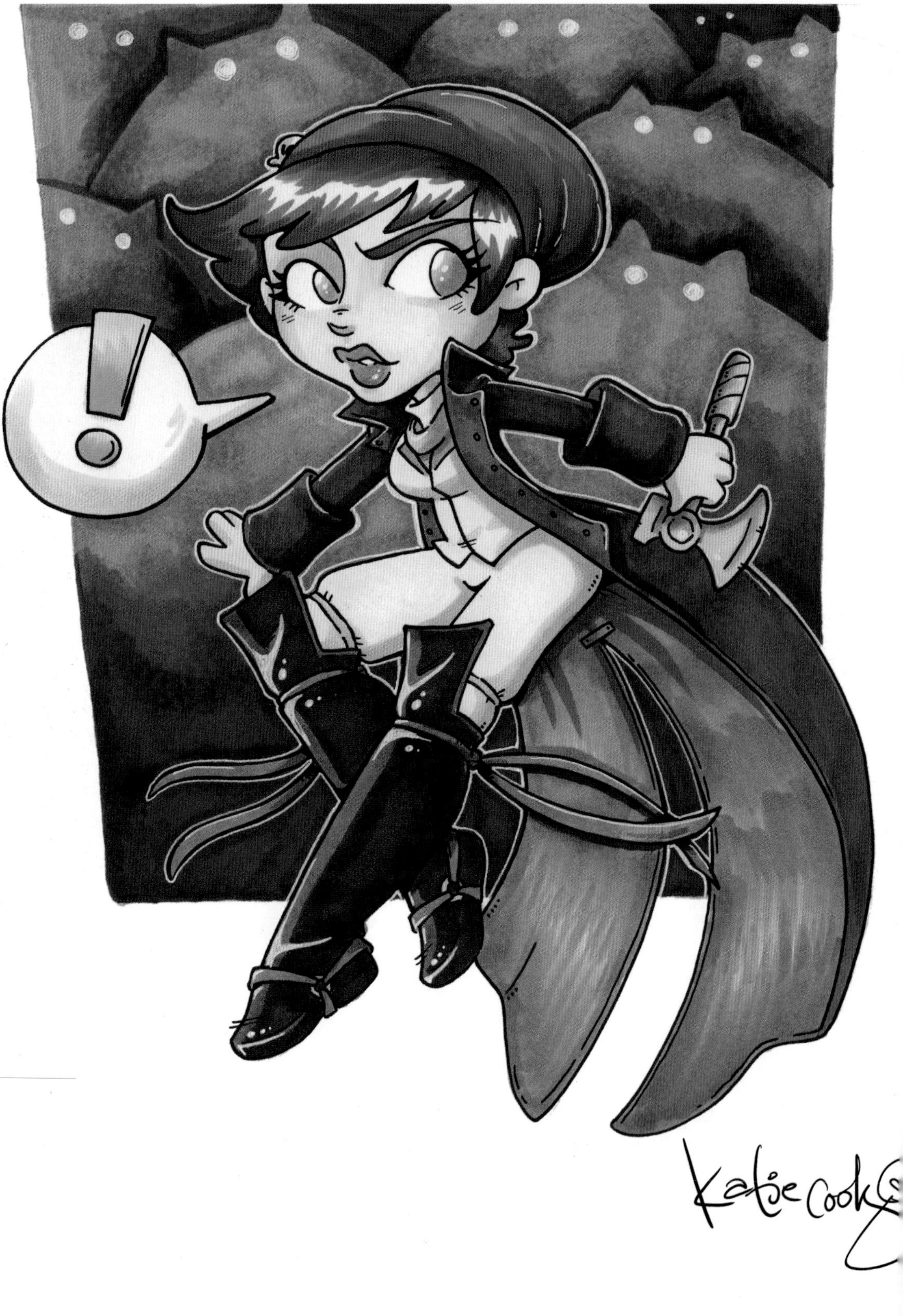
!

KATIE COOK

MARK BUCKINGHAM

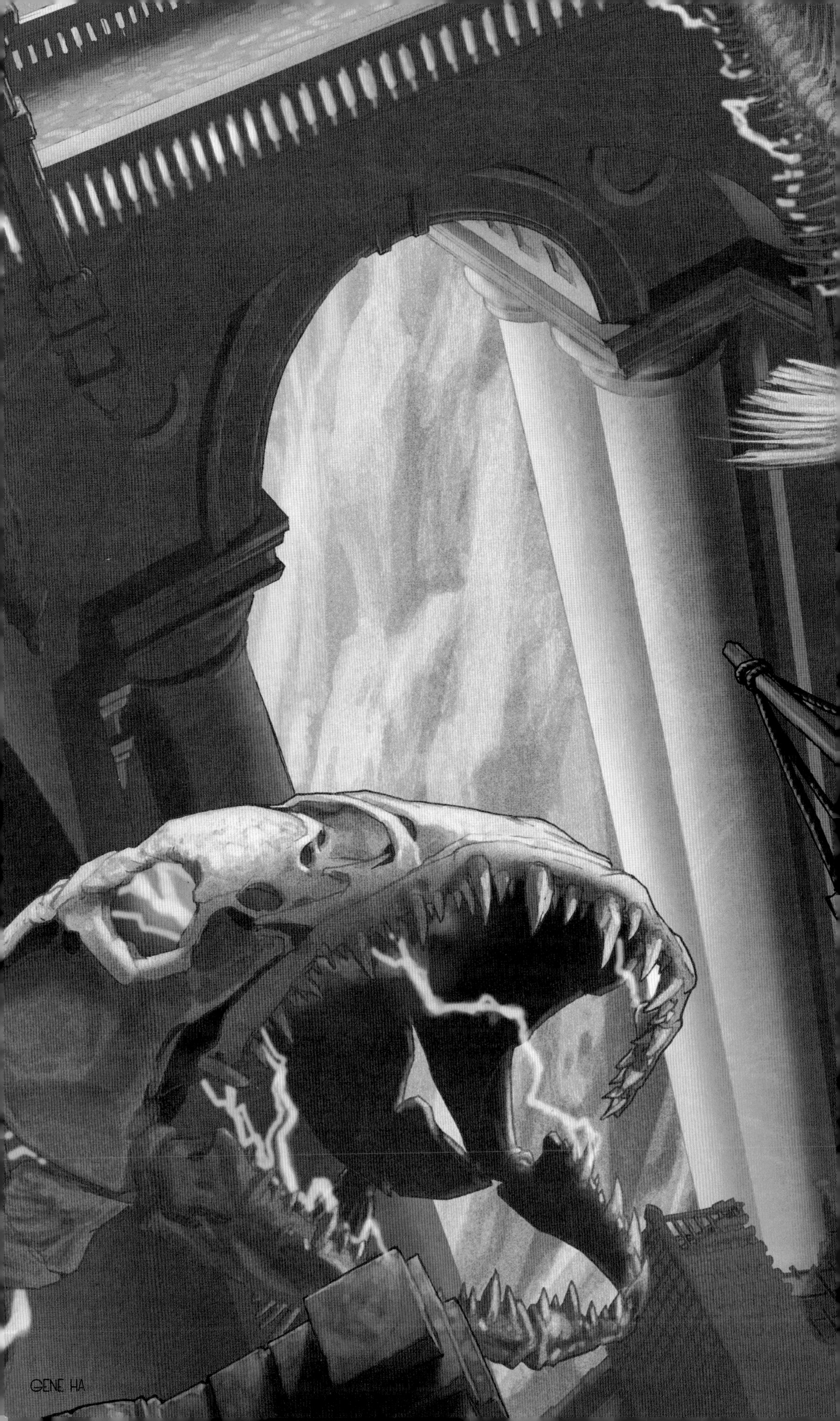
GENE HA

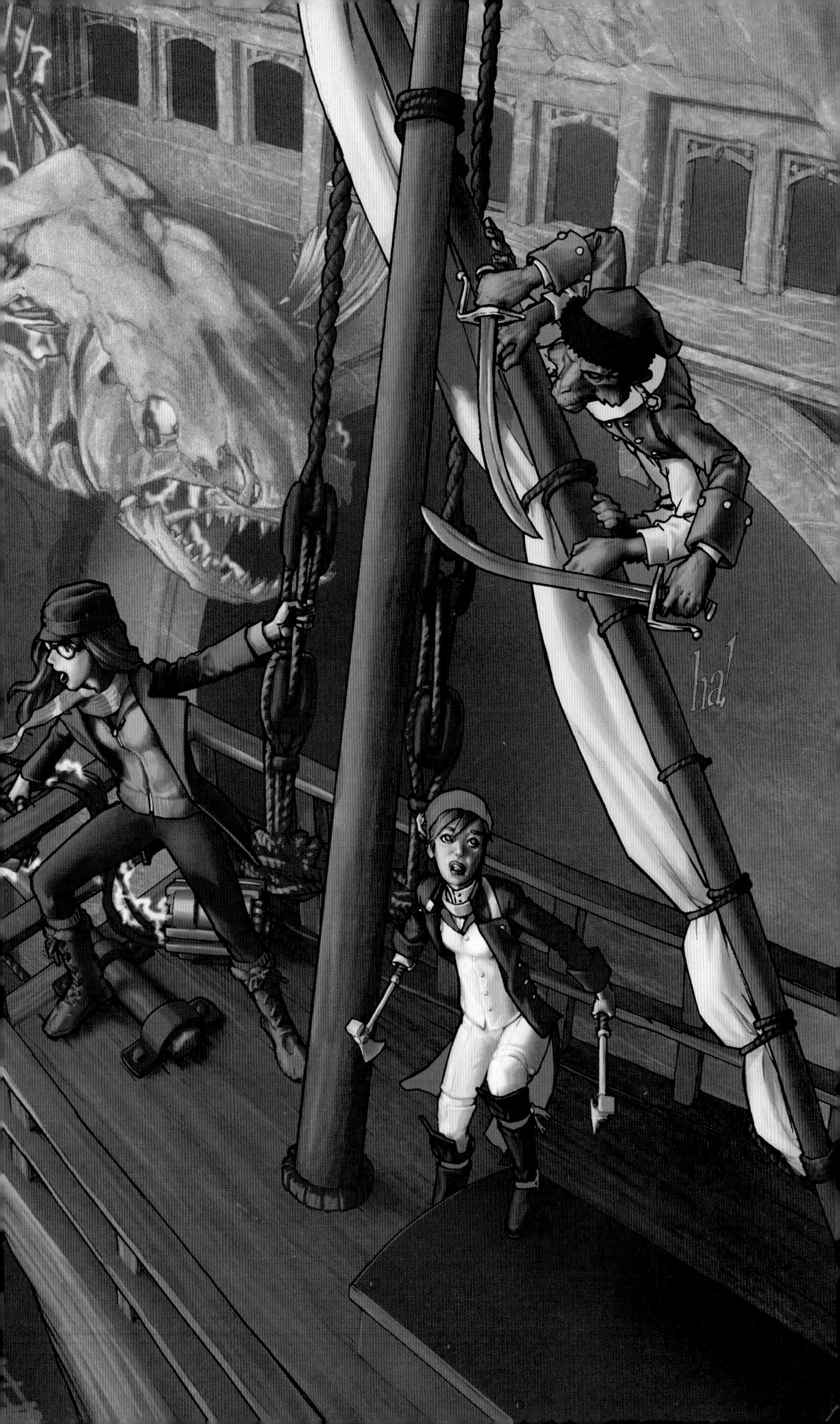
ha!

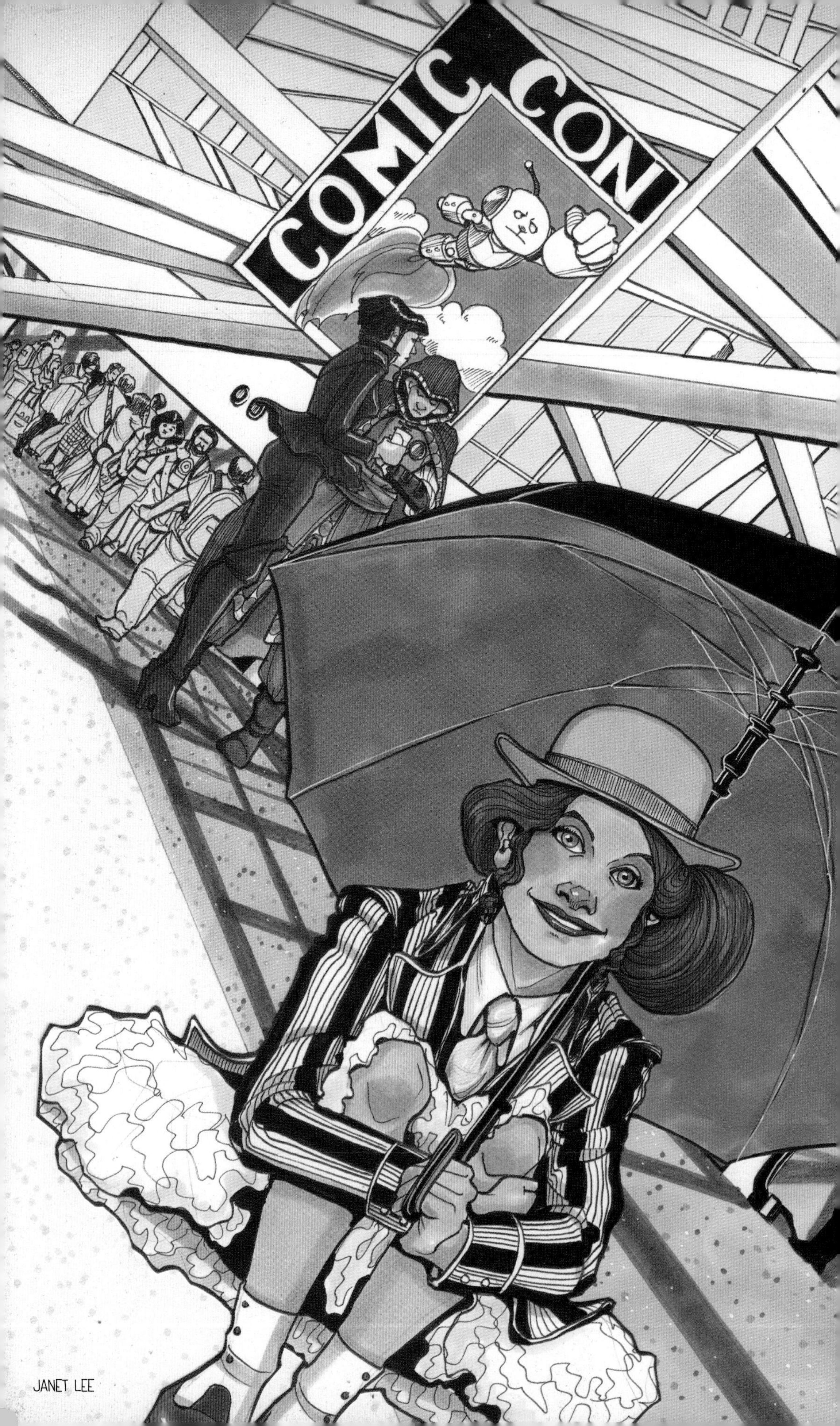
COMIC CON
JANET LEE

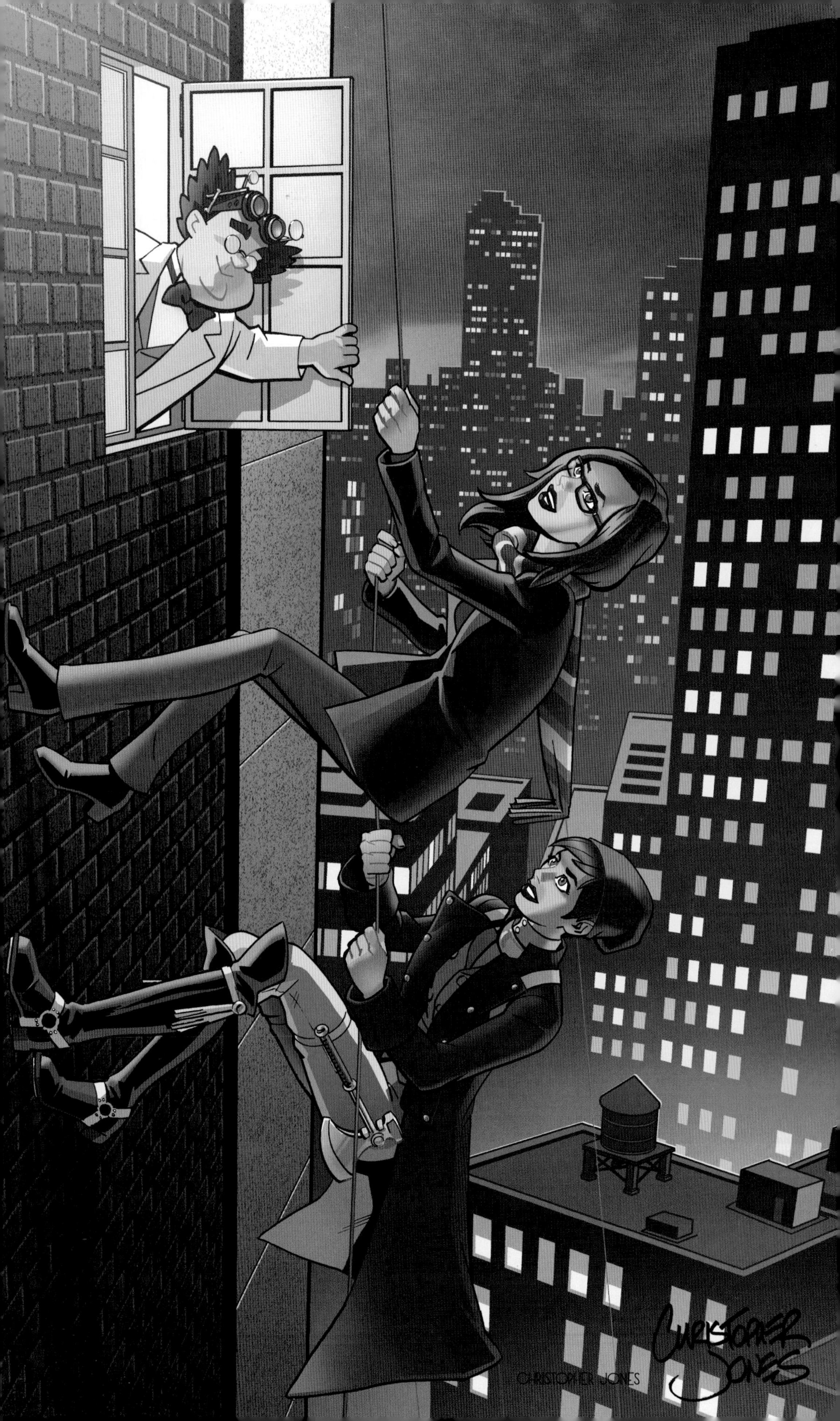
CHRISTOPHER JONES
©CHRISTOPHER JONES

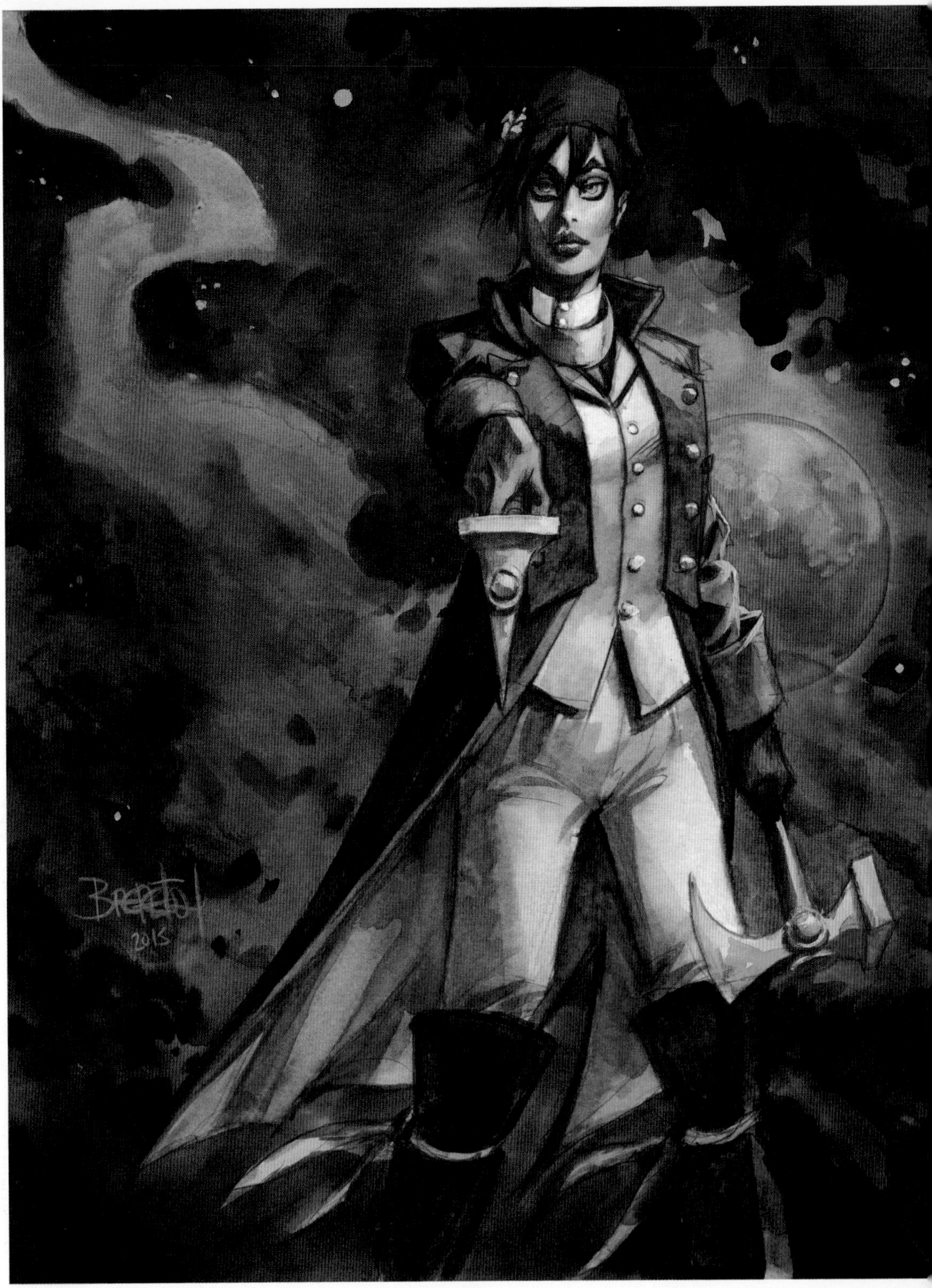

DAN BRERETON

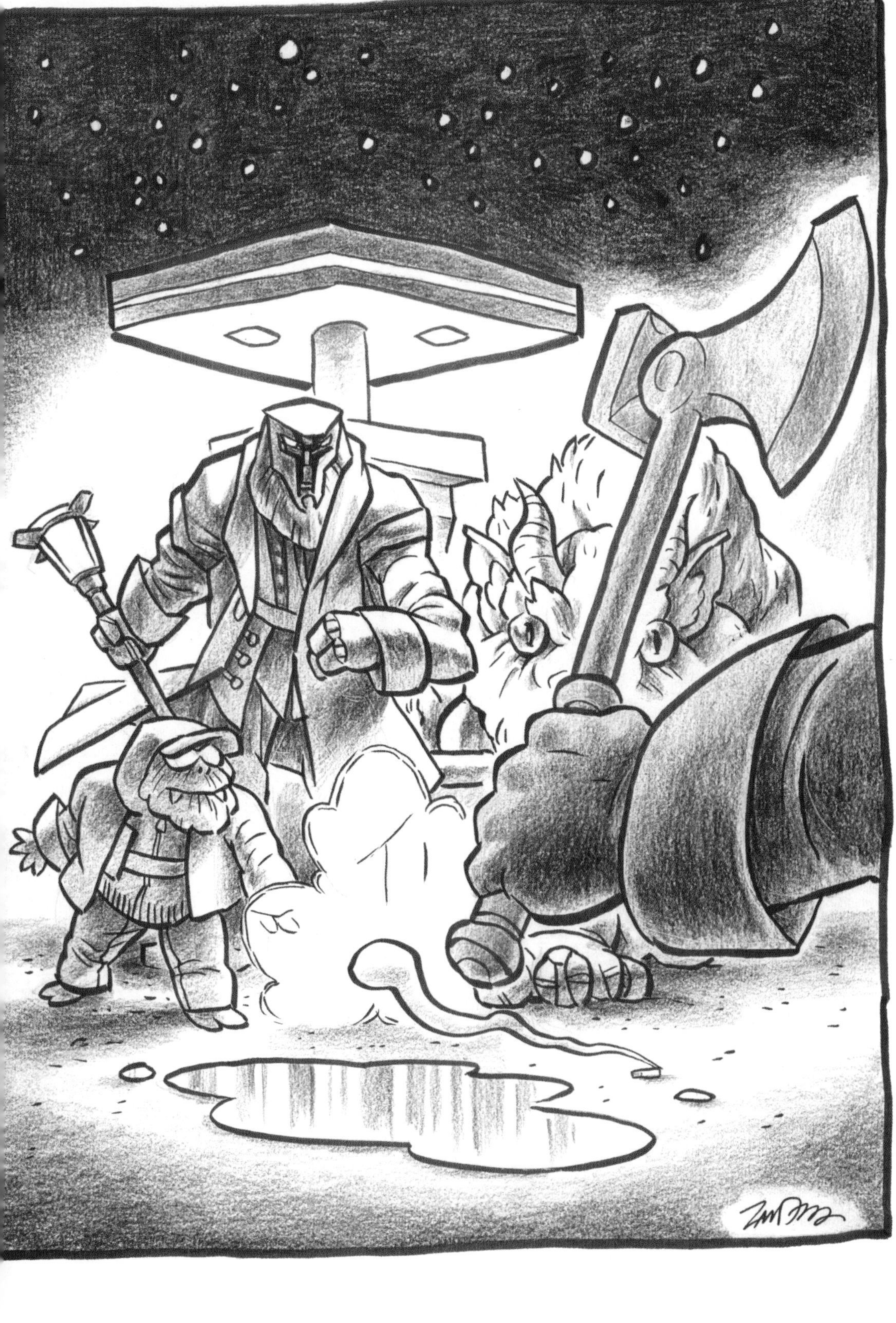

ZANDER CANNON

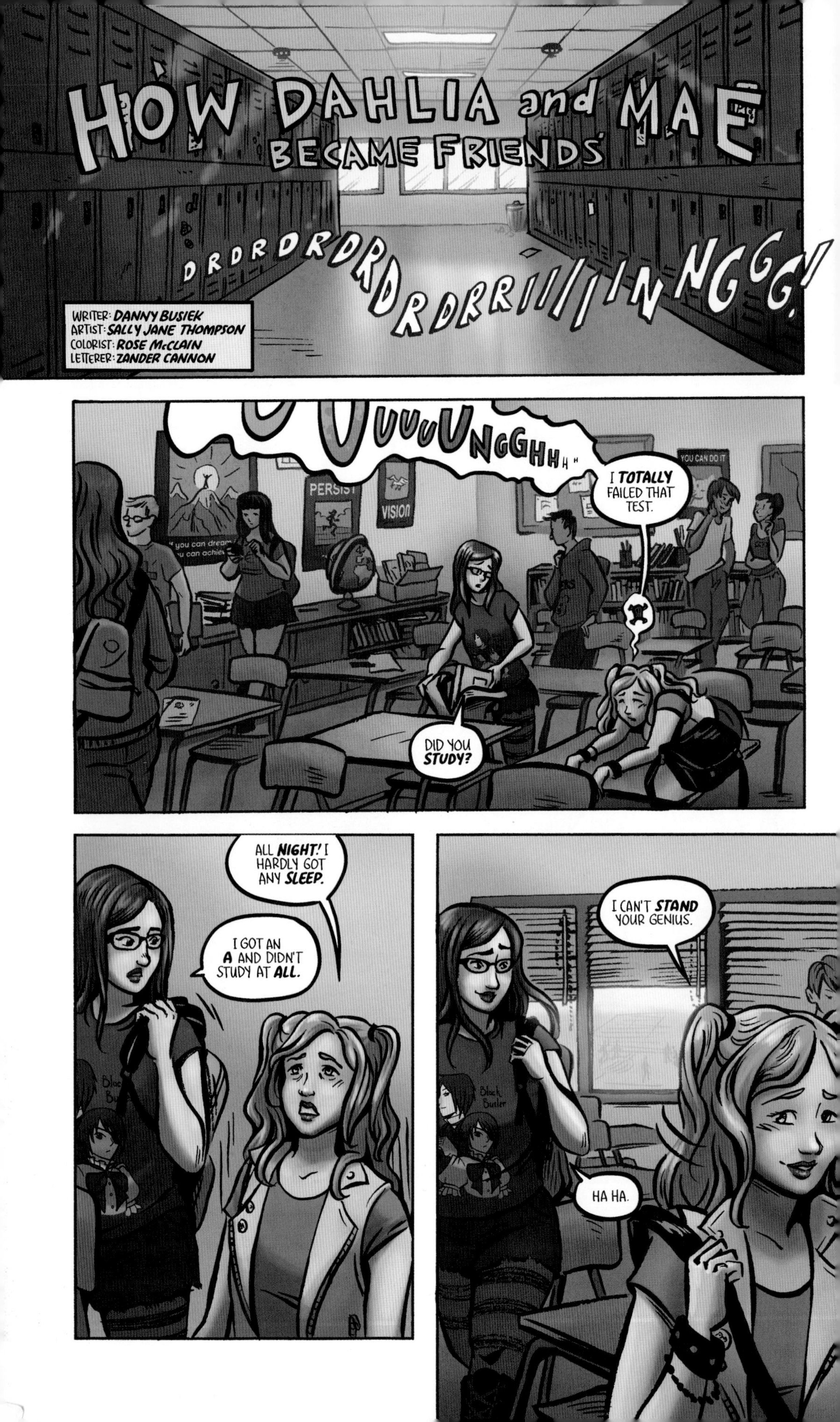
HOW DAHLIA and MAE BECAME FRIENDS
DRDRDRDRDRDRDRRIIIIIINNGGG!
WRITER: DANNY BUSIEK
ARTIST: SALLY JANE THOMPSON
COLORIST: ROSE McCLAIN
LETTERER: ZANDER CANNON
UUUUUNGGHHHH
PERSIST
VISION
YOU CAN DO IT
I TOTALLY FAILED THAT TEST.
DID YOU STUDY?
ALL NIGHT! I HARDLY GOT ANY SLEEP.
I GOT AN A AND DIDN'T STUDY AT ALL.
Black Butler
I CAN'T STAND YOUR GENIUS.
HA HA.

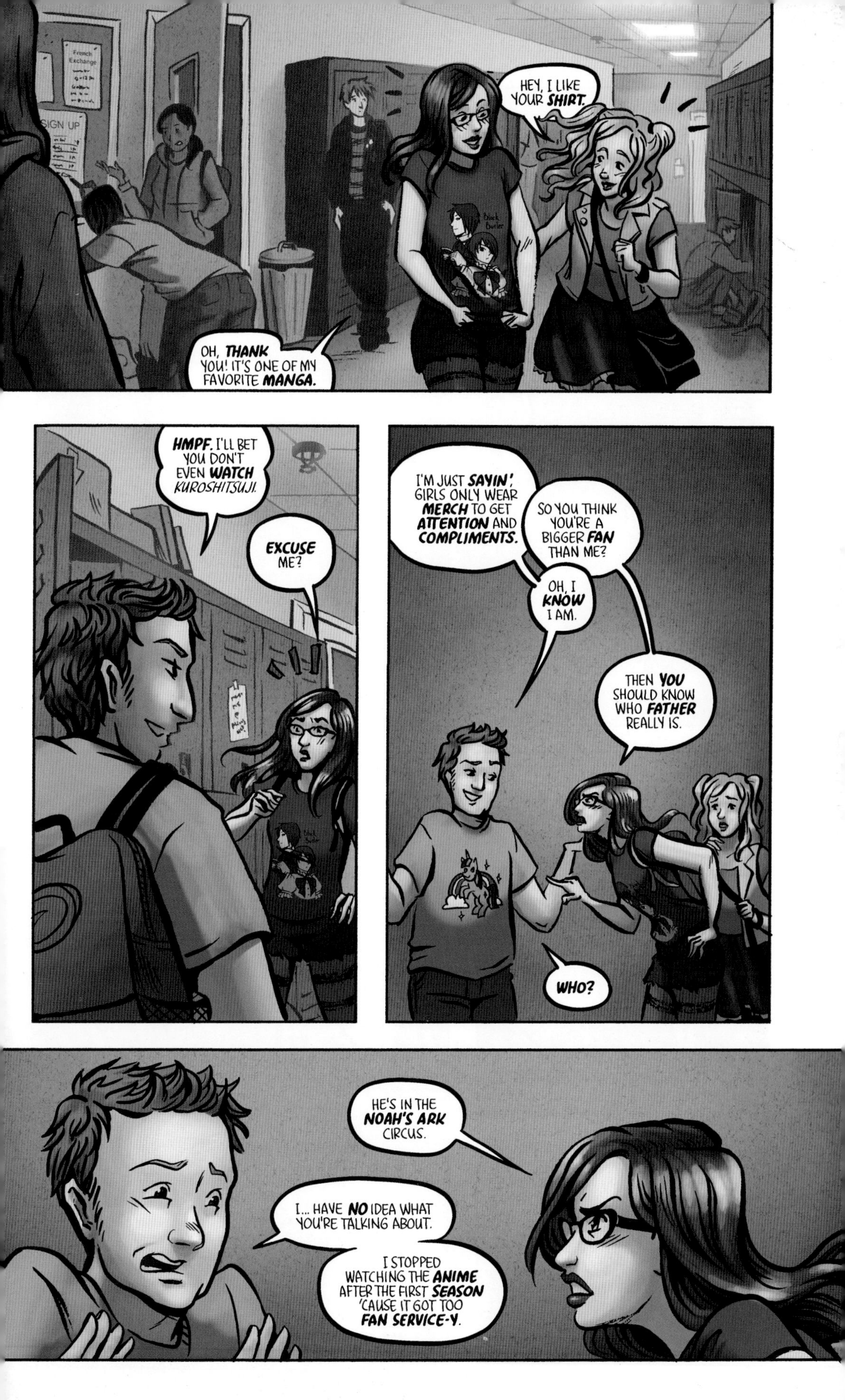

HEY, I LIKE YOUR SHIRT.
OH, THANK YOU! IT'S ONE OF MY FAVORITE MANGA.
HMPF. I'LL BET YOU DON'T EVEN WATCH KUROSHITSUJI.
EXCUSE ME?
I'M JUST SAYIN', GIRLS ONLY WEAR MERCH TO GET ATTENTION AND COMPLIMENTS.
SO YOU THINK YOU'RE A BIGGER FAN THAN ME?
OH, I KNOW I AM.
THEN YOU SHOULD KNOW WHO FATHER REALLY IS.
WHO?
HE'S IN THE NOAH'S ARK CIRCUS.
I... HAVE NO IDEA WHAT YOU'RE TALKING ABOUT.
I STOPPED WATCHING THE ANIME AFTER THE FIRST SEASON 'CAUSE IT GOT TOO FAN SERVICE-Y.

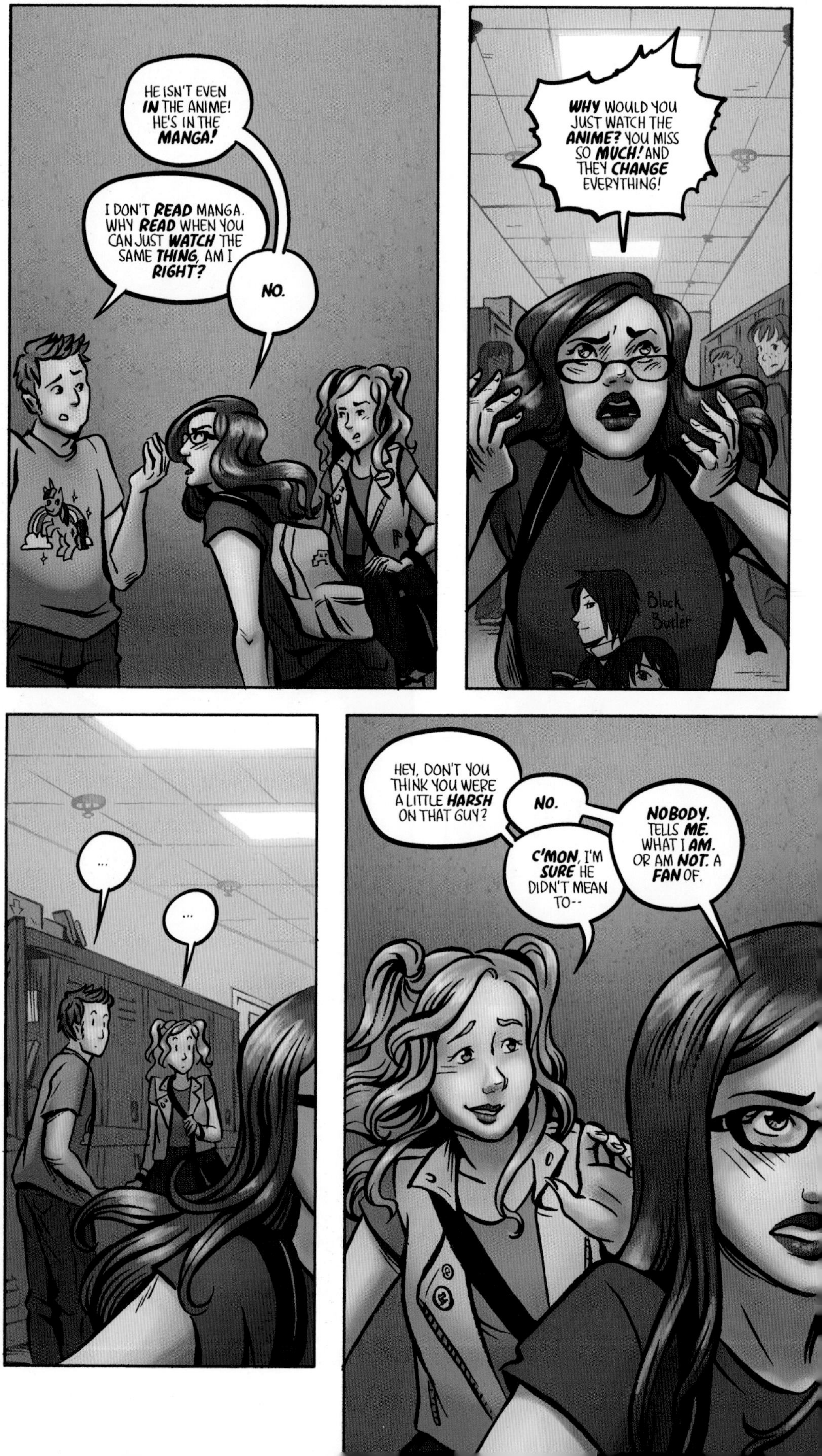
HE ISN'T EVEN **IN** THE ANIME! HE'S IN THE **MANGA!**
I DON'T **READ** MANGA. WHY **READ** WHEN YOU CAN JUST **WATCH** THE SAME **THING**, AM I **RIGHT?**
NO.
WHY WOULD YOU JUST WATCH THE **ANIME?** YOU MISS SO **MUCH!** AND THEY **CHANGE** EVERYTHING!
Black Butler
...
...
HEY, DON'T YOU THINK YOU WERE A LITTLE **HARSH** ON THAT GUY?
NO.
C'MON, I'M **SURE** HE DIDN'T MEAN TO--
NOBODY. TELLS **ME.** WHAT I **AM.** OR AM **NOT.** A **FAN** OF.

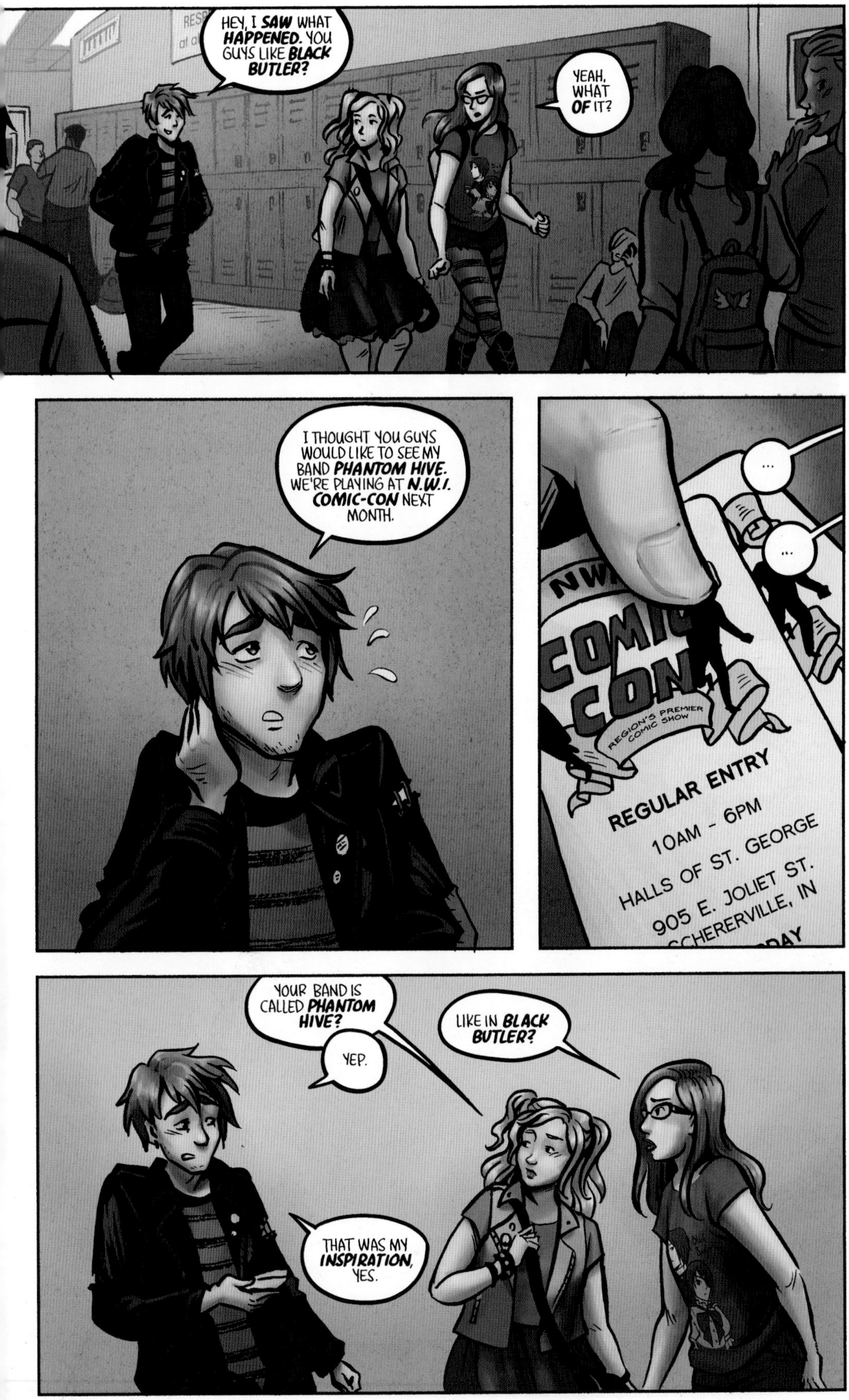
HEY, I SAW WHAT HAPPENED. YOU GUYS LIKE BLACK BUTLER?
YEAH, WHAT OF IT?
I THOUGHT YOU GUYS WOULD LIKE TO SEE MY BAND PHANTOM HIVE. WE'RE PLAYING AT N.W.I. COMIC-CON NEXT MONTH.
...
...
NWI
COMIC CON
REGION'S PREMIER COMIC SHOW
REGULAR ENTRY
10AM - 6PM
HALLS OF ST. GEORGE
905 E. JOLIET ST.
SCHERERVILLE, IN
YOUR BAND IS CALLED PHANTOM HIVE?
YEP.
LIKE IN BLACK BUTLER?
THAT WAS MY INSPIRATION, YES.

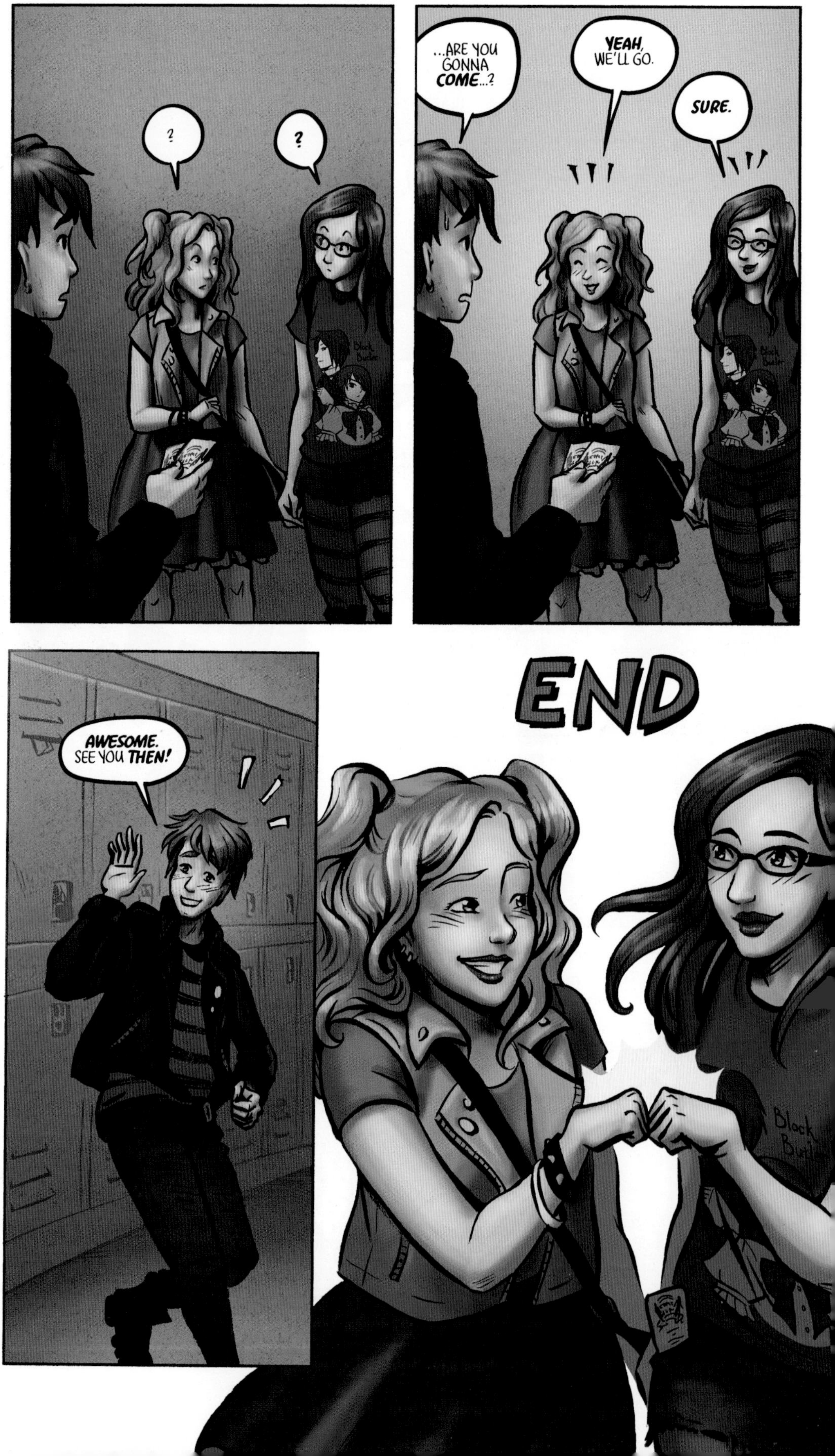
?
?
...ARE YOU GONNA COME...?
YEAH, WE'LL GO.
SURE.
AWESOME. SEE YOU THEN!
END

Mae BE SO, Mae BE NOT

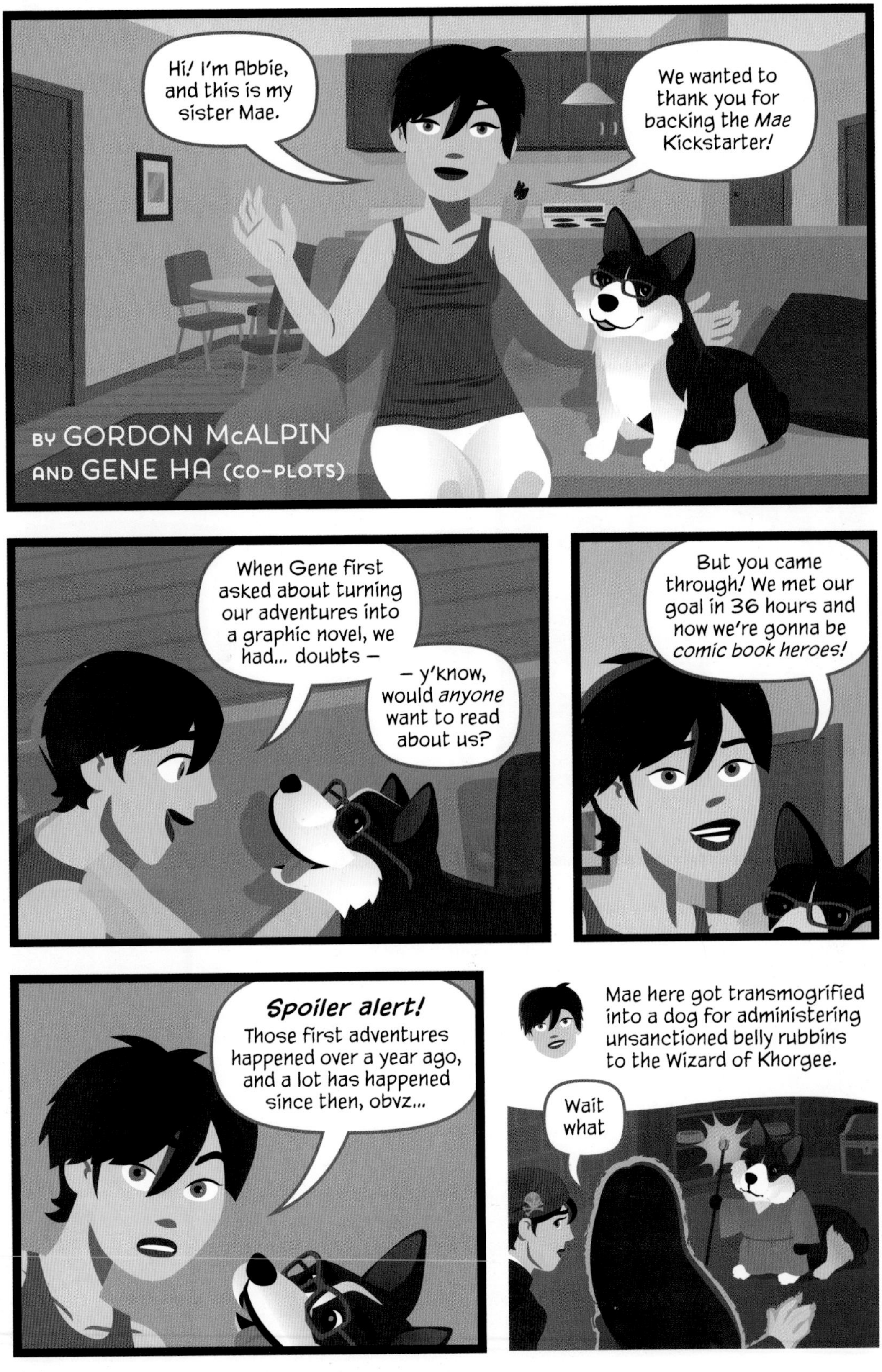

Hi! I'm Abbie, and this is my sister Mae.
We wanted to thank you for backing the *Mae* Kickstarter!
BY GORDON McALPIN AND GENE HA (CO-PLOTS)
When Gene first asked about turning our adventures into a graphic novel, we had... doubts –
– y'know, would *anyone* want to read about us?
But you came through! We met our goal in 36 hours and now we're gonna be *comic book heroes!*
Spoiler alert! Those first adventures happened over a year ago, and a lot has happened since then, obvz...
Mae here got transmogrified into a dog for administering unsanctioned belly rubbins to the Wizard of Khorgee.
Wait what

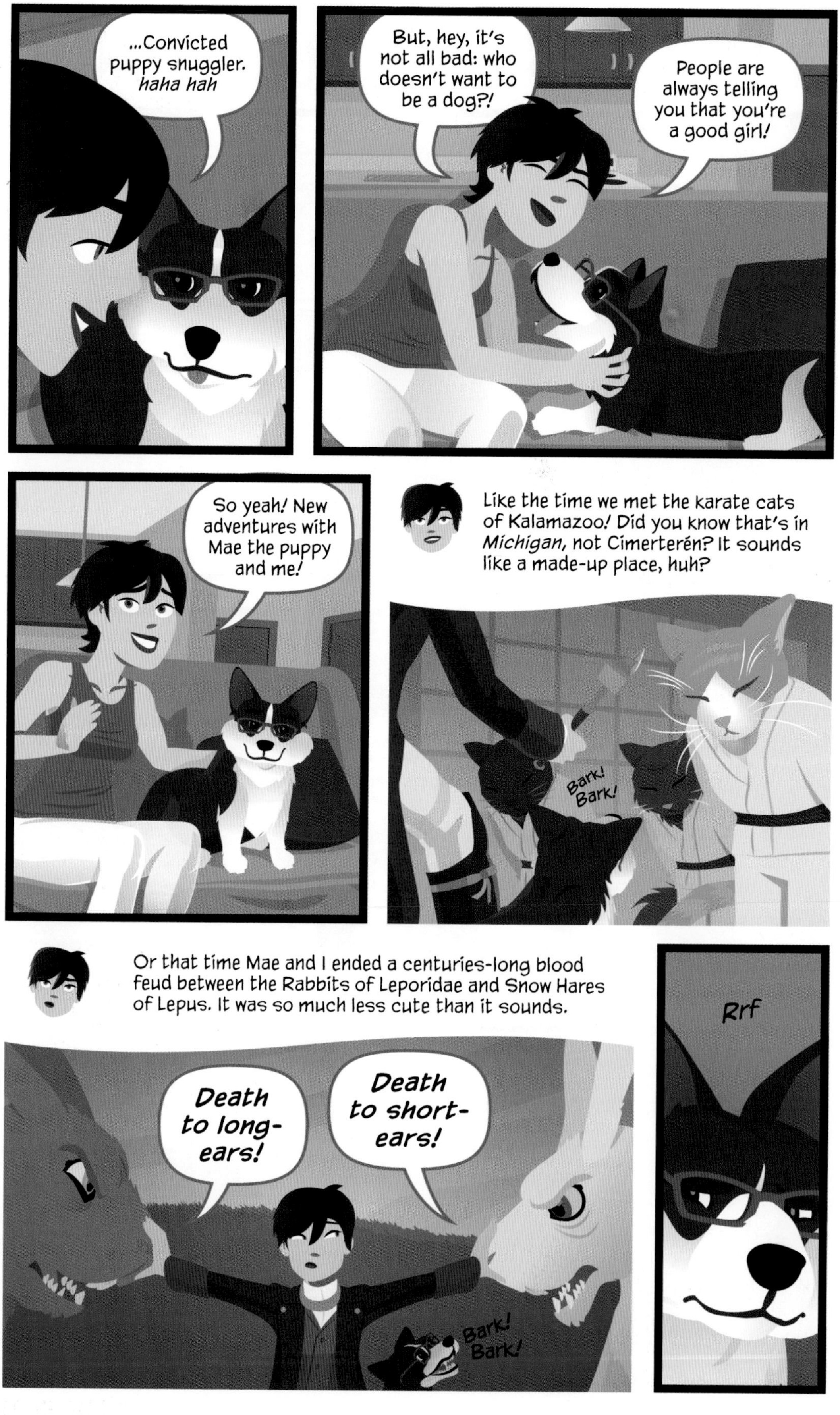

...Convicted puppy snuggler. *haha hah*
But, hey, it's not all bad: who doesn't want to be a dog?!
People are always telling you that you're a good girl!
So yeah! New adventures with Mae the puppy and me!
Like the time we met the karate cats of Kalamazoo! Did you know that's in *Michigan*, not Cimerterén? It sounds like a made-up place, huh?
Bark! Bark!
Or that time Mae and I ended a centuries-long blood feud between the Rabbits of Leporidae and Snow Hares of Lepus. It was so much less cute than it sounds.
Death to long-ears!
Death to short-ears!
Bark! Bark!
Rrf

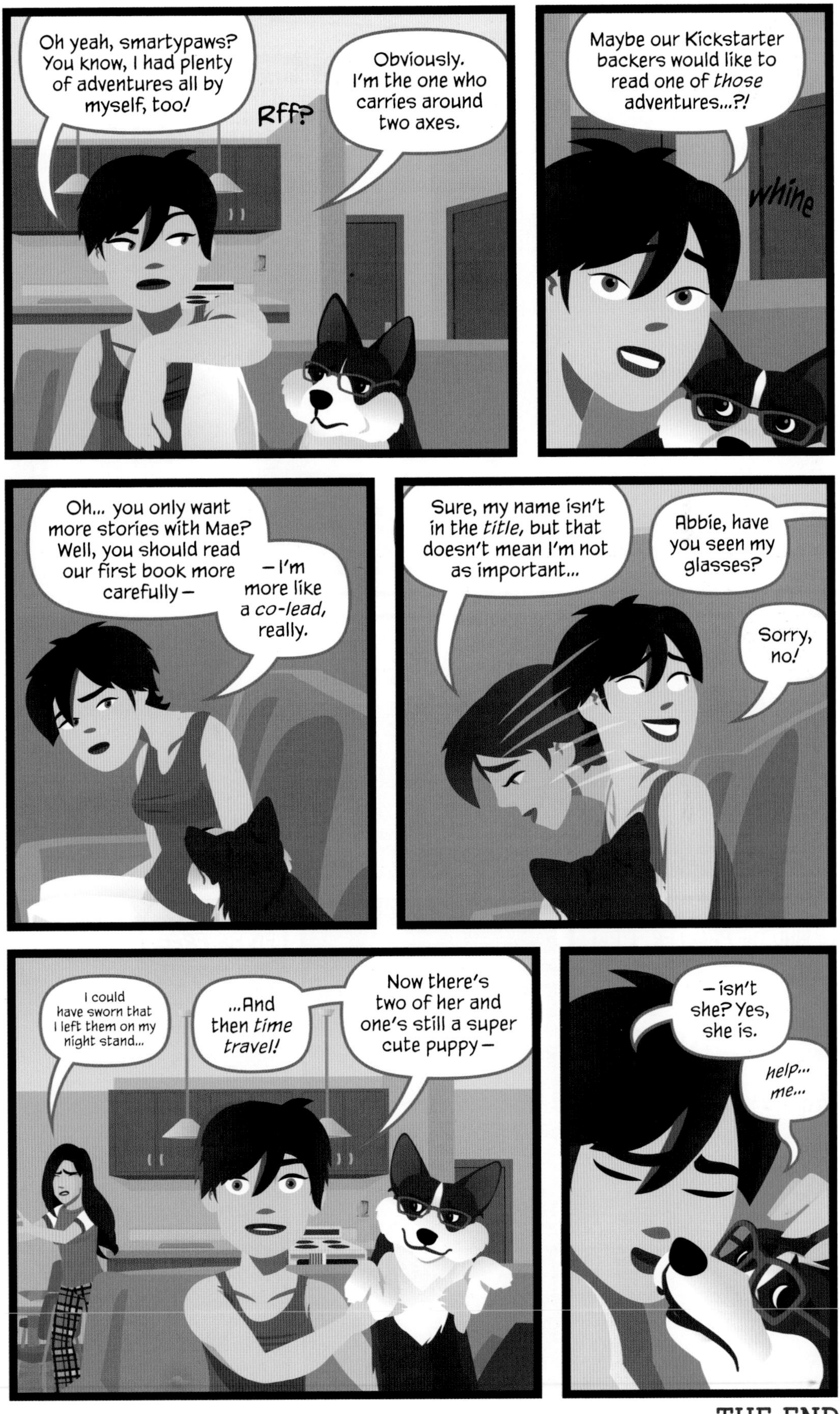
Oh yeah, smartypaws? You know, I had plenty of adventures all by myself, too!
Rff?
Obviously. I'm the one who carries around two axes.
Maybe our Kickstarter backers would like to read one of *those* adventures...?!
whine
Oh... you only want more stories with Mae? Well, you should read our first book more carefully—
—I'm more like a *co-lead,* really.
Sure, my name isn't in the *title,* but that doesn't mean I'm not as important...
Abbie, have you seen my glasses?
Sorry, no!
I could have sworn that I left them on my night stand...
...And then *time travel!*
Now there's two of her and one's still a super cute puppy—
—isn't she? Yes, she is.
help... me...

THE END

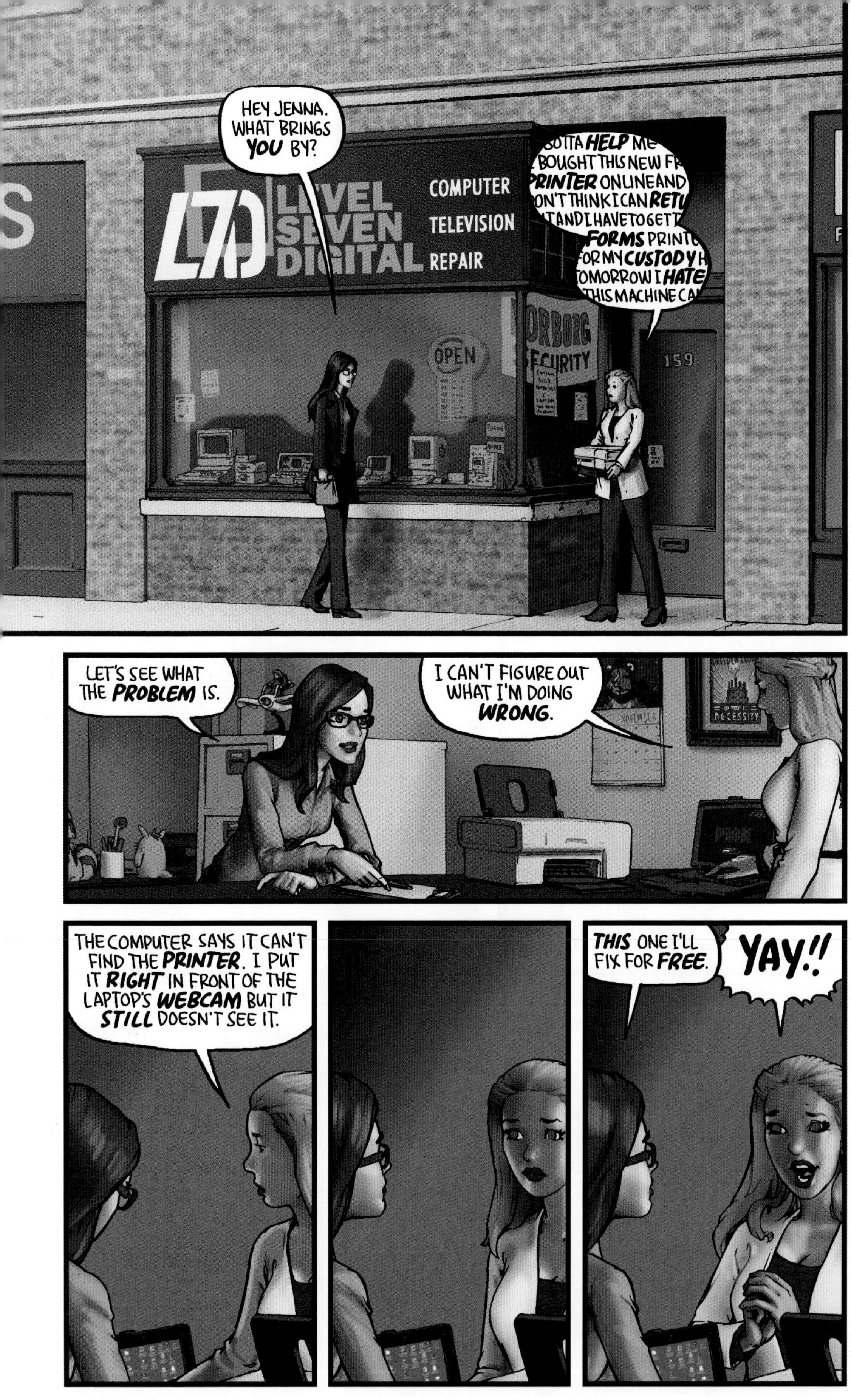
HEY JENNA. WHAT BRINGS YOU BY?
LEVEL SEVEN DIGITAL
COMPUTER
TELEVISION
REPAIR
OPEN
SECURITY
159
OTTA HELP ME
BOUGHT THIS NEW
PRINTER ONLINE AND
ON'T THINK I CAN
T AND I HAVE TO GET
FORMS PRINT
FOR MY CUSTODY
TOMORROW I HATE
THIS MACHINE
LET'S SEE WHAT THE PROBLEM IS.
I CAN'T FIGURE OUT WHAT I'M DOING WRONG.
NECESSITY
THE COMPUTER SAYS IT CAN'T FIND THE PRINTER. I PUT IT RIGHT IN FRONT OF THE LAPTOP'S WEBCAM BUT IT STILL DOESN'T SEE IT.
THIS ONE I'LL FIX FOR FREE.
YAY!!

Mae™

Sketchbook
Notes by Gene Ha

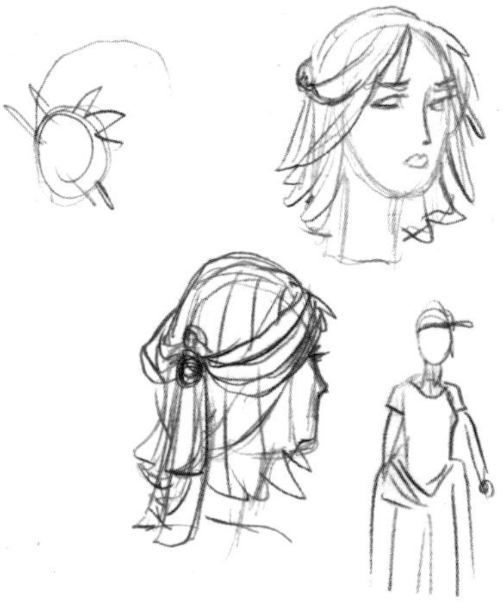

hen I first imagined this story, Mae was t the main character. The hero was Ani orrow, and her down-to-earth techie sister, ae, was a sidekick.

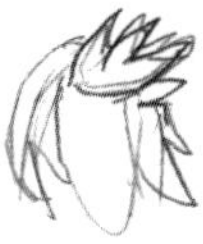

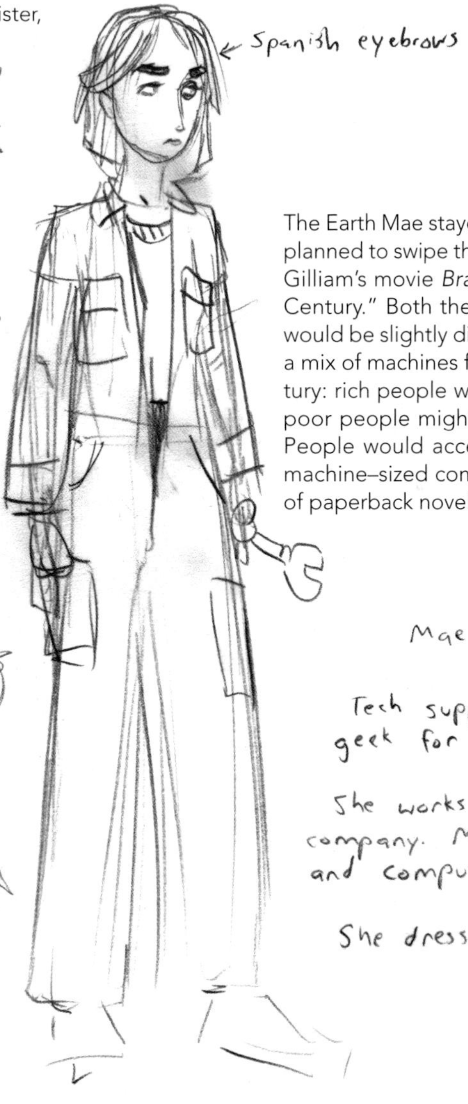

Spanish eyebrows
Tech support- a computer geek for vacuum tube pcs.
She works for the phone company. Ma Bell leases phones and computers to the public.
She dresses like a plumber.
Mae

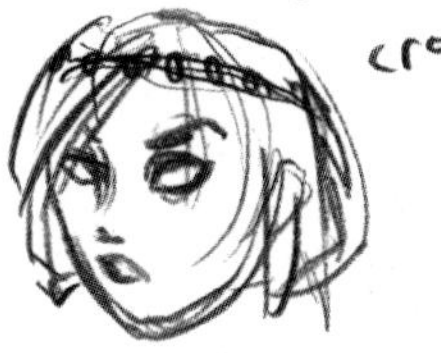

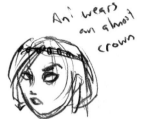

Ani wears an almost crown

The Earth Mae stayed on wasn't quite our Earth. I planned to swipe the opening caption from Terry Gilliam's movie *Brazil*: "Somewhere in the 20th Century." Both the history and the technology would be slightly different from ours. There'd be a mix of machines from throughout the last century: rich people would drive luxury 1930s cars; poor people might have small, boxy '50s cars. People would access the Internet on washing machine–sized computers with screens the size of paperback novels.

sible last name - Quillion
Cricket
Christmas

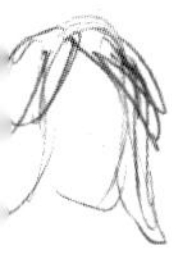

ni was an Indiana girl who, years go, ventured into space after nding a hidden rocket ship. Mae as her less glamorous sister who orked for the phone company.

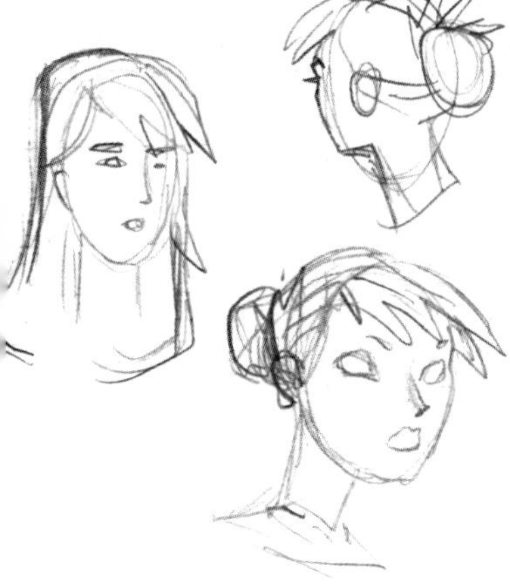

My wife, Lisa, asked what the point was to all this alternate history. There really wasn't any, and it got in the way of the larger adventure. As much as I loved playing with the setting, it had to go. The Indiana that Mae lives in is very much like ours. The only bizarre retro tech is Mae's flip phone: those were still popular when I drew the first story pages in my free time.

The town of Zenith and Raintree County are made up but have roots in the real world. Zenith used to be a popular American TV brand built in Indiana factories. *Raintree County* is an epic 1948 novel set in a fictional corner of the Hoosier State.

Doors Ani
Old library books someone else will check out

In these notes and sketches, you can see a lot of discarded ideas. But this is also where I found the heart of the tale.

She returns to earth after escaping from a POW camp. Tho they knew 10 POWs would be killed as punishment, they elected to sneak Ani out to go for help.
When she got to the rebel tribal camp, she found it destroyed by Imperial forces, littered with rebel dead.
Unable to free her friends she comes home bitter and angry. It's the early morning after Halloween when Mae bails her out.

Has an invisible friend she talks to—She claims it's an artificially induced hallucinatory assistant.

In part, it's about Ani's (PDA). Never shown visually. new appreciation for the planet she left. The taste of beer, or strawberries. The smell of old basements and newspaper clippings. Walking on a gravel driveway barefoot.

Friend Allison Jukebox (there's a community center in B-town called Allison-Jukebox)

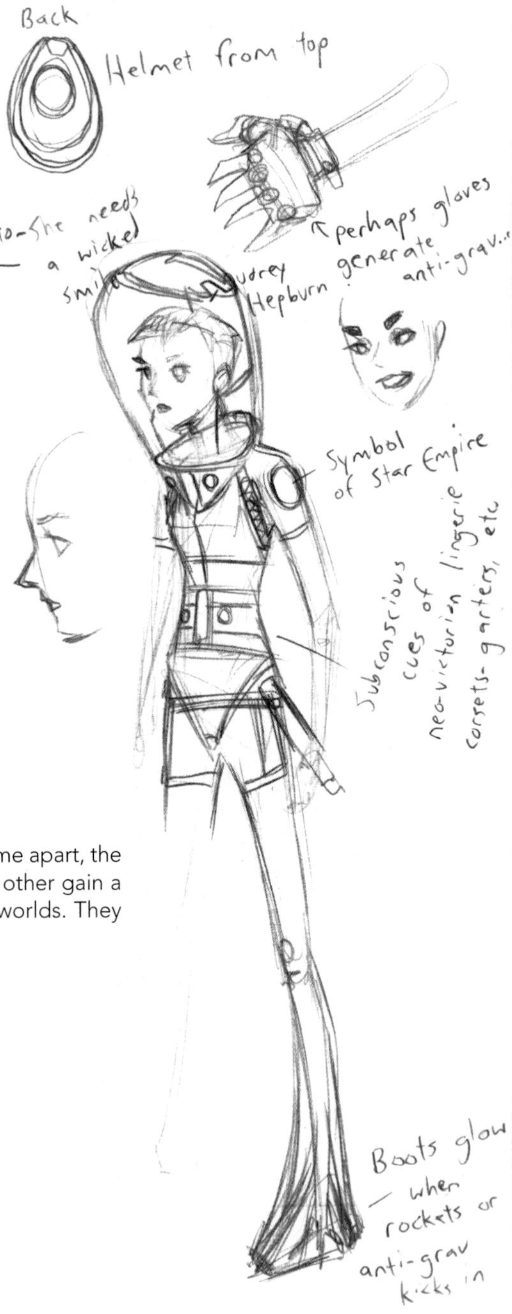

Back
Helmet from top
perhaps gloves generate anti-grav...
She needs a wicked smile
Audrey Hepburn
Symbol of Star Empire
Subconscious cues of neo-victorian lingerie corsets-garters, etc
Boots glow — when rockets or anti-grav kicks in

After spending so much time apart, the reunited sisters help each other gain a new appreciation for the worlds. They rediscover wonder.

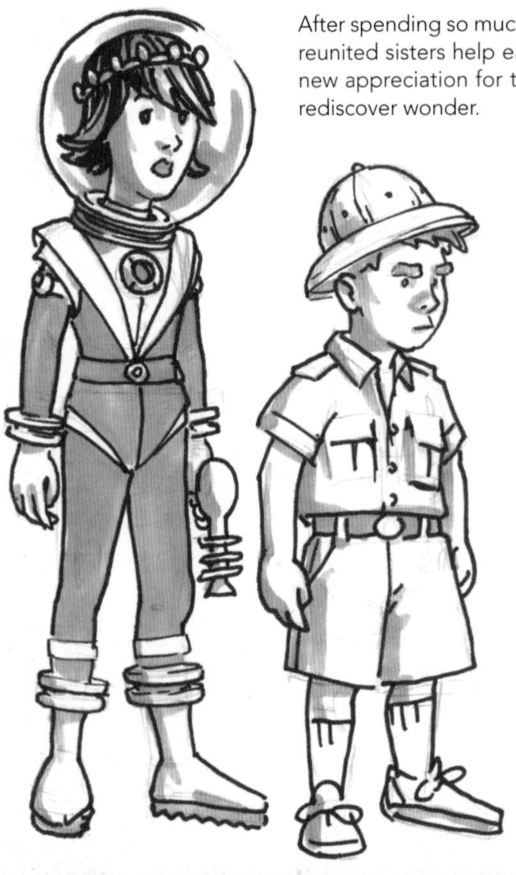

Much of the inspiration for *Mae* came from Kyle Baker's graphic novel *Why I Hate Saturn*, which is about Anne and Laura Merkel, sisters living in New York. Laura is also convinced she's the Queen of the Leather Astro-Girls of Saturn. That's why Ani began as a space hero. In a very real sense *Mae* started out as a fanfic.

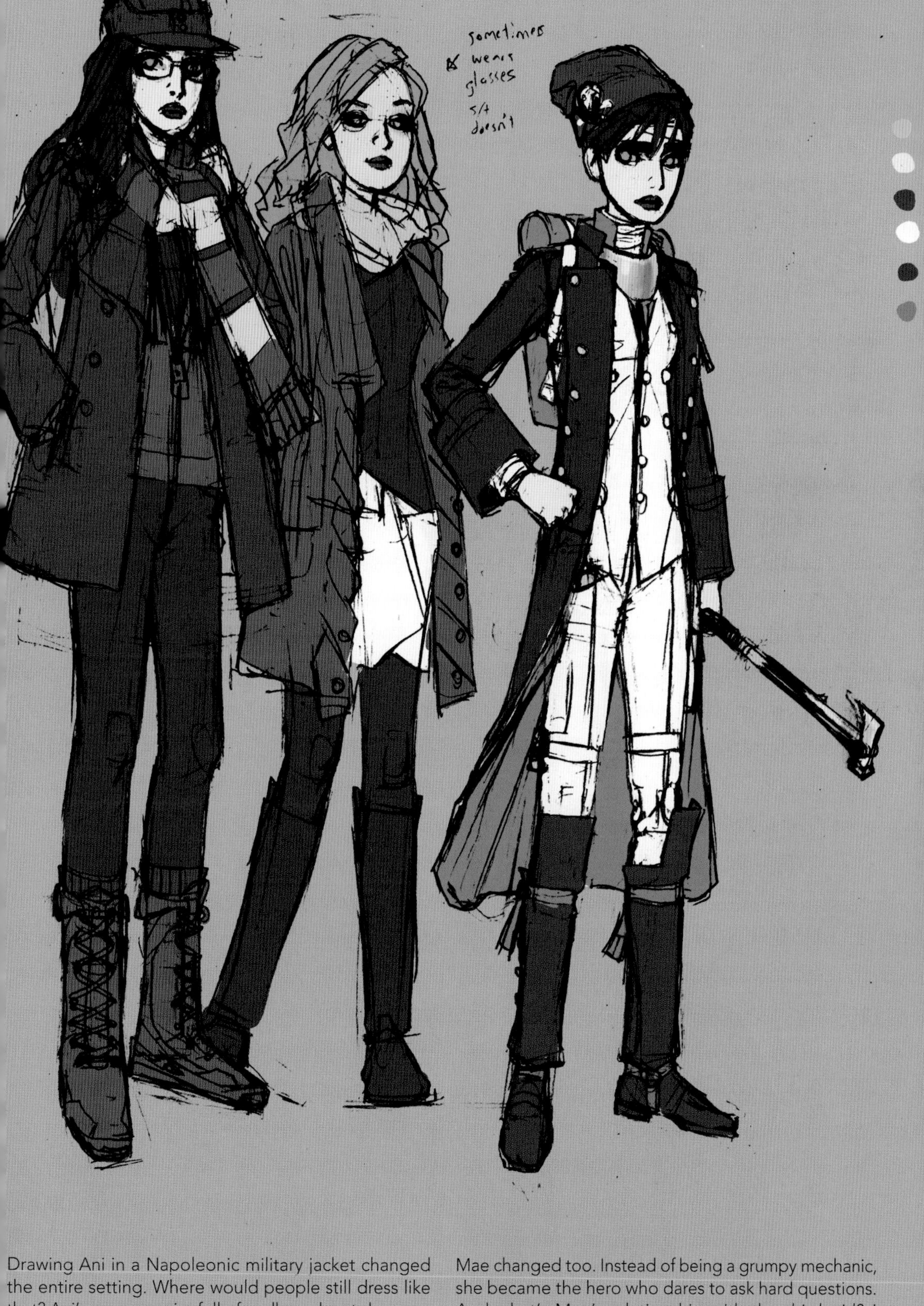
sometimes
wears
glasses
s/t
doesn't

Drawing Ani in a Napoleonic military jacket changed the entire setting. Where would people still dress like that? Ani's space empire full of endless planets became Abbie's lost world of Cimerterěn. That world was first colonized by mad scientists during the Napoleonic era and then cut off before the First World War.

Mae changed too. Instead of being a grumpy mechanic, she became the hero who dares to ask hard questions. And what's Mae's relationship with the third girl? I decided Dahlia was a giant nerd, and the two bonded over geek trivia and goofy humor.

Everything that followed came from this sketch.

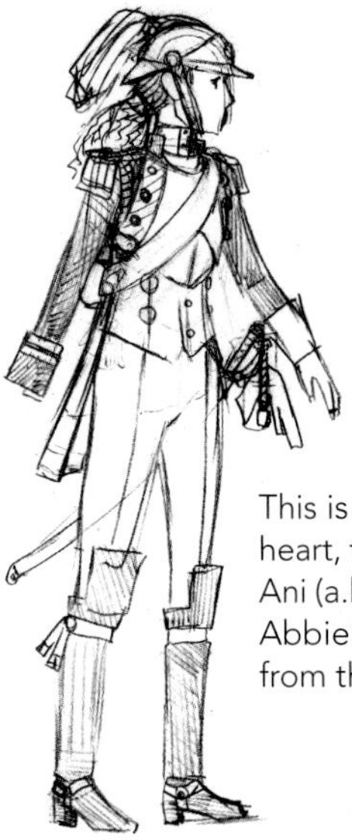

This is my first sketch of Petra Stoneheart, the military officer who enlisted Ani (a.k.a. Abbie Fortell) into her unit. Abbie's costume is her old uniform from this force.

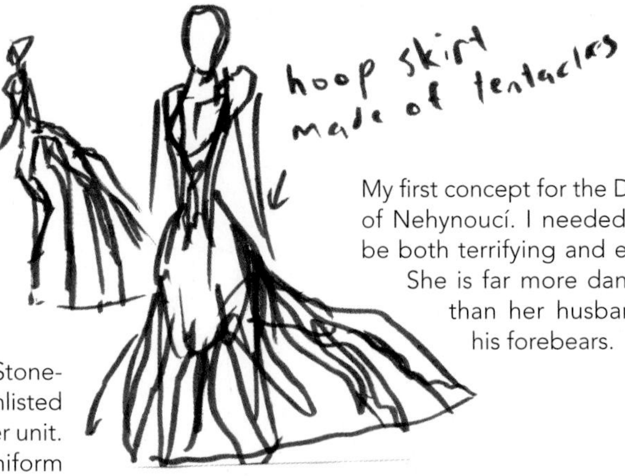
hoop skirt
made of tentacles

My first concept for the Duche
of Nehynoucí. I needed her
be both terrifying and elegar
She is far more dangero
than her husband ar
his forebears.

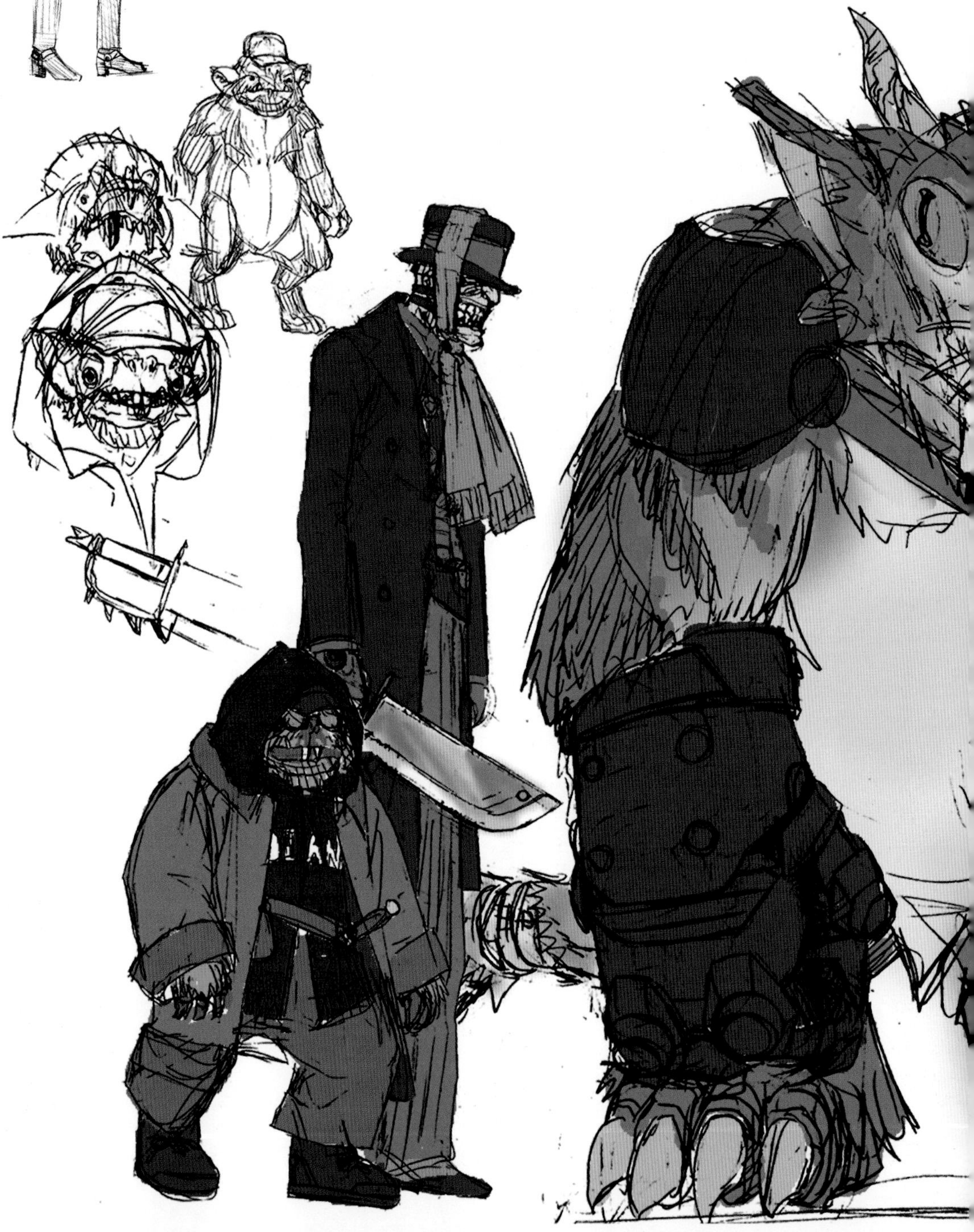

The design for the Dukes of Nehynoucí looks like a skull if you squint. A giant skull with tiny arms and legs (Thank you, Jack Kirby!).

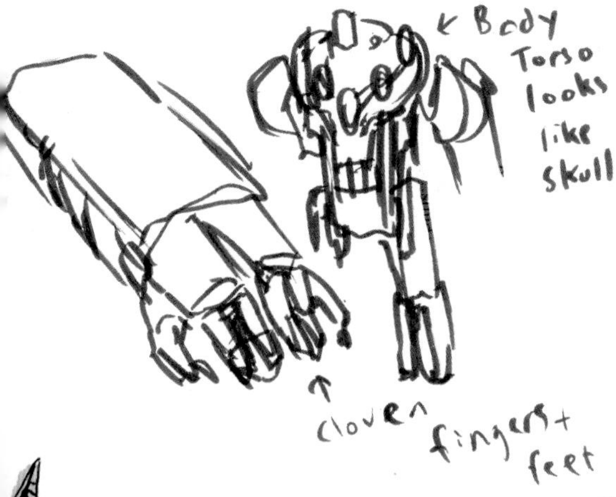
Body
Torso looks like skull
cloven fingers + feet

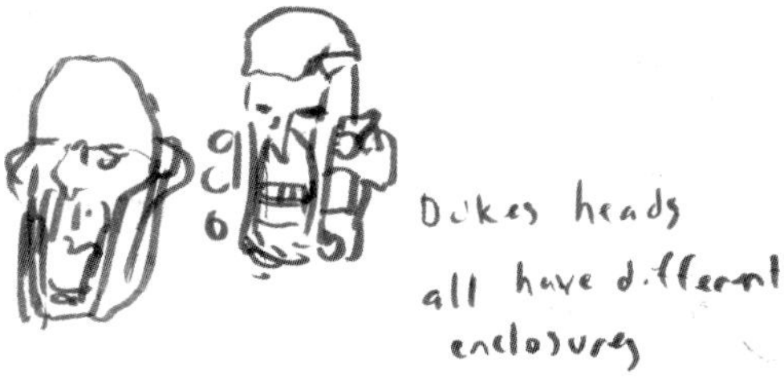
Dukes heads all have different enclosures

The Dukes are severed living-dead heads sharing a single robotic body. They include the current duke, and his father, and his father's father, and so on. That empty spot at ten o'clock is reserved for the son.

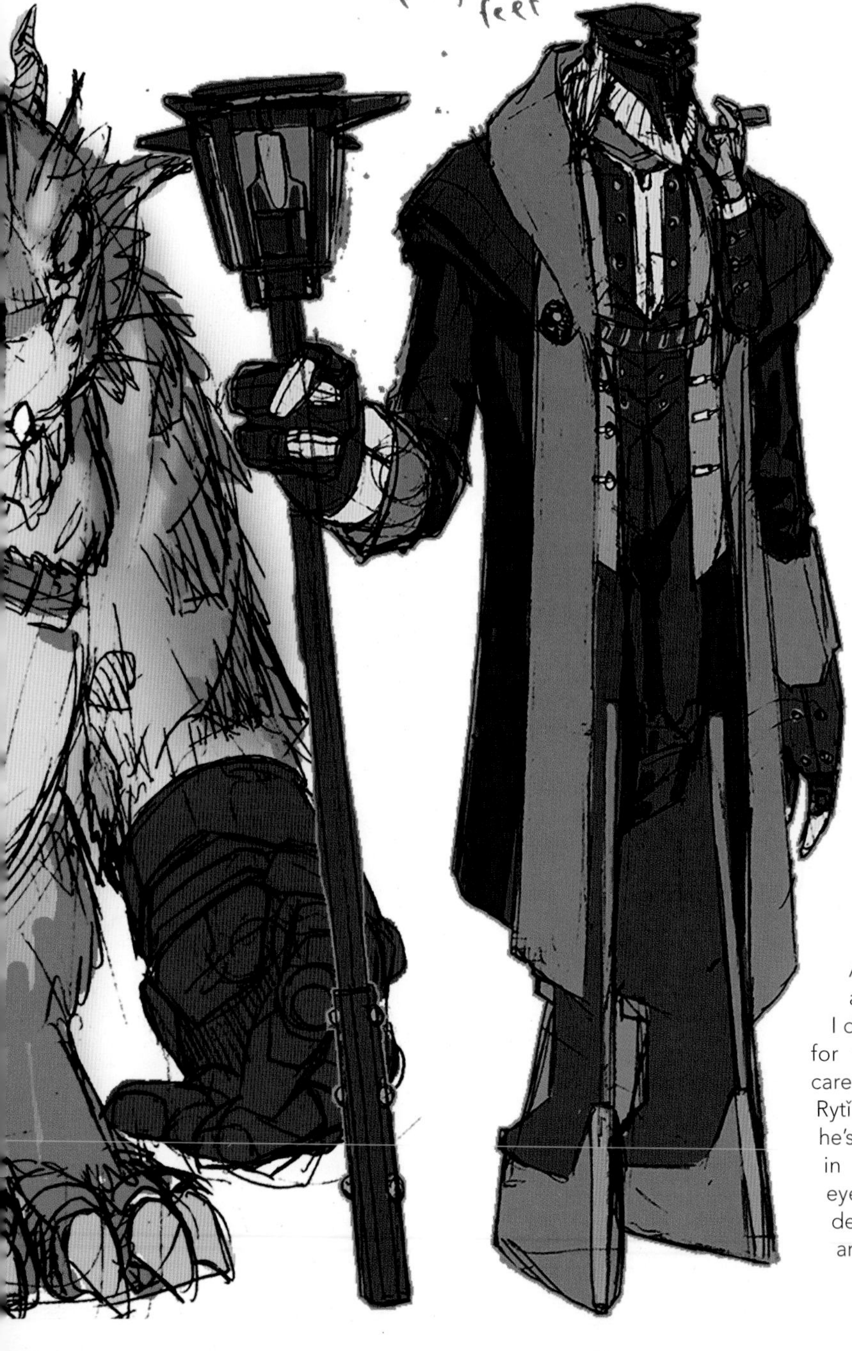

After I designed Mae's and Abbie's current looks, I drew this—my first villains for the book. If you look carefully at the tall, robotic Rytíř Kazisvet, you'll see that he's actually a very short man in a stilt suit. The upper eye slits on the helmet are decorative; the lower ones are where his eyes are.

NON-POLARIA

The other world is a sci-fi fantasy world. Dinosaurs and barbarians and space ships and jet packs and rapiers.

Ani's mother was a ~~bab~~ barbarian princess, her father a ~~b~~ dashing space pilot. When the Witch Kings took over, they escaped to earth on a space ship, along with a mad scientist

Eventually, Ani began hanging around the scientist, who taught her how to fly, and how to travel back to the home worlds,

By the time the story starts, the mother and the scientist have died. The father is bitter and crippled, and hates Ani for disobeying his orders and visiting the other world.

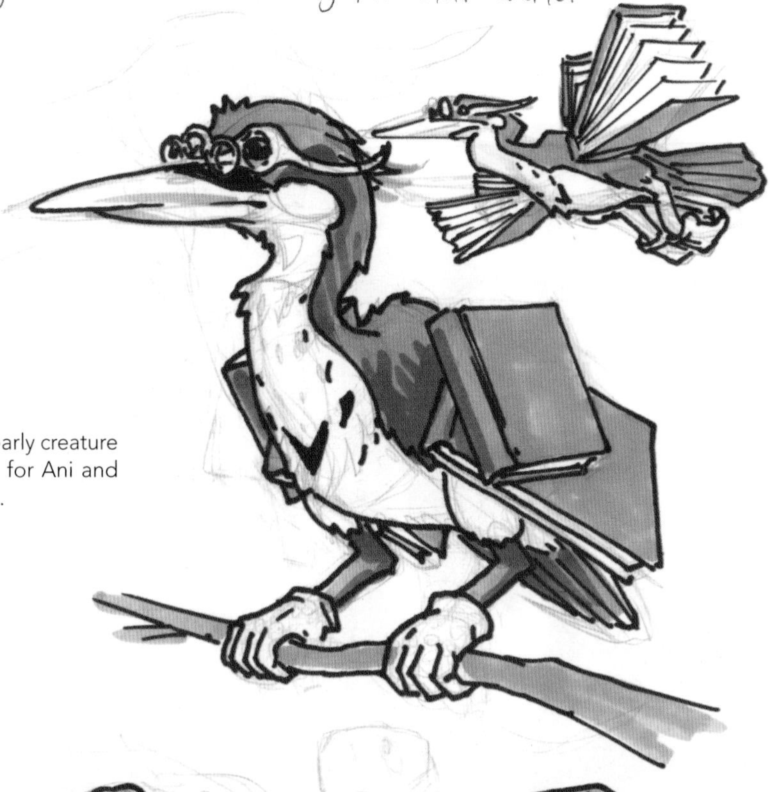

These are some early creature concepts I made for Ani and Mae's adventures.

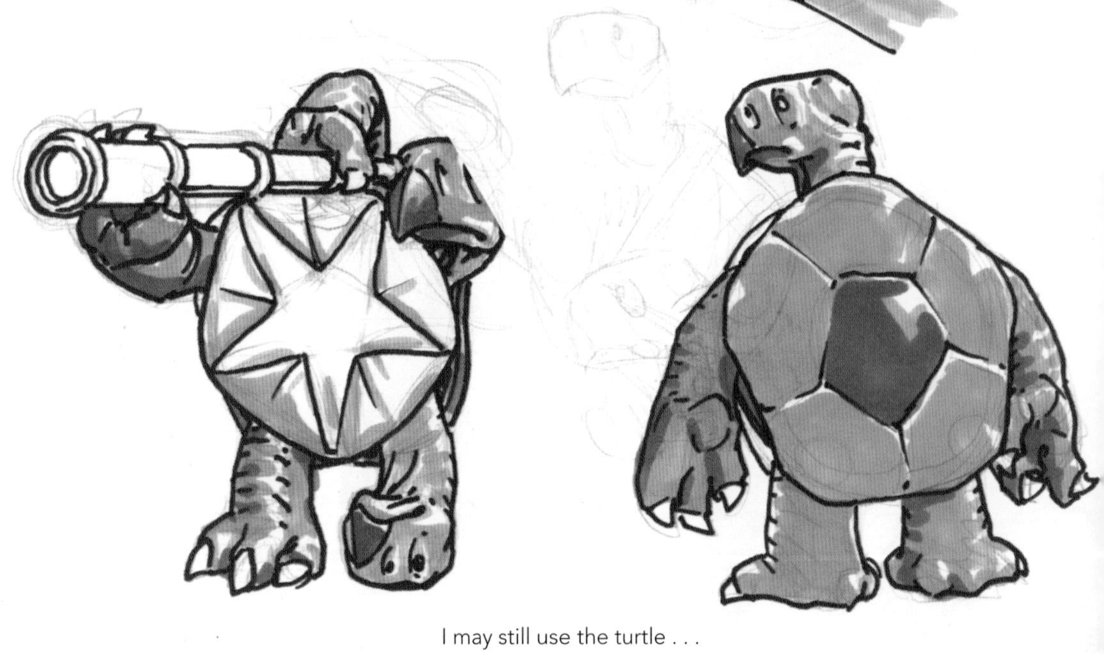

I may still use the turtle . . .

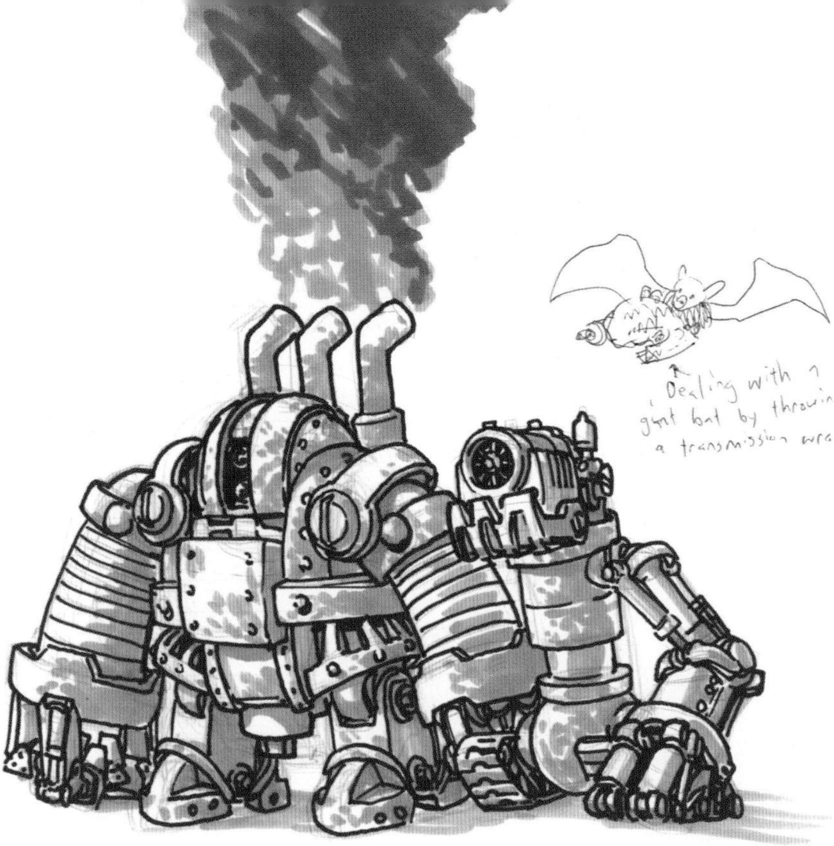
make chest into boiler
Dealing with a
giant bat by throwing
a transmission wrapped in a sweater

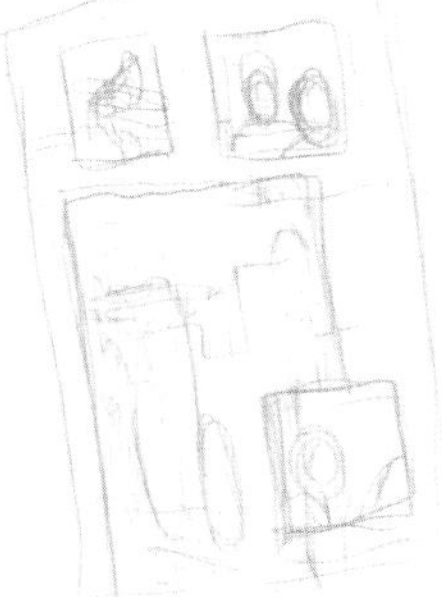

Later I tightened up my technobabble for the mad science of Cimerterěn. It doesn't include the magic needed to allow a book-winged bird to fly, or to let a monkey instantly unwind coaxial cable from its butt. The mad scientists definitely haven't mastered electronic or mechanical computers, so there are no adorable little steam robots there.

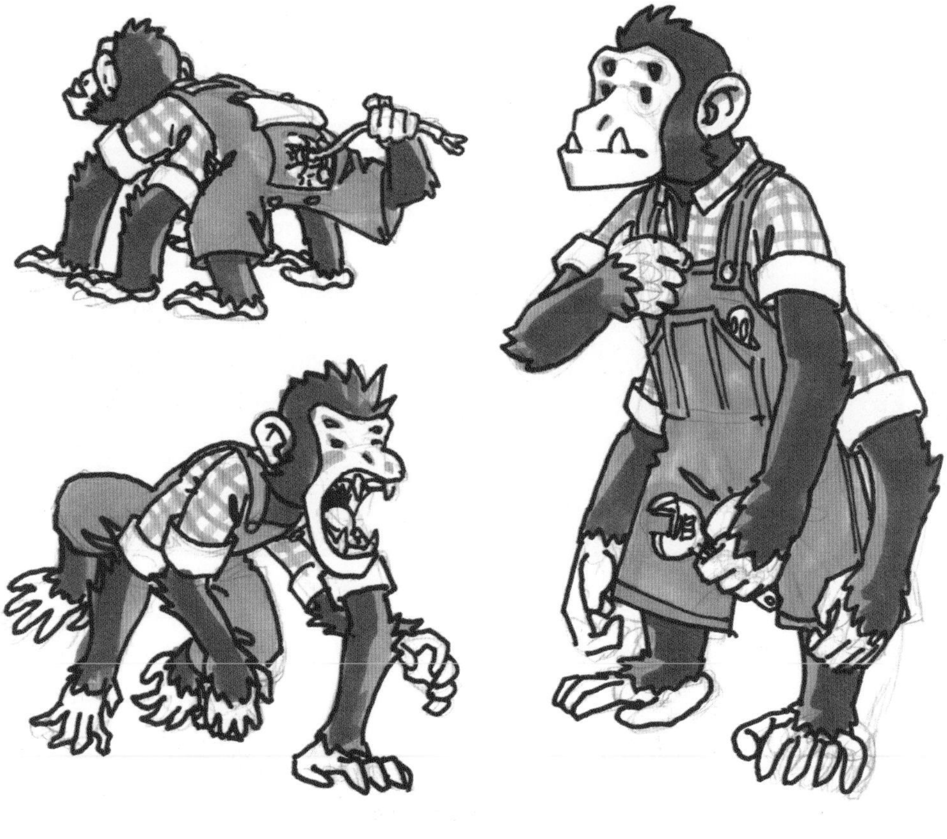

When I'm the artist and the writer, I like to script in doodles instead of words. I start off with thumb-sized "thumbnail" pencil doodles. I scan them into the computer and add drafts of the speech bubble dialogue over the art in Manga Studio. Then I figure out the black-and-white shading in Photoshop.

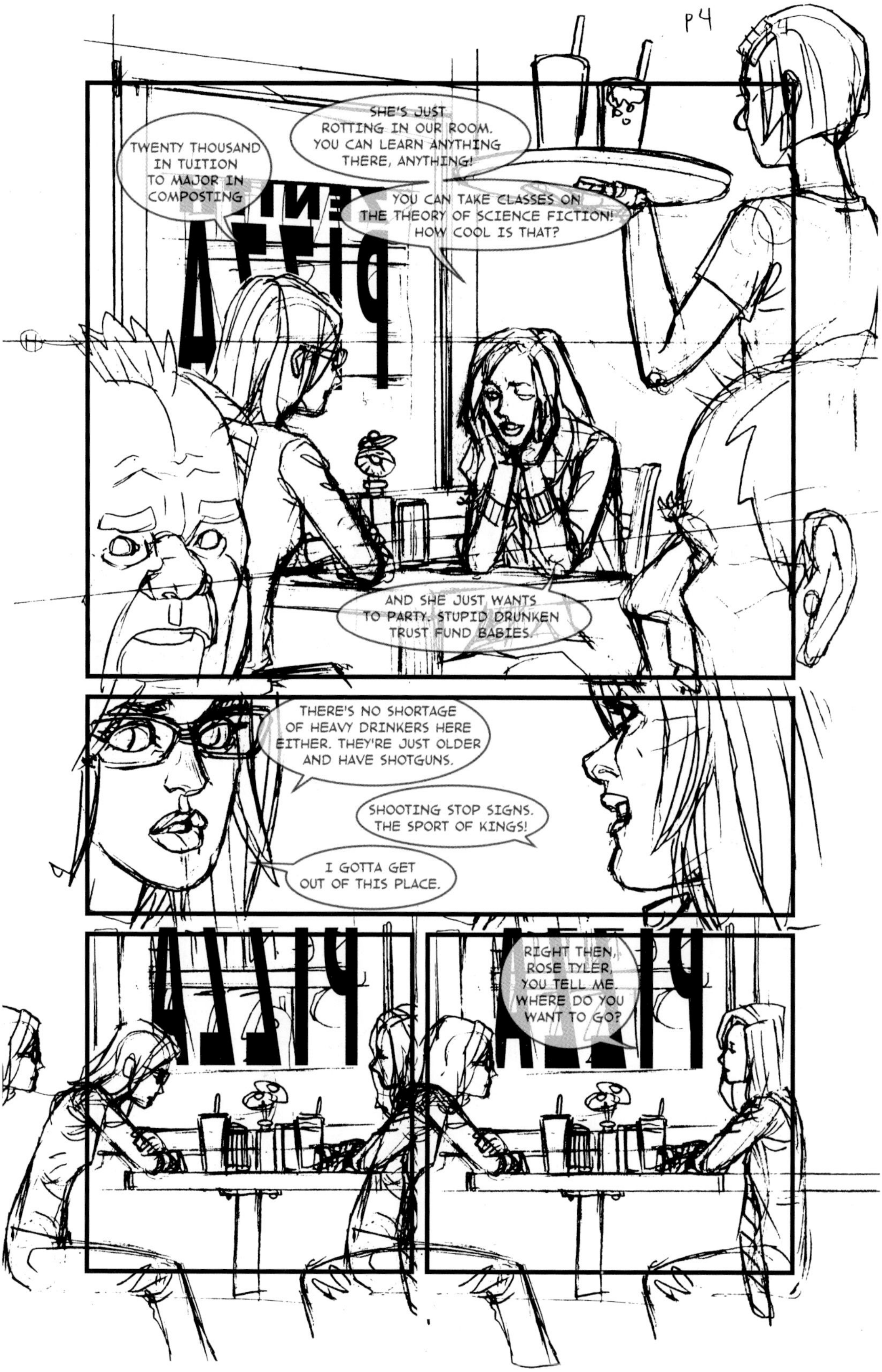
p4
TWENTY THOUSAND IN TUITION TO MAJOR IN COMPOSTING
SHE'S JUST ROTTING IN OUR ROOM. YOU CAN LEARN ANYTHING THERE, ANYTHING!
YOU CAN TAKE CLASSES ON THE THEORY OF SCIENCE FICTION! HOW COOL IS THAT?
AND SHE JUST WANTS TO PARTY. STUPID DRUNKEN TRUST FUND BABIES.
THERE'S NO SHORTAGE OF HEAVY DRINKERS HERE EITHER. THEY'RE JUST OLDER AND HAVE SHOTGUNS.
SHOOTING STOP SIGNS. THE SPORT OF KINGS!
I GOTTA GET OUT OF THIS PLACE.
RIGHT THEN, ROSE TYLER, YOU TELL ME. WHERE DO YOU WANT TO GO?

Next I take the grayscale rough art and inkjet print it in blueline on 8½ x 11–inch paper. A blueline is a faint image in "nonphoto blue" that will disappear when scanned. I draw tight pencils over the blueline rough.

Hopefully some day I'll draw on a computer screen, but it feels clumsy. It would cut out all the scanning and blueline inkjet prints and save a lot of time, *sigh*. Young artists, jump at your first chance to learn how to draw on a computer!

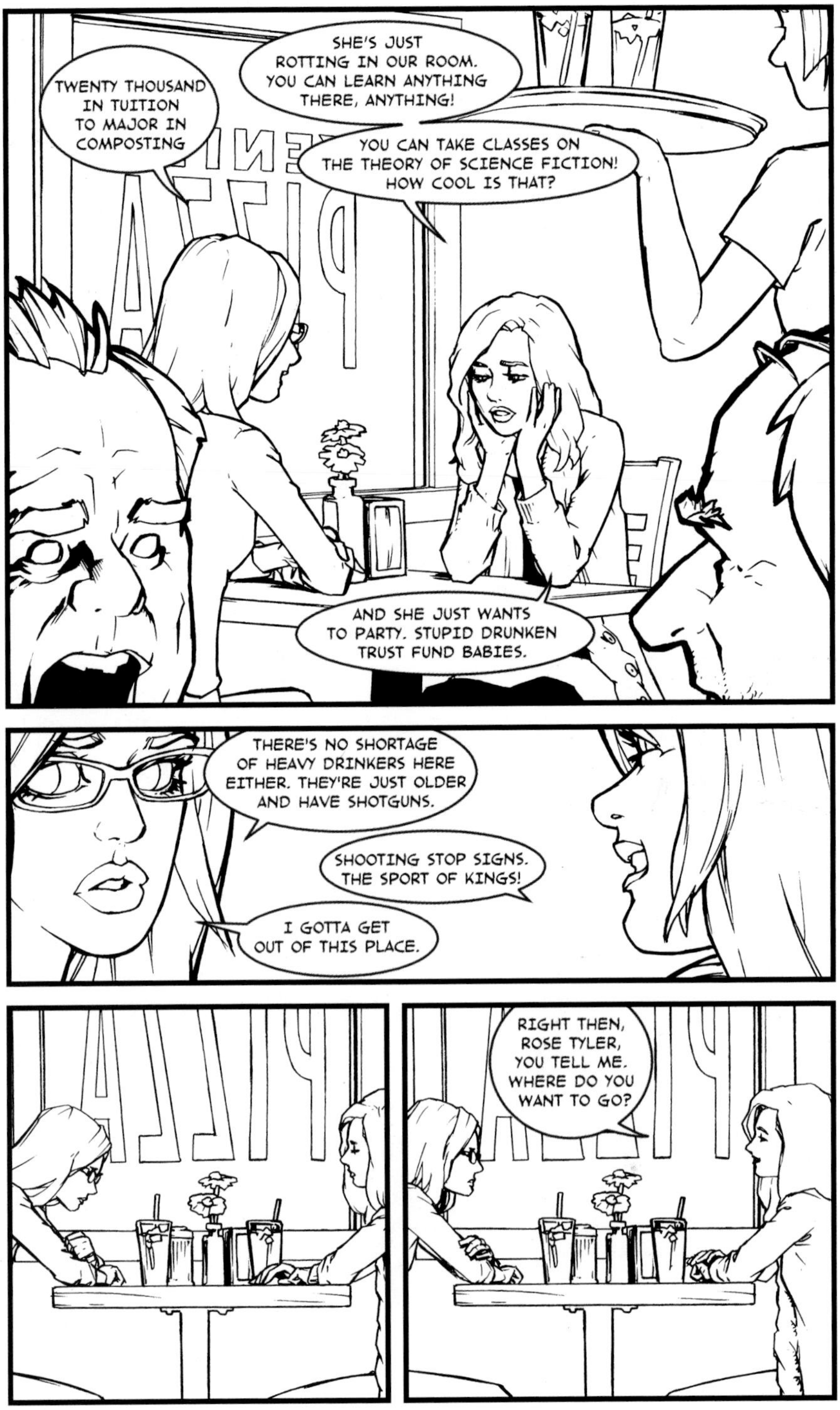
SHE'S JUST ROTTING IN OUR ROOM. YOU CAN LEARN ANYTHING THERE, ANYTHING!
TWENTY THOUSAND IN TUITION TO MAJOR IN COMPOSTING
YOU CAN TAKE CLASSES ON THE THEORY OF SCIENCE FICTION! HOW COOL IS THAT?
AND SHE JUST WANTS TO PARTY. STUPID DRUNKEN TRUST FUND BABIES.
THERE'S NO SHORTAGE OF HEAVY DRINKERS HERE EITHER. THEY'RE JUST OLDER AND HAVE SHOTGUNS.
SHOOTING STOP SIGNS. THE SPORT OF KINGS!
I GOTTA GET OUT OF THIS PLACE.
RIGHT THEN, ROSE TYLER, YOU TELL ME. WHERE DO YOU WANT TO GO?

Once again, I scan in the art and then blueline print it bigger, on 11 x 17–inch paper.

The drawings I make at this stage are called the "inks," but I use both dark 2B pencil and Copic Sketch brush marker for these, in addition to Pitt ink pens.

You'll notice I don't draw the black pupils on the eyes or highlights and twinkles. I sometimes make last-minute changes to the lighting on a scene, and I like the location of the highlights to match the direction of the light.

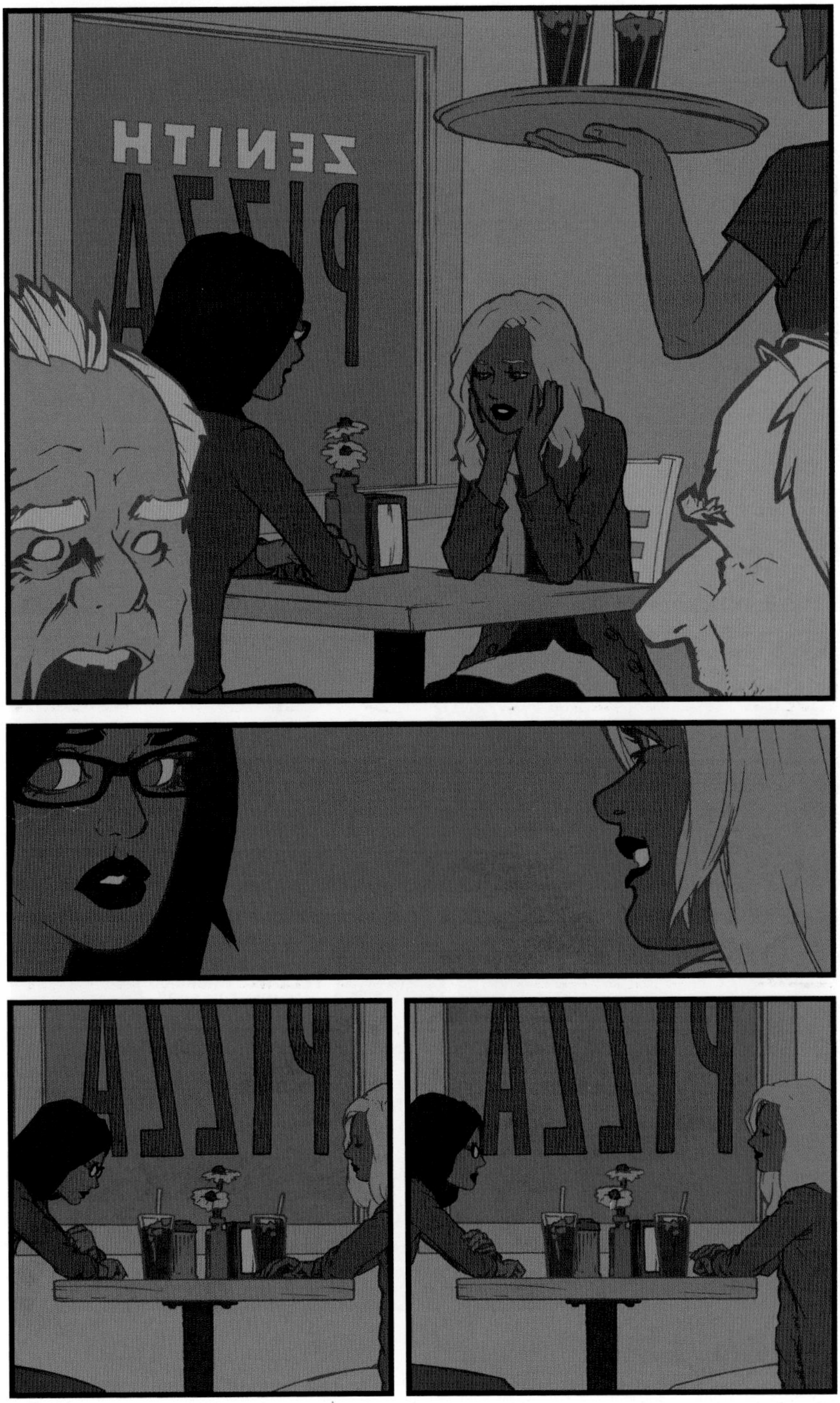
ZENITH
PIZZA

These are the flats by my color assistant, Rose McClain. The flats are useful in Photoshop, allowing me to use the Magic Wand tool to select an area. As long as an area is selected, you can't color beyond its borders, which means you can't "color outside the lines" until you deselect.

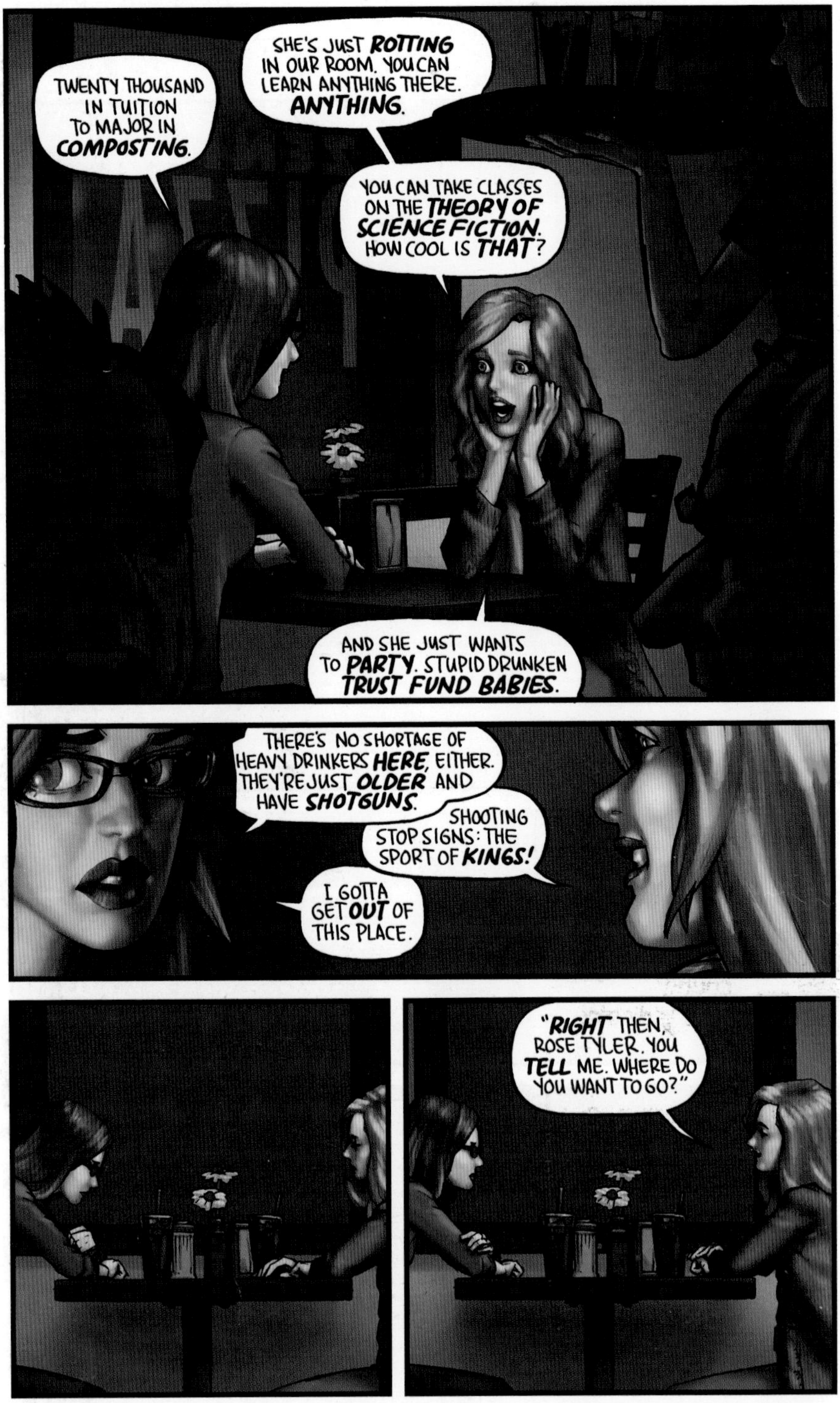

TWENTY THOUSAND IN TUITION TO MAJOR IN COMPOSTING.
SHE'S JUST ROTTING IN OUR ROOM. YOU CAN LEARN ANYTHING THERE. ANYTHING.
YOU CAN TAKE CLASSES ON THE THEORY OF SCIENCE FICTION. HOW COOL IS THAT?
AND SHE JUST WANTS TO PARTY. STUPID DRUNKEN TRUST FUND BABIES.
THERE'S NO SHORTAGE OF HEAVY DRINKERS HERE, EITHER. THEY'RE JUST OLDER AND HAVE SHOTGUNS.
SHOOTING STOP SIGNS: THE SPORT OF KINGS!
I GOTTA GET OUT OF THIS PLACE.
"RIGHT THEN, ROSE TYLER. YOU TELL ME. WHERE DO YOU WANT TO GO?"

The final color art, with Zander Cannon's lettering! I dislike overly tight lettering, even if the font is designed to look hand drawn. Zander's letters are a little loose, and that makes the page friendly and inviting.

I commonly use several tricks to draw the eye to where I want you to look. I give the most important parts the highest contrast. They ideally have both the brightest brights and the darkest darks. They should also have the most vivid colors. Usually this means the main characters, but not always.

I also like to throw a bright spotlight on the center of attention and let the rest of the image fade into darkness. A line drawing in a comic can get very complicated. Good colors make sense of the scene.

I hope you've enjoyed this little peek behind the scenes. Feel free to ask me questions at my website GeneHa.com!

AVENGERS WORLD

ASCENSION

AVENGERS WORLD VOL. 2: ASCENSION. Contains material originally published in magazine form as AVENGERS WORLD #6-9 and AVENGERS #34.1. First printing 2014. ISBN# 978-0-7851-9094-3. Published by MARVEL WORLDWIDE, INC., a subsidiary of MARVEL ENTERTAINMENT, LLC. OFFICE OF PUBLICATION: 135 West 50th Street, New York, NY 10020. Copyright © 2014 Marvel Characters, Inc. All rights reserved. All characters featured in this issue and the distinctive names and likenesses thereof, and all related indicia are trademarks of Marvel Characters, Inc. No similarity between any of the names, characters, persons, and/or institutions in this magazine with those of any living or dead person or institution is intended, and any such similarity which may exist is purely coincidental. **Printed in Canada.** ALAN FINE, EVP - Office of the President, Marvel Worldwide, Inc. and EVP & CMO Marvel Characters B.V.; DAN BUCKLEY, Publisher & President - Print, Animation & Digital Divisions; JOE QUESADA, Chief Creative Officer; TOM BREVOORT, SVP of Publishing; DAVID BOGART, SVP of Operations & Procurement, Publishing; C.B. CEBULSKI, SVP of Creator & Content Development; DAVID GABRIEL, SVP Print, Sales & Marketing; JIM O'KEEFE, VP of Operations & Logistics; DAN CARR, Executive Director of Publishing Technology; SUSAN CRESPI, Editorial Operations Manager; ALEX MORALES, Publishing Operations Manager; STAN LEE, Chairman Emeritus. For information regarding advertising in Marvel Comics or on Marvel.com, please contact Niza Disla, Director of Marvel Partnerships, at ndisla@marvel.com. For Marvel subscription inquiries, please call 800-

Avengers World #6-9

WRITER: **NICK SPENCER**
ARTISTS: **MARCO CHECCHETTO** (#6 & #8) &
STEFANO CASELLI (#7 & #9)
COLOR ARTIST: **ANDRES MOSSA**
LETTERER: **VC'S JOE CARAMAGNA**
COVER ART: **NEAL ADAMS** &
PAUL MOUNTS (#6), **MARK BROOKS** (#7),
GABRIELE DELL'OTTO (#8) AND
RYAN STEGMAN & EDGAR DELGADO (#9)

Avengers #34.1

WRITER: **AL EWING**
PENCILER: **DALE KEOWN**
INKER: **NORMAN LEE**
COLOR ARTIST: **JASON KEITH**
LETTERER: **VC'S CORY PETIT**
COVER ART: **DALE KEOWN & JASON KEITH**

ASSISTANT EDITOR: **JAKE THOMAS**
EDITOR: **WIL MOSS**
EXECUTIVE EDITOR: **TOM BREVOORT**

Collection Editor: **Jennifer Grünwald** • Assistant Editor: **Sarah Brunstad** • Associate Managing Editor: **Alex Starbuck**
Editor, Special Projects: **Mark D. Beazley** • Senior Editor, Special Projects: **Jeff Youngquist**
SVP Print, Sales & Marketing: **David Gabriel** • Book Design: **Nelson Ribeiro**

Editor in Chief: **Axel Alonso** • Chief Creative Officer: **Joe Quesada** • Publisher: **Dan Buckley** • Executive Producer: **Alan Fine**

S.H.I.E.L.D. MISSION REPORT

● FILE 4V3NG3R5
● FILE M47V3L

TROUBLE MAP/LOCATION ALPHA:
BARBUDA, CAPITAL CITY.
A.I.M. EMPIRE.

Barbuda, the sovereign-island home to the science-focused terrorist organization A.I.M. (Advanced Idea Mechanics), appeared to be "evolving," growing at an alarming rate. S.H.I.E.L.D. sent in a team of Avengers to investigate. Cannonball, Sunspot and Smasher were captured. The Scientist Supreme and Jude the Entropic Man forced Smasher to undergo their strange transformative process, turning her into their "Messenger."

Captain America assembled a rescue team composed of Thor, Hyperion and Captain Marvel, but the island's evolving defenses had created an impenetrable force field. Manifold was brought in to perform an extremely risky teleportation maneuver to gain them access to the island, where A.I.M. had recently extracted Hyperion from his dying universe.

● FILE 74345345Y
● FILE 63453T

TROUBLE MAP/LOCATION CHARLIE:
THE ISLAND NATION OF MADRIPOOR.
CURRENTLY ATOP A CENTURIES-OLD DRAGON,
SEVERAL HUNDRED FEET ABOVE SOUTHEAST ASIA.

Avengers assets Falcon, Black Widow, Wolverine and Shang-Chi were dispatched to the crime haven of Madripoor, where chaos and riots were erupting on the streets.

Shang-Chi broke off from the group to find the Gorgon, who was in the midst of a ceremony to raise the great dragon on whose head the island of Madripoor rests. Before Shang-Chi could stop him, the dragon awakened, launching the entire island out of the ocean. In their fight, the Gorgon grievously wounded Shang-Chi, then tossed him off the airborne island!

● FILE 5413LD
● FILE 1337

TROUBLE MAP/LOCATION BRAVO:
BENEATH VELLETRI, ITALY.
THE CITY OF THE DEAD.

Starbrand, Spider-Woman, Hawkeye and Nightmask were dispatched to Velletri, Italy, where the town's entire population and a fact-finding team had both disappeared. While exploring the town, they came across a strange stone object that, when touched, transported them underneath Velletri to the City of the Dead, a place that traps tormented souls. Over the years, the sheer number of such souls trapped there has imbued the place with great power.

While his teammates fought strange creatures rising from the black river that runs through the city, Starbrand was called away by the voices of the classmates killed in the event that gave him his powers. The voices were a trap, leading Starbrand to the new ruler of the City of the Dead, the powerful sorceress known as Morgan Le Fay.

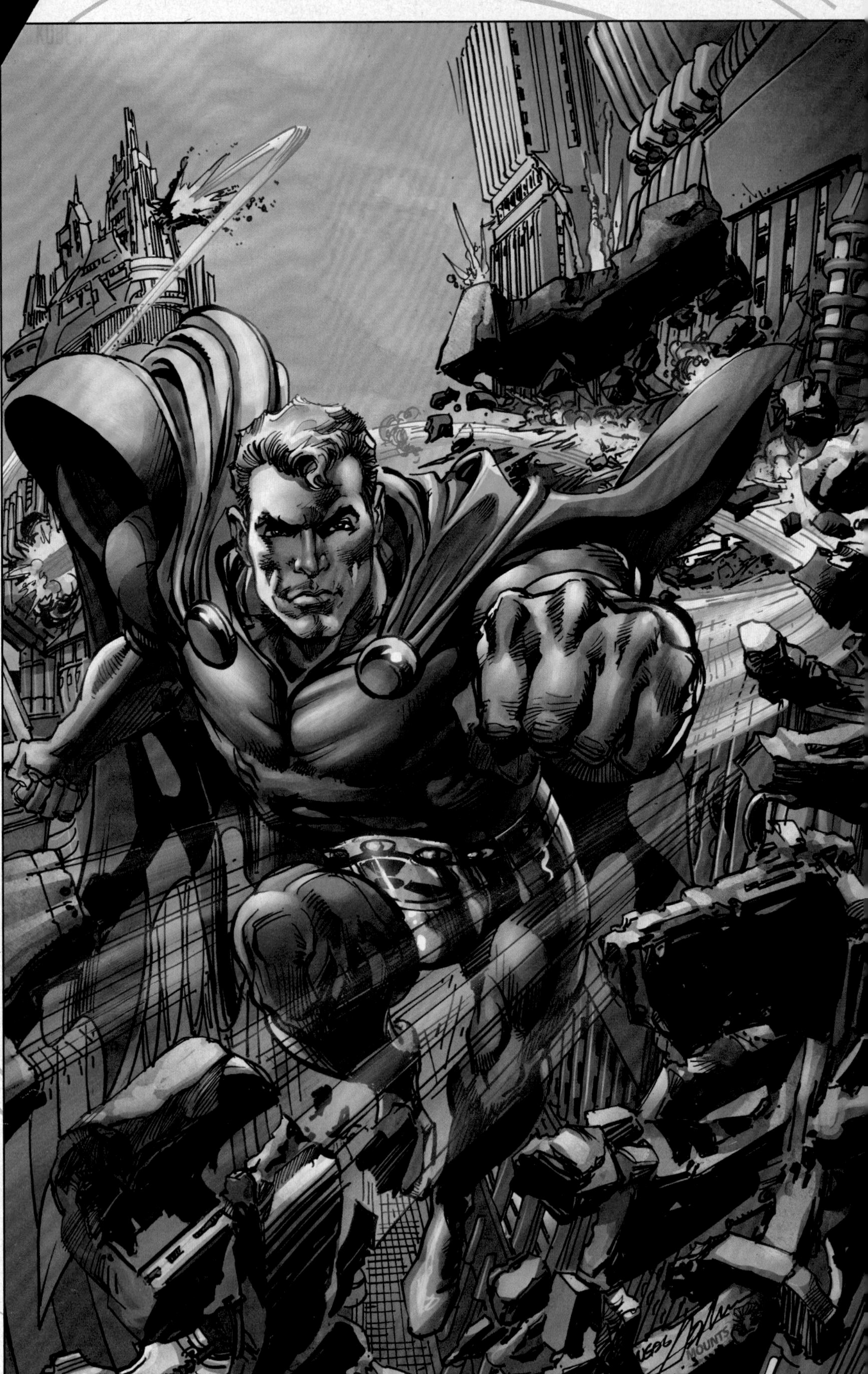

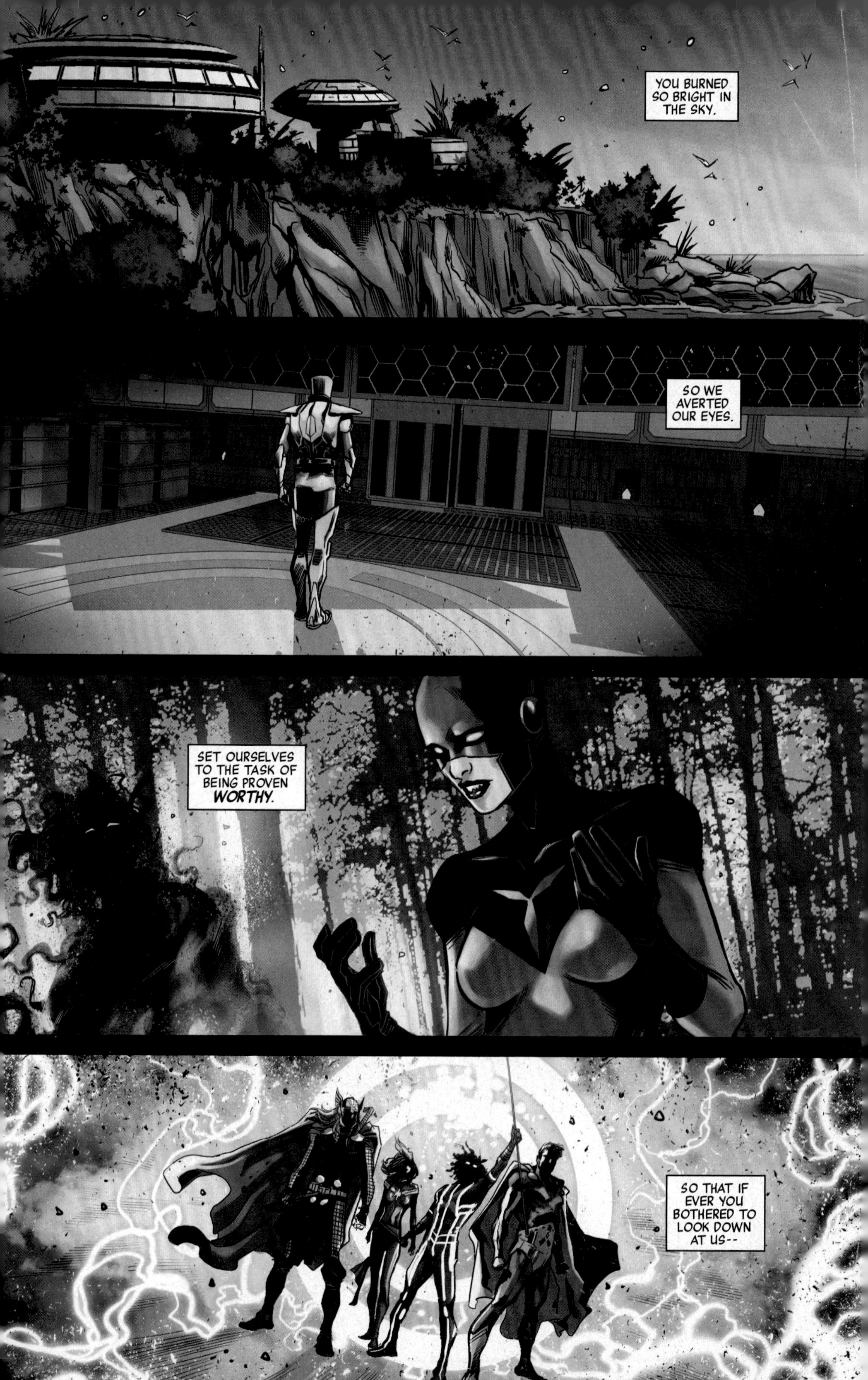
YOU BURNED SO BRIGHT IN THE SKY.
SO WE AVERTED OUR EYES.
SET OURSELVES TO THE TASK OF BEING PROVEN *WORTHY*.
SO THAT IF EVER YOU BOTHERED TO LOOK DOWN AT US--

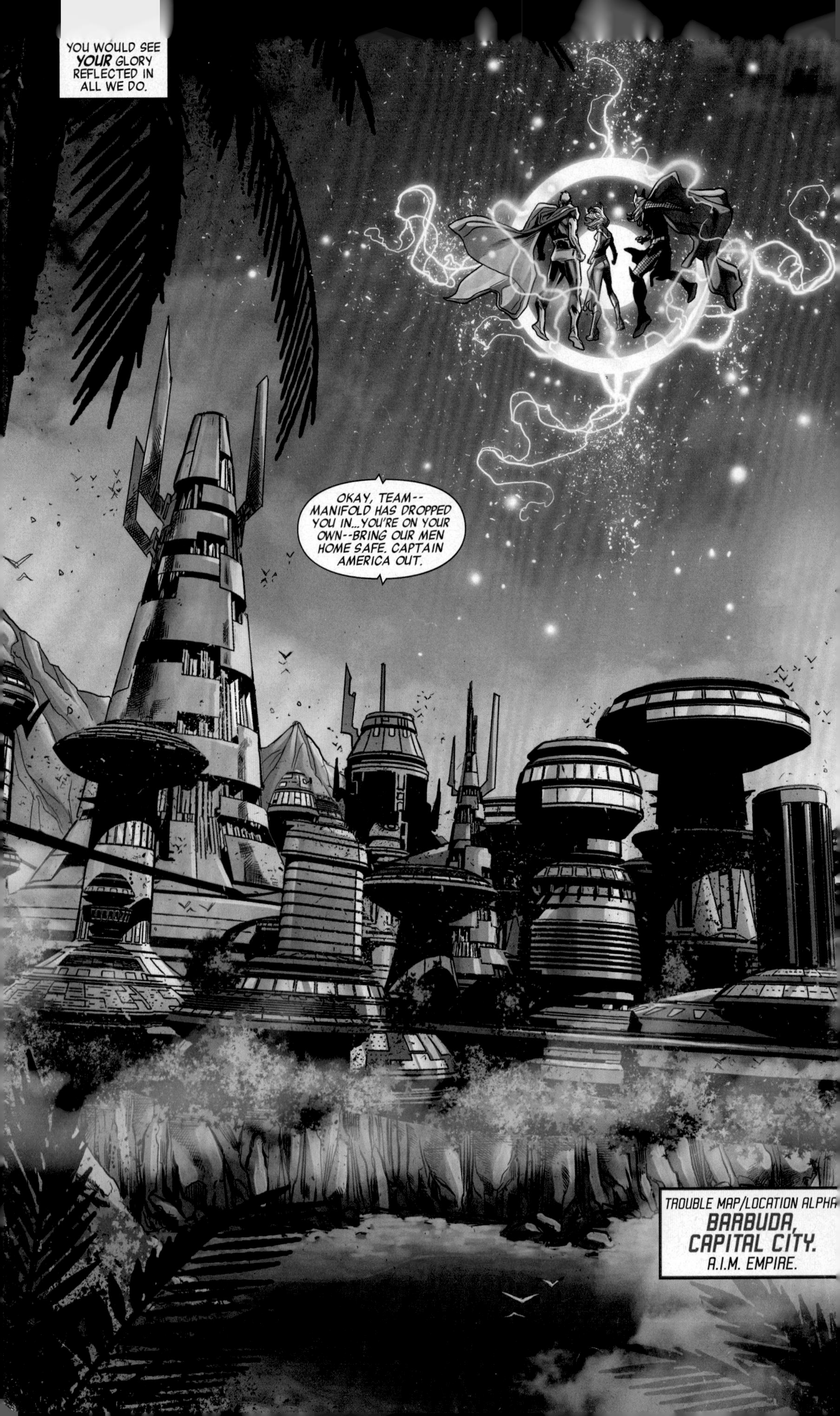
YOU WOULD SEE YOUR GLORY REFLECTED IN ALL WE DO.
OKAY, TEAM--MANIFOLD HAS DROPPED YOU IN...YOU'RE ON YOUR OWN--BRING OUR MEN HOME SAFE. CAPTAIN AMERICA OUT.
TROUBLE MAP/LOCATION ALPHA
BARBUDA, CAPITAL CITY.
A.I.M. EMPIRE.

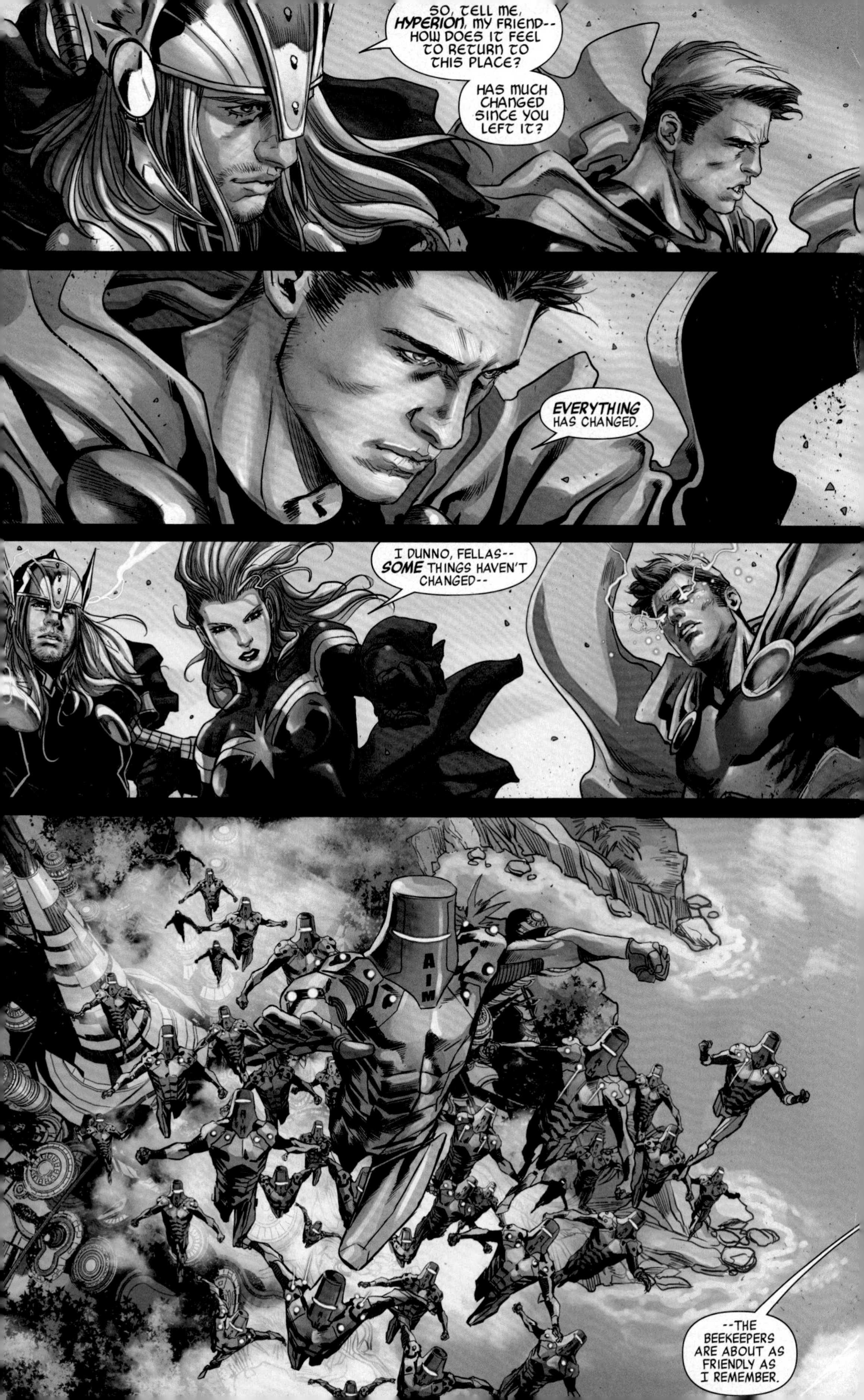
SO, TELL ME, **HYPERION**, MY FRIEND-- HOW DOES IT FEEL TO RETURN TO THIS PLACE?
HAS MUCH CHANGED SINCE YOU LEFT IT?
EVERYTHING HAS CHANGED.
I DUNNO, FELLAS-- **SOME** THINGS HAVEN'T CHANGED--
A I M
--THE BEEKEEPERS ARE ABOUT AS FRIENDLY AS I REMEMBER.

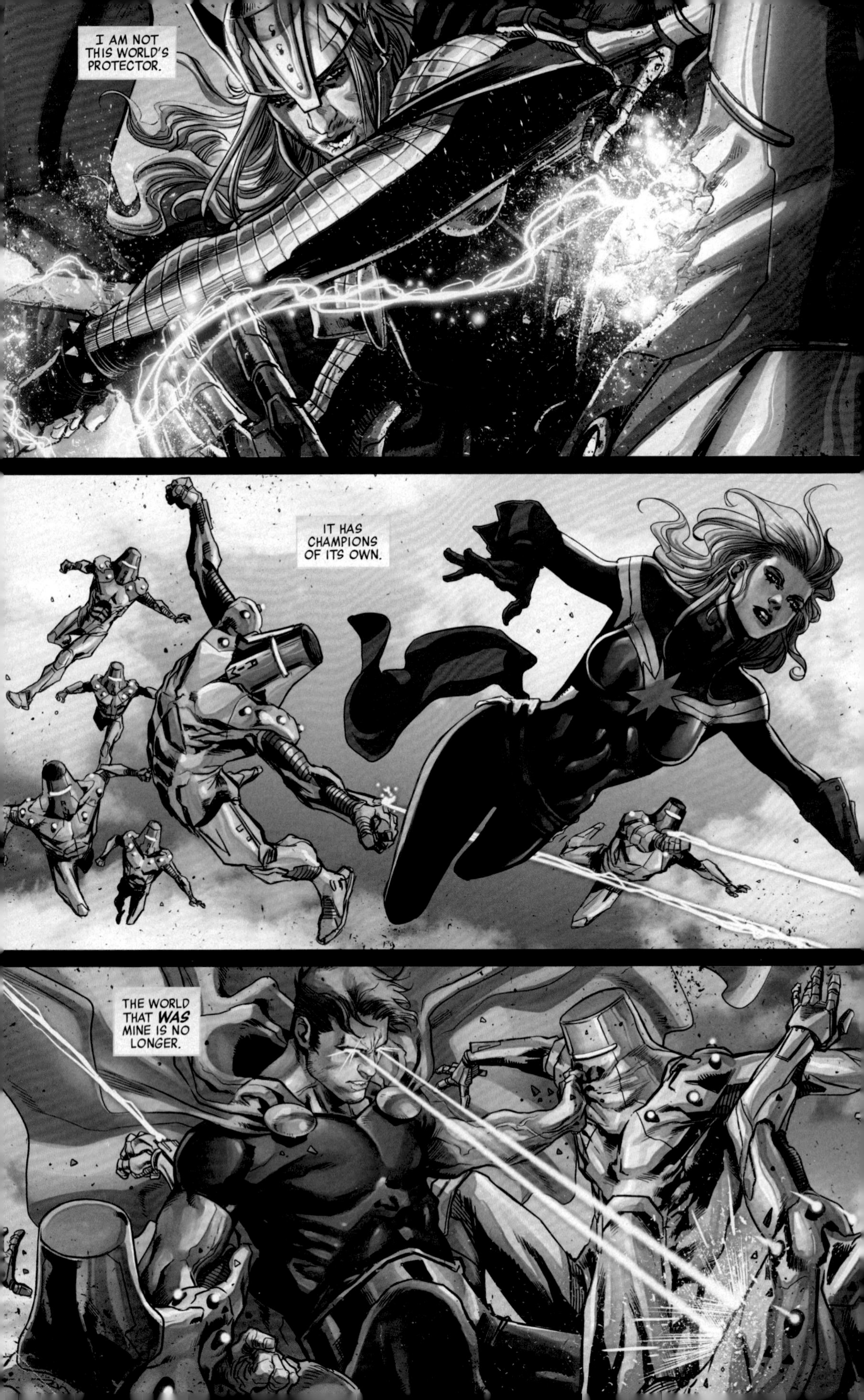
I AM NOT THIS WORLD'S PROTECTOR.
IT HAS CHAMPIONS OF ITS OWN.
THE WORLD THAT WAS MINE IS NO LONGER.

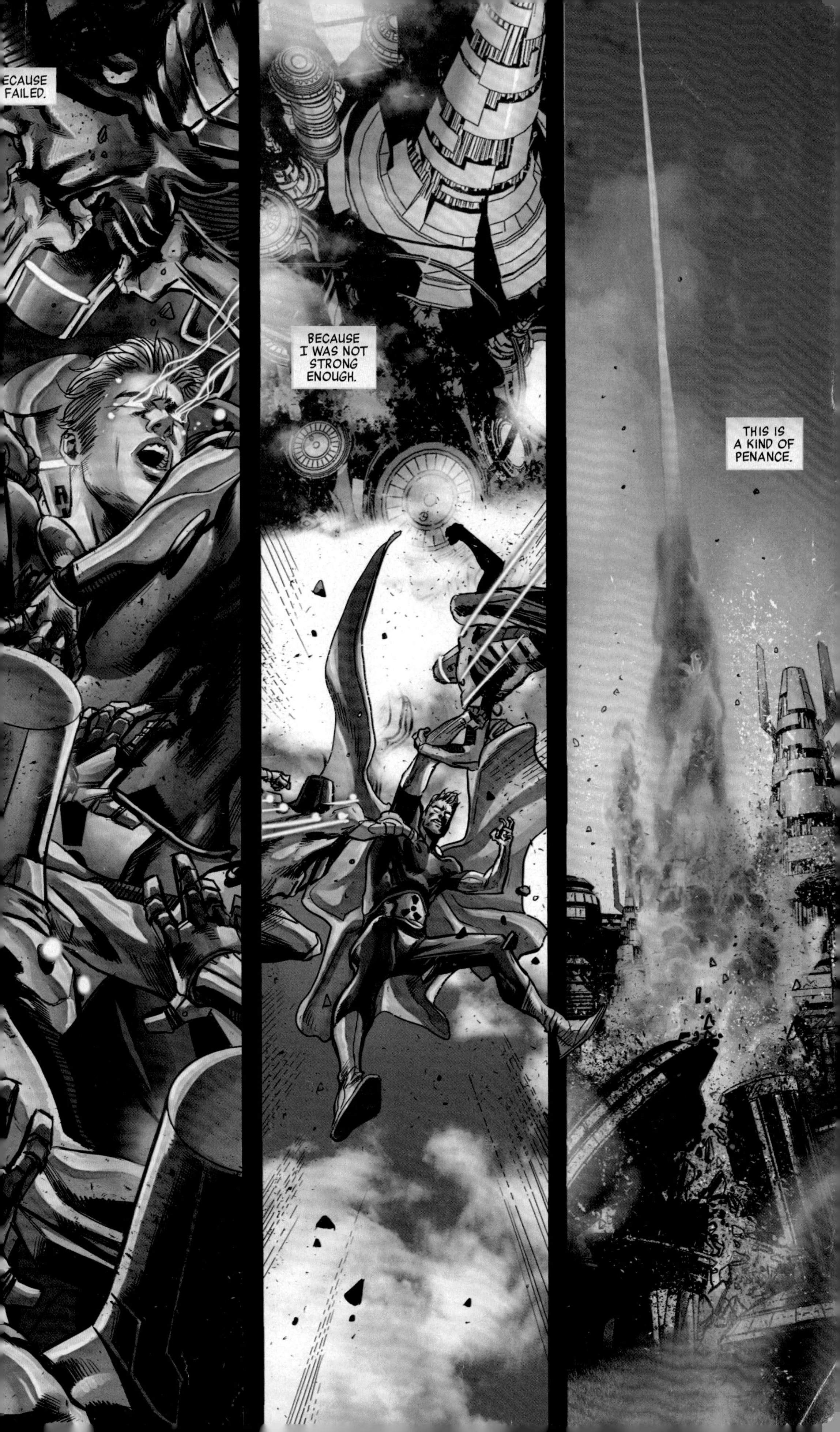
ECAUSE
FAILED.
BECAUSE
I WAS NOT
STRONG
ENOUGH.
THIS IS
A KIND OF
PENANCE.

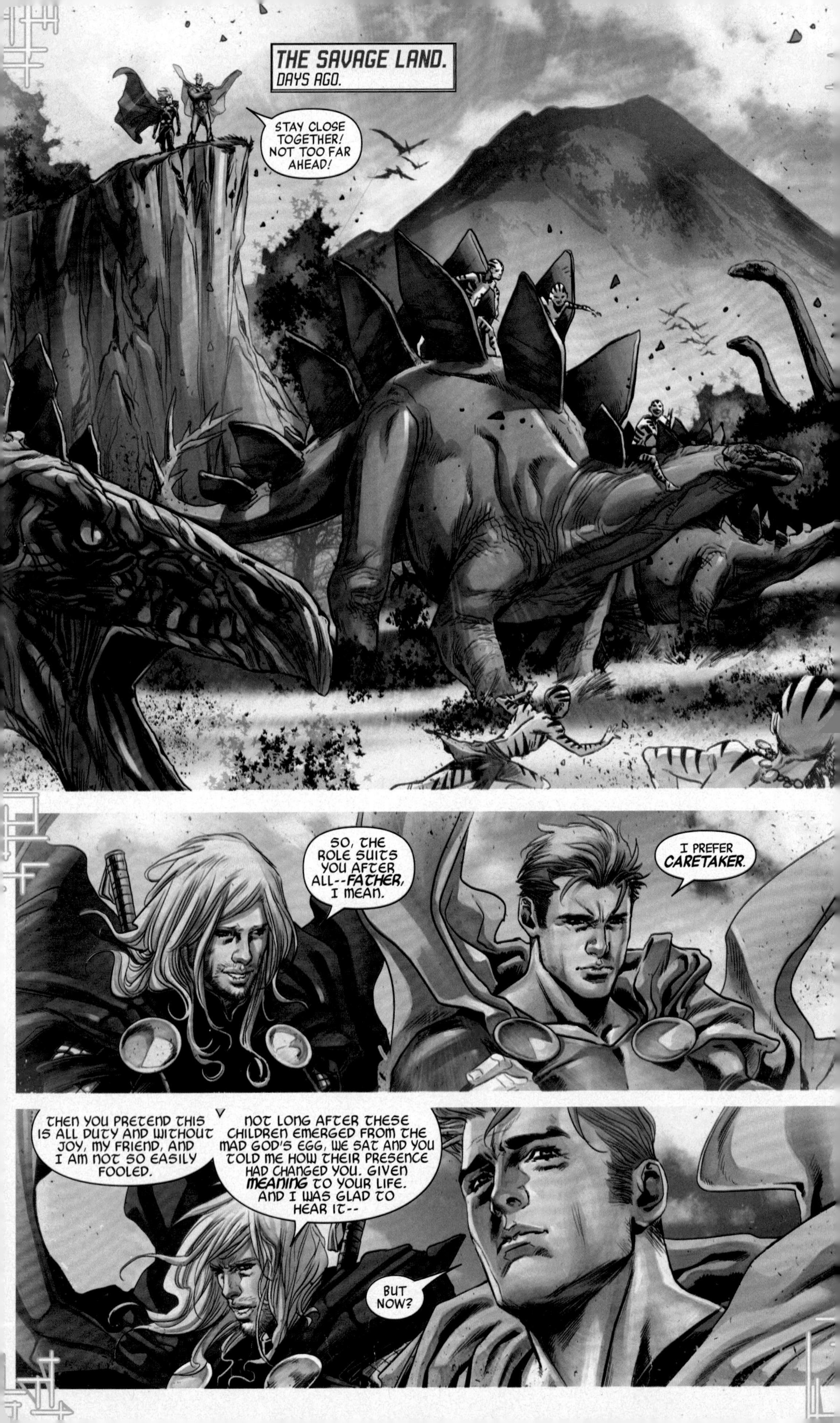
THE SAVAGE LAND. DAYS AGO.
STAY CLOSE TOGETHER! NOT TOO FAR AHEAD!
SO, THE ROLE SUITS YOU AFTER ALL--FATHER, I MEAN.
I PREFER CARETAKER.
THEN YOU PRETEND THIS IS ALL DUTY AND WITHOUT JOY, MY FRIEND, AND I AM NOT SO EASILY FOOLED.
NOT LONG AFTER THESE CHILDREN EMERGED FROM THE MAD GOD'S EGG, WE SAT AND YOU TOLD ME HOW THEIR PRESENCE HAD CHANGED YOU. GIVEN MEANING TO YOUR LIFE. AND I WAS GLAD TO HEAR IT--
BUT NOW?

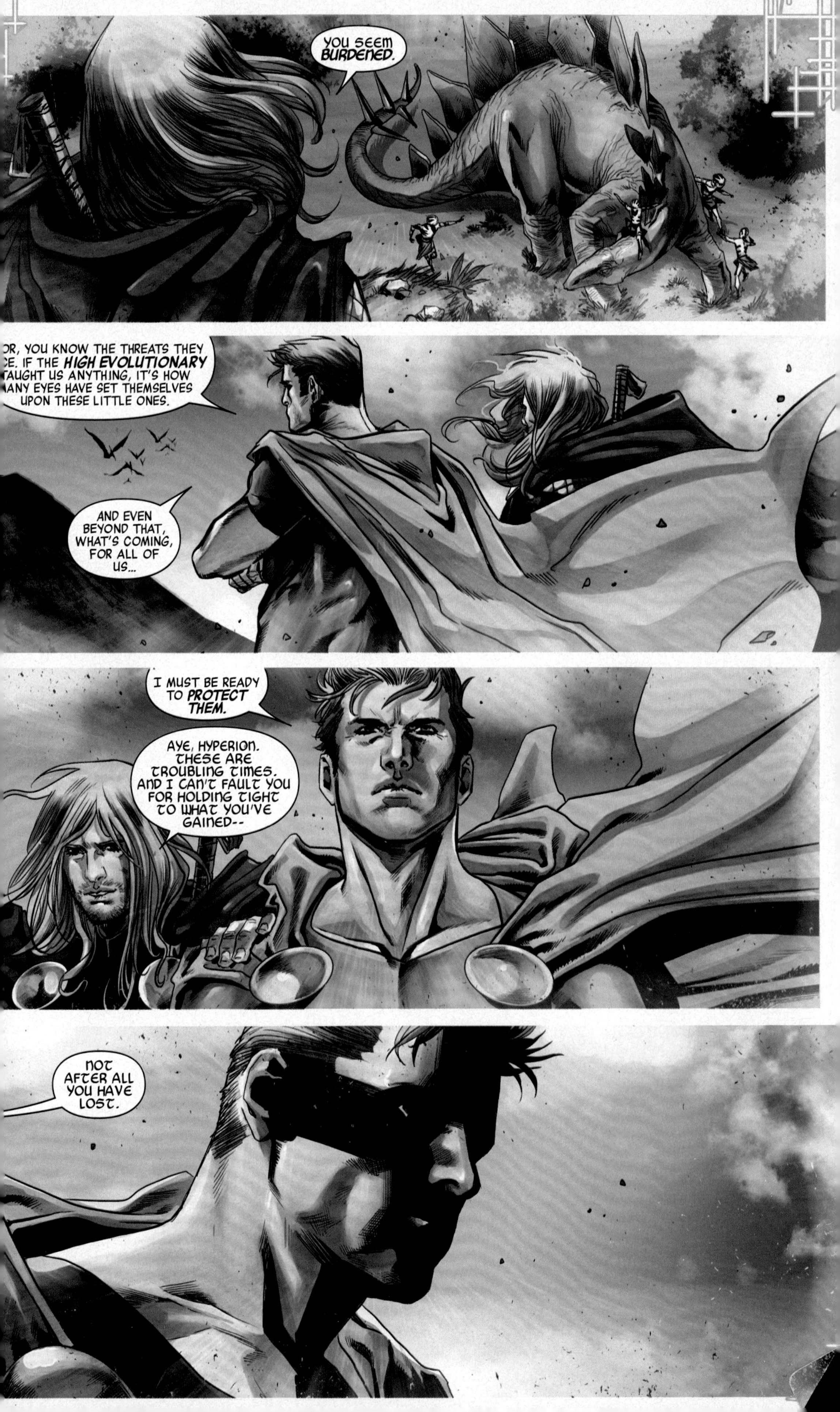
YOU SEEM **BURDENED**.
OR, YOU KNOW THE THREATS THEY CE. IF THE ***HIGH EVOLUTIONARY*** TAUGHT US ANYTHING, IT'S HOW ANY EYES HAVE SET THEMSELVES UPON THESE LITTLE ONES.
AND EVEN BEYOND THAT, WHAT'S COMING, FOR ALL OF US...
I MUST BE READY TO ***PROTECT THEM.***
AYE, HYPERION. THESE ARE TROUBLING TIMES. AND I CAN'T FAULT YOU FOR HOLDING TIGHT TO WHAT YOU'VE GAINED--
NOT AFTER ALL YOU HAVE LOST.

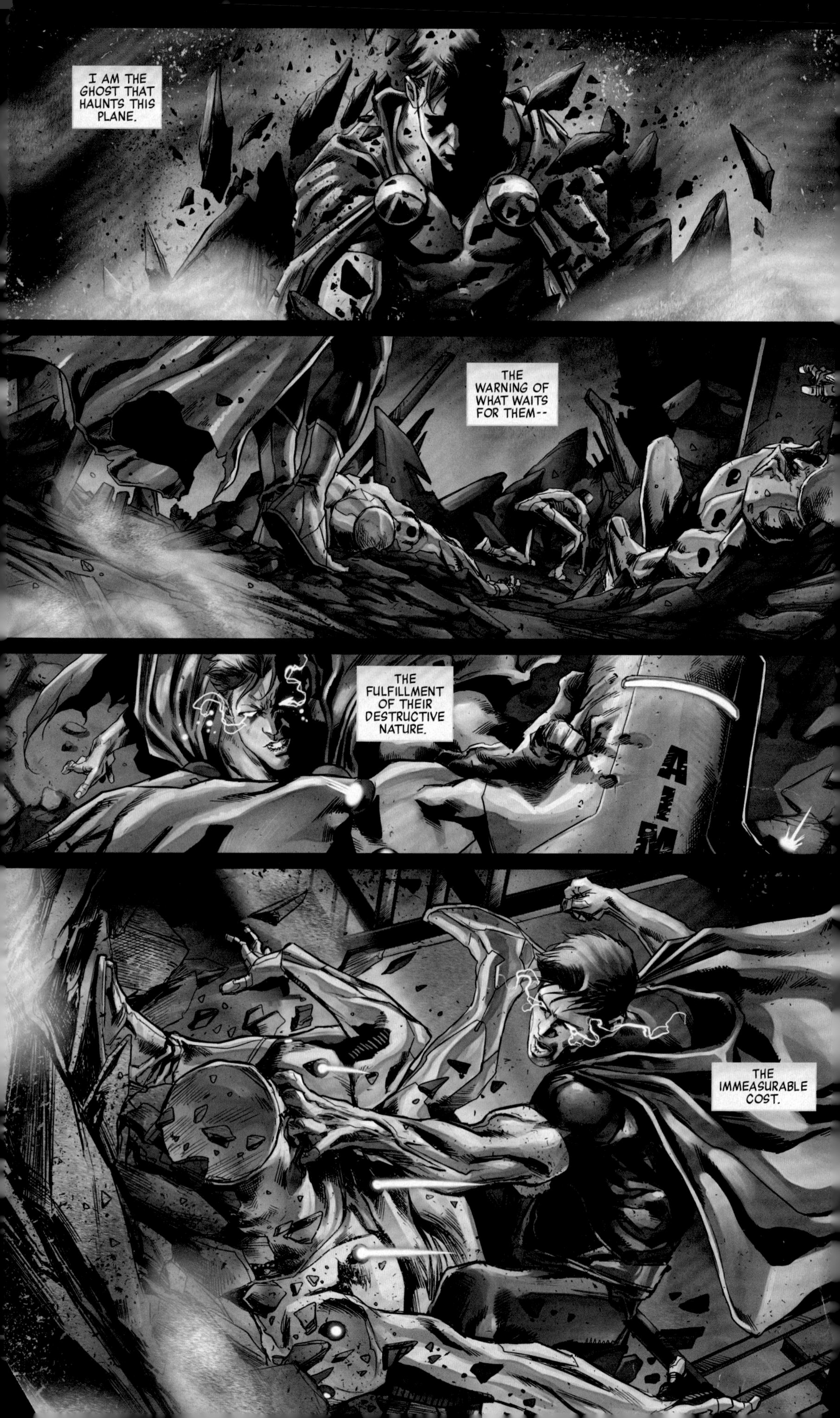
I AM THE GHOST THAT HAUNTS THIS PLANE.
THE WARNING OF WHAT WAITS FOR THEM--
THE FULFILLMENT OF THEIR DESTRUCTIVE NATURE.
A.I.M.
THE IMMEASURABLE COST.

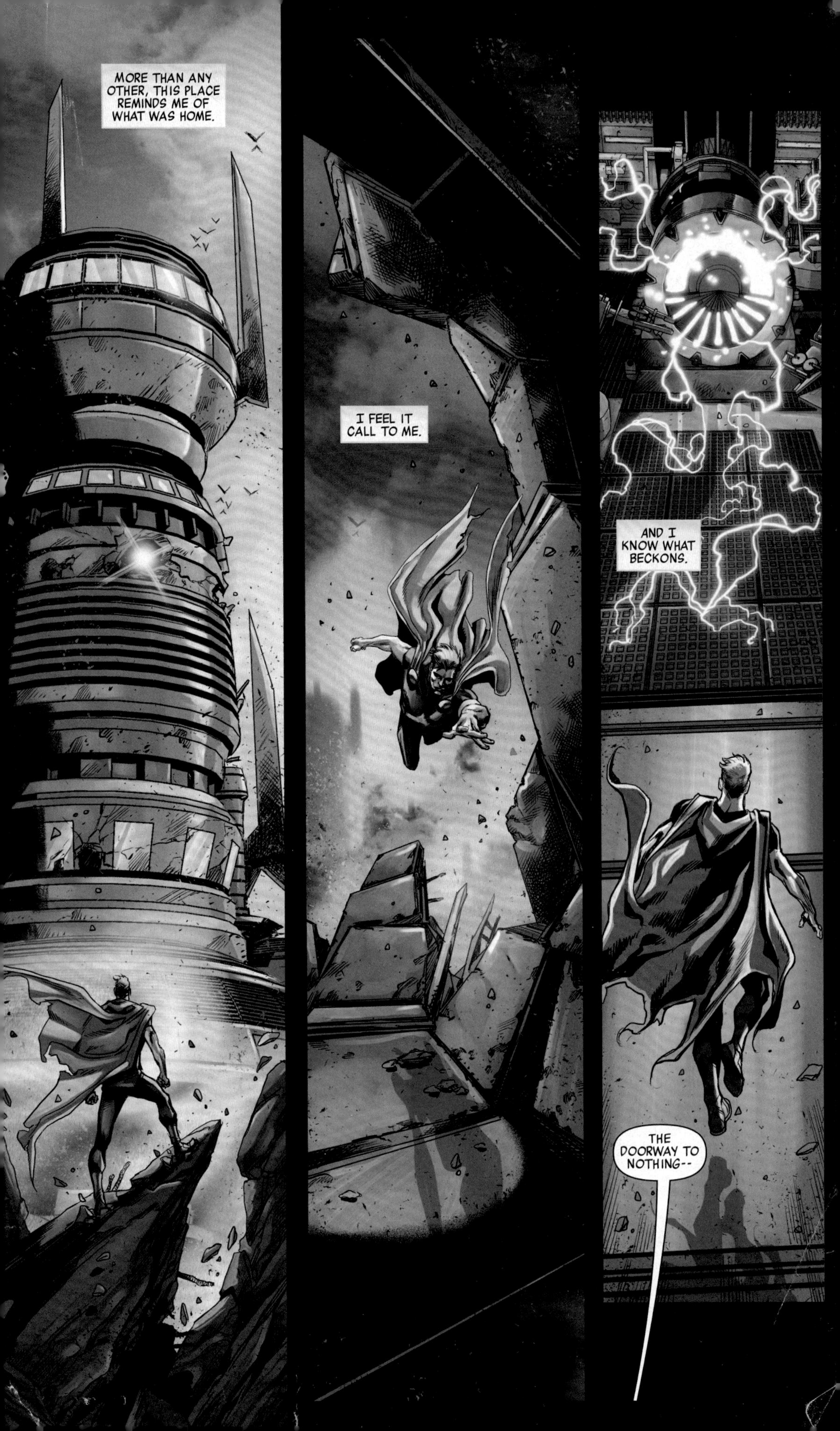
MORE THAN ANY OTHER, THIS PLACE REMINDS ME OF WHAT WAS HOME.
I FEEL IT CALL TO ME.
AND I KNOW WHAT BECKONS.
THE DOORWAY TO NOTHING--

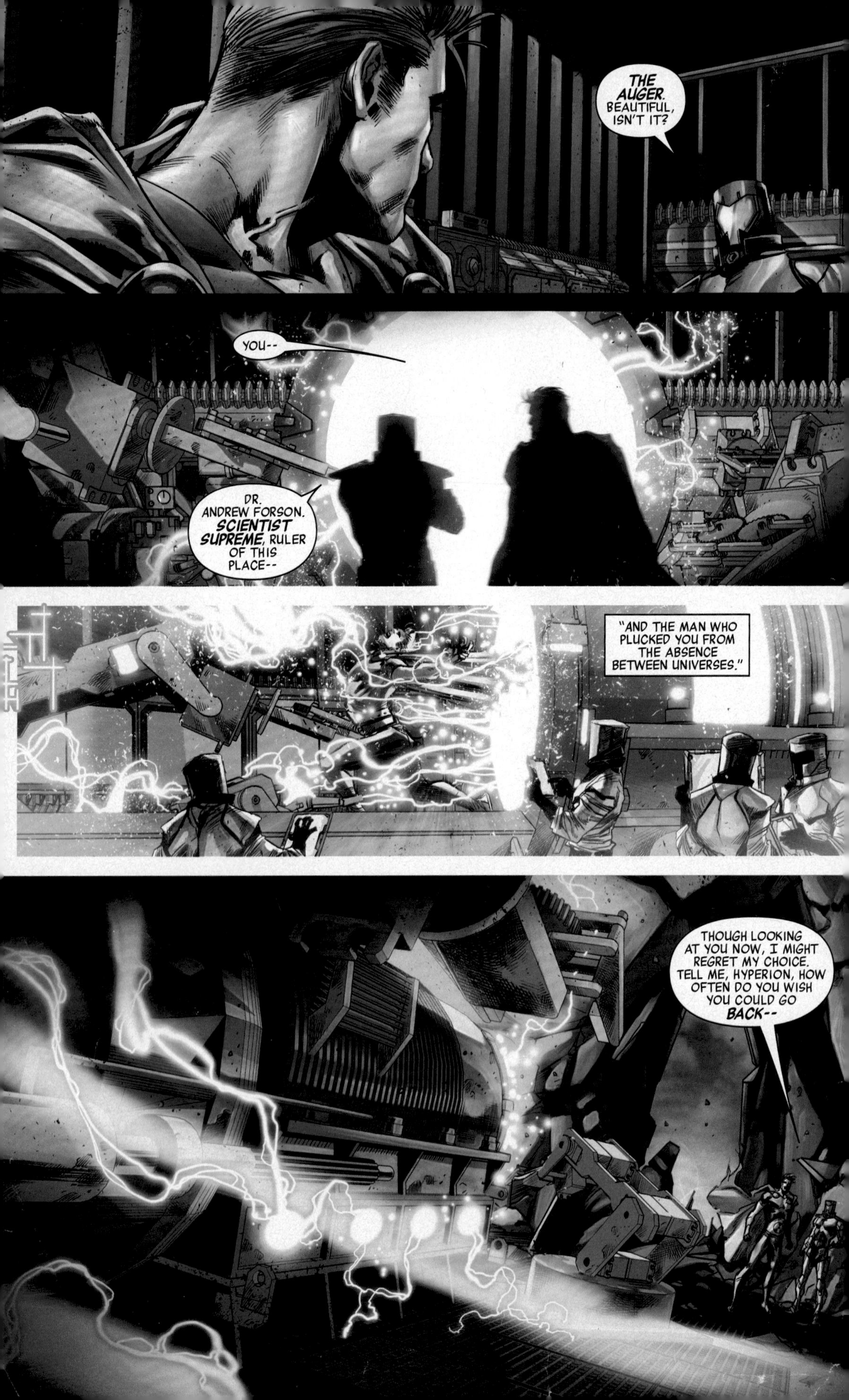
THE AUGER. BEAUTIFUL, ISN'T IT?
YOU--
DR. ANDREW FORSON. SCIENTIST SUPREME, RULER OF THIS PLACE--
"AND THE MAN WHO PLUCKED YOU FROM THE ABSENCE BETWEEN UNIVERSES."
THOUGH LOOKING AT YOU NOW, I MIGHT REGRET MY CHOICE. TELL ME, HYPERION, HOW OFTEN DO YOU WISH YOU COULD GO BACK--

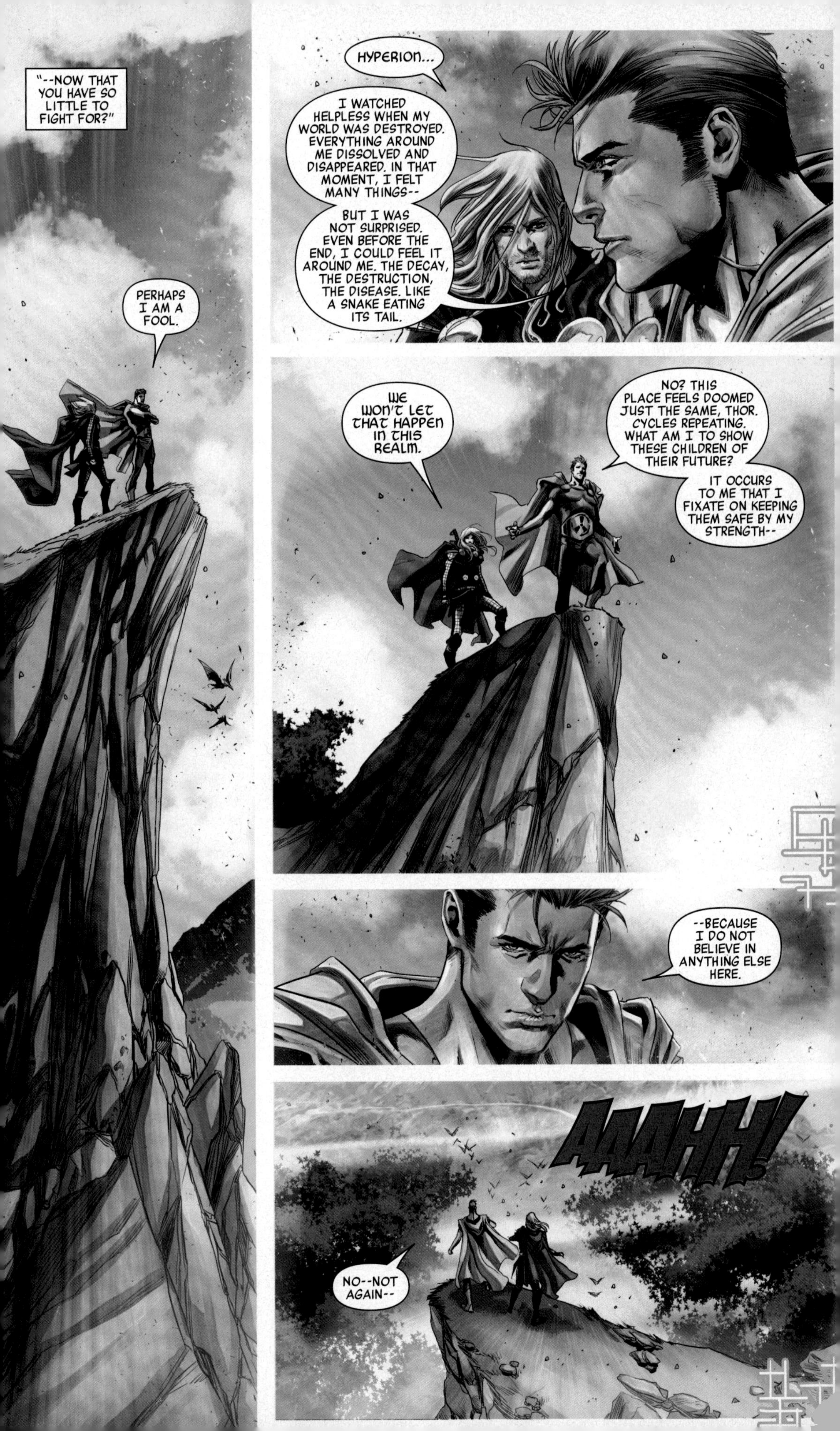
"--NOW THAT YOU HAVE SO LITTLE TO FIGHT FOR?"
PERHAPS I AM A FOOL.
HYPERION...
I WATCHED HELPLESS WHEN MY WORLD WAS DESTROYED. EVERYTHING AROUND ME DISSOLVED AND DISAPPEARED. IN THAT MOMENT, I FELT MANY THINGS--
BUT I WAS NOT SURPRISED. EVEN BEFORE THE END, I COULD FEEL IT AROUND ME. THE DECAY, THE DESTRUCTION, THE DISEASE. LIKE A SNAKE EATING ITS TAIL.
WE WON'T LET THAT HAPPEN IN THIS REALM.
NO? THIS PLACE FEELS DOOMED JUST THE SAME, THOR. CYCLES REPEATING. WHAT AM I TO SHOW THESE CHILDREN OF THEIR FUTURE?
IT OCCURS TO ME THAT I FIXATE ON KEEPING THEM SAFE BY MY STRENGTH--
--BECAUSE I DO NOT BELIEVE IN ANYTHING ELSE HERE.
AAAHH!
NO--NOT AGAIN--

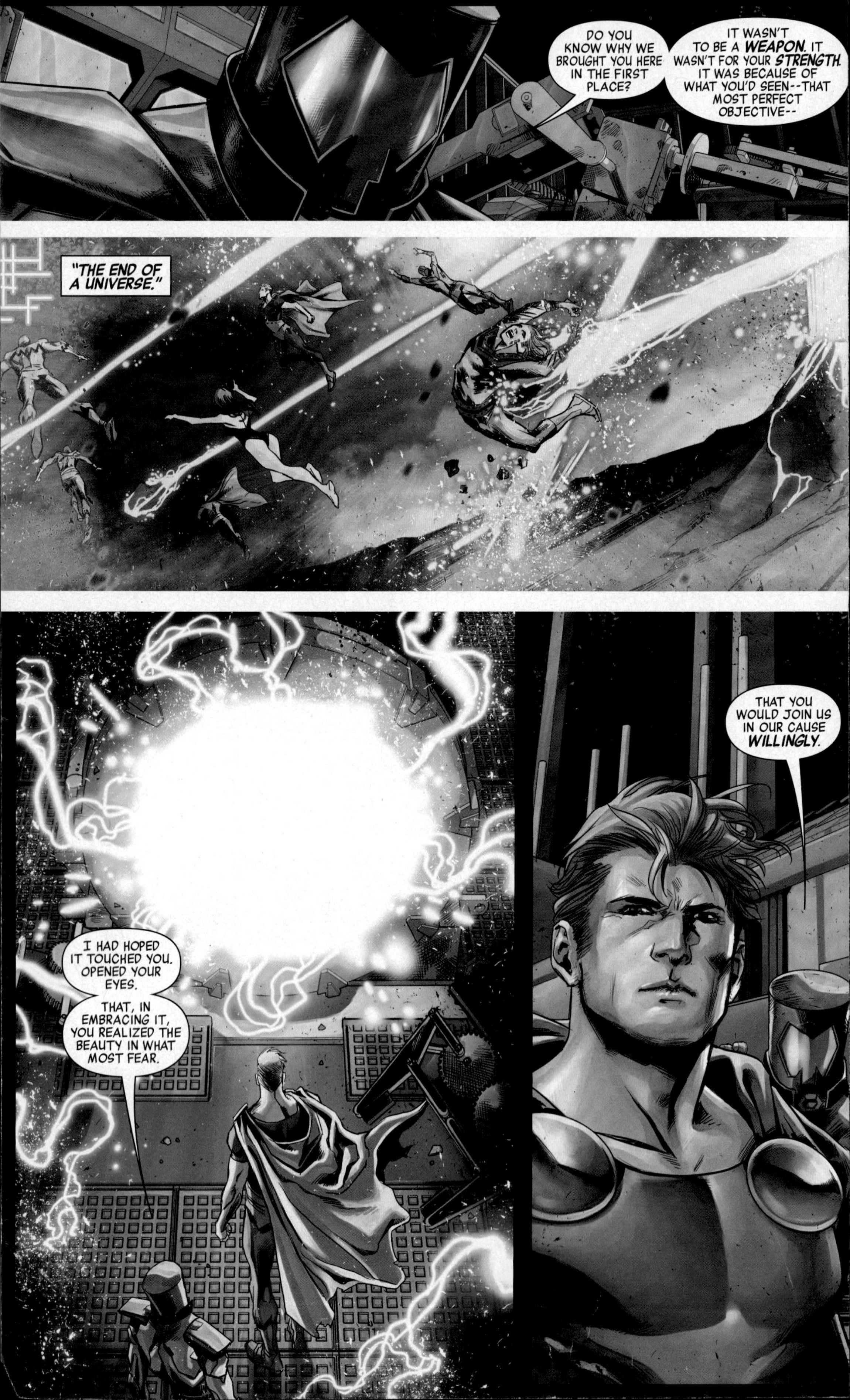

DO YOU KNOW WHY WE BROUGHT YOU HERE IN THE FIRST PLACE?
IT WASN'T TO BE A **WEAPON**. IT WASN'T FOR YOUR **STRENGTH**. IT WAS BECAUSE OF WHAT YOU'D SEEN--THAT MOST PERFECT OBJECTIVE--
"THE END OF A UNIVERSE."
I HAD HOPED IT TOUCHED YOU. OPENED YOUR EYES.
THAT, IN EMBRACING IT, YOU REALIZED THE BEAUTY IN WHAT MOST FEAR.
THAT YOU WOULD JOIN US IN OUR CAUSE **WILLINGLY**.

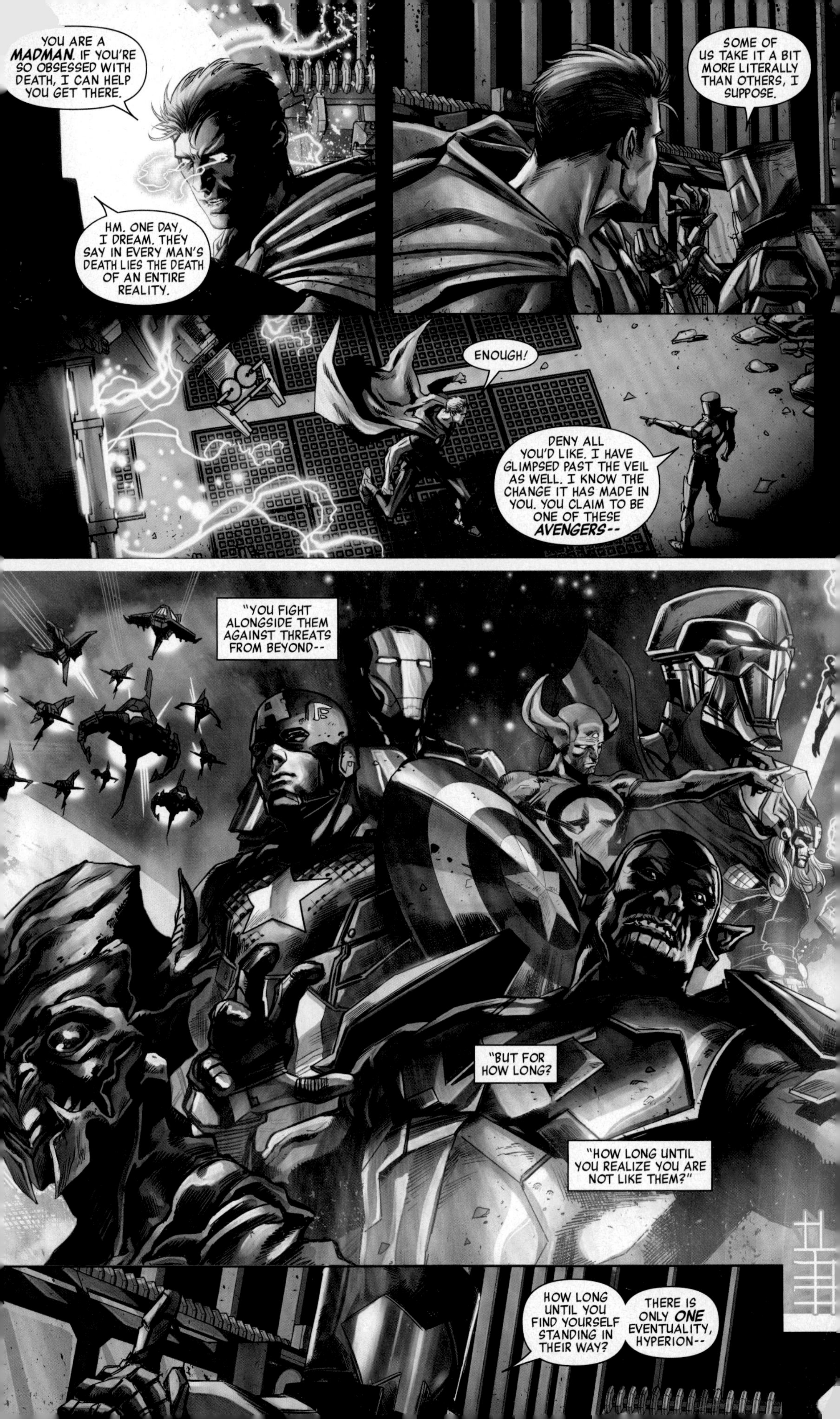
YOU ARE A MADMAN. IF YOU'RE SO OBSESSED WITH DEATH, I CAN HELP YOU GET THERE.
HM. ONE DAY, I DREAM. THEY SAY IN EVERY MAN'S DEATH LIES THE DEATH OF AN ENTIRE REALITY.
SOME OF US TAKE IT A BIT MORE LITERALLY THAN OTHERS, I SUPPOSE.
ENOUGH!
DENY ALL YOU'D LIKE. I HAVE GLIMPSED PAST THE VEIL AS WELL. I KNOW THE CHANGE IT HAS MADE IN YOU. YOU CLAIM TO BE ONE OF THESE AVENGERS--
"YOU FIGHT ALONGSIDE THEM AGAINST THREATS FROM BEYOND--
"BUT FOR HOW LONG?
"HOW LONG UNTIL YOU REALIZE YOU ARE NOT LIKE THEM?"
HOW LONG UNTIL YOU FIND YOURSELF STANDING IN THEIR WAY?
THERE IS ONLY ONE EVENTUALITY, HYPERION--

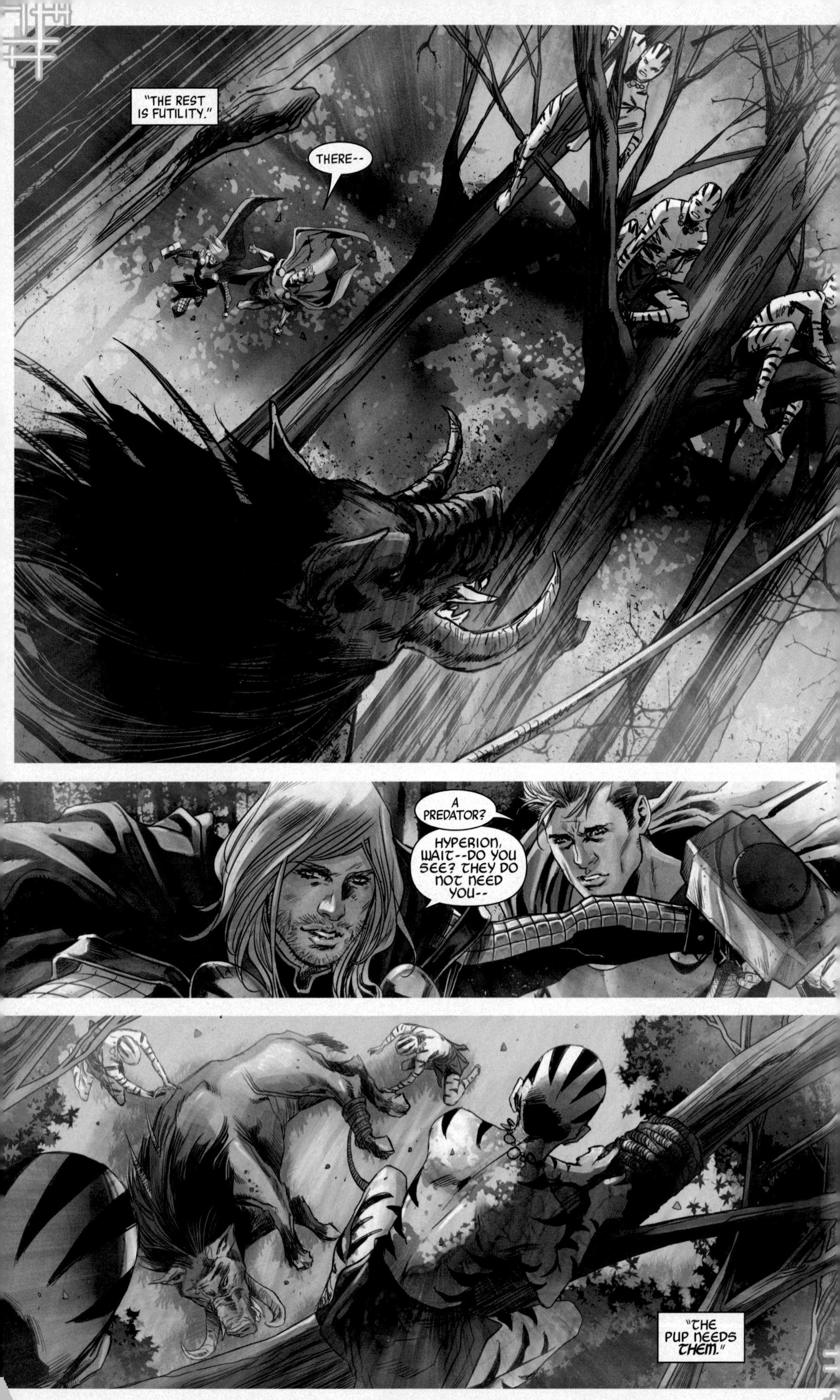
"THE REST IS FUTILITY."
THERE--
A PREDATOR?
HYPERION, WAIT--DO YOU SEE? THEY DO NOT NEED YOU--
"THE PUP NEEDS THEM."

YOUR INSPIRATION AT WORK.

TO SEE YOURSELF REFLECTED IN THEIR ACTIONS--IT IS A REWARD, I'LL ADMIT THAT.

THEN LET THAT BE THE HOPE YOU LOST, FRIEND--WHEN I SAID EARLIER THAT THIS REALM WILL BE DIFFERENT, IT WAS NOT ARROGANCE. I DO NOT THINK US ANY BETTER.

T THEY D NOT VE YOUR RNING. AND IF YOU ARE A FFERENT MAN AN YOU WERE BEFORE ITS END, AS YOU CLAIM--

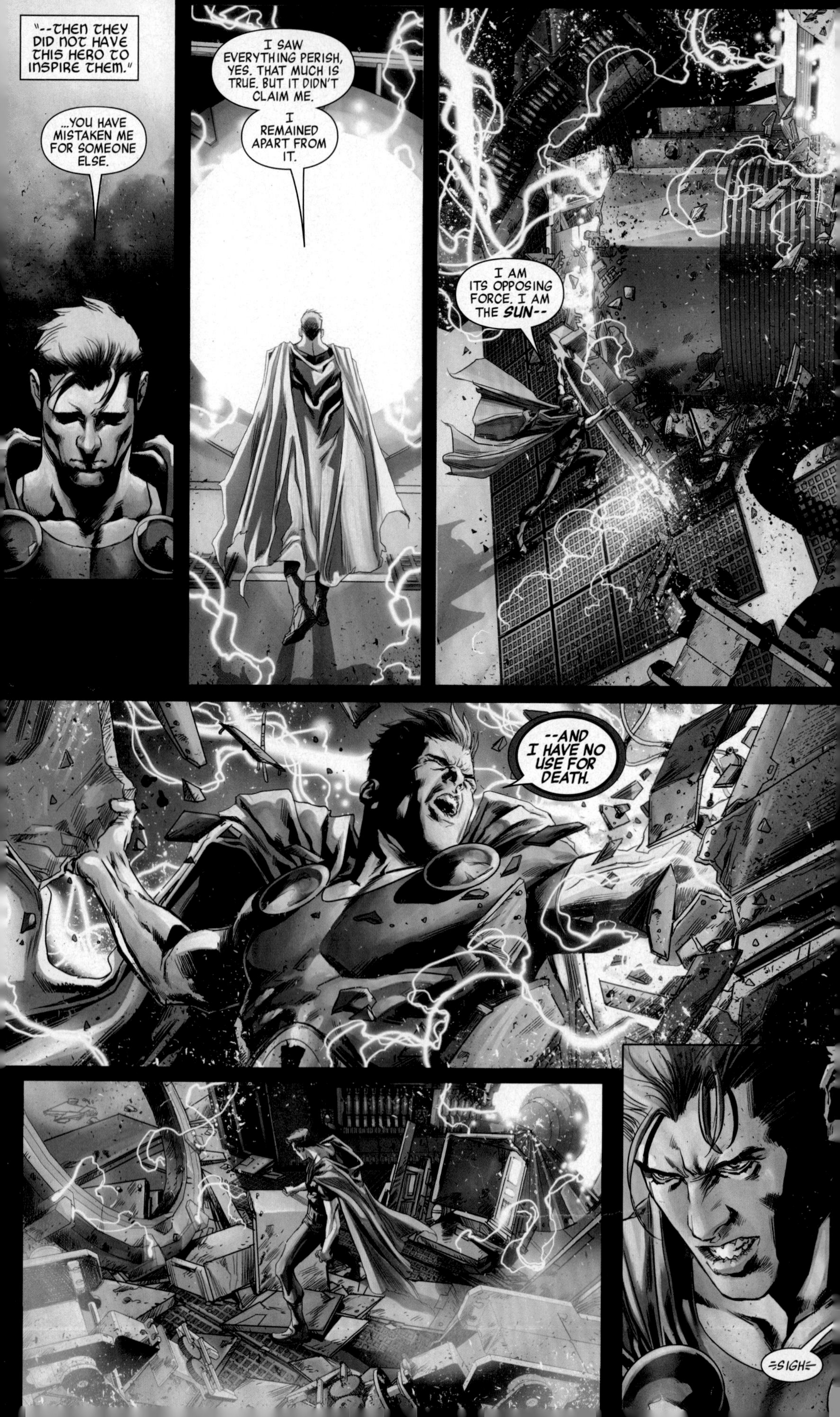
"--THEN THEY DID NOT HAVE THIS HERO TO INSPIRE THEM."
...YOU HAVE MISTAKEN ME FOR SOMEONE ELSE.
I SAW EVERYTHING PERISH, YES. THAT MUCH IS TRUE. BUT IT DIDN'T CLAIM ME.
I REMAINED APART FROM IT.
I AM ITS OPPOSING FORCE. I AM THE SUN--
--AND I HAVE NO USE FOR DEATH.
=SIGH=

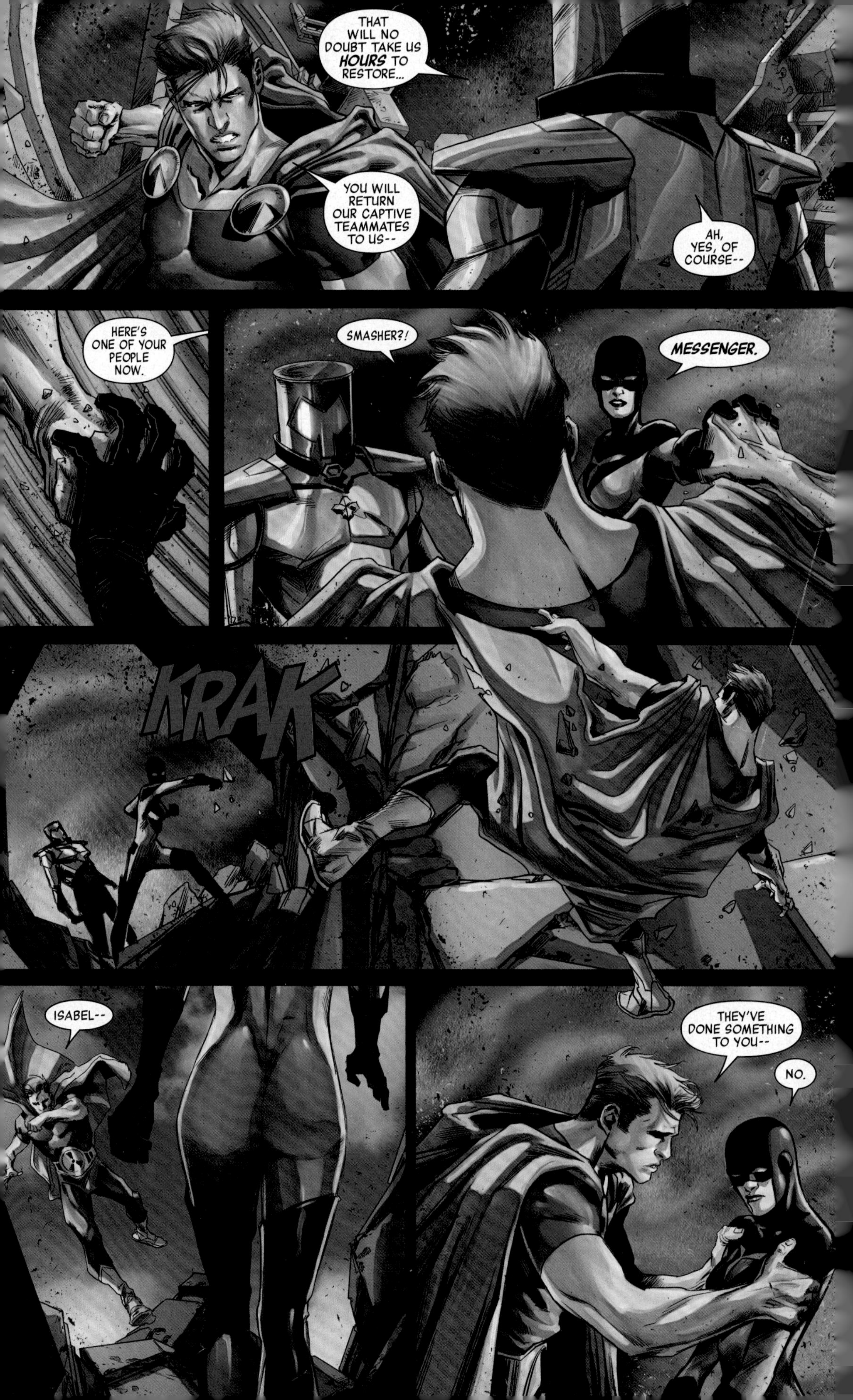
THAT WILL NO DOUBT TAKE US HOURS TO RESTORE...
YOU WILL RETURN OUR CAPTIVE TEAMMATES TO US--
AH, YES, OF COURSE--
HERE'S ONE OF YOUR PEOPLE NOW.
SMASHER?!
MESSENGER.
KRAK
ISABEL--
THEY'VE DONE SOMETHING TO YOU--
NO.

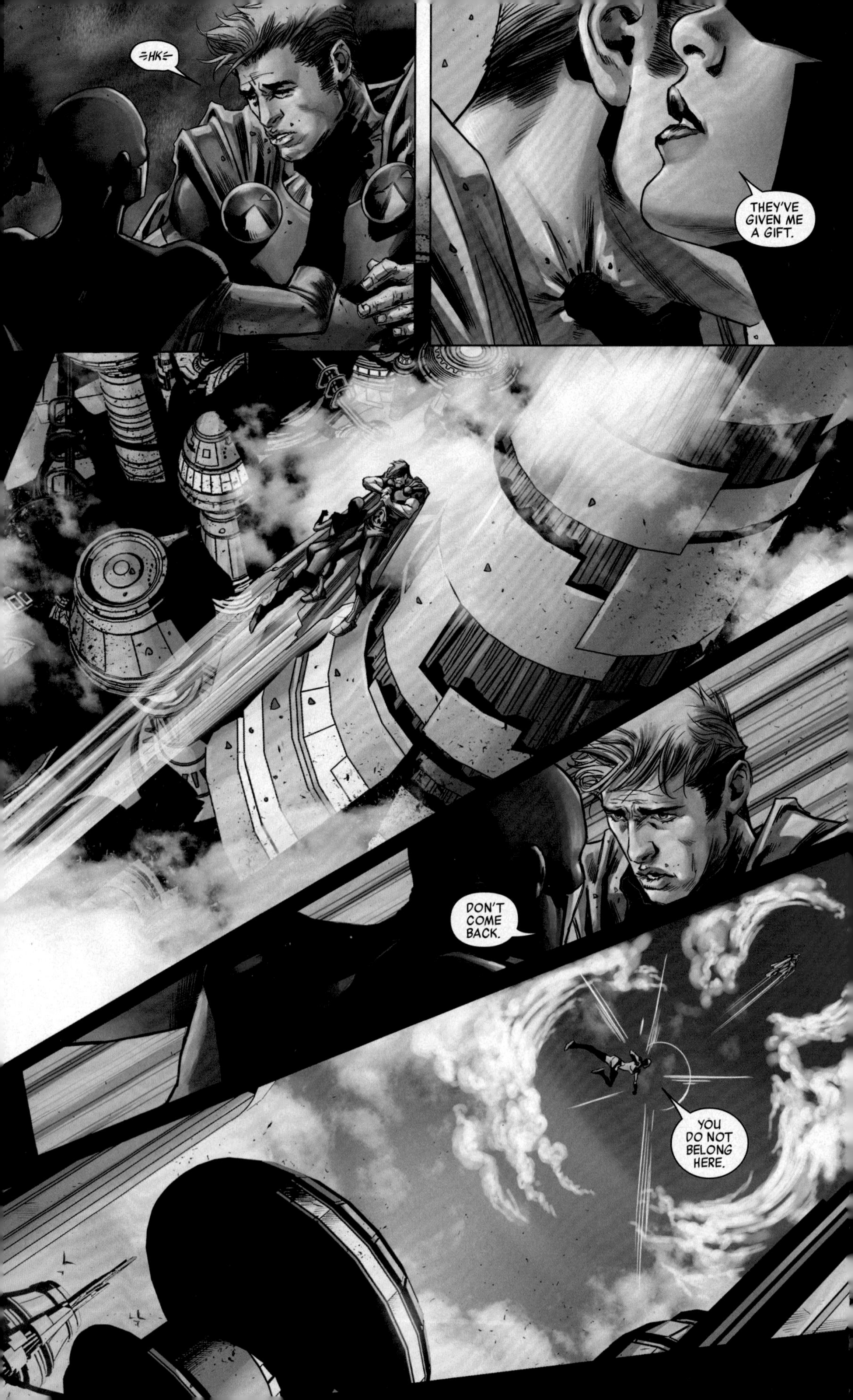
HK
THEY'VE GIVEN ME A GIFT.
DON'T COME BACK.
YOU DO NOT BELONG HERE.

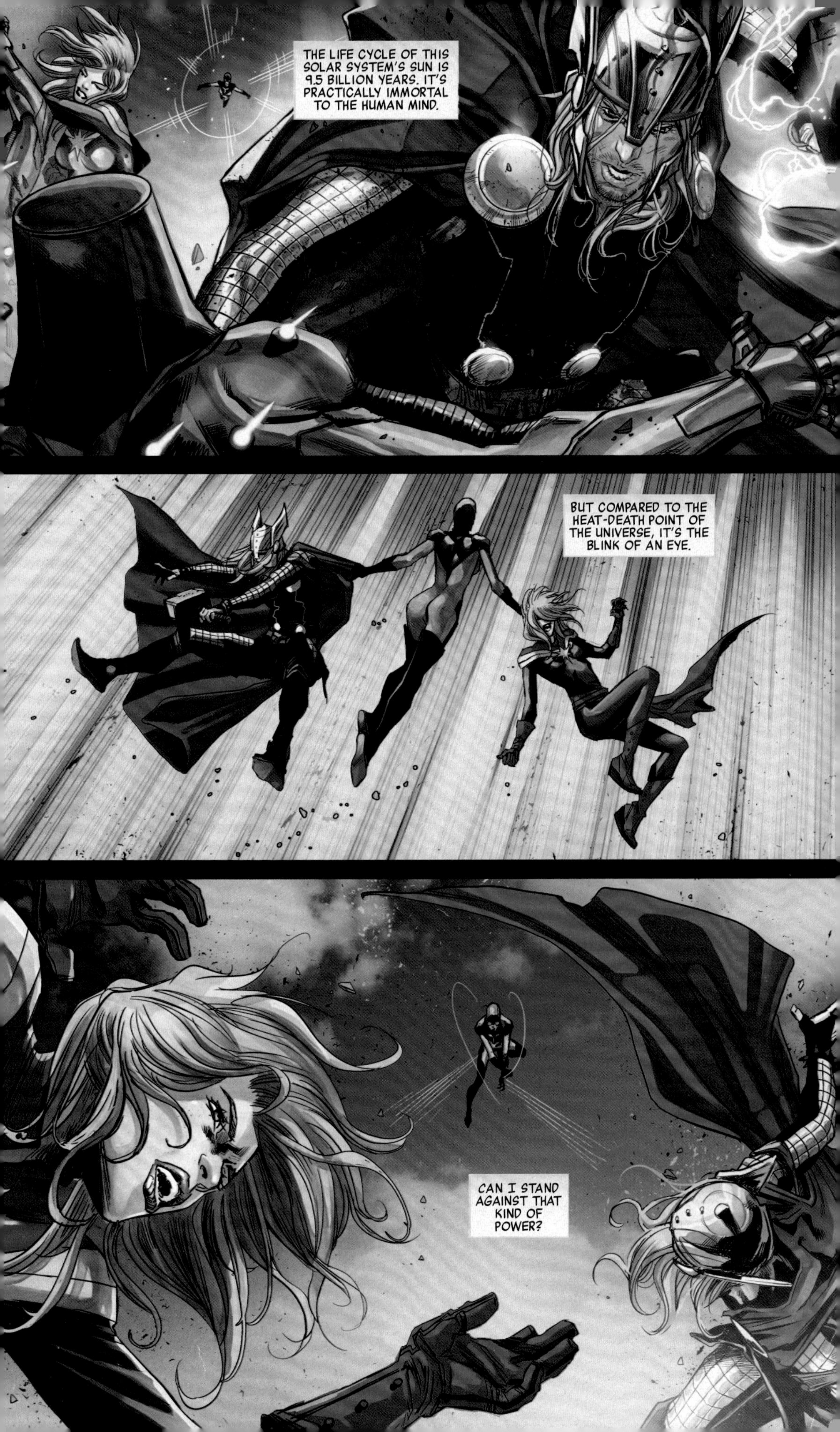
THE LIFE CYCLE OF THIS SOLAR SYSTEM'S SUN IS 9.5 BILLION YEARS. IT'S PRACTICALLY IMMORTAL TO THE HUMAN MIND.
BUT COMPARED TO THE HEAT-DEATH POINT OF THE UNIVERSE, IT'S THE BLINK OF AN EYE.
CAN I STAND AGAINST THAT KIND OF POWER?

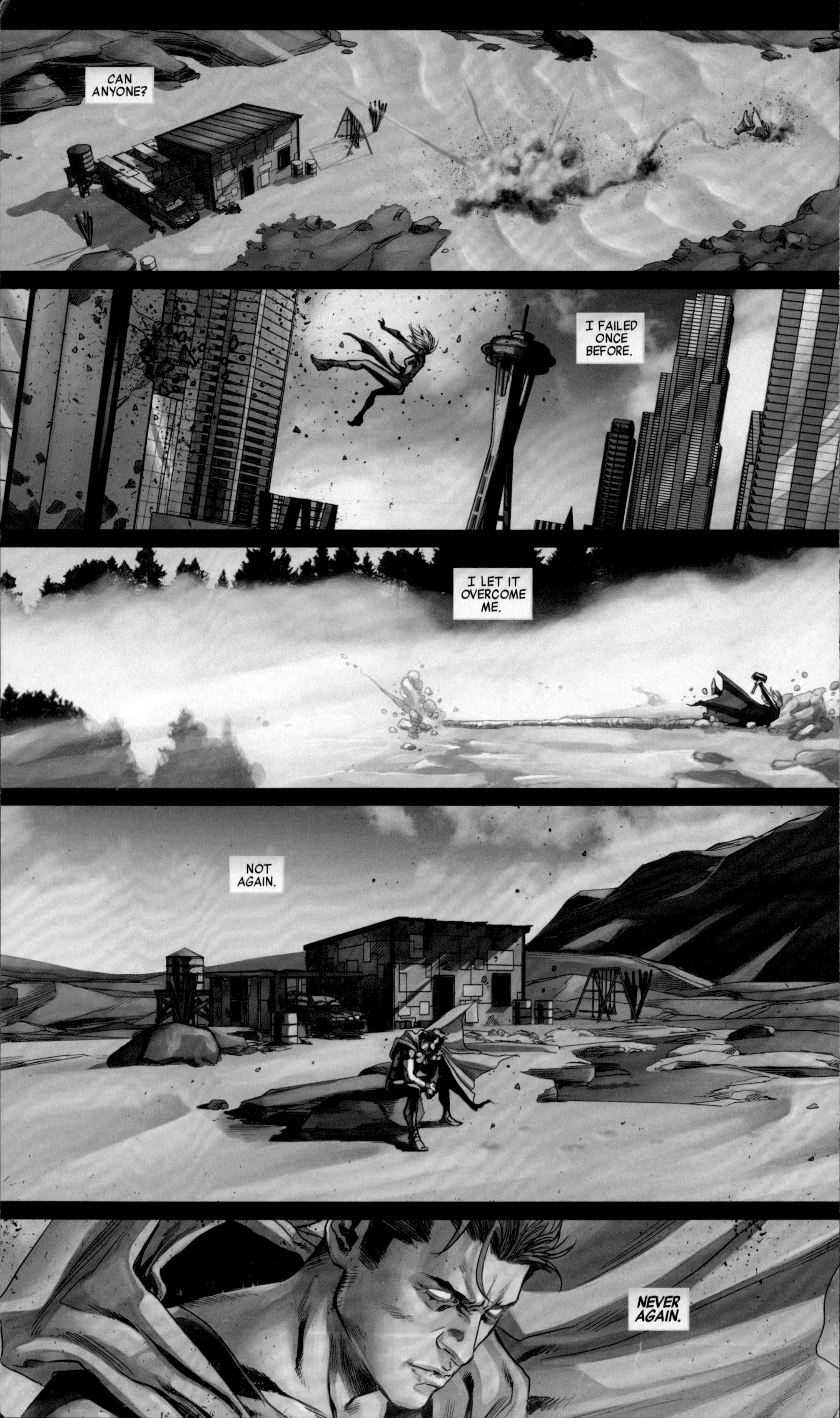

CAN ANYONE?
I FAILED ONCE BEFORE.
I LET IT OVERCOME ME.
NOT AGAIN.
NEVER AGAIN.

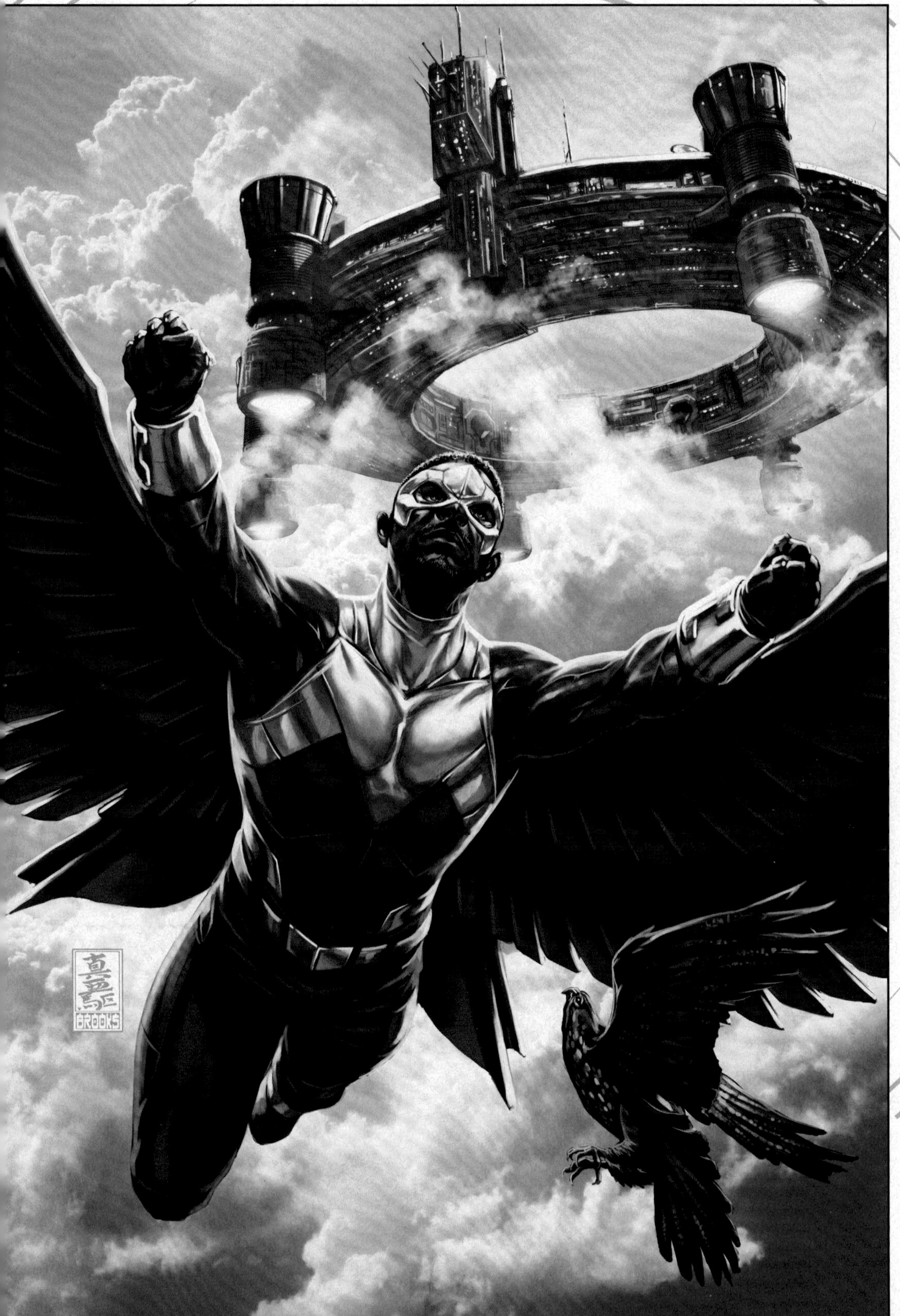
BROOKS

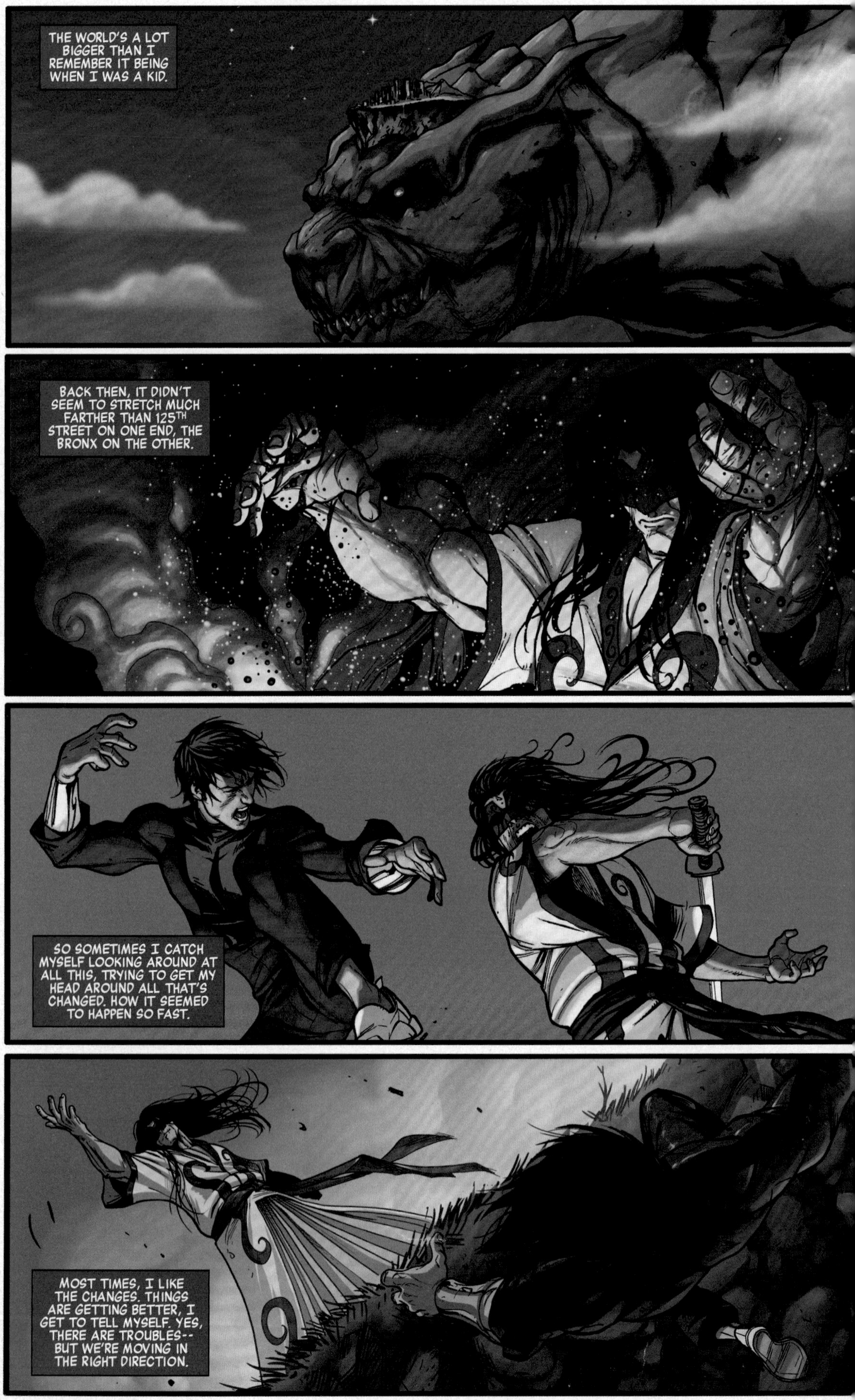
THE WORLD'S A LOT BIGGER THAN I REMEMBER IT BEING WHEN I WAS A KID.
BACK THEN, IT DIDN'T SEEM TO STRETCH MUCH FARTHER THAN 125TH STREET ON ONE END, THE BRONX ON THE OTHER.
SO SOMETIMES I CATCH MYSELF LOOKING AROUND AT ALL THIS, TRYING TO GET MY HEAD AROUND ALL THAT'S CHANGED. HOW IT SEEMED TO HAPPEN SO FAST.
MOST TIMES, I LIKE THE CHANGES. THINGS ARE GETTING BETTER, I GET TO TELL MYSELF. YES, THERE ARE TROUBLES-- BUT WE'RE MOVING IN THE RIGHT DIRECTION.

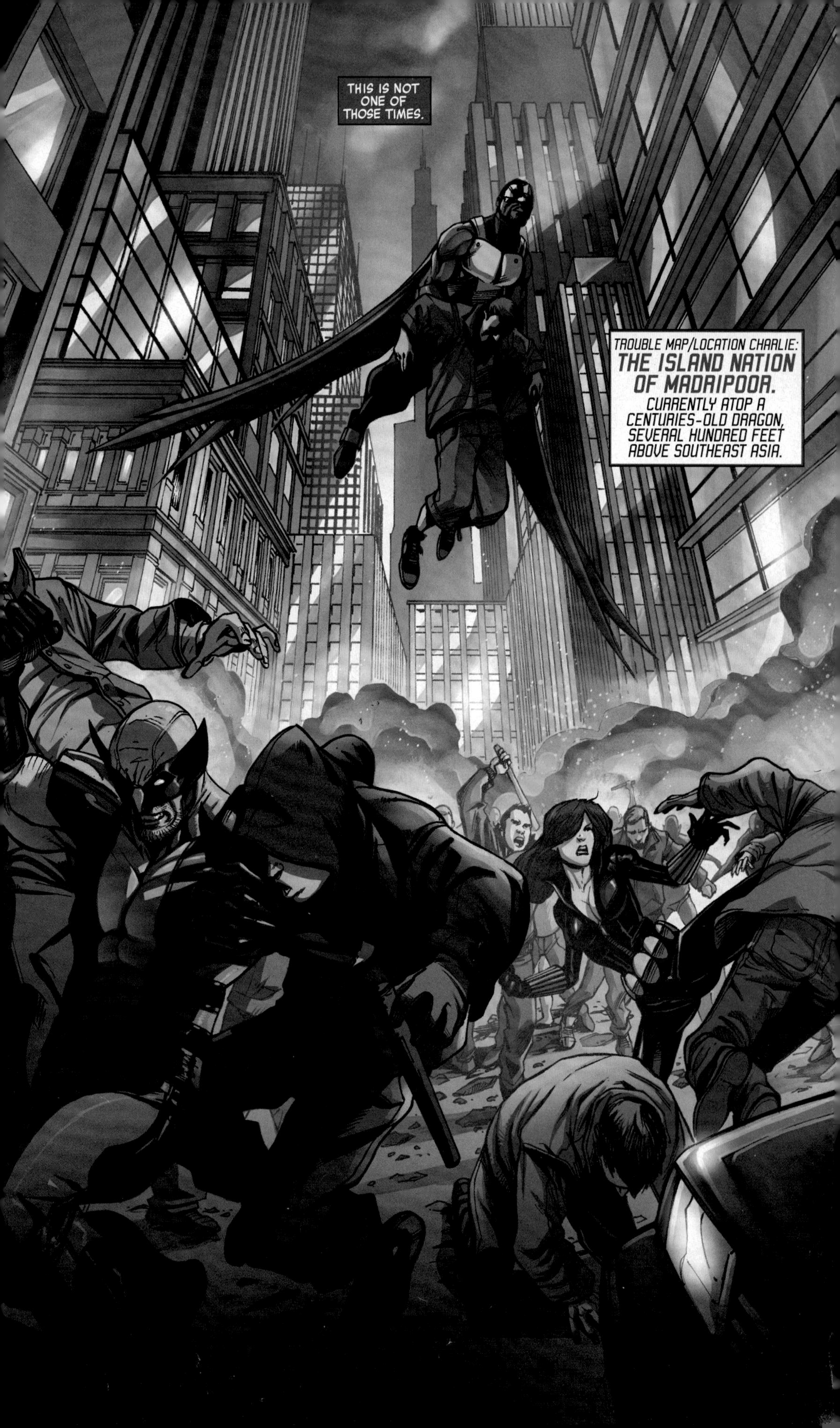
THIS IS NOT ONE OF THOSE TIMES.
TROUBLE MAP/LOCATION CHARLIE: THE ISLAND NATION OF MADRIPOOR. CURRENTLY ATOP A CENTURIES-OLD DRAGON, SEVERAL HUNDRED FEET ABOVE SOUTHEAST ASIA.

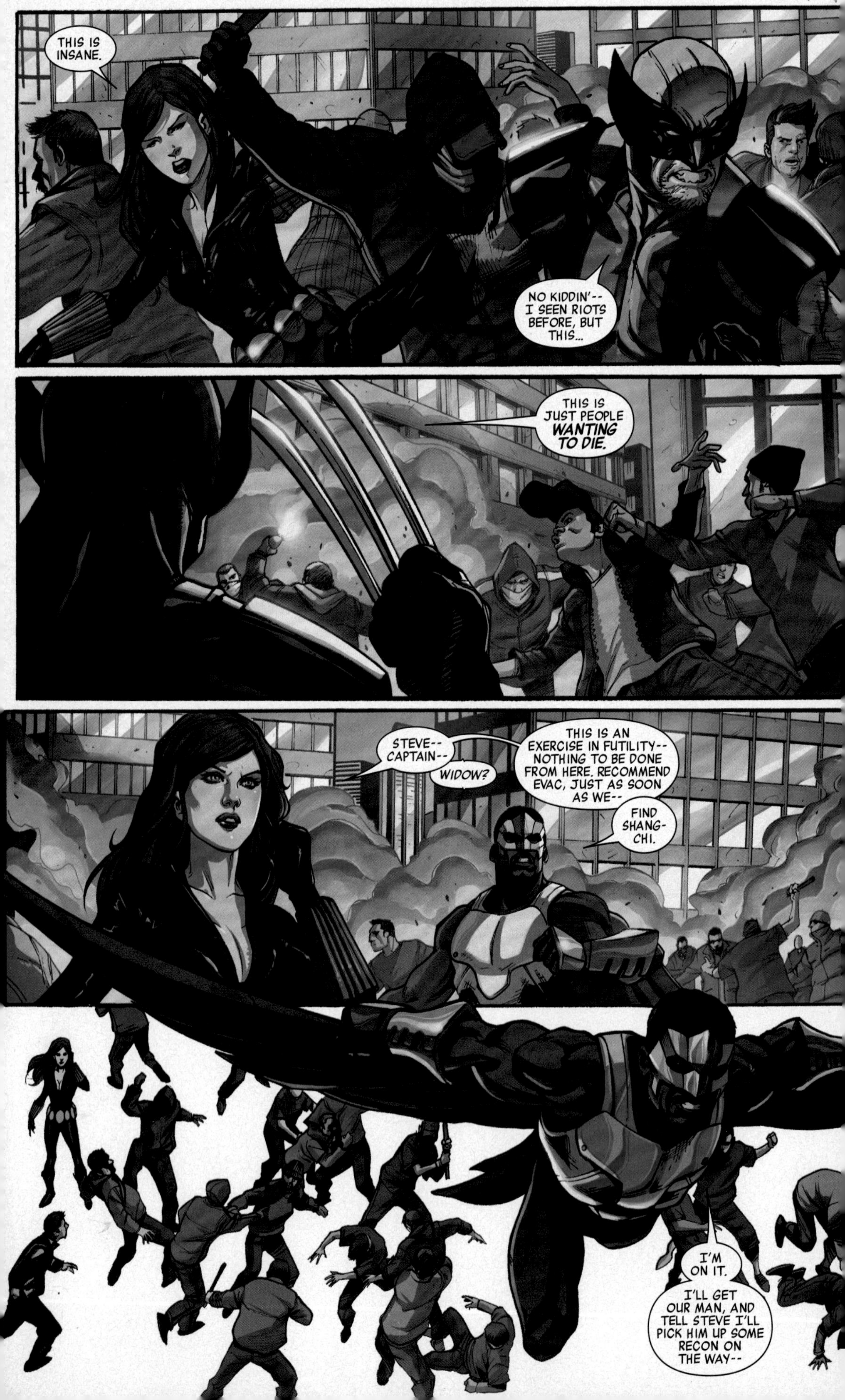
THIS IS INSANE.
NO KIDDIN'-- I SEEN RIOTS BEFORE, BUT THIS...
THIS IS JUST PEOPLE *WANTING TO DIE.*
STEVE-- CAPTAIN--
WIDOW?
THIS IS AN EXERCISE IN FUTILITY-- NOTHING TO BE DONE FROM HERE. RECOMMEND EVAC, JUST AS SOON AS WE--
FIND SHANG-CHI.
I'M ON IT.
I'LL GET OUR MAN, AND TELL STEVE I'LL PICK HIM UP SOME RECON ON THE WAY--

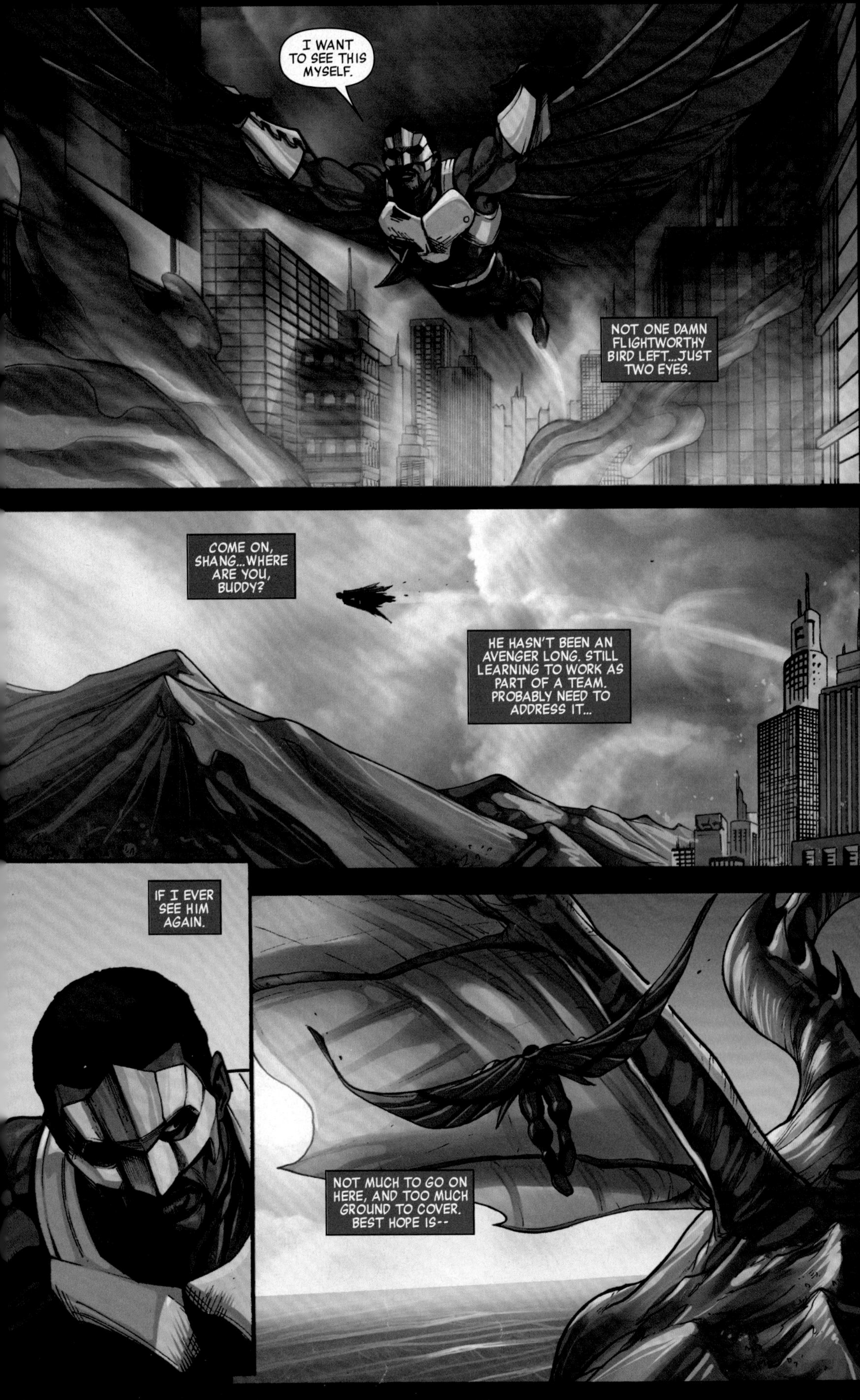
I WANT TO SEE THIS MYSELF.
NOT ONE DAMN FLIGHTWORTHY BIRD LEFT...JUST TWO EYES.
COME ON, SHANG...WHERE ARE YOU, BUDDY?
HE HASN'T BEEN AN AVENGER LONG. STILL LEARNING TO WORK AS PART OF A TEAM. PROBABLY NEED TO ADDRESS IT...
IF I EVER SEE HIM AGAIN.
NOT MUCH TO GO ON HERE, AND TOO MUCH GROUND TO COVER. BEST HOPE IS--

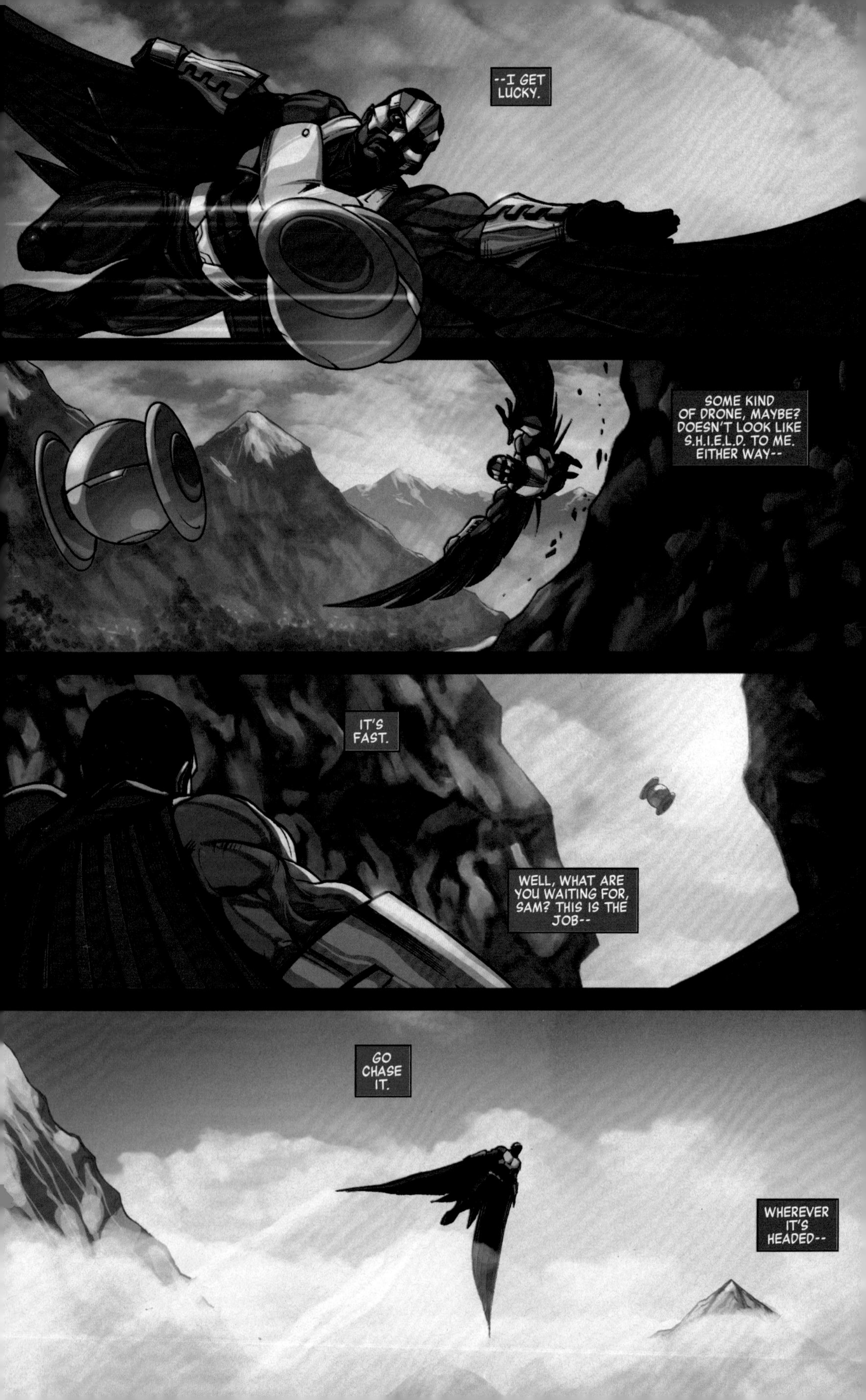
--I GET LUCKY.
SOME KIND OF DRONE, MAYBE? DOESN'T LOOK LIKE S.H.I.E.L.D. TO ME. EITHER WAY--
IT'S FAST.
WELL, WHAT ARE YOU WAITING FOR, SAM? THIS IS THE JOB--
GO CHASE IT.
WHEREVER IT'S HEADED--

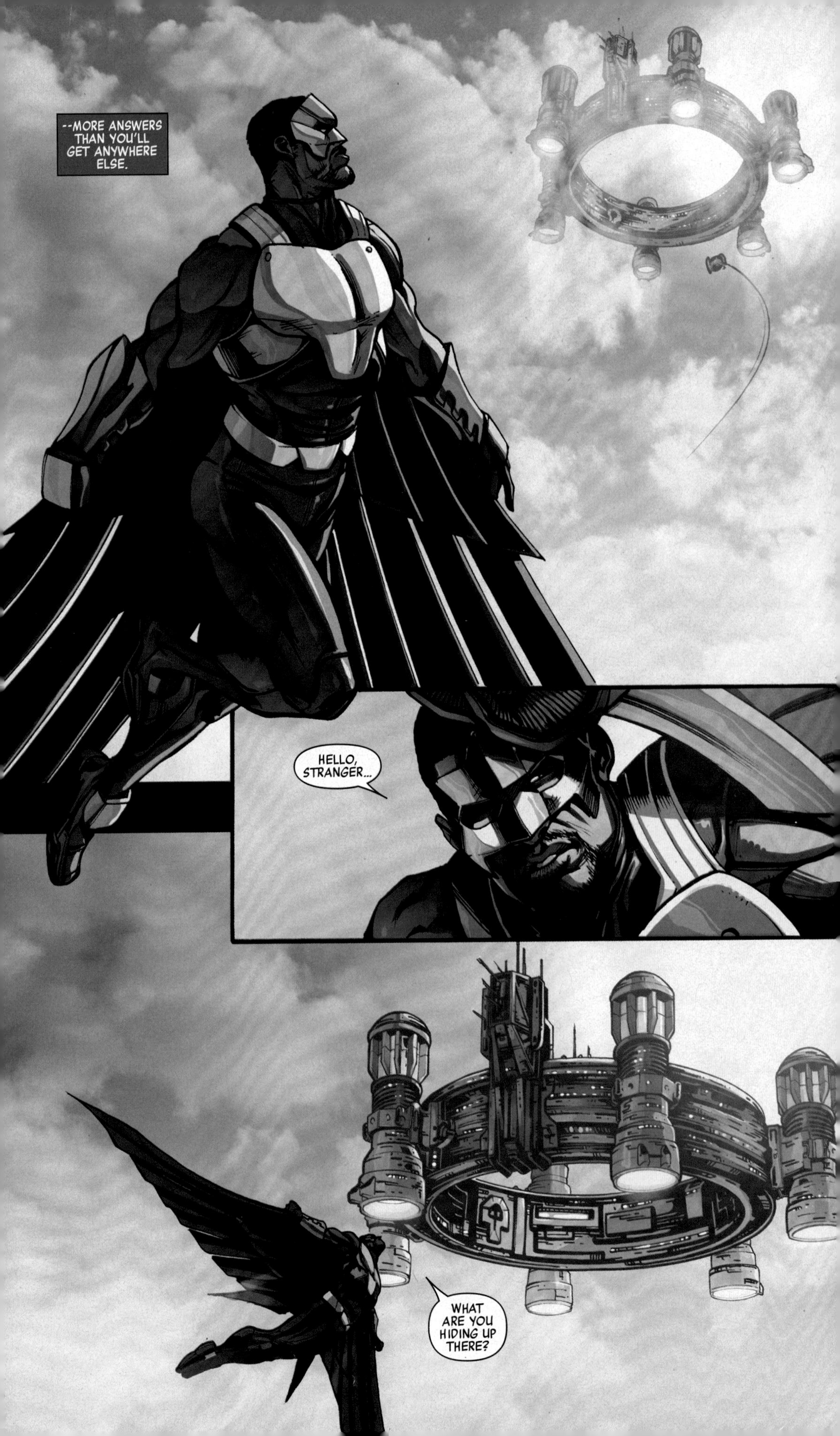

--MORE ANSWERS THAN YOU'LL GET ANYWHERE ELSE.
HELLO, STRANGER...
WHAT ARE YOU HIDING UP THERE?

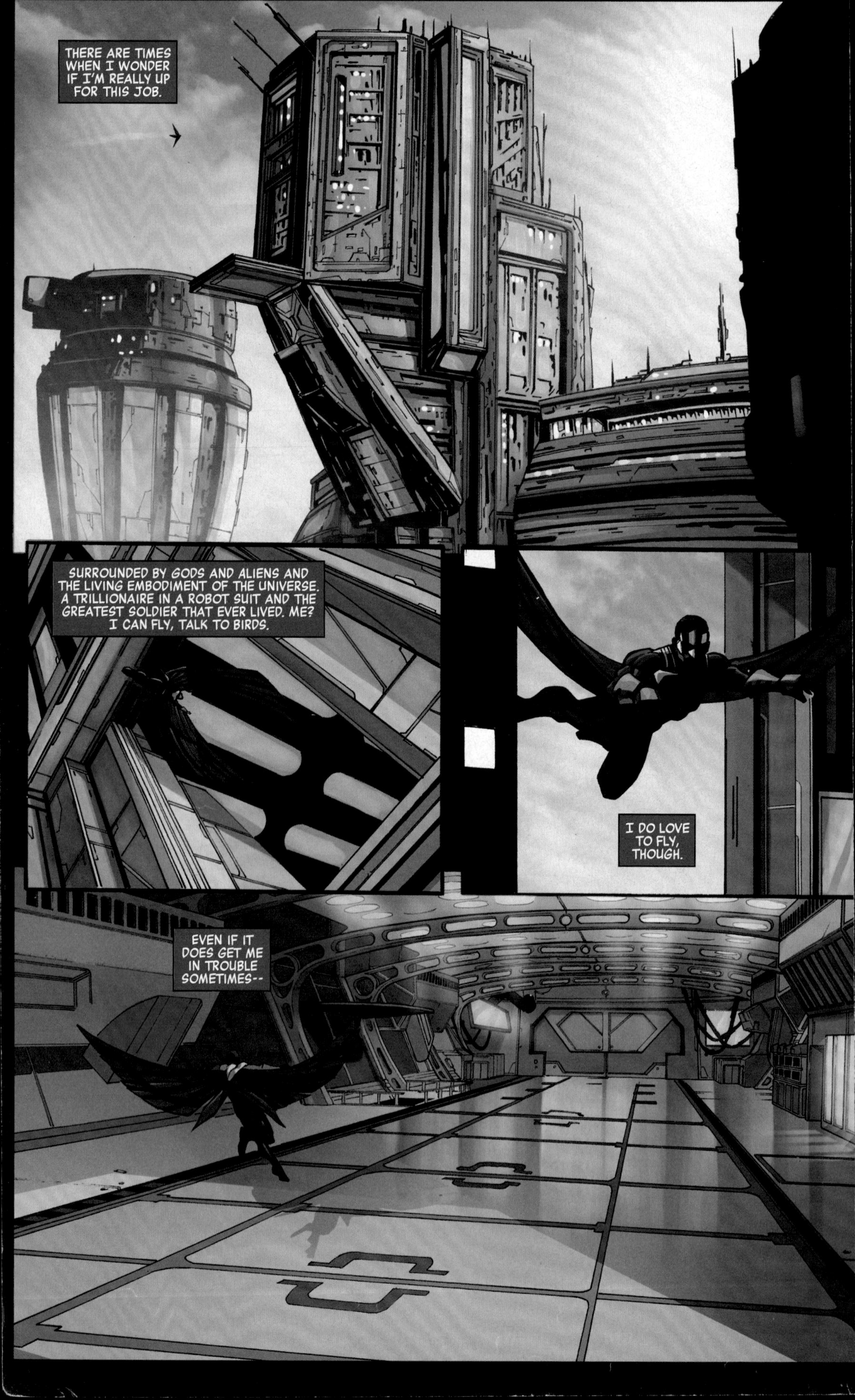
THERE ARE TIMES WHEN I WONDER IF I'M REALLY UP FOR THIS JOB.
SURROUNDED BY GODS AND ALIENS AND THE LIVING EMBODIMENT OF THE UNIVERSE. A TRILLIONAIRE IN A ROBOT SUIT AND THE GREATEST SOLDIER THAT EVER LIVED. ME? I CAN FLY, TALK TO BIRDS.
I DO LOVE TO FLY, THOUGH.
EVEN IF IT DOES GET ME IN TROUBLE SOMETIMES--

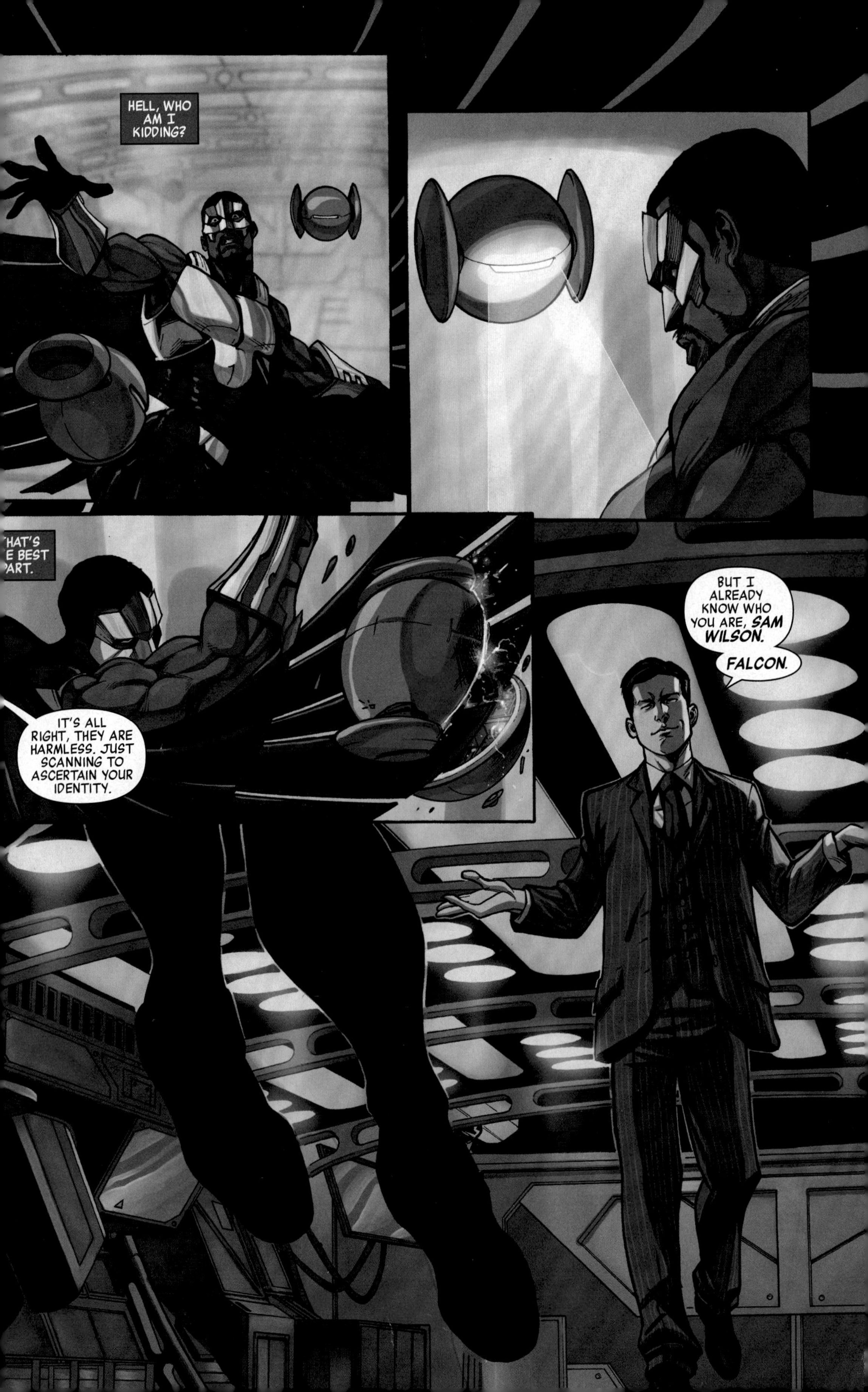
HELL, WHO AM I KIDDING?
HAT'S E BEST ART.
IT'S ALL RIGHT, THEY ARE HARMLESS. JUST SCANNING TO ASCERTAIN YOUR IDENTITY.
BUT I ALREADY KNOW WHO YOU ARE, SAM WILSON.
FALCON.

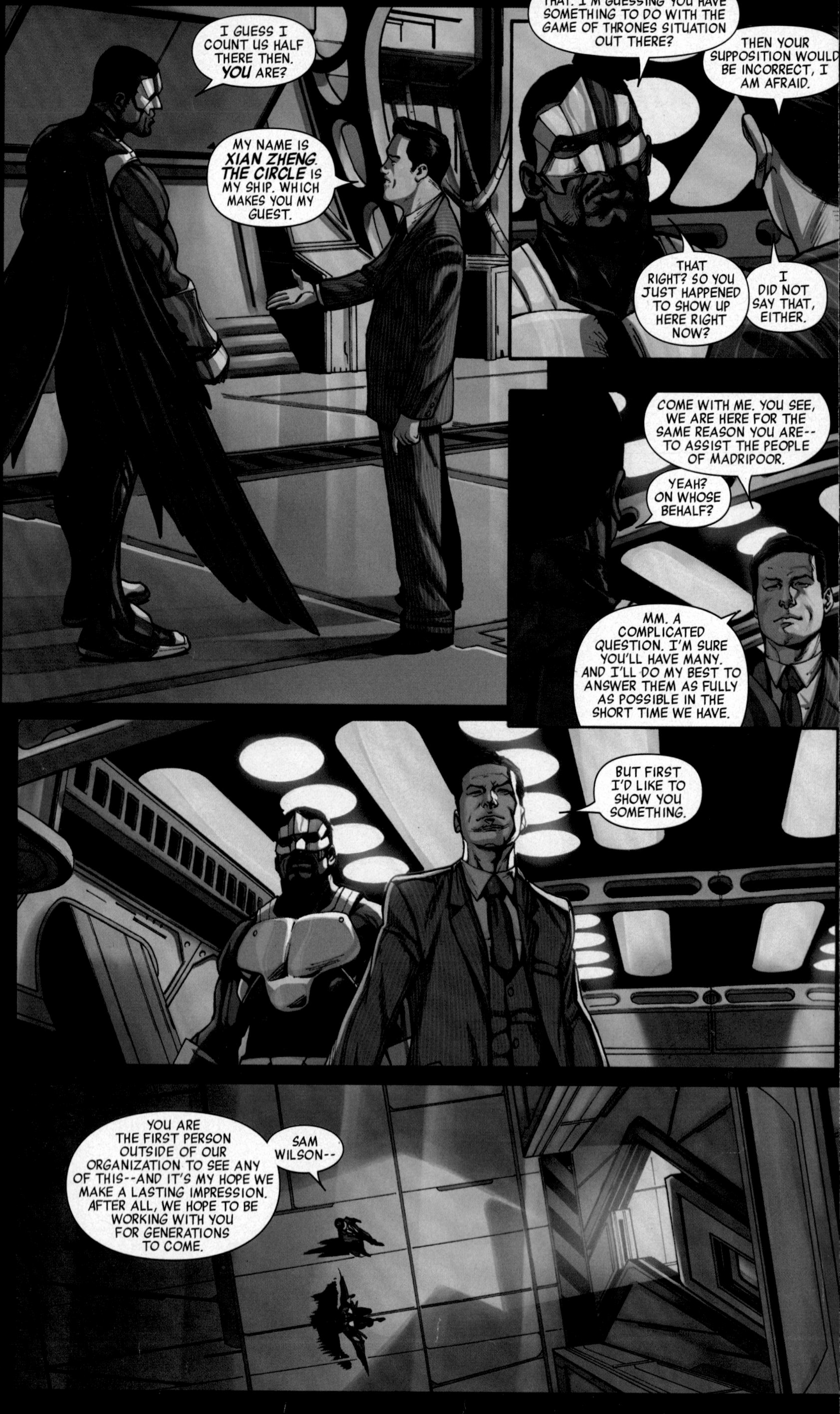
I GUESS I COUNT US HALF THERE THEN. YOU ARE?
MY NAME IS XIAN ZHENG. THE CIRCLE IS MY SHIP. WHICH MAKES YOU MY GUEST.
...SOMETHING LIKE THAT. I'M GUESSING YOU HAVE SOMETHING TO DO WITH THE GAME OF THRONES SITUATION OUT THERE?
THEN YOUR SUPPOSITION WOULD BE INCORRECT, I AM AFRAID.
THAT RIGHT? SO YOU JUST HAPPENED TO SHOW UP HERE RIGHT NOW?
I DID NOT SAY THAT, EITHER.
COME WITH ME. YOU SEE, WE ARE HERE FOR THE SAME REASON YOU ARE--TO ASSIST THE PEOPLE OF MADRIPOOR.
YEAH? ON WHOSE BEHALF?
MM. A COMPLICATED QUESTION. I'M SURE YOU'LL HAVE MANY. AND I'LL DO MY BEST TO ANSWER THEM AS FULLY AS POSSIBLE IN THE SHORT TIME WE HAVE.
BUT FIRST I'D LIKE TO SHOW YOU SOMETHING.
SAM WILSON--
YOU ARE THE FIRST PERSON OUTSIDE OF OUR ORGANIZATION TO SEE ANY OF THIS--AND IT'S MY HOPE WE MAKE A LASTING IMPRESSION. AFTER ALL, WE HOPE TO BE WORKING WITH YOU FOR GENERATIONS TO COME.

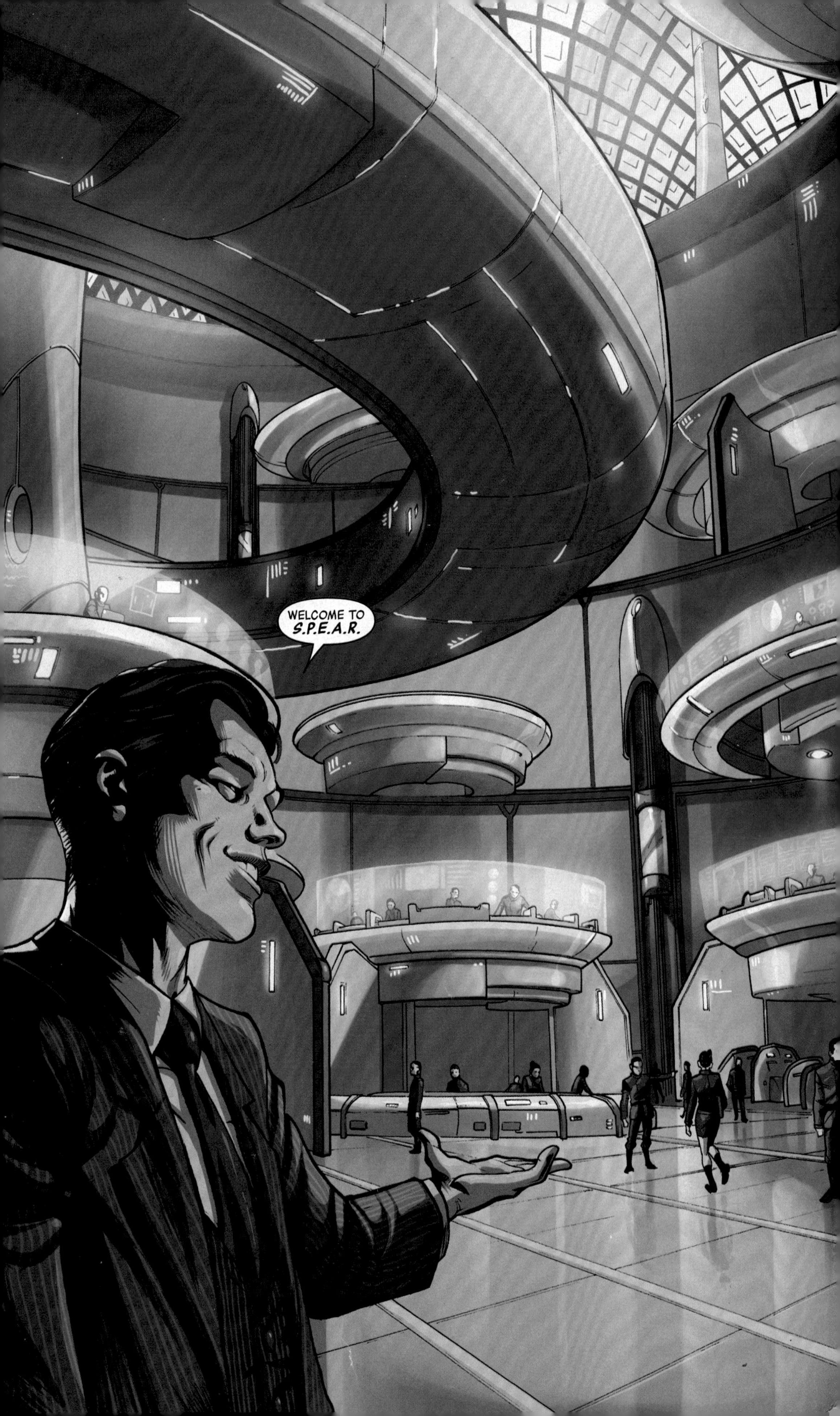
WELCOME TO S.P.E.A.R.

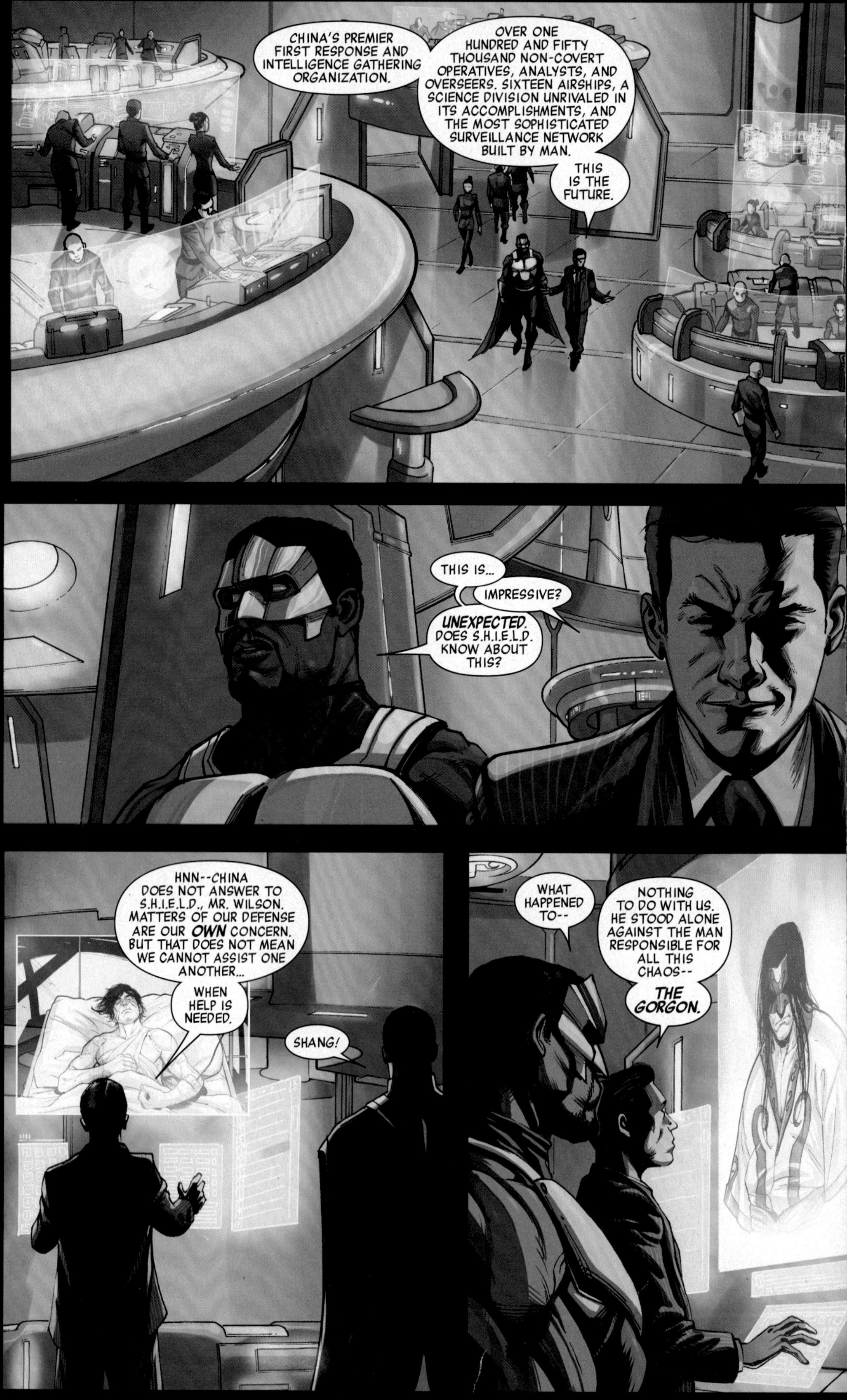
CHINA'S PREMIER FIRST RESPONSE AND INTELLIGENCE GATHERING ORGANIZATION.
OVER ONE HUNDRED AND FIFTY THOUSAND NON-COVERT OPERATIVES, ANALYSTS, AND OVERSEERS. SIXTEEN AIRSHIPS, A SCIENCE DIVISION UNRIVALED IN ITS ACCOMPLISHMENTS, AND THE MOST SOPHISTICATED SURVEILLANCE NETWORK BUILT BY MAN.
THIS IS THE FUTURE.
THIS IS...
IMPRESSIVE?
UNEXPECTED. DOES S.H.I.E.L.D. KNOW ABOUT THIS?
HNN--CHINA DOES NOT ANSWER TO S.H.I.E.L.D., MR. WILSON. MATTERS OF OUR DEFENSE ARE OUR OWN CONCERN. BUT THAT DOES NOT MEAN WE CANNOT ASSIST ONE ANOTHER...
WHEN HELP IS NEEDED.
SHANG!
WHAT HAPPENED TO--
NOTHING TO DO WITH US. HE STOOD ALONE AGAINST THE MAN RESPONSIBLE FOR ALL THIS CHAOS--
THE GORGON.

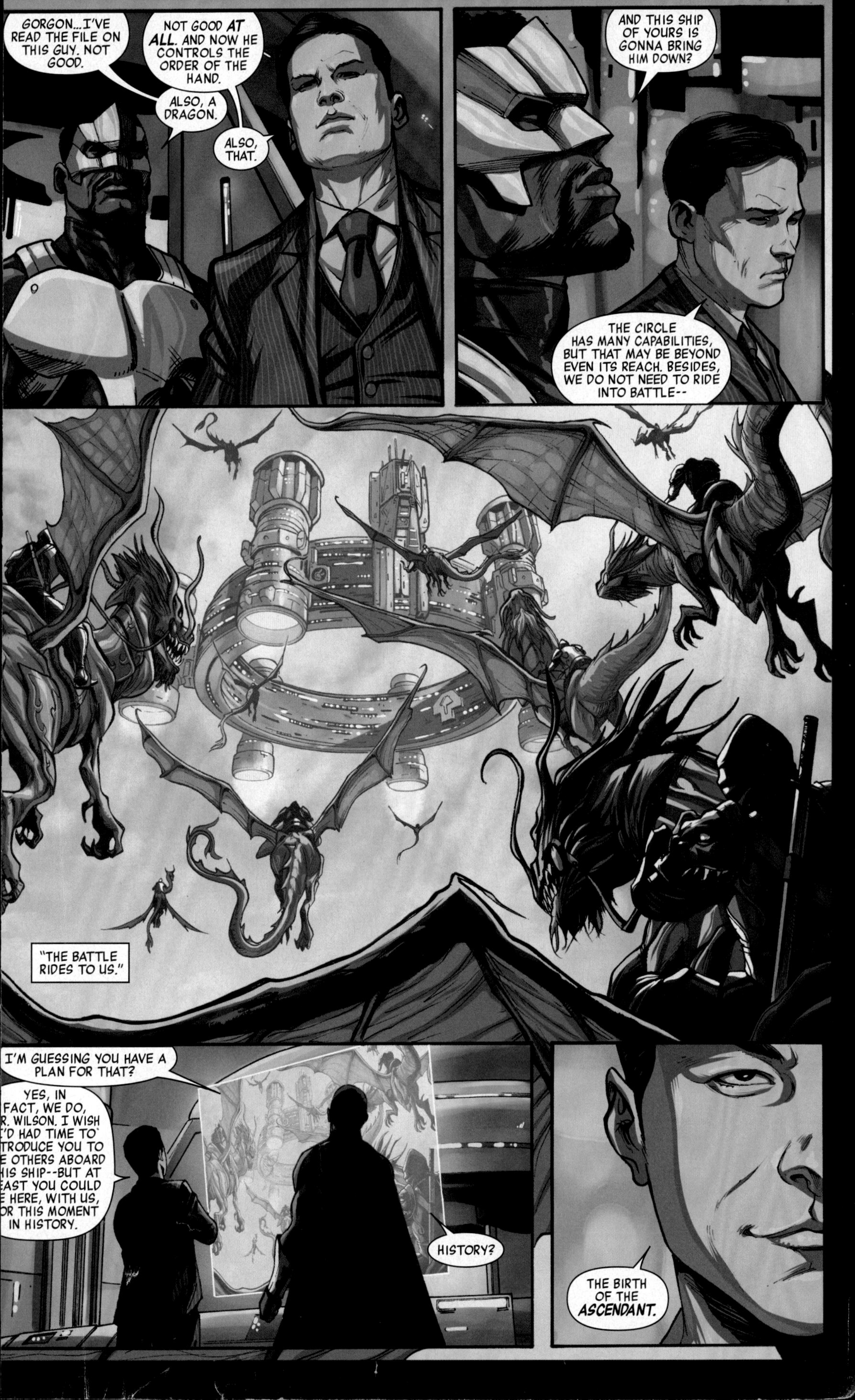
GORGON...I'VE READ THE FILE ON THIS GUY. NOT GOOD.
NOT GOOD AT ALL. AND NOW HE CONTROLS THE ORDER OF THE HAND.
ALSO, A DRAGON.
ALSO, THAT.
AND THIS SHIP OF YOURS IS GONNA BRING HIM DOWN?
THE CIRCLE HAS MANY CAPABILITIES, BUT THAT MAY BE BEYOND EVEN ITS REACH. BESIDES, WE DO NOT NEED TO RIDE INTO BATTLE--
"THE BATTLE RIDES TO US."
I'M GUESSING YOU HAVE A PLAN FOR THAT?
YES, IN FACT, WE DO, R. WILSON. I WISH 'D HAD TIME TO TRODUCE YOU TO E OTHERS ABOARD HIS SHIP--BUT AT EAST YOU COULD E HERE, WITH US, OR THIS MOMENT IN HISTORY.
HISTORY?
THE BIRTH OF THE ASCENDANT.

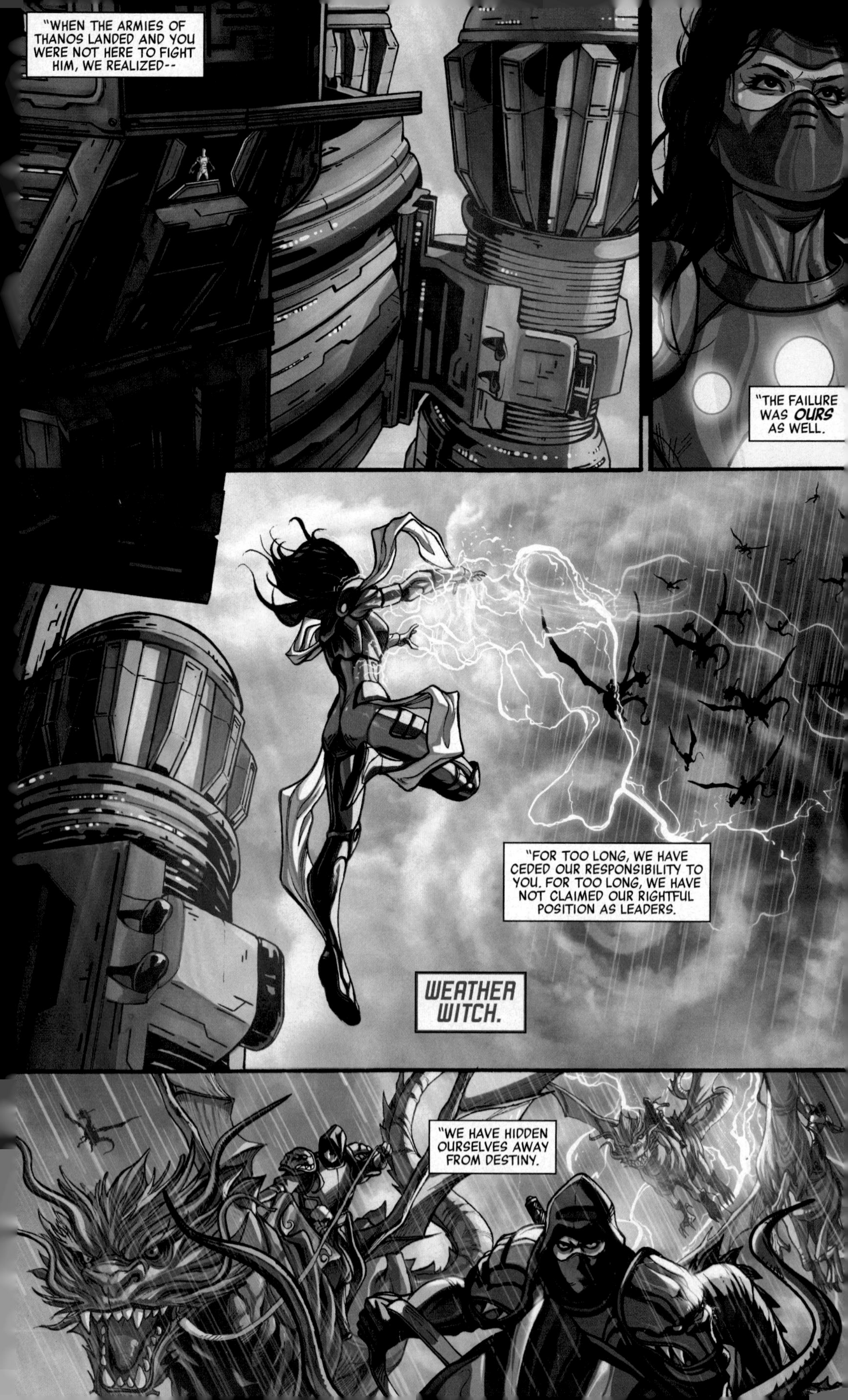
"WHEN THE ARMIES OF THANOS LANDED AND YOU WERE NOT HERE TO FIGHT HIM, WE REALIZED--
"THE FAILURE WAS OURS AS WELL.
"FOR TOO LONG, WE HAVE CEDED OUR RESPONSIBILITY TO YOU. FOR TOO LONG, WE HAVE NOT CLAIMED OUR RIGHTFUL POSITION AS LEADERS.
WEATHER WITCH.
"WE HAVE HIDDEN OURSELVES AWAY FROM DESTINY.

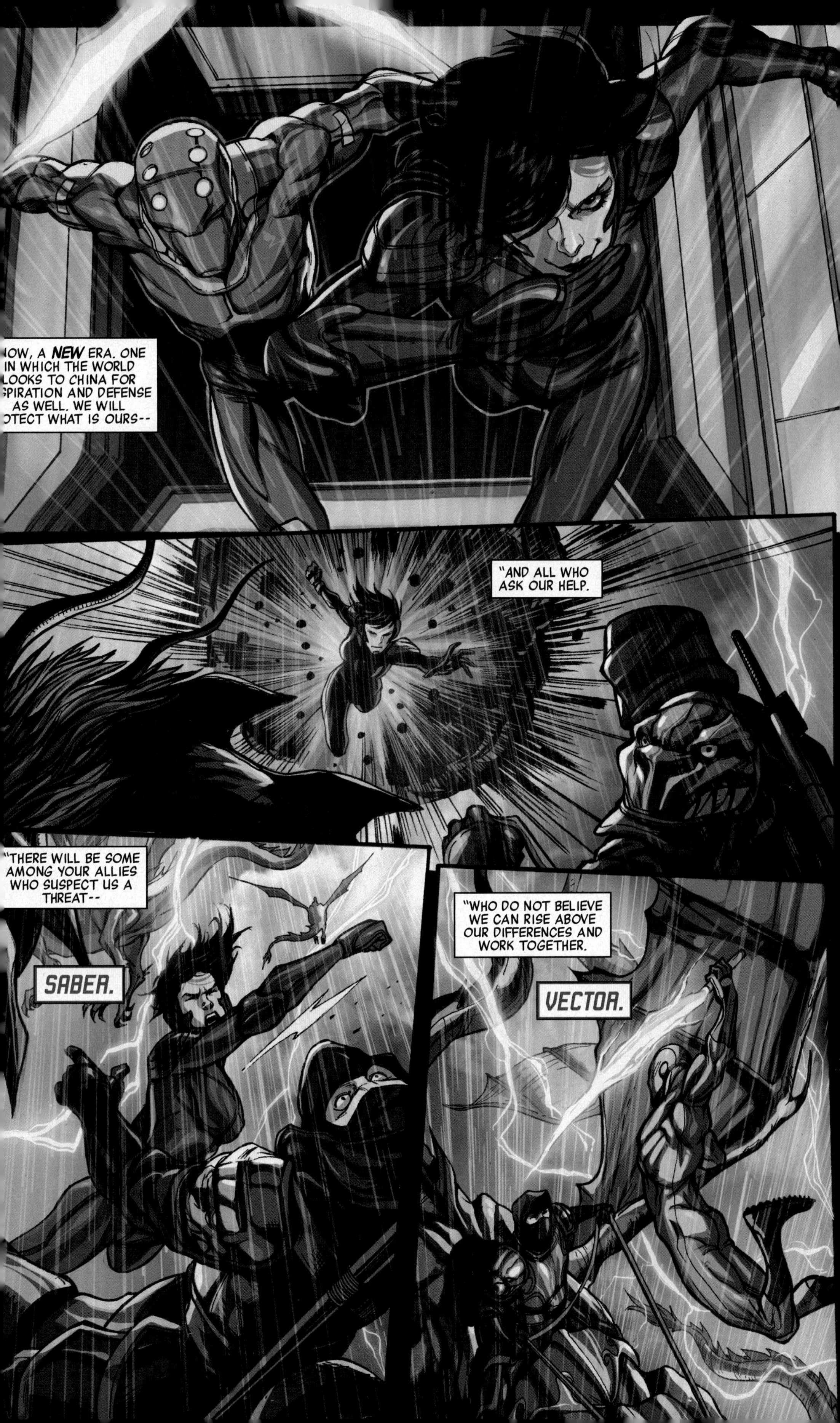

NOW, A NEW ERA. ONE IN WHICH THE WORLD LOOKS TO CHINA FOR SPIRATION AND DEFENSE AS WELL. WE WILL OTECT WHAT IS OURS--
"AND ALL WHO ASK OUR HELP.
"THERE WILL BE SOME AMONG YOUR ALLIES WHO SUSPECT US A THREAT--
SABER.
"WHO DO NOT BELIEVE WE CAN RISE ABOVE OUR DIFFERENCES AND WORK TOGETHER.
VECTOR.

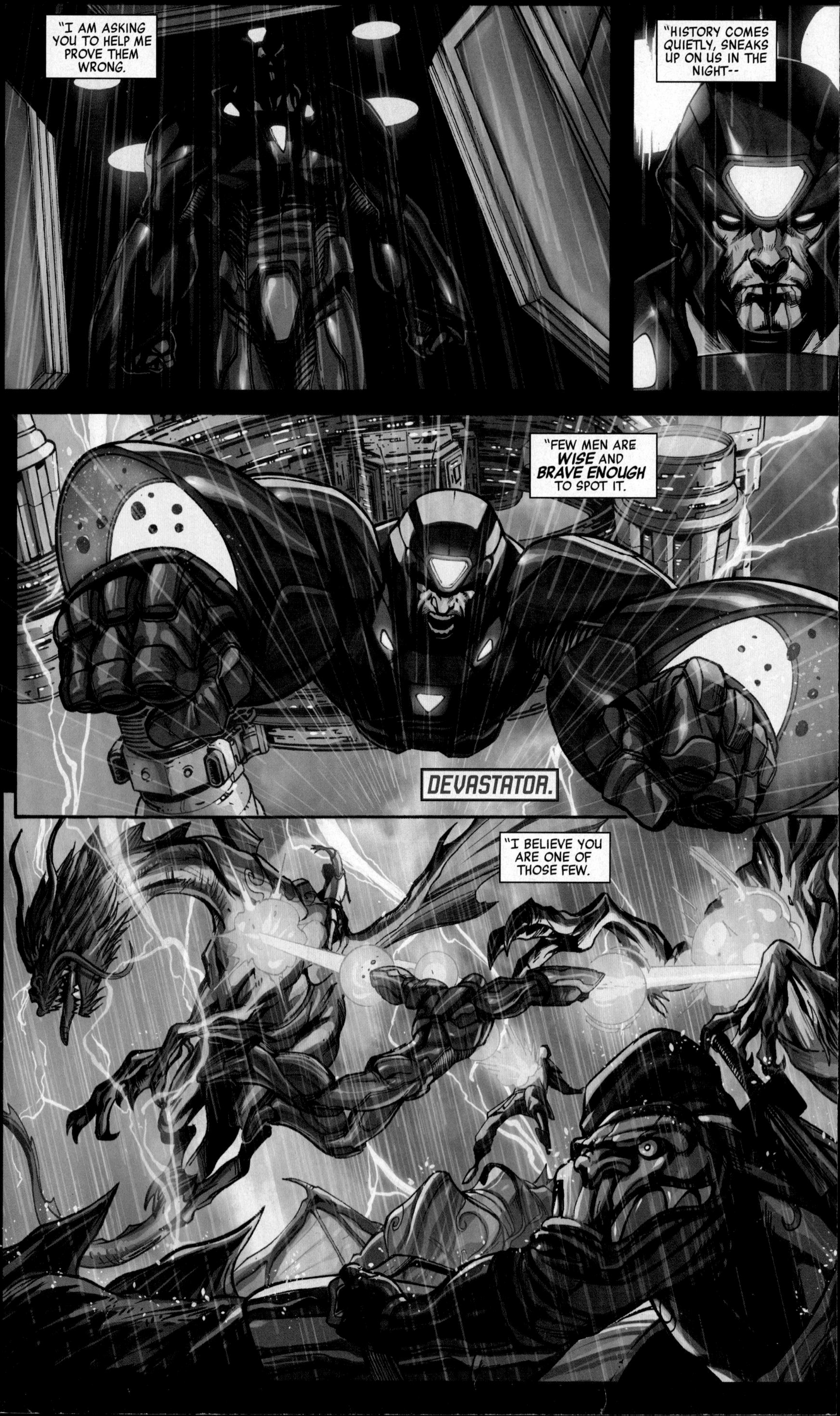
"I AM ASKING YOU TO HELP ME PROVE THEM WRONG.
"HISTORY COMES QUIETLY, SNEAKS UP ON US IN THE NIGHT--
"FEW MEN ARE **WISE** AND **BRAVE ENOUGH** TO SPOT IT.
DEVASTATOR.
"I BELIEVE YOU ARE ONE OF THOSE FEW.

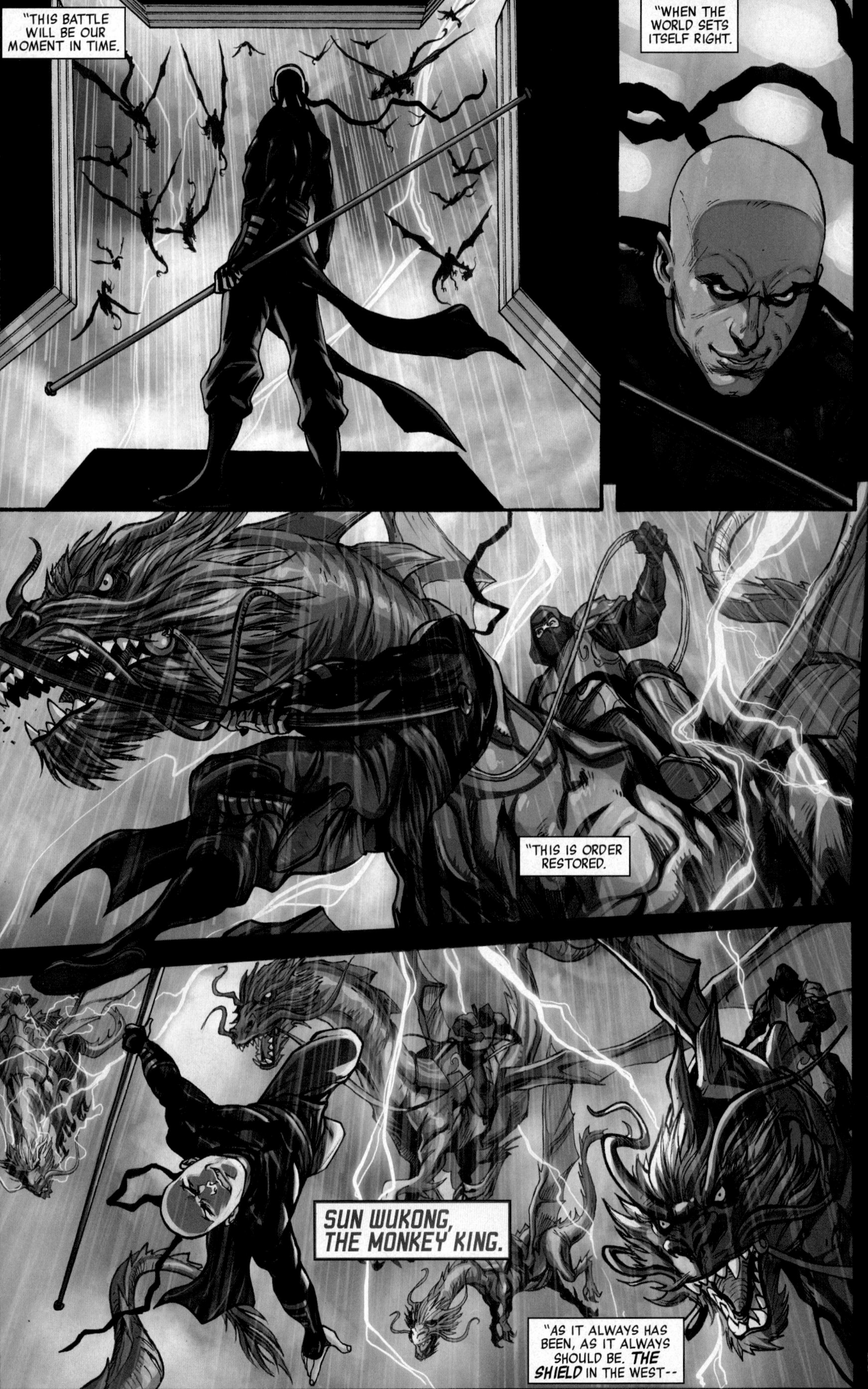
"THIS BATTLE WILL BE OUR MOMENT IN TIME.
"WHEN THE WORLD SETS ITSELF RIGHT.
"THIS IS ORDER RESTORED.
SUN WUKONG, THE MONKEY KING.
"AS IT ALWAYS HAS BEEN, AS IT ALWAYS SHOULD BE. THE SHIELD IN THE WEST--

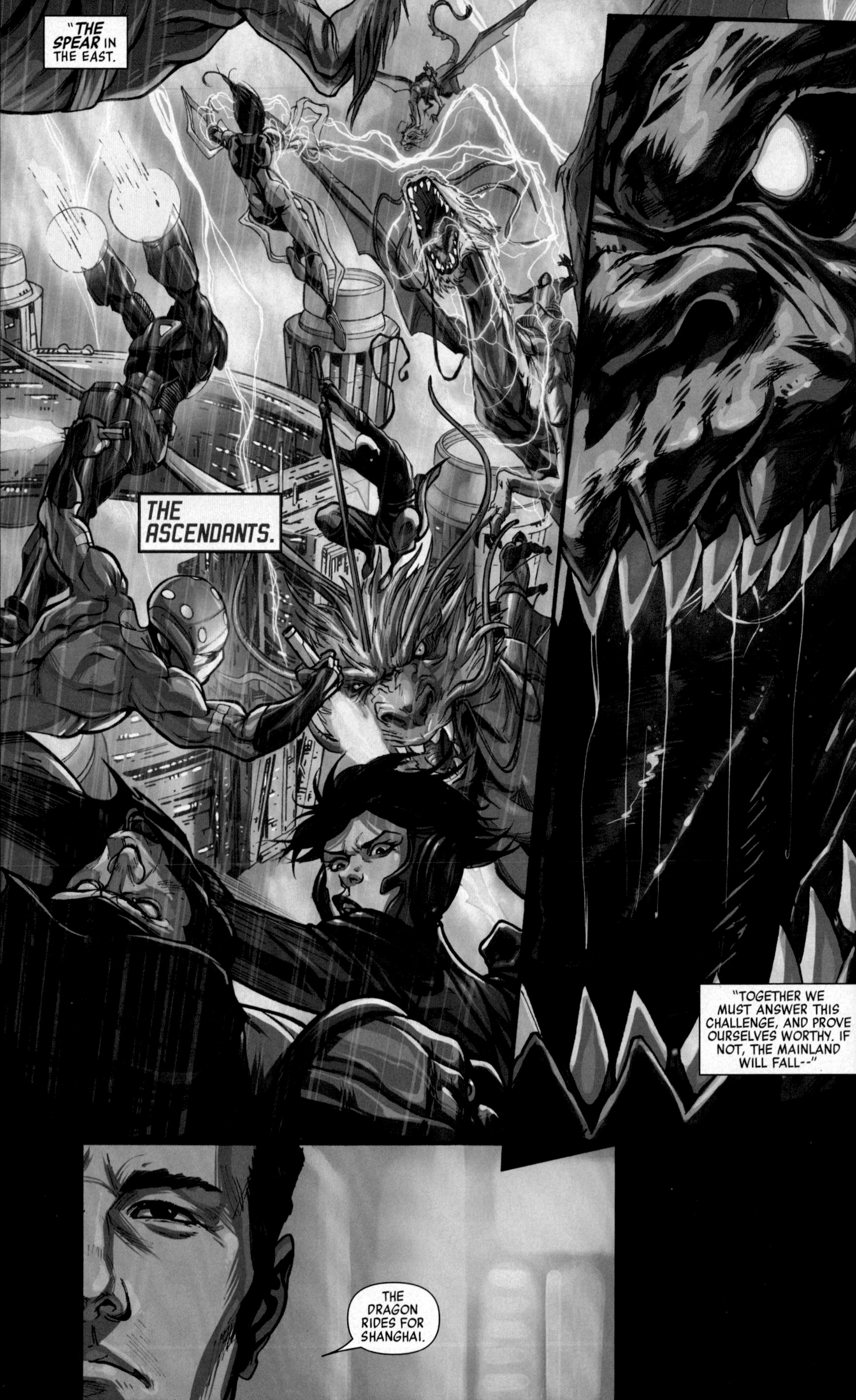
"THE SPEAR IN THE EAST.
THE ASCENDANTS.
"TOGETHER WE MUST ANSWER THIS CHALLENGE, AND PROVE OURSELVES WORTHY. IF NOT, THE MAINLAND WILL FALL--"
THE DRAGON RIDES FOR SHANGHAI.

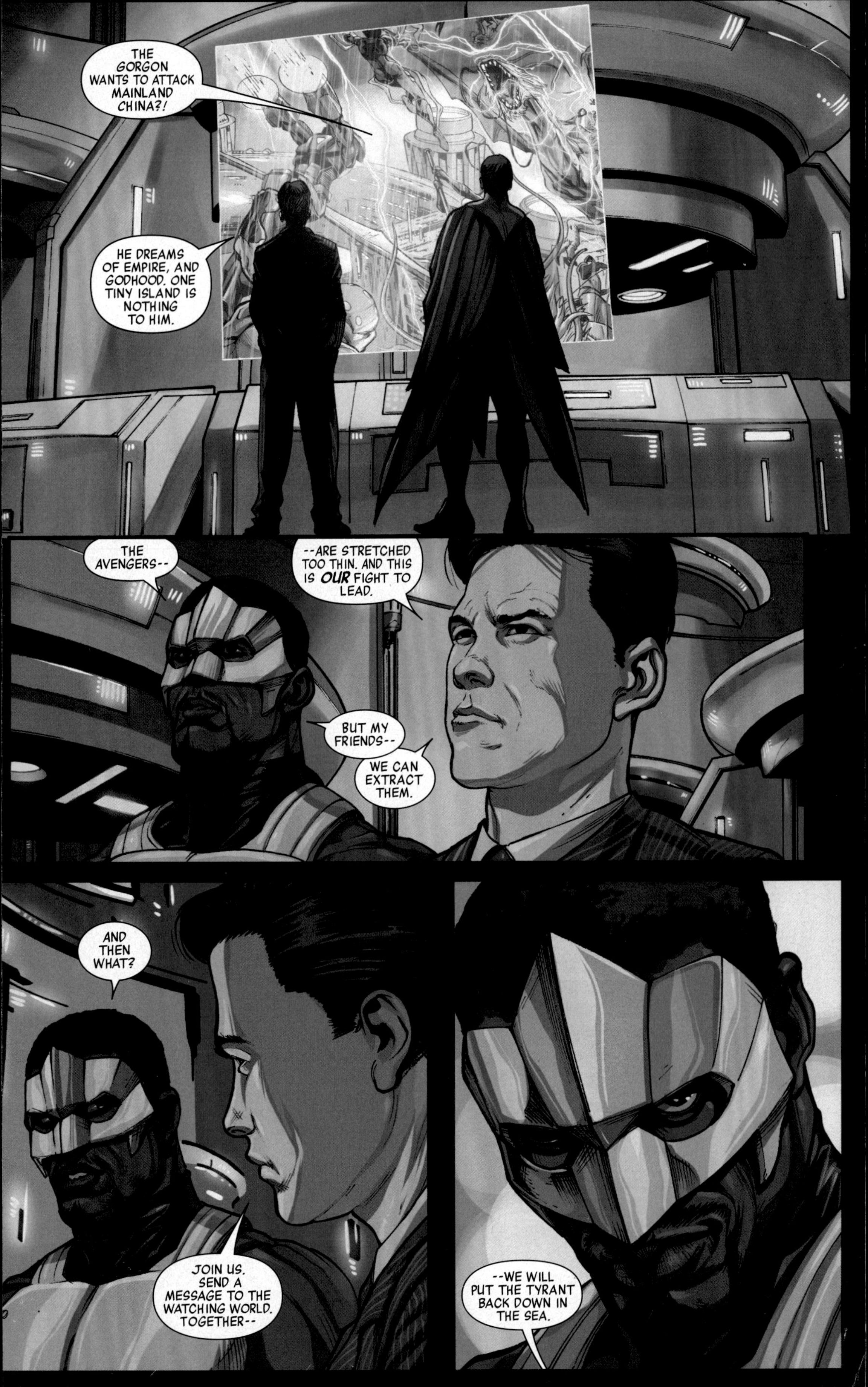
THE GORGON WANTS TO ATTACK MAINLAND CHINA?!
HE DREAMS OF EMPIRE, AND GODHOOD. ONE TINY ISLAND IS NOTHING TO HIM.
THE AVENGERS--
--ARE STRETCHED TOO THIN. AND THIS IS OUR FIGHT TO LEAD.
BUT MY FRIENDS--
WE CAN EXTRACT THEM.
AND THEN WHAT?
JOIN US. SEND A MESSAGE TO THE WATCHING WORLD. TOGETHER--
--WE WILL PUT THE TYRANT BACK DOWN IN THE SEA.

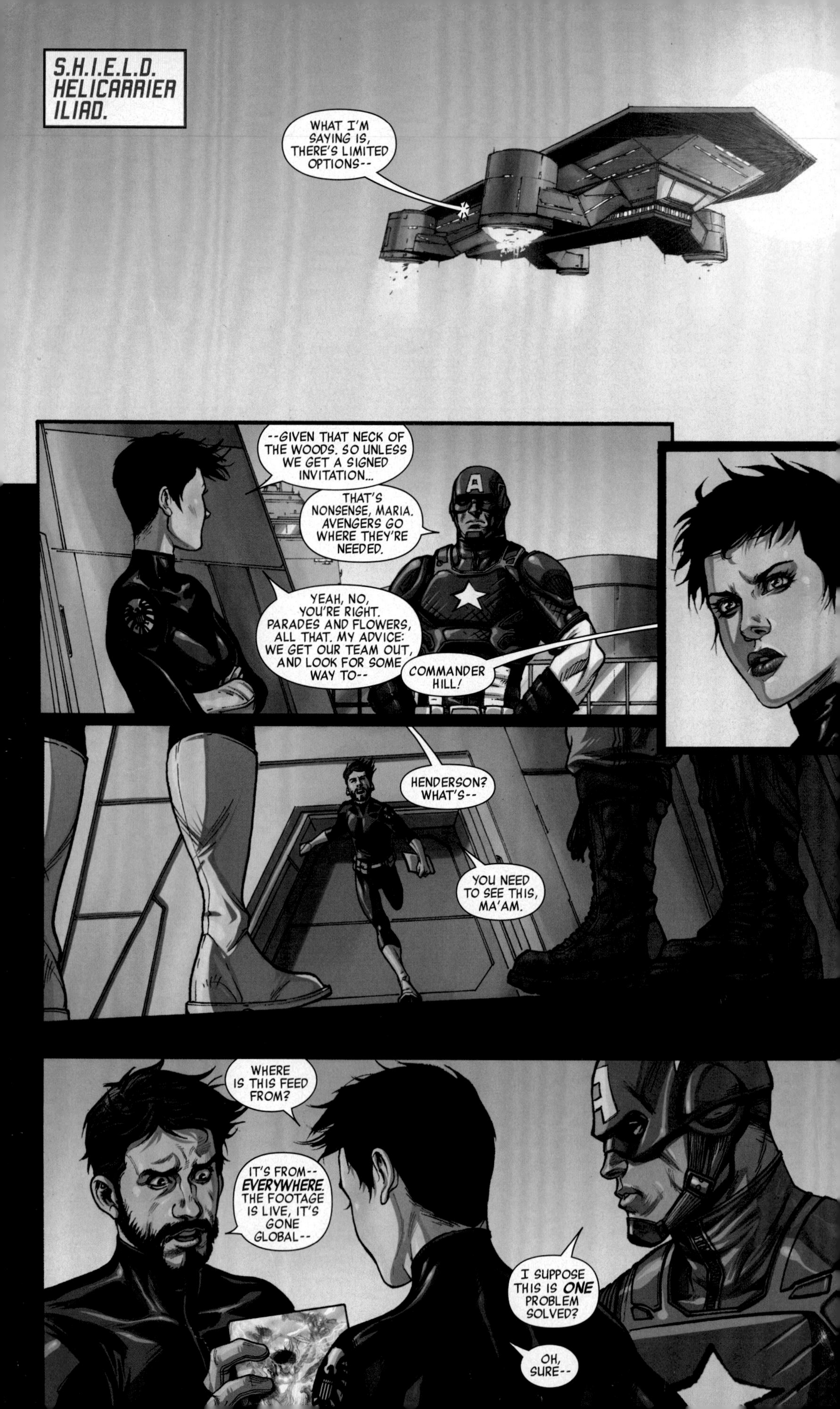
S.H.I.E.L.D. HELICARRIER ILIAD.
WHAT I'M SAYING IS, THERE'S LIMITED OPTIONS--
--GIVEN THAT NECK OF THE WOODS. SO UNLESS WE GET A SIGNED INVITATION...
THAT'S NONSENSE, MARIA. AVENGERS GO WHERE THEY'RE NEEDED.
YEAH, NO, YOU'RE RIGHT. PARADES AND FLOWERS, ALL THAT. MY ADVICE: WE GET OUR TEAM OUT, AND LOOK FOR SOME WAY TO--
COMMANDER HILL!
HENDERSON? WHAT'S--
YOU NEED TO SEE THIS, MA'AM.
WHERE IS THIS FEED FROM?
IT'S FROM-- EVERYWHERE. THE FOOTAGE IS LIVE, IT'S GONE GLOBAL--
I SUPPOSE THIS IS ONE PROBLEM SOLVED?
OH, SURE--

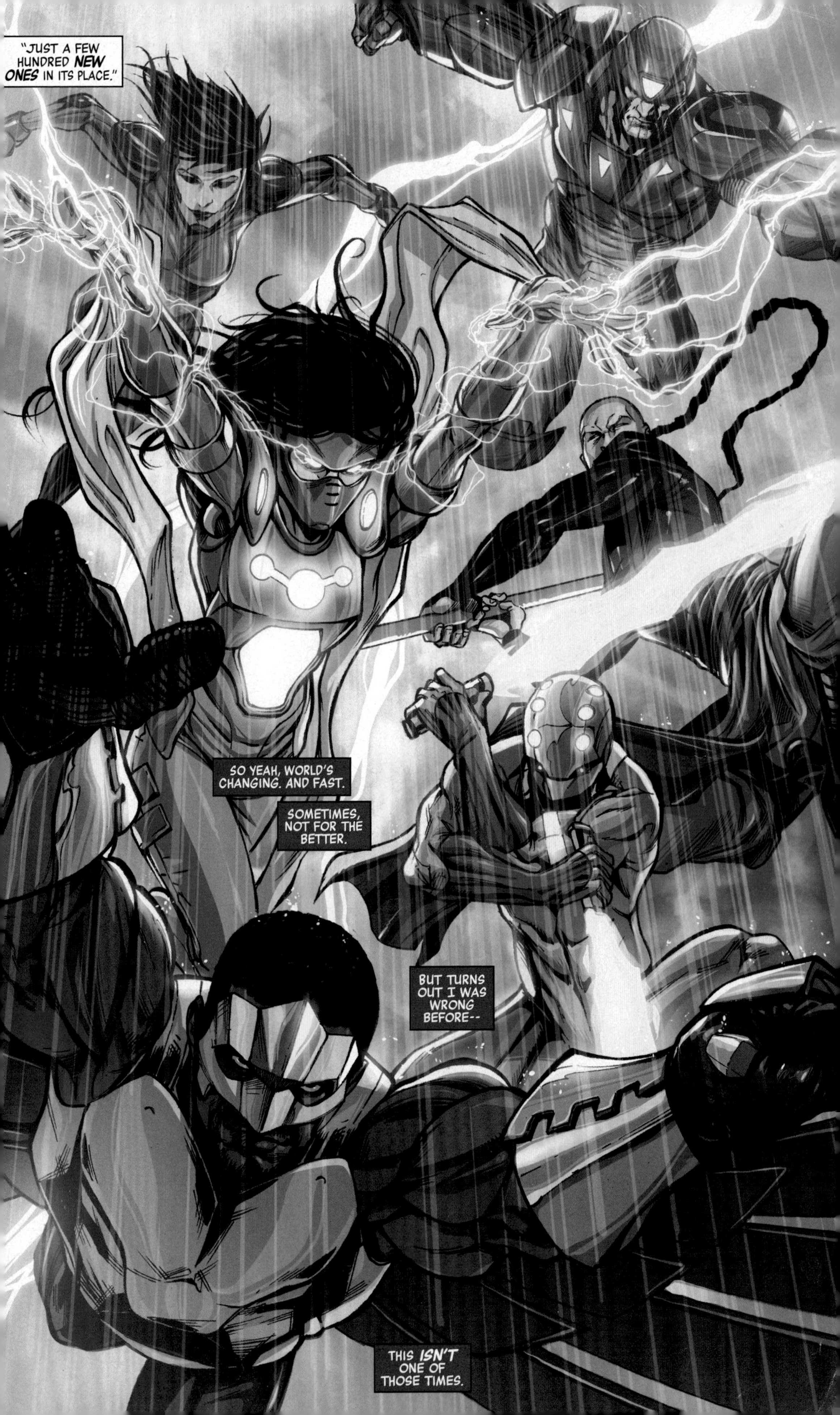
"JUST A FEW HUNDRED NEW ONES IN ITS PLACE."
SO YEAH, WORLD'S CHANGING. AND FAST.
SOMETIMES, NOT FOR THE BETTER.
BUT TURNS OUT I WAS WRONG BEFORE--
THIS ISN'T ONE OF THOSE TIMES.

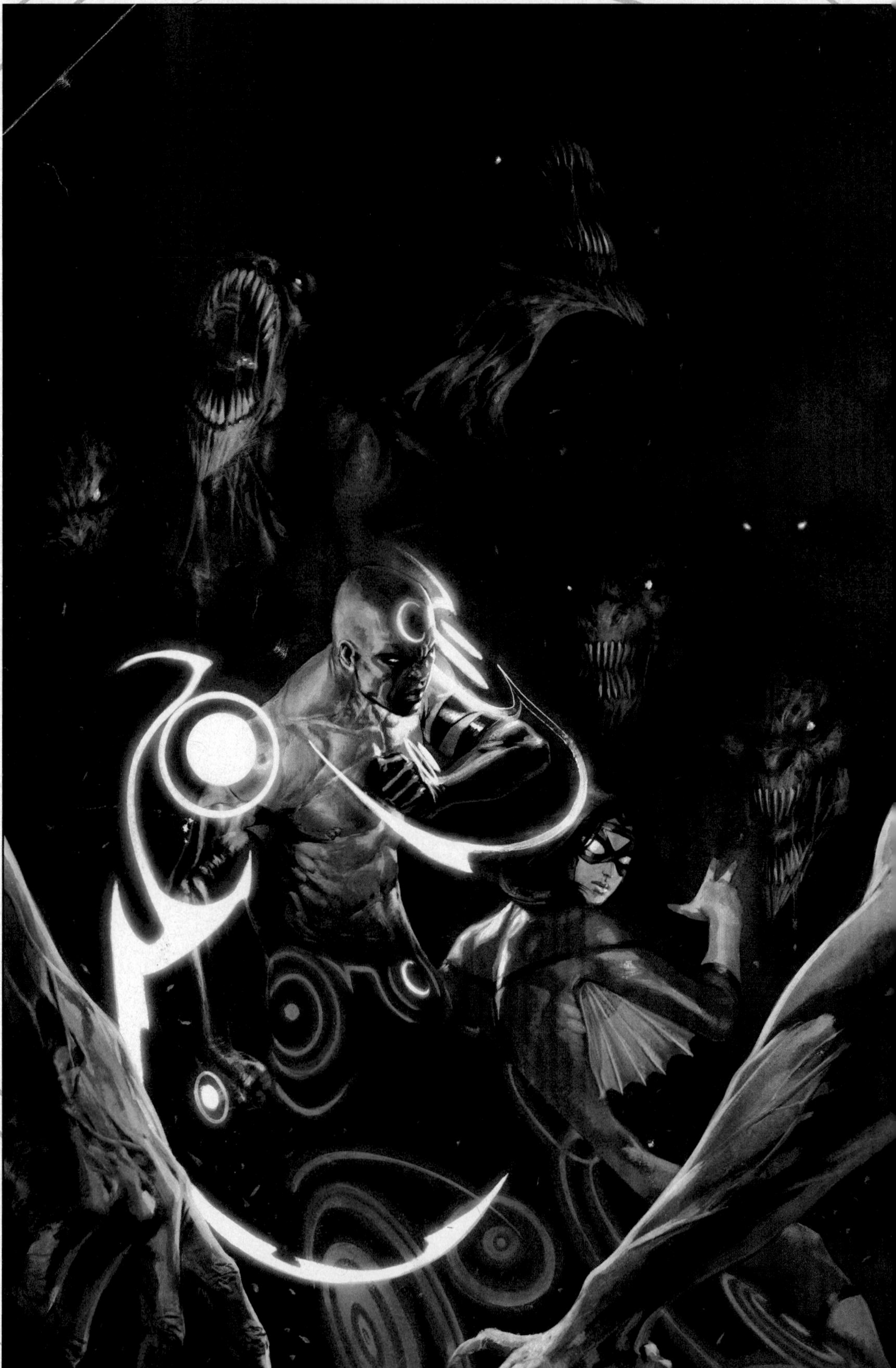

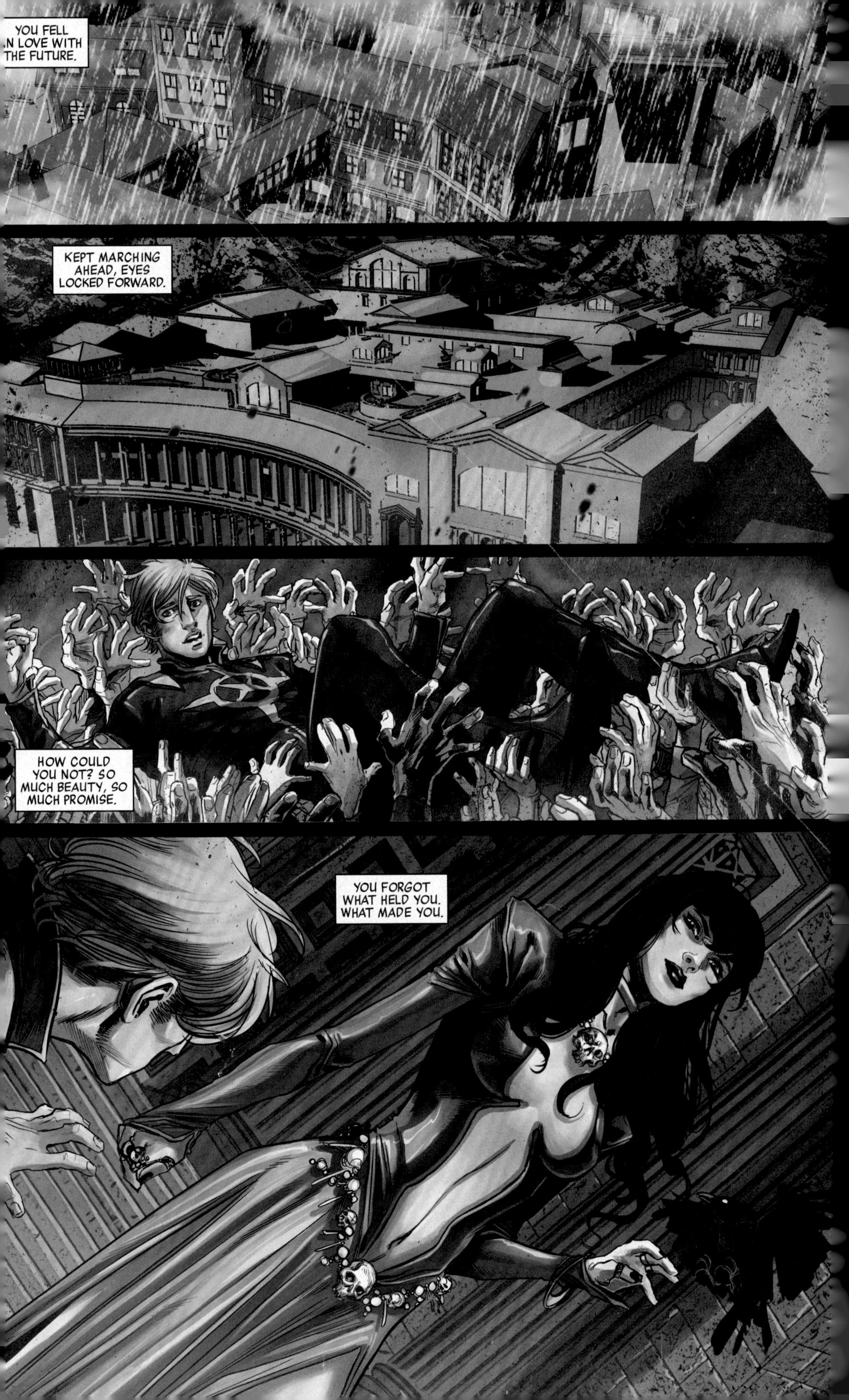
YOU FELL
N LOVE WITH
THE FUTURE.
KEPT MARCHING AHEAD, EYES LOCKED FORWARD.
HOW COULD YOU NOT? SO MUCH BEAUTY, SO MUCH PROMISE.
YOU FORGOT WHAT HELD YOU. WHAT MADE YOU.

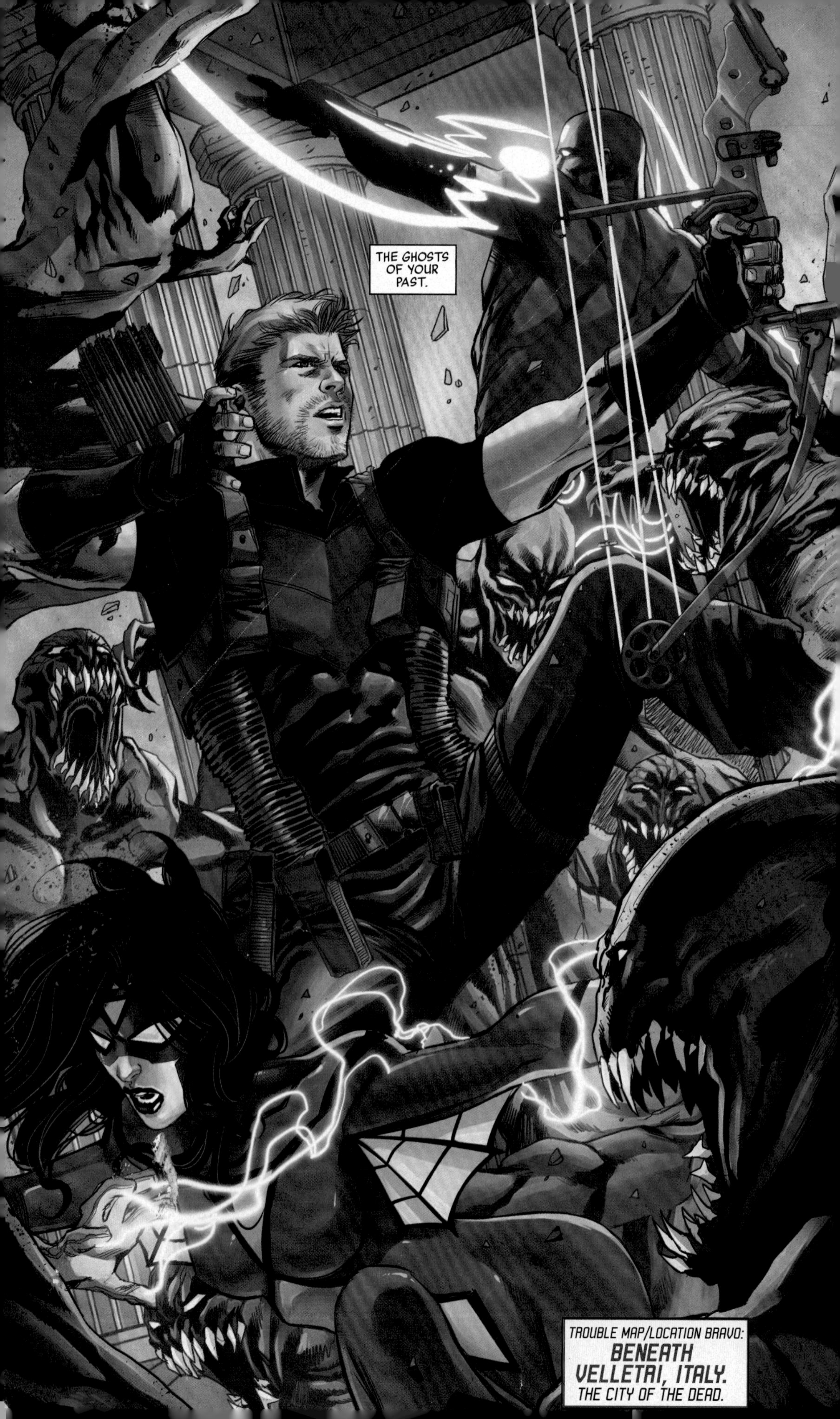
THE GHOSTS OF YOUR PAST.
TROUBLE MAP/LOCATION BRAVO:
BENEATH VELLETRI, ITALY.
THE CITY OF THE DEAD.

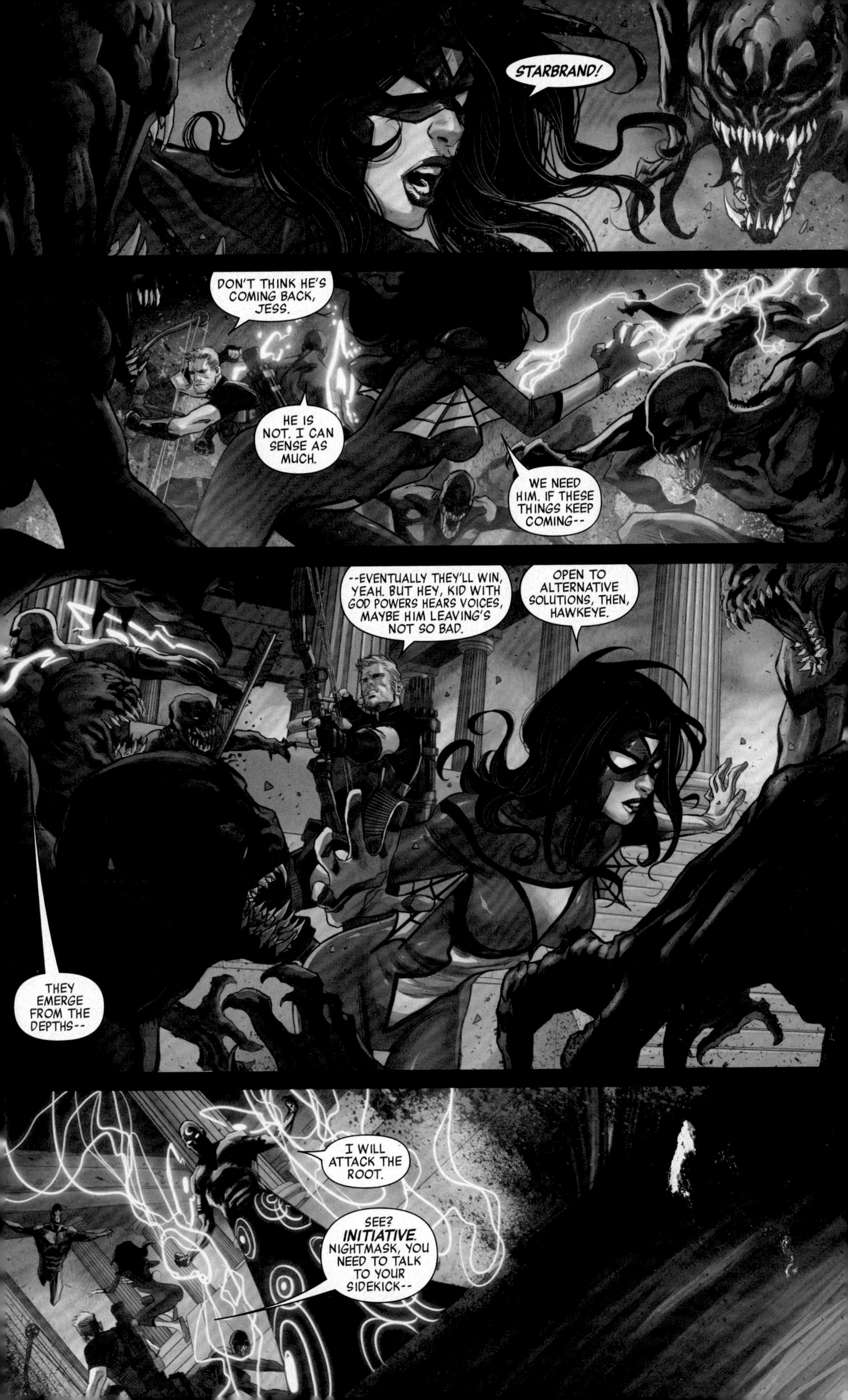
STARBRAND!
DON'T THINK HE'S COMING BACK, JESS.
HE IS NOT. I CAN SENSE AS MUCH.
WE NEED HIM. IF THESE THINGS KEEP COMING--
--EVENTUALLY THEY'LL WIN, YEAH. BUT HEY, KID WITH GOD POWERS HEARS VOICES, MAYBE HIM LEAVING'S NOT SO BAD.
OPEN TO ALTERNATIVE SOLUTIONS, THEN, HAWKEYE.
THEY EMERGE FROM THE DEPTHS--
I WILL ATTACK THE ROOT.
SEE? INITIATIVE. NIGHTMASK, YOU NEED TO TALK TO YOUR SIDEKICK--

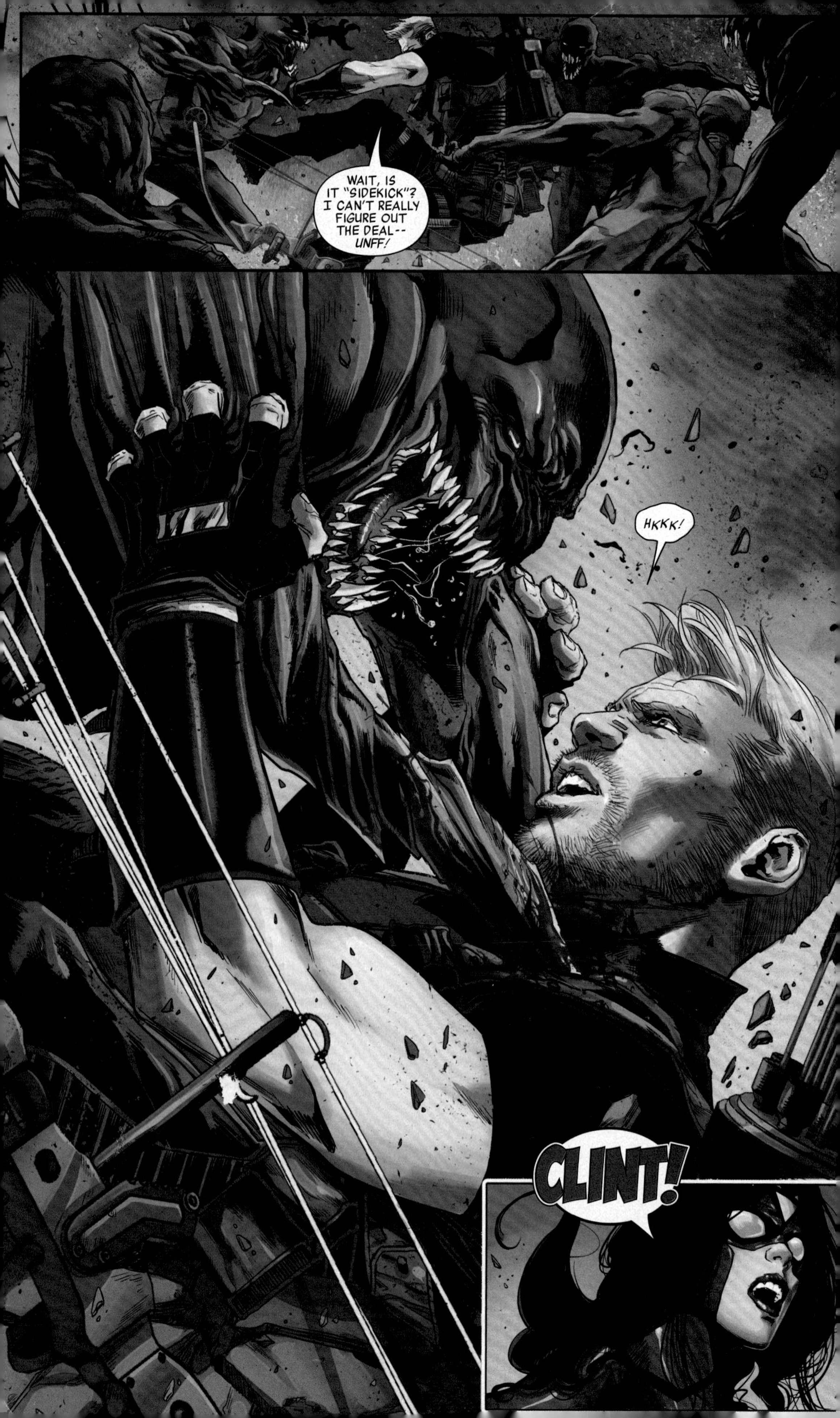
WAIT, IS IT "SIDEKICK"? I CAN'T REALLY FIGURE OUT THE DEAL-- UNFF!
HKKK!
CLINT!

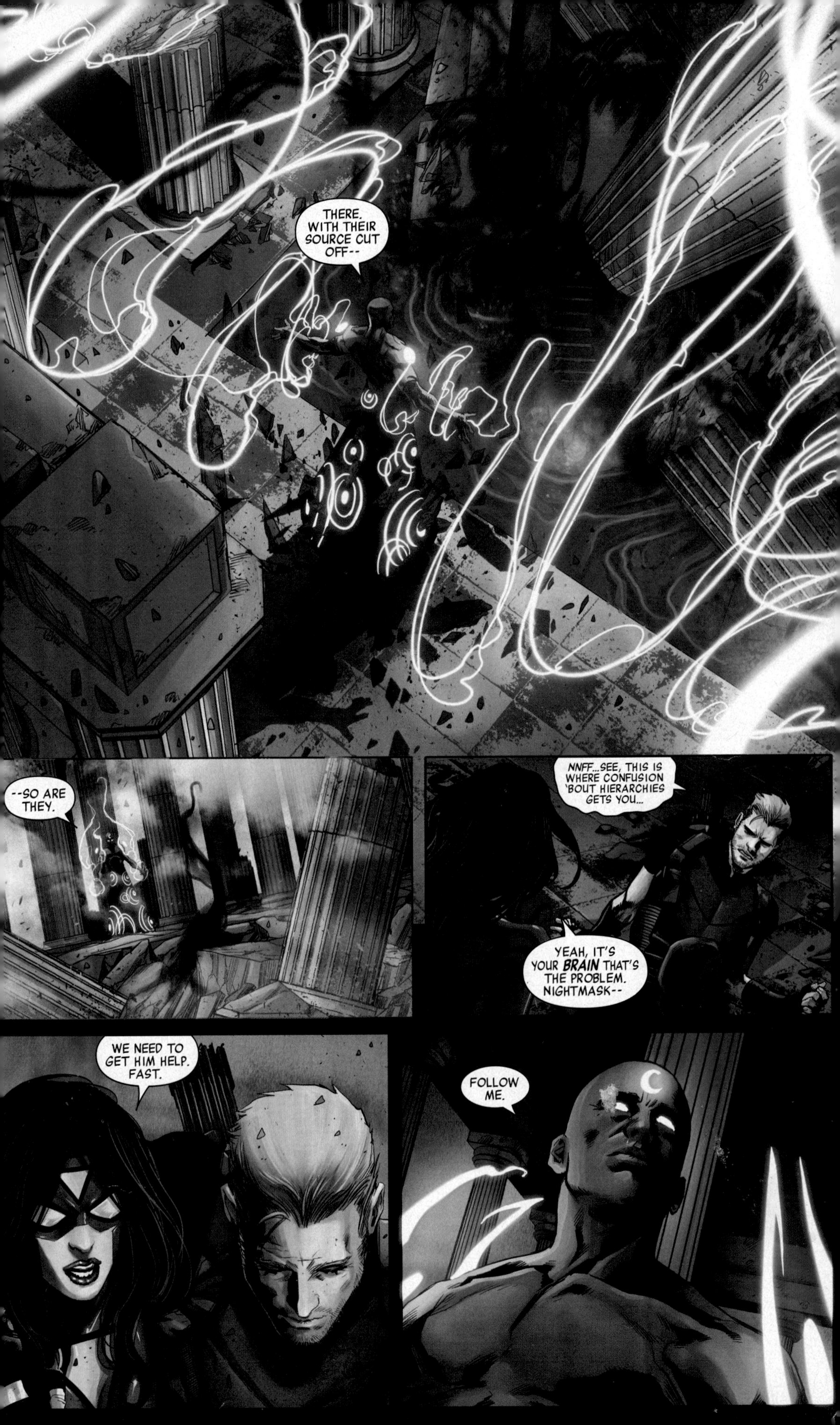
THERE. WITH THEIR SOURCE CUT OFF--
--SO ARE THEY.
NNFF...SEE, THIS IS WHERE CONFUSION 'BOUT HIERARCHIES GETS YOU...
YEAH, IT'S YOUR BRAIN THAT'S THE PROBLEM. NIGHTMASK--
WE NEED TO GET HIM HELP. FAST.
FOLLOW ME.

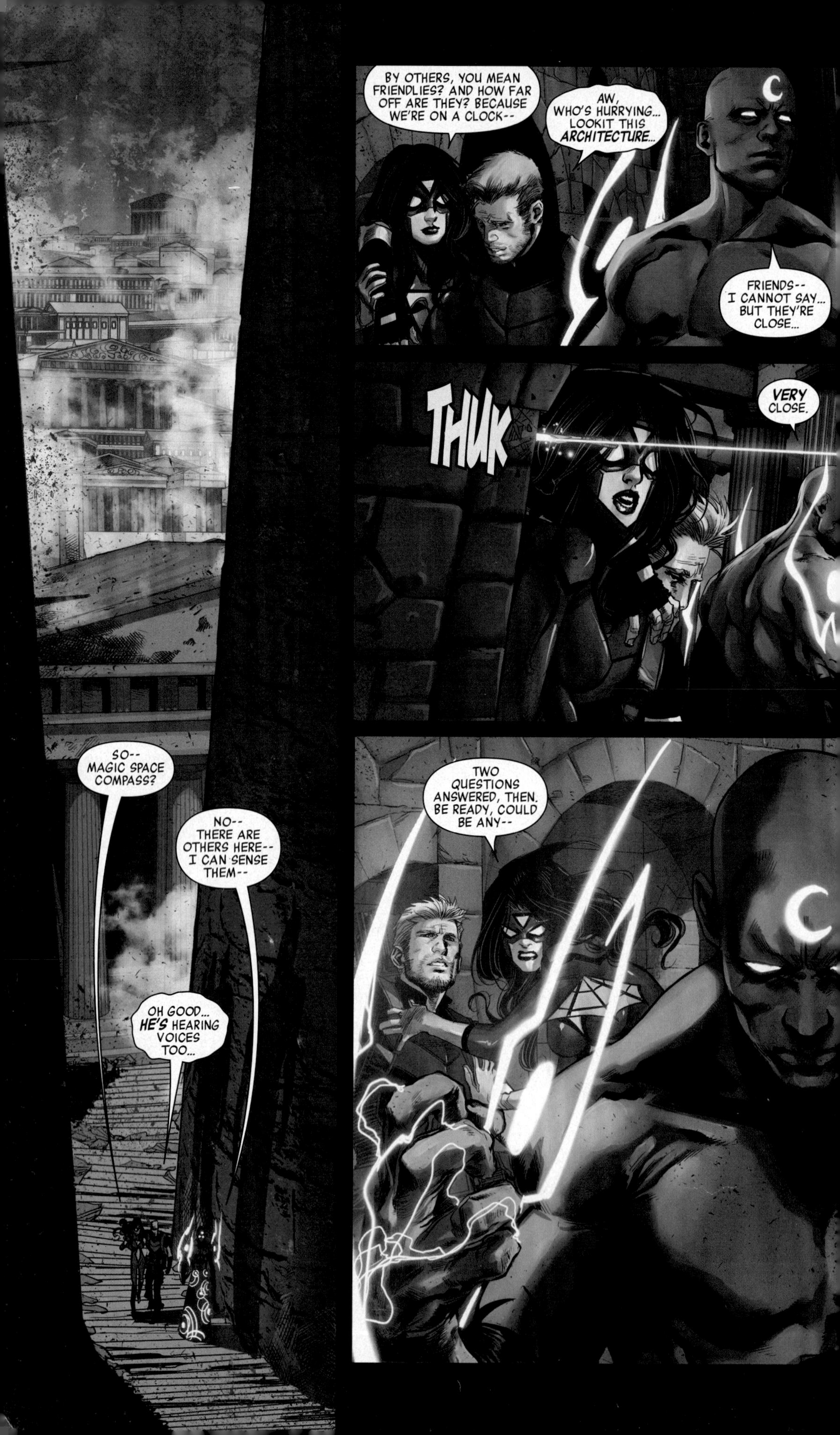
SO-- MAGIC SPACE COMPASS?
NO-- THERE ARE OTHERS HERE-- I CAN SENSE THEM--
OH GOOD... HE'S HEARING VOICES TOO...
BY OTHERS, YOU MEAN FRIENDLIES? AND HOW FAR OFF ARE THEY? BECAUSE WE'RE ON A CLOCK--
AW, WHO'S HURRYING... LOOKIT THIS ARCHITECTURE...
FRIENDS-- I CANNOT SAY... BUT THEY'RE CLOSE...
THUK
VERY CLOSE.
TWO QUESTIONS ANSWERED, THEN. BE READY, COULD BE ANY--

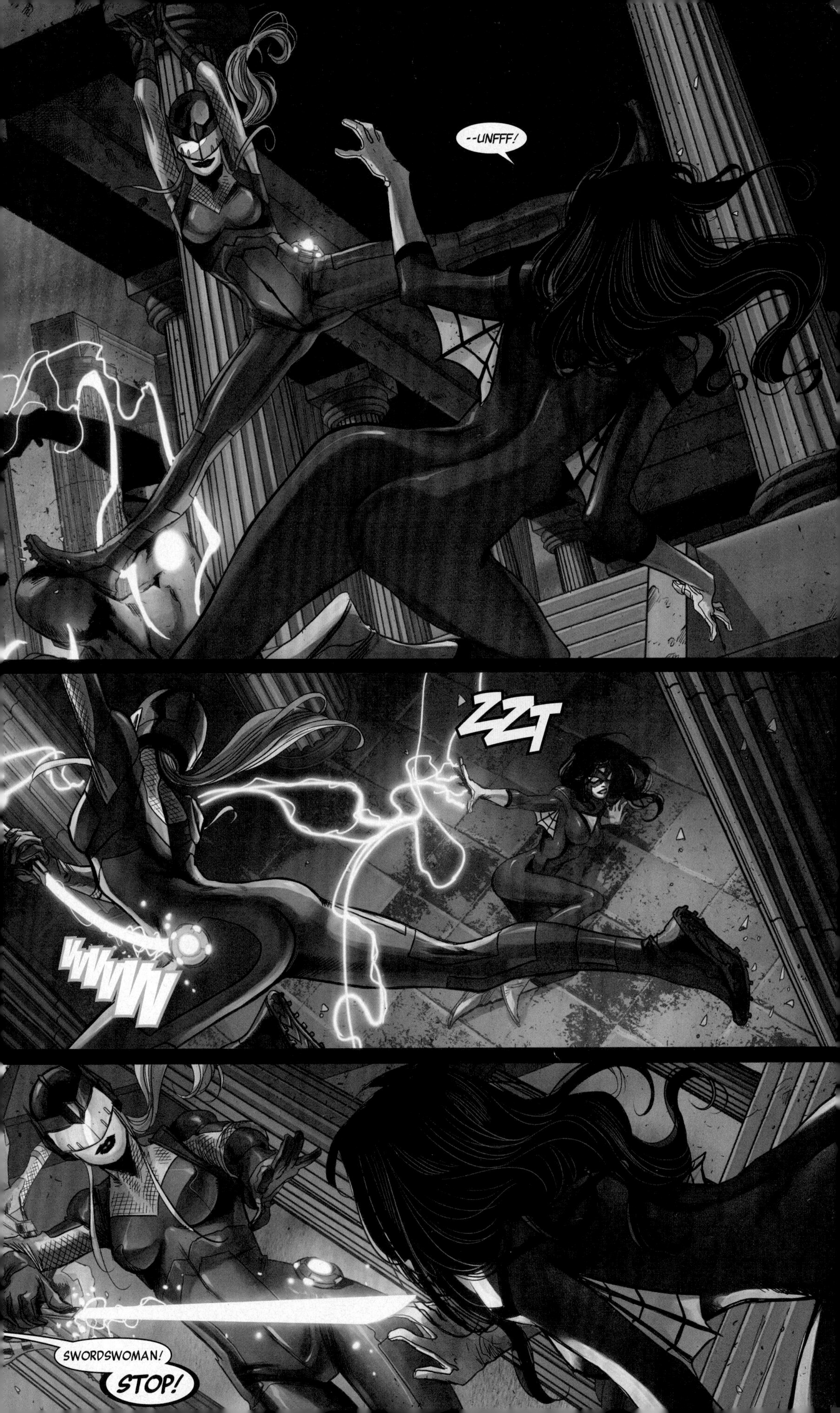
--UNFFF!
ZZZT
WWWW
SWORDSWOMAN!
STOP!

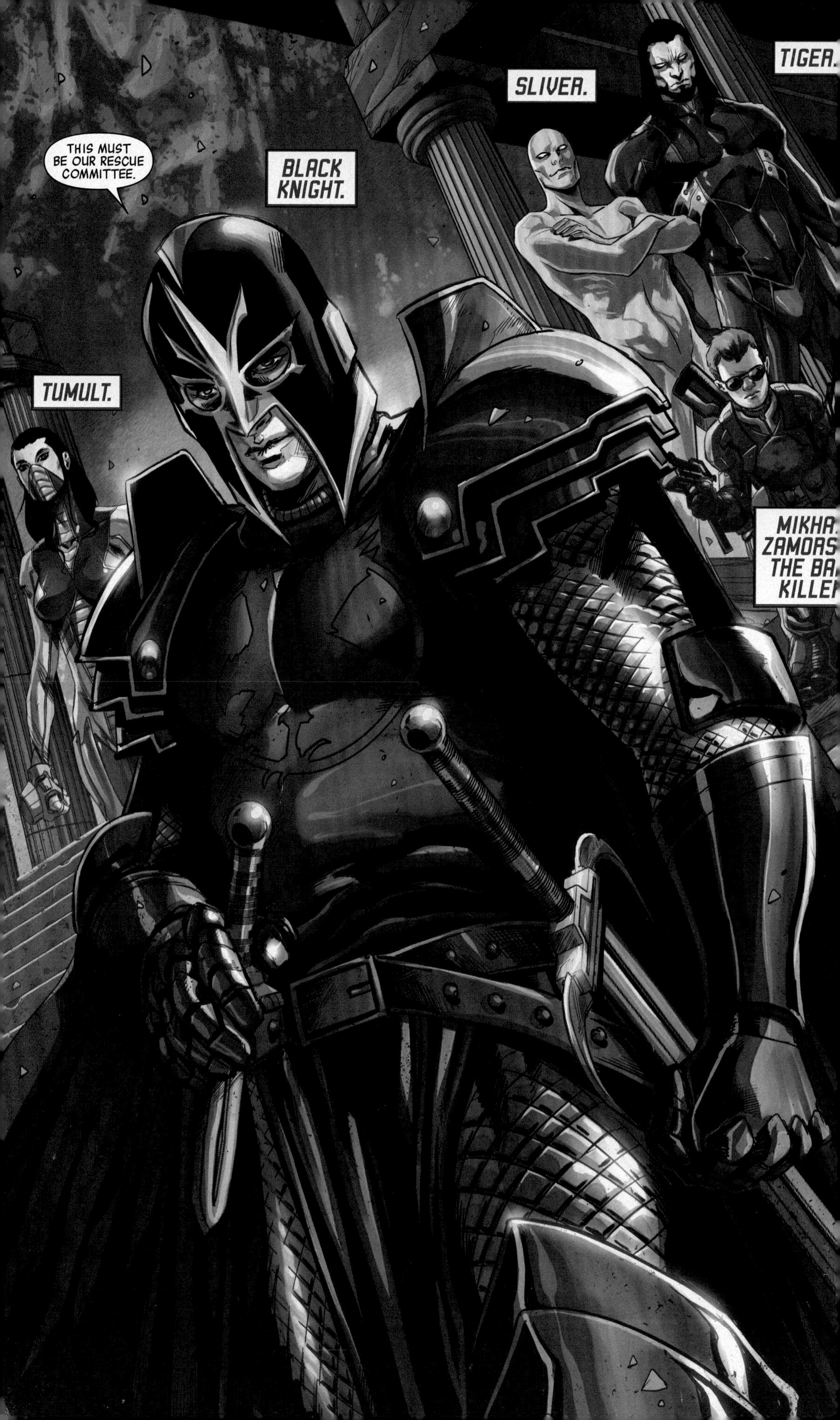
THIS MUST BE OUR RESCUE COMMITTEE.
BLACK KNIGHT.
SLIVER.
TIGER.
TUMULT.

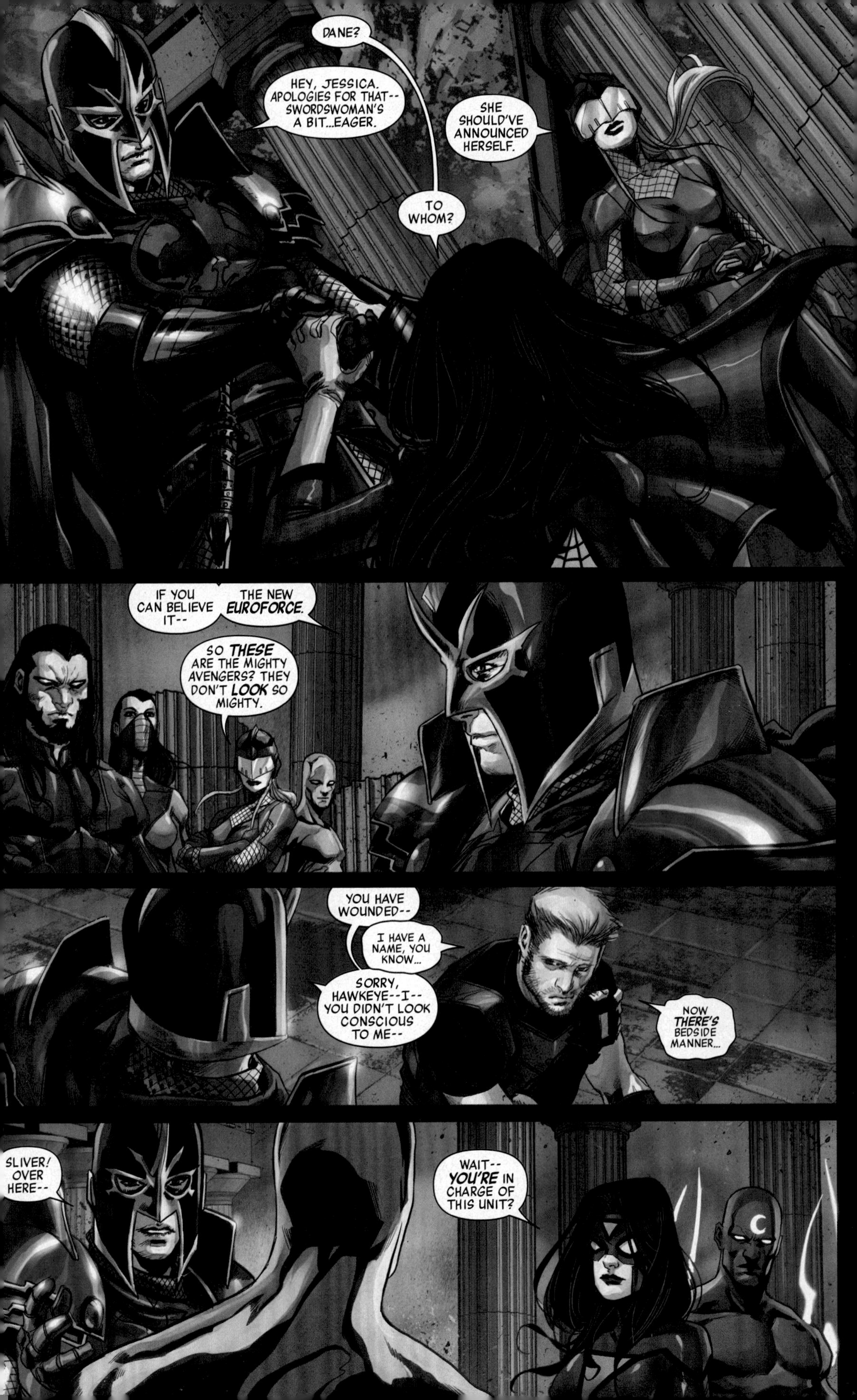
DANE?
HEY, JESSICA. APOLOGIES FOR THAT-- SWORDSWOMAN'S A BIT...EAGER.
SHE SHOULD'VE ANNOUNCED HERSELF.
TO WHOM?
IF YOU CAN BELIEVE IT--
THE NEW EUROFORCE.
SO THESE ARE THE MIGHTY AVENGERS? THEY DON'T LOOK SO MIGHTY.
YOU HAVE WOUNDED--
I HAVE A NAME, YOU KNOW...
SORRY, HAWKEYE--I-- YOU DIDN'T LOOK CONSCIOUS TO ME--
NOW THERE'S BEDSIDE MANNER...
SLIVER! OVER HERE--
WAIT-- YOU'RE IN CHARGE OF THIS UNIT?

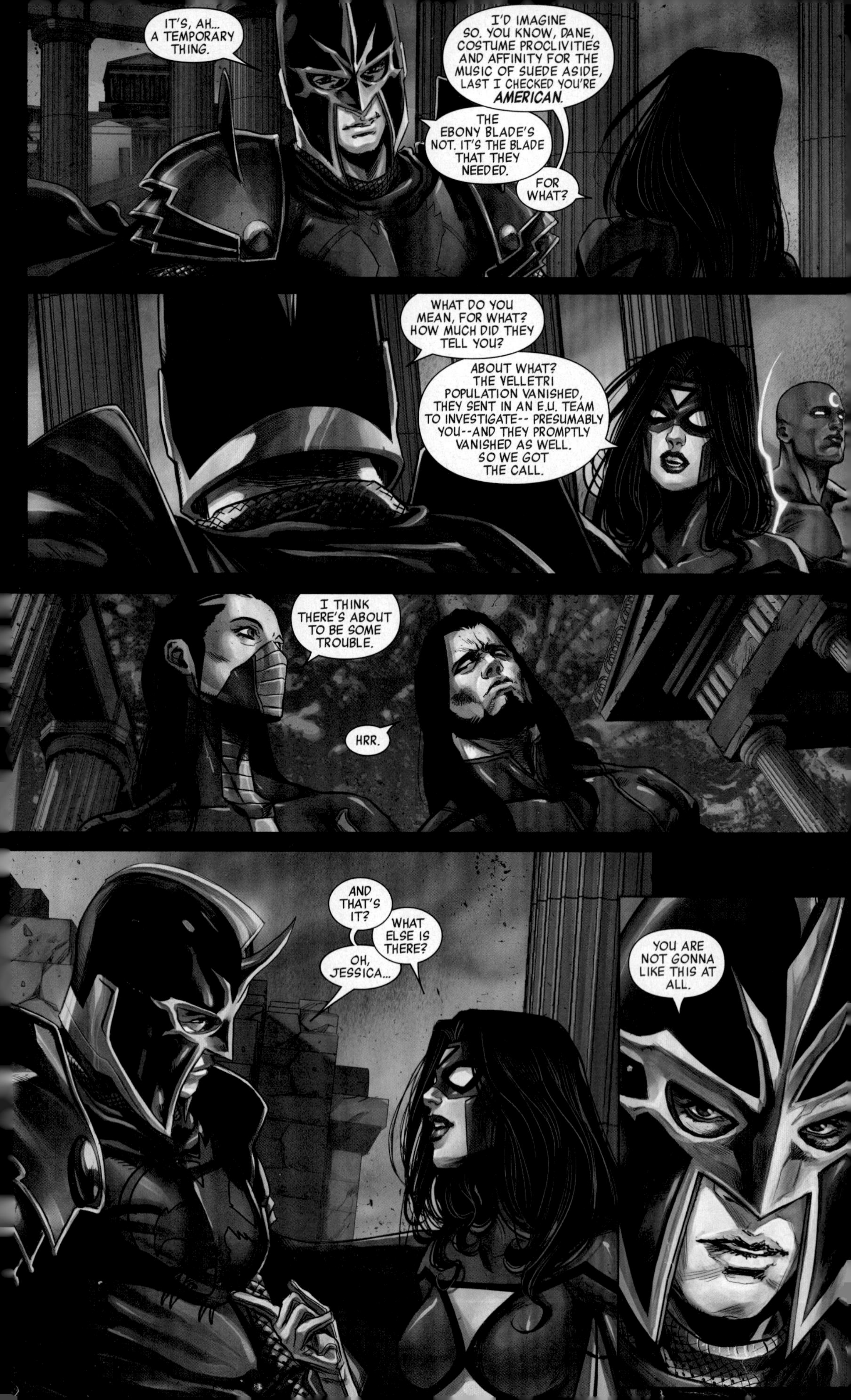

IT'S, AH... A TEMPORARY THING.
I'D IMAGINE SO. YOU KNOW, DANE, COSTUME PROCLIVITIES AND AFFINITY FOR THE MUSIC OF SUEDE ASIDE, LAST I CHECKED YOU'RE AMERICAN.
THE EBONY BLADE'S NOT. IT'S THE BLADE THAT THEY NEEDED.
FOR WHAT?
WHAT DO YOU MEAN, FOR WHAT? HOW MUCH DID THEY TELL YOU?
ABOUT WHAT? THE VELLETRI POPULATION VANISHED, THEY SENT IN AN E.U. TEAM TO INVESTIGATE-- PRESUMABLY YOU--AND THEY PROMPTLY VANISHED AS WELL. SO WE GOT THE CALL.
I THINK THERE'S ABOUT TO BE SOME TROUBLE.
HRR.
AND THAT'S IT?
WHAT ELSE IS THERE?
OH, JESSICA...
YOU ARE NOT GONNA LIKE THIS AT ALL.

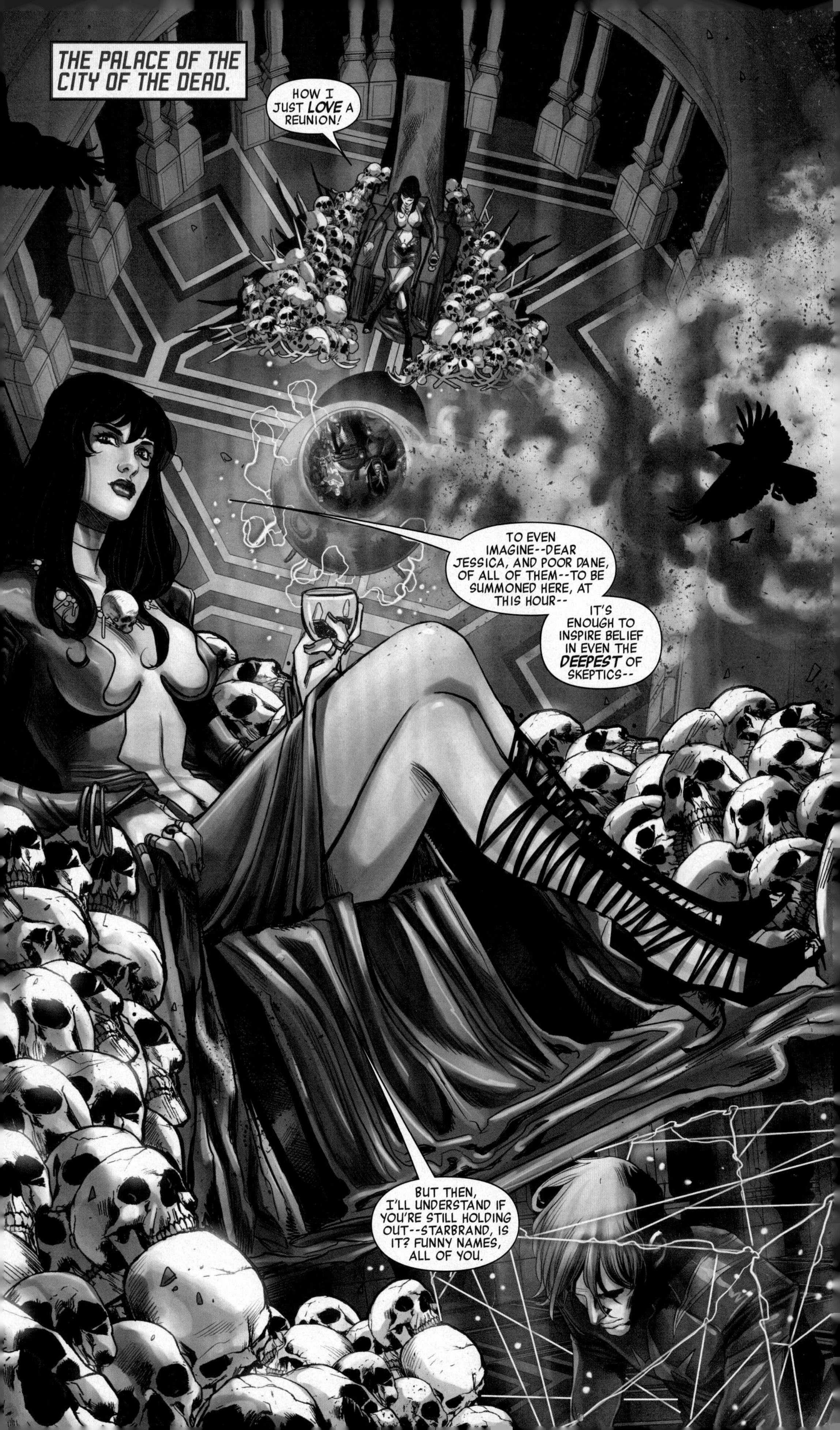
THE PALACE OF THE CITY OF THE DEAD.
HOW I JUST LOVE A REUNION!
TO EVEN IMAGINE--DEAR JESSICA, AND POOR DANE, OF ALL OF THEM--TO BE SUMMONED HERE, AT THIS HOUR--
IT'S ENOUGH TO INSPIRE BELIEF IN EVEN THE DEEPEST OF SKEPTICS--
BUT THEN, I'LL UNDERSTAND IF YOU'RE STILL HOLDING OUT--STARBRAND, IS IT? FUNNY NAMES, ALL OF YOU.

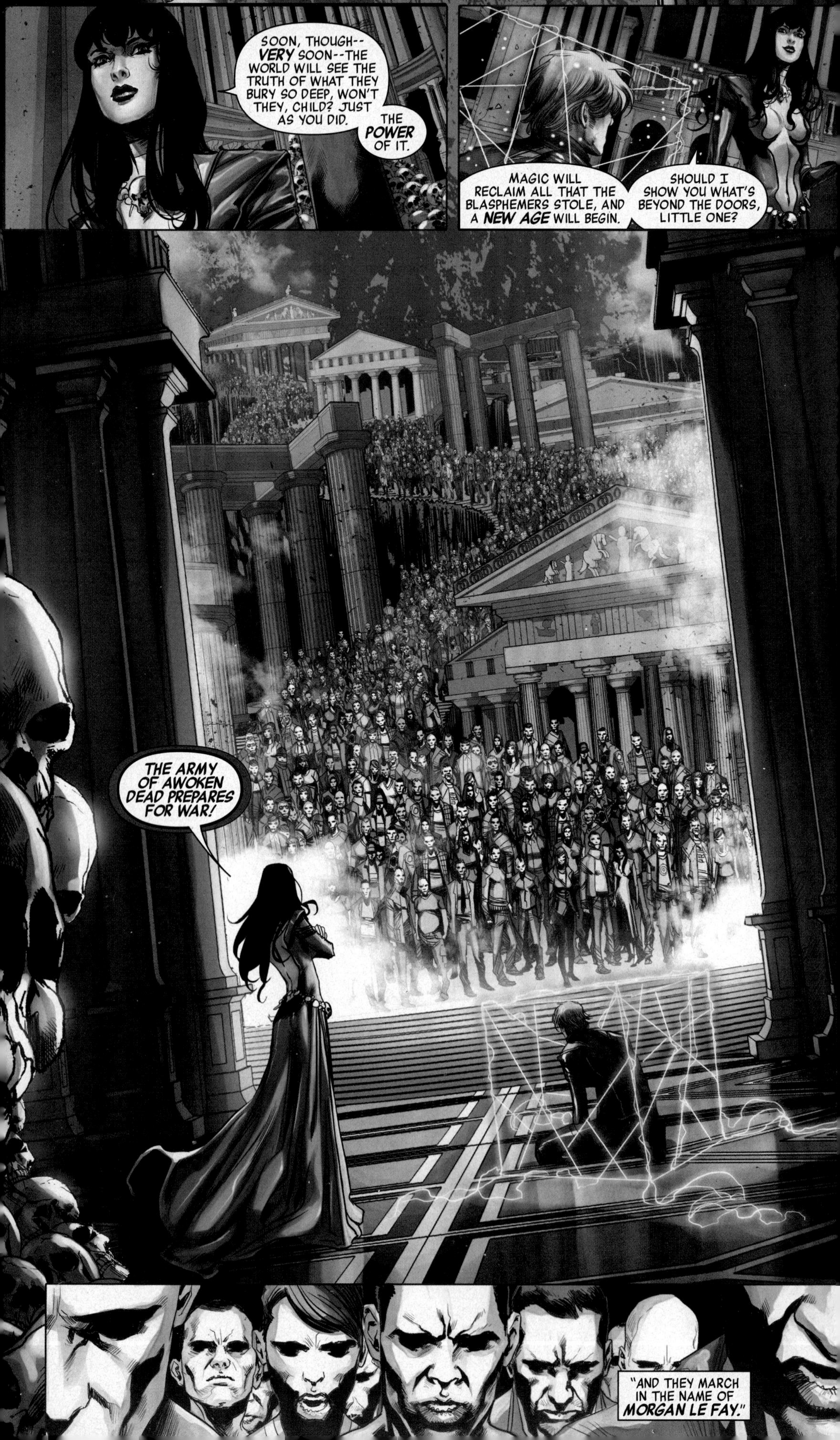
SOON, THOUGH-- VERY SOON--THE WORLD WILL SEE THE TRUTH OF WHAT THEY BURY SO DEEP, WON'T THEY, CHILD? JUST AS YOU DID.
THE POWER OF IT.
MAGIC WILL RECLAIM ALL THAT THE BLASPHEMERS STOLE, AND A NEW AGE WILL BEGIN.
SHOULD I SHOW YOU WHAT'S BEYOND THE DOORS, LITTLE ONE?
THE ARMY OF AWOKEN DEAD PREPARES FOR WAR!
"AND THEY MARCH IN THE NAME OF MORGAN LE FAY."

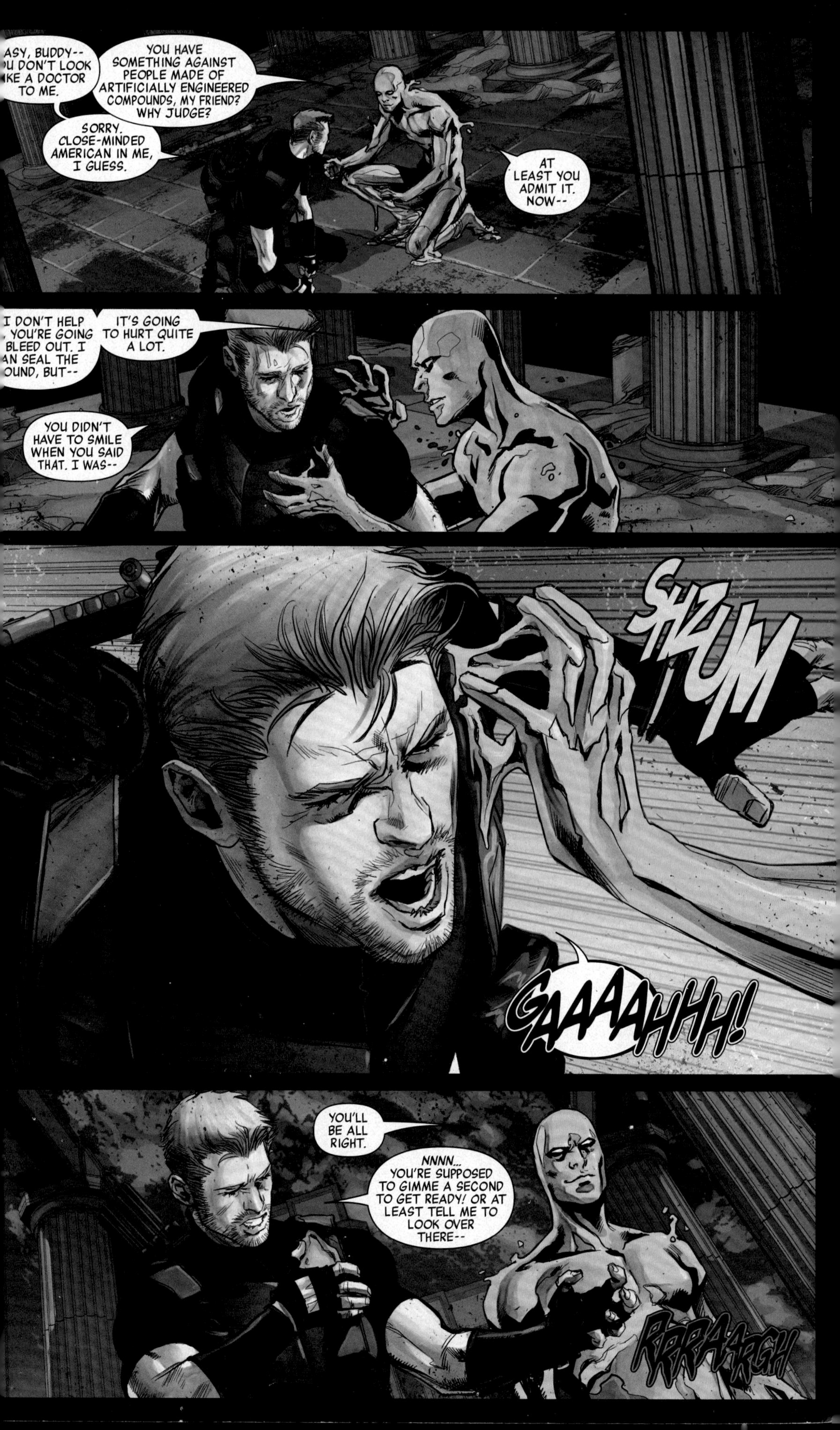

ASY, BUDDY-- U DON'T LOOK IKE A DOCTOR TO ME.
YOU HAVE SOMETHING AGAINST PEOPLE MADE OF ARTIFICIALLY ENGINEERED COMPOUNDS, MY FRIEND? WHY JUDGE?
SORRY. CLOSE-MINDED AMERICAN IN ME, I GUESS.
AT LEAST YOU ADMIT IT. NOW--
I DON'T HELP , YOU'RE GOING BLEED OUT. I AN SEAL THE OUND, BUT--
IT'S GOING TO HURT QUITE A LOT.
YOU DIDN'T HAVE TO SMILE WHEN YOU SAID THAT. I WAS--
SHZUM
GAAAAHHH!
YOU'LL BE ALL RIGHT.
NNNN... YOU'RE SUPPOSED TO GIMME A SECOND TO GET READY! OR AT LEAST TELL ME TO LOOK OVER THERE--
RRRAARGH

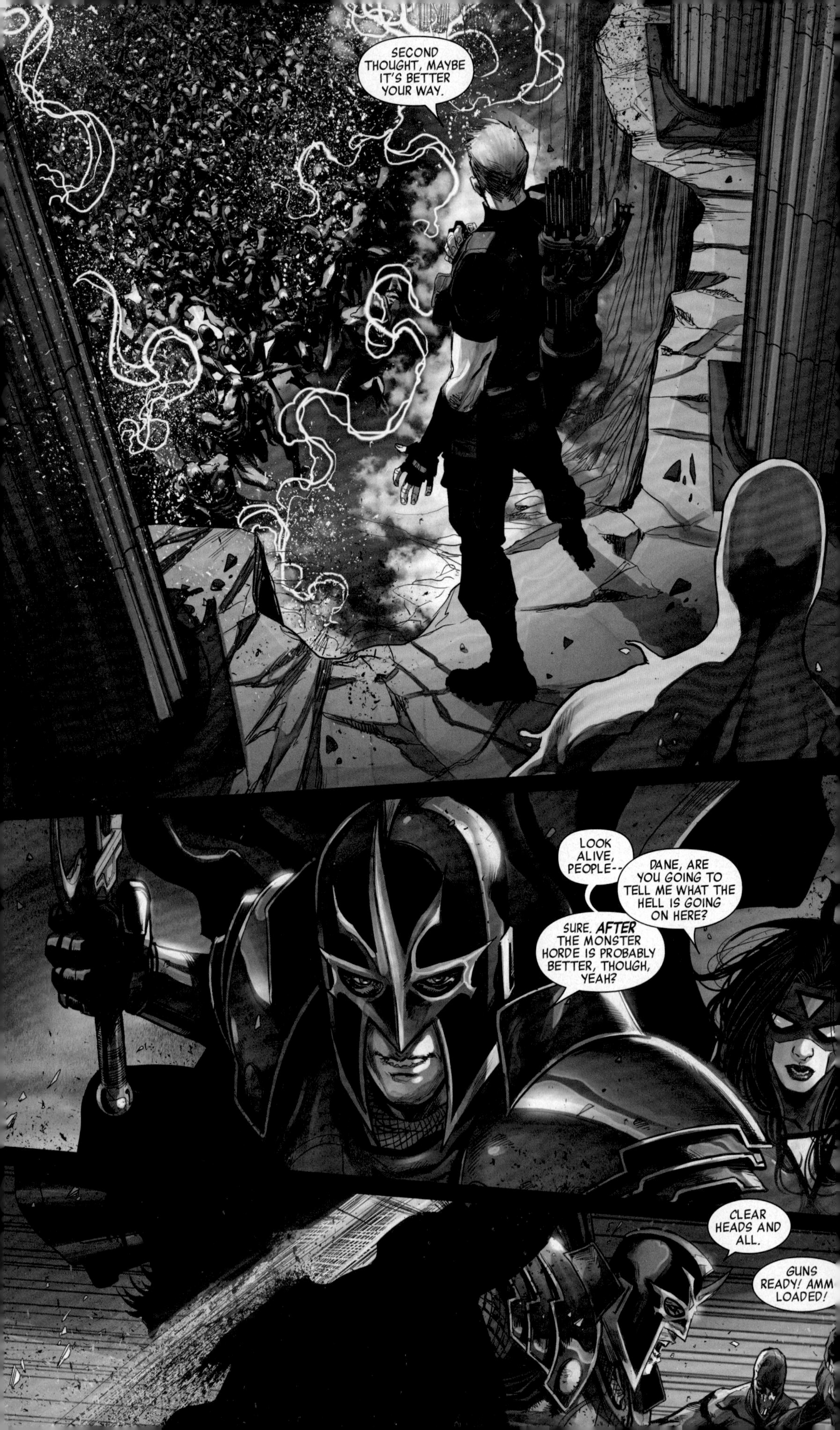
SECOND THOUGHT, MAYBE IT'S BETTER YOUR WAY.
LOOK ALIVE, PEOPLE--
DANE, ARE YOU GOING TO TELL ME WHAT THE HELL IS GOING ON HERE?
SURE. AFTER THE MONSTER HORDE IS PROBABLY BETTER, THOUGH, YEAH?
CLEAR HEADS AND ALL.
GUNS READY! AMM LOADED!

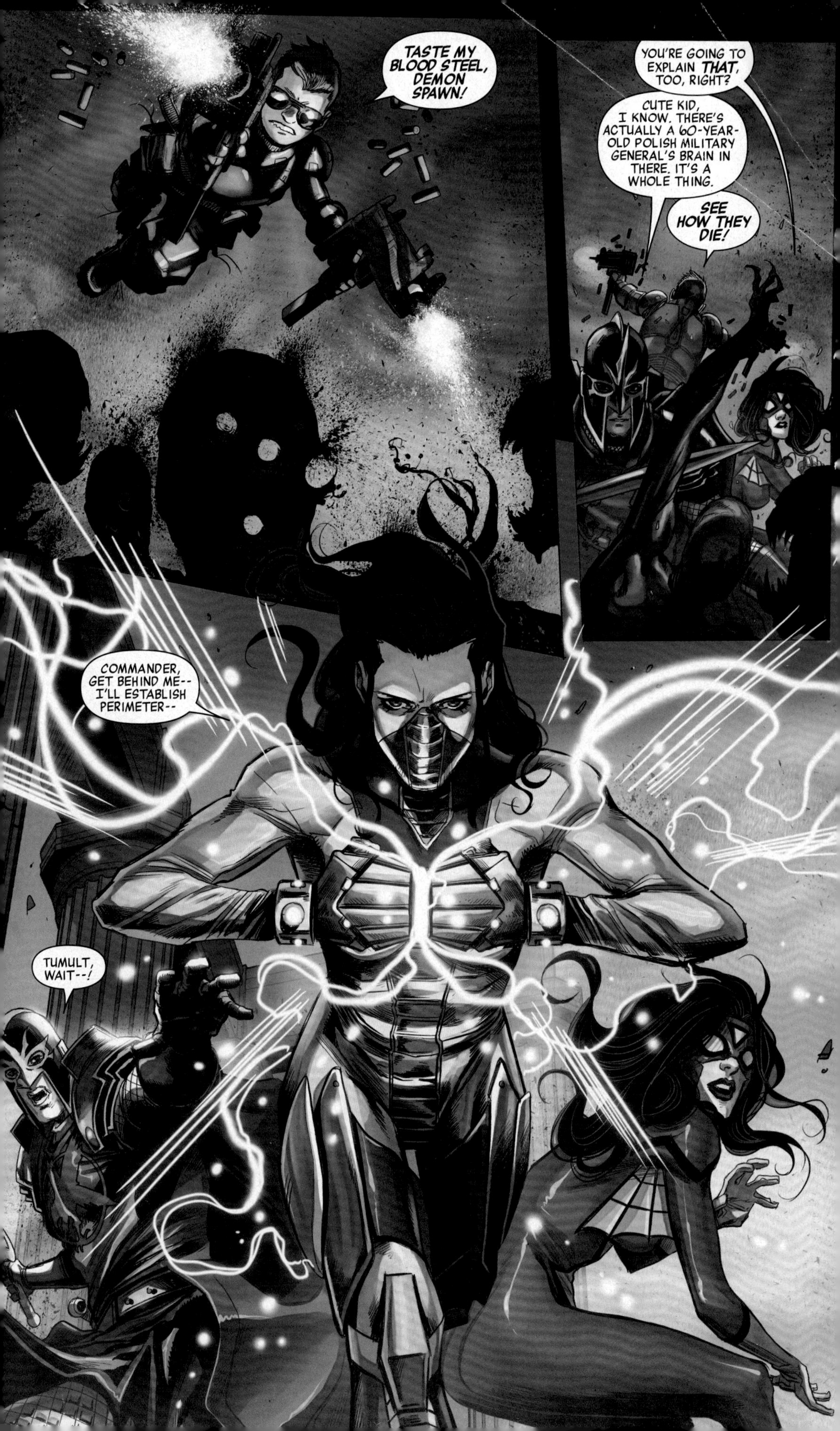
TASTE MY BLOOD STEEL, DEMON SPAWN!
YOU'RE GOING TO EXPLAIN THAT, TOO, RIGHT?
CUTE KID, I KNOW. THERE'S ACTUALLY A 60-YEAR-OLD POLISH MILITARY GENERAL'S BRAIN IN THERE. IT'S A WHOLE THING.
SEE HOW THEY DIE!
COMMANDER, GET BEHIND ME-- I'LL ESTABLISH PERIMETER--
TUMULT, WAIT--!

THOOOOOOOOOOM

RRMMMKRKKK

THIS ISN'T EXACTLY A *STABLE* ENVIRONMENT--

I-- I'M SORRY, SIR--

DON'T APOLOGIZE TO HIM--

--HE FEEDS OFF WEAKNESS. ADELYNN-- SWORDSWOMAN!

I RECOGNIZE THE CONCEPT...

SWORDSMAN'S DAUGHTER, THOUGH DUQUESNE DIDN'T EXACTLY KNOW ABOUT HER. SHE'S GOT POTENTIAL--

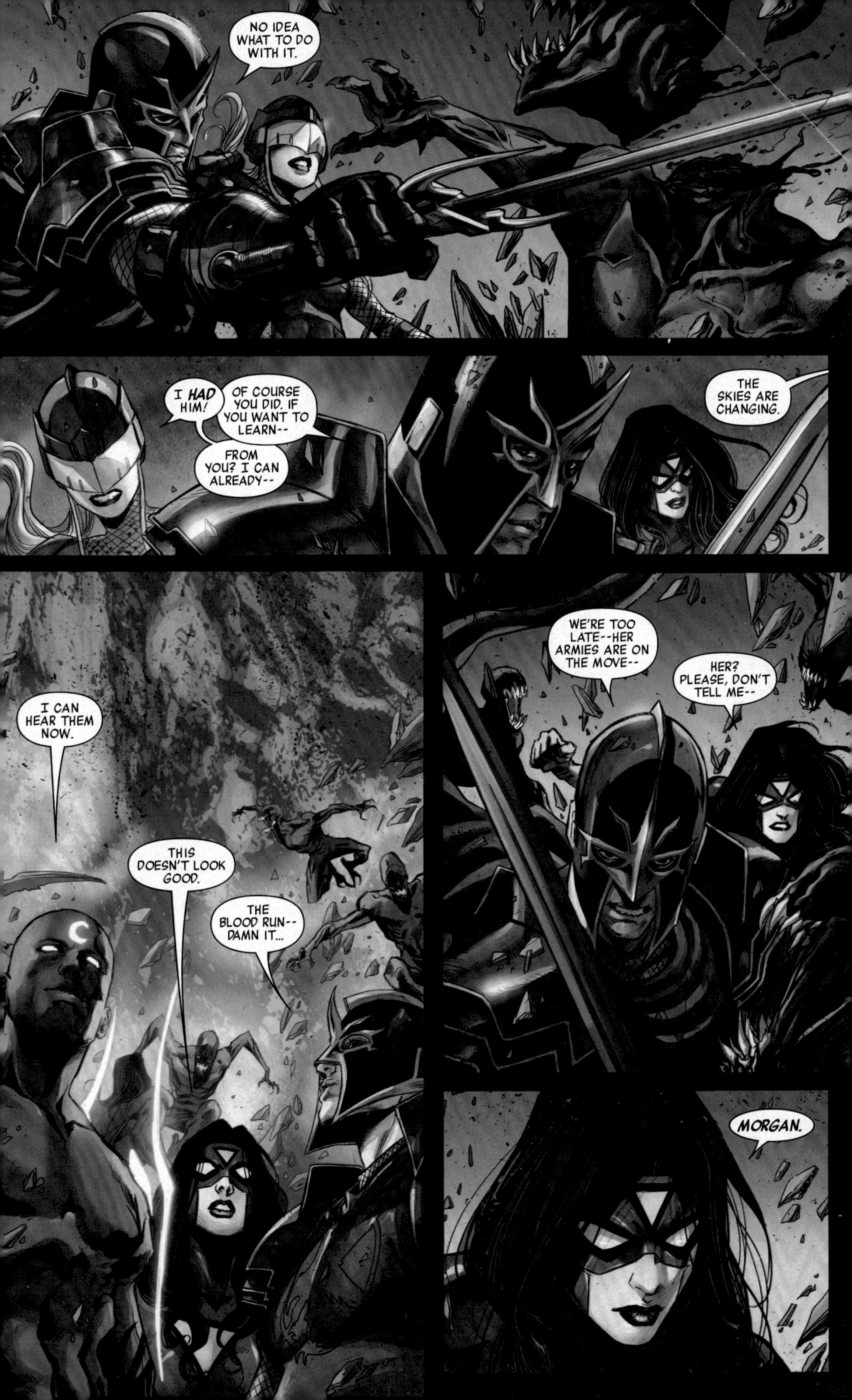
NO IDEA WHAT TO DO WITH IT.
I HAD HIM!
OF COURSE YOU DID. IF YOU WANT TO LEARN--
FROM YOU? I CAN ALREADY--
THE SKIES ARE CHANGING.
I CAN HEAR THEM NOW.
THIS DOESN'T LOOK GOOD.
THE BLOOD RUN--DAMN IT...
WE'RE TOO LATE--HER ARMIES ARE ON THE MOVE--
HER? PLEASE, DON'T TELL ME--
MORGAN.

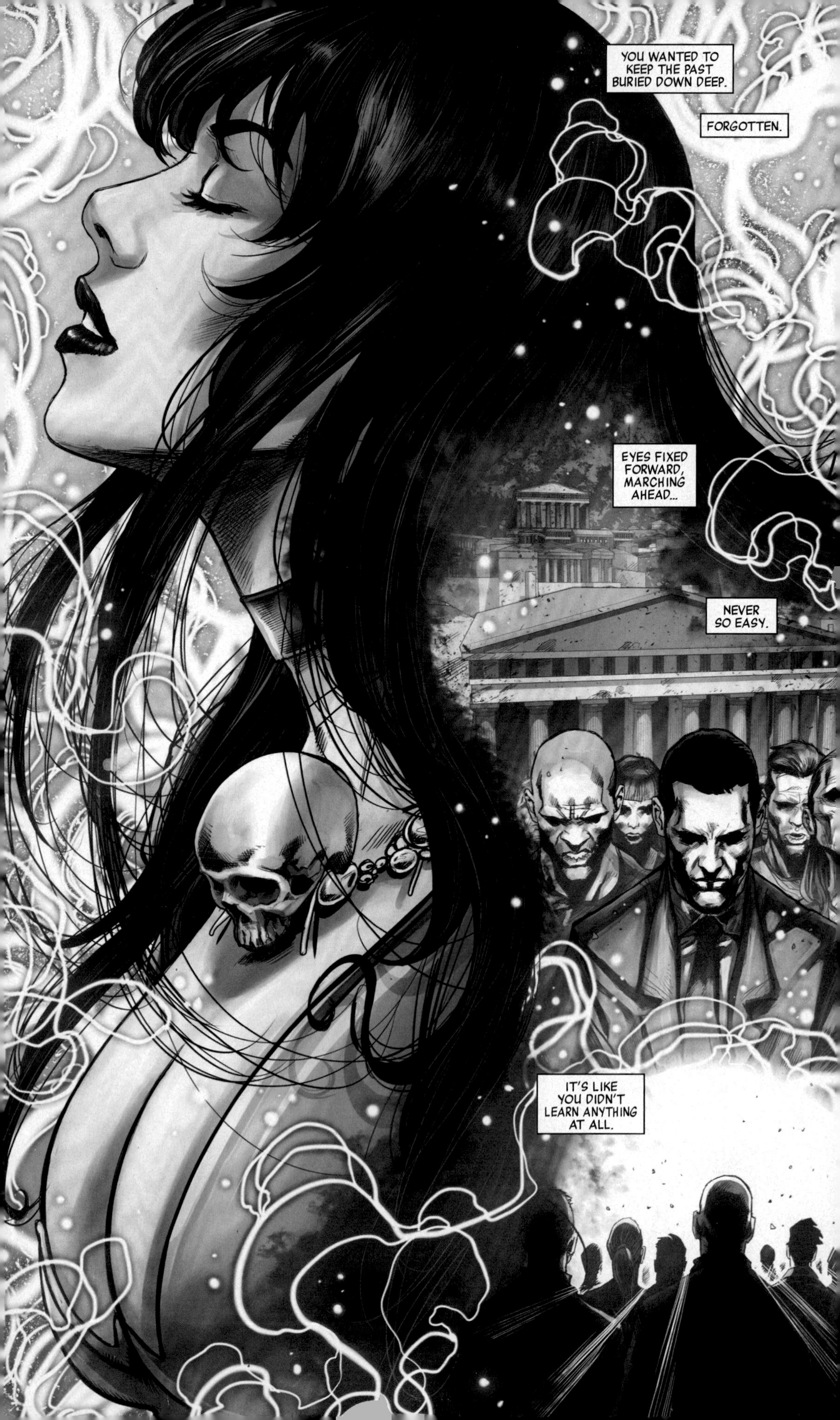

YOU WANTED TO KEEP THE PAST BURIED DOWN DEEP.
FORGOTTEN.
EYES FIXED FORWARD, MARCHING AHEAD...
NEVER SO EASY.
IT'S LIKE YOU DIDN'T LEARN ANYTHING AT ALL.

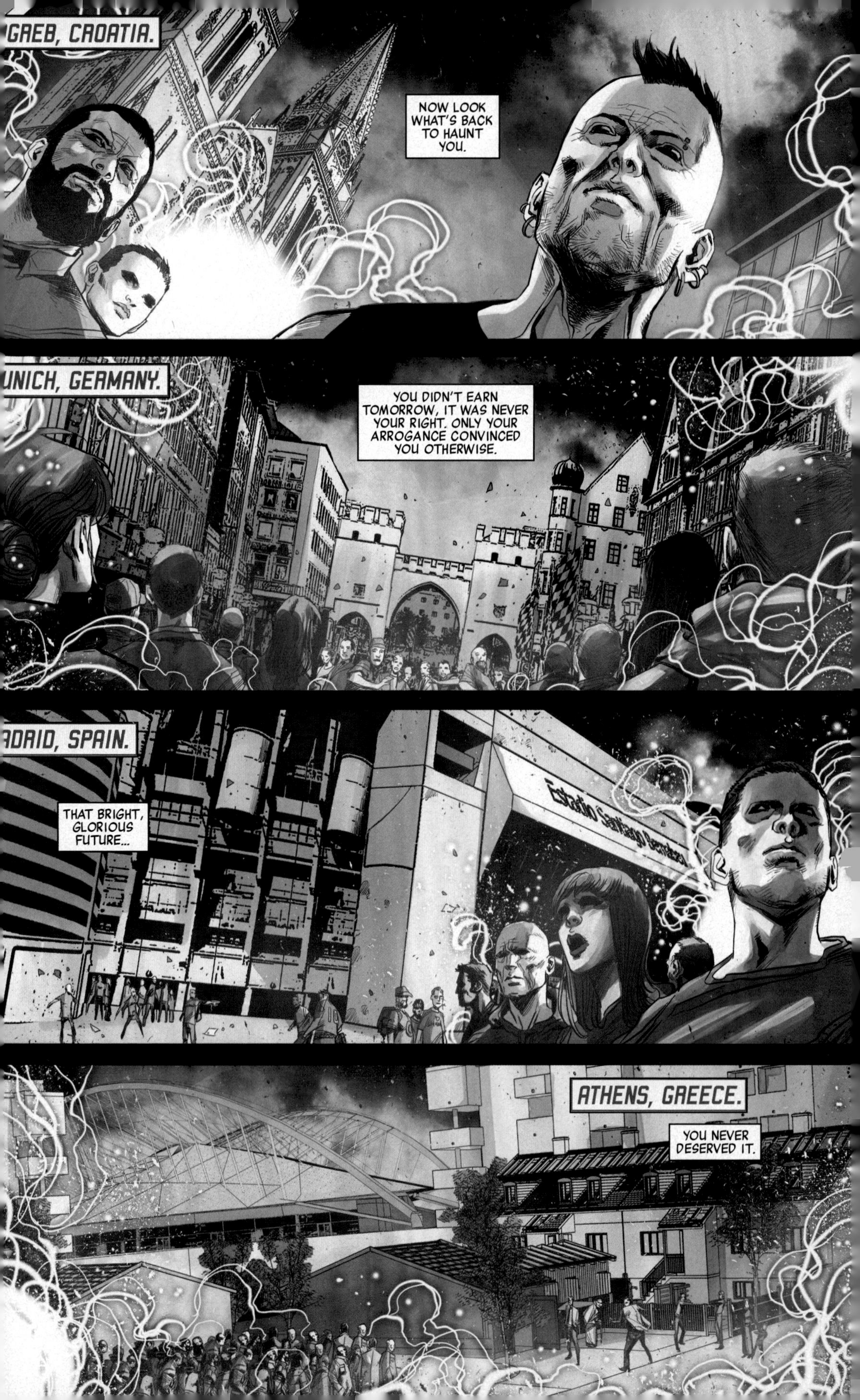
GREB, CROATIA.
NOW LOOK WHAT'S BACK TO HAUNT YOU.
UNICH, GERMANY.
YOU DIDN'T EARN TOMORROW, IT WAS NEVER YOUR RIGHT. ONLY YOUR ARROGANCE CONVINCED YOU OTHERWISE.
ADRID, SPAIN.
THAT BRIGHT, GLORIOUS FUTURE...
Estadio Santiago Bernabeu
ATHENS, GREECE.
YOU NEVER DESERVED IT.

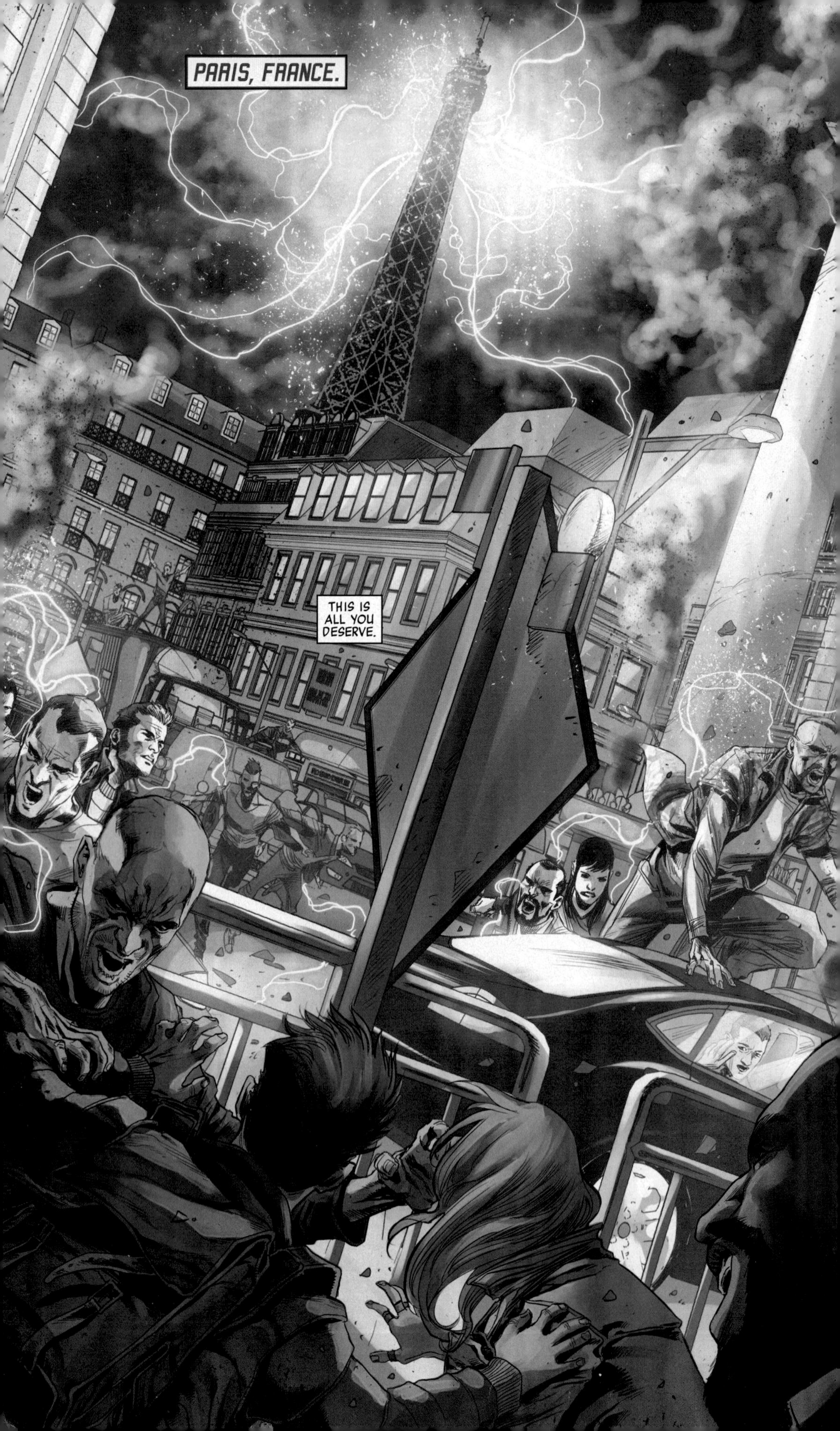
PARIS, FRANCE.
THIS IS ALL YOU DESERVE.

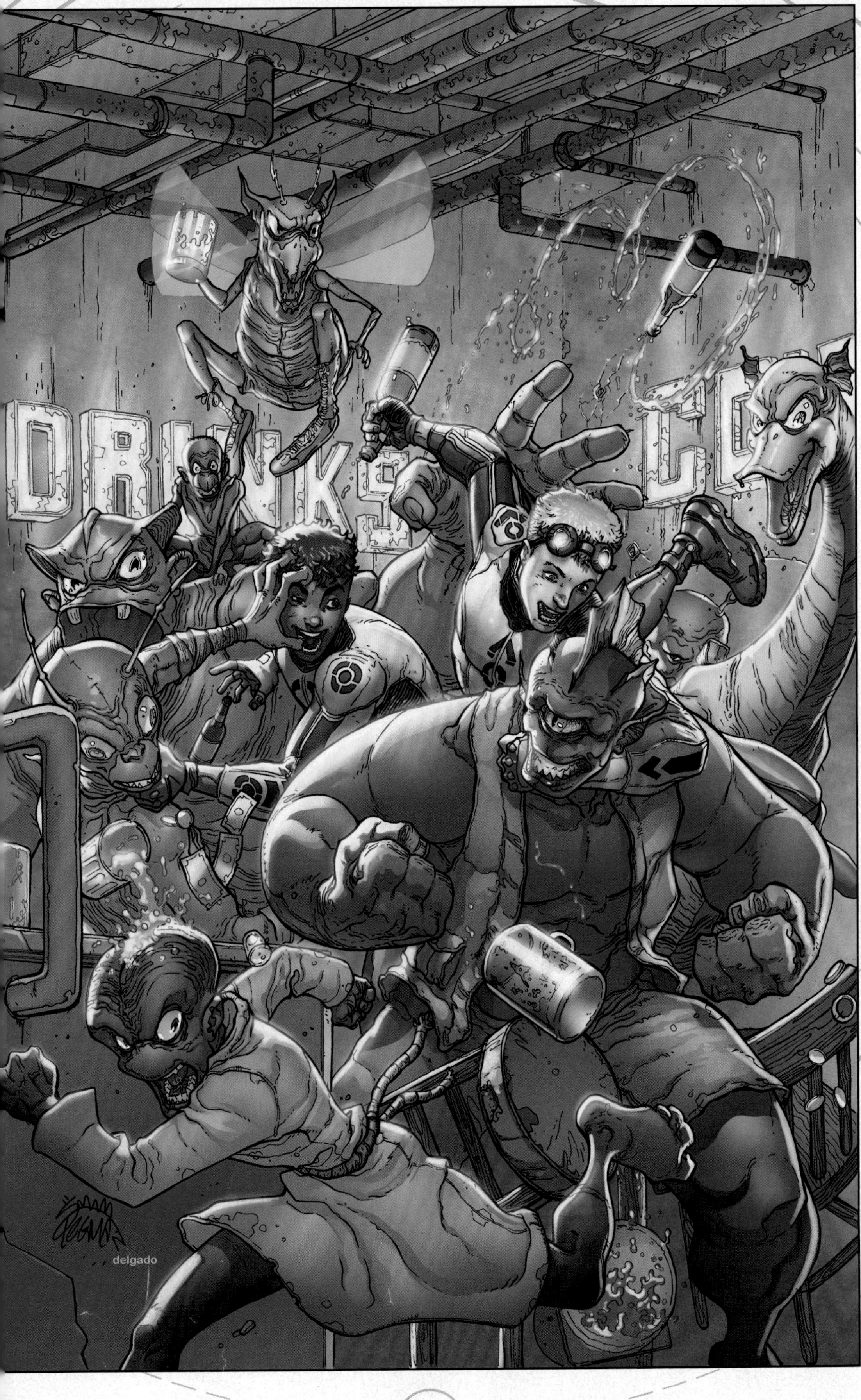
delgado

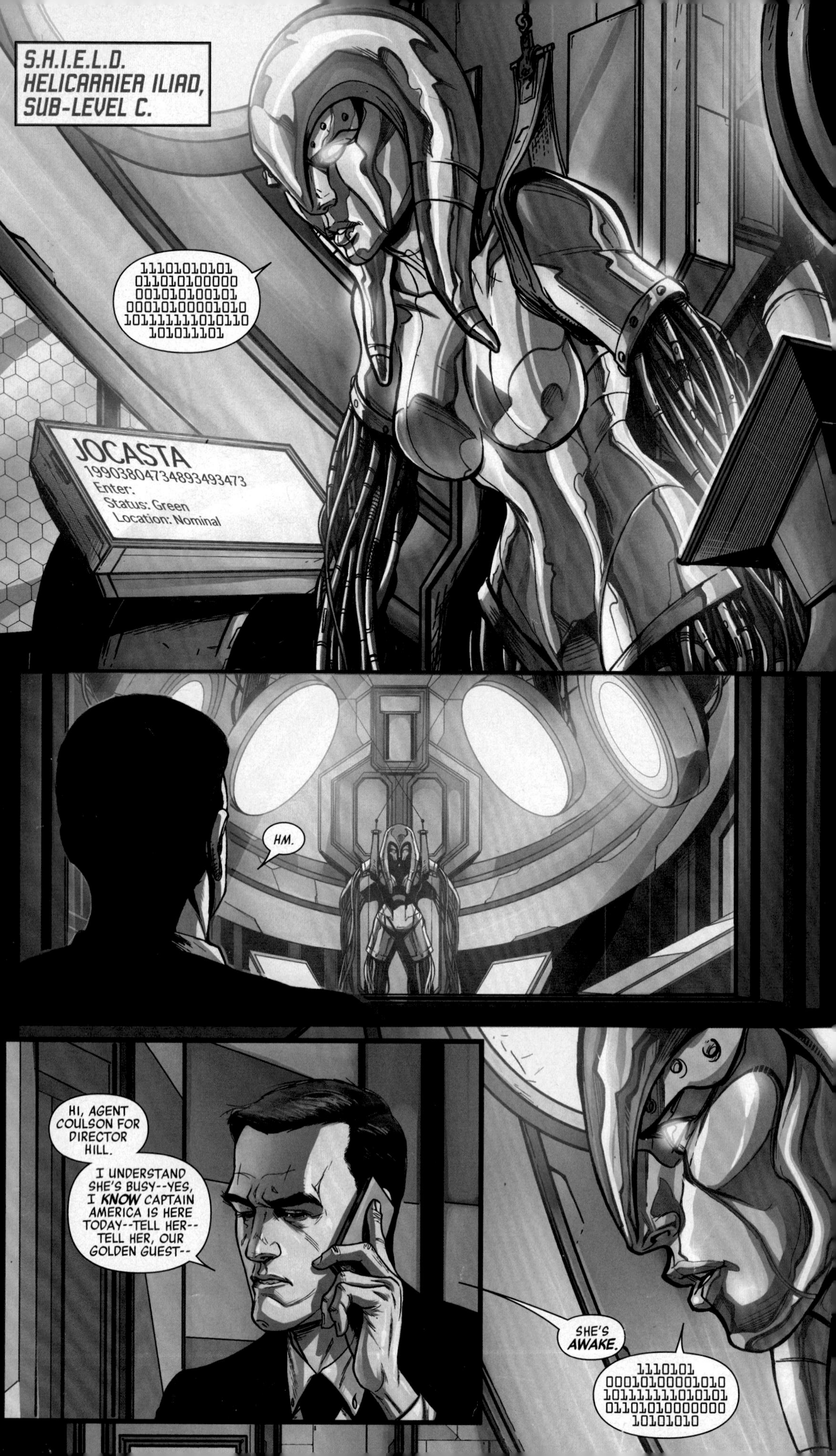

S.H.I.E.L.D. HELICARRIER ILIAD, SUB-LEVEL C.
11101010101 01101010000 00101010 0101 0001010000 1010 101111111010110 101011101
JOCASTA
19903804734893493473
Enter:
Status: Green
Location: Nominal
HM.
HI, AGENT COULSON FOR DIRECTOR HILL.
I UNDERSTAND SHE'S BUSY--YES, I **KNOW** CAPTAIN AMERICA IS HERE TODAY--TELL HER--TELL HER, OUR GOLDEN GUEST--
SHE'S **AWAKE.**
1110101 0001010000 1010 101111111010101 01101010000000 10101010

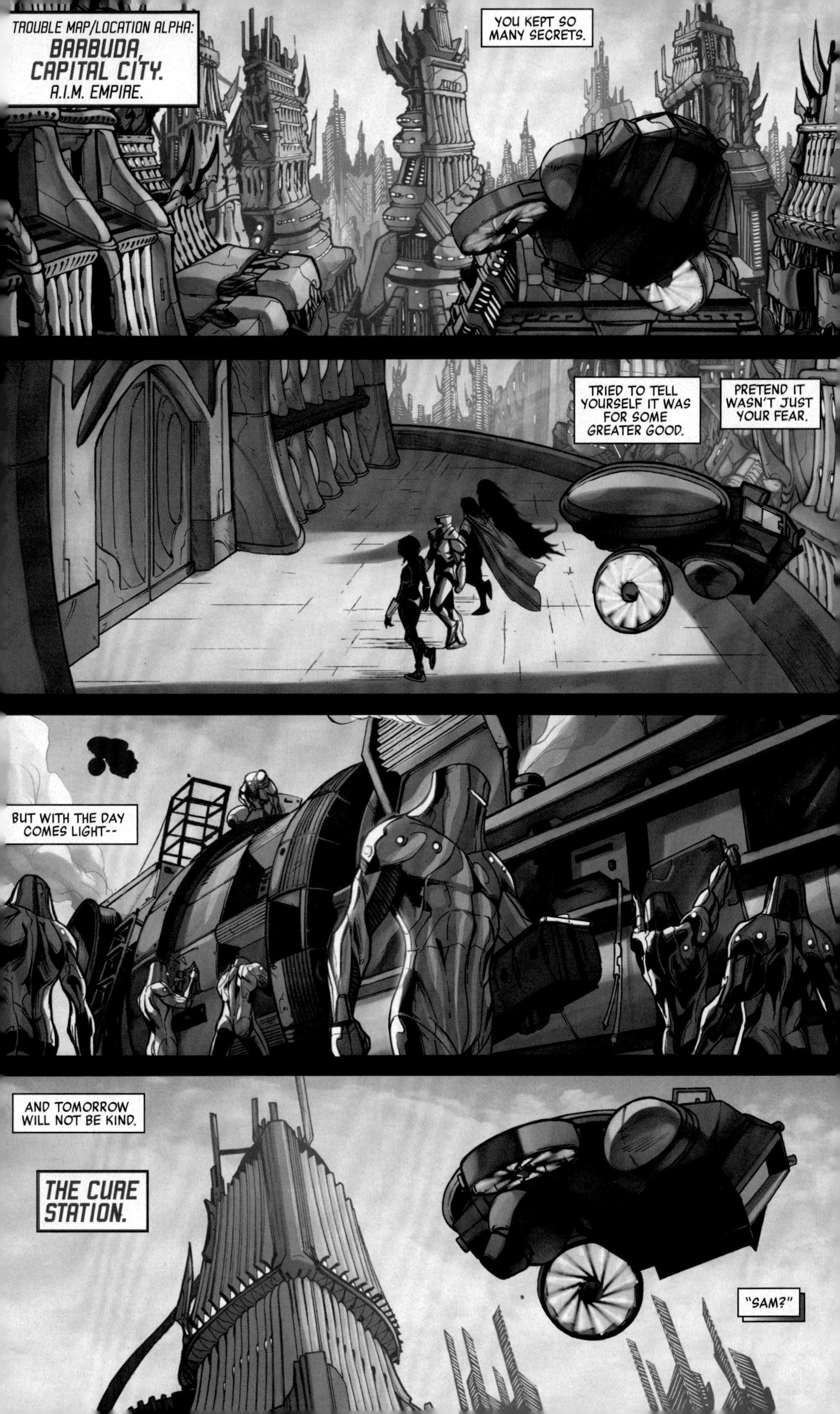
TROUBLE MAP/LOCATION ALPHA:
BARBUDA, CAPITAL CITY.
A.I.M. EMPIRE.
YOU KEPT SO MANY SECRETS.
TRIED TO TELL YOURSELF IT WAS FOR SOME GREATER GOOD.
PRETEND IT WASN'T JUST YOUR FEAR.
BUT WITH THE DAY COMES LIGHT--
AND TOMORROW WILL NOT BE KIND.
THE CURE STATION.
"SAM?"

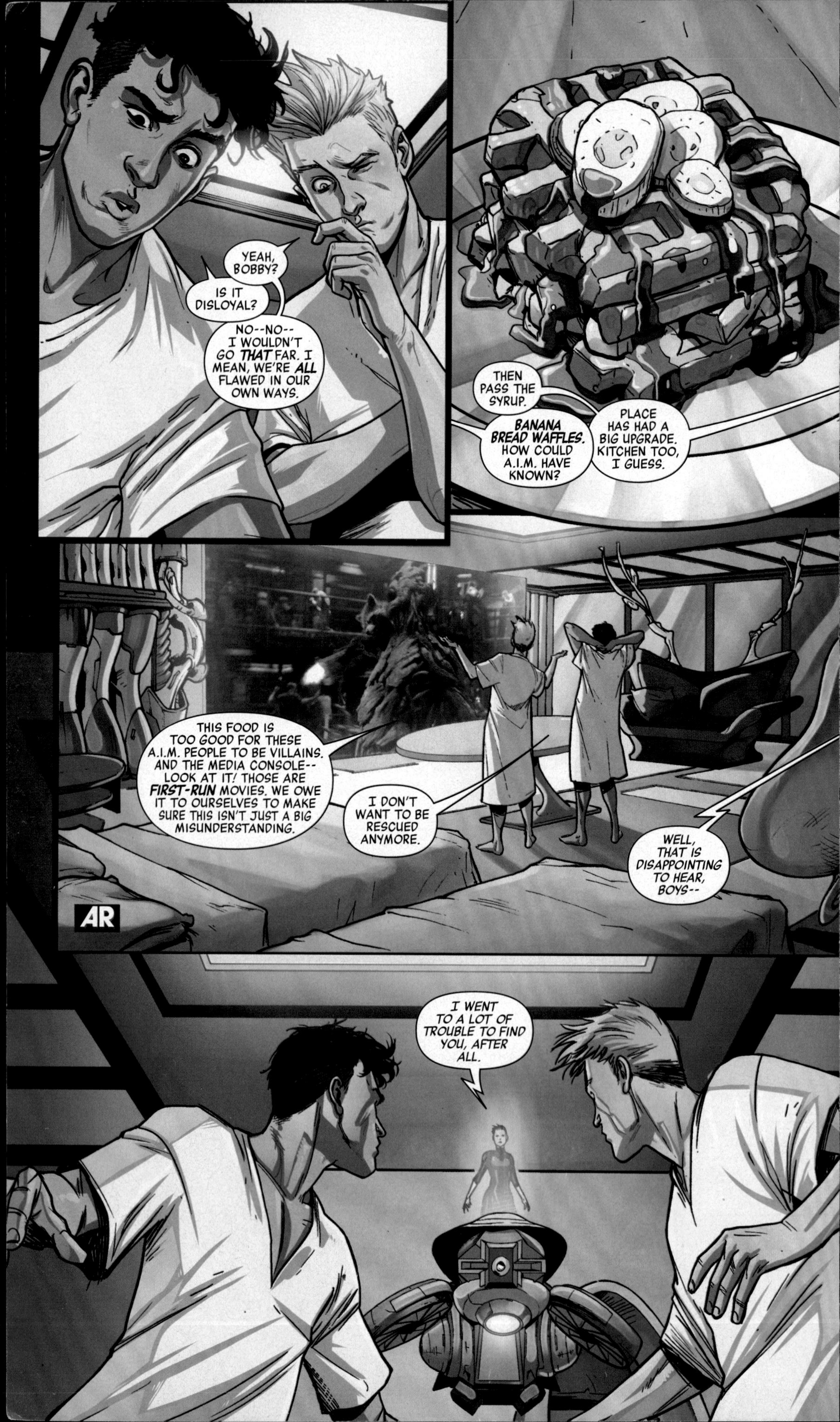
YEAH, BOBBY?
IS IT DISLOYAL?
NO--NO-- I WOULDN'T GO THAT FAR. I MEAN, WE'RE ALL FLAWED IN OUR OWN WAYS.
THEN PASS THE SYRUP.
BANANA BREAD WAFFLES. HOW COULD A.I.M. HAVE KNOWN?
PLACE HAS HAD A BIG UPGRADE. KITCHEN TOO, I GUESS.
THIS FOOD IS TOO GOOD FOR THESE A.I.M. PEOPLE TO BE VILLAINS. AND THE MEDIA CONSOLE-- LOOK AT IT! THOSE ARE FIRST-RUN MOVIES. WE OWE IT TO OURSELVES TO MAKE SURE THIS ISN'T JUST A BIG MISUNDERSTANDING.
I DON'T WANT TO BE RESCUED ANYMORE.
WELL, THAT IS DISAPPOINTING TO HEAR, BOYS--
AR
I WENT TO A LOT OF TROUBLE TO FIND YOU, AFTER ALL.

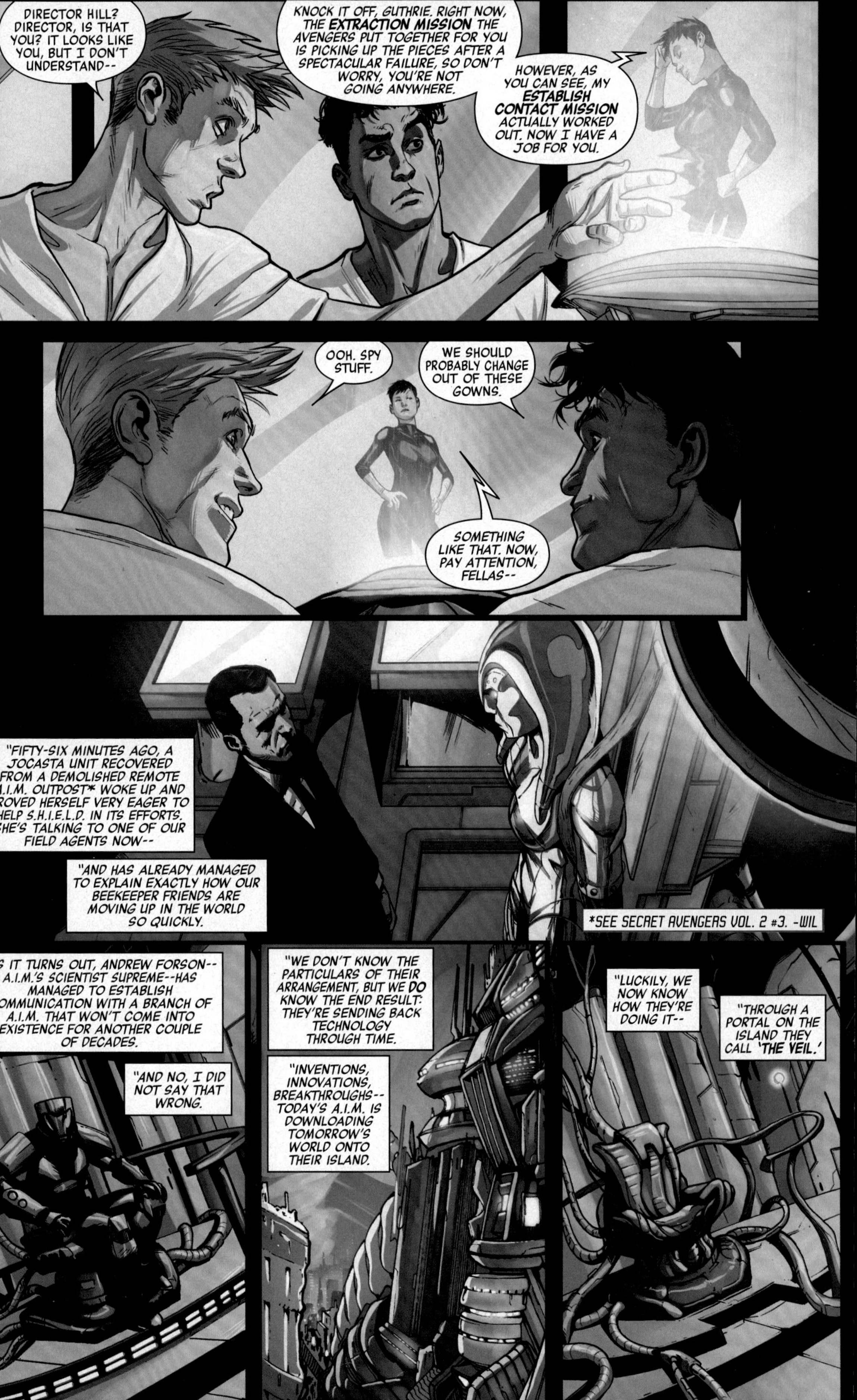
DIRECTOR HILL? DIRECTOR, IS THAT YOU? IT LOOKS LIKE YOU, BUT I DON'T UNDERSTAND--
KNOCK IT OFF, GUTHRIE. RIGHT NOW, THE EXTRACTION MISSION THE AVENGERS PUT TOGETHER FOR YOU IS PICKING UP THE PIECES AFTER A SPECTACULAR FAILURE, SO DON'T WORRY, YOU'RE NOT GOING ANYWHERE.
HOWEVER, AS YOU CAN SEE, MY ESTABLISH CONTACT MISSION ACTUALLY WORKED OUT. NOW I HAVE A JOB FOR YOU.
OOH. SPY STUFF.
WE SHOULD PROBABLY CHANGE OUT OF THESE GOWNS.
SOMETHING LIKE THAT. NOW, PAY ATTENTION, FELLAS--
"FIFTY-SIX MINUTES AGO, A JOCASTA UNIT RECOVERED FROM A DEMOLISHED REMOTE A.I.M. OUTPOST* WOKE UP AND PROVED HERSELF VERY EAGER TO HELP S.H.I.E.L.D. IN ITS EFFORTS. SHE'S TALKING TO ONE OF OUR FIELD AGENTS NOW--
"AND HAS ALREADY MANAGED TO EXPLAIN EXACTLY HOW OUR BEEKEEPER FRIENDS ARE MOVING UP IN THE WORLD SO QUICKLY.
*SEE SECRET AVENGERS VOL. 2 #3. -WIL
AS IT TURNS OUT, ANDREW FORSON--A.I.M.'S SCIENTIST SUPREME--HAS MANAGED TO ESTABLISH COMMUNICATION WITH A BRANCH OF A.I.M. THAT WON'T COME INTO EXISTENCE FOR ANOTHER COUPLE OF DECADES.
"AND NO, I DID NOT SAY THAT WRONG.
"WE DON'T KNOW THE PARTICULARS OF THEIR ARRANGEMENT, BUT WE DO KNOW THE END RESULT: THEY'RE SENDING BACK TECHNOLOGY THROUGH TIME.
"INVENTIONS, INNOVATIONS, BREAKTHROUGHS--TODAY'S A.I.M. IS DOWNLOADING TOMORROW'S WORLD ONTO THEIR ISLAND.
"LUCKILY, WE NOW KNOW HOW THEY'RE DOING IT--
"THROUGH A PORTAL ON THE ISLAND THEY CALL 'THE VEIL.'

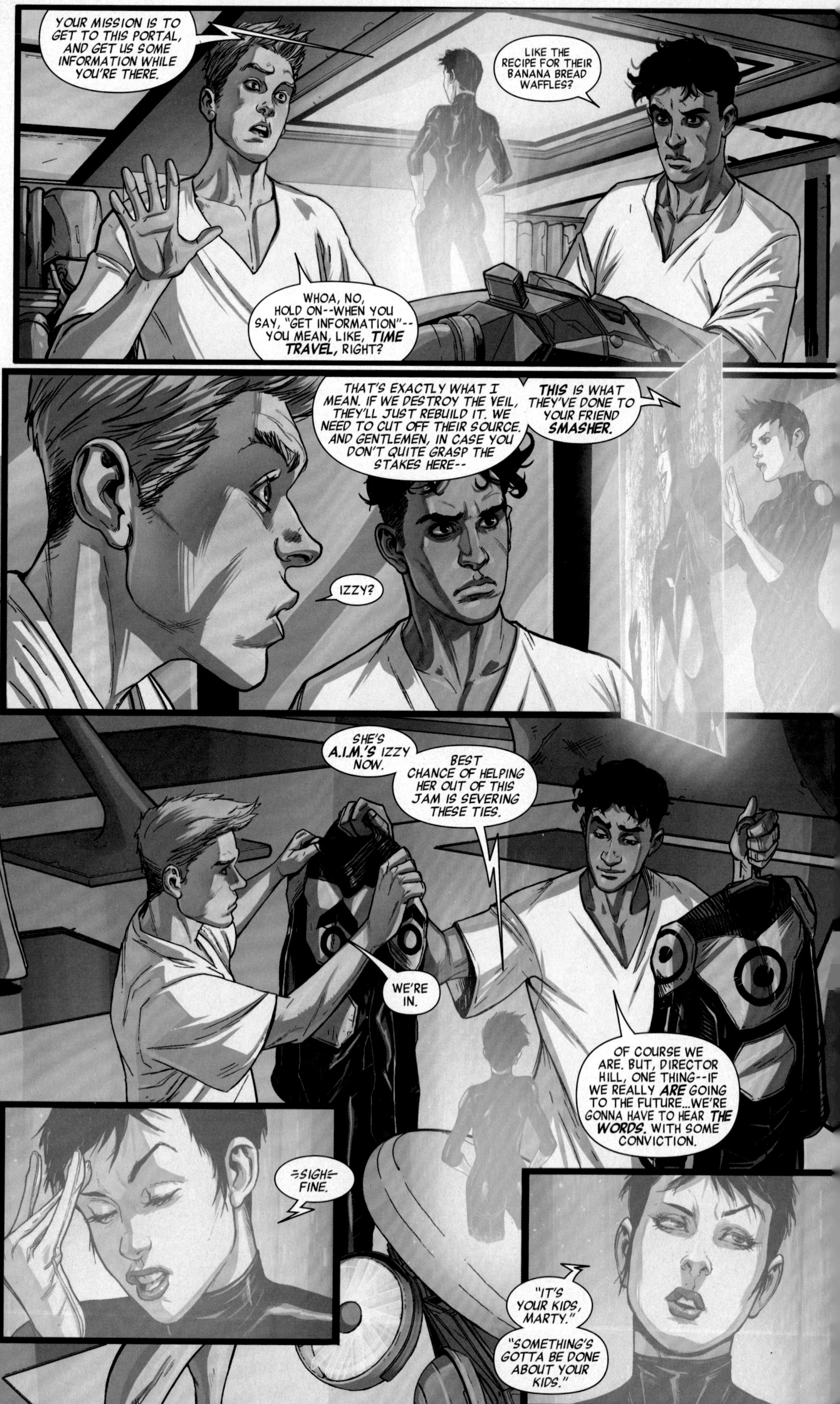

YOUR MISSION IS TO GET TO THIS PORTAL, AND GET US SOME INFORMATION WHILE YOU'RE THERE.
LIKE THE RECIPE FOR THEIR BANANA BREAD WAFFLES?
WHOA, NO, HOLD ON--WHEN YOU SAY, "GET INFORMATION"--YOU MEAN, LIKE, TIME TRAVEL, RIGHT?
THAT'S EXACTLY WHAT I MEAN. IF WE DESTROY THE VEIL, THEY'LL JUST REBUILD IT. WE NEED TO CUT OFF THEIR SOURCE. AND GENTLEMEN, IN CASE YOU DON'T QUITE GRASP THE STAKES HERE--
THIS IS WHAT THEY'VE DONE TO YOUR FRIEND SMASHER.
IZZY?
SHE'S A.I.M.'S IZZY NOW.
BEST CHANCE OF HELPING HER OUT OF THIS JAM IS SEVERING THESE TIES.
WE'RE IN.
OF COURSE WE ARE. BUT, DIRECTOR HILL, ONE THING--IF WE REALLY ARE GOING TO THE FUTURE...WE'RE GONNA HAVE TO HEAR THE WORDS. WITH SOME CONVICTION.
=SIGH= FINE.
"IT'S YOUR KIDS, MARTY."
"SOMETHING'S GOTTA BE DONE ABOUT YOUR KIDS."

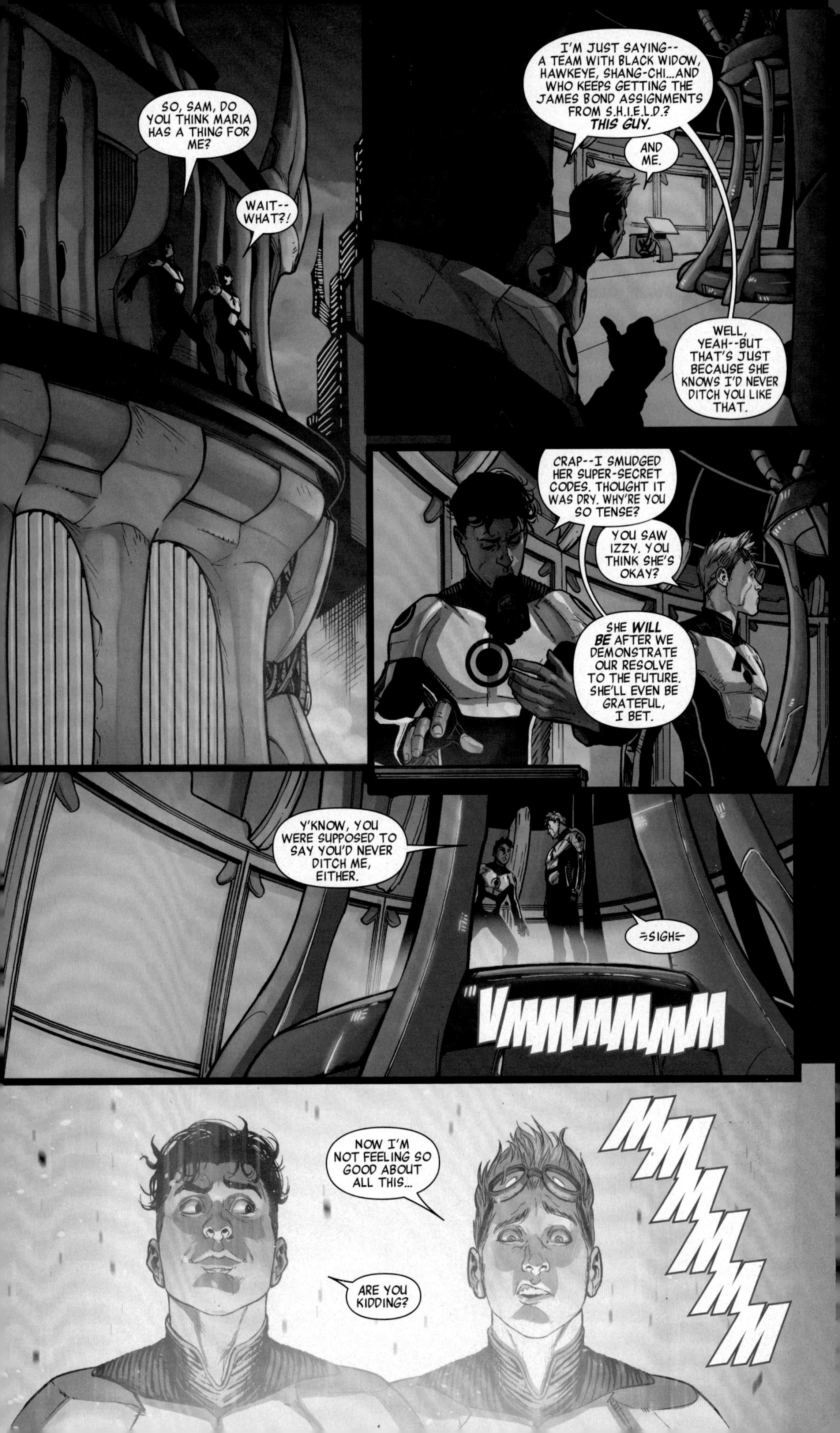
SO, SAM, DO YOU THINK MARIA HAS A THING FOR ME?
WAIT-- WHAT?!
I'M JUST SAYING-- A TEAM WITH BLACK WIDOW, HAWKEYE, SHANG-CHI...AND WHO KEEPS GETTING THE JAMES BOND ASSIGNMENTS FROM S.H.I.E.L.D.? THIS GUY.
AND ME.
WELL, YEAH--BUT THAT'S JUST BECAUSE SHE KNOWS I'D NEVER DITCH YOU LIKE THAT.
CRAP--I SMUDGED HER SUPER-SECRET CODES. THOUGHT IT WAS DRY. WHY'RE YOU SO TENSE?
YOU SAW IZZY. YOU THINK SHE'S OKAY?
SHE WILL BE AFTER WE DEMONSTRATE OUR RESOLVE TO THE FUTURE. SHE'LL EVEN BE GRATEFUL, I BET.
Y'KNOW, YOU WERE SUPPOSED TO SAY YOU'D NEVER DITCH ME, EITHER.
=SIGH=
VMMMMMMMM
MMMMMMMMM
NOW I'M NOT FEELING SO GOOD ABOUT ALL THIS...
ARE YOU KIDDING?

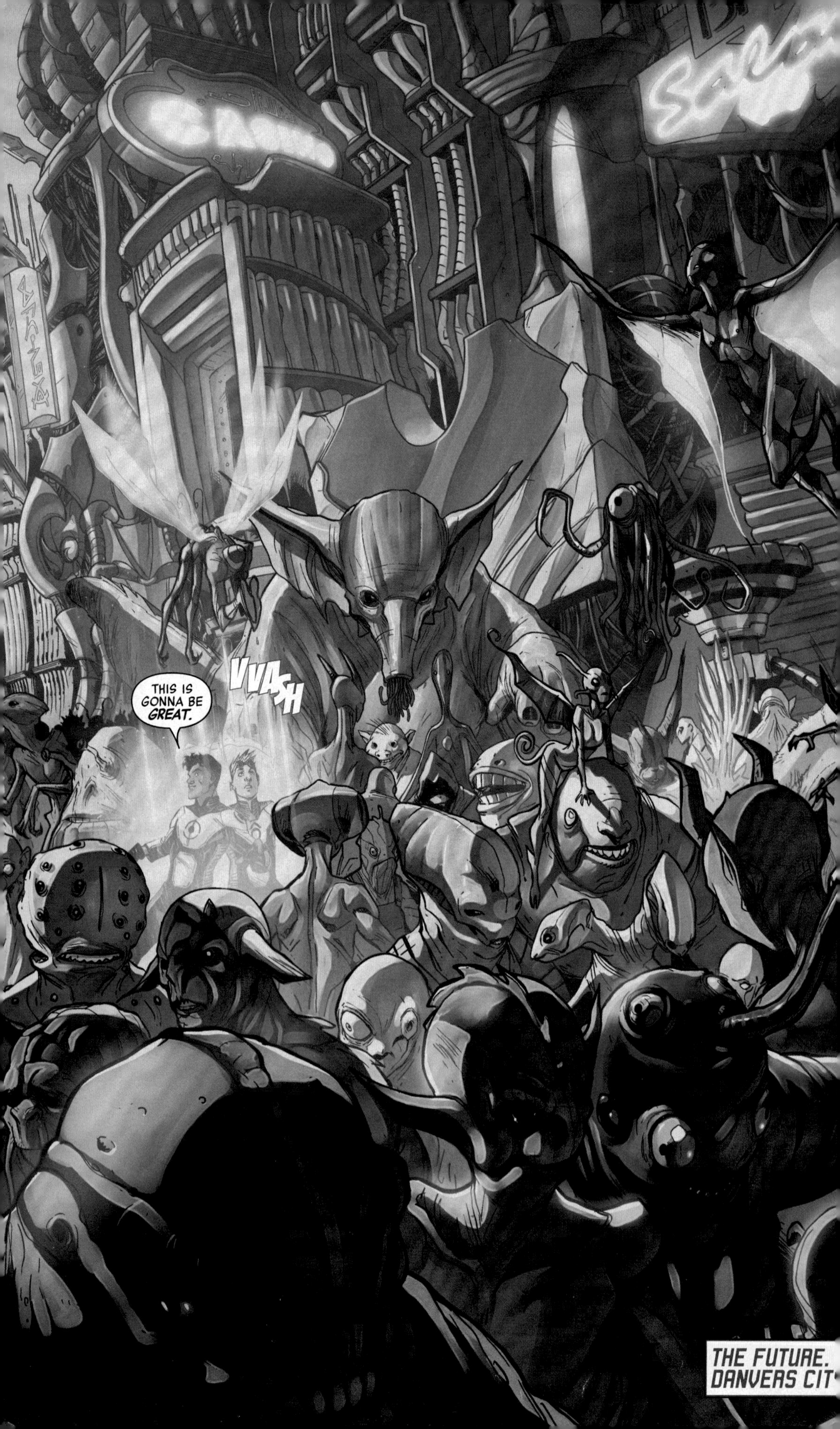
THIS IS GONNA BE GREAT.
VVASH
THE FUTURE. DANVERS CIT

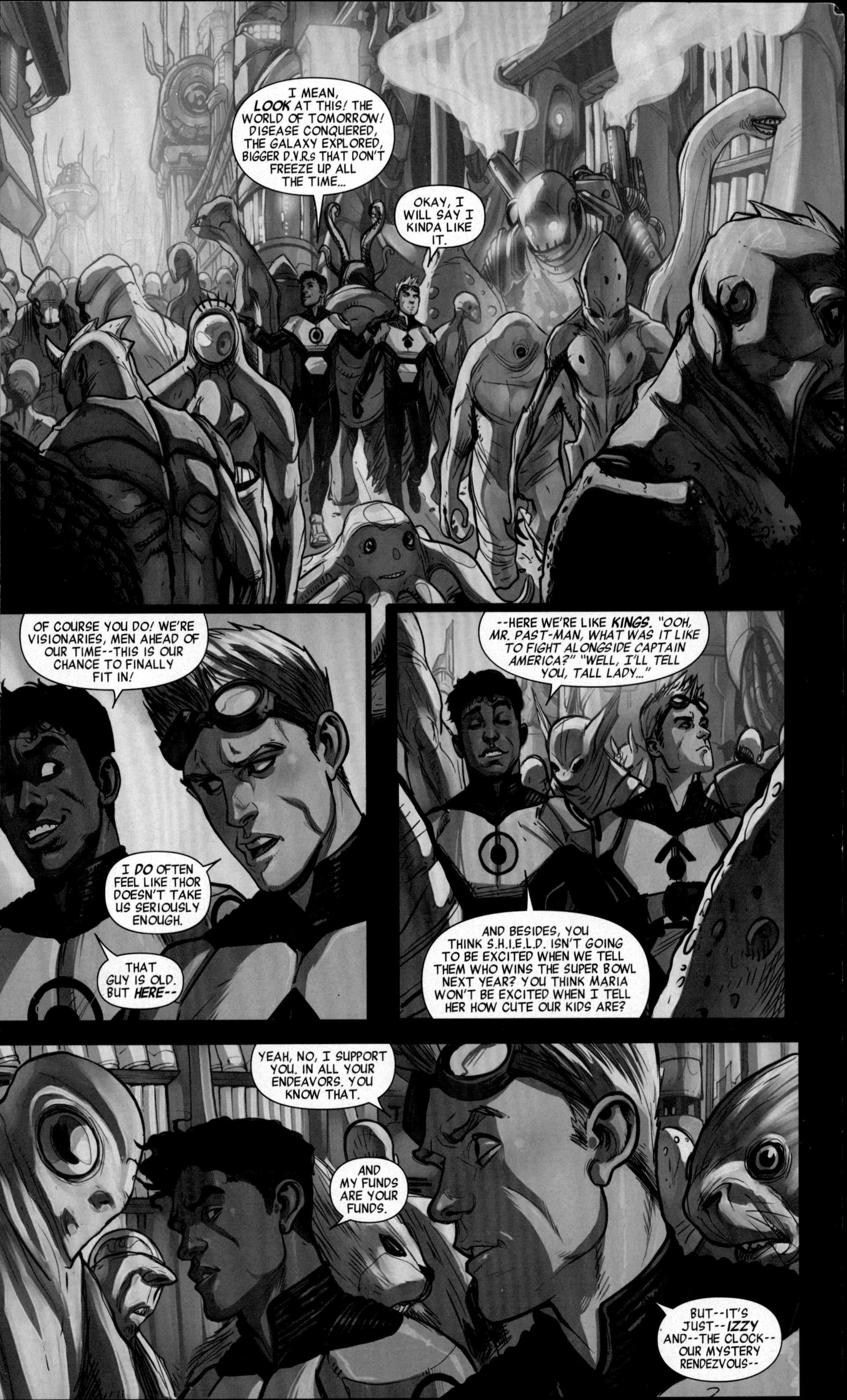
I MEAN, LOOK AT THIS! THE WORLD OF TOMORROW! DISEASE CONQUERED, THE GALAXY EXPLORED, BIGGER D.V.R.s THAT DON'T FREEZE UP ALL THE TIME...
OKAY, I WILL SAY I KINDA LIKE IT.
OF COURSE YOU DO! WE'RE VISIONARIES, MEN AHEAD OF OUR TIME--THIS IS OUR CHANCE TO FINALLY FIT IN!
I DO OFTEN FEEL LIKE THOR DOESN'T TAKE US SERIOUSLY ENOUGH.
THAT GUY IS OLD. BUT HERE--
--HERE WE'RE LIKE KINGS. "OOH, MR. PAST-MAN, WHAT WAS IT LIKE TO FIGHT ALONGSIDE CAPTAIN AMERICA?" "WELL, I'LL TELL YOU, TALL LADY..."
AND BESIDES, YOU THINK S.H.I.E.L.D. ISN'T GOING TO BE EXCITED WHEN WE TELL THEM WHO WINS THE SUPER BOWL NEXT YEAR? YOU THINK MARIA WON'T BE EXCITED WHEN I TELL HER HOW CUTE OUR KIDS ARE?
YEAH, NO, I SUPPORT YOU. IN ALL YOUR ENDEAVORS. YOU KNOW THAT.
AND MY FUNDS ARE YOUR FUNDS.
BUT--IT'S JUST--IZZY AND--THE CLOCK--OUR MYSTERY RENDEZVOUS--

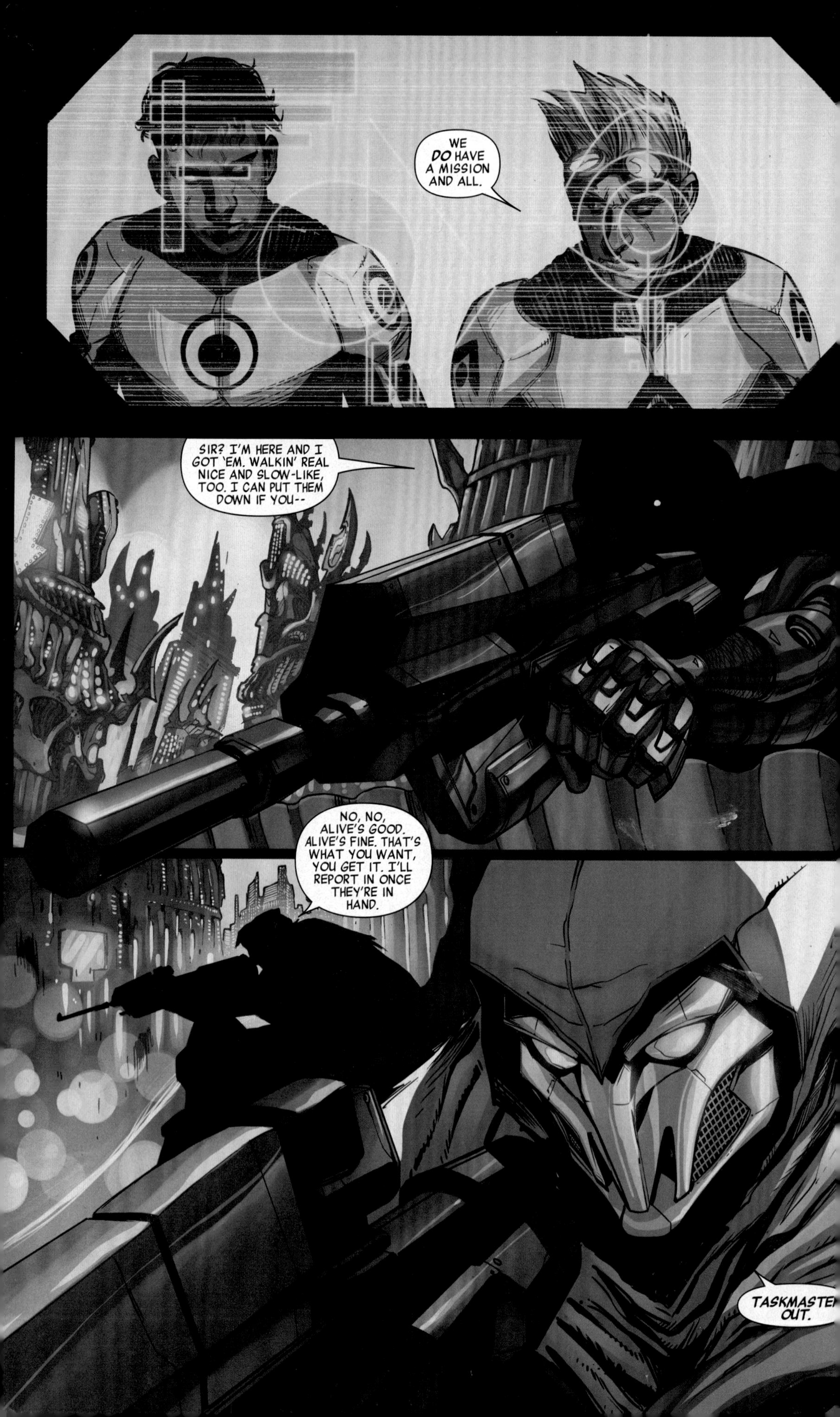
WE DO HAVE A MISSION AND ALL.
SIR? I'M HERE AND I GOT 'EM. WALKIN' REAL NICE AND SLOW-LIKE, TOO. I CAN PUT THEM DOWN IF YOU--
NO, NO, ALIVE'S GOOD. ALIVE'S FINE. THAT'S WHAT YOU WANT, YOU GET IT. I'LL REPORT IN ONCE THEY'RE IN HAND.
TASKMASTE OUT.

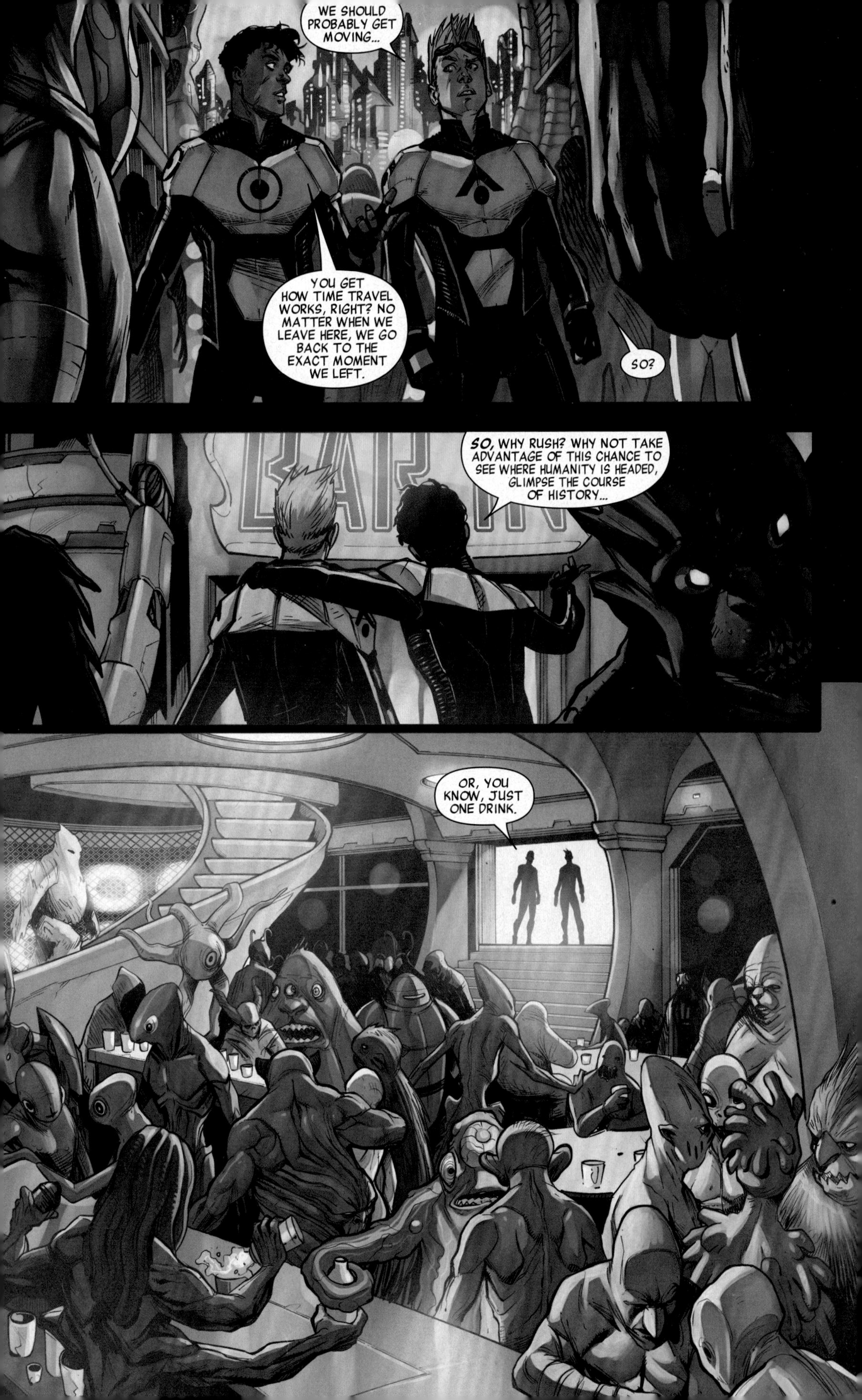
WE SHOULD PROBABLY GET MOVING...
YOU GET HOW TIME TRAVEL WORKS, RIGHT? NO MATTER WHEN WE LEAVE HERE, WE GO BACK TO THE EXACT MOMENT WE LEFT.
SO?
SO, WHY RUSH? WHY NOT TAKE ADVANTAGE OF THIS CHANCE TO SEE WHERE HUMANITY IS HEADED, GLIMPSE THE COURSE OF HISTORY...
OR, YOU KNOW, JUST ONE DRINK.

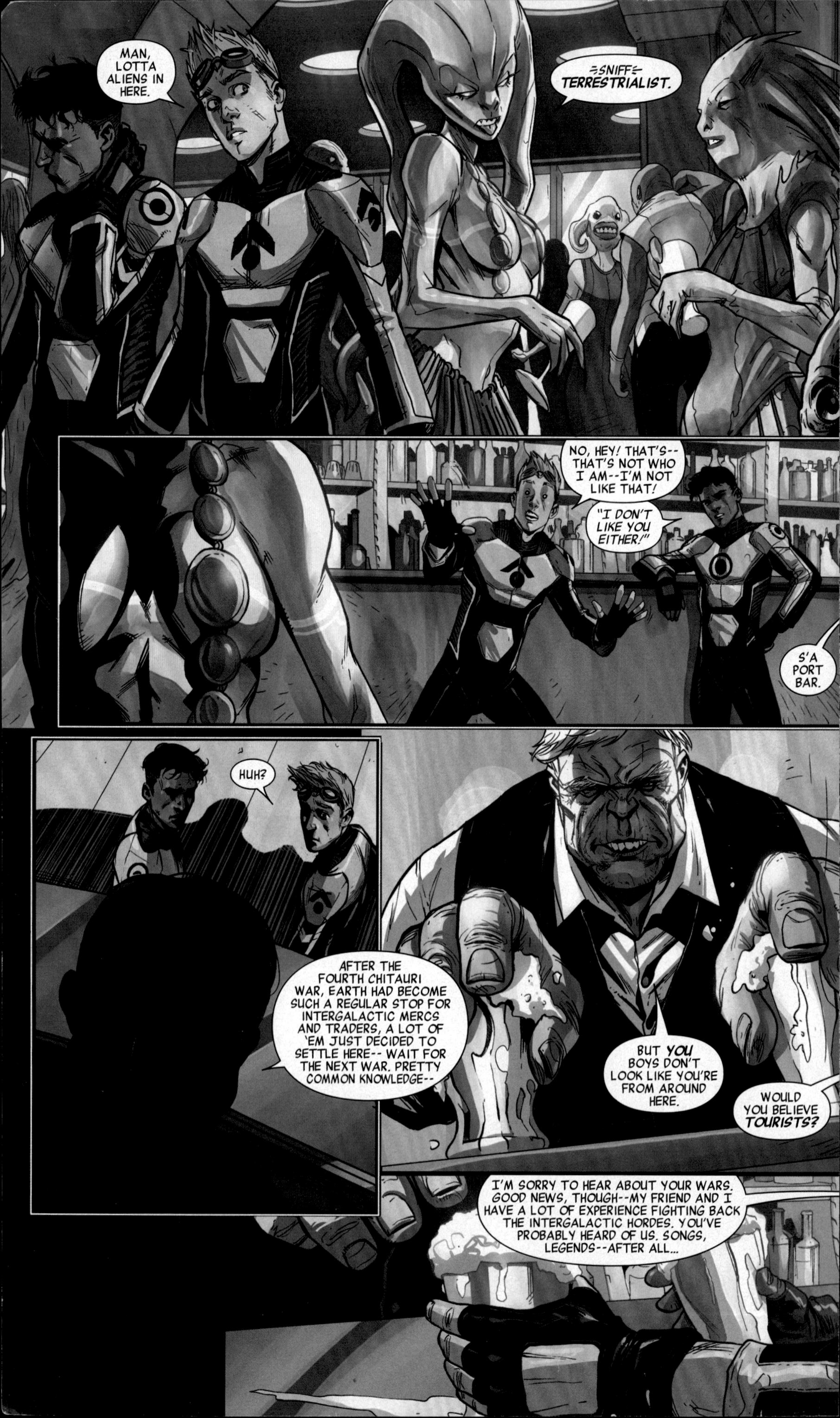
MAN, LOTTA ALIENS IN HERE.
=SNIFF= TERRESTRIALIST.
NO, HEY! THAT'S-- THAT'S NOT WHO I AM--I'M NOT LIKE THAT!
"I DON'T LIKE YOU EITHER!"
S'A PORT BAR.
HUH?
AFTER THE FOURTH CHITAURI WAR, EARTH HAD BECOME SUCH A REGULAR STOP FOR INTERGALACTIC MERCS AND TRADERS, A LOT OF 'EM JUST DECIDED TO SETTLE HERE-- WAIT FOR THE NEXT WAR. PRETTY COMMON KNOWLEDGE--
BUT YOU BOYS DON'T LOOK LIKE YOU'RE FROM AROUND HERE.
WOULD YOU BELIEVE TOURISTS?
I'M SORRY TO HEAR ABOUT YOUR WARS. GOOD NEWS, THOUGH--MY FRIEND AND I HAVE A LOT OF EXPERIENCE FIGHTING BACK THE INTERGALACTIC HORDES. YOU'VE PROBABLY HEARD OF US. SONGS, LEGENDS--AFTER ALL...

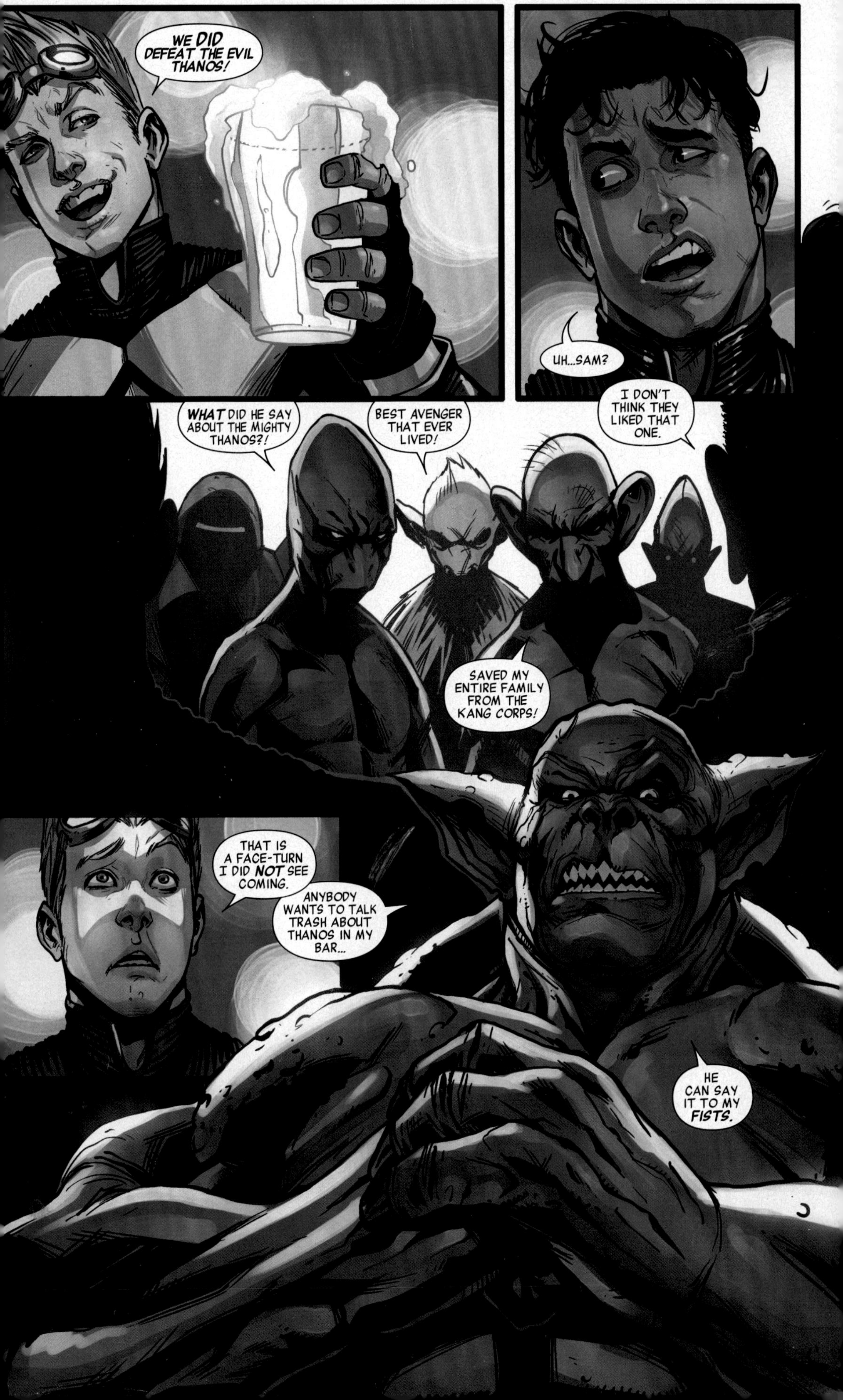
WE DID DEFEAT THE EVIL THANOS!
UH...SAM?
WHAT DID HE SAY ABOUT THE MIGHTY THANOS?!
BEST AVENGER THAT EVER LIVED!
I DON'T THINK THEY LIKED THAT ONE.
SAVED MY ENTIRE FAMILY FROM THE KANG CORPS!
THAT IS A FACE-TURN I DID NOT SEE COMING.
ANYBODY WANTS TO TALK TRASH ABOUT THANOS IN MY BAR...
HE CAN SAY IT TO MY FISTS.

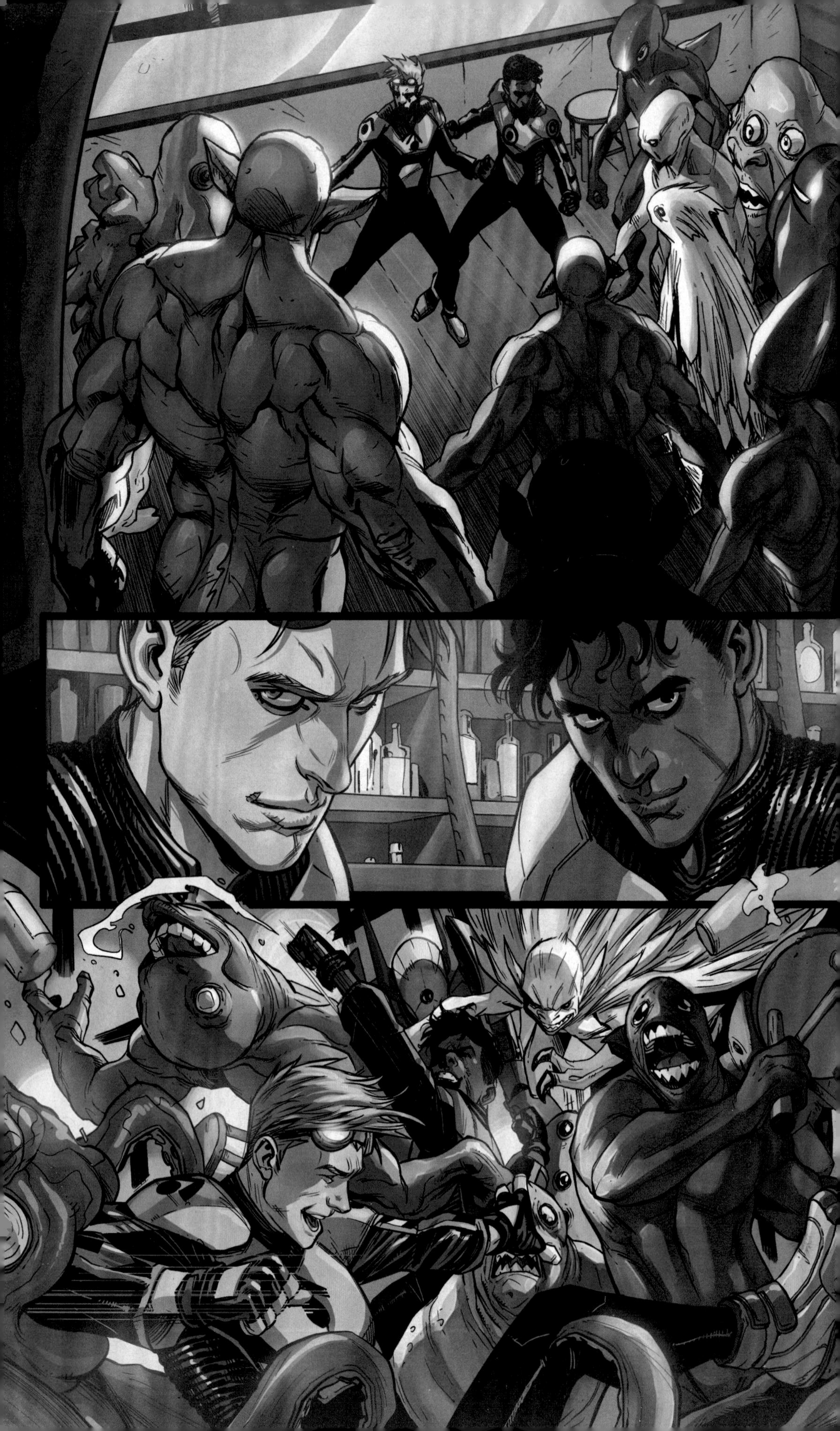

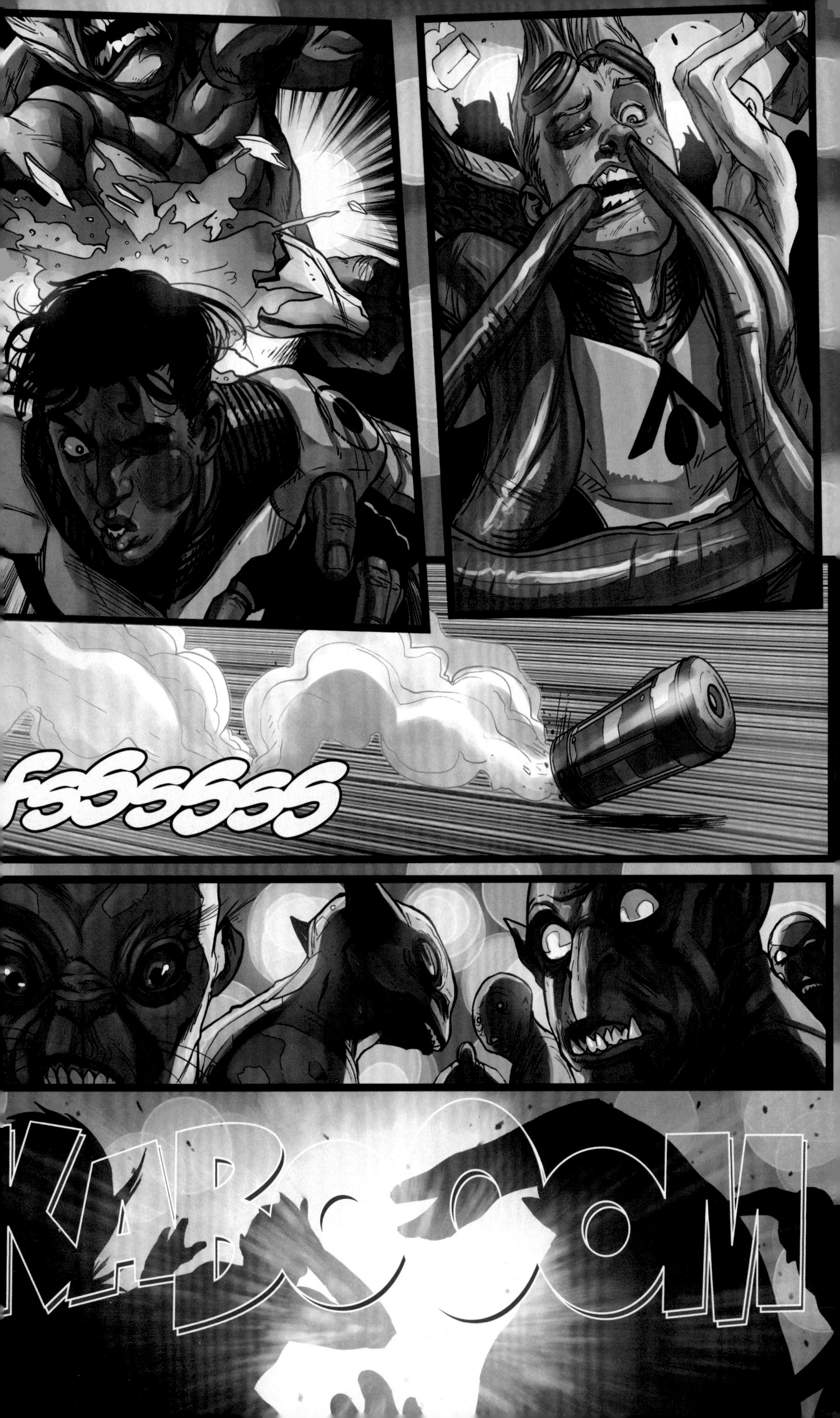
fSSSSSS
KABOOOM

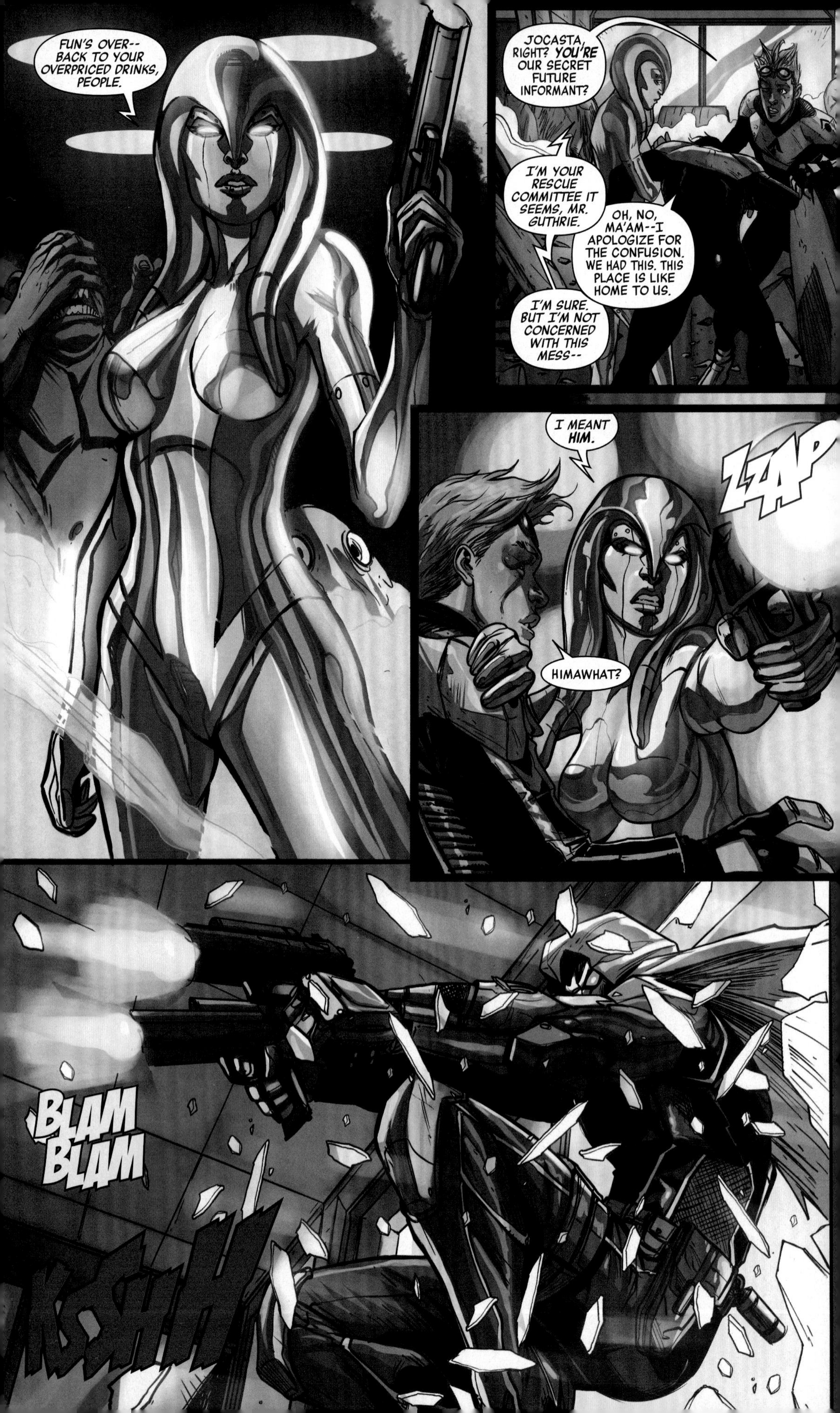
FUN'S OVER-- BACK TO YOUR OVERPRICED DRINKS, PEOPLE.
JOCASTA, RIGHT? YOU'RE OUR SECRET FUTURE INFORMANT?
I'M YOUR RESCUE COMMITTEE IT SEEMS, MR. GUTHRIE.
OH, NO, MA'AM--I APOLOGIZE FOR THE CONFUSION. WE HAD THIS. THIS PLACE IS LIKE HOME TO US.
I'M SURE. BUT I'M NOT CONCERNED WITH THIS MESS--
I MEANT HIM.
ZZAP
HIMAWHAT?
BLAM BLAM
TKSHH

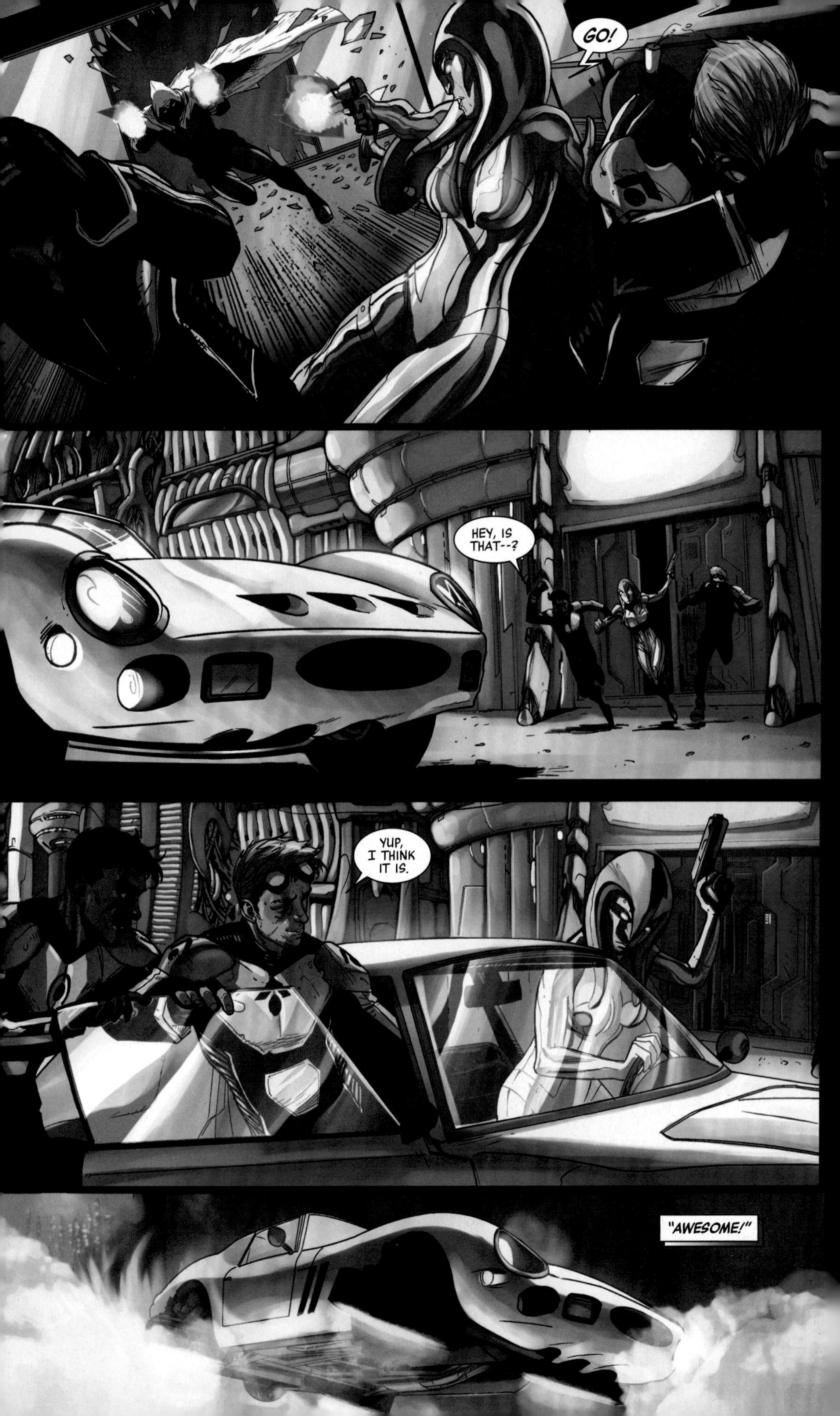
GO!
HEY, IS THAT--?
YUP, I THINK IT IS.
"AWESOME!"

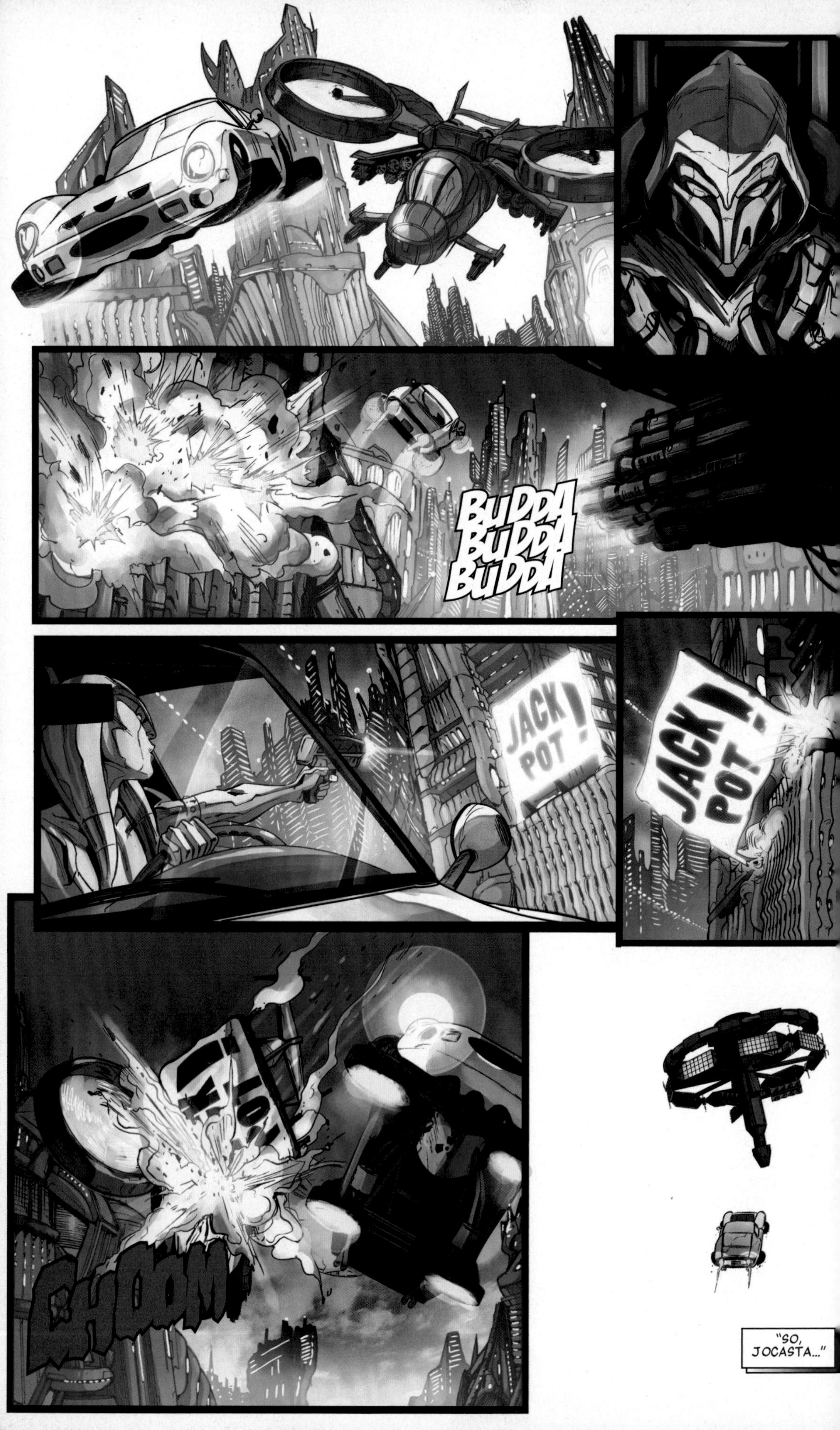
BUDDA
BUDDA
BUDDA
JACK POT!
JACK POT!
CHOOM
"SO, JOCASTA..."

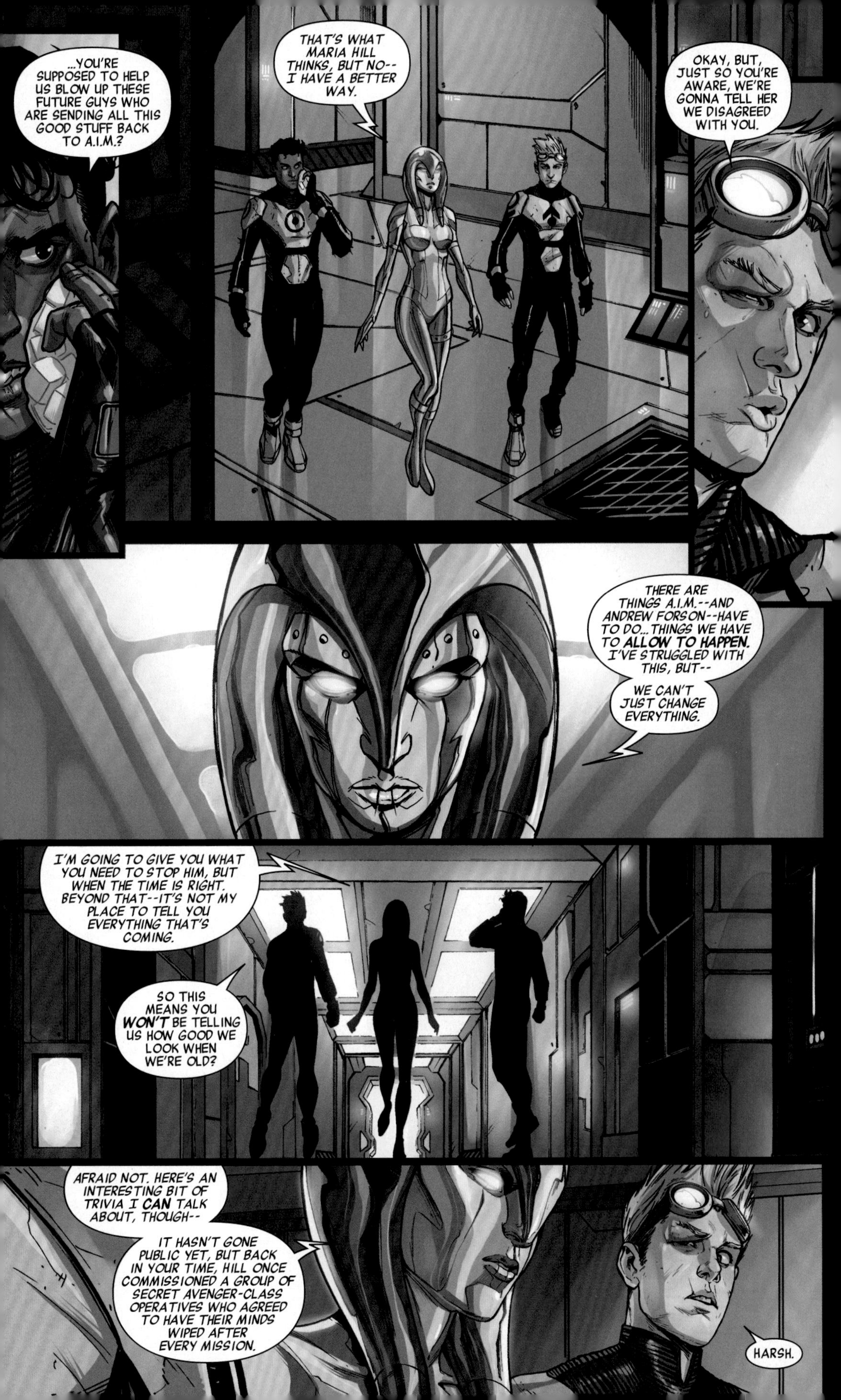

...YOU'RE SUPPOSED TO HELP US BLOW UP THESE FUTURE GUYS WHO ARE SENDING ALL THIS GOOD STUFF BACK TO A.I.M.?
THAT'S WHAT MARIA HILL THINKS, BUT NO-- I HAVE A BETTER WAY.
OKAY, BUT, JUST SO YOU'RE AWARE, WE'RE GONNA TELL HER WE DISAGREED WITH YOU.
THERE ARE THINGS A.I.M.--AND ANDREW FORSON--HAVE TO DO...THINGS WE HAVE TO **ALLOW TO HAPPEN.** I'VE STRUGGLED WITH THIS, BUT--
WE CAN'T JUST CHANGE EVERYTHING.
I'M GOING TO GIVE YOU WHAT YOU NEED TO STOP HIM, BUT WHEN THE TIME IS RIGHT. BEYOND THAT--IT'S NOT MY PLACE TO TELL YOU EVERYTHING THAT'S COMING.
SO THIS MEANS YOU **WON'T** BE TELLING US HOW GOOD WE LOOK WHEN WE'RE OLD?
AFRAID NOT. HERE'S AN INTERESTING BIT OF TRIVIA I **CAN** TALK ABOUT, THOUGH--
IT HASN'T GONE PUBLIC YET, BUT BACK IN YOUR TIME, HILL ONCE COMMISSIONED A GROUP OF SECRET AVENGER-CLASS OPERATIVES WHO AGREED TO HAVE THEIR MINDS WIPED AFTER EVERY MISSION.
HARSH.

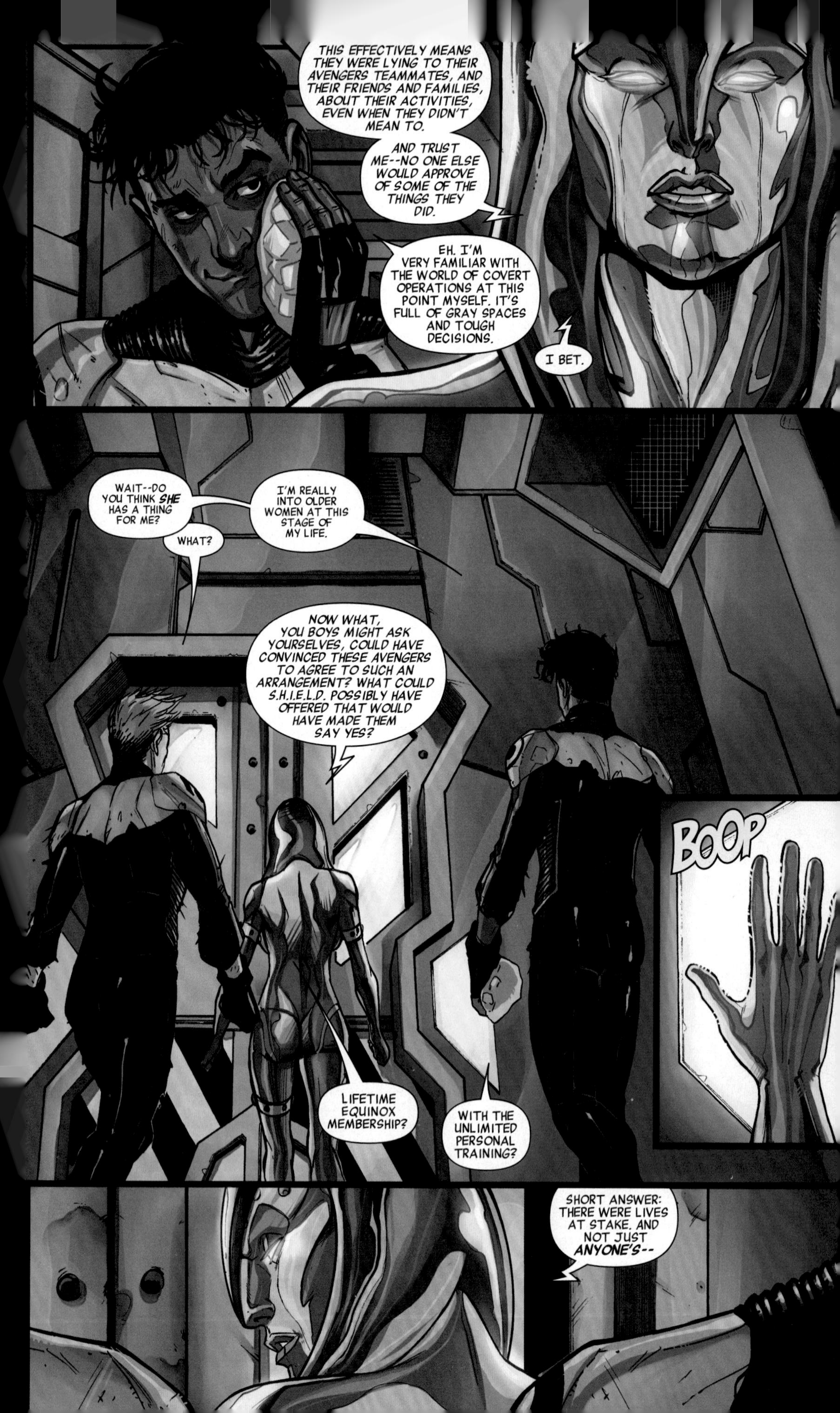
THIS EFFECTIVELY MEANS THEY WERE LYING TO THEIR AVENGERS TEAMMATES, AND THEIR FRIENDS AND FAMILIES, ABOUT THEIR ACTIVITIES, EVEN WHEN THEY DIDN'T MEAN TO.
AND TRUST ME--NO ONE ELSE WOULD APPROVE OF SOME OF THE THINGS THEY DID.
EH. I'M VERY FAMILIAR WITH THE WORLD OF COVERT OPERATIONS AT THIS POINT MYSELF. IT'S FULL OF GRAY SPACES AND TOUGH DECISIONS.
I BET.
WAIT--DO YOU THINK SHE HAS A THING FOR ME?
WHAT?
I'M REALLY INTO OLDER WOMEN AT THIS STAGE OF MY LIFE.
NOW WHAT, YOU BOYS MIGHT ASK YOURSELVES, COULD HAVE CONVINCED THESE AVENGERS TO AGREE TO SUCH AN ARRANGEMENT? WHAT COULD S.H.I.E.L.D. POSSIBLY HAVE OFFERED THAT WOULD HAVE MADE THEM SAY YES?
LIFETIME EQUINOX MEMBERSHIP?
WITH THE UNLIMITED PERSONAL TRAINING?
BOOP
SHORT ANSWER: THERE WERE LIVES AT STAKE. AND NOT JUST ANYONE'S--

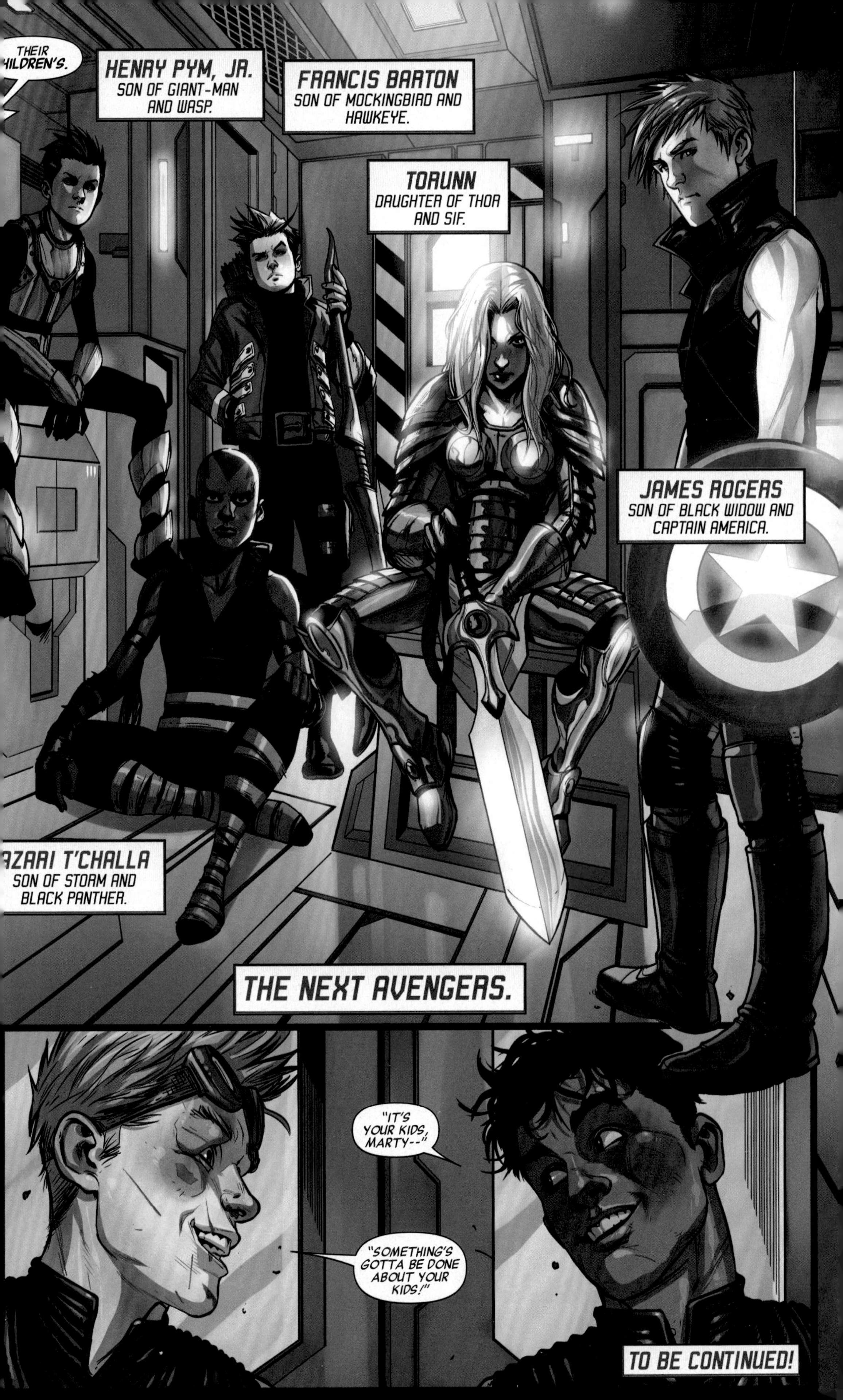

THEIR CHILDREN'S.
HENRY PYM, JR. SON OF GIANT-MAN AND WASP.
FRANCIS BARTON SON OF MOCKINGBIRD AND HAWKEYE.
TORUNN DAUGHTER OF THOR AND SIF.
JAMES ROGERS SON OF BLACK WIDOW AND CAPTAIN AMERICA.
AZARI T'CHALLA SON OF STORM AND BLACK PANTHER.
THE NEXT AVENGERS.
"IT'S YOUR KIDS, MARTY--"
"SOMETHING'S GOTTA BE DONE ABOUT YOUR KIDS!"
TO BE CONTINUED!

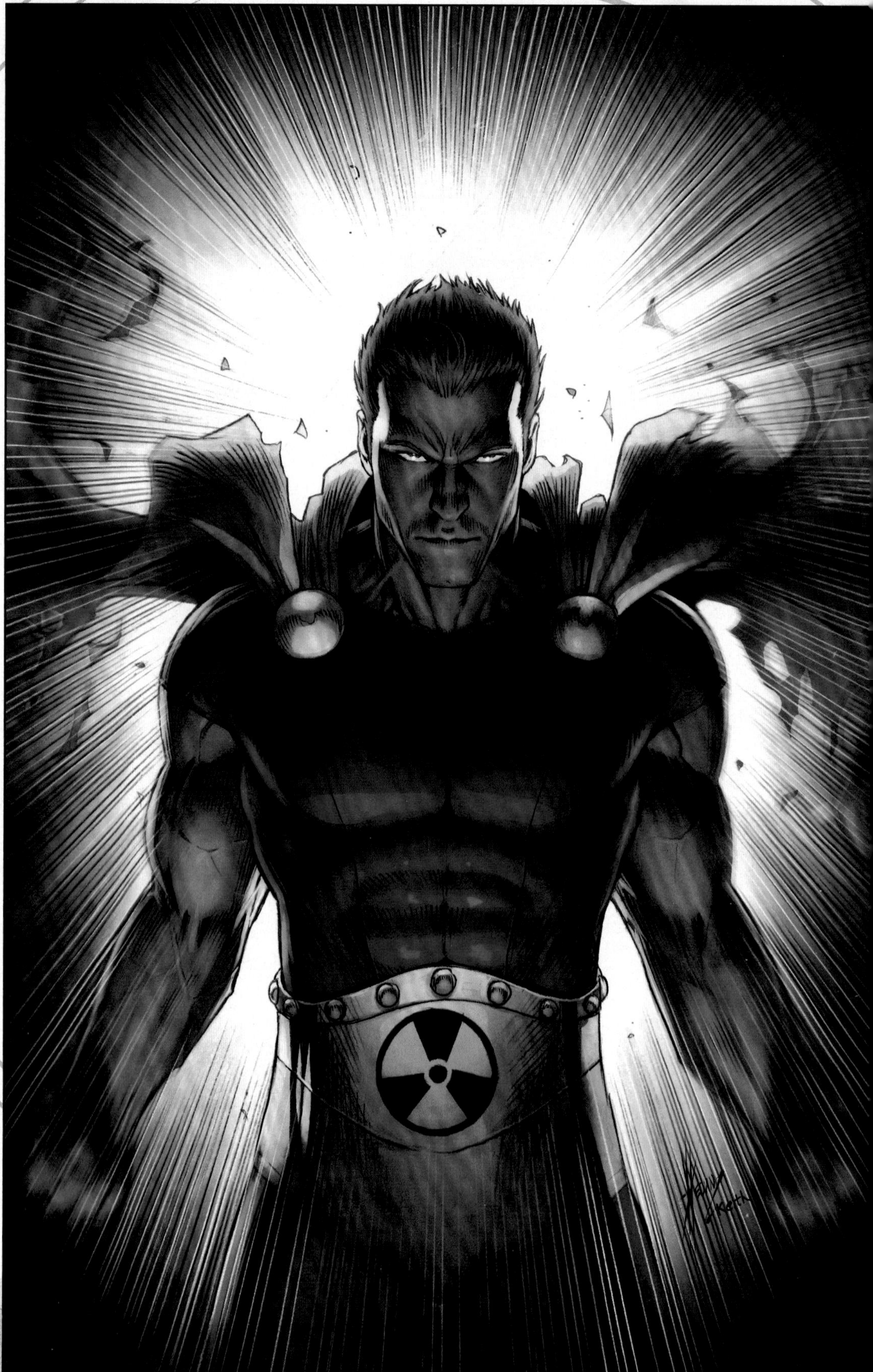

AVENGERS 34.1

PREVIOUSLY IN AVENGERS

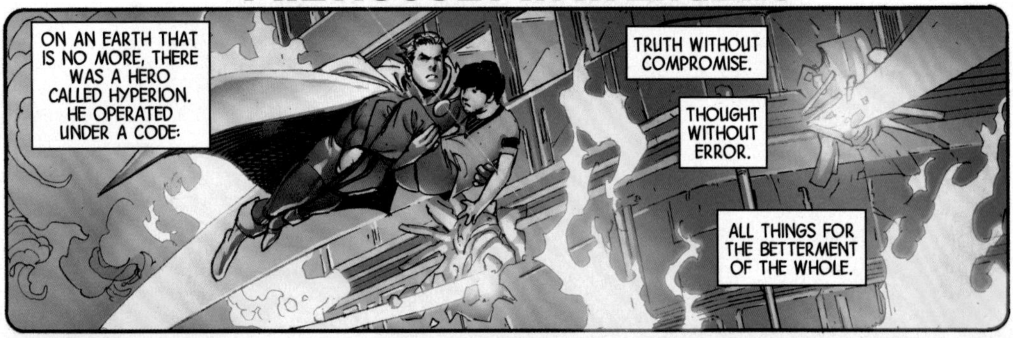
ON AN EARTH THAT IS NO MORE, THERE WAS A HERO CALLED HYPERION. HE OPERATED UNDER A CODE:
TRUTH WITHOUT COMPROMISE.
THOUGHT WITHOUT ERROR.
ALL THINGS FOR THE BETTERMENT OF THE WHOLE.

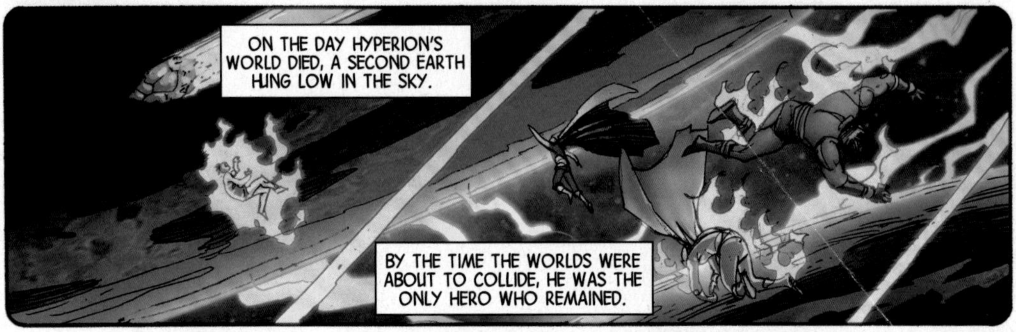
ON THE DAY HYPERION'S WORLD DIED, A SECOND EARTH HUNG LOW IN THE SKY.
BY THE TIME THE WORLDS WERE ABOUT TO COLLIDE, HE WAS THE ONLY HERO WHO REMAINED.

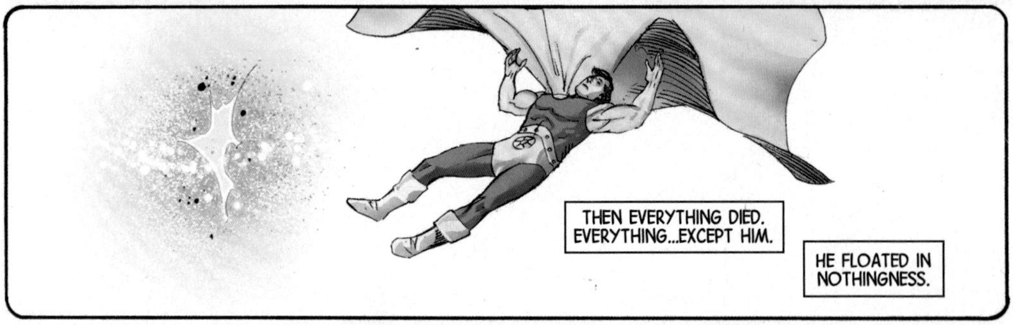
THEN EVERYTHING DIED. EVERYTHING...EXCEPT HIM.
HE FLOATED IN NOTHINGNESS.

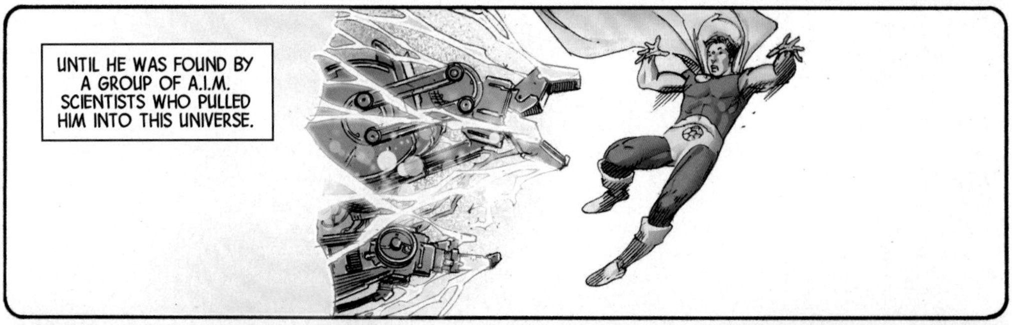
UNTIL HE WAS FOUND BY A GROUP OF A.I.M. SCIENTISTS WHO PULLED HIM INTO THIS UNIVERSE.

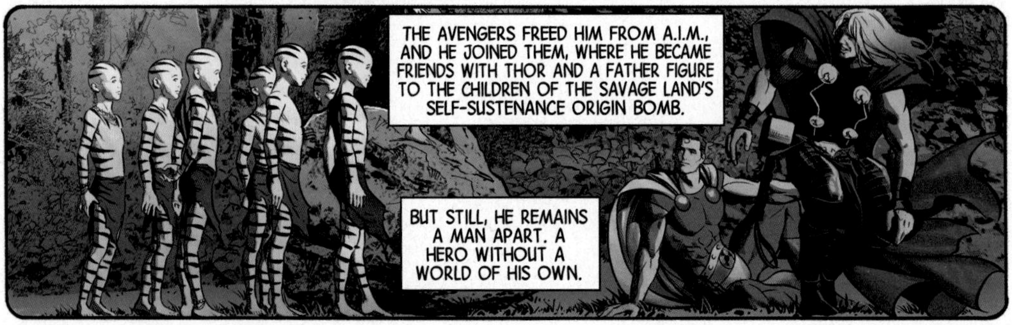
THE AVENGERS FREED HIM FROM A.I.M., AND HE JOINED THEM, WHERE HE BECAME FRIENDS WITH THOR AND A FATHER FIGURE TO THE CHILDREN OF THE SAVAGE LAND'S SELF-SUSTENANCE ORIGIN BOMB.
BUT STILL, HE REMAINS A MAN APART. A HERO WITHOUT A WORLD OF HIS OWN.

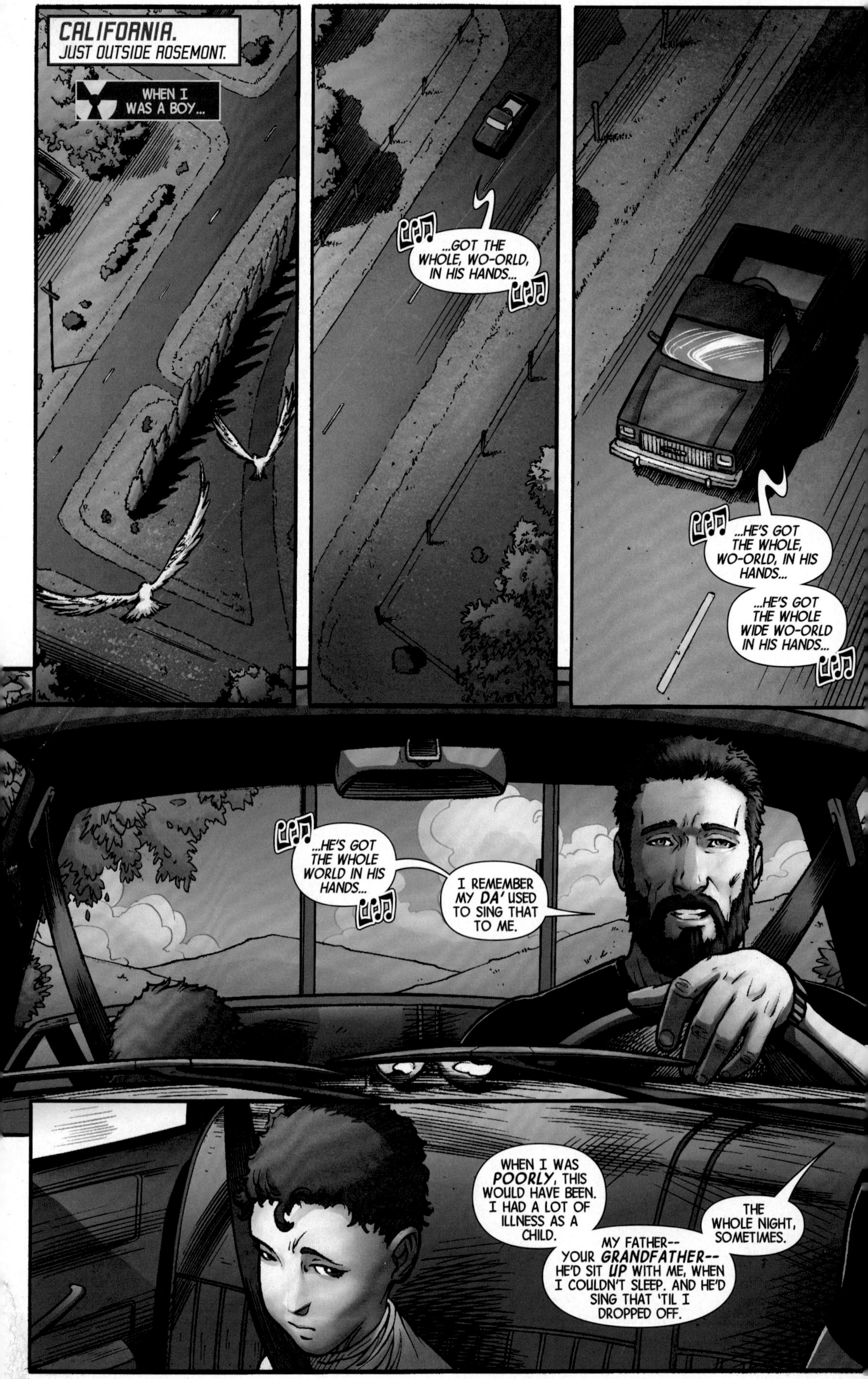
CALIFORNIA.
JUST OUTSIDE ROSEMONT.
WHEN I WAS A BOY...
...GOT THE WHOLE, WO-ORLD, IN HIS HANDS...
...HE'S GOT THE WHOLE, WO-ORLD, IN HIS HANDS...
...HE'S GOT THE WHOLE WIDE WO-ORLD IN HIS HANDS...
...HE'S GOT THE WHOLE WORLD IN HIS HANDS...
I REMEMBER MY DA' USED TO SING THAT TO ME.
WHEN I WAS POORLY, THIS WOULD HAVE BEEN. I HAD A LOT OF ILLNESS AS A CHILD.
MY FATHER-- YOUR GRANDFATHER-- HE'D SIT UP WITH ME, WHEN I COULDN'T SLEEP. AND HE'D SING THAT 'TIL I DROPPED OFF.
THE WHOLE NIGHT, SOMETIMES.

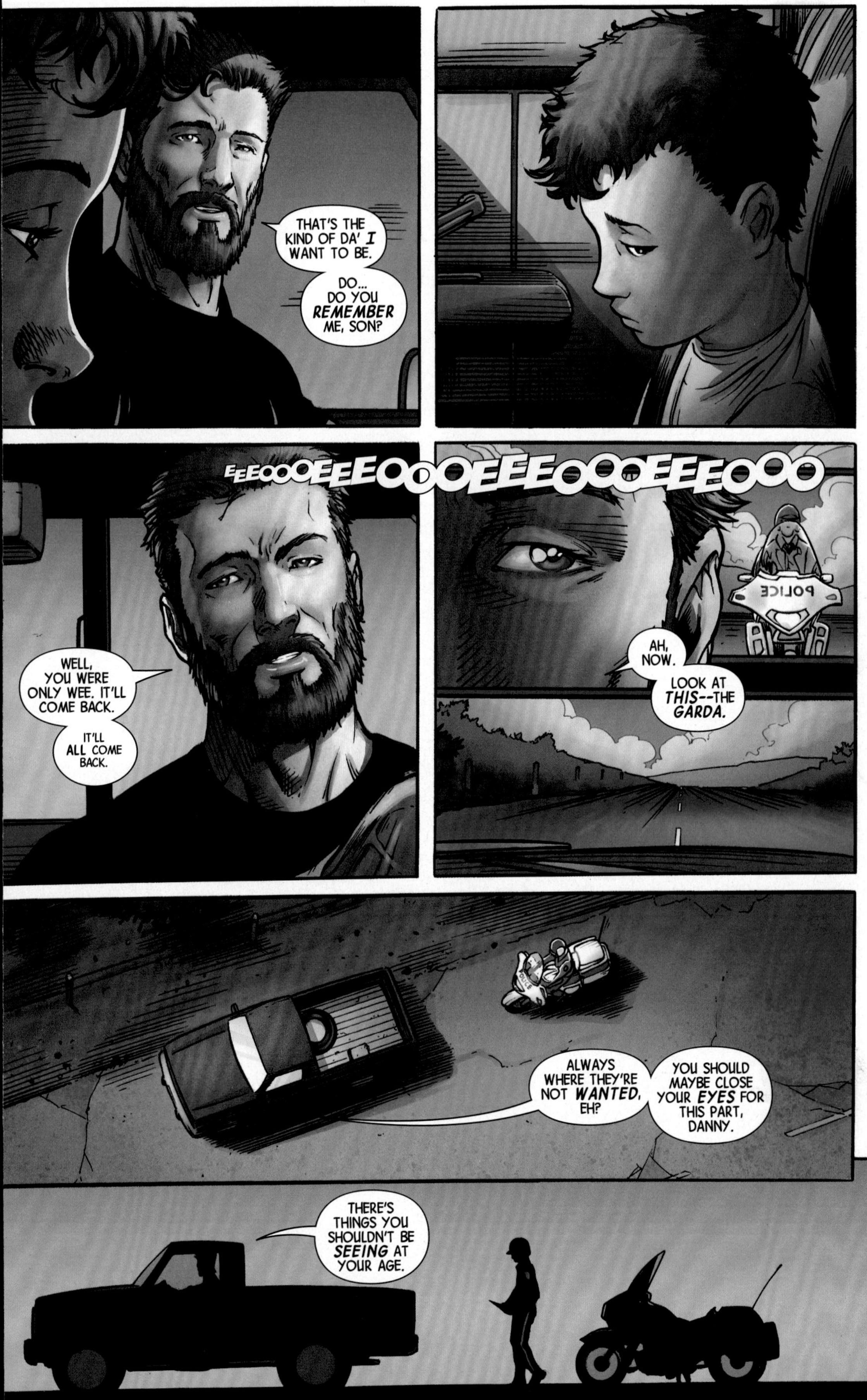
THAT'S THE KIND OF DA' I WANT TO BE.
DO... DO YOU REMEMBER ME, SON?
EEEOOOEEEOOOEEEOOOEEEOOO
WELL, YOU WERE ONLY WEE. IT'LL COME BACK.
IT'LL ALL COME BACK.
POLICE
AH, NOW.
LOOK AT THIS--THE GARDA.
POLICE
ALWAYS WHERE THEY'RE NOT WANTED, EH?
YOU SHOULD MAYBE CLOSE YOUR EYES FOR THIS PART, DANNY.
THERE'S THINGS YOU SHOULDN'T BE SEEING AT YOUR AGE.

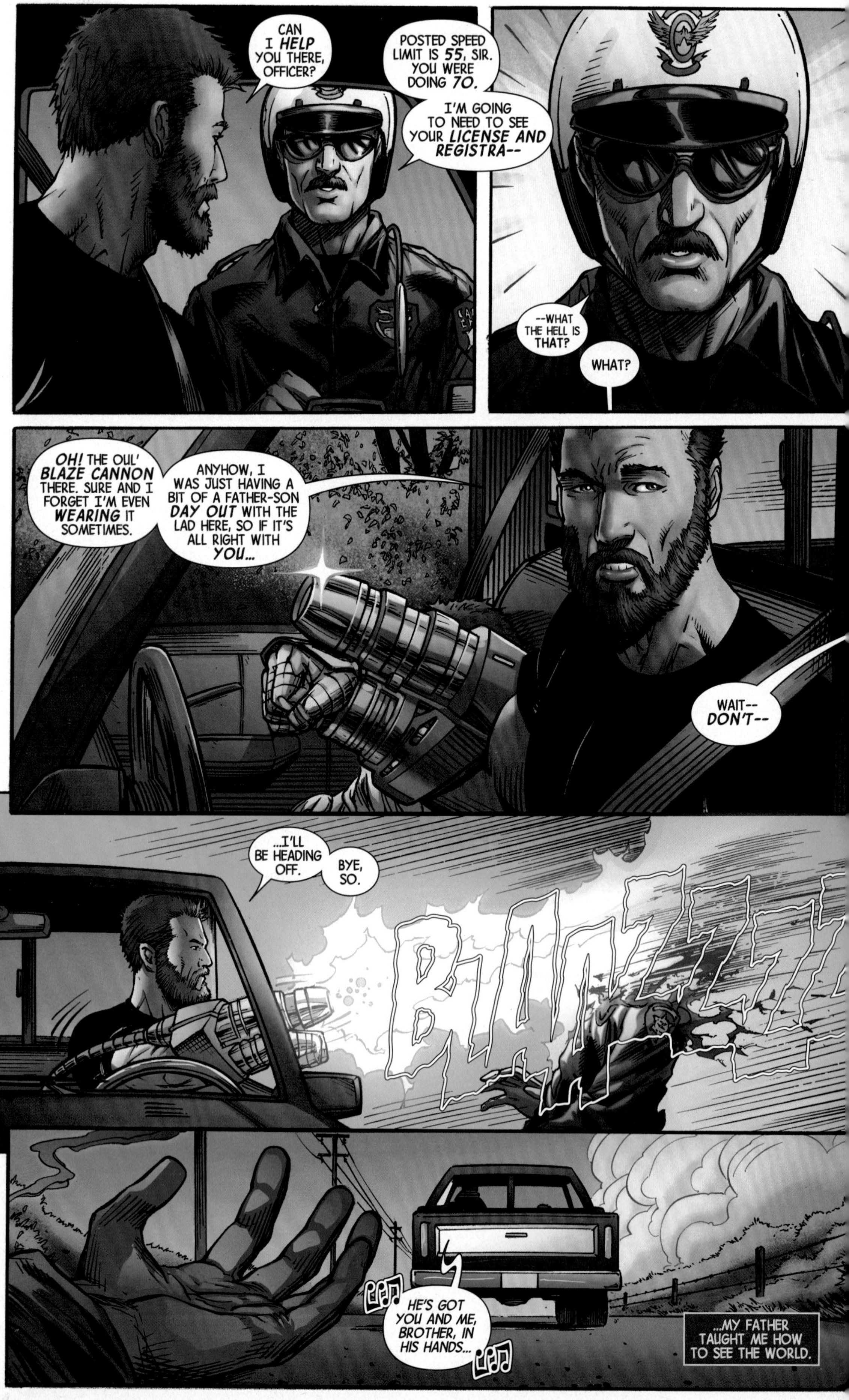

CAN I HELP YOU THERE, OFFICER?
POSTED SPEED LIMIT IS 55, SIR. YOU WERE DOING 70.
I'M GOING TO NEED TO SEE YOUR LICENSE AND REGISTRA--
--WHAT THE HELL IS THAT?
WHAT?
OH! THE OUL' BLAZE CANNON THERE. SURE AND I FORGET I'M EVEN WEARING IT SOMETIMES.
ANYHOW, I WAS JUST HAVING A BIT OF A FATHER-SON DAY OUT WITH THE LAD HERE, SO IF IT'S ALL RIGHT WITH YOU...
WAIT-- DON'T--
...I'LL BE HEADING OFF.
BYE, SO.
HE'S GOT YOU AND ME, BROTHER, IN HIS HANDS...
...MY FATHER TAUGHT ME HOW TO SEE THE WORLD.

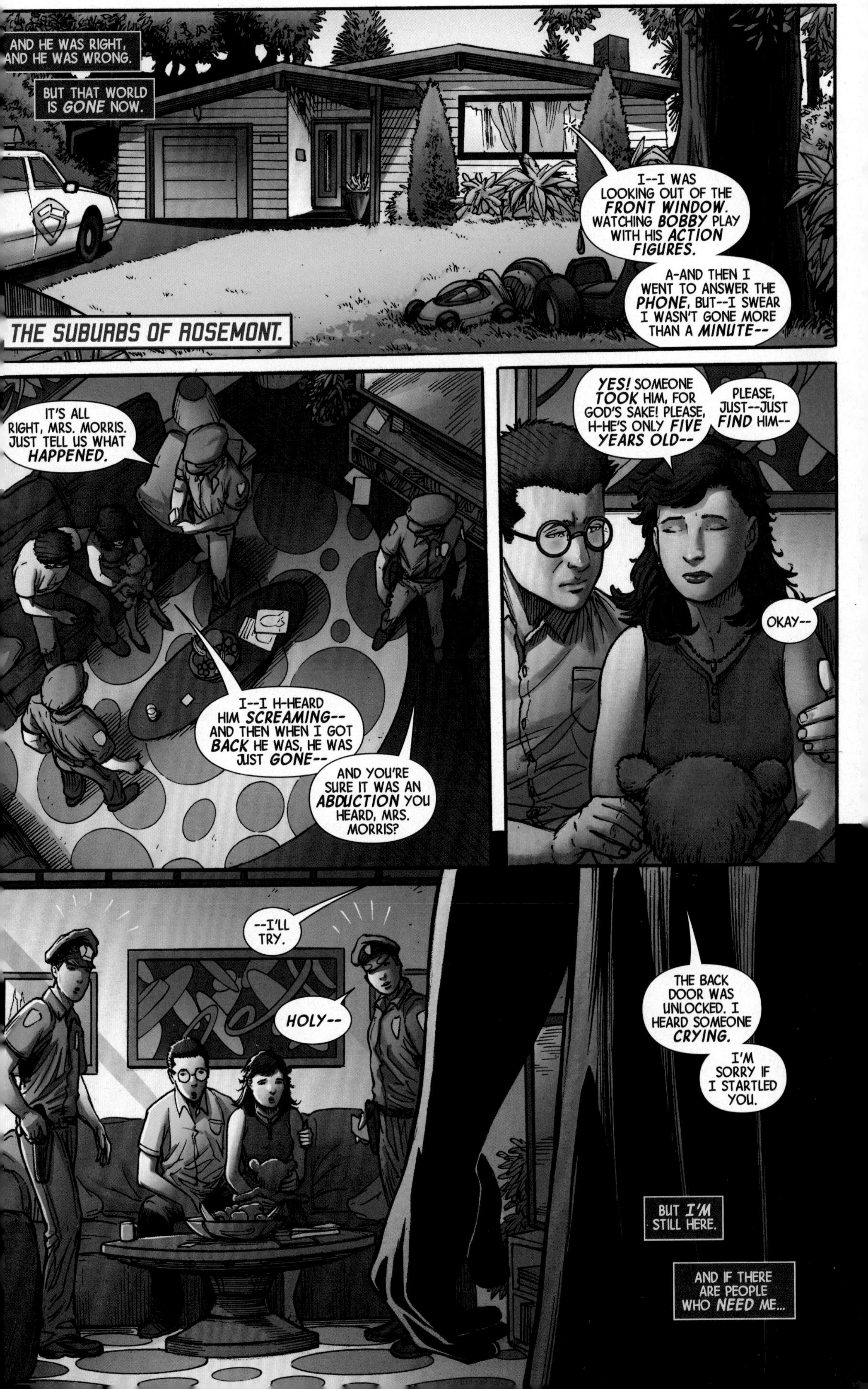
AND HE WAS RIGHT, AND HE WAS WRONG.
BUT THAT WORLD IS GONE NOW.
I--I WAS LOOKING OUT OF THE FRONT WINDOW. WATCHING BOBBY PLAY WITH HIS ACTION FIGURES.
A-AND THEN I WENT TO ANSWER THE PHONE, BUT--I SWEAR I WASN'T GONE MORE THAN A MINUTE--
THE SUBURBS OF ROSEMONT.
IT'S ALL RIGHT, MRS. MORRIS. JUST TELL US WHAT HAPPENED.
I--I H-HEARD HIM SCREAMING-- AND THEN WHEN I GOT BACK HE WAS, HE WAS JUST GONE--
AND YOU'RE SURE IT WAS AN ABDUCTION YOU HEARD, MRS. MORRIS?
YES! SOMEONE TOOK HIM, FOR GOD'S SAKE! PLEASE, H-HE'S ONLY FIVE YEARS OLD--
PLEASE, JUST--JUST FIND HIM--
OKAY--
--I'LL TRY.
HOLY--
THE BACK DOOR WAS UNLOCKED. I HEARD SOMEONE CRYING.
I'M SORRY IF I STARTLED YOU.
BUT I'M STILL HERE.
AND IF THERE ARE PEOPLE WHO NEED ME...

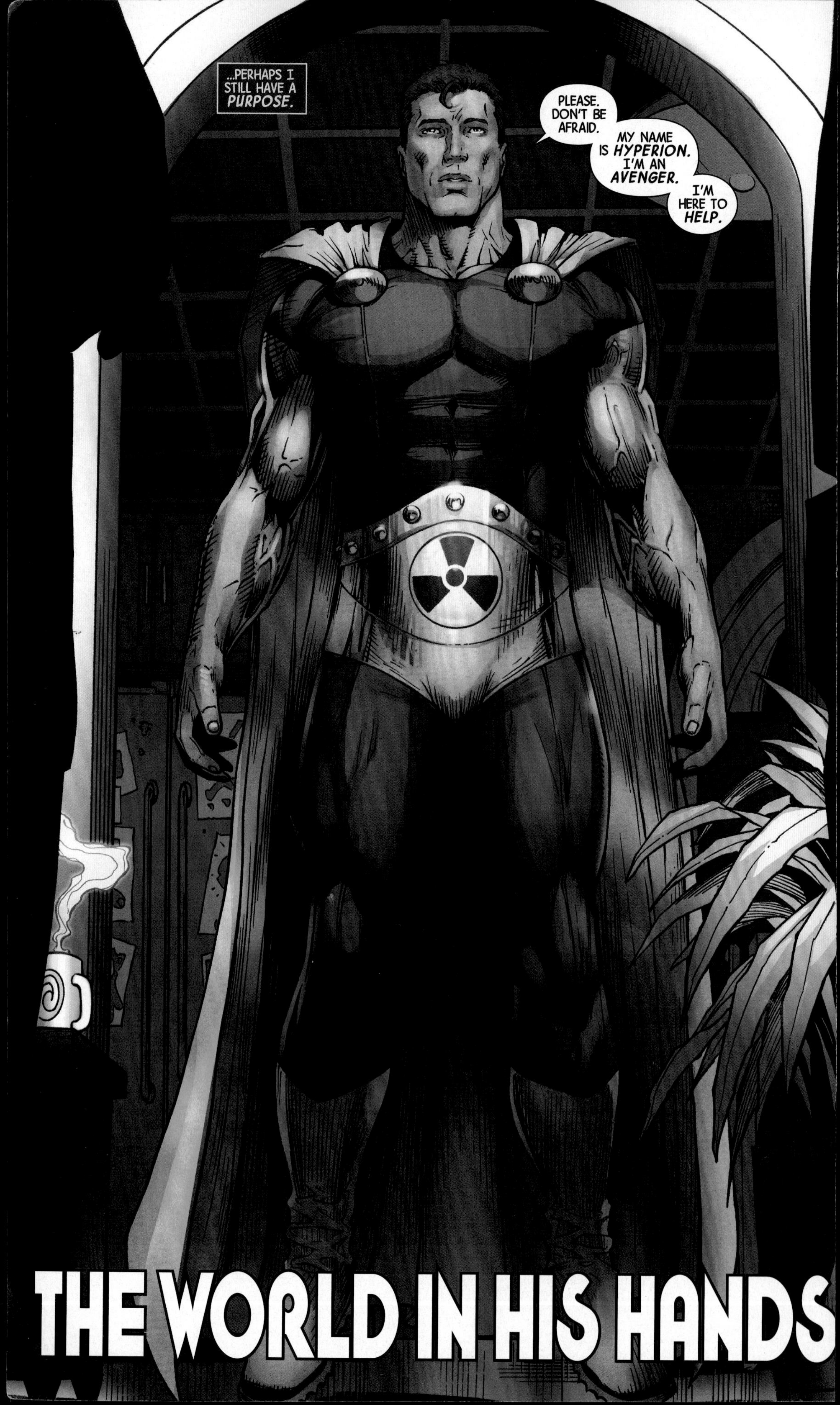

...PERHAPS I STILL HAVE A PURPOSE.
PLEASE. DON'T BE AFRAID.
MY NAME IS HYPERION. I'M AN AVENGER.
I'M HERE TO HELP.
THE WORLD IN HIS HANDS

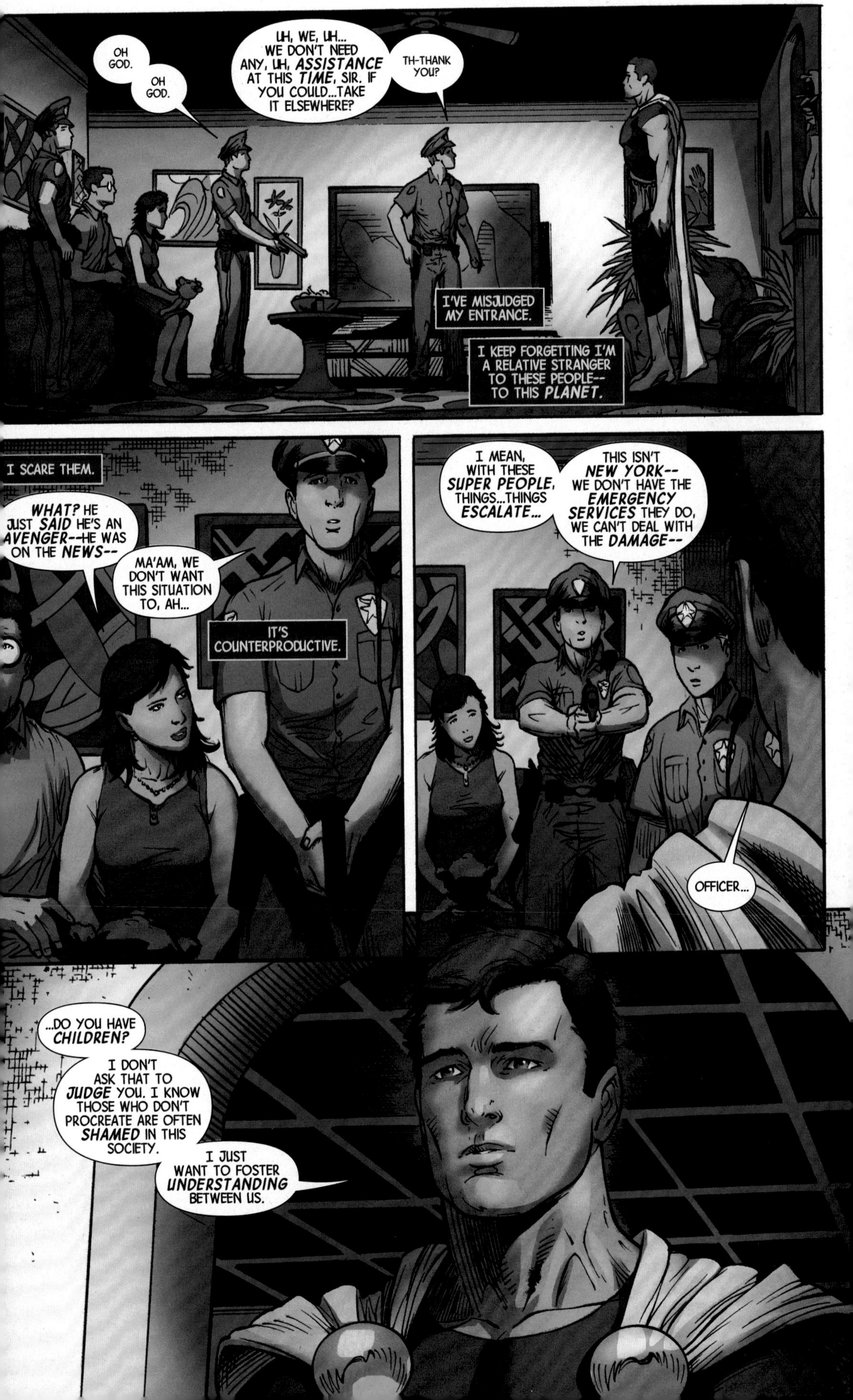
OH GOD.
OH GOD.
UH, WE, UH... WE DON'T NEED ANY, UH, ASSISTANCE AT THIS TIME, SIR. IF YOU COULD...TAKE IT ELSEWHERE?
TH-THANK YOU?
I'VE MISJUDGED MY ENTRANCE.
I KEEP FORGETTING I'M A RELATIVE STRANGER TO THESE PEOPLE-- TO THIS PLANET.
I SCARE THEM.
WHAT? HE JUST SAID HE'S AN AVENGER--HE WAS ON THE NEWS--
MA'AM, WE DON'T WANT THIS SITUATION TO, AH...
IT'S COUNTERPRODUCTIVE.
I MEAN, WITH THESE SUPER PEOPLE, THINGS...THINGS ESCALATE...
THIS ISN'T NEW YORK-- WE DON'T HAVE THE EMERGENCY SERVICES THEY DO, WE CAN'T DEAL WITH THE DAMAGE--
OFFICER...
...DO YOU HAVE CHILDREN?
I DON'T ASK THAT TO JUDGE YOU. I KNOW THOSE WHO DON'T PROCREATE ARE OFTEN SHAMED IN THIS SOCIETY.
I JUST WANT TO FOSTER UNDERSTANDING BETWEEN US.

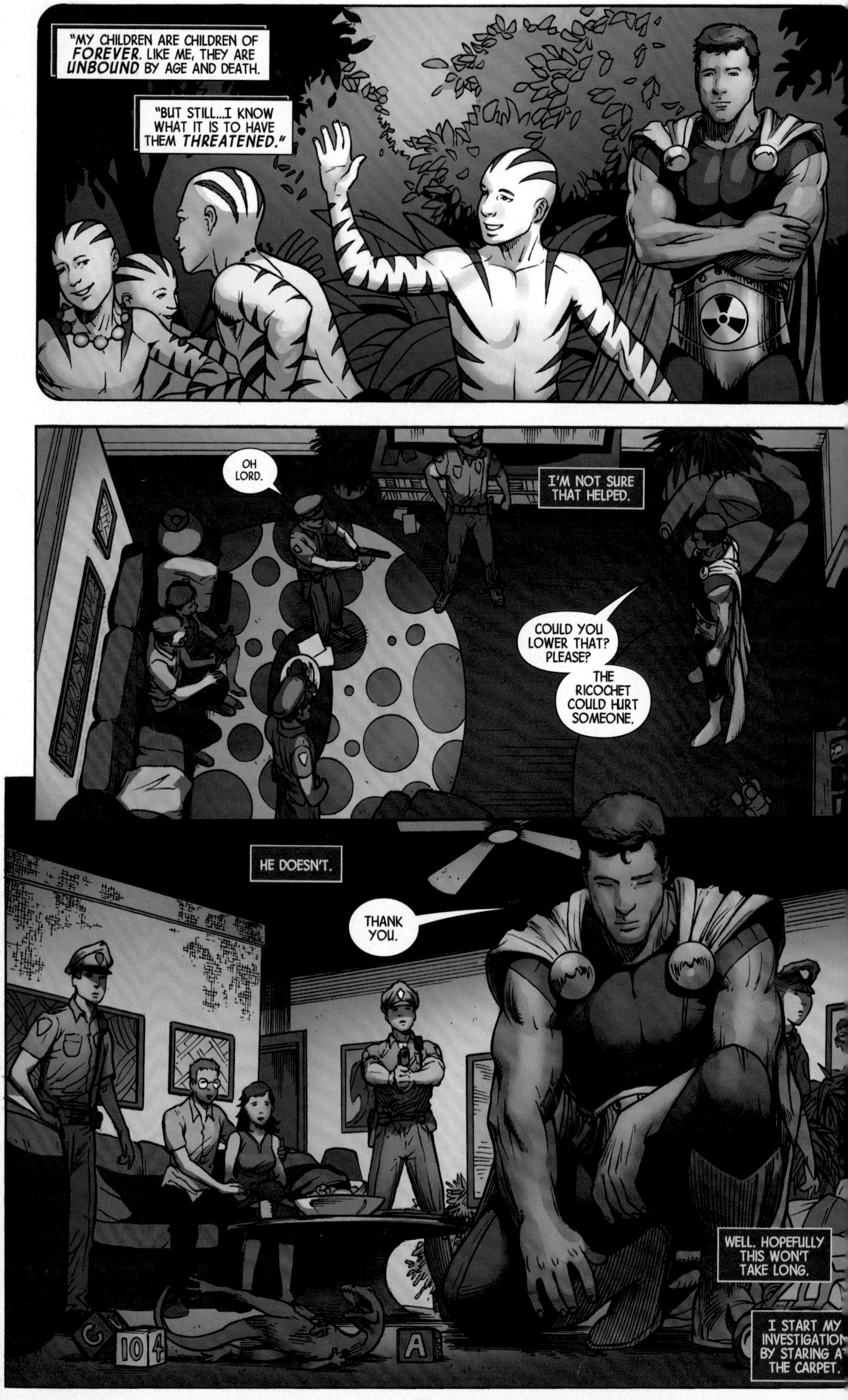
"MY CHILDREN ARE CHILDREN OF FOREVER. LIKE ME, THEY ARE UNBOUND BY AGE AND DEATH.
"BUT STILL...I KNOW WHAT IT IS TO HAVE THEM THREATENED."
OH LORD.
I'M NOT SURE THAT HELPED.
COULD YOU LOWER THAT? PLEASE?
THE RICOCHET COULD HURT SOMEONE.
HE DOESN'T.
THANK YOU.
WELL. HOPEFULLY THIS WON'T TAKE LONG.
I START MY INVESTIGATION BY STARING AT THE CARPET.

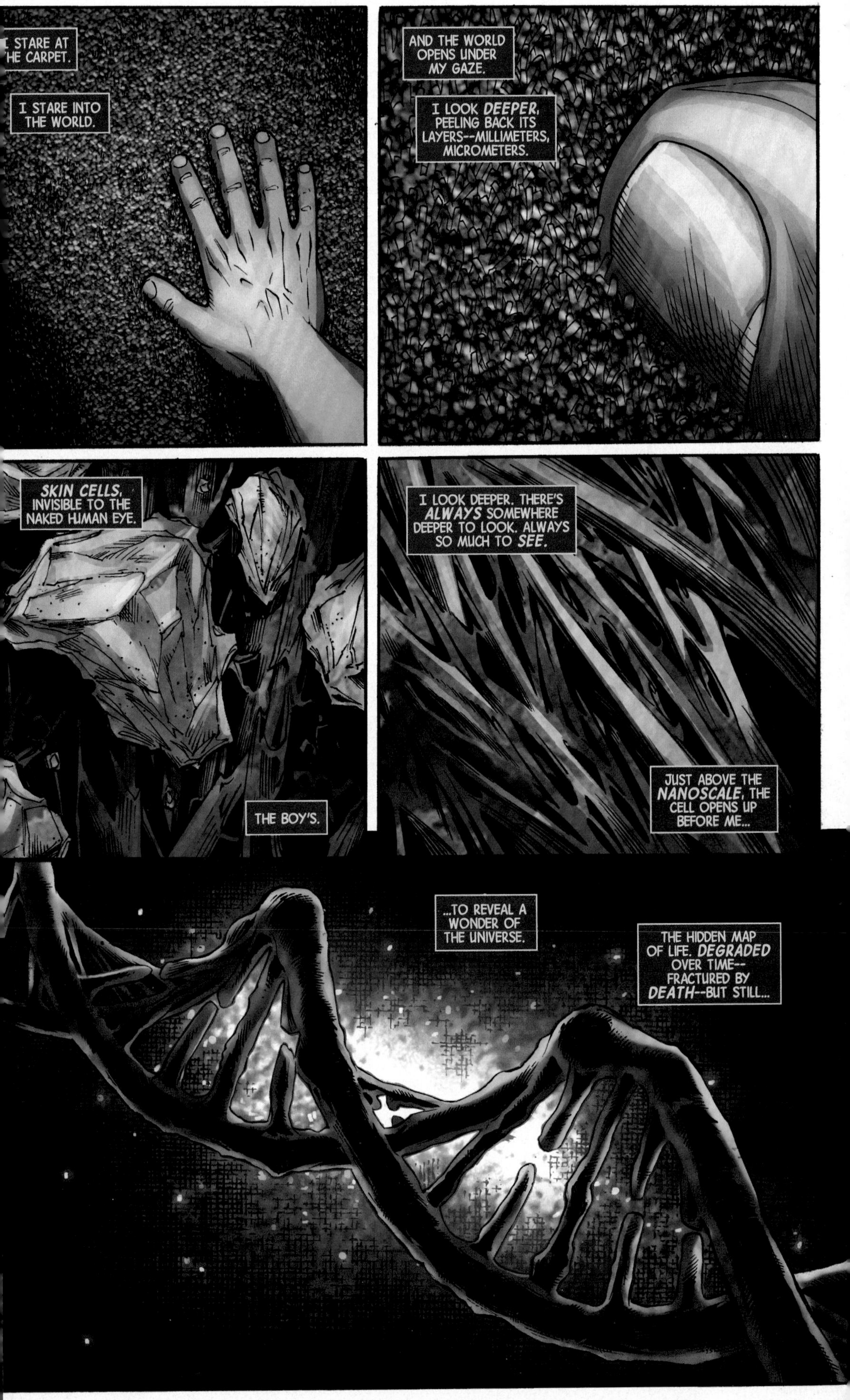
I STARE AT THE CARPET.
I STARE INTO THE WORLD.
AND THE WORLD OPENS UNDER MY GAZE.
I LOOK DEEPER, PEELING BACK ITS LAYERS--MILLIMETERS, MICROMETERS.
SKIN CELLS, INVISIBLE TO THE NAKED HUMAN EYE.
THE BOY'S.
I LOOK DEEPER. THERE'S ALWAYS SOMEWHERE DEEPER TO LOOK. ALWAYS SO MUCH TO SEE.
JUST ABOVE THE NANOSCALE, THE CELL OPENS UP BEFORE ME...
...TO REVEAL A WONDER OF THE UNIVERSE.
THE HIDDEN MAP OF LIFE. DEGRADED OVER TIME--FRACTURED BY DEATH--BUT STILL...

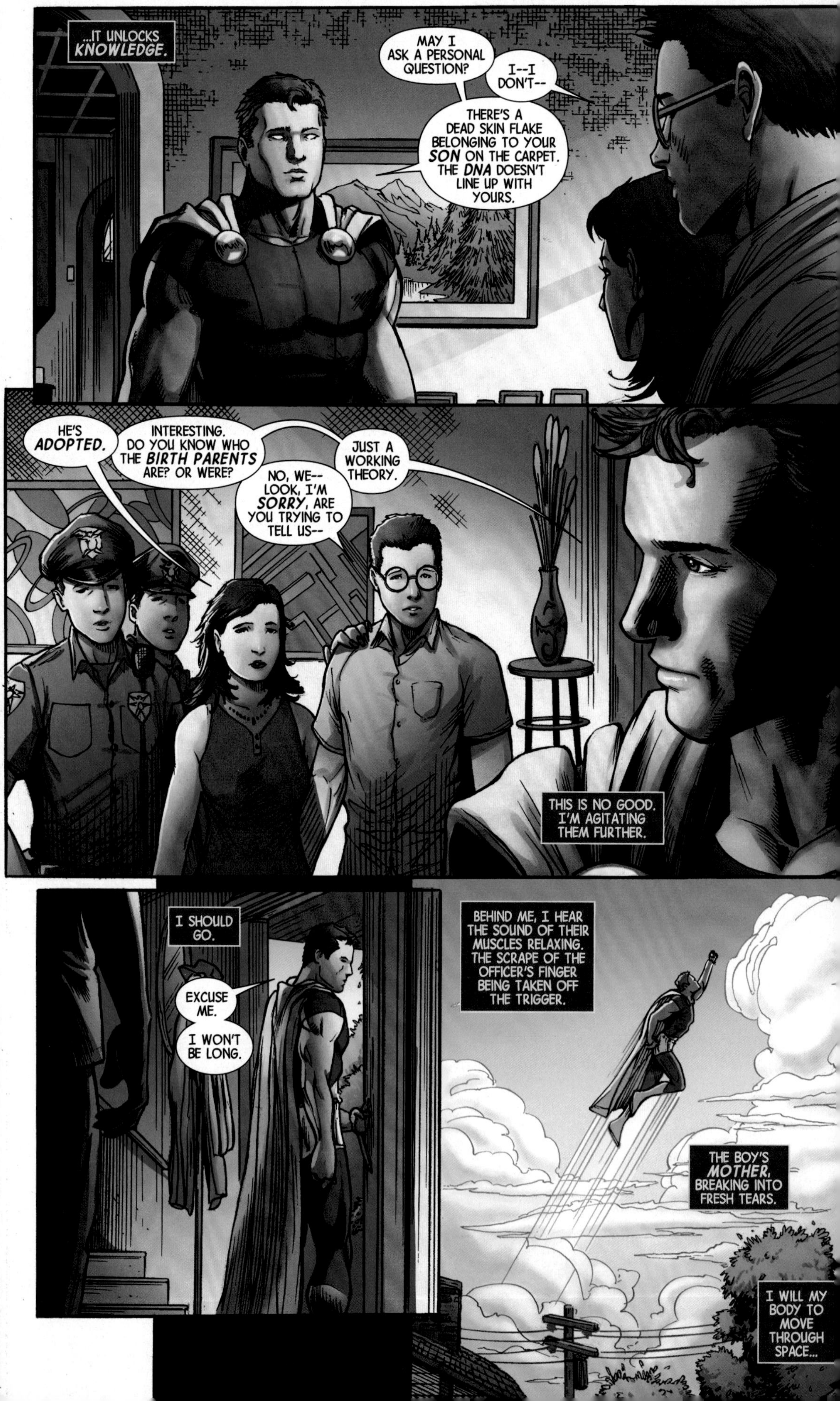
...IT UNLOCKS KNOWLEDGE.
MAY I ASK A PERSONAL QUESTION?
I--I DON'T--
THERE'S A DEAD SKIN FLAKE BELONGING TO YOUR SON ON THE CARPET. THE DNA DOESN'T LINE UP WITH YOURS.
HE'S ADOPTED.
INTERESTING. DO YOU KNOW WHO THE BIRTH PARENTS ARE? OR WERE?
NO, WE-- LOOK, I'M SORRY, ARE YOU TRYING TO TELL US--
JUST A WORKING THEORY.
THIS IS NO GOOD. I'M AGITATING THEM FURTHER.
I SHOULD GO.
EXCUSE ME.
I WON'T BE LONG.
BEHIND ME, I HEAR THE SOUND OF THEIR MUSCLES RELAXING. THE SCRAPE OF THE OFFICER'S FINGER BEING TAKEN OFF THE TRIGGER.
THE BOY'S MOTHER, BREAKING INTO FRESH TEARS.
I WILL MY BODY TO MOVE THROUGH SPACE...

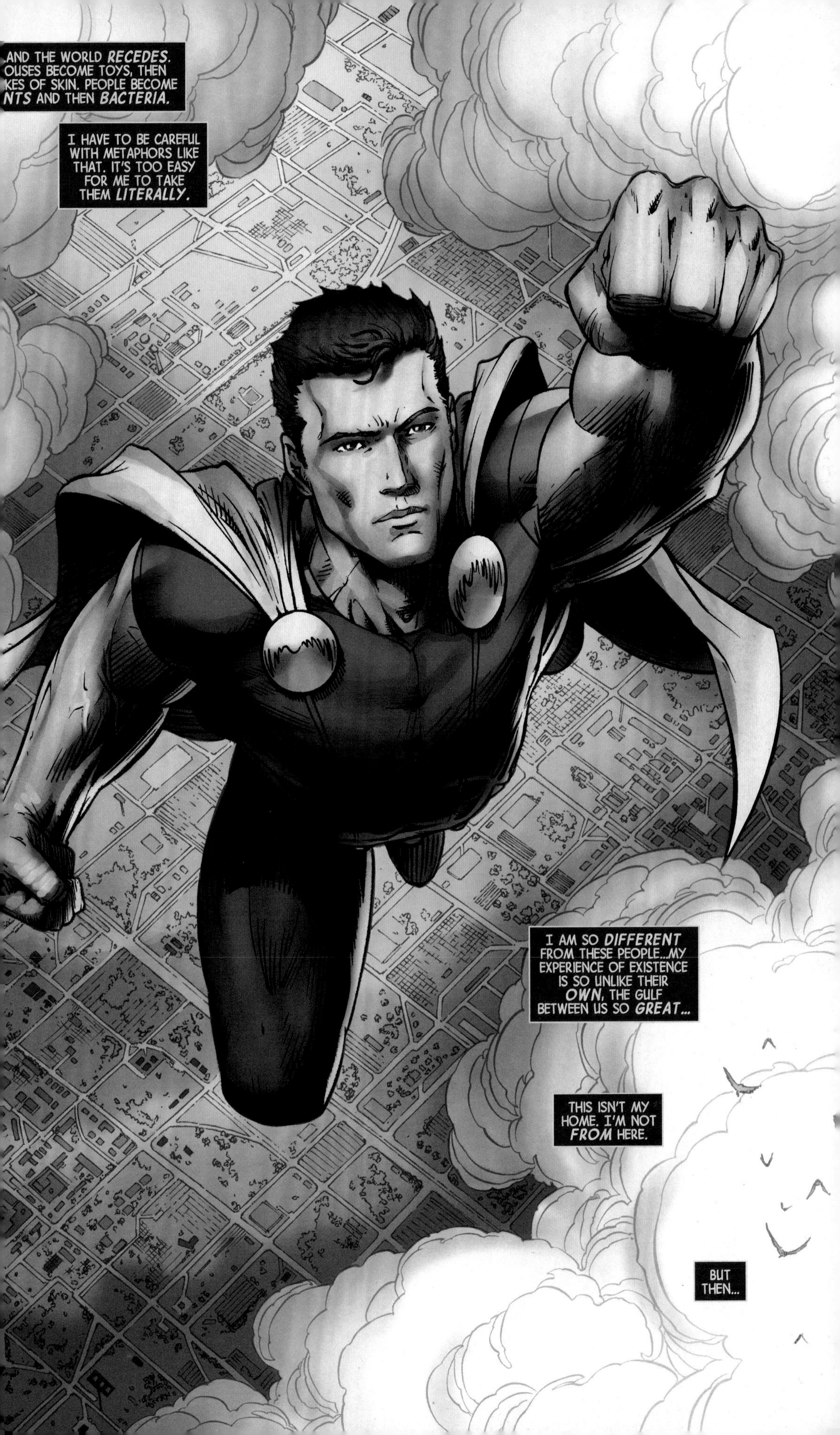

.AND THE WORLD RECEDES. OUSES BECOME TOYS, THEN KES OF SKIN. PEOPLE BECOME NTS AND THEN BACTERIA.
I HAVE TO BE CAREFUL WITH METAPHORS LIKE THAT. IT'S TOO EASY FOR ME TO TAKE THEM LITERALLY.
I AM SO DIFFERENT FROM THESE PEOPLE...MY EXPERIENCE OF EXISTENCE IS SO UNLIKE THEIR OWN, THE GULF BETWEEN US SO GREAT...
THIS ISN'T MY HOME. I'M NOT FROM HERE.
BUT THEN...

...I WASN'T FROM *THERE* EITHER.

I WAS BORN ON A WORLD THAT *DIED*. SENT INTO THE VOID ON A WING AND A PRAYER, TO FIND A *NEW* HOME.

A NEW *FATHER*...

...WHO TAUGHT ME HOW TO SEE THE WORLD.

WE'LL CALL YOU...HOW ABOUT *MARCUS?* WELCOME TO THE *EARTH*, YOUNG MARCUS.

WHAT WILL YOUR ROLE BE?

TRUTH WITHOUT COMPROMISE. THOUGHT WITHOUT ERROR. ALL THINGS FOR THE BETTERMENT OF THE WHOLE.

IF WE KEEP TO THOSE *PRINCIPLES*-- IF WE REMAIN TRUE TO THAT *CODE*--THEN *BETWEEN* US...WHAT *CAN'T* WE DO?

WHEN YOU SEE THE WORLD, TRY TO SEE IT AS A *WHOLE*.

AS ONE GREAT, EVER-EVOLVING *ORGANISM*-- AN ORGANISM WITH A SIMPLE SET OF *NEEDS*.

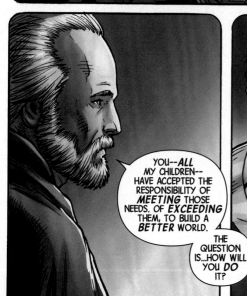

YOU--*ALL* MY CHILDREN-- HAVE ACCEPTED THE RESPONSIBILITY OF *MEETING* THOSE NEEDS. OF *EXCEEDING* THEM, TO BUILD A *BETTER* WORLD.

THE QUESTION IS...HOW WILL YOU *DO* IT?

WHAT WILL YOUR ROLE BE?

"WHAT ARE YOU *FOR?*"

WHAT AM I FOR?

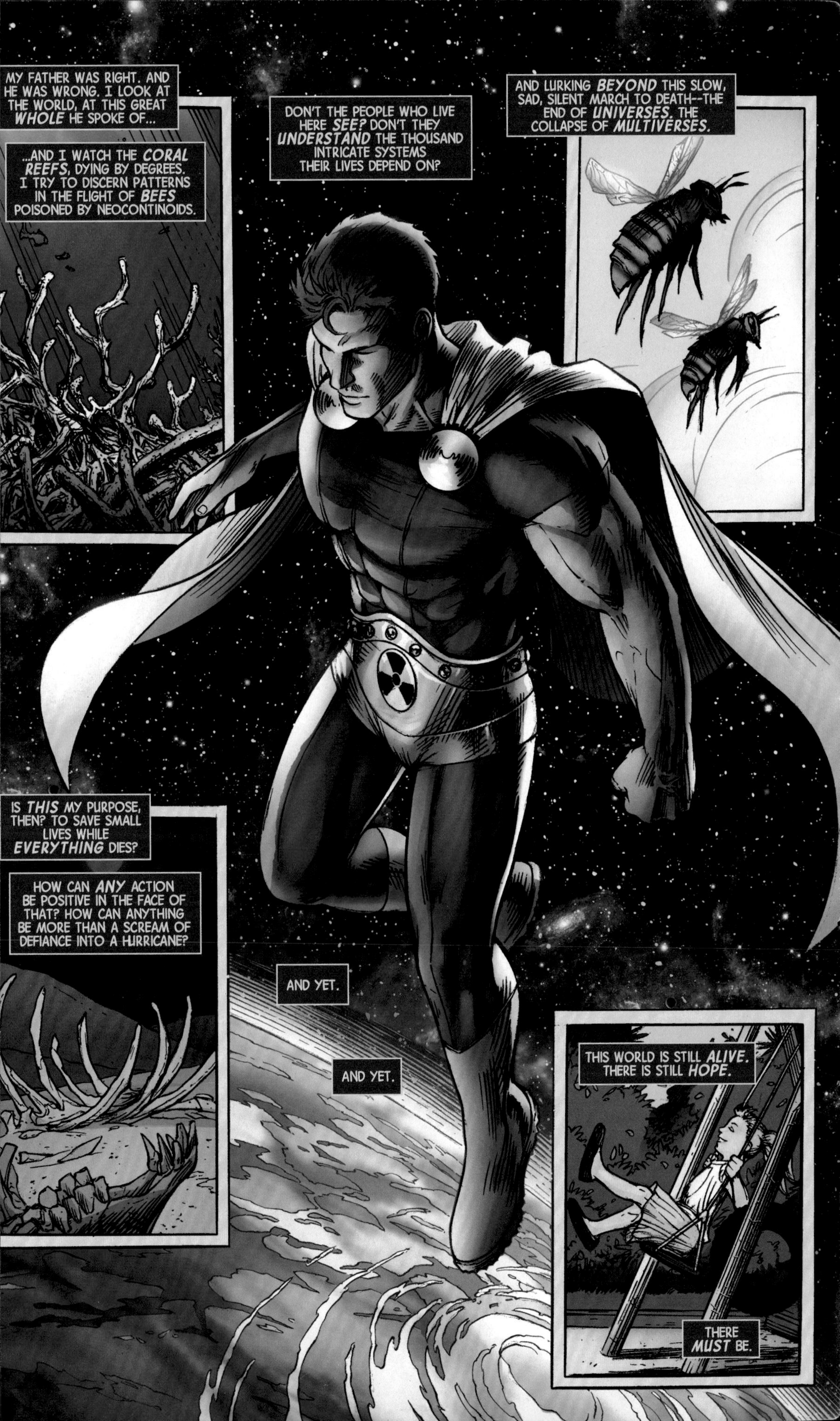

MY FATHER WAS RIGHT. AND HE WAS WRONG. I LOOK AT THE WORLD, AT THIS GREAT *WHOLE* HE SPOKE OF...
...AND I WATCH THE *CORAL REEFS*, DYING BY DEGREES. I TRY TO DISCERN PATTERNS IN THE FLIGHT OF *BEES* POISONED BY NEOCONTINOIDS.
DON'T THE PEOPLE WHO LIVE HERE *SEE?* DON'T THEY *UNDERSTAND* THE THOUSAND INTRICATE SYSTEMS THEIR LIVES DEPEND ON?
AND LURKING *BEYOND* THIS SLOW, SAD, SILENT MARCH TO DEATH--THE END OF *UNIVERSES*. THE COLLAPSE OF *MULTIVERSES*.
IS *THIS* MY PURPOSE, THEN? TO SAVE SMALL LIVES WHILE *EVERYTHING* DIES?
HOW CAN *ANY* ACTION BE POSITIVE IN THE FACE OF THAT? HOW CAN ANYTHING BE MORE THAN A SCREAM OF DEFIANCE INTO A HURRICANE?
AND YET.
AND YET.
THIS WORLD IS STILL *ALIVE*. THERE IS STILL *HOPE*.
THERE *MUST* BE.

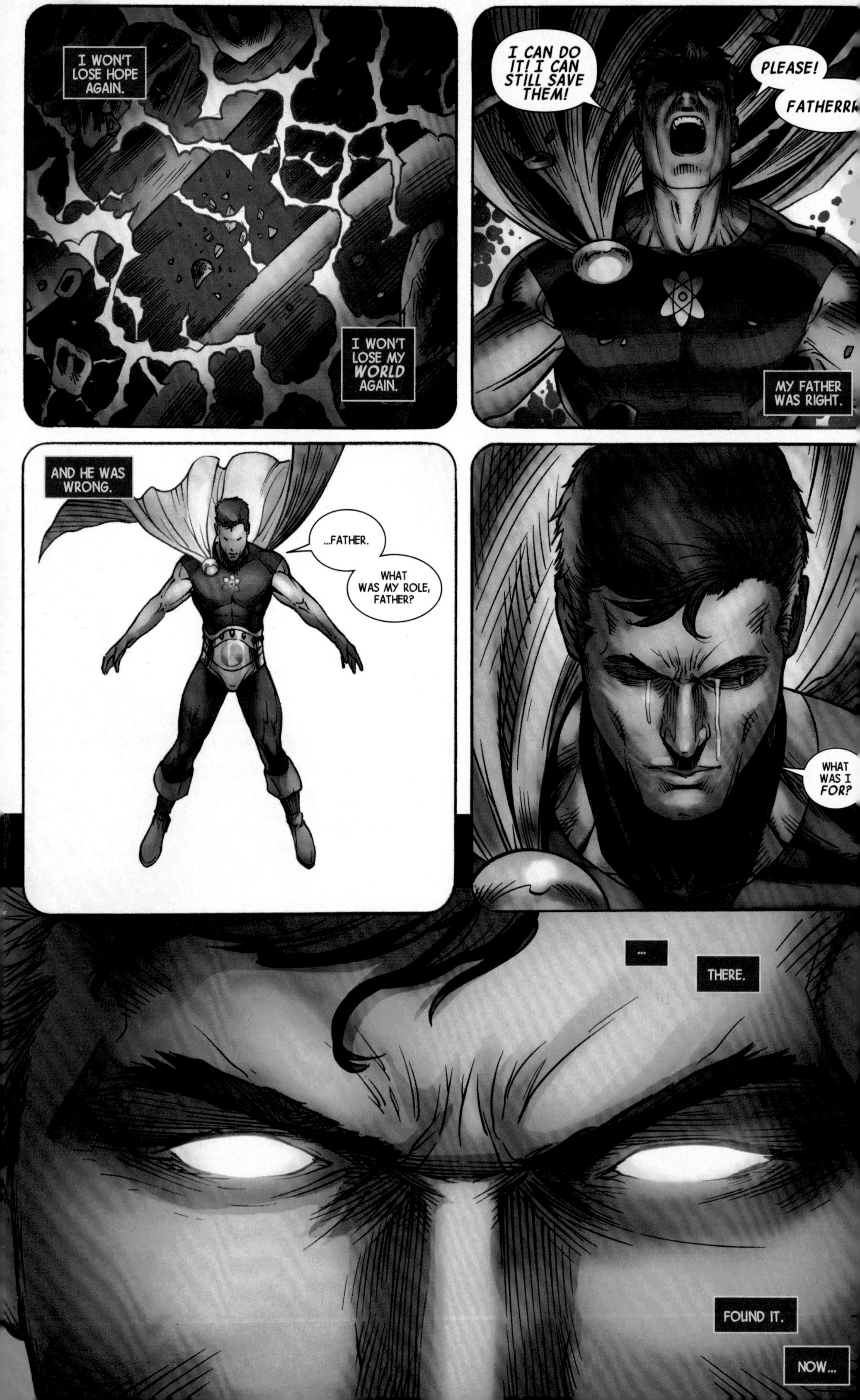

I WON'T LOSE HOPE AGAIN.
I WON'T LOSE MY WORLD AGAIN.
I CAN DO IT! I CAN STILL SAVE THEM!
PLEASE!
FATHERR
MY FATHER WAS RIGHT.
AND HE WAS WRONG.
...FATHER.
WHAT WAS MY ROLE, FATHER?
WHAT WAS I FOR?
...
THERE.
FOUND IT.
NOW...

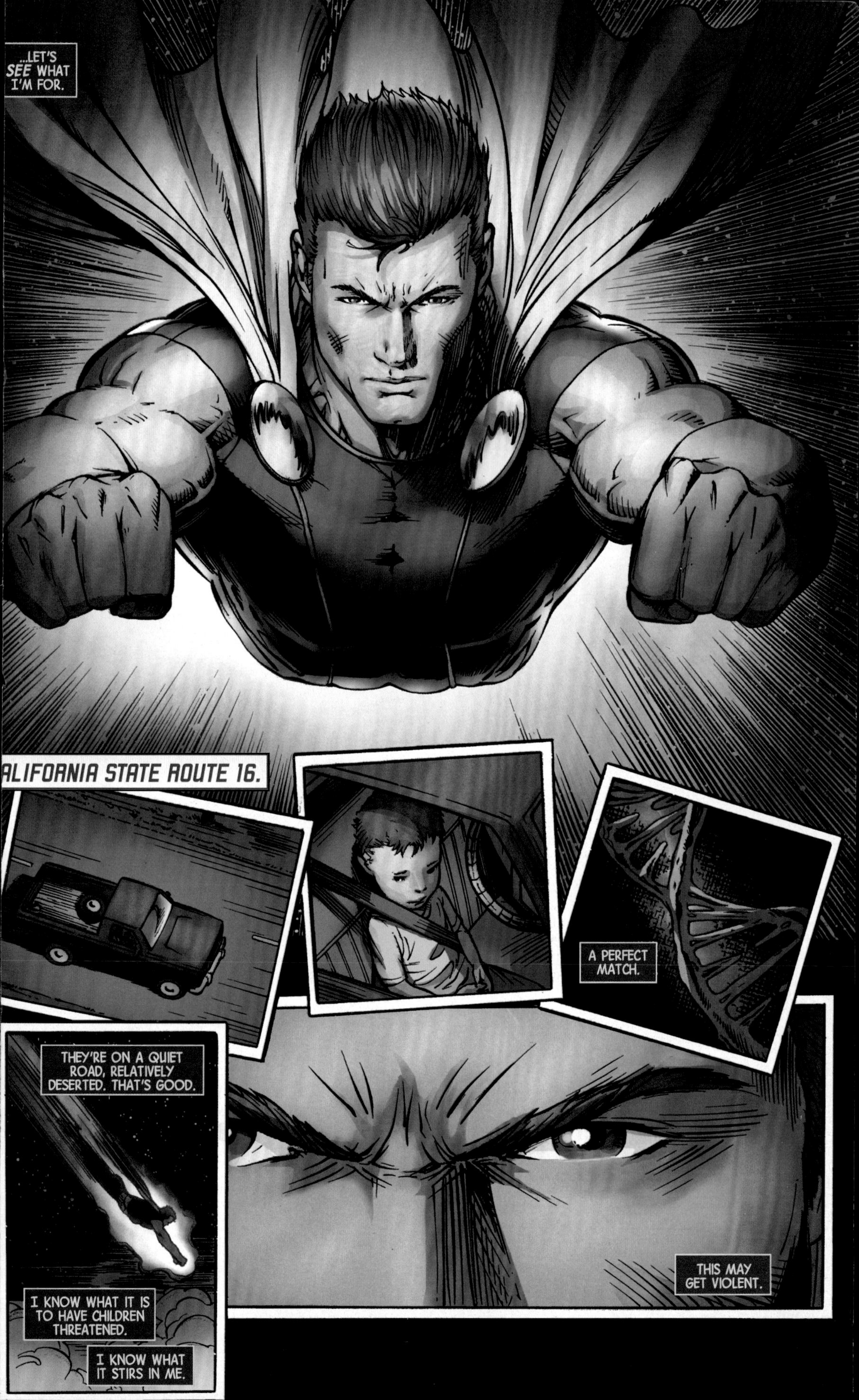
...LET'S SEE WHAT I'M FOR.
ALIFORNIA STATE ROUTE 16.
A PERFECT MATCH.
THEY'RE ON A QUIET ROAD, RELATIVELY DESERTED. THAT'S GOOD.
THIS MAY GET VIOLENT.
I KNOW WHAT IT IS TO HAVE CHILDREN THREATENED.
I KNOW WHAT IT STIRS IN ME.

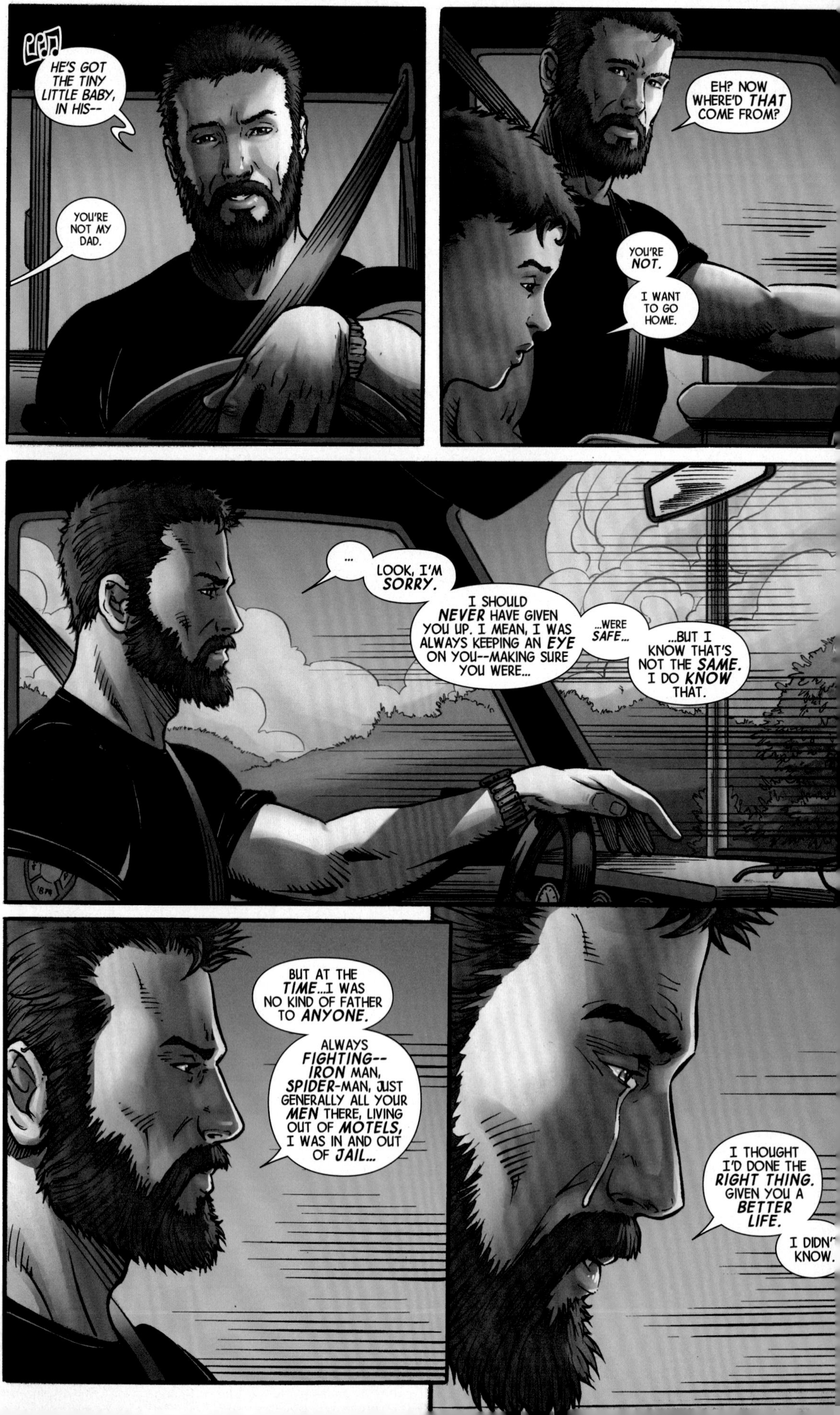

HE'S GOT THE TINY LITTLE BABY, IN HIS--
YOU'RE NOT MY DAD.
EH? NOW WHERE'D THAT COME FROM?
YOU'RE NOT.
I WANT TO GO HOME.
...
LOOK, I'M SORRY.
I SHOULD NEVER HAVE GIVEN YOU UP. I MEAN, I WAS ALWAYS KEEPING AN EYE ON YOU--MAKING SURE YOU WERE...
...WERE SAFE...
...BUT I KNOW THAT'S NOT THE SAME. I DO KNOW THAT.
BUT AT THE TIME...I WAS NO KIND OF FATHER TO ANYONE.
ALWAYS FIGHTING-- IRON MAN, SPIDER-MAN, JUST GENERALLY ALL YOUR MEN THERE, LIVING OUT OF MOTELS, I WAS IN AND OUT OF JAIL...
I THOUGHT I'D DONE THE RIGHT THING. GIVEN YOU A BETTER LIFE.
I DIDN'T KNOW.

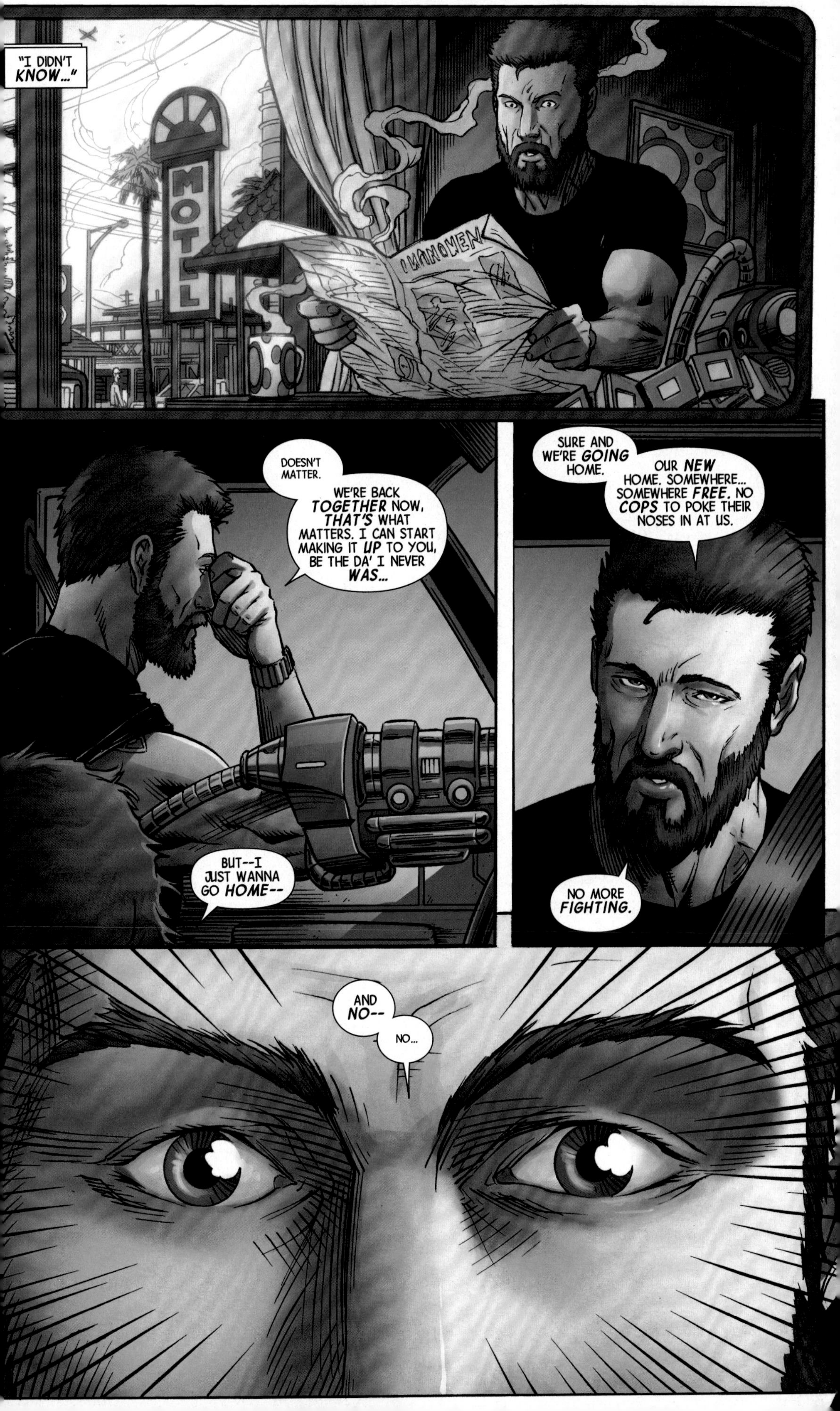
"I DIDN'T KNOW..."
DOESN'T MATTER.
WE'RE BACK TOGETHER NOW, THAT'S WHAT MATTERS. I CAN START MAKING IT UP TO YOU, BE THE DA' I NEVER WAS...
BUT--I JUST WANNA GO HOME--
SURE AND WE'RE GOING HOME.
OUR NEW HOME. SOMEWHERE... SOMEWHERE FREE. NO COPS TO POKE THEIR NOSES IN AT US.
NO MORE FIGHTING.
AND NO--
NO...

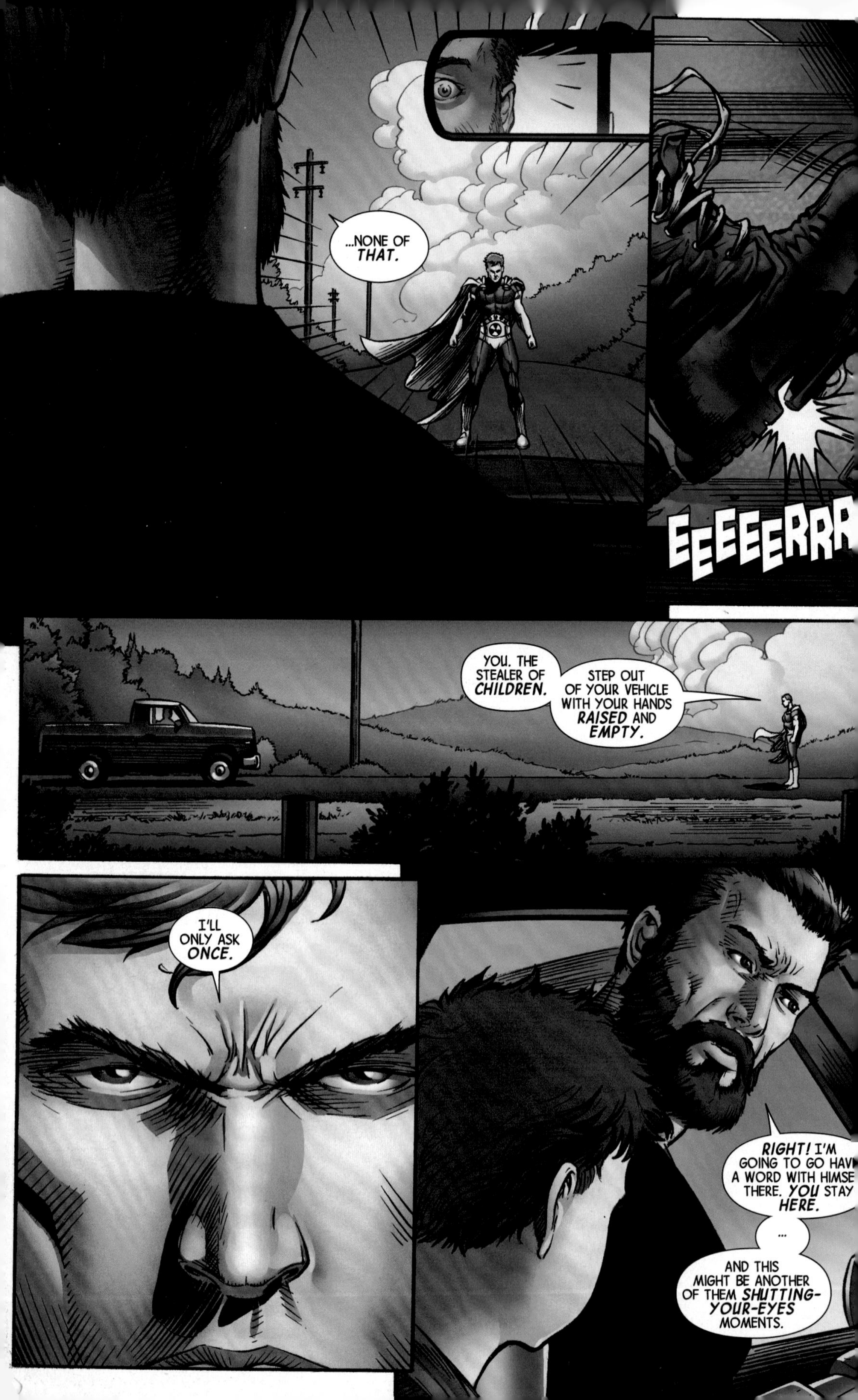

...NONE OF THAT.
EEEEERRR
YOU. THE STEALER OF CHILDREN.
STEP OUT OF YOUR VEHICLE WITH YOUR HANDS RAISED AND EMPTY.
I'LL ONLY ASK ONCE.
RIGHT! I'M GOING TO GO HAV A WORD WITH HIMSE THERE. YOU STAY HERE.
...
AND THIS MIGHT BE ANOTHER OF THEM SHUTTING-YOUR-EYES MOMENTS.

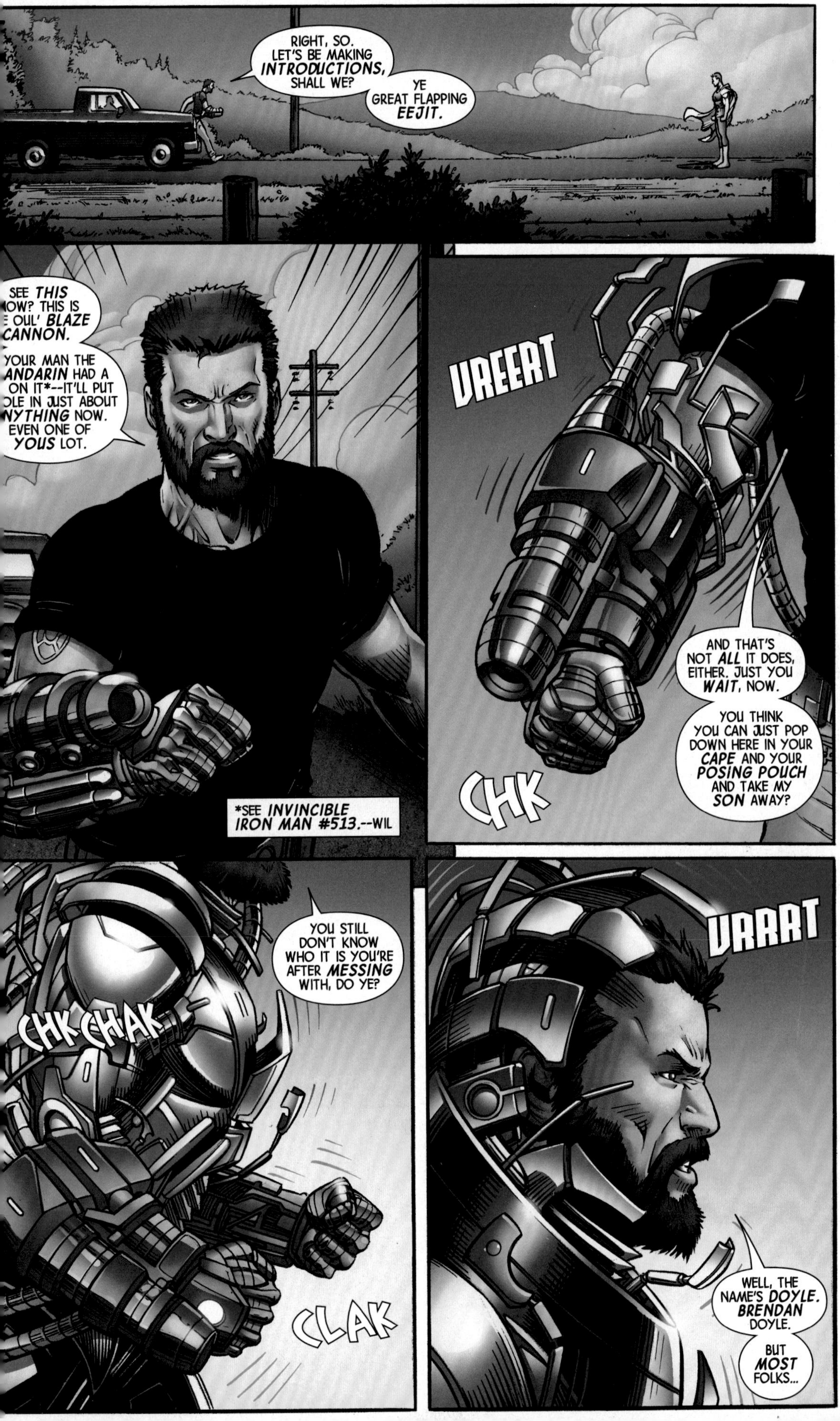
RIGHT, SO. LET'S BE MAKING INTRODUCTIONS, SHALL WE?
YE GREAT FLAPPING EEJIT.
SEE THIS OW? THIS IS E OUL' BLAZE CANNON.
YOUR MAN THE ANDARIN HAD A ON IT*--IT'LL PUT OLE IN JUST ABOUT NYTHING NOW. EVEN ONE OF YOUS LOT.
*SEE INVINCIBLE IRON MAN #513.--WIL
VREERT
AND THAT'S NOT ALL IT DOES, EITHER. JUST YOU WAIT, NOW.
YOU THINK YOU CAN JUST POP DOWN HERE IN YOUR CAPE AND YOUR POSING POUCH AND TAKE MY SON AWAY?
CHK
YOU STILL DON'T KNOW WHO IT IS YOU'RE AFTER MESSING WITH, DO YE?
CHKCHAK
CLAK
VRRRT
WELL, THE NAME'S DOYLE. BRENDAN DOYLE.
BUT MOST FOLKS...

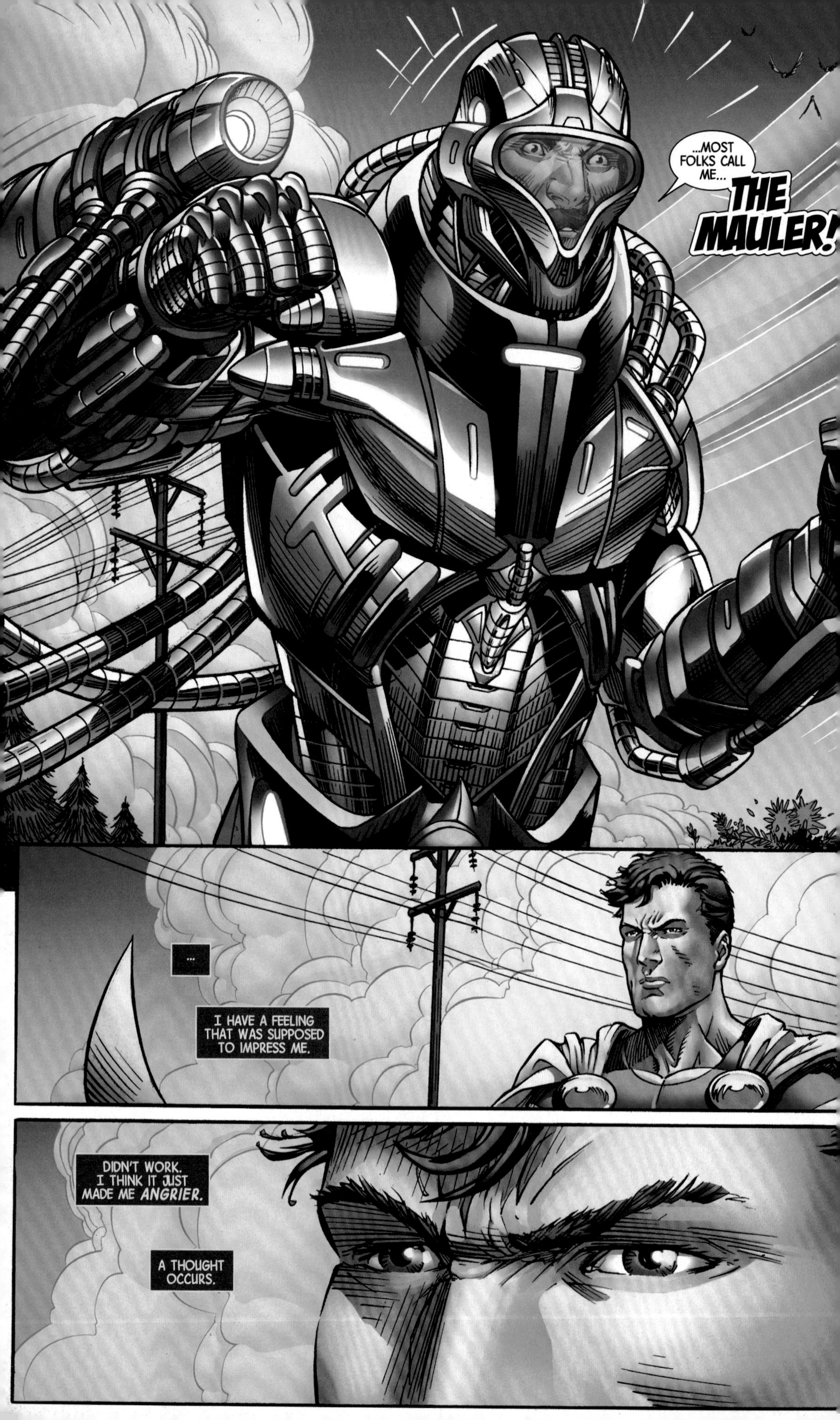
...MOST FOLKS CALL ME... THE MAULER!
...
I HAVE A FEELING THAT WAS SUPPOSED TO IMPRESS ME.
DIDN'T WORK. I THINK IT JUST MADE ME ANGRIER.
A THOUGHT OCCURS.

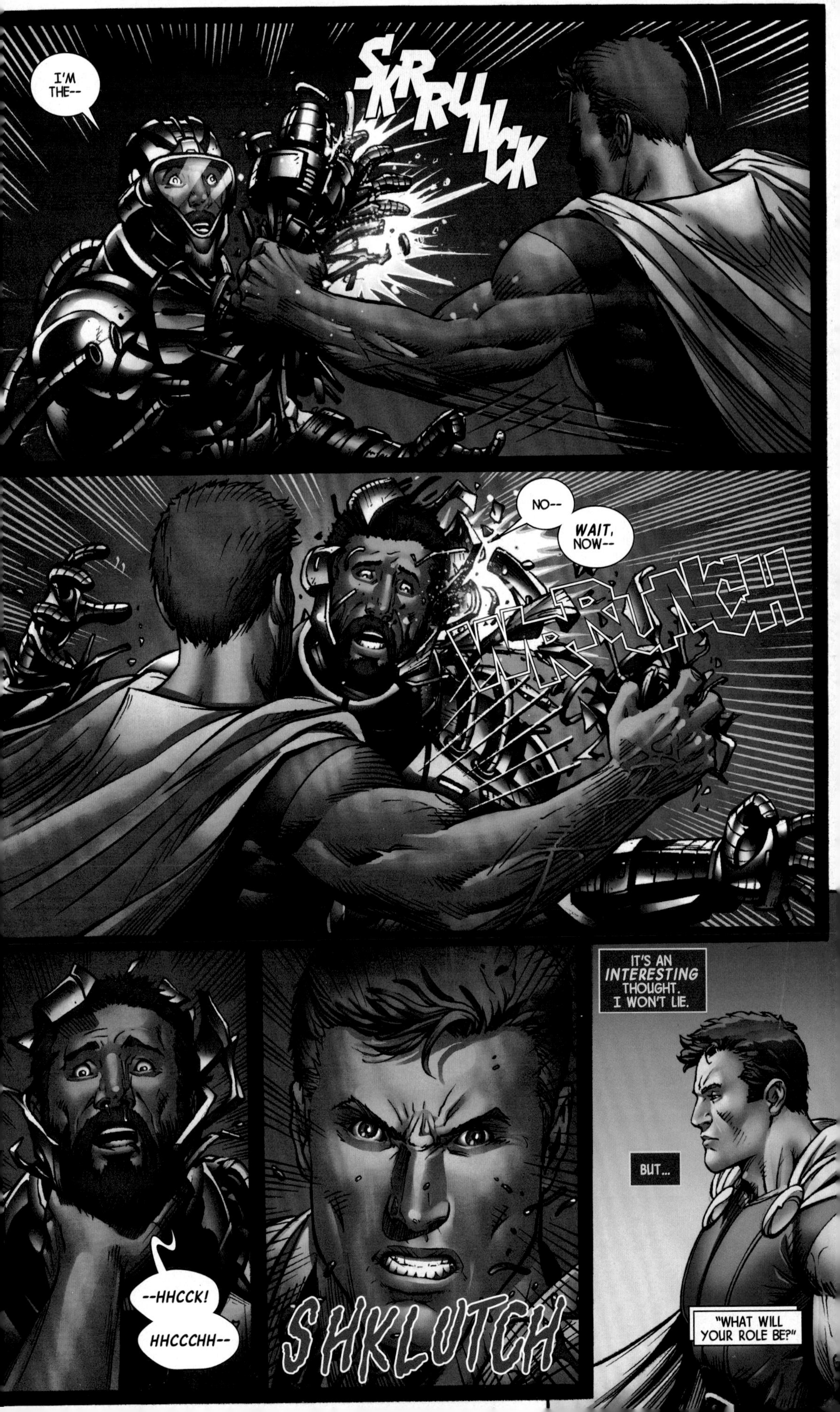
I'M THE--
SKRRUNCK
NO--
WAIT, NOW--
WHRRUNCH
--HHCCK!
HHCCCHH--
SHKLUTCH
IT'S AN INTERESTING THOUGHT. I WON'T LIE.
BUT...
"WHAT WILL YOUR ROLE BE?"

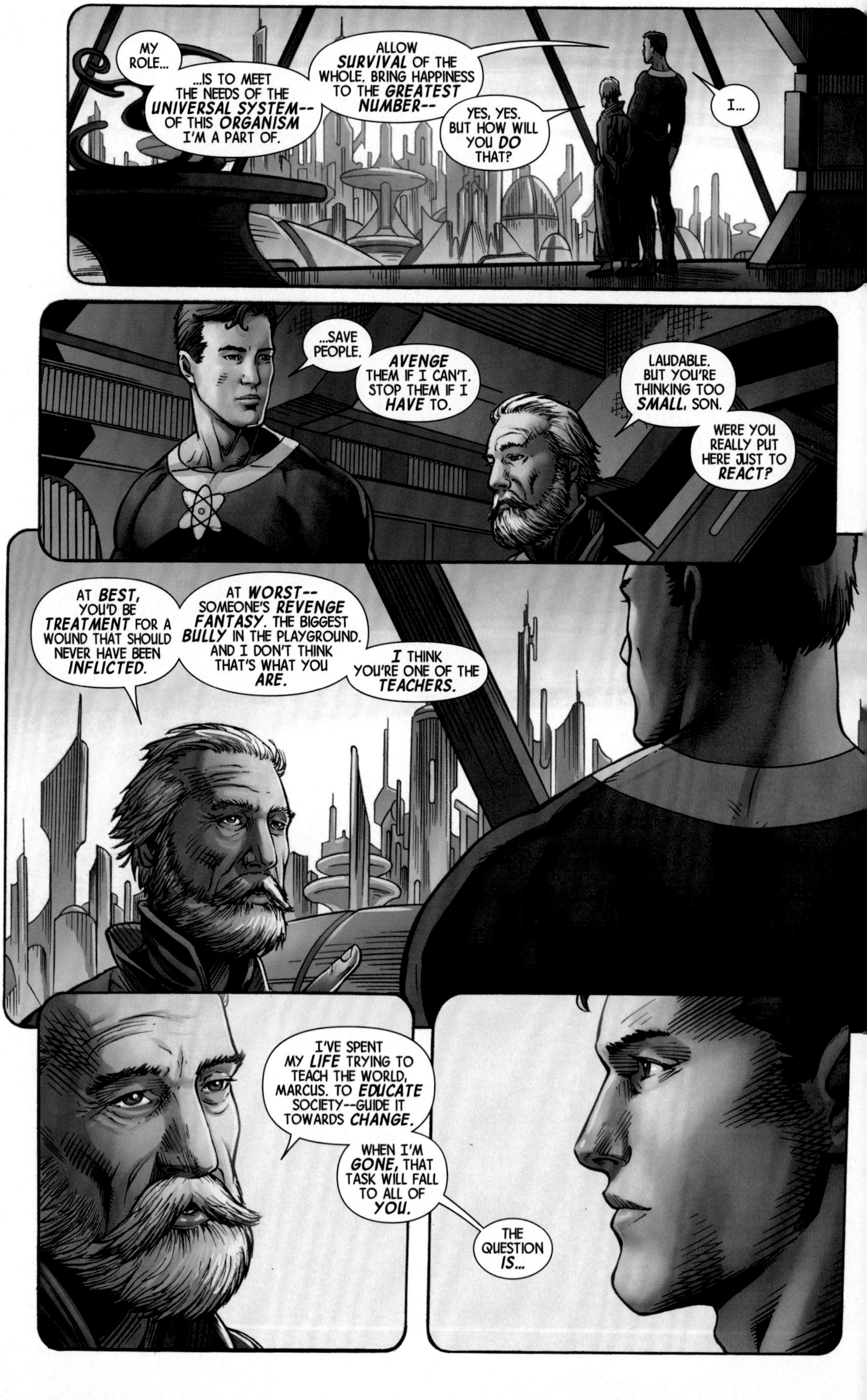
MY ROLE...
...IS TO MEET THE NEEDS OF THE UNIVERSAL SYSTEM-- OF THIS ORGANISM I'M A PART OF.
ALLOW SURVIVAL OF THE WHOLE. BRING HAPPINESS TO THE GREATEST NUMBER--
YES, YES. BUT HOW WILL YOU DO THAT?
I...
...SAVE PEOPLE.
AVENGE THEM IF I CAN'T. STOP THEM IF I HAVE TO.
LAUDABLE. BUT YOU'RE THINKING TOO SMALL, SON.
WERE YOU REALLY PUT HERE JUST TO REACT?
AT BEST, YOU'D BE TREATMENT FOR A WOUND THAT SHOULD NEVER HAVE BEEN INFLICTED.
AT WORST-- SOMEONE'S REVENGE FANTASY. THE BIGGEST BULLY IN THE PLAYGROUND. AND I DON'T THINK THAT'S WHAT YOU ARE.
I THINK YOU'RE ONE OF THE TEACHERS.
I'VE SPENT MY LIFE TRYING TO TEACH THE WORLD, MARCUS. TO EDUCATE SOCIETY--GUIDE IT TOWARDS CHANGE.
WHEN I'M GONE, THAT TASK WILL FALL TO ALL OF YOU.
THE QUESTION IS...

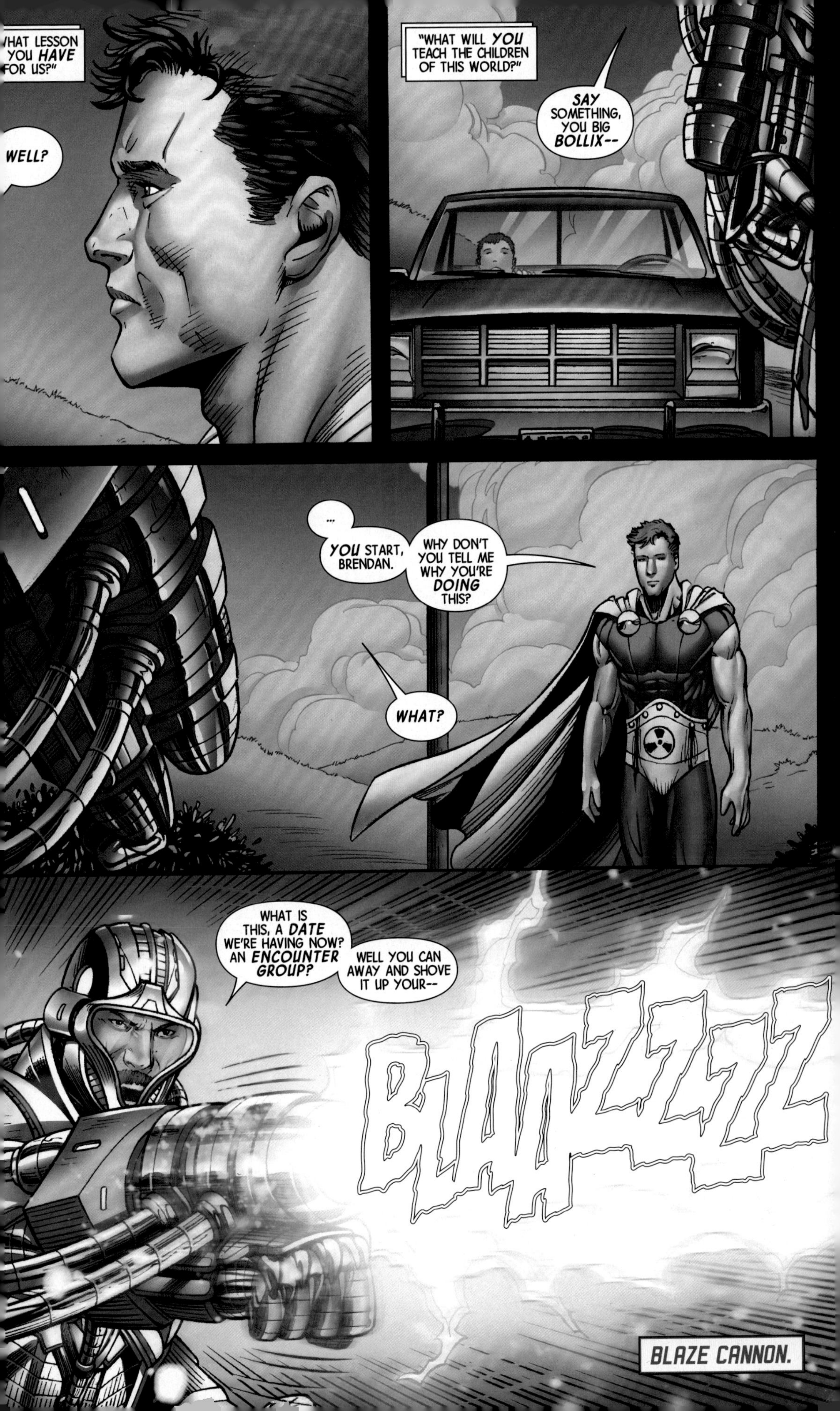
"WHAT LESSON YOU HAVE FOR US?"
WELL?
"WHAT WILL YOU TEACH THE CHILDREN OF THIS WORLD?"
SAY SOMETHING, YOU BIG BOLLIX--
...
YOU START, BRENDAN.
WHY DON'T YOU TELL ME WHY YOU'RE DOING THIS?
WHAT?
WHAT IS THIS, A DATE WE'RE HAVING NOW? AN ENCOUNTER GROUP?
WELL YOU CAN AWAY AND SHOVE IT UP YOUR--
BLAZZZZZ
BLAZE CANNON.

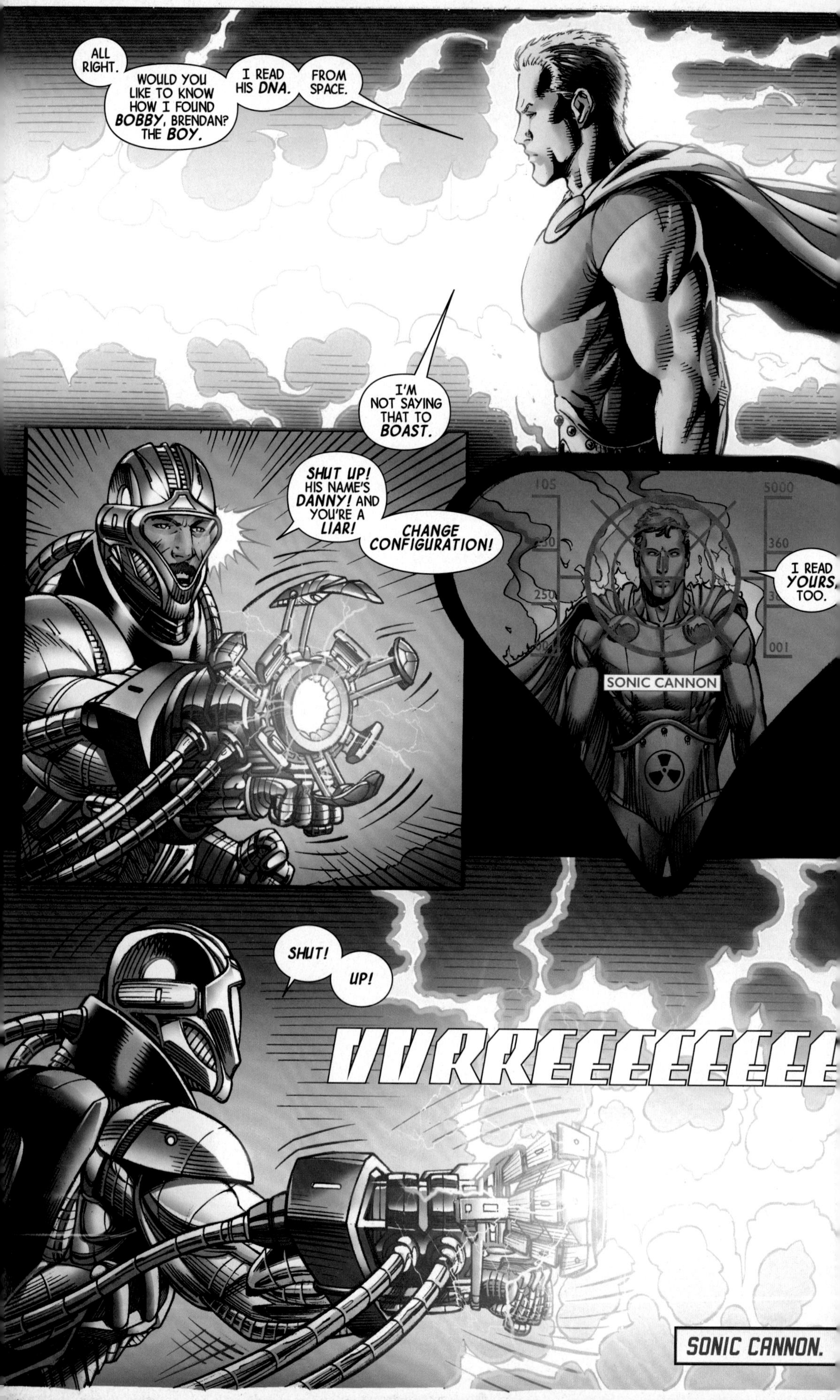
ALL RIGHT.
WOULD YOU LIKE TO KNOW HOW I FOUND BOBBY, BRENDAN? THE BOY.
I READ HIS DNA.
FROM SPACE.
I'M NOT SAYING THAT TO BOAST.
SHUT UP! HIS NAME'S DANNY! AND YOU'RE A LIAR!
CHANGE CONFIGURATION!
SONIC CANNON
I READ YOURS, TOO.
SHUT!
UP!
VVRREEEEEEEEE
SONIC CANNON.

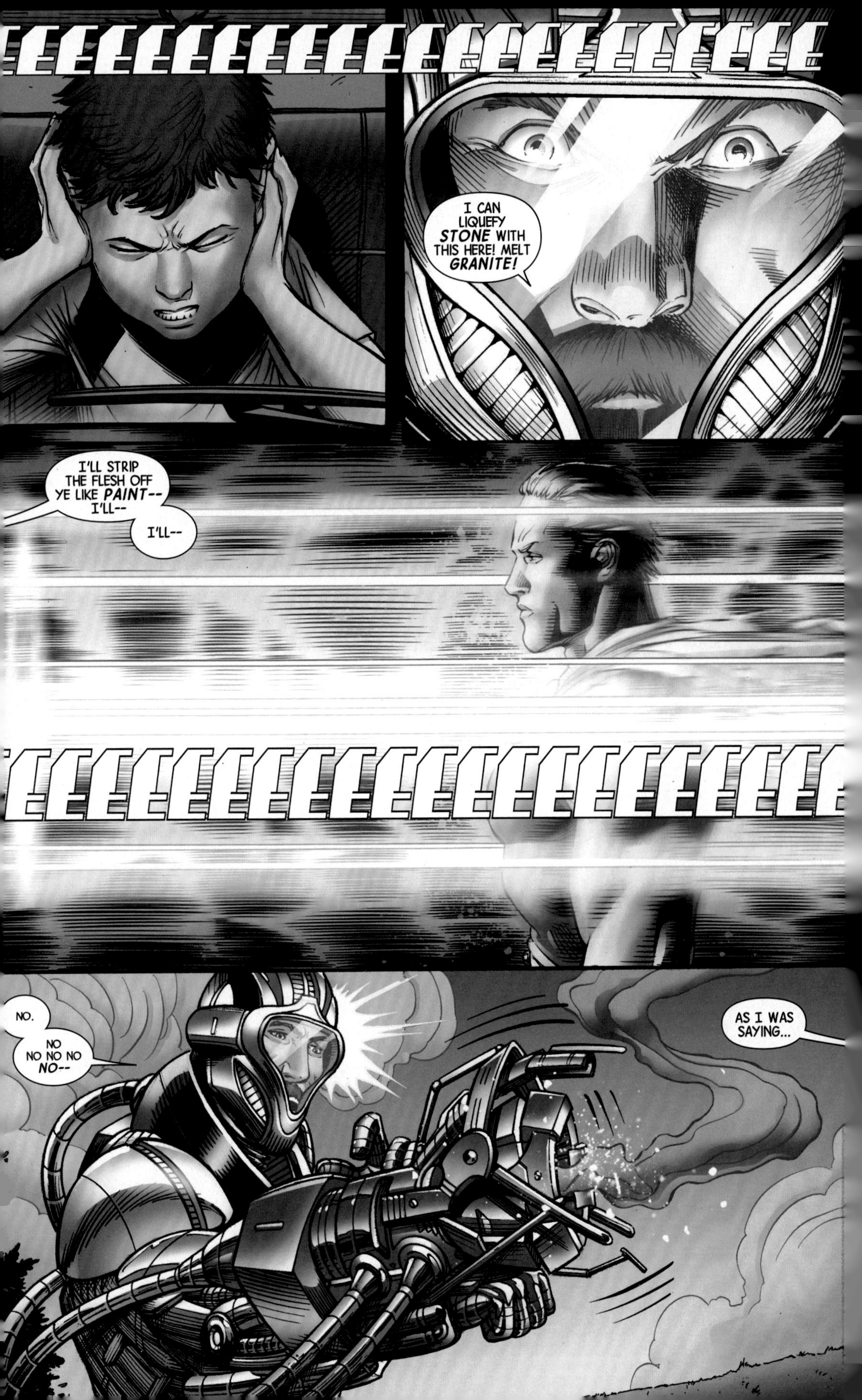
EEEEEEEEEEEEEEEEEEEEEEE
I CAN LIQUEFY STONE WITH THIS HERE! MELT GRANITE!
I'LL STRIP THE FLESH OFF YE LIKE PAINT-- I'LL--
I'LL--
EEEEEEEEEEEEEEEEEEEEEEE
NO.
NO NO NO NO NO--
AS I WAS SAYING...

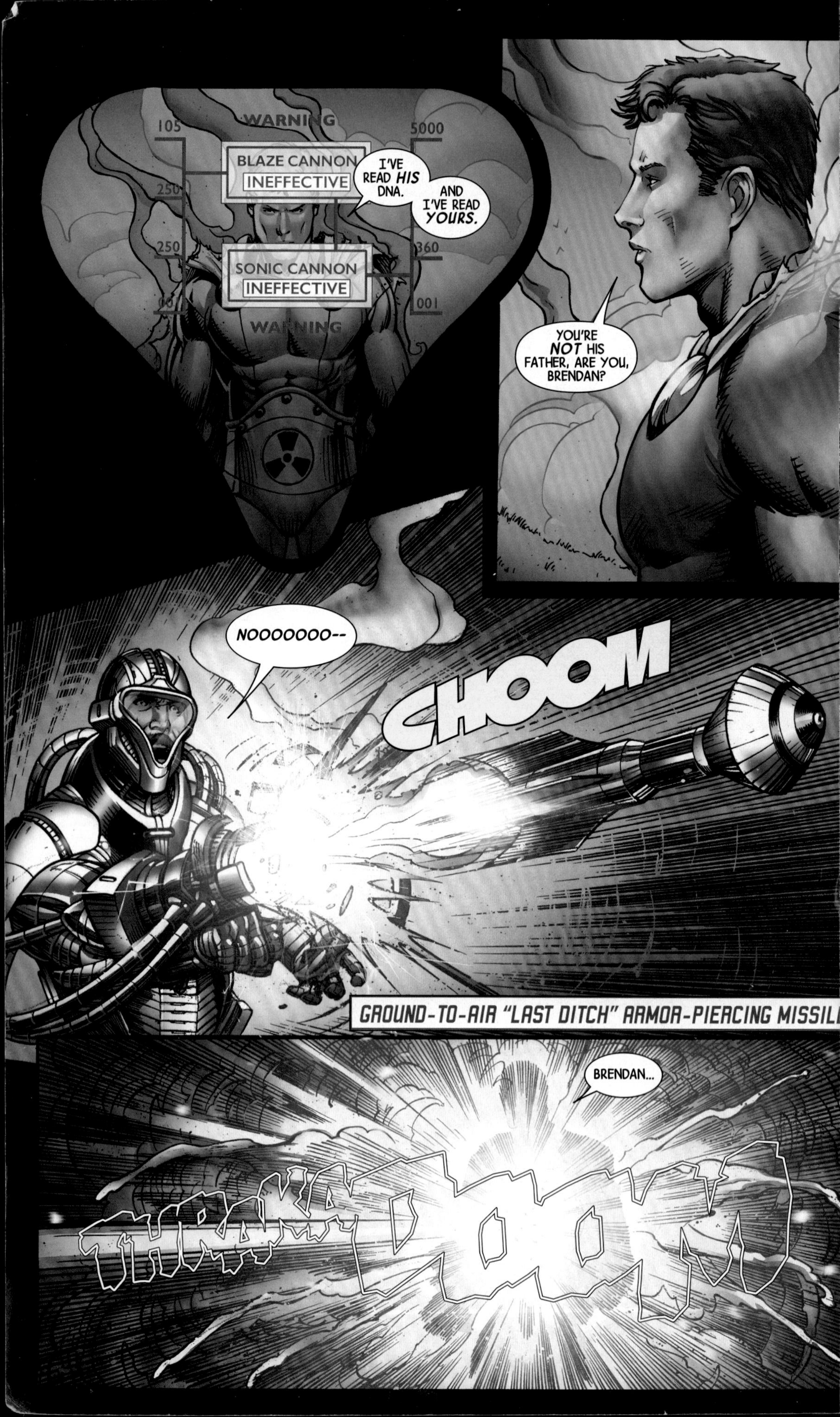
WARNING
105
5000
BLAZE CANNON
INEFFECTIVE
250
I'VE READ HIS DNA.
AND I'VE READ YOURS.
250
360
SONIC CANNON
INEFFECTIVE
001
WARNING
YOU'RE NOT HIS FATHER, ARE YOU, BRENDAN?
NOOOOOOO--
CHOOM
GROUND-TO-AIR "LAST DITCH" ARMOR-PIERCING MISSILE
BRENDAN...

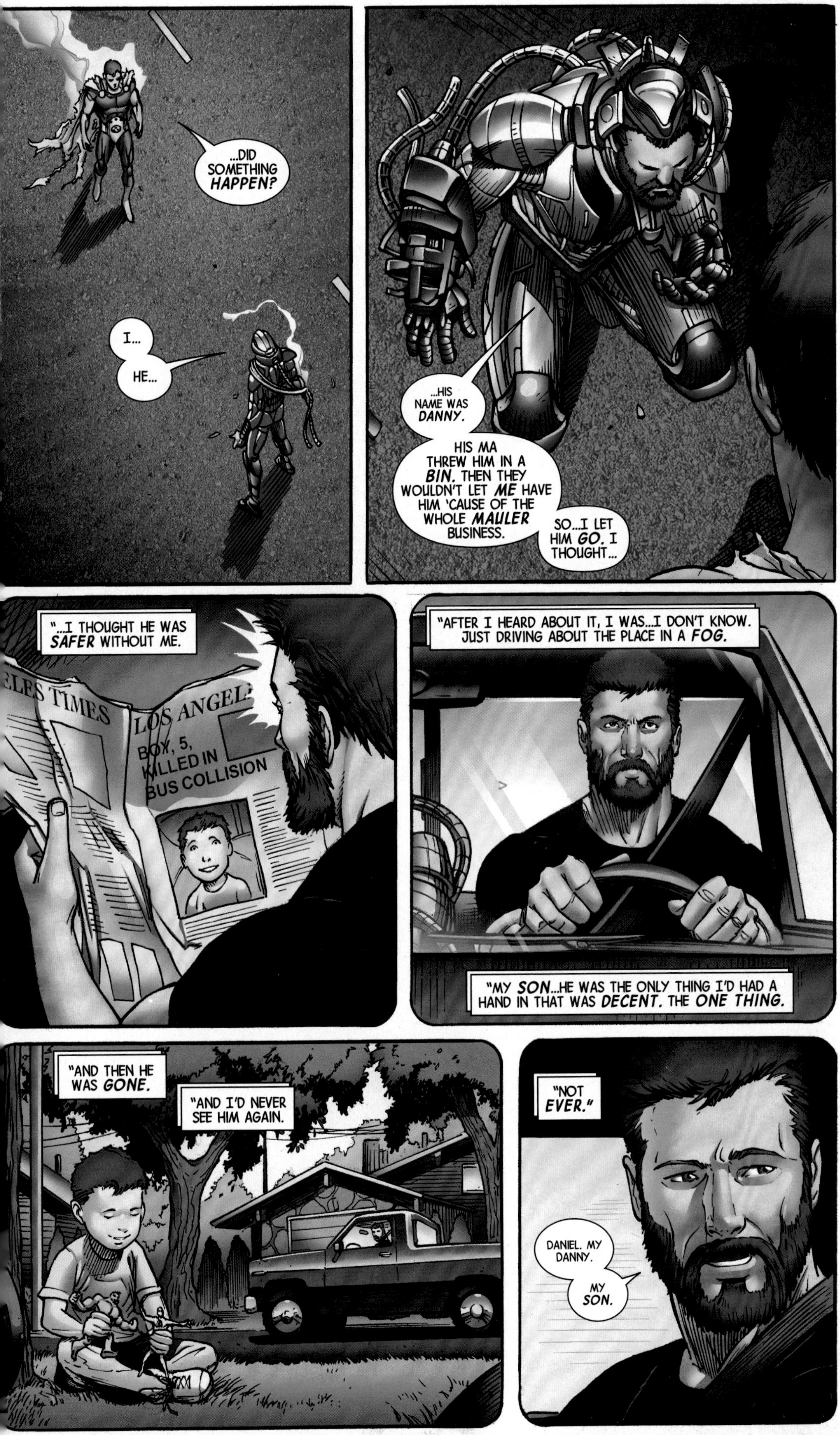
...DID SOMETHING HAPPEN?
I...
HE...
...HIS NAME WAS DANNY.
HIS MA THREW HIM IN A BIN. THEN THEY WOULDN'T LET ME HAVE HIM 'CAUSE OF THE WHOLE MAULER BUSINESS.
SO...I LET HIM GO. I THOUGHT...
"...I THOUGHT HE WAS SAFER WITHOUT ME.
LOS ANGELES TIMES
BOY, 5, KILLED IN BUS COLLISION
"AFTER I HEARD ABOUT IT, I WAS...I DON'T KNOW. JUST DRIVING ABOUT THE PLACE IN A FOG.
"MY SON...HE WAS THE ONLY THING I'D HAD A HAND IN THAT WAS DECENT. THE ONE THING.
"AND THEN HE WAS GONE.
"AND I'D NEVER SEE HIM AGAIN.
"NOT EVER."
DANIEL. MY DANNY.
MY SON.

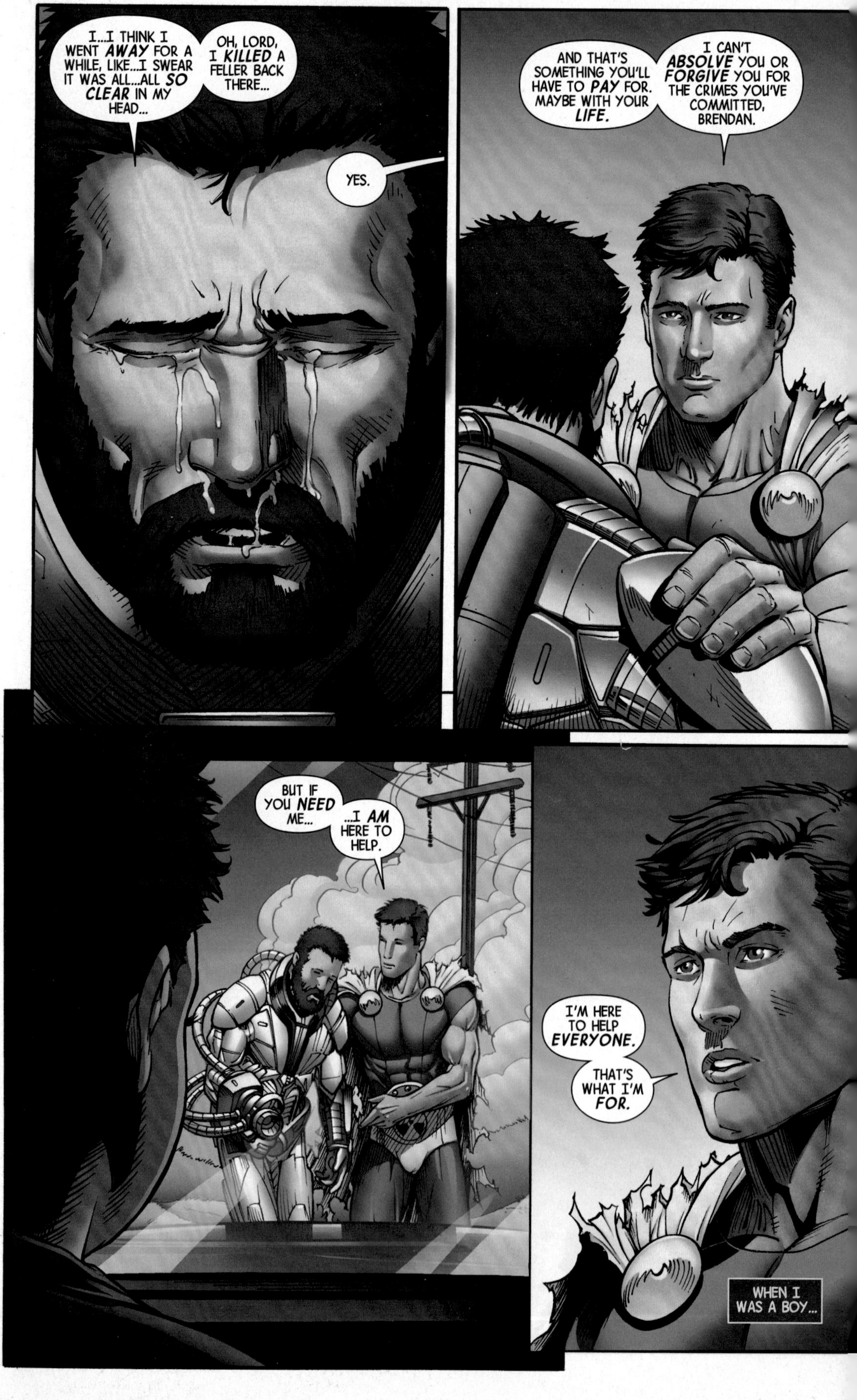
I...I THINK I WENT AWAY FOR A WHILE, LIKE...I SWEAR IT WAS ALL...ALL SO CLEAR IN MY HEAD...
OH, LORD, I KILLED A FELLER BACK THERE...
YES.
I CAN'T ABSOLVE YOU OR FORGIVE YOU FOR THE CRIMES YOU'VE COMMITTED, BRENDAN.
AND THAT'S SOMETHING YOU'LL HAVE TO PAY FOR. MAYBE WITH YOUR LIFE.
BUT IF YOU NEED ME...
...I AM HERE TO HELP.
I'M HERE TO HELP EVERYONE.
THAT'S WHAT I'M FOR.
WHEN I WAS A BOY...

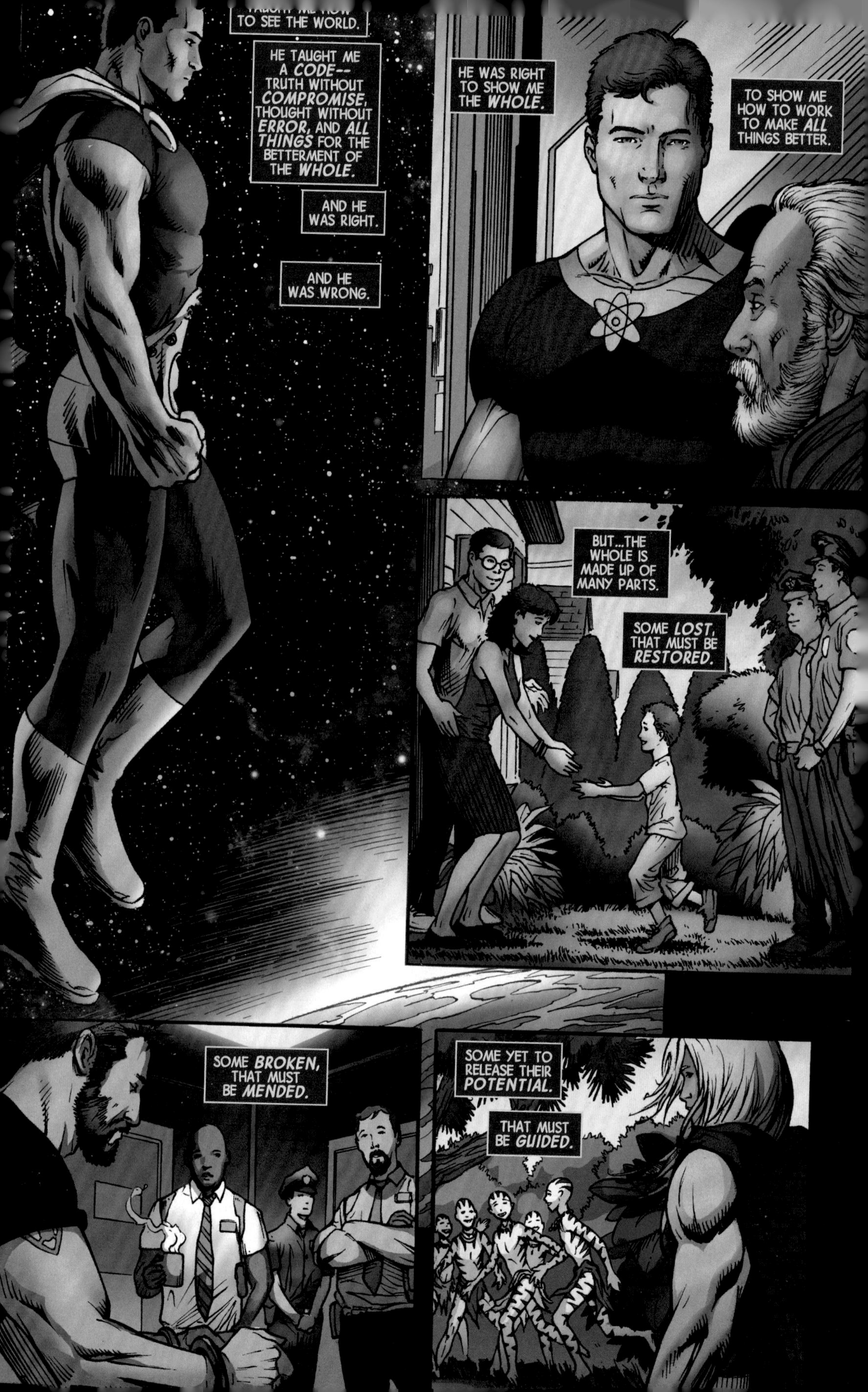

TO SEE THE WORLD.
HE TAUGHT ME A *CODE*-- TRUTH WITHOUT *COMPROMISE*, THOUGHT WITHOUT *ERROR*, AND *ALL THINGS* FOR THE BETTERMENT OF THE *WHOLE*.
AND HE WAS RIGHT.
AND HE WAS WRONG.
HE WAS RIGHT TO SHOW ME THE *WHOLE*.
TO SHOW ME HOW TO WORK TO MAKE *ALL* THINGS BETTER.
BUT...THE WHOLE IS MADE UP OF MANY PARTS.
SOME *LOST*, THAT MUST BE *RESTORED*.
SOME *BROKEN*, THAT MUST BE *MENDED*.
SOME YET TO RELEASE THEIR *POTENTIAL*.
THAT MUST BE *GUIDED*.

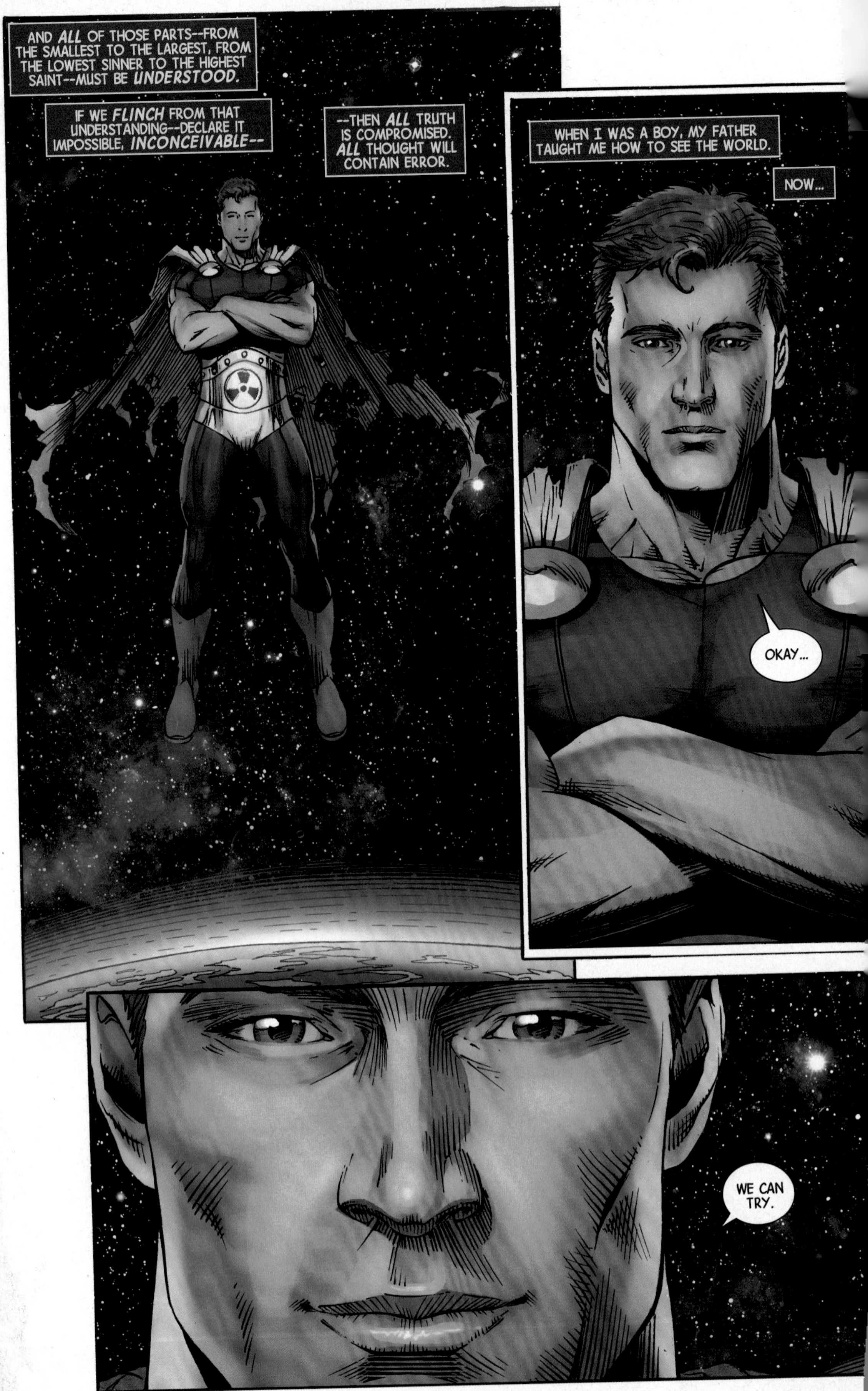

AND ALL OF THOSE PARTS--FROM THE SMALLEST TO THE LARGEST, FROM THE LOWEST SINNER TO THE HIGHEST SAINT--MUST BE UNDERSTOOD.
IF WE FLINCH FROM THAT UNDERSTANDING--DECLARE IT IMPOSSIBLE, INCONCEIVABLE--
--THEN ALL TRUTH IS COMPROMISED. ALL THOUGHT WILL CONTAIN ERROR.
WHEN I WAS A BOY, MY FATHER TAUGHT ME HOW TO SEE THE WORLD.
NOW...
OKAY...
WE CAN TRY.

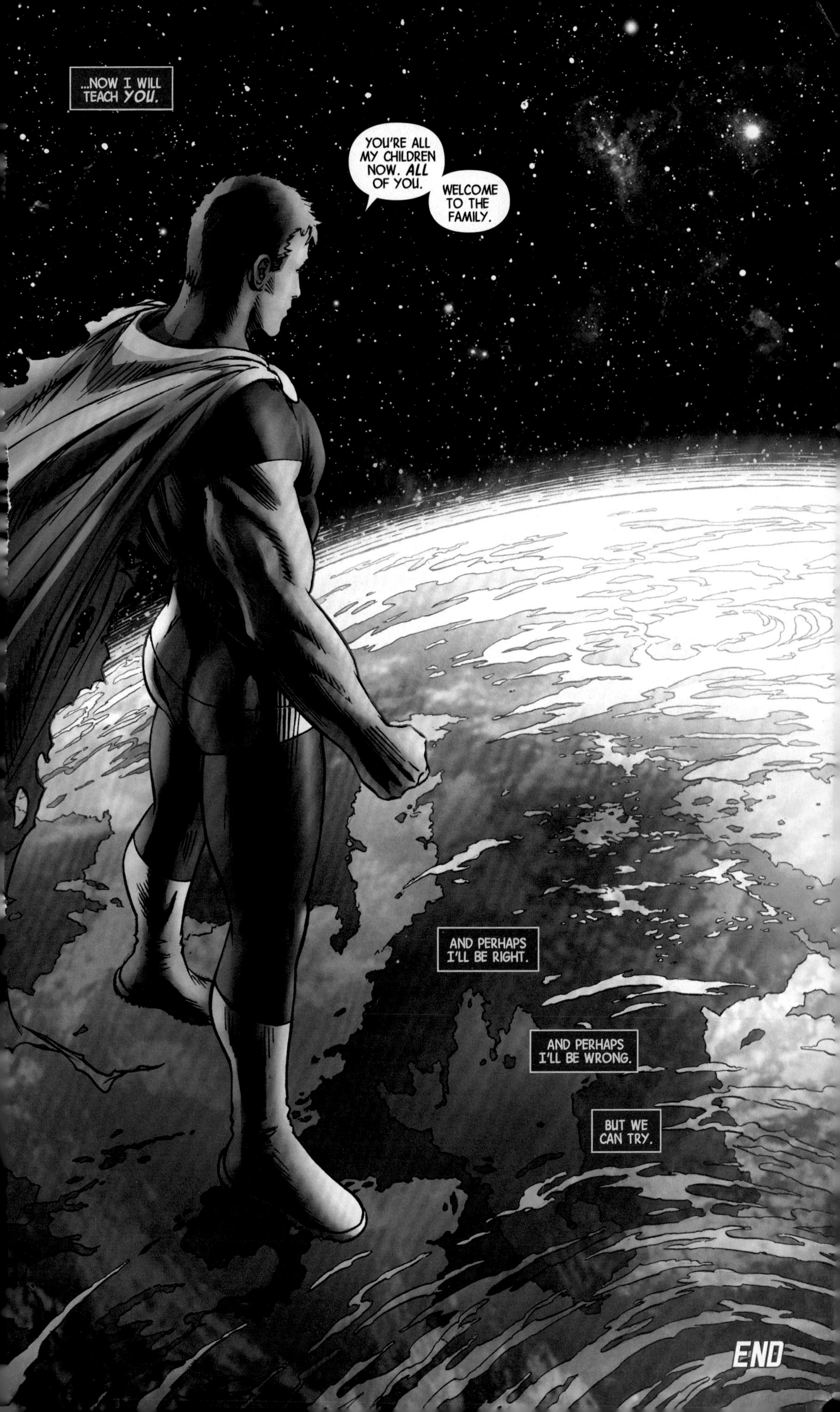
...NOW I WILL TEACH *YOU.*
YOU'RE ALL MY CHILDREN NOW. *ALL* OF YOU.
WELCOME TO THE FAMILY.
AND PERHAPS I'LL BE RIGHT.
AND PERHAPS I'LL BE WRONG.
BUT WE CAN TRY.
END

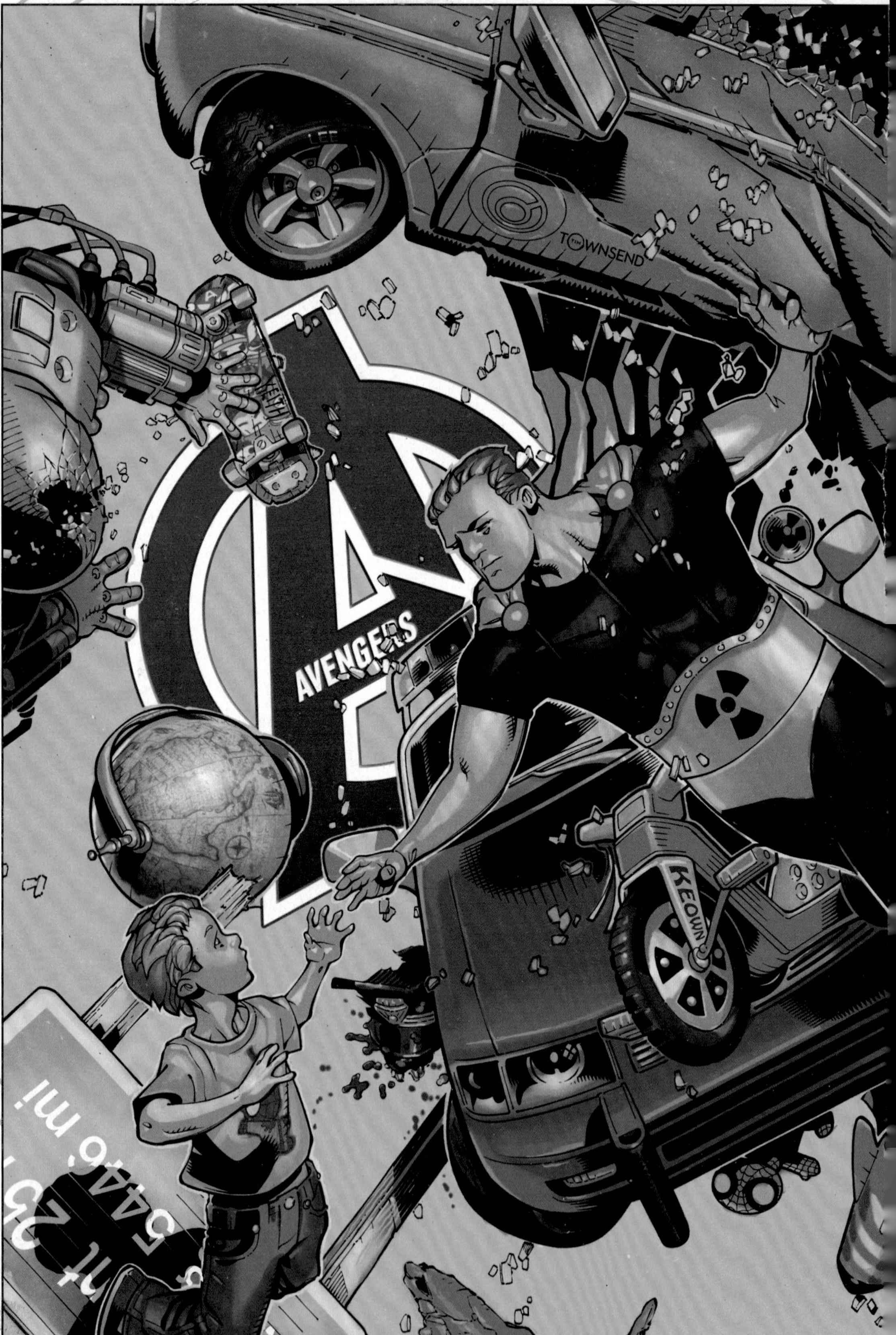
AVENGERS
KEOWN
TIM TOWNSEND

AVENGERS 34.1 VARIANT BY CHRIS BACHALO & TIM TOWNSEND